W9-ARU-068

ESSENTIAL Shakespeare HANDBOOK

ESSENTIAL
Shakespeare
HANDBOOK

Leslie Dunton-Downer
Alan Riding

London, New York, Munich,
Melbourne, and Delhi

Senior Designers Mabel Chan, Karen Wilkes
Designers Victoria Clark, Elaine Hewson, Alison Gardner, Colin Goody, Jerry Udall, Ann Burnham
Design Assistance
Kathrine Gammon, Claire-Louise Armitt.
DTP Designer John Goldsmid

Project Editors Sam Atkinson, Liz Wyse
Editors Victoria Heyworth-Dunne, Belinda Wilkinson
Editorial Assistance
Michelle Crane, Catherine Day, Michelle Pickering

Quantitative Analysis Andrew Berry

Managing Art Editor Louise Dick
Managing Editor Debra Clapson
Art Director Bryn Walls
Editorial Director Andrew Heritage

Production Jo Bull
Picture Research Franziska Marking
DK Picture Librarians Claire Bowers, Neale Chamberlaine, Richard Dabb
Index Jane Horton

First American Edition, 2004
04 05 06 10 9 8 7 6 5 4 3 2

Published in the United States by
DK Publishing, Inc.
375 Hudson Street
New York, New York 10014

A CIP catalog record for this book is available from the Library of Congress.

ISBN: 0-7894-9333-0

Reproduced by Colourscan, Singapore

Printed and bound in Slovakia by TBB (s.r.o)

See our complete product line at
www.dk.com

CONTENTS

Shakespeare's Globe, Bankside, London.

Placido Domingo plays the leading role in Franco Zeffirelli's film of Verdi's opera *Otello*, based on Shakespeare's *Othello*.

HOW TO USE THIS HANDBOOK

THE ESSENTIAL SHAKESPEARE HANDBOOK is a one-stop guide to the life and work of William Shakespeare. It is organized into three sections: the first is an overview of Shakespeare's early life in Stratford, his subsequent career as a playwright and poet, and his cultural influence; the second is a survey of all 39 of his plays, arranged by genre, then chronologically; the third is an exploration of his non-dramatic work – the narrative and lyric poems.

COLOR CODING

This book is color-coded to help the reader find a specific play, poem or background essay with ease.

Introduction

The History Plays

The Comedies

The Tragedies

The Romances

Non Dramatic Poetry

Global Shakespeare

INTRODUCING SHAKESPEARE

An opening section gives a biographical, cultural, historical, literary, and cultural reference to the life, work and times of William Shakespeare, including a discussion of Elizabethan and Jacobean theater and explanations of literary terms such as verse, prose, and meter.

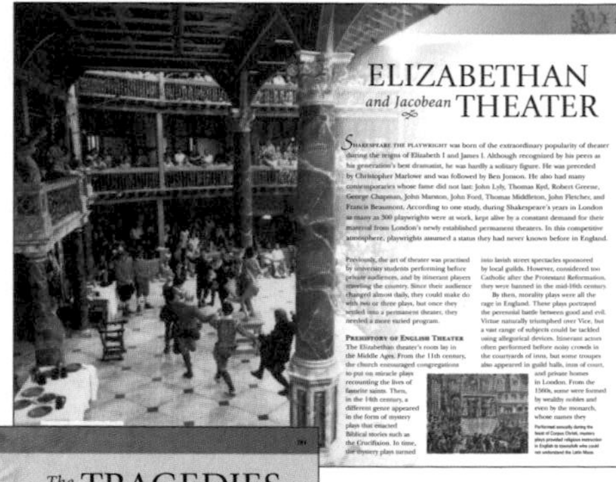

GENRE OVERVIEW

Each of the four types of Shakespeare play: history play, comedy, tragedy, and romance is introduced by a detailed discussion of the genre as a whole. The overlap between genres is discussed and the Bard's historical and literary sources explored.

THE PLAYS

The plays are organized first by genre, then by the approximate date of their composition. Each of the plays is discussed in great detail over a number of pages, which are divided into distinct sections.

1 Introduction *The top half of this page looks at the genesis of the play, from Shakespeare's sources to its probable first performance and early production history. The bottom half looks at the background story to the plot of the play itself.*

Graphics give at-a-glance, statistical information which can be used to compare certain features of the plays, such as the number of lines per act and a comparison of verse to prose language.

2 Dramatis Personae
This page lists every character in the play, giving a short description of their role within the plot, and the number of lines that they speak on stage. Six icons add an extra level of detail.

3 Plot Summary
Here the plot of the play itself is outlined, act-by-act. Icons and citations from the text orient the reader to specific points within the story.

Role Profile boxes highlight one or two of the most important roles within each play.

4 Reading the Play
This page looks at approaching the play as a text and gives special attention to aspects of the plot known to cause frustration among first-time readers.

5 Seeing the Play
This provides an overview of the play's performance history and discusses the issues surrounding performing the play on stage, from characterization to set design and visual effects.

Who's Who boxes explain in shorthand form the relationships between characters in many of the more complex plays.

6 Beyond the Play
The most frequently performed plays feature an additional page which looks at the play's wider cultural significance.

Boxes scattered throughout the plays section give additional information about each play, organized into the seven topics *(below)*.

- HISTORICAL SOURCES
- LITERARY SOURCES
- PLAY HISTORY
- LANGUAGE NOTE
- ON STAGE
- ON SCREEN
- PLAYER PROFILE

NON-DRAMATIC POETRY

This section is split into two parts. *The Narrative Poems* gives an overview of Shakespeare's story-based poetry, such as *Venus and Adonis* and *The Rape of Lucrece*. The next section looks at *The Lyric Poems*: verse which expresses emotional states rather than telling stories. The Sonnets can be found in this category.

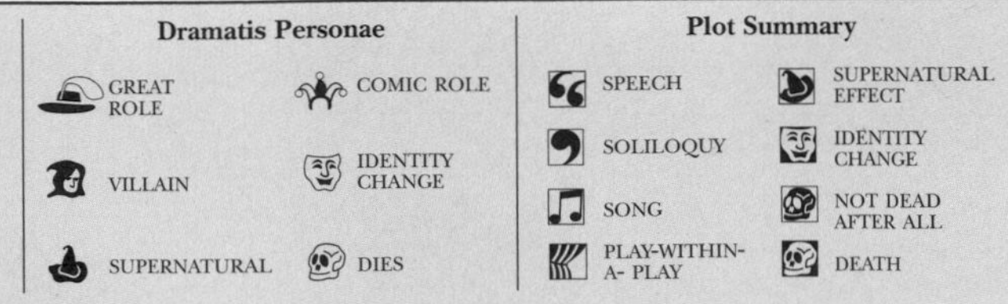

ICONS
The Dramatis Personae and the Plot Summary for each play use icons to assist the reader or theatergoer in following the action of each play. The meaning of each icon is listed to the right.

Dramatis Personae
- GREAT ROLE
- COMIC ROLE
- VILLAIN
- IDENTITY CHANGE
- SUPERNATURAL
- DIES

Plot Summary
- SPEECH
- SUPERNATURAL EFFECT
- SOLILOQUY
- IDENTITY CHANGE
- SONG
- NOT DEAD AFTER ALL
- PLAY-WITHIN-A-PLAY
- DEATH

John Shakespeare and Mary Arden's impressive house on Henley Street in Stratford-upon-Avon is better known today as Shakespeare's birthplace.

The Life of WILLIAM SHAKESPEARE

RARELY HAS SO MUCH BEEN WRITTEN about a man about whom so little is known. Indeed, biographers are forced to invent their own Shakespeare, just as he created characters on stage. The extreme position is that "Shakespeare" was not written by Shakespeare at all, but by another author who preferred to hide his name. Yet even scholars, theatergoers and readers who revere the poet-playwright called William Shakespeare feel a need to seek out the secret Shakespeare: Shakespeare the hidden Catholic, the closet gay, the misogynist, the revolutionary, the racist, the imperialist. The secret of Shakespeare's universal appeal is far simpler: he serves as a mirror in which human beings see themselves. In the 18th century, Samuel Johnson put it elegantly: "His Works may be considered a Map of Life."

GIVEN THE FEW available facts about Shakespeare's life and personality, it is inevitable that biographers should fill the gaps with deduction, speculation, and imagination. Many scan his plays for clues to his life: for instance, they say, to write so convinignly about nature, he must have explored the fields and forests surrounding the small town of Stratford-upon-Avon where he was born. But nothing can explain his genius.

The "Chandos Portrait" is one of several paintings which are believed to portray likenesses of William Shakespeare, though none has been verified beyond all doubt.

SHAKESPEARE'S CHILDHOOD

The proven facts about Shakespeare's early years all come from church documents. Parish records indicate that he was baptized in Holy Trinity Church in Stratford on April 26, 1564, close enough to April 23 to give rise to the legend that he was born on St. George's Day. The next reference to him comes on November 28, 1582, when the Bishop of Winchester granted him dispensation to marry Anne Hathaway, who was eight years his senior. Six months later, on May 26, 1583, they baptized their first child, Susanna, in Holy Trinity Church, where they also baptized their new-born twins, Judith and Hamnet, on February 2, 1585.

More can be deduced about Shakespeare's childhood from records about his father. The son of a farmer, John Shakespeare was raised in

Little documentary evidence exists about Shakespeare's early life in Stratford, but it is reasonable to assume that he started earning his keep by helping in his father's glove-making business.

the village of Snitterfield. In 1550, when he was around 20, he moved to nearby Stratford to start a glove-making business. It must have prospered, because in 1556 he bought the house on Henley Street known today as Shakespeare's birthplace.

The following year, John married Mary Arden, the daughter of a wealthy local landowner. The couple's first two daughters died in infancy, but these were followed by William, three more sons, and two daughters. John also became something of a local worthy: in 1557, he joined the town council, rising to the position of high bailiff in 1568.

A classroom at Stratford grammar school. It may have been here that Shakespeare received a grounding in Latin, used by the Roman writers who strongly influenced both his dramatic and narrative works.

Shakespeare could have done worse. He was raised in a comfortable home in a prosperous town of some 1,500 people, its thriving market the main outlet for farming products in all of central Warwickshire. Stratford also had a grammar school, or secondary school, with a reputation for excellence thanks to a teaching staff of Oxford graduates. No extant document links Shakespeare to any school, but it seems reasonable to suppose that, after learning to read and write at "petty" school, he attended the grammar school.

At the age of 15 or 16, good students from wealthy families would move on to Oxford or Cambridge universities. Shakespeare did not, an omission that university-educated rival playwrights never allowed him to forget. What he did when he left school is not known for certain. By then, around 1579 or 1580, records show that his father's fortunes had turned sour. Heavily in debt, John Shakespeare had stopped attending the town council and was embroiled in various lawsuits. Under such circumstances, young William presumably started earning his keep. He was certainly living in Stratford in 1582, when Anne Hathaway was carrying their first child. And he was present for the birth of his children in 1583 and 1585. How, then, did Shakespeare find himself a rising star in London's theater world in 1592?

Then, the whining schoolboy, with his satchel/ And shining morning face, creeping like snail/ Unwillingly to school...

As You Like It, 2.7

The Lost Years

The undocumented period of Shakespeare's life, from 1585 to 1592, is known as the "lost years," but there is also a mystery about what Shakespeare was up to before then, in his late teens. Did he, like many young men of his day, spend time fighting the Spanish occupation of the Low Countries? Did he work as a lawyer's clerk? There is one legend that he was caught stealing a deer from a wealthy squire and was forced to flee town.

Certain biographers have argued that, although the Protestant regime was persecuting Roman Catholics, John Shakespeare remained a secret Catholic. Some of the grammar school teachers were also recusant Catholics from Lancashire in northern England. A case is made that Shakespeare was sent as a tutor to the home of Alexander Hoghton who, in a will dated

August 3, 1581, asked his neighbor, Sir Thomas Hesketh, to be friendly to one "William Shakeshafte."

In 1575, when Shakespeare was just 11, there was a great occasion: a visit by Queen Elizabeth to Kenilworth Castle, near Stratford, where the Earl of Leicester organized three weeks of festivities to celebrate her birthday. These included a water-pageant in the castle's lake in which Arion rode a dolphin's back. A line in *Twelfth Night*, "Like Arion on the dolphin's back," suggests that young Shakespeare attended the pageant. More importantly, among well established theater groups visiting Stratford were Lord Strange's Men in 1579, the Earl of Essex's Men in 1584 and the Queen's Men in 1587. Could Shakespeare have gone to London with one of these companies?

Some literary detectives conjecture that to create a character like the disreputable Falstaff, Shakespeare must have frequented London's taverns.

POET AND PLAYWRIGHT

The first reference to Shakespeare in London in 1592 indicates clearly that he was already making his mark as a playwright, which implies that he had been working as an actor for some time before trying his hand at writing. By 1592, he had probably completed his tetralogy on the Wars of the Roses as well as *The Two Gentlemen of Verona*. He had also awakened the envy of Robert Greene, an embittered writer who in *Groatsworth of Wit Bought with a Million of Repentance* warned three fellow playwrights, Christopher Marlowe, George Peele, and Thomas Nashe, against the uneducated newcomer who was invading their turf: "There is an upstart crow, beautified with our feathers, that with his "Tiger's heart wrapt in a player's hide" supposes he is well able to bombast out blank verse as the best of you; and being an absolute *Johannes factotum*, is in his own conceit the only Shake-scene in a country." Greene died soon afterward but his publisher, Henrye Chettle, apologized to Shakespeare, noting "his uprightedness of dealing, which argues his honesty, and his facetious grace in writing, that approves his art."

Bands of strolling players frequently toured the countryside, complementing the celebrations, parades, and performances that took place routinely on feast days.

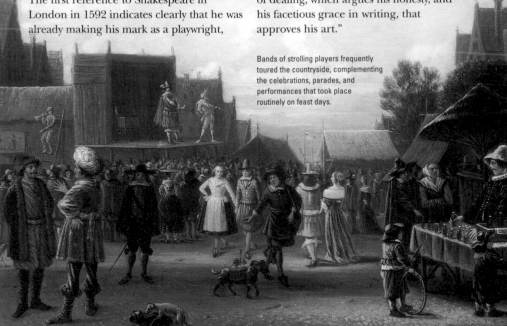

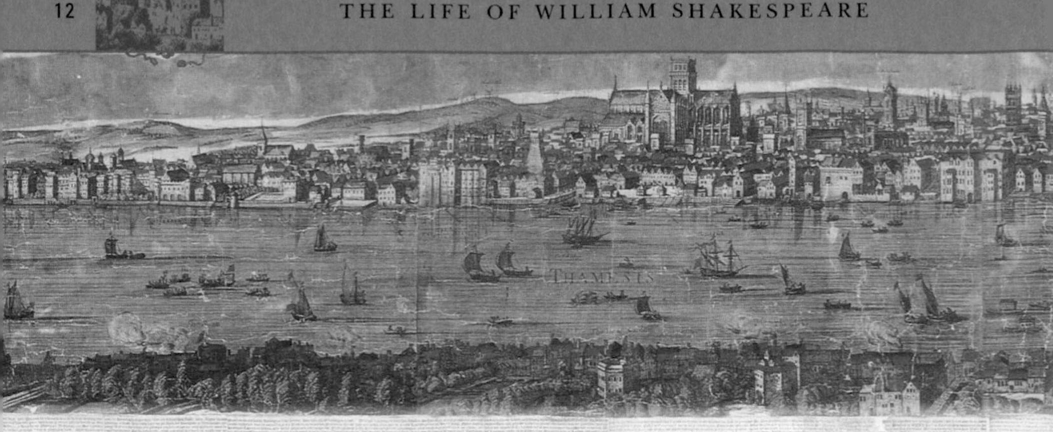

When Shakespeare arrived in London sometime before 1592, London Bridge was the only means of land transport across the River Thames. Queen Elizabeth and her court would have used boats and barges to travel between her palaces at Whitehall and Greenwich.

Shakespeare was only one of scores of playwrights trying to satisfy the needs of the new permanent theaters that had recently been built in London. Shakespeare, though, was apparently quickly noticed, as his early plays were presented at the Rose, London's most popular theater in the early 1590's. Another sign that he was faring well was that the Rose's owner, Philip Henslowe, reported a good take for "harey the vi"—one of the *Henry VI* plays—on March 3, 1592.

That summer, an outbreak of the plague prompted many theater companies to resume their tours of the provinces. Shakespeare chose not to join them, instead trying his hand at poetry. His good fortune was to find a patron in Henry Wriothesley, 3rd Earl of Southampton, to whom he dedicated two long narrative poems, *Venus and Adonis* and *The Rape of Lucrece*, both of which were quickly published.

Success in London

By the fall of 1594, the plague had abated. Some players found a new patron in Henry Carey, Baron Hunsdon, the new Lord Chamberlain. In October that year, the Lord Chamberlain's Men was founded, its shareholders including Shakespeare and his actor friends Will Kemp and Richard Burbage. For the rest of Shakespeare's career as an actor and playwright he belonged to this company, which was soon considered London's best (it became the King's Men after James I succeeded Elizabeth in 1603). Not reputed to be a great actor, Shakespeare focused on play-writing.

In the 1590's, Shakespeare devoted himself principally to history plays and comedies, yet little is known of his personal life. With lodgings in Bishopsgate near the Theatre playhouse, Shakespeare was well settled in London. He presumably returned to Stratford when his only son, Hamnet, died and was buried on August 11, 1596. But, with the

Outbreaks of plague often forced the closure of London's theaters. During one such closure in 1592, Shakespeare chose to gamble on becoming a poet, a profession that enjoyed greater esteem than that of a playwright.

In 1596 Shakespeare obtained the coat-of-arms his father had failed to receive 27 years earlier. His chosen motto: *Non Sanz Droict* ("Not Without Right").

Lord Chamberlain's Men frequently invited to perform before Queen Elizabeth, his stature as a playwright was growing. As a shareholder in the Lord Chamberlain's Men, he was also for the first time making money; soon he had bought New Place, one of Stratford's grandest houses, and his wife and two daughters moved there from Henley Street.

A key turning point came in 1599, with the opening of the Globe, near the Rose and Swan theaters. It was soon recognized as London's best playhouse, with space for over 2,000 spectators. Over the next decade, almost all of Shakespeare's new plays were presented at the Globe. In Richard Burbage, he also had an actor capable of handling the great tragic roles he would soon write.

The Jacobean Era

In March 1603, Queen Elizabeth died and was succeeded by James VI of Scotland, who became James I of England. For the Lord Chamberlain's Men, this also brought change. Shakespeare and his colleagues had performed regularly before Elizabeth at her palaces at Greenwich and Whitehall, but they were to prove even more popular with James. Just days after he succeeded to the throne, he adopted the Lord Chamberlain's Men. During Elizabeth's last nine years, the Lord Chamberlain's Men performed at court 32 times, roughly three times per year; between 1603 and Shakespeare's death in 1616, as the King's Men, his company appeared before James on 177 occasions, more than all other troupes put together.

Since the King's Men continued to perform almost daily at the Globe, this royal appetite added to the pressure on its writers. A fresh outbreak of the plague closed theaters for much of 1603, but Shakespeare kept working, producing an average of two new plays a year. With his monumental *Hamlet* in 1600–01, he began turning his energy toward tragedies. In an explosion of creativity between 1604 and 1607, he wrote *Othello*, *King Lear*, and *Macbeth*, which, with *Hamlet*, are considered the pinnacles of his genius.

What cause prompted this shift toward these dark explorations of the human soul? Some biographers suggest that his father's death in 1601 or perhaps his own 40th birthday in 1604 brought on a life crisis that stirred new intimations of

SEDUCER?

John Manningham, a law student, is the source of a perhaps apocryphal story that a spectator, taking a liking to Burbage as Richard III, invited him to visit her later. Shakespeare went first to the woman's home. When Burbage arrived, "message being brought that Richard III was at the door, Shakespeare caused return to be made that William the Conqueror was before Richard the Third."

mortality. Others speculate that years of hard living in London, far from his family, spawned a sense of personal failure. He was not, however, the only playwright to turn his pen to tragedies under King James.

Shakespeare was now at the height of his fame and fortune. But documentary evidence of his life is still minimal. There is one record that Shakespeare and Ben Jonson engaged in public "wit-combats" in taverns. Some references survive of performances of his plays at court, at Gray's Inn or at the Globe. Most other records of Shakespeare's life are more mundane. Thanks to a law suit a decade later, it is known that from 1604 he was lodging with a family called Mountjoy on Silver Street in Cripplegate, north of St. Paul's Cathedral. Property records suggest he travelled frequently to Stratford; he was investing heavily in farming land near the town. On these trips, he would often spend a night at Oxford with his old London friends, John and Jeannette Davenant; he was also godfather to their son, William (decades later, Sir William Davenant, himself a prominent writer, liked to hint that Shakespeare was his real father).

He was a man, take him for all in all/ I shall not look upon his like again...

Hamlet, 1.2

These gardens are the site of New Place in Stratford, the house in which Shakespeare spent his final years.

The Final Plays

From 1608, the King's Men recovered the lease for the main hall of the old Dominican monastery at Blackfriars, which had been used by "boy companies." The theaters had the same repertoires, but Blackfriars offered exciting new staging possibilities, which probably suited what became known as Shakespeare's romances, plays like *The Winter's Tale* and *The Tempest* that were rife with magic, storms, and divine interventions.

The Tempest, first performed before King James in November 1611, is thought to be the last play that Shakespeare wrote on his own. Indeed, it is tempting to see Prospero's Epilogue as Shakespeare's own farewell to the stage. Property records and lawsuits over debts place him in Stratford from 1612, but he returned frequently to London. He was there for the wedding of James's daughter, Elizabeth, in February 1613, when several of his plays were presented. The following month, he bought the gatehouse of the former Blackfriars monastery, and perhaps lived there. That year, he also collaborated with John Fletcher, the new chief playwright of the King's Men, in writing *Cardenio* (now lost), *Henry VIII,* and *The Two Noble Kinsmen,* which contain only flashes of Shakespeare at his best. *Henry VIII* would be remembered as the play that set fire to and destroyed the Globe on June 29, 1613.

Return to Stratford

The Globe was rebuilt, but the fire marks Shakespeare's break with the King's Men. While he visited London in 1614, everything suggests that he had finally made New Place in Stratford his permanent home. There are

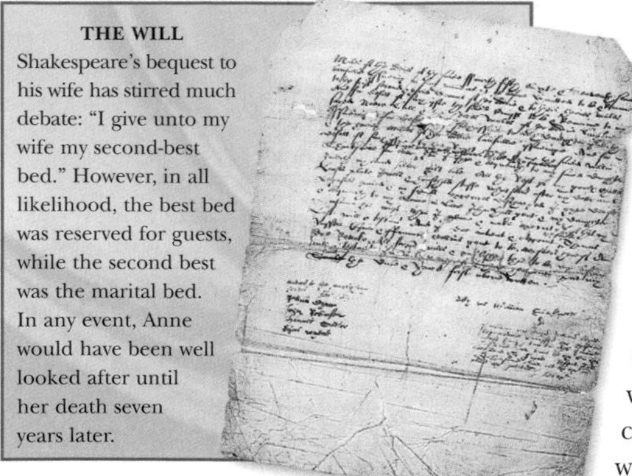

THE WILL
Shakespeare's bequest to his wife has stirred much debate: "I give unto my wife my second-best bed." However, in all likelihood, the best bed was reserved for guests, while the second best was the marital bed. In any event, Anne would have been well looked after until her death seven years later.

records of property deals and of a complex dispute related to demarcation of farming land. For the first time, perhaps reluctantly, he also became a family man. In June 1607, his eldest daughter, Susanna, had married a local doctor, John Hall, and seven months later they gave him his first grandchild, Elizabeth. His other daughter, Judith, now 31, lived at home until she finally met Thomas Quiney, a local vintner of some disrepute five years her junior. They were married at Holy Trinity Church on February 10, 1616. Shakespeare's fellow playwrights, Ben Jonson and Michael Drayton, attended the celebrations.

Ten weeks later, on April 23, 1616, St. George's Day, Shakespeare was dead. The only records of his illness link it to festivities at the wedding. A year after his death, Dr. Hall suggested his father-in-law drank too much at the wedding, "sweated in a hot room, walked out hatless and cloakless" and caught a chill. "A quick attack of pneumonia, which his son-in-law's emetics and electuaries would do nothing to relieve, was enough to affect his quietus." This explanation was evidently widely accepted. A half-century later, John Ward, a local doctor, wrote: "Shakespeare, Drayton, and Ben Jonson, had a merry meeting, and it seems drank too much, for Shakespeare died of a fever there contracted."

Shakespeare was not unprepared. Six months earlier, he had made a will, which in March 1616 he revised to take account of Judith's marriage and, in effect, to reduce her legacy. He looked after his family, but clearly favored Susanna: she inherited New Place and many other properties, while Judith received some money. He also gave money and objects to friends in Stratford as well as to his three closest King's Men colleagues, Richard Burbage, John Hemminge, and Henry Condell.

Shakespeare was buried beneath the stone floor of Holy Trinity Church, where he had been baptized 52 years earlier.

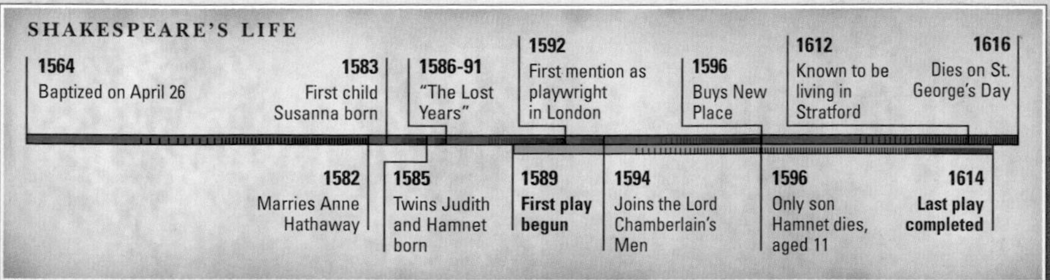
SHAKESPEARE'S LIFE
1564
Baptized on April 26
1583
First child Susanna born
1586-91
"The Lost Years"
1592
First mention as playwright in London
1596
Buys New Place
1612
Known to be living in Stratford
1616
Dies on St. George's Day
1582
Marries Anne Hathaway
1585
Twins Judith and Hamnet born
1589
First play begun
1594
Joins the Lord Chamberlain's Men
1596
Only son Hamnet dies, aged 11
1614
Last play completed

GOOD FREND FOR IESVS SAKE FORBEARE,
TO DIGG THE DVST ENCLOASED HEARE.
BLESE BE Y MAN Y SPARES THES STONES
AND CVRST BE HE Y MOVES MY BONES.

It is said that, in a moment of levity some years before his death, Shakespeare himself wrote the epitaph inscribed on his tomb.

Under Elizabeth I, England not only earned new respect in Europe when it defeated Spain's 'invincible' Armada in 1588, but it also began eyeing potential colonies in the New World and exploring lands and markets in the East.

SHAKESPEARE *in his* TIME

SHAKESPEARE'S LIFETIME COINCIDES with a remarkable period of English history. The flowering of dramatic literature in the late 16th-century was just one signal of the country's new sophistication. Under Elizabeth I, as change became the leitmotif of the times, England crossed the bridge from medieval to modern society. London emerged as a vibrant metropolis, its bustling economic, political, and cultural life a magnet for migrants. New paths of social mobility were opened by the weakening of baronial fiefdoms and the consolidation of Protestantism. Scientific discoveries and a publishing boom expanded the horizons of knowledge, while a powerful merchant class started trading far beyond England's shores. In a strikingly short period, a backward and underpopulated island began its transformation into a global power.

ELIZABETH WAS NOT GROOMED to become queen. When her father, Henry VIII, died in 1547, the crown passed to her half-brother, Edward VI, who was ten at the time and would die six years later. The Duke of Northumberland then maneuvered to install his daughter-in-law, Lady Jane Grey, Henry VIII's great-niece, but her reign lasted only nine days. The country rallied instead to Elizabeth's older half-sister, Mary. During Mary Tudor's reign, Catholicism was restored and Protestants were persecuted. Mary even briefly imprisoned Elizabeth on false charges of plotting. In 1556, aged 40 and still hoping to produce a Catholic heir, Mary married Philip II of Spain. But she died two years later and Elizabeth assumed the throne. Few would have gambled that she would rule England for the next 45 years.

Just 25 when she acceeded to the English throne, Elizabeth was well-educated and said to be fluent in six languages, but she had spent her life in reclusion and had no experience of government.

The queen repeatedly proved her mettle in times of crisis, but her reign was disturbed by food riots, outbreaks of the plague, Catholic and other conspiracies, threats of invasion by both Spain and France, war in the Netherlands, trouble in Ireland, and mounting anxiety that the unmarried queen had no heir. That Elizabeth survived all this *and* strengthened the monarchy is a measure of her political and diplomatic skills, her devotion to duty, and her resolute personality. Visiting troops preparing to confront the Spanish Armada, she told them: "I know I have the body of a weak and feeble woman, but I have the heart and stomach of a king, and a King of England too."

Religious Strife

Religion demanded Elizabeth's immediate attention. Henry VIII had rebelled against Rome, prompted by the Vatican's refusal to approve his divorce from Catherine of Aragon, but he felt little sympathy for the radical Protestant message expounded by Martin Luther. Under Edward VI, the Church became more openly Protestant, with religious statues and stained-glass windows often destroyed as symbols of Catholicism. Then, after Mary's violent lurch back to Catholicism, Elizabeth immediately restored Protestantism and formalized the new Church of England. The Act of Supremacy of 1559 made her its titular head, while church doctrine was enunciated in the 39 Articles of 1563. Elizabeth's approach was more moderate than that of Edward. Her Anglican Church was a hybrid between Roman Catholicism and northern European Protestantism, a "broad church" born of a political and religious need for compromise.

The Puritans were particularly noted for their strict moral beliefs. Among their strongholds was the City of London, which in due course banned all theatrical performances as sinful.

For much of Elizabeth's reign, though, England's religious landscape was confused. Some regions—and some nobility—remained devoutly Catholic, while even those who accepted the break with Rome often continued to follow Catholic rituals. In some counties, not least Shakespeare's native Warwickshire, Catholics were actively persecuted, with hefty fines imposed on those who failed to attend Anglican services. At the other extreme were the Puritans, who considered the Church of England's structure and doctrine still too close to that of Rome. Alarmed by the religious wars raging in France, however, Elizabeth worked hard to preserve the fragile armistice between Catholics, Anglicans, and Puritans. Wisely, Shakespeare steered clear of religion in his plays.

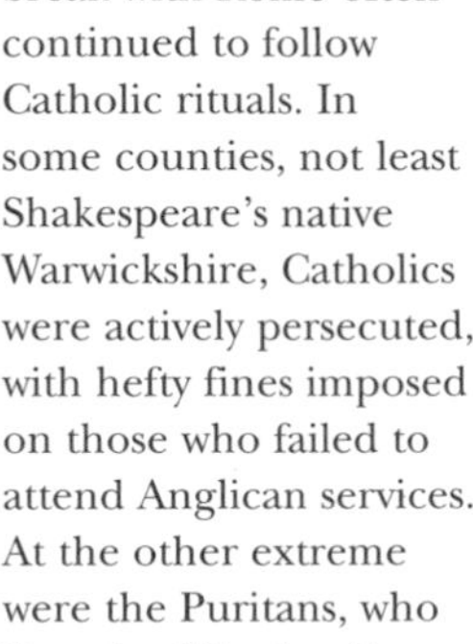

In 16th century Europe, politics revolved around court life. In England, leading nobles would curry Elizabeth's favor, though true favorites also assumed risks.

Domestic Affairs

A Parliament formed by commoners, albeit landed gentry, had authority to approve taxes, but Elizabeth called it into session only 16 times during her long reign. She governed through a handful of key advisers, notably Lord Burghley as Secretary of State, Sir Christopher Hatton as Lord Chancellor, and Sir Francis Walsingham as chief spymaster. Her administration numbered no more than 600 officials, with another 600 or so managing the Crown lands that financed the court. There was no standing army, so money had to be raised for every expeditionary force. Without a powerful centralized state, much of England was self-governed. The authority of the aristocracy stemmed from its ownership of land worked by peasants or tenant farmers. Law and order were maintained by sheriffs, Justices of the Peace, and an efficient court system.

The country as a whole was poor and, with around three million inhabitants at the time of Shakespeare's birth, sparsely populated. Apart from London, only three other cities had more than 10,000 inhabitants (Stratford-upon-Avon had some 1,500). During much of Elizabeth's reign, the economy fared badly, weakened by inflation, food shortages, and high rents for farming land.

Elizabeth could do little about this. There was no national economy as such: there were simply socioeconomic strata. Yet, unlike today's rulers, Elizabeth's popularity was detached from the state of the economy. Even as many of her subjects suffered, she personified success and stability. Variously hailed as "Gloriana," "Good Queen Bess," and "The Virgin Queen," she regularly traveled the country on tours known as "progresses," riding on horseback and wearing the finest trappings of royalty. With each trip, her image was reinforced.

Most of the British population lived in market towns and small farming communities, which were vulnerable to bad harvests. Northern England was shaken by food riots in 1569–70 and again in 1597.

Urban Life

Change was most apparent in London, with migration from the countryside and from Europe more than doubling its population to 200,000 during Elizabeth's reign. The walled City of London was a warren of narrow streets and dirty alleys, a perfect breeding ground for the plague epidemics of 1564, 1592–93, 1603, and 1623. But London's inhabitants were now also settling outside the city, encroaching on farming land to the north and occupying the south bank of the Thames River at Southwark, home to bear- and bull-baiting, and dog- and cock-fighting.

Not all the water in the rough rude sea/ Can wash the balm off from an anointed king…

Richard II, 3.2

Freed from the strictures of Catholicism, cultural life blossomed. Centered around the book stores located in the courtyard of St. Paul's Cathedral, publishing expanded rapidly, with the poetry of Sir Philip Sidney and Edmund Spenser reaching a wide public, and many European classics available for the first time in translation. In 1576, construction of the city's first permanent theater turned theatergoing into an important

During Elizabeth's reign, England began amassing a commercial empire which accelerated the growth of the nation's shipping and trading companies.

new form of public entertainment, with Shakespeare one of scores of playwrights keeping London's stages busy. What gave Elizabethan theater its political and social weight, though, was that it cut across class lines: the same play performed before the queen in Whitehall would be seen by rich merchants and down-at-heel "groundlings" at the Globe Theatre.

Foreign Affairs

London's new prosperity also began affecting England's relations with the world. The loss of Calais in 1558 and the failed attempt to recover it in 1562 symbolized the end of England's territorial ambitions in France. Far more important now was Antwerp, the Flemish port through which English wool merchants exported their goods to Europe. It was the need to keep this port open that led England to support recurrent Dutch efforts to drive the Spanish occupiers out of the Netherlands. For the first time, England showed a readiness to use military force to defend its economic welfare, proof that it now saw foreign trade as a key to its prosperity. The blending of England's foreign policy with its commercial interests became even more apparent with the formation of the English East India Company in 1600. Created to give England a share of the East Indian spice trade, it was soon drawn into politics and, by the 18th century, was forging the British Empire in Asia.

Age cannot wither her/ Nor custom stale her infinite variety...

Antony and Cleopatra, 2.2

However, while English buccaneers and explorers, like Sir Francis Drake, Sir Walter Raleigh, and Humphrey Gilbert, operated freely in both West and East Indies, Elizabeth managed England's relations with Europe. Commercial interests were certainly a factor when it came to keeping Antwerp open to English exports, but the queen's attention was more consumed by three seemingly domestic issues—England's religion, her own possible marriage, and the succession—in which continental Europe's dynasties kept interfering.

When Elizabeth came to the throne, Philip II of Spain ruled a gigantic empire comprising much of Italy, part of France, most of the Americas, the Netherlands, and Spain itself. He had also taken it upon himself to stop the expansion of Protestantism. As Mary Tudor's widower, he proposed marriage to Elizabeth, believing that their heir would return England to Catholicism, but he was rebuffed. England's Catholicism again became an issue in 1570 when Pope Pius V excommunicated Elizabeth and, 10 years later, when Pope Gregory XIII decreed that she could be murdered as a heretic.

Meanwhile, at least in part because of the activities of English privateers, relations with Spain deteriorated to the point of open war in 1585. England was ill-prepared for a lengthy conflict in the

Netherlands, but its navy was well-equipped. In 1588, when Philip prepared to invade England with a huge naval force bolstered by troops from the Netherlands, English warships defeated the Spanish Armada in the English Channel. The war would continue sporadically for another 15 years, with Spain launching new armadas, England raiding ports in Spain and Spanish-ruled Portugal, and with Spain establishing a beachhead in Ireland for a fresh invasion attempt. But England was no longer easily intimidated.

SIR FRANCIS DRAKE

The methods employed by England to promote its foreign interests were close to impudent. As early as 1572, Elizabeth gave Sir Francis Drake a privateering commission. In other words, she authorized a private fleet of warships to plunder Spanish ships carrying New World riches to Spain. Six years later, when Drake set off on his round-the-world voyage, his purpose was to discover new markets and sign trading treaties. And, again, Drake was free to take the law into his own hands.

Mary, Queen of Scots

England was also threatened by France which, like Spain, seemed intent on restoring Catholicism in England. France's campaign was built around the claim of Mary Stuart, Queen of Scots, to the English throne through her Tudor grandmother, Henry VIII's sister. When Mary Tudor was succeeded by Elizabeth, the French king, Henry II, claimed the English throne for his daughter-in-law.

Mary represented a palpable Catholic threat. Her marriage to a cousin, Henry Stewart, Earl of Darnley, set in motion the events that would lead to her overthrow. After they had a child in 1566, Mary embarked on an adulterous affair with the Earl of Bothwell who, it is said, arranged Darnley's murder in February 1567. Three months later, she married Bothwell, but she was immediately deposed by the Protestant lords who named her baby son, James, in her place. In May 1568, Mary fled to England and sought the protection of her cousin, Elizabeth I, who promptly imprisoned her. But Mary soon became the focus of English plotting to restore Catholicism. A serious plot in 1586, in which Mary was implicated, finally convinced Elizabeth that her Scottish cousin had to die. Even then, wary of the precedent of executing legitimate monarchs, she hesitated before ordering Mary beheaded and, in a letter to Mary's son, James VI of Scotland, she expressed grief over her action.

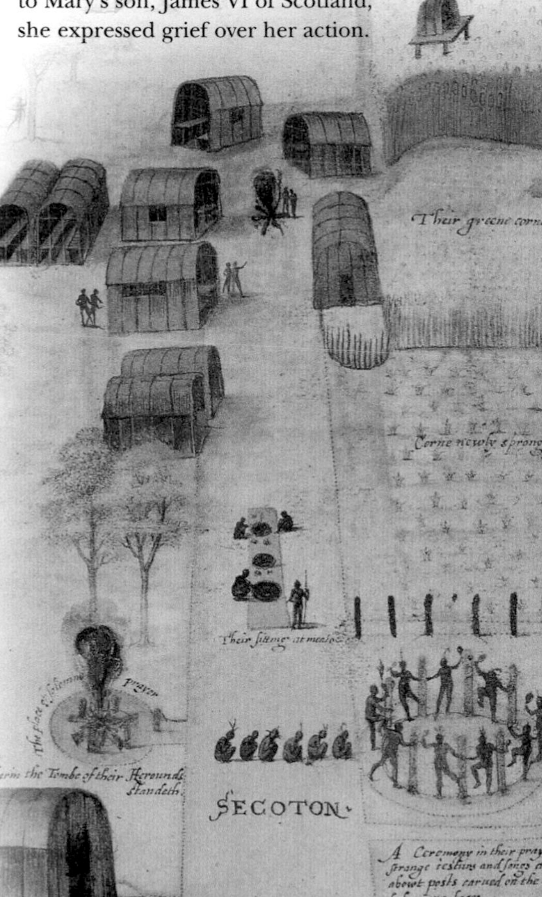

English exploration and exploitation of the East and West Indies began in earnest during the reign of Elizabeth. The artist and explorer John White made numerous expeditions to the New World, during which he made many sketches of the native peoples, flora, and fauna.

Elizabeth's Last Years

It would be one of many letters that she exchanged with James, who inherited Mary's claim to the English throne and who would eventually become Elizabeth's successor. By then, the English queen was in her mid-forties and still unmarried. After the proposal from Philip II of Spain, she received marriage offers from several foreign kings and princes, including the Archduke Charles of Austria; Erik XIV of Sweden; Henry Duke of Anjou (later Henry III of France); and François, Duke of Alençon. She turned them all down. Despite her undisguised affection for Robert Dudley, Earl of Leicester, she also refused to contemplate marrying an English noble. Everything suggests that she believed any marriage would both weaken her power and create unnecessary conflicts: a foreign consort could draw England into European disputes; an English consort would create fierce rivalries within the nobility. Fearing a chaotic succession and a return to Catholicism, the English Parliament frequently urged her to marry and produce an heir. Similarly, Shakespeare's history plays, written in the 1590's, constantly evoke the perils of uncertain successions and the need for English unity. Even as Elizabeth's power waned in her final years, she refused to name a successor until she was on her deathbed. But the warm welcome given in 1603 to James VI of Scotland as James I of England helped to insure a smooth transition.

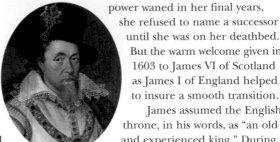

After the supremely regal Elizabeth, James cut an unimpressive figure, clever yet strangely undignified.

James assumed the English throne, in his words, as "an old and experienced king." During his childhood, Scotland was governed by a succession of powerful regents, but by the time James was 16 he had assumed real power and, in the two decades that followed, proved to be a skilled and conciliatory monarch. He appointed himself head of the Presbyterian church, but he was tolerant of Catholic factions among the Scottish nobility. Even before the execution of his mother, Mary Queen of Scots, he cultivated Elizabeth with a view to succeeding her, thus ensuring peace between England and Scotland.

England Under James I

Yet James was to prove a far less successful English ruler than he had been king of Scotland. He quickly and wisely made peace with Spain, but he was far less adept at managing his relations with Parliament than he had been in controlling the Scottish nobility. He inherited an economic crisis as well as a crown badly indebted by the war with Spain. When Parliament refused to approve new taxes, he stirred hostility by imposing new customs duties. Further, by ignoring Parliament and ruling through a series of unpopular favorites, he

James I was forced to clamp down on Catholic dissidents after the Gunpowder Plot in 1605, when his court narrowly escaped being blown up during a visit to Parliament. The Catholic plotters were hanged, drawn and quartered.

alienated both the House of Commons and the House of Lords, setting the stage for the parliamentary rebellion against his son, Charles I, in 1642. James's nickname, "the wisest fool in Christendom," was well earned.

His own personality did not help. He had a strong Scottish accent, walked with a shuffling gait, reportedly never bathed, and was a fervent believer in the power of witchcraft. After he and his Danish-born queen, Anne, began hosting extravagant parties at Whitehall, he also earned a reputation for decadence. These parties, which often included performances of plays, were good news for the King's Men: plays by Shakespeare and other writers were presented at court on average once a month. But, with the economy doing poorly, such excesses did not help James's image. Puritans were also offended by his undisguised affection for handsome young men, some of whom later became powerful favorites.

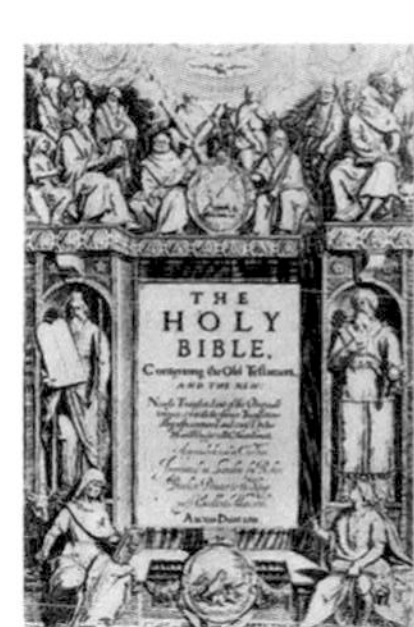
THE
HOLY
BIBLE,
As a sacred work from the same period as the writings of Shakespeare, the King James version of the Bible illustrates the rich language used by Jacobean writers.

Still, James was not without his merits. He kept England out of the Thirty Years War in Europe and averted any religious conflict at home. He also sponsored one of the most important books ever published in the English language, the King James Bible, personally approving the 47 scholars who spent seven years preparing the translation. Published in 1611, this "authorized version" became the standard English-language text for the Bible for well over three centuries.

Shakespeare in His Time

While Shakespeare was a product of this era, however, he was never a chronicler of his times. The traumas of royal succession recorded in his history plays may have echoed concerns about Elizabeth's own succession; the bucolic world evoked in some of his comedies is perhaps Elizabethan; his tragedies mirror the country's darkening mood after James came to the throne; and his romances certainly include magical and supernatural effects pleasing to James and Jacobean audiences. But few contemporary references are found in Shakespeare's plays. For his plots, the playwright drew freely on earlier writers and earlier epochs.

In other ways, though, Shakespeare did speak for his age. By mirroring the turbulence, innovation, excitement, and soul-searching of a fast-changing society, he captured the new theatricality of English life. Using his uniquely sonorous language and exceptional dramatic skills, he portrayed the English inventing new roles for themselves in their search for a modern identity. Yet if Shakespeare's influence far outlived his era, it is also because he could see beyond Elizabethan and Jacobean England to the enduring quandaries of human existence. If the words and predicaments of his characters still move people throughout the world, it is because, in Ben Jonson's phrase, "he was not of an age, but for all time!"

HISTORIC TIMELINE
1558 Mary I dies; Elizabeth I becomes queen
1564 Birth of Shakespeare
1566 Birth of James VI of Scotland, later James I of England
1572 Sir Francis Drake is given privateering commission
1587 Mary Queen of Scots is executed
1588 English forces defeat the Spanish Armada
1589 First play begun
1603 Elizabeth I dies; James I accedes to the throne
1605 The Gunpowder Plot
1611 King James Bible is published
1614 Last play completed
1616 Shakespeare's death
1625 James I dies; Charles I becomes king

Shakespeare's Globe on Bankside in London is a modern recreation of the Globe of Elizabethan times, with its apron stage, galleries, and open arena.

ELIZABETHAN *and Jacobean* THEATER

SHAKESPEARE THE PLAYWRIGHT was born of the extraordinary popularity of theater during the reigns of Elizabeth I and James I. Although recognized by his peers as his generation's best dramatist, he was hardly a solitary figure. He was preceded by Christopher Marlowe and was followed by Ben Jonson. He also had many contemporaries whose fame did not last: John Lyly, Thomas Kyd, Robert Greene, George Chapman, John Marston, John Ford, Thomas Middleton, John Fletcher, and Francis Beaumont. According to one study, during Shakespeare's years in London as many as 300 playwrights were at work, kept alive by a constant demand for their material from London's newly established permanent theaters. In this competitive atmosphere, playwrights assumed a status they had never known before in England.

Previously, the art of theater was practised by university students performing before private audiences, and by itinerant players traveling the country. Since their audience changed almost daily, they could make do with two or three plays, but once they settled into a permanent theater, they needed a more varied program.

Prehistory of English Theater

The Elizabethan theater's roots lay in the Middle Ages. From the 11th century, the church encouraged congregations to put on miracle plays recounting the lives of favorite saints. Then, in the 14th century, a different genre appeared in the form of mystery plays that enacted Biblical stories such as the Crucifixion. In time, the mystery plays turned into lavish street spectacles sponsored by local guilds. However, considered too Catholic after the Protestant Reformation, they were banned in the mid-16th century.

By then, morality plays were all the rage in England. These plays portrayed the perennial battle between good and evil. Virtue naturally triumphed over Vice, but a vast range of subjects could be tackled using allegorical devices. Itinerant actors often performed before noisy crowds in the courtyards of inns, but some troupes also appeared in guild halls, inns of court, and private homes in London. From the 1560s, some were formed by wealthy nobles and even by the monarch, whose names they

Performed annually during the feast of Corpus Christi, mystery plays provided religious instruction in English to townsfolk who could not understand the Latin Mass.

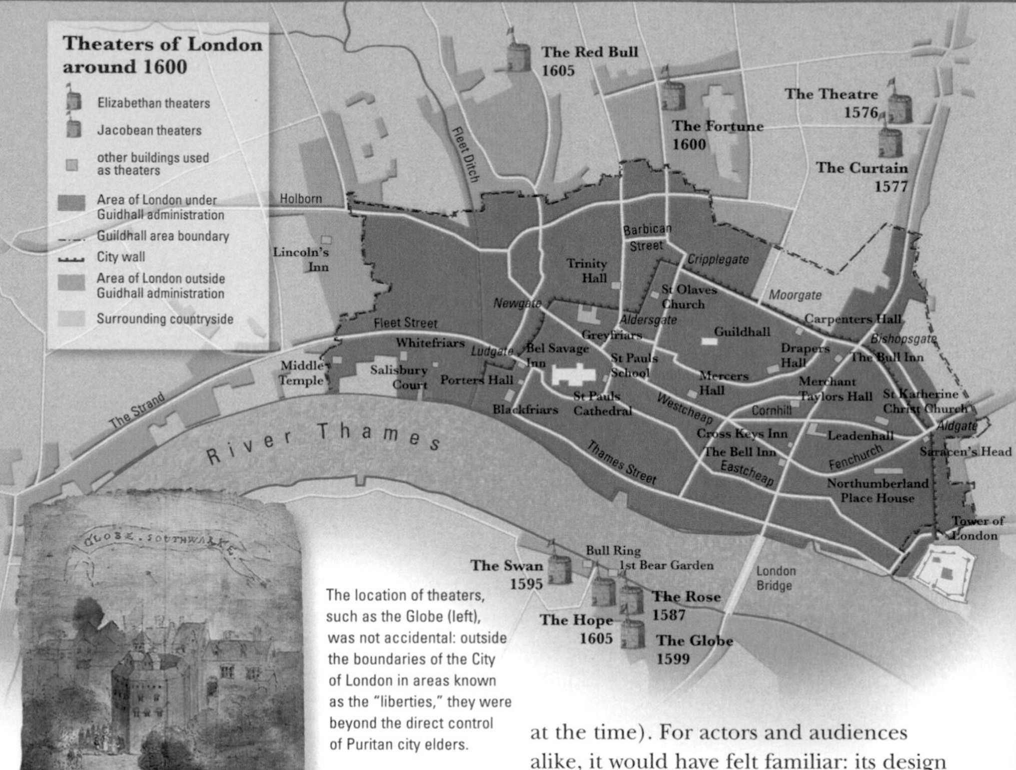

The location of theaters, such as the Globe (left), was not accidental: outside the boundaries of the City of London in areas known as the "liberties," they were beyond the direct control of Puritan city elders.

adopted. When they toured the provinces, they could now boast of being, say, the Queen's Men or the Earl of Derby's Players. Some actors tried their hand at writing, and plays began to move beyond the narrow focus of morality plays. Quite separately, a group of graduates from Oxford and Cambridge, the so-called "University Wits," began writing plays for the informal London theater circuit.

The Theater Districts

In 1576 Elizabethan drama entered an entirely new era. James Burbage, a prosperous joiner, built a theater in the style of an amphitheater near Bishopsgate in London and called it the Theatre (the word "theater" was not in common usage at the time). For actors and audiences alike, it would have felt familiar: its design was inspired by the courtyards of country inns that had long served as temporary theaters. Within a year, the Curtain opened nearby, giving London its first modest theater district. Later, two other theaters opened north of the City of London: the Fortune in 1600 and the Red Bull in 1605. By then, another theater district had appeared on the south bank of the Thames on Bankside with the opening of the Rose in 1587, the Swan in 1595, the Globe in 1599, and the Hope in 1605. Smaller indoor playhouses were also established in the former monasteries of Blackfriars and Whitefriars, where popular children's theater groups performed. In 1608, Blackfriars was taken over by Shakespeare's own company.

Puritan city elders regarded theaters as cradles of vice, and actors as unrepentant low-lifes. No new play could be performed without the consent of the Master of the

The Swan had a typical apron stage, partly covered by a roof, that thrust out into the arena, allowing 'groundlings' to crowd around it on three sides.

Revels, a post held by Edmund Tilney from 1579 to 1610. To the distress of Puritans, however, Tilney seemed less interested in suppressing lewdness than in spotting "seditious matter" that could stir unrest. The rules were clear: sensitive political and religious questions were off limits, and no living public figure could be depicted on stage. More than one writer ended up in jail for not taming his pen.

Round in appearance, the new theaters were generally 14- or even (as the Globe itself) 20-sided, with benches in three tiers of galleries, where seats cost up to sixpence. Poorer theatergoers, or "groundlings," paid one penny to stand in an arena that was open to the sky. The stage had a gallery that was used by musicians or hired by wealthy spectators eager to be seen. Some theaters, it is said, could squeeze in 3,000 people.

Performances, held in all but the coldest winter months, took place in daylight, and the actors had to compete for attention with the comings and goings of groundlings, and the disruptions of people selling food and drink. London's moody weather was another variable. The stage, about 40 feet (12 meters) wide, with room for as many as 20 actors at a time, usually had a trap-door to facilitate the apparition of spirits or the disappearance of corpses, but otherwise it would be bare. Because of the rapid turnover of plays and lack of storage space, companies rarely built sets or used props other than, say, swords, torches, or pots of pigs' blood. The actors, all men or boys, wore the fashions of the day, their more ornate costumes sometimes donated by their wealthy patrons. But the actors counted mostly on the words of the playwright to convey what was happening when and where. Occasionally, an actor would inform the audience of a change of location; more often, the playwright provided the key information in his text. A flag flying above the theater announced that a performance was under way.

BOY PLAYERS

There were no actresses in Shakespeare's day and young female roles were all played by boys. Cross-dressing (boys playing girls who are disguised as boys) was common in Elizabethan and Jacobean drama, and is central to the plots of *As You Like It*, *The Merchant of Venice*, and *Twelfth Night*.

The theaters on Bankside did not have a salubrious location. Home to bull- and bear-baiting arenas, the district opposite St Paul's Cathedral was crowded with prostitutes and petty thieves, brothels, inns, and prisons.

Life Behind the Curtain

Rivalry between the theaters was intense. When Shakespeare arrived in London, probably several years before the first surviving reference to him in 1592, the Rose, owned by Philip Henslowe, was the most successful, with Marlowe among its playwrights. It was there that Shakespeare presented his first plays, notably the *Henry VI* trilogy. Theater owners hired different troupes depending on what they had to offer, but the closure of all theaters during the plague epidemic of 1592 and 1593 led to a shake-up of the companies, with some forced to find new patrons. From 1594, the Admiral's Men settled at the Rose, while Shakespeare joined the newly formed Lord Chamberlain's Men at the Theatre. Four years later, the lease on the land where the Theatre stood ran out and, after fruitless negotiations with the landowner, Richard Burbage and his brother, Cuthbert, decided to move it. From the night of 28 December 1598 they surreptitiously dismantled the playhouse and shipped it to Bankside on the south bank of the Thames. There, in the summer of 1599, it was reopened as the Globe. Unhappy with the new competition, Henslowe allowed the Rose to fall into disrepair. In 1600, he built the Fortune in northern London to seek out new audiences, only returning to Bankside in 1613 after the Globe burned down. Although the Globe was quickly rebuilt, Henslowe founded the Hope theater nearby.

The theaters were primarily business ventures, and if Shakespeare eventually became quite prosperous, it was as a shareholder of both the Lord Chamberlain's Men and the Globe, not as a writer or actor: the writer was there to serve the actor, the actor to enrich the "sharer," as the company's owners were known. Actor-playwrights attached to companies would discuss their ideas with their colleagues, while outside writers would "pitch" their plays by reading them to the sharers. Once a play was accepted, actors were given only sheets of paper with their own speeches and the "cue" lines preceding them. Since time was short, there was minimal rehearsal, and since the notion of the all-powerful stage director was still centuries away, the play was what the dramatist wrote and the actors interpreted. It would be given a short run on stage and was rarely revived.

Elizabethan Theater

By the time Shakespeare reached London, the English literary Renaissance was well under way, fed by a revival of interest in Greek and Roman classics and new curiosity about more recent Italian and French literature. It was poetry that led the way. The first figure of note, Sir

The Workes of William Shakeſpeare, containing all his Comedies, Hiſtories, and Tragedies: Truely ſet forth, according to their firſt ORIGINALL.

The Names of the Principall Actors in all theſe Playes.

William Shakeſpeare.	Samuel Gilburne.
Richard Burbadge.	Robert Armin.
John Hemmings.	William Oſtler.
Auguſtine Phillips.	Nathan Field.
William Kempt.	John Underwood.
Thomas Poope.	Nicholas Tooley.
George Bryan.	William Eccleſtone.
Henry Condell.	Joſeph Taylor.
William Slye.	Robert Benfield.
Richard Cowly.	Robert Goughe.
John Lowine.	Richard Robinſon.
Samuell Croſſe.	John Shancke.
Alexander Cooke.	John Rice.

The *First Folio* lists the actors from Shakespeare's company.

Richard Burbage was the first great Shakespearean actor.

ACTORS OF SHAKESPEARE'S DAY

No less than in today's movie world, actors were the real stars, celebrities whose on- and off-stage antics were followed by the public. Richard Tarlton was an immensely popular clown, applauded by Queen Elizabeth herself. After he died in 1588, his place was taken by Will Kemp. In what might now be considered a publicity stunt, he famously danced for nine days as he traveled from London to Norwich. When Kemp left the Lord Chamberlain's Men (the company to which Shakespeare belonged) in 1600, he was replaced by Robert Armin, who played in Shakespeare's later comedies and was the fool in *King Lear*. Some male leads were like matinee idols. Richard Burbage, Shakespeare's friend and colleague at the Lord Chamberlain's Men, and Edward Alleyn of the Admiral's Men, drew crowds no matter what their role. When Alleyn retired in 1603, Burbage then ruled the London stage alone as he successively portrayed *Hamlet, Othello, King Lear* and *Macbeth*. Parts in plays were often written specifically for these and other actors.

Will Kemp

Philip Sidney, was himself a Renaissance man: courtier, statesman, soldier, patron of scholars and poet. His *Astrophel and Stella*, written in 1582, is considered second only to Shakespeare's sonnets among Elizabethan sonnet cycles. Sidney's contemporary, Edmund Spenser, gained still greater renown with his epic poem *The Faerie Queene*, published in 1590, which recounts the adventures of Queen Gloriana's knights in the land of Faerie (Gloriana representing Elizabeth, and Faerie a mythical England or Ireland).

Thomas Kyd's *The Spanish Tragedie* may have inspired Shakespeare to write *Hamlet*. Some scholars believe Kyd to be the author of an earlier version of *Hamlet*, known as the *Ur-Hamlet*.

While poetry was a vocation worthy of gentlemen, drama was not held in the same high esteem, but the new playwrights had one advantage: Elizabeth enjoyed theater as entertainment and propaganda. The playwrights' main concern was to fill the theaters that bought their works, but the queen's support served as a traditional incentive. The message of the morality play did not entirely disappear – Falstaff, for instance, is modeled after Vice – but London's regular theatergoers came to expect more. Soon, everything from comedies and farces to history plays and melodramas were being staged, with little heed paid to the rules of classical drama. Many elements now identified with Shakespeare, such as cross-dressing, ribald but insightful clowns and easy movement between prose and verse, were common to much of this drama.

Our revels now are ended: these our actors/ (As I foretold you) were all spirits, and/ Are melted into air, into thin air...

The Tempest, 4.1

John Lyly was a prose stylist. His prose romances, *Euphues: The Anatomy of Wit* and *Euphues and His England*, earned him immense popularity in London. He then turned his energies to writing prose comedies. Lyly's *Euphues* is said to have influenced Robert Greene, whose plot for *Pandosto: The Triumph of Time* was adapted by Shakespeare in writing *The Winter's Tale*. Of more immediate impact on Shakespeare was Thomas Kyd. His play *The Spanish Tragedy* introduced revenge tragedy to English theater and it was presented regularly throughout the 1590s. However, Kyd's own life was less happy. He was arrested and tortured for suspected treason in 1593 and died penniless the following year, aged 36.

The true master of the London stage in the late 1580s and early 1590s was "Kit" Marlowe, born just two months before Shakespeare, but already famous when Shakespeare was still an apprentice. He was only 23 when the two parts of his *Tamburlaine the Great*, set in 14th-century Central Asia, were first performed. In quick succession, he wrote *Dr Faustus*, structured like a morality play; *The Jew of Malta*, about Barabas's conflicts in Christian Malta; and *Edward II*, the first important history play of the Elizabethan era. Marlowe led a dangerous life, spending time in rough taverns and rumoured to be a royalist spy. On 30 May 1593, aged just 29, he was killed in a brawl at a lodging house in Deptford. There is no record that Shakespeare met either Kyd or Marlowe, although London's lively theater scene could well have brought them together. With Marlowe's death, Shakespeare's star soon rose. Scores of other playwrights were also busily supplying the new theaters, but many of their names are not known.

The final years of Queen Elizabeth's long reign represented anxious days for the London theater. Ignoring the objections of the Puritans, she had been a firm supporter of theater, summoning troupes to her palaces to entertain her with plays (the Lord Chamberlain's Men appeared before her at least three times a year). It is believed that, after enjoying Falstaff in *Henry IV Part I*, she asked Shakespeare to write a play showing the fat knight in love (he promptly penned *The Merry Wives of Windsor*). However, when she refused to name a successor until her final hours, actors and playwrights could only hope that the next monarch would also be partial to theater.

Christopher Marlowe's *Edward II* was a model for Shakespeare's early history plays.

JACOBEAN THEATER

Their concerns were unfounded. In almost his first act as king in 1603, James I offered his patronage to the Lord Chamberlain's Men. Known as the King's Majesty's Players or, more commonly, the King's Men, in the years that followed they averaged 20 performances at court per year. Other companies were also favored: the Admiral's Men became Prince Henry's Men and, after the prince's death in 1612, the Elector Palatine's Men.

Theater did change under the new monarch, however. The difference between Elizabethan and Jacobean drama lay not in the names of the companies, but in the kinds of plays that were popular. Elizabethan theater was in the main optimistic, with even history plays suggesting that a better future lay ahead. Shakespeare's Elizabethan comedies were typically light-hearted. In contrast, the Jacobean theater was often more sombre, moralizing and introspective. This mood may have influenced Shakespeare's late comedies, which are far darker than those of the 1590s. Some of these changes in tone can be attributed to Whitehall, a venue popular with James's court. This candlelit hall drastically affected the staging of the plays. Night scenes could be portrayed more realistically, while the use of special effects, like flying spirits and descending gods, became common practise.

Just as Shakespeare wrote his great tragedies early in James's reign, a darker undertone also appeared in the work of his contemporaries, with violence, evil, lust, and madness overwhelming love, beauty, and hope. Ben Jonson is remembered for the serious dramas *Volpone, The Alchemist* and *Bartholomew Fair.* John Webster won recognition as a tragedian for

Witches and other supernatural forces feature in several Shakespeare plays.

THE SUPERNATURAL

Educated in Greek, Latin, and French, James I was a man of considerable intellect and something of a scholar. He was also fascinated by witchcraft, magic, and the supernatural. In 1597, he wrote his own treatise on the subject, *Daemonologie*, in which he declared his belief in the power of evil spirits. When he came to the throne, he would certainly have appreciated the supernatural elements in *Macbeth* and Shakespeare's later romances.

The White Devil and *The Duchess of Malfi.* George Chapman, who earned his place in English literature as a translator of Homer's *Iliad* and *Odyssey,* also wrote several tragedies. John Marston, whose best known play was *The Malcontent,* was a fierce satirist. Playwrights also often collaborated on writing projects. Indeed, Marston worked with Jonson and Chapman on *Eastward Ho,* a comedy that mocked Scottish social climbers at court and earned the three men a brief spell in prison. Other writers also worked in teams, perhaps in

BELL'S EDITION.
Every Man in his Humour.
A COMEDY, by BEN JOHNSON.
By D. GARRICK,
Theatre-Royal in Drury-Lane.
By PERMISSION of the MANAGERS,
LONDON,

Ben Jonson's *Every Man in His Humour* was written for the Lord Chamberlain's Men in 1598. Shakespeare and Jonson remained lifelong friends, and Jonson's reputation would be consolidated under James I.

response to the pressure to deliver material to the theaters, although not with publication in mind. Thomas Middleton was probably sole author of his boisterous comedy *A Chaste Maid in Cheapside,* but he often worked with Webster, Thomas Dekker, Philip Massinger, and William Rowley. For instance, Middleton wrote *The Changeling,* one of his best known tragedies, with Rowley. John Ford also wrote with Dekker and Rowley, although his love tragedy *'Tis Pity She's a Whore* was his own work. The most famous collaboration was between Francis Beaumont and John Fletcher, who together wrote at least a score of plays between 1607 and 1613. Their best works, *Philaster, The Maides Tragedy* and *A King and No King,* were first presented at the Globe. This connection to the King's Men explains how Fletcher came to collaborate with Shakespeare on *Henry VIII* and *The Two Noble Kinsmen.* When Shakespeare finally retired, Fletcher took over as the Globe's chief playwright.

MASQUES

Under King James I, Ben Jonson and the architect Inigo Jones developed a new version of the masque, drawing on French court practises. Music, dance, and drama combined with an elaborate set to recount otherworldly tales in which the king and his court were assigned key roles. Shakespeare is not known to have written any masque, but he included one in *Henry VIII.* Starting with *The Masque of Blackness* in 1605, Jonson wrote no fewer than 30 masques for King James.

Theater after Shakespeare

Although the London theater boom outlived Shakespeare, this singular chapter in English drama lost much of its verve after King James's death in 1625: his ill-fated son, Charles I, was more interested in art than in theater. Then, in 1642, under Puritan influence, Parliament ordered the closure of all theaters. During the Civil War and Interregnum that followed, most theaters were torn down. When public entertainment returned with the Restoration of the monarchy in 1660, not one theater remained standing. Yet somehow London's love of theater survived. New plays were written and old plays revived.

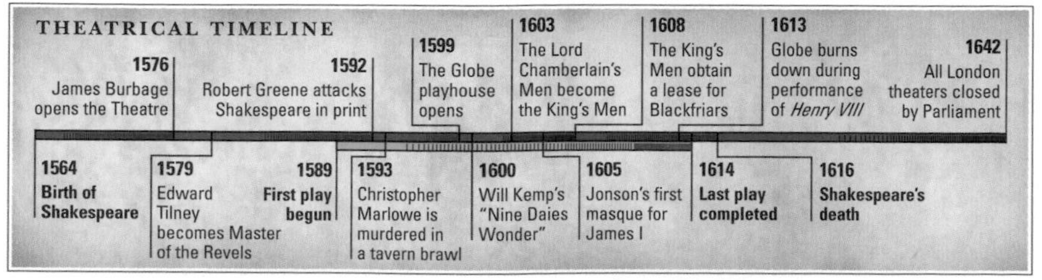
THEATRICAL TIMELINE
1564 Birth of Shakespeare
1576 James Burbage opens the Theatre
1579 Edward Tilney becomes Master of the Revels
1589 First play begun
1592 Robert Greene attacks Shakespeare in print
1593 Christopher Marlowe is murdered in a tavern brawl
1599 The Globe playhouse opens
1600 Will Kemp's "Nine Daies Wonder"
1603 The Lord Chamberlain's Men become the King's Men
1605 Jonson's first masque for James I
1608 The King's Men obtain a lease for Blackfriars
1613 Globe burns down during performance of Henry VIII
1614 Last play completed
1616 Shakespeare's death
1642 All London theaters closed by Parliament

SHAKESPEARE'S CANON

SHAKESPEARE MIGHT NEVER HAVE TAKEN HIS PLACE as the greatest writer in the English language if the *First Folio* had not been published in 1623. Of the 36 plays attributed to him at his death, 18 existed in quarto editions of varying reliability and the rest had not been published. Shakespeare's good fortune was to have loyal friends and admirers eager to secure his reputation. Two colleagues from the King's Men, John Hemminge and Henry Condell, tracked down and edited 36 of his "Comedies, Histories & Tragedies," which were published by Isaac Jaggard and Edward Blount in a large format book known as a folio. Ben Jonson had previously published his complete works in a single volume in 1616. Shakespeare's 907-page edition had far greater impact. With the *First Folio,* "Shakespeare"—concept and creed—was born.

Mr. WILLIAM
SHAKESPEARES
COMEDIES,
HISTORIES, &
TRAGEDIES.
Published according to the True Originall Copies.

LONDON
Printed by Isaac Iaggard, and Ed. Blount.

The title page of the *First Folio,* decorated with an engraving of a stern-looking Shakespeare, declares that the plays are "Published according to the True Originall Copies."

Shakespeare would have earned nothing from publishing his plays himself since they were owned by his theater company. As a shareholder of the company, he would even lose money if, once published, his plays were staged by a rival company. Another problem was that the unauthorized versions were often unreliable. Popular myth had it that publishers infiltrated audiences with spies who took down dialogue, but there is no reliable evidence to support this. Many sixpenny quarto editions were nonetheless full of mistakes.

PUBLISHING THE PLAYS

The editors of the *First Folio* appear to have worked from several sources. They had the flawed texts of six plays, the so-called "bad" quartos; one "doubtful" quarto; and 11 "good" quartos. They used Shakespeare's own manuscripts, known as "foul papers" for a first draft, and "fair copy" for an edited transcript; loose sheets kept by actors; and the "prompt book" approved by the royal censor. The editors or publishers also had to negotiate the right to print plays that existed in quarto editions that had not sold out: *Troilus and Cressida,* for instance, is not listed in the contents of the *First Folio* because that page was printed before permission to include the play was obtained. There are even different versions of the *First Folio,* since the 750 to 1200 first run was printed over at least 18 months. Copies cost around one pound each.

QUARTOS

On occasion, the first surviving mention of a play is when it was published in a pirate "quarto" edition, at first anonymously (as with *Titus Andronicus* in 1594), later with Shakespeare's name (as with *Love's Labour's Lost* in 1598), but always without his permission. Indeed, in the absence of effective copyright laws, theater companies discouraged publication of their plays since they could then be used by rival companies. Eighteen of Shakespeare's plays were never published in his lifetime.

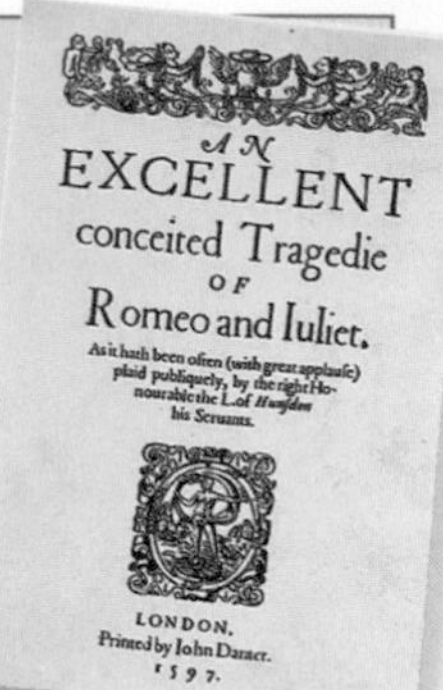

AN
EXCELLENT
conceited Tragedie
OF
Romeo and Iuliet.
LONDON.
Printed by Iohn Danter.
1597.

The frontispiece of a 1597 quarto edition of *Romeo and Juliet*.

A *Second Folio* was printed in 1632 and a *Third Folio* in 1663. In 1664 seven new plays were added to the *Third Folio*, although of these only *Pericles* would eventually be accepted as authentic. This "contaminated" edition was reprinted as the *Fourth Folio* in 1685 and was the basis for the complete works published by Nicholas Rowe in 1709.

An Authoritative Shakespeare

Shakespeare's reputation suffered when some of his plays were "improved" in adaptations. Some tragedies were thought to be more palatable to audiences if "happy endings" were added, for instance. By the mid-18th century, however, thanks to Samuel Johnson and Edward Capell, attention turned back to the *First Folio* as the most authentic version. The great actor-manager David Garrick, who proclaimed Shakespeare to be England's own genius, also preferred Shakespeare's texts to indifferent adaptations. But the search for authoritative texts for the plays did not end. Throughout the 19th century, new editions of the complete works of Shakespeare were published, with the spelling modernized and corrections, modifications, and fresh interpretations added. Even now, major Shakespeare publishers routinely review their texts in the light of new research.

The debate over the Shakespeare canon continues. *Pericles* was omitted from the *First Folio*, less because of doubts over its authorship than because of the editors' dissatisfaction with the available text, but after it was added to the reissued *Third Folio* in 1664, it was never removed. In contrast, while *The Two Noble Kinsmen* was jointly attributed to Shakespeare and John Fletcher when published outside the folios in 1634, it was another three centuries before it was included in the collected plays. *Cardenio*, a play performed on several occasions in 1613, was also attributed to Shakespeare and Fletcher when it was registered for publication in 1653, but no text survives. Then, in the 1990s, publishers decided to include *Edward III* as a 39th play, albeit recognizing it as a collaborative effort. Still not included in the canon is *Sir Thomas More*, which includes 147 lines thought to be in Shakespeare's handwriting. Written around 1595, the play was initially banned in the theaters, but Shakespeare may have been brought in to rewrite one controversial scene.

The playwright Ben Jonson was a great friend of Shakespeare (here, the two men are imagined playing chess), but he was impartial in his critiques of the Bard's work.

Early Criticism

The first substantial commentaries about Shakespeare came from Ben Jonson. In a poem in the *First Folio*, he proclaimed Shakespeare to be "the Soul of the Age." Jonson recognized that nature alone could not explain Shakespeare's achievement: "Yet must I not give Nature all: Thy art/My gentle Shakespeare, must enjoy a part./For though the poet's matter, Nature be,/His Art doth give the fashion." In other words, the playwright was also a craftsman using his skills to express what he observed in the world. However, Jonson did not find Shakespeare's talent flawless. Years later, recalling that Hemminge and Condell had noted in the *First Folio* that "we have scarce received from him a blot in his papers," Jonson responded tartly: "My answer hath been, would he had blotted a thousand" lines. Shakespeare, he believed, should have edited himself more strictly. However, he concluded: "There was ever more in him to be praised than to be pardoned."

Tear him for his bad verses, tear him for his bad verses!

Julius Caesar, 3.3

Barely 40 years later, John Dryden, another poet-playwright, noted that Shakespeare was not consistent, "at times flat, insipid" and far too devoted to puns, "but he is always great, when some great occasion is presented to him."

Problems of Genre

Some of Dryden's successors, however, were troubled by Shakespeare's disregard of the classical rules, and they struggled to fit his plays into the *First Folio*'s categories of comedies, histories, and tragedies. "Those which are called histories, and even some of his comedies, are really tragedies, with a run or mixture of comedy amongst them," wrote Nicholas Rowe in 1709. This was evidently something that never worried Shakespeare, who cheerfully blended genres within a single play. It probably helped readers when at the end of the 19th century a new category was created to accommodate some of the later plays: *Pericles, Cymbeline, The Winter's Tale,* and *The Tempest* became known as romances. Yet three plays—*Troilus and Cressida, All's Well That Ends Well,* and *Measure for Measure*—are still considered "problem plays."

Dr. Samuel Johnson (1709–84) wrote: "Shakespeare is above all writers, at least above all modern writers, the poet of nature; the poet that holds up to his readers the faithful mirror and manners and life."

Playwright or Poet

Shakespeare lovers were no less divided over whether he should be read as a poet or seen and heard as a playwright. English

Actor-manager David Garrick (1717–79) gave Shakespeare fresh life for a new generation of theatergoers with a return to the texts of the *First Folio*.

DID SOMEONE ELSE WRITE "SHAKESPEARE"?

The case against Shakespeare's authorship of the works attributed to him is built around disbelief that a man from a provincial town with no university education could have wielded a vocabulary of over 15,000 words and displayed such expertise in fields as diverse as law, medicine, astronomy, history, military affairs, and court etiquette. It is reinforced by the fact that none of his manuscripts exists and that surviving references to him are fewer than those to lesser contemporaries.

The Case For Others

In the 19th century, Sir Francis Bacon, the Elizabethan essayist and statesman, was promoted as the phantom Shakespeare because his references to the Bible and the ancient classics

Sir Francis Bacon, essayist.

were thought similar to those found in some Shakespeare plays. But his candidacy did not prosper and, by the end of the century, Christopher Marlowe was offered as the new "Shakespeare." To explain Marlowe's murder in 1593, his advocates claimed that he faked his death, fled to Italy, and sent his work to a middleman called William Shakespeare.

Today, a stronger case is made for Edward de Vere, 17th Earl of Oxford, whose writings are echoed in some of Shakespeare's early work. He had the education, class, and experience necessary to write "Shakespeare" and, it is argued, had good reason to use a different name: it would have been improper for a nobleman to be associated with the ungentlemanly craft of playwriting. To the counter argument that he died in 1604 and that 10 of Shakespeare's plays are dated after that, Oxfordians respond that, at most, only *The Tempest* and *Henry VIII* were written after 1604.

Edward de Vere, 17th Earl of Oxford.

The Case For Shakespeare

The Stratfordians—as defenders of the Bard of Avon are known—point to at least 50 surviving references linking Shakespeare to his plays, starting with the envious outburst of Robert Greene in 1592. But they rest their case with the *First Folio*. Introducing the plays, the actors John Hemminge and Henry Condell, as well as the playwright Ben Jonson, speak of Shakespeare with fondness and admiration. Would they really have gone to the trouble of perpetuating the lie that Shakespeare was the author of poetry and plays written by someone else? In the gossipy world of London's theaters, such a hoax would soon have been exposed.

TIMELINE OF THE PLAYS

1589–90
First play
Henry VI Part I

1591
Henry VI Part II
Henry VI Part III

1593
Richard III

1594
Edward III
Titus Andronicus
The Comedy of Errors
The Taming of the Shrew
The Two Gentlemen of Verona

1595
Love's Labour's Lost
Richard II

1596
King John
Romeo and Juliet
A Midsummer Night's Dream

1597
The Merchant of Venice
The Merry Wives of Windsor
Henry IV Part I

1598
Henry IV Part II

1599
Much Ado About Nothing
As You Like It
Julius Caesar
Henry V
Hamlet

critics were long smitten with his poetry, but Shakespeare's theatrical "excesses" disturbed some critics. However, in the late 18th century, the idea of Shakespeare as above all a dramatic artist gained ground in Germany and this view gradually caught on in England. In the early 19th century, after some hesitation, the poet and philosopher Samuel Taylor Coleridge agreed that Shakespeare's "irregularities" were not the result of indiscipline, but the product of subtle intelligence. Early in the 20th century, the English critic A. C. Bradley found in Shakespeare's major characters reflections of the human condition, even noting that "his tragic characters are made of the stuff we find within ourselves."

Even as Shakespeare's greatness became widely accepted, though, some prominent writers refused to join the chorus. In the 18th century, Voltaire said Shakespeare was "natural and sublime, but had not so much as a single spark of good taste, or knew one rule of the drama." A century later, Tolstoy recalled being disappointed when he first read Shakespeare. "Not only did I feel no delight, but I felt an irresistible repulsion and tedium," he wrote.

Reinterpretation

In the 20th century, Shakespeare proved more dominant than ever and his plays were constantly reinterpreted by literary critics and theater directors. Freud's contribution was among the most innovative when he focused on Hamlet's supposed Oedipal complex. His approach in turn freed scholars and critics to study Shakespeare and his characters through every imaginable prism, from Marxism to feminism. Indeed, in recent decades, near-scientific analysis has come to dominate academia's view of Shakespeare.

Modern directors and actors continue to explore new ways of staging Shakespeare's plays, such as this all-female production of *Richard III* at Shakespeare's Globe Theatre in London, 2003.

Today, some traditionalists fear that literary theory and "concept" productions have undermined appreciation of both the music of Shakespeare's poetry and the raw excitement of his plots. But there are also signs that the pendulum may be swinging back to the essence of Shakespearean drama: the stage, and the ability of actors to move audiences with Shakespeare's words. Clearly, Shakespeare is what every generation makes of him.

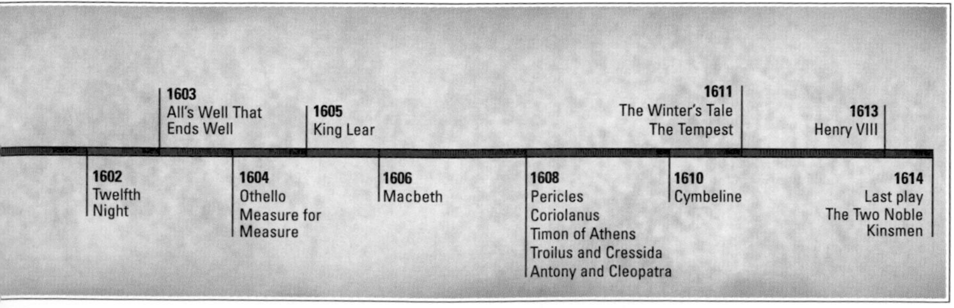

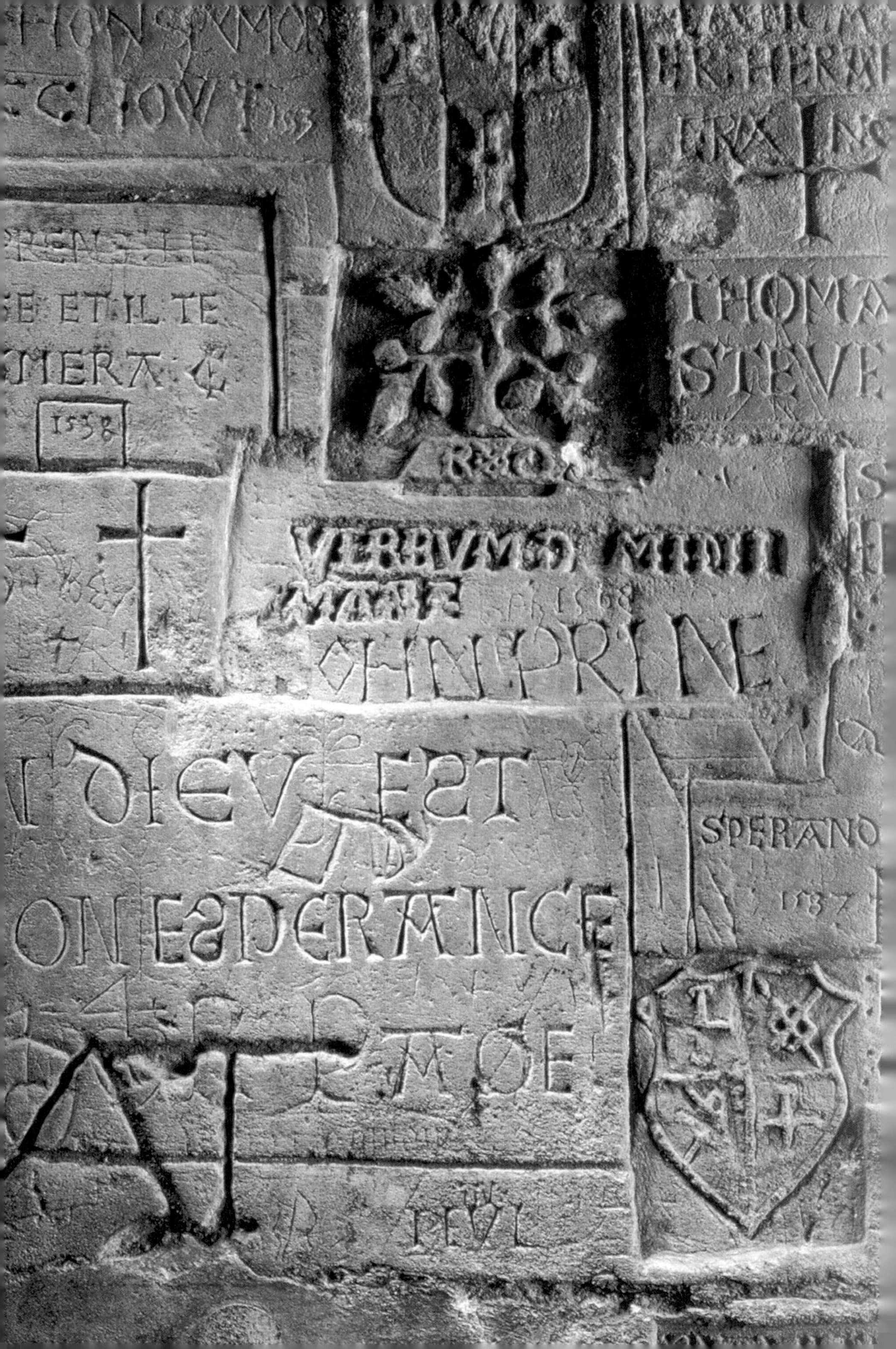

ET IL TE
1558
THOMA
STEVE
SPERANO

SHAKESPEARE'S LANGUAGE

THE RICH TEXTURE OF SHAKESPEARE'S ENGLISH reflects the colorful history of the language. From its early Anglo-Saxon roots, English has been a dynamic language of multiple heritages. Born of invasions and raids, reshaped by more raids and invasions, even Old English, the earliest known form of English, represents a mixture of West Germanic and Scandinavian tongues. The Elizabethan and Jacobean eras witnessed the emergence of Modern English, a language registering the unprecedented mobility and ideas of its speakers. No poet displays the vocabulary explosion more fully than Shakespeare, who introduced around 1,500 new English words among the 20,000 used in his corpus. Many well-known phrases still in use today also appeared for the first time in his plays and poetry.

BEFORE THE ROMAN EMPEROR Claudius began his conquest of Britain in 43 AD, the Celtic inhabitants of the British Isles spoke languages akin to modern Irish, Welsh, and Scottish Gaelic. But when the Romans departed four centuries later, in *c.* 410, the languages of some Germanic peoples, mainly the Angles and Saxons, gradually came to dominate, forming Anglo-Saxon, also called Old English. At the end of the 6th century, Pope Gregory the Great began to convert the Anglo-Saxons to Christianity. Latin, the church's lingua franca, was employed in pockets throughout the British Isles. Gradually, Latin words entered Old English and the Roman alphabet was used to record early English literature, until then spoken but unwritten.

The Vikings, who raided and formed settlements in England in the 8th and 9th centuries, added their Scandinavian words to Old English. Even *Beowulf*, the first major work of English literature, conveys Scandinavian influence. The great epic poem tells how Beowulf rescued the Danish people from man-eating monsters and saved his own people, in Geatland, from a devastating dragon.

Old English is a Germanic language. Its syntax, grammar, and vocabulary define the core of current-day English. But Old English was altered radically by the Norman Conquest of 1066. With a

When the Normans landed in 1066, they brought ashore more than their horses, seen here in the Bayeux Tapestry (1082). With them came a wealth of new words that greatly enriched the language.

French-speaking court then established in England by William the Conqueror, elite poets wrote in French or Latin until the mid-14th century. Spoken English nevertheless borrowed around 10,000 words from French, many reflecting courtly ideals, such as "courtesy," "diplomacy" and "virtue."

When English regained status as a literary language in the 14th century, it only distantly resembled Old English. The Middle English of Chaucer's *The Canterbury Tales* (1399) shows how extensively the Germanic language had been reshaped by French, a Romance language.

Middle English changed in the late 15th century, when William Caxton set up the first English printing press to publish works written in or translated into English. Equivalents in English were found for ideas originally expressed in Italian, Portuguese, and Spanish as well as French, by then a foreign language. Translations of works from antiquity, especially in Latin, further enriched English with words of classical heritage.

Not long after Caxton's press began to run in 1476, Columbus landed in the New World, heralding an era of broader horizons and linguistic contacts. By the time the English had formed settlements in Virginia and repelled the Spanish Armada in 1588, theirs was no longer the language of an oft-invaded island. Instead, English ships were plying the seas of the spice-rich East and transporting colonists to the West. Just as Shakespeare embarked on his career, English entered the most volatile phase of its history.

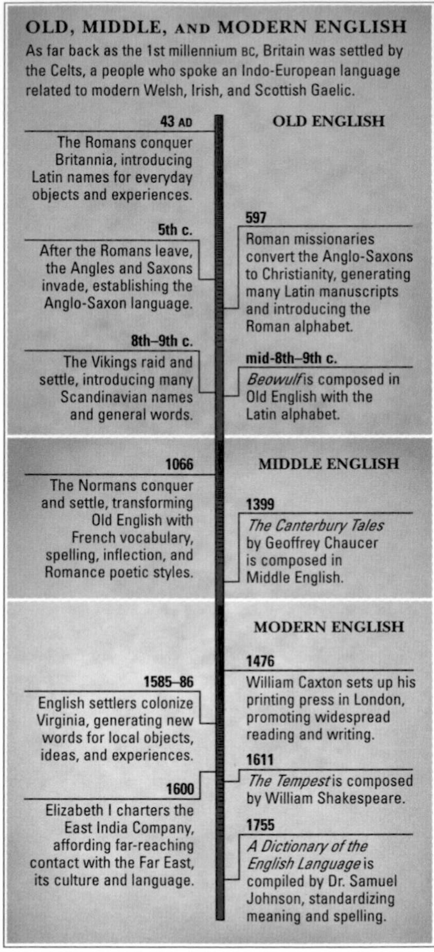

OLD, MIDDLE, AND MODERN ENGLISH
As far back as the 1st millennium BC, Britain was settled by the Celts, a people who spoke an Indo-European language related to modern Welsh, Irish, and Scottish Gaelic.
OLD ENGLISH
43 AD
The Romans conquer Britannia, introducing Latin names for everyday objects and experiences.
597
Roman missionaries convert the Anglo-Saxons to Christianity, generating many Latin manuscripts and introducing the Roman alphabet.
5th c.
After the Romans leave, the Angles and Saxons invade, establishing the Anglo-Saxon language.
8th–9th c.
The Vikings raid and settle, introducing many Scandinavian names and general words.
mid-8th–9th c.
Beowulf is composed in Old English with the Latin alphabet.
MIDDLE ENGLISH
1066
The Normans conquer and settle, transforming Old English with French vocabulary, spelling, inflection, and Romance poetic styles.
1399
The Canterbury Tales by Geoffrey Chaucer is composed in Middle English.
MODERN ENGLISH
1476
William Caxton sets up his printing press in London, promoting widespread reading and writing.
1585–86
English settlers colonize Virginia, generating new words for local objects, ideas, and experiences.
1611
The Tempest is composed by William Shakespeare.
1600
Elizabeth I charters the East India Company, affording far-reaching contact with the Far East, its culture and language.
1755
A Dictionary of the English Language is compiled by Dr. Samuel Johnson, standardizing meaning and spelling.

SHAKESPEARE'S CREATIVE ENGLISH

When Shakespeare began writing plays and poems, the English language was absorbing new words more rapidly than ever before or since. Contact between speakers of English and those of other languages increased dramatically through wars, trade, exploration, diplomacy, colonization, pirating. With the arrival of goods and ideas from places as far as the East Indies and the New World, new words were needed to express them. Among thousands entering English during the Elizabethan period alone was "tobacco," from the Spanish pronunciation of the leaf which Columbus had observed Caribbeans smoking; "mandolin" from the Italian name for the instrument; "madeira," from the Portuguese island's wine; and "furlough," from the Dutch maritime code.

OLD ENGLISH: *c.* 500–1150

Old English poetry captures the culture and ideals of pagan Germanic warriors alongside the later Christian beliefs of the monks and scholars setting down the poems in Latin script. The heroic poem ***Beowulf*** uses liberal alliteration, and each half-line usually contains two beats. In keeping with Germanic poetics, there is no fixed number of syllables per line.

The mythical, man-eating troll Grendel terrorized the Danes until slain by the hero from Geatland named Beowulf.

Beowulf (mid-8th to end 10th century)

Set in 6th-century Scandinavia, the epic poem recounts the exploits of Beowulf. Here, his men advance toward the Danish palace of Heorot:

Stræt wæs stān-fāh, stīg wīsode
The street was stone-paved, a narrow path that pulled
gummum ætgædere. Gūð-byrne scan,
the men together. Their mail coats flashed,
heard, hond-locen; hring-iren scīr
hard, hand-fastened; and the shining iron rings
song in searwum.
sounded in their armor.

MIDDLE ENGLISH: 1150–1500

Middle English literature reflects the influence of Old French on English following the Norman Invasion of 1066. The basic structure of English remains Germanic, but it gains a vastly enriched vocabulary from the French. ***The Canterbury Tales,*** influenced by Romance poetry, uses rhyming couplets, each line of which is usually 10 syllables long. Some traces of Old English alliteration survive.

This 14th-century manuscript depicts pilgrims setting out from Canterbury on their homeward journies.

The Canterbury Tales (1399)
by Geoffrey Chaucer

A narrator describes the Prioress, one of the pilgrims bound for Canterbury; she sings in Latin and speaks French.

Ful weel she soong the service dyvyne,
Old French *service*, Latin *servitium*

Entuned in hir nose ful semely;
Old English *nosu.*

And Frenssh she spak ful faire and fetishly,
Old English *fægre.*

After the scole of Stratford atte Bowe,
For Frenssh of Parys was to hire unknowe.

MODERN ENGLISH: 1500–PRESENT

Modern English reflects the rapid expansion of the language during the Renaissance through contact with both ancient classical cultures and the contemporary, rapidly developing fields of science, medicine, and the arts. In every line Shakespeare reveals his enthusiasm for the evolving ideas, words, and literary traditions of his time. In his plays, the alliteration of Old English is just one of many optional poetic effects. In ***The Tempest***, as in *The Canterbury Tales*, lines are built of 10 syllables containing five stresses, but rhyming couplets have given way to blank verse, composed in non-rhyming meter (see page 45) With its relative freedom and lack of structure, blank verse can express layered subtleties and nuances, making it ideal for pensive soliloquies.

The Tempest (1611)
by William Shakespeare

Caliban, the child of a witch and sea monster, describes the natural sounds of his island home.

Be not afeard; the isle is full of noises,
Old French *noise*, Latin *nausea*, "seasickness."

Sounds, and sweet airs, that give delight and hurt not.
Sometimes a thousand twangling instruments
Poetic, imitating sound described.

Will hum about mine ears…
Middle English *hummen*,
Dutch *hommel*, "bumblebee."

Shakespeare by Martin Droeshout, 1623.

Many of Shakespeare's new words reflect vigorous contact between English and other living languages, as well the English passion for classical antiquity. From the Italian *bandito* Shakespeare coined "bandit." From Dutch words, he formed "rant" and "switch," the twig used for striking. From Ancient Greek, the Bard generated the verb "metamorphose" and the nouns "dialogue," "mimic" and "ode," as well as that abiding nemesis of playwrights, the "critic." From Latin, whose influence on public life was enormous, he coined the words "negotiate," "circumstantial," "premeditated," "marketable," and one of the most important words for theater professionals to this day, "manager."

EXPRESSIONS CREATED BY SHAKESPEARE

Some of Shakespeare's invented phrases have become such everyday expressions in English that they no longer strike speakers as creative.

A fool's paradise	Milk of human kindness
A foregone conclusion	More fool you
A tower of strength	My own flesh and blood
An eye-sore	Neither a borrower nor a lender be
Ay, there's the rub	Never-ending
Bag and baggage	One fell swoop
Bated breath	Play fast and loose
Budge an inch	Pomp and circumstance
Cold comfort	Puppy dog
Come full circle	Shooting star
Dead as a doornail	Short and the long of it
Elbow room	Skim milk
Every inch a king	Short shrift
For goodness sake	Something in the wind
Good riddance	Sorry sight
Green-eyed monster	Star-crossed lovers
Hold a candle to	Throw cold water on it
Household words	To the manner born
I have not slept a wink	To thine own self be true
In my heart of hearts	Too much of a good thing
Into thin air	Wear my heart on my sleeve
It was Greek to me	Well-behaved
Kill with kindness	What the dickens
Laughing-stock	Wild goose chase
Love is blind	
Love letter	
Marriage bed	

Shakespeare's lexical creativity was not limited to languages from distant lands or times. From existing English of Germanic origin he formed the adjective "kissing," the nouns "amazement," "eyeball" and "scuffle," the verb "swagger" and another whose straightforwardness still shocks: "puke." From new English words, he built newer ones, forming "assassination" from "assassin," a word picked up on the Crusades and derived from the Arabic for "eaters of hashish," referring to legendary murderers for hire. He also created words from scratch, such as his "buzzer," an amusing onomatopoeia for a gossiper.

But new words alone cannot sum up the coltish energies of Shakespeare's English. Even as it expanded, the language also changed, offering poets options soon to be obsolete. The "goeth" and "doth" of Middle English had not yet been fully replaced by the modern "goes" and "does." These happily coexist in Shakespeare's English, as do "thou," "thee," and "ye" alongside the modern counterpart: "you."

Elizabethan Wordplay

Shakespeare's English displays numerous symptoms of a language undergoing profound shifts in order to accommodate the changing world of its speakers. One of the most prominent, particularly in his Elizabethan texts, is wordplay, as when Costard of *Love's Labour's Lost* says of the word "enigma":

> ***No egma, no riddle, no l'envoy, no salve in the mail, sir! O, sir, plantain, a plain plantain! No l'envoy, no l'envoy, no salve, sir, but a plantain!*** *3.1*

Much of Shakespeare's most extravagant wordplay, delightful to his peers, has become as enigmatic as Costard's speech. But wordplay invariably expresses the Bard's fondness for pushing the senses of words to their limits, as if to explore the very process by which words are given new meanings. In his soliloquies and dialogues, he often examines relationships between words and meanings, as when Juliet ponders Romeo's name.

> ***What's in a name? That which we call a rose***
> ***By any other word would smell as sweet.*** *2.2*

Shakespeare's language can rarely be taken at face value. Meanings of words were highly negotiable, as was their spelling. With the first important dictionary of the English language published only in 1755, both the sense and appearance of words were more fluid in Shakespeare's day. Spellings of his own name, which run to at least 26, from Shagspere to Shexpere, document the erratic renderings of words before the age of the dictionary. This does not mean that Shakespeare's English was held to no formal standards. Most writers of his day, including Shakespeare's famous attacker Robert Greene, consciously imitated the regulated decorum of Latin authors. A passage from Christopher Marlowe's play *Tamburlaine The Great* (1590) illustrates the contrasting style of a university-educated playwright:

> ***Nature, that framed us of four elements***
> ***Warring within our breasts for regiment,***
> ***Doth teach us all to have aspiring minds.***

WORDS COINED BY SHAKESPEARE

Shakespeare introduced more words into English than all other poets of his lifetime combined. Some of Shakespeare's words still in frequent use include:

academe *n.*	**luggage** *n.*
advertising *n.*	**misquote** *v.*
cater *v.*	**mountaineer** *n.*
circumstantial *adj.*	**numb** *adj.*
cold-blooded *adj.*	**outbreak** *n.*
courtship *n.*	**partner** *n.*
drug *v.*	**premeditated** *adj.*
embrace *n.*	**petition** *v.*
employer *n.*	**retirement** *n.*
engagement *n.*	**rival** *adj.*
epileptic *adj.*	**roadway** *n.*
fashionable *adj.*	**soft-hearted** *adj.*
glow *n.*	**traditional** *adj.*
gossip *v.*	**vastly** *adv.*
grovel *v.*	**watchdog** *n.*
investment *n.*	**wormhole** *n.*
laughable *adj.*	**zany** *adj.*

adj. = adjective; adv. = adverb; n. = noun; v. = verb

Following Shakespeare's death in 1616, fellow playwright Ben Jonson complained amicably of Shakespeare's English: "His wit was in his owne power; would the rule of it had beene so too." But the Bard's lack of self-editing may have been among his greatest literary assets: English was simply

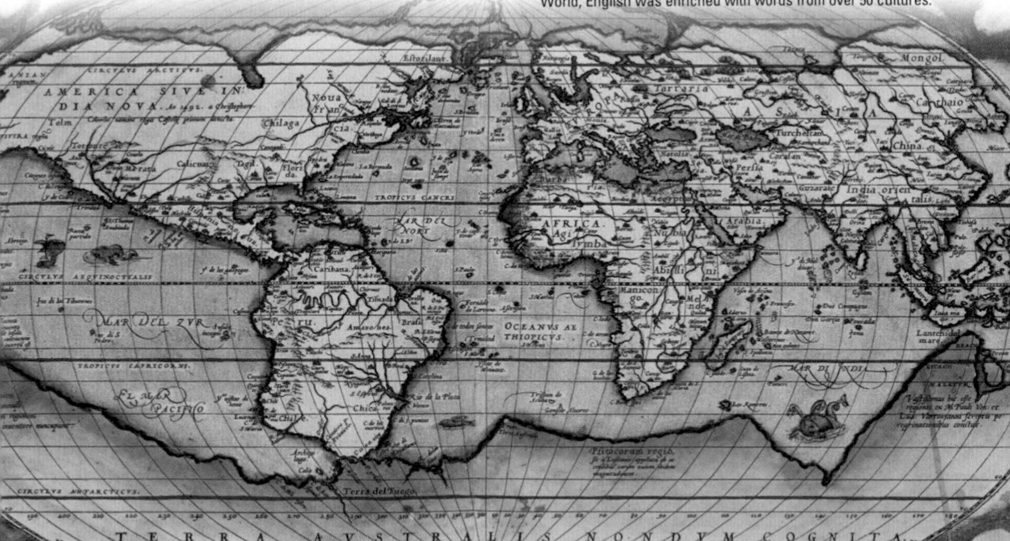

The expanding world of the Elizabethans, as mapped by Abraham Ortelius in 1574. Through contact with the New World, English was enriched with words from over 50 cultures.

SHAKESPEARE'S PROSE AND VERSE

While Shakespeare's poems are composed in verse, his plays employ verse and prose alike. The two are easy to tell apart. Verse lines are printed with line breaks, and the first word of each line is capitalized, as in *Hamlet*:

> ***To be, or not to be—that is the question;***
> ***Whether 'tis nobler in the mind to suffer...*** 3.1

In prose, one sentence flows into another, without line breaks, as in *Henry IV Part II*:

> ***I have a whole school of tongues in this belly of mine, and not a tongue of them all...*** 4.3

No play is free of verse, but four of the history plays are free of prose: *Henry VI Part I, Henry VI Part III, Richard II,* and *King John.* From *Othello* on, verse became more prominent than prose. Some verse lines are composed of rhyming couplets, as in *A Midsummer Night's Dream:*

> ***Dark night that from the eye his function takes***
> ***The ear more quick of apprehension makes.*** 3.2

More frequently, Shakespeare preferred "blank verse," in which metrical lines do not rhyme. With its comparative lack of rigidity, blank verse conveys more subtle thoughts and feelings, as in Iago's soliloquy in *Othello:*

> ***And what's he then that says I play the villain,***
> ***When this advice is free I give, and honest,***
> ***Probal to thinking, and indeed the course***
> ***To win the Moor again?*** 2.3

Shakespeare's verse was usually reserved for noble speakers, his prose for common or comical parts. Some characters, such as Prince Hal, alternate between verse and prose, depending on the context; whether, for instance, at court or in a tavern.

Falstaff and his friends speak in prose.

changing too quickly for more restrained authors to keep up with it. Poetry was to be found well beyond libraries and lectures halls; Shakespeare found it in voices from his native Warwickshire, and in the heart of his adopted London: its streets and taverns, shops and stalls, docks and yards, noble homes, courthouses, churches, brothels, prisons, public spaces filled by processions and ceremonies and hangings, and, of course, in its theaters.

SHAKESPEARE'S LIVING DRAMA

No literary form was better suited than drama to charting and inventing the English of Shakespeare's time. Unlike lyric or narrative poetry, drama calls for voices to be fully impersonated. With the playwright's own work helping to change conventions, plays were no longer narrowly focused on speakers of noble stature or stock characters, like the Virtue and Vice of morality plays. Shakespearean roles range from kings and queens, through middle-class constables and artisans, to household servants and battlefield riff-raff.

The English of Shakespeare's plays is also augmented by the inclusion of other languages or varieties of speech. The pedant Holofernes of *Love's Labour's Lost* impresses interlocutors with his command of Latin (in fact comically hopeless) and Constable Shallow of *The Merry Wives of Windsor* speaks with such a strong regional accent that even Falstaff, who of all Shakespearean characters most loves to experiment with English, is unable to understand him.

But Shakespeare's English did more than reflect a changing world in a changing language. The Bard also contributed to that world and its language. In the Elizabethan theaters of his London, Shakespeare's English became inseparable from the roles he invented for its performers. And to this day, albeit often unknowingly, English speakers continue to describe their feelings and their lives in Shakespeare's language.

THE METERS OF SHAKESPEAREAN VERSE

Whether they rhyme or not, verse lines are metrical, meaning simply that they follow regulated patterns of speech. The patterns of Shakespearean verse language are composed of five kinds of building blocks, known as meters, combining syllables and stresses in different variations. Pronounced naturally, the words below illustrate specific meters. Slashes indicate breaks between syllables of one metrical beat each. And syllables in bold show where emphasis usually falls when the words are uttered. Syllables receiving emphasis are said to be stressed.

METERS

Iamb	*re/**venge***	*mis/**take***
Trochee	***mid**/night*	***butch**/er*
Dactyl	***doc**/u/ment*	***mock**/er/y*
Spondee	***a/men***	
Anapest	*un/der/**neath***	*af/ter/**noon***

Most Shakespearean verse lines contain ten syllables each, and their meters are determined simply by reading the lines aloud in a natural voice. Each syllable produces one beat, and some syllables produce stressed beats.

The most natural sounding meter in Shakespearean English is the one the Bard most frequently employed: iambic pentameter. This meter is built of five iambs in a row (the penta of "pentameter" comes from the Greek for "five".) Often, characters speaking in iambic pentameter produce sensations of comfort and well-being. In *Romeo and Juliet*, Friar Lawrence speaks in this meter to reassuring effect, adding to the impression that he is able to solve the lovers' dilemmas:

*Care **keeps** his **watch** in **every** **old** man's **eye**,*
*And **where** care **lodges**, **sleep** will **never** **lie**.* 2.3

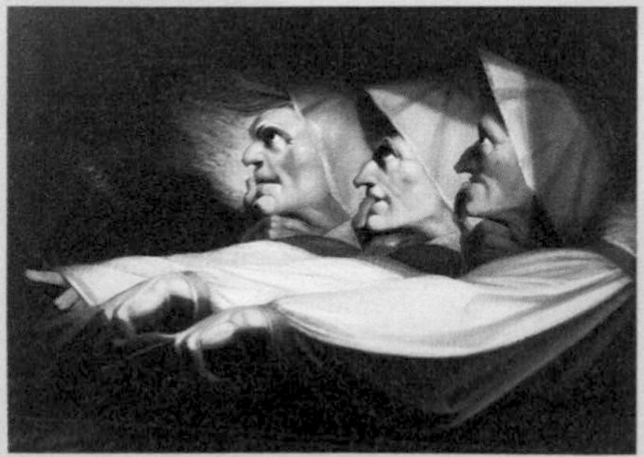

Speaking in the calm and measured tones of iambic pentameter, Friar Lawrence soothes the troubled lovers Romeo and Juliet.

The first syllable is unstressed, the second is stressed, the third unstressed, and so on as the metre see-saws back and forth in easy iambs. But while iambic pentameter often conveys natural harmony or lyrical beauty, it may also produce disturbing intensity, as when Macbeth speaks in soliloquy:

*To-**morrow**, **and** to-**morrow**, **and** to-**morrow**,*
*Creeps **in** this **petty** **pace** from **day** to **day**...* 5.5

An extra syllable has been added to the first line, but this in no way changes the basic meter. Iambic pentameter here amplifies Macbeth's observation by pairing stressed syllables with repeated sounds. Meters lie at the heart of Shakespeare's verse language, and frequently offer the best means to measure a character's disposition or evolving state of mind. For instance, when witches chant spells in *Macbeth*, their trochees resound with wickedness:

***Dou**ble, **dou**ble, **toil** and **trou**ble...* 4.1

But the meters of unhinged human speakers can be even more unsettling. In *Richard III*, Richard awakens from a nightmare to speak in mixed meters that leave his audience as unbalanced as himself. One way to scan Richard's speech is:

*The **lights burn blue**. It is **now dead mid**night.*
*Cold **fear**ful **drops** stand **on** my **trembl**ing **flesh**.*
***What do I fear?** My**self**? There's **none else by**.*
***Rich**ard loves **Rich**ard: that is, **I am I**.*
*Is **there** a **mur**derer **here? No. Yes, I** am.* 5.3

Macbeth's weird witches chant their wicked incantations in an unnerving trochee meter, which clearly spells "**dou**ble, **trou**ble." *The Three Witches* by Henry Fuseli, *c.* 1810.

Shakespeare

THE WORKS

SHAKESPEARE WAS A PROLIFIC PLAYWRIGHT AND POET. HIS SURVIVING WORKS CONSIST OF 39 PLAYS, FOUR NARRATIVE POEMS, THE SONNETS, AND OTHER POETRY.

The HISTORY PLAYS

EACH OF SHAKESPEARE'S HISTORY PLAYS TREATS ENGLAND'S PAST UNDER THE REIGN OF AN HISTORICAL KING WHOSE NAME GIVES THE PLAY ITS TITLE.

With his history plays, Shakespeare proved England's past to be a subject worthy of great theater. For the first time in English drama, historical events were treated as grandly as timeless themes such as love and death. Elizabethans of the 1590s were swelling with patriotism and military pride. In 1588, Sir Francis Drake had defeated the Spanish Armada against all odds. By then, too, England had established a presence in the New World and on maritime trade routes. Elizabethans began to view themselves as subjects not merely of a monarch but also of a historical process whose precarious shape could be changed by their actions. Nowhere is this more evident than in Shakespeare's history plays. All but *Henry VIII* were written during the most optimistic years of Queen Elizabeth's reign. Yet even in these plays, Shakespeare is less interested in historical accuracy than in compelling drama. And it is a testament to the playwright's priorities that the history plays include many of his most enduring and universally engaging dramas.

A Troubled Past Revisited

Ten of the eleven history plays—*Edward III* was only recently admitted into the Shakespearean corpus—are listed as "Histories" in the *First Folio.* They are not difficult to distinguish from other kinds of Shakespearean plays: comedies, tragedies, and romances. Each play is set principally in England and addresses the political challenges confronted by a specific English king, whose name figures as the play's title. Each king's troubles are usually covered in a single play, although two Lancastrian monarchs receive more than one play each: three early plays treat the reign of Henry VI and two somewhat later plays the reign of Henry IV. *Macbeth* and *King Lear* are not counted among the history plays, for while King Macbeth in Scotland and King Lear in England were historically attested rulers, these plays, like *Julius Caesar* and the other Roman tragedies, focus instead on the tragic fall of a heroic person who only happened to be a historical ruler.

The history plays examine not a single person or thread of action but rather a sequence of historical events related to the theme of the unification of England. However, while these plays form a distinct category of Shakespearean drama, they contain elements of other kinds of drama. Most history plays present a character similar to the central figure of a tragedy: the heroic figure who falls. And, with the final scenes of many history plays offering cause for celebration, their conclusions resemble those of the comedies. Indeed, few of Shakespeare's characters are more comical than Falstaff and his associates, who nevertheless make their first and most enduring appearances not in a comedy but in a history play. Yet Shakespeare's history plays do not merely combine aspects of comedy and tragedy. They form an independent genre characterized by specific themes, dramatic structures, and political implications.

In Elizabethan times, these plays were also enormously topical: audiences were assured by the history plays that, thanks to their ruler's Tudor bloodline, they dwelled in a country providentially united. But at the same time, they were cautioned not to be complacent, for the calamitous civil wars of pre-Tudor England could one day return. Thus, the ideological stance of the history plays is consistent: were England divided internally, it could again face defeat both at home and overseas.

Early Historical Dramas

The history play was not the first dramatic genre in England to resemble political propaganda. Even before Shakespeare flourished, morality plays treated political themes, often in a didactic manner. In John Bale's *King John* (*c.*1530) and Thomas Sackville & Thomas Norton's *Gorboduc* (*c.*1562), tyranny and rebellion unravel the national unity inevitably restored to England by the end of each play. But after the defeat of the Spanish Armada in 1588, the morality play, with its simplified worlds of good and evil, no longer satisfied Elizabethans eager to celebrate England's grand successes and ambitions. Cardboard cut-out figures of Virtue and Vice needed to be given flesh and bones.

George Peele, Robert Greene, Thomas Lodge, and Christopher Marlowe first turned to English history for dramatic material appealing to new audiences. As in Elizabeth's England, where the vulnerable succession of her crown was coveted by rulers overseas and upstarts at home, the England of past monarchs was also plagued by foreign and domestic threats to stability and continuity. Thus, the past offered ample material mirroring the present. Further, English history was well documented by the 1590s, when the fad for plays about historic defeats and conquests was peaking.

The stage was set for a talented new playwright to satisfy spectators of a changed London theater scene and of a new English political reality. Shakespeare's earliest works in this genre were not radically different from the linear chronicle plays then popular in London. But as his plays began to explore historical figures as individuals with inner worlds and dimensional passions, they came to form their own kind of English drama.

Shakespeare's History Plays

For all but three history plays, Shakespeare set action during reigns associated with the rise and fall of the House of Lancaster. Following the deposition of Richard II in 1399 by the Lancastrian Henry IV through to the usurpation of the throne by Henry VII in 1485, sons of the House of Lancaster struggled to gain and then hold onto the English crown. In using reigns associated with Lancastrians and their Yorkist rivals as dramatic settings, Shakespeare was making a politically astute and even ideologically charged choice. For it was Queen Elizabeth's Tudor grandfather, Henry VII, who brought an end to the bloody Wars of the Roses by uniting the dynastic lines of Lancaster and York. The legacy of Henry VII left its mark on the Elizabethans, who believed not only that English rulers were vice-regents of God, but also that history itself unfolded according to divine design. God may have intended for England to suffer through foreign and civil wars but, with Henry VII, Elizabethans believed God had interceded to end an era of devastating strife and bloodshed.

King Henry VII shrewdly called for chroniclers to recount England's history from the new, Tudor viewpoint. He commissioned the Italian humanist Polydore Vergil to write *Historia Anglica*, which in turn served as the basis for the two chief sources for Shakespeare's history plays. The first was Edward Hall's 1548 *The Union of the Two Noble and Illustre Families of Lancaster and York*, whose very title refers to Henry VII and the Tudor line that brought peace to England by unifying opposed claimants to the crown. The second and most important was Raphael Holinshed's *The Chronicles of England, Ireland and Scotland*, published first in 1578 and again in 1587, when the work served as a major source for London playwrights responding to the post-Armada thirst for plays about English history. Equipped with these and other chronicles, and drawing on such diverse materials as classical Senecan tragedies and more recent political morality plays, Shakespeare addressed in some of his earliest plays the reigns of the Wars of the Roses.

The First Tetralogy

Known collectively as the "first tetralogy" because they were written early and around the same time (1589–93) are: *Henry VI Part I, Henry VI Part II, Henry VI Part III*, and *Richard III*. Henry VI and Richard III reigned during three decades of civil wars pitting the House of Lancaster (symbolized by a red rose) against that of York (symbolized by a white rose). The reign of Lancastrian Henry VI is handled in linear episodic fashion, the work of a playwright trying his hand at a new form.

THE HISTORY PLAYS AT A GLANCE

	Play	Reign of King	Subject
First Tetralogy	1 Henry VI	1422–61	100 Years' War
	2 Henry VI		Wars of Roses
	3 Henry VI		Wars of Roses
	Richard III	1483–85	Wars of Roses ends
	King John	1199–1216	War in France and usurpation of throne
	Edward III	1327–77	100 Years' War
Second Tetralogy	Richard II	1377–99	Usurpation of throne
	1 Henry IV	1399–1413	Rebellion/Falstaff
	2 Henry IV		Rebellion/Falstaff
	Henry V	1413–22	100 Years' War/ Victory at Agincourt
	Henry VIII	1509–47	Tudor father of Queen Elizabeth

WEAPONS IN THE HISTORY PLAYS

The history plays abound in battle scenes, often challenging for theater directors to stage. Some update weaponry for modern interpretations, but most directors prefer to employ stage props resembling weapons of the play's period.

Shafted weapons. The prehistoric spear was a wooden shaft whose tip was strengthened by fire. Later, points of flint or metal were added. The pike, a spear tipped with steel, was often hooked to one side. An axlike cutting blade crowned the halberd *(left)*.

Sword. The sword was among the most widespread weapons of antiquity and the Middle Ages. In the 16th century, a lighter sword, the rapier, was introduced into England.

Dagger or poniard. A hand weapon with a short blade, the medieval dagger was used chiefly to pierce the armor of unhorsed adversaries.

Bow. The crossbow *(below)* fired arrows, darts, and stones. It was replaced by the lighter, more precise, and less expensive longbow, a favorite English weapon well into the 14th century. Longbows won the day in 1346 at the battle of Crécy and in 1415 at Agincourt, where outnumbered English troops defeated the superior French forces.

Firearms. In the 14th century, firearms gradually replaced more primitive weapons. The pistol, a light firearm, was held in one hand. Heavy firearms such as the cannon made castle fortifications obsolete, bringing feudalism to an end in Europe. A cannon fired during a performance of *Henry VIII*, Shakespeare's last history play, marked the end of another era when it burned down the Globe Theatre in 1613.

Richard III portrays a villain of the House of York, who murders and marries his way to the throne held by his Yorkist brother Edward IV as the play begins. In this play, certain rigid and repetitive elements drawn from Senecan tragedy are overwhelmed by the dazzling fiendishness of Richard's persona. In dialogues of intense dramatic irony and in riveting soliloquies, *Richard III* distinctly shows Shakespeare making the history play his own kind of drama.

THE "HENRIAD"

From 1595 to 1599, Shakespeare wrote another grouping of four history plays, known as the "second tetralogy," or the "Henriad": *Richard II, Henry IV Part I, Henry IV Part II,* and *Henry V.* While written after the first tetralogy, these plays are set in the earlier era of the Hundred Years War between England and France. The "Henriad" takes as its broad theme the rise of the House of Lancaster, and the glory achieved by England when Henry V finally defeated France. *Richard II*, notable for its lyrical language, treats the reign of the deposed and murdered Yorkist king as a man who failed to rule effectively. Turning to the reigns of Lancastrians Henry IV (1399–1413) and Henry V (1413–22), Shakespeare moved from high lyricism to a remarkable mixture of prose and poetic language, and tragic and comic modes. The playwright's most grandiose creation, Sir John Falstaff, enters in *Henry IV Part I* with his feisty associates and remains in *Henry IV Part II*, with his death mourned in *Henry V*. For Falstaff and his entourage, Shakespeare found an English of entirely new energies, which he balanced against the more formal language of other speakers to render both parts of *Henry IV* among his most extraordinarily innovative plays. *Henry V* changes stylistic tempos yet again, following in a highly patriotic register the rise to the throne of the rebellious young Hal, who as Henry V is represented as the most successful of Shakespeare's English rulers, achieving an ideal balance between man and king, soldier, and lover.

King John, Edward III, Henry VIII

During the interval between the composition of the two tetralogies, Shakespeare wrote two other history plays: *King John*, set in the early 13th century, portrays the English monarch as an incompetent usurper who loses most English territories in France, murders the rightful heir to the throne, and is then poisoned to death; and *Edward III*, set in the mid-14th century, is principally a vehicle for exhibiting the heroism of the king's son, Edward the Black Prince, in defeating the French in the battles of Crécy and Poitiers. Fourteen years after writing his last Elizabethan history play, *Henry V*, Shakespeare returned to the genre with *Henry VIII*, based on the reign of Queen Elizabeth's Tudor father. Written with John Fletcher while King James held the throne, *Henry VIII* treats Henry's break with Rome after the pope refused to sanction his divorce from Katherine of Aragon and his marriage to Anne Boleyn, Queen Elizabeth's mother. The play is among the very last written by Shakespeare.

Literature Rewriting History

Readers and audiences in and beyond Britain frequently mistake the history plays for accurate representations of the reigns of their eponymous kings. But Shakespeare took immense liberties in recasting history for the stage. The plays abound in historical errors: chronologies are freely compressed and sometimes wildly altered, locations are changed, anachronisms inserted, motivations fabricated, and characterizations invented. Shakespeare's concern was not to represent historical events with accuracy. He sought to make great theater, but he paid heed to the political sensibilities of Queen Elizabeth and King James. Nevertheless, his influence on perceptions of the historical English kings is so far-reaching that even today Richard III is thought to have been as much a wicked plotter as the real Henry V is believed to have been a national savior.

The history plays are proof that literature can overwhelm history even in a sphere as carefully documented and closely studied as the dynastic rule of England.

DATES OF THE HISTORY PLAYS

1589–90	Henry VI Part I
1590–91	Henry VI Part II
1590–91	Henry VI Part III
1590–1594	Edward III
1592–1593	Richard III
1595	Richard II
1595–1596	King John
1596–1597	Henry IV Part I
1598	Henry IV Part II
1598–99	Henry V
1612–1613	Henry VIII
1614	Last play

HENRY VI PART I

HENRY VI PART I, the opening play of the tetralogy devoted to the Wars of the Roses, shows Shakespeare's emerging talent and exhibits his daring in taking on a vast sweep of history. Although the first play in the *Henry VI* trilogy, it was probably written after *Part II* and *Part III*, with its first recorded performance at the Rose Theatre in Southwark, London, in 1592. *Henry VI Part I* lacks the narrative clarity of Shakespeare's later plays, and was long thought to be the work of several dramatists. However, since all three parts of *Henry VI* were included in the *First Folio*, the trilogy's authorship was not in doubt in 1623. Based on Holinshed's *Chronicles* and Hall's *Union of the Two Noble and Illustrious Families of Lancaster and York*, the play is distinguished from its sources by its emphasis on contemporary issues: the need for political stability, the legitimacy of the monarchy, and the vagaries of royal succession.

BEHIND THE PLAY

THE PLAY, SET BETWEEN 1422 AND 1445, covers the final battles of the Hundred Years' War with France and the early stirrings of the Wars of the Roses. It captures the mood of the time, but it is not an accurate chronicle of the period. To extract drama from the blur of history, Shakespeare ignores dates and telescopes events. He is accurate in presenting Henry VI as a child-king, with real power exercised by two competing relatives: Humphrey, Duke of Gloucester, as Protector, and Henry Beaufort, Bishop of Winchester. Shakespeare also respects the historical record by showing that, while Henry claimed the French crown, the Dauphin was crowned Charles VII after Joan of Arc's troops defeated the English at Orleans in 1429. But Shakespeare also takes many liberties. He treats Joan with singular unfairness, ignoring her stature in France as the saintly heroine who helped to drive out the English invaders. He builds up Talbot as an English hero, but then kills him off eight years before he died in reality. Shakespeare also creates mischief by having Suffolk seduce Margaret of Anjou before she marries Henry in 1445, although there is no evidence that this happened.

Sad tidings bring I to you out of France/ Of loss, of slaughter, and discomfiture…
1.1

DATE OF PLAY

1589–90
HENRY VI PART I

1589 first play begun
HENRY VI PART I

last play completed 1614
THE TWO NOBLE KINSMEN

LENGTH OF PLAY

2,702 lines
HENRY VI PART I

0 lines

shortest play: 1,786 lines
THE COMEDY OF ERRORS

longest play: 4,024 lines
HAMLET

DRAMATIS PERSONAE

Henry VI (Alan Howard) cannot stop the English from feuding.

THE ENGLISH

KING HENRY VI
178 lines
A young man who cannot stop the feuding at court.

DUKE OF GLOUCESTER
184 lines
Henry's uncle and Protector.

DUKE OF BEDFORD
76 lines
Henry's uncle and Regent of France.

DUKE OF EXETER
59 lines
Great-uncle and personal guardian to the king.

BEAUFORT, BISHOP OF WINCHESTER
96 lines
Henry's great-uncle.

DUKE OF SOMERSET
64 lines
A Lancastrian leader.

RICHARD PLANTAGENET, DUKE OF YORK
184 lines
Son of Richard, Earl of Cambridge, he quietly plots to take the throne.

EARL OF WARWICK
72 lines
Supporter of York.

EARL OF SALISBURY
15 lines
An English noble.

EARL OF SUFFOLK
174 lines
He seduces Margaret of Anjou.

LORD TALBOT
407 lines
A heroic English general, feared by the French, he dies in battle; he may have been Shakespeare's model for Henry V.

JOHN TALBOT
47 lines
Lord Talbot's son.

EDMUND MORTIMER
88 lines
Richard's imprisoned uncle and pretender to the throne, he proclaims Richard as his heir.

Joan la Pucelle (Charlotte Cornwell) believes that divine forces will lead her to drive the English out of France.

The Duke of York (Emrys James), whose father was executed by Henry V, prepares to bid for Henry VI's throne.

SIR JOHN FALSTAFF
8 lines
A cowardly English officer.

SIR WILLIAM LUCY
77 lines
He condemns the English bickering that leads to the death of both Talbots.

SIR WILLIAM GLANSDALE
1 line
Companion to Salisbury.

SIR THOMAS GARGRAVE
2 lines
He dies with Salisbury.

MAYOR OF LONDON
21 lines
A peacemaker.

WOODVILLE
5 lines
Keeper of the Tower of London.

VERNON AND BASSET
29; 25 lines
English knights.

THE FRENCH

CHARLES
134 lines
Dauphin and later King Charles VII.

REIGNIER
59 lines
Duke of Anjou, his daughter marries Henry.

DUKE OF BURGUNDY
44 lines
An English ally, he is persuaded to rejoin the French side.

DUKE OF ALENÇON
49 lines
A French noble.

BASTARD OF ORLEANS
29 lines
He presents Joan la Pucelle to Charles.

AN OLD SHEPHERD
24 lines
He claims to be Joan la Pucelle's father.

MARGARET OF ANJOU
33 lines
Duke of Anjou's daughter, she marries Henry.

COUNTESS OF AUVERGNE
45 lines
She tries to capture Talbot.

JOAN LA PUCELLE
255 lines
Also Joan of Arc, she is executed by the English.

OTHER PLAYERS
Lords, Ambassadors, the Governor of Paris, Warders, Legate, Lawyer, Master Gunner, Boy, Officers, Scout, Watch, Soldiers, Porter, Servants, Gaolers, Messengers, and Fiends.

PLOT SUMMARY

SIZE OF ACTS

ACT 1	ACT 2	ACT 3	ACT 4	ACT 5
605 lines	495 lines	479 lines	558 lines	565 lines

ACT ONE 605 lines

LONDON AND OUTSIDE ORLEANS

At Henry V's funeral, Gloucester, Bedford, and other lords are lamenting the young king's death when they learn that English forces have been defeated in France. Talbot, the English commander, has been captured; Salisbury is besieged at Orleans; and the Dauphin, Charles, has been crowned at Rheims. Bedford, Regent of France, sets off with reinforcements, while Gloucester as Protector proclaims Henry's infant son England's new king.

In France, Charles tries to retake Orleans, but is beaten back by Salisbury's forces. His cousin, the Bastard of Orleans, introduces a "holy maid," Joan la Pucelle, or Joan of Arc, who boasts that she can defeat the English. Charles is sceptical and challenges her to a duel, but he quickly proclaims "thou art an Amazon." Joan tells him that, with Henry V dead, it is time to drive out the English.

Dauphin, I am by birth a shepherd's daughter,/ My wit untrained in any kind of art... 1.2

Gloucester arrives at the Tower of London to collect weapons, but a fight erupts when he is refused entry on orders of the Bishop of Winchester. In France, Talbot has been freed after paying a ransom, but Joan's French troops kill Salisbury and occupy Orleans. Meeting Talbot on the battlefield, Joan tells him "thy hour is not yet come." Charles, now entranced by Joan, proclaims that she "shall be France's saint".

'Tis Joan, not we, by whom the day is won;/ For which I will divide my crown with her... 1.6

ACT TWO 495 lines

ORLEANS, AUVERGNE AND LONDON

After the English retake Orleans under the command of Talbot, Charles turns his anger on Joan, but she blames his "improvident soldiers." Talbot accepts an invitation to visit the Countess of Auvergne, ignoring warnings from his French ally, the Duke of Burgundy. The countess promptly orders Talbot's arrest, but his own soldiers free him.

In London, lords from the Lancastrian and Yorkist factions are arguing in Temple

King Henry the Fifth, too famous to live long!/ England ne'er lost a king of so much worth... 1.1

Garden. Richard Plantagenet symbolically plucks a white rose of York, entreating others to do the same. Warwick and Vernon also pluck white roses, but Somerset and Suffolk each pick a red Lancastrian rose and remind Richard that his father was executed for treason. Warwick announces that the next Parliament will call a truce between Gloucester and Winchester and restore Richard's title as Duke of York.

Since you are tongue-tied and so loath to speak,/In dumb significants proclaim your thoughts... 2.4

Richard visits his uncle, Edmund Mortimer, in the Tower of London, where he has been jailed for seeking the crown. His claim dates back to 1399, when Henry IV, the present king's grandfather, overthrew Richard II. On his deathbed, Mortimer declares Richard to be the new pretender to the throne, but he warns him to act cautiously: "With silence, nephew, be thou politic".

I will, if that my fading breath permit/ And death approach not ere my tale be done... 2.5

ACT THREE

479 lines

LONDON, NEAR ROUEN, AND PARIS

Alarmed by feuding between Gloucester and Winchester, the young king warns of the perils of "civil dissension". Warwick proposes that Richard Plantagenet be restored "to his blood" and the king agrees, naming him Duke of York. When Gloucester announces that Henry will travel to Paris to be crowned King of France, Exeter predicts greater conflict in England between warring lords.

Uncles of Gloucester, and of Winchester,/The special watchmen of our English weal, I would prevail... 3.1

Ay, we may march in England or in France,/Not seeing what is likely to ensue/ This late dissension grown betwixt the peers... 3.1

After Joan drives Talbot out of Rouen, the English retake the city, but Bedford, Regent of France, dies. Talbot buries him before traveling to Paris for Henry's coronation. Near Rouen, Joan reassures Charles that the fight is not lost and she convinces Burgundy to rejoin the French forces. In Paris, Talbot informs the king of his conquests and is named Earl of Shrewsbury. When the king leaves, Vernon, a Yorkist, and Basset, a Lancastrian, turn on each other.

Look on thy country, look on fertile France,/ And see the cities and the towns defaced/By wasting ruin of the cruel foe... 3.3

ACT FOUR

558 lines

PARIS AND NEAR BORDEAUX

After Henry is crowned King of France, he learns that Burgundy has joined Charles's forces. He orders Talbot to march on the French, urging Somerset and York to put aside their differences for the present and remember they are "amongst a fickle, wavering nation". Henry, himself a Lancastrian, puts on a Lancastrian red rose, which York angrily identifies as "the badge of Somerset." The king names York as new Regent of France and orders Somerset to help York's troops.

Come hither, you that would be combatants./Henceforth I charge you, as you love our favour,/Quite to forget this quarrel and the cause... 4.1

Camped outside Bordeaux, Talbot learns that Charles is approaching with 10,000 men. Recognizing his forces to be greatly outnumbered, Talbot appeals to York and Somerset, but neither responds in time to save him.

He fables not; I hear the enemy./Out, some light horsemen, and peruse their wings./O negligent and heedless discipline!... 4.2

Surrounded by French forces, Talbot is joined by his son, who refuses to flee. In the ensuing battle, both Talbot and his son are fatally wounded. Holding his son's body, the old man dies.

Thou antic death, which laughest us here to scorn,/ Anon, from thy insulting tyranny... 4.7

ACT FIVE

565 lines

LONDON, NEAR THE CITY OF ANGIERS, AND IN THE REGION OF ANJOU

Gloucester announces that the Pope and Holy Roman Emperor have called for peace between England and France, and that the Earl of Armagnac, a close relative of Charles, has offered Henry his daughter in marriage. Henry agrees to end the war and accepts the marriage proposal. Winchester is sent with a gift for Armagnac's daughter, but first he sends money to Rome to thank the pope for raising him to cardinal.

Near Angiers in France, learning that English forces have finally united, Joan calls on spirits to help her. When they appear, but ignore her appeals, she knows she is doomed. After a brief combat with York, she is seized by the English. Nearby, Suffolk captures Margaret, the daughter of the Duke of Anjou, and is struck by her "gorgeous beauty." Tempted to take her as his own, he instead proposes that she marry Henry. When Anjou agrees, Suffolk kisses her passionately and returns to London.

The Regent conquers and the Frenchmen fly./ Now help, ye charming spells and periapts... 5.3

At the English camp, Joan begs for her life, first saying she is a virgin, then claiming she is pregnant, but York insults her savagely and orders her burned at the stake. As she is led away, she curses England, wishing upon it "darkness and the gloomy shade of death". The French king agrees to make peace, but York worries that England will lose its territories in France. In London, Henry decides to marry Margaret instead of Armagnac's daughter. Sent to get Margaret, Suffolk boasts that "I will rule both her, the King, and realm."

Will nothing turn your unrelenting hearts?/Then, Joan, discover thy infirmity,/ That warranteth by law to be thy privilege... 5.4

Damsel of France, I think I have you fast./ Unchain your spirits now with spelling charms,/ And try if they can gain your liberty... 5.3

READING THE PLAY

COMPARISON OF PROSE TO VERSE

prose: 0% verse: 100%

The play is written in blank verse and, in the tradition of historical pageants, many speeches are devoted to providing the necessary background, such as Mortimer's long explanation of his—and therefore Richard of York's—claim to the throne. This background is particularly helpful to anyone tackling the complex narrative of the entire trilogy.

This late 18th-century engraving by James Northcote depicts the death of Edmund Mortimer in the Tower of London, attended by his nephew Richard.

Already in this early play, Shakespeare shares secret information with his audiences through the use of "asides" in which evil characters—York and Suffolk—reveal their darkest thoughts. It is a technique Shakespeare used in many subsequent plays, most dramatically in *Richard III* and *Othello*. In the clash between Gloucester and Winchester in Act 3 and the final confrontation of Joan of Arc and York in Act 5, Shakespeare also displays his talent for florid epithets.

Although the play carries his name, Henry VI is too young to play a major part in government or in the narrative. However, in the king's only important speech, when he tries to bring peace between his warring nobles, Shakespeare develops what will become an underlying theme of all his history plays: the need for unity to protect England's greater interests.

HISTORICAL SOURCES

JOAN OF ARC

Born *c.* 1412, Joan of Arc was a peasant girl from Lorraine. Claiming to have heard the voices of saints, she persuaded both the dauphin and the religious authorities to engage the English at Orleans, rather than Poitiers. Armed as a soldier, she led the French to a string of victories. Following her capture in 1430, she was tried by the English and burned at the stake as a heretic.

A 15th-century French illustration showing Joan of Arc clad in armor.

WHO'S WHO

Henry VI is king of England, but he is too young to control his feuding nobles. Meanwhile **Joan la Pucelle** (Joan of Arc), the visionary maid of Orleans, believes that divine forces will lead her to drive the English out of France. At home **Richard Plantagenet**, Duke of York, quietly prepares his claim to the throne. In France, the brave English general, **Lord Talbot**, having inflicted defeat on the French, dies in battle. His appeals for help are ignored by the Duke of York and the **Duke of Somerset**, a leader of the Lancastrian faction. Joan of Arc is executed by York, while the ambitious **Earl of Suffolk**, a foe of York, chooses **Margaret of Anjou** as young Henry's queen.

SEEING THE PLAY

Wallace Acton (Richard) and Philip Goodwin (King Henry VI) in The Shakespeare Theatre's 1996 production of *Henry VI, Parts 1, 2, and 3.*

POPULAR IN SHAKESPEARE'S LIFETIME, *Henry VI Part I* was then largely ignored until the 20th century. Today, it is usually performed as part of a cycle depicting all of the plays set during the Wars of the Roses. The play is not easy to follow. Unlike later history plays, where the king is at the center of the action, Henry VI is a peripheral character. The story jumps constantly between London and different French cities and between battlefields; it has a large cast of characters, for the most part, English nobles who are always squabbling; and there is no clear narrative beyond the passage of time. Even its two parallel plots—the gradual "loss:"of France and the growing power struggles within the English court—suggest that Shakespeare is largely setting the stage for the next two parts of the trilogy.

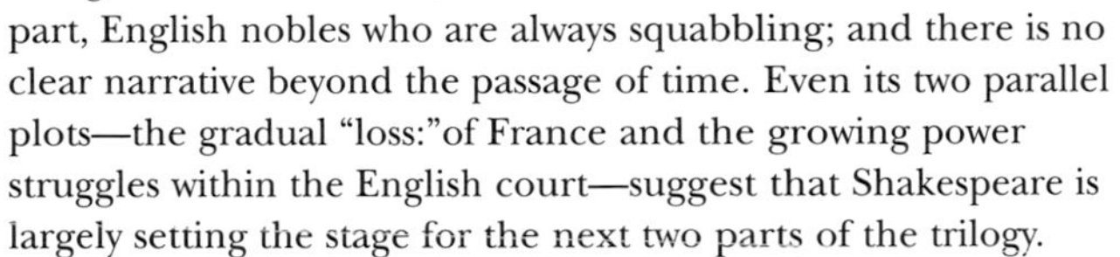

Still, while always a headache to present, the battle scenes are important in order to focus attention on the two warrior-heroes: Talbot, who represents English honor, and the "witch," Joan of Arc, who personifies French wiles. Yet, in the Manicheistic tradition of the medieval morality plays, even these characters display little psychological depth. The conflict between virtue and vice continues in London, where the saintly young king contrasts with Winchester who, following Elizabethan tradition, is portrayed as a corrupt and evil Catholic prelate. By the end of the play Shakespeare has ensured that the audience's eyes are fixed on Richard of York, the devious conspirator who is preparing his moment to reach for the crown.

"See, see the pining malady of France" (3.3), a stirring speech from Joan la Pucelle (Julia Ford) in the RSC 1988–89 *Plantagenets* tetralogy.

HISTORICAL SOURCES

ROSES

The scene in Temple Garden where the York and Lancaster factions pick roses as their symbols is a bold piece of theater and an example of hindsight in action. The white rose had long been a Yorkist emblem, but the red rose of Lancaster was invented by Henry VII, who blended the two to create the Tudor rose. Thus the Wars of the Roses acquired their name only after they were over.

The symbolic scene in Temple Garden in which Richard Plantagenet plucks a white rose of York was Shakespeare's own invention.

Henry

HENRY VI PART II

GENERALLY CONSIDERED THE BEST PLAY in the *Henry VI* trilogy, *Henry VI Part II* led Shakespeare into the dangerous waters of domestic politics by charting the rise of the Yorkist challenge to the Lancastrian monarchy. Thought to have been written in 1590–91, followed immediately by *Part III*, it was initially named *The First Part of the Contention betwixt the two famous houses of Yorke and Lancaster*, with *Part III* called *The True Tragedie of Richard Duke of York and the death of good king Henrie the Sixt.* The switch of focus from wars in France to feuding inside the court represented real risks for the young playwright. He now touched on the delicate questions of royal legitimacy and succession, which had spawned the Wars of the Roses. With Queen Elizabeth I moving into old age without a direct heir or even an appointed successor, these issues were again highly topical and politically explosive.

BEHIND THE PLAY

SET BETWEEN 1445 AND 1455, the play announces the start of the Wars of the Roses. It is accurate in its portrayal of Henry VI as a weak, pious, and malleable monarch who, after his marriage, quickly fell under the sway of his French wife, Queen Margaret, and the Earl of Suffolk. By 1450, when Suffolk was impeached and murdered en route to exile in France, Richard, Duke of York, was openly seeking the crown. While Shakespeare offers a true picture of the endless squabbling within the court, he does, however, alter events and dates to suit his needs. Jack Cade, a small landowner whose 1450 rebellion against high taxes was of some historic importance, is painted here as a buffoon. Still, Henry VI's England was unquestionably in disarray. Normandy was lost in 1450; three years later, the king became temporarily insane and York assumed the office of Protector. As soon as Henry recovered in 1454, Margaret drove York from the king's council. Shakespeare, however, ignores events between 1450 and 1455, when York finally took up arms and defeated the Lancastrians at the Battle of St. Albans. The Wars of the Roses had begun and would continue sporadically for the next 30 years.

Seems he a dove? His feathers are but borrowed,/ For he's disposèd as the hateful raven… 3.1

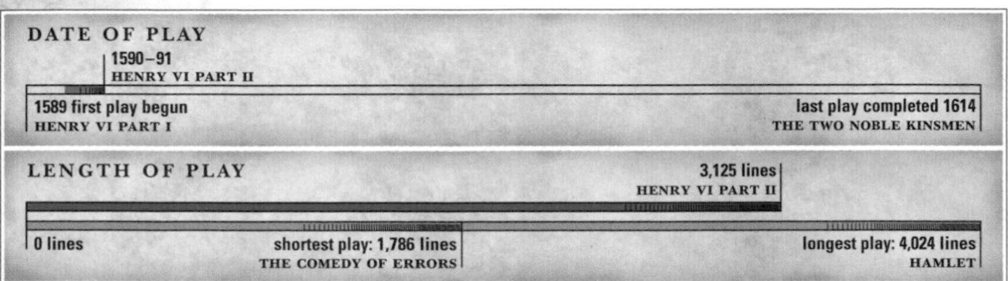

DRAMATIS PERSONAE

KING HENRY VI
315 lines
A devout, but weak, young monarch.

DUKE OF GLOUCESTER
307 lines
Henry's uncle and Protector, he is murdered in his bed.

CARDINAL BEAUFORT, BISHOP OF WINCHESTER
108 lines
Henry's great-uncle, he plots against Gloucester.

DUKE OF YORK
385 lines
Yorkist pretender to the throne, he wins the Battle of St. Albans and marches on London.

EDWARD AND RICHARD
1; 24 lines
York's sons.

DUKE OF SOMERSET
26 lines
A Lancastrian, he plots against Gloucester.

DUKE OF SUFFOLK
297 lines
He orders Gloucester's murder, but is banished.

19th-century engraving of Shakespeare's Gloucester.

DUKE OF BUCKINGHAM
76 lines
An ally of Somerset, he backs the king.

LORD CLIFFORD
57 lines
Loyal to the king, he dies in battle against York.

YOUNG CLIFFORD
46 lines
Lord Clifford's son and cofighter.

EARL OF SALISBURY
96 lines
A Yorkist supporter.

Henry VI (David Oyelowo) can neither control his nobles or his queen, nor prevent Gloucester's murder or York's rebellion.

EARL OF WARWICK
132 lines
Salisbury's son, a Yorkist.

LORD SCALES
8 lines
Loyal to the king, he tries to crush Cade's revolt.

LORD SAY
48 lines
Loyal to Henry VI, he is murdered by followers of Cade.

SIR HUMPHREY AND WILLIAM STAFFORD
16; 7 lines
They die fighting Cade.

SIR JOHN STANLEY
7 lines
He escorts the Duchess of Gloucester into exile.

VAUX
11 lines
He reports Cardinal Beaufort's illness.

ALEXANDER IDEN
51 lines
He kills the fugitive Cade.

WALTER WHITMORE, A SEA CAPTAIN, MASTER, AND MASTER'S MATE
19; 64; 1; 1 lines
They capture and kill Suffolk as a traitor.

JOHN HUME AND JOHN SOUTHWELL
31; 0 lines
Two priests, they organize a witchcraft session.

ROGER BOLINGBROKE
23 lines
A conjurer, he participates in the witchcraft session.

THOMAS HORNER
20 lines
An armorer, he is accused of proclaiming York's right to be king.

PETER THUMP
25 lines
Horner's assistant and accuser, he kills Horner.

Queen Margaret (Penny Downie) holding the severed head of her lover, Suffolk.

SAUNDER SIMPCOX
24 lines
An impostor, he claims his sight has been restored.

JACK CADE
242 lines
He leads a commoners' rebellion on behalf of York.

BEVIS, HOLLAND, DICK, SMITH AND MICHAEL
16; 18; 43; 20; 4 lines
Followers of Jack Cade.

TWO MURDERERS
5; 2 lines
Suffolk's henchmen.

QUEEN MARGARET
317 lines
French-born queen, also Suffolk's mistress, she mocks the king and backs Gloucester's murder.

ELEANOR
119 lines
Gloucester's ambitious wife, she is banished after being caught using witchcraft.

MARGERY JOURDAIN
4 lines
A witch burned at the stake.

OTHER PLAYERS
Lords, Ladies, Attendants, Aldermen, Sheriff, Officers, Soldiers, Guards, Messengers, and a Spirit.

PLOT SUMMARY

SIZE OF ACTS

ACT 1	ACT 2	ACT 3	ACT 4	ACT 5
669 lines	510 lines	835 lines	768 lines	343 lines

ACT ONE 669 lines

THE KING'S PALACE AND GLOUCESTER'S HOME IN LONDON

Suffolk arrives from France with Margaret, Henry VI's future queen. As part of a truce, England agrees to return the duchy of Anjou and the county of Maine to Margaret's father, Duke of Anjou. Henry is happy, but Gloucester, Warwick, and York object to Suffolk's concessions. As Gloucester leaves, his enemies begin plotting against him. Cardinal Beaufort leads the conspiracy, while Buckingham and Somerset covet Gloucester's powerful post as Protector. Salisbury and Warwick feel sure the plotters will soon turn against each other. Alone, York dreams of seizing the throne, but he knows he must still "sit and fret and bite his tongue".

Anjou and Maine are given to the French;/Paris is lost; the state of Normandy stands on a tickle point… 1.1

In Gloucester's London home, the old duke chides his wife Eleanor for imagining that one day she will be queen. When they are summoned by the king to St. Albans, Eleanor promises to follow her husband there. Two priests in Suffolk's pay lead her to a witch and a conjurer who can summon spirits. At the palace, Queen Margaret complains about power-hungry noblemen, adding that no one irritates her more than "that proud dame," Gloucester's wife. Suffolk, Margaret's ally and lover, promises that first Eleanor and then the others will be removed, and "you yourself shall steer the happy helm." Eleanor watches the witch and the conjurer summon a spirit prophesying that the king will be overthrown and Suffolk will die "by water". The session is broken up by York, Buckingham, and guards, who arrest Eleanor and her cronies.

Madam, myself have limed a bush for her,/And placed a choir of such enticing birds/That she will light to listen to the lays… 1.3

ACT TWO 510 lines

ST. ALBANS AND LONDON

The king, queen, and nobles are hunting at St. Albans when a townsman announces a miracle: a blind and lame man has recovered his sight at St. Alban's shrine. The king is impressed, but the man is unmasked as an impostor. Buckingham reports that Eleanor has been caught "Raising up wicked spirits from under ground," news that alarms Gloucester but delights his enemies.

But all his mind is bent to holiness,/ To number Ave-Maries on his beads;/ His champions are the prophets and apostles… 1.3

In London, York explains his claim to the throne to Salisbury and Warwick, recalling that his family's rights were usurped by the present king's grandfather, Henry IV. Impressed, the two nobles kneel before "our rightful sovereign," but York warns that he must first defeat the House of Lancaster.

The king orders the death of Eleanor's accomplices in witchcraft, but she, "more nobly born," must instead parade in rags through London before being banished. The king also strips Gloucester of his title of Protector. As Eleanor walks through London in a white sheet, incredulous that her husband has allowed her humiliation, Gloucester tells her to be patient. Called to Bury St. Edmunds, Gloucester begs her escort to treat her kindly.

Ah, Gloucester, teach me to forget myself;/For while I think I am your married wife,/And thou a prince... 2.4

ACT THREE 835 lines

BURY ST. EDMUNDS AND LONDON

As the king awaits Gloucester, Queen Margaret warns him of the old duke's pride. Others also accuse Gloucester of theft and treason, but the king dismisses the charges. News of the loss of all English territories in France goes almost unnoticed as England's domestic troubles mount. When Gloucester appears, Suffolk arrests him for treason, although the king again defends the duke. As Gloucester is led away, he warns Henry of the plotting around him. The king withdraws, leaving the queen to tell the cardinal and Suffolk that she wishes Gloucester dead.

Can you not see? Or will you not observe/ The strangeness of his altered countenance?... 3.1

Ah, gracious lord, these days are dangerous;/ Virtue is choked with foul ambition... 3.1

York is ordered to suppress a new uprising in Ireland; while away, he promotes a rebellion led by John Cade of Kent, a former soldier who resembles John Mortimer, a distant cousin of York, as a way of testing the Yorkist strength.

Suffolk reports Gloucester's death to the king, who faints with shock. As Henry recovers, he turns against Suffolk, but the queen jumps to her ally's defense and complains of the king's abuse. After Warwick confirms that Gloucester has been murdered in his bed by "violent hands," he accuses Suffolk of the crime. With the Commons demanding Suffolk's death or banishment, the king chooses banishment, leaving the queen in tears. On his deathbed, Cardinal Beaufort asks to see the king and rambles incoherently before expiring. "So bad a death argues a monstrous life," Warwick notes coldly.

Be woe for me, more wretched than he is./ What, dost thou turn away and hide thy face?... 3.2

ACT FOUR

768 lines

THE COAST OF KENT, BLACKHEATH, LONDON, KENILWORTH CASTLE, AND A GARDEN IN KENT

After a battle at sea, Suffolk and two gentlemen are captured by a boat captain and his crew. Suffolk arrogantly identifies himself as William de la Pole. Recognizing him as Suffolk, the captain orders him beheaded, while the gentlemen accompanying him are freed to carry his head to the queen.

Poole! Sir Poole! Lord!/ Ay, kennel, puddle, sink, whose filth and dirt/ Troubles the silver spring where England drinks… 4.1

In Blackheath, Jack Cade, claiming to be Sir John Mortimer, defeats loyalist forces under Humphrey Stafford and heads for London, where the queen, with Suffolk's head on her lap, is mourning her dead lover. Cade and his men score more victories as they arrive in London. However, by promising an amnesty, Buckingham and Clifford finally persuade Cade's followers to abandon the rebel. A messenger arrives with news that York has landed from Ireland and is marching on London to demand Somerset's arrest as a traitor. Cade, on the run, enters a garden in Kent where he is confronted by the owner of the house. They fight and Cade is killed.

ACT FIVE

343 lines

BETWEEN DARTFORD AND BLACKHEATH, AND ST. ALBANS

York marches on London, confident that the crown of England is within his reach. When Buckingham brings him a message from the king, York pretends that his only demand is Somerset's removal. Informed that Somerset has indeed been arrested, he then feels obliged to announce the demobilization of his army and pledge his loyalty to the king. But when he discovers that Somerset is still free, he explodes in anger and warns the king that "thou shalt rule no more". Somerset in turn orders York's arrest. York calls on his sons, Edward and Richard, to stand surety for him and take his place in detention. Lord Clifford rules that York himself must be sent to the Tower of London.

How now? Is Somerset at liberty?/Then, York, unloose thy long-imprisoned thoughts… 5.1

When Salisbury and Warwick endorse York's claim to the throne, however, war becomes inevitable. At the Battle of St. Albans, York kills Lord Clifford and his son Richard slays Somerset. As Clifford's son mourns his father, the queen sends the king to the safety of London. Nearby, York celebrates his victory and prepares to pursue the king.

Saint Albans battle, won by famous York,/ Shall be eternized in all age to come… 5.3

READING THE PLAY

COMPARISON OF PROSE TO VERSE

prose: 15% | verse: 85%

HISTORICAL SOURCES

JOHN CADE

In 1450, John Cade of Kent led a revolt against high taxes. He demanded the removal of several of the king's chief ministers, and seized London before being captured and killed. His uprising contributed to the breakdown in royal authority that presaged civil war.

Jack Cade in Cannon Street declaring himself Lord of the City of London.

THE PLAY IS WRITTEN in blank verse, although with Cade's mutiny Shakespeare for the first time has lowly citizens involved in comic scenes speak in prose, a common practice in Elizabethan theater. Much of the play is given over to advancing and resolving a series of power struggles and conspiracies, with few characters given moments of introspection. York reveals his inner thoughts only when he is alone, but even these are only variations on his ongoing maneuvers to seize the throne. York's language, though, anticipates the still greater guile and hypocrisy of his son, Richard. Indeed, when in Act 5 Clifford insults young Richard as a "foul ingested lump,/As crookèd in thy manners as thy shape!" it is apparent that Shakespeare is building the monster of *Richard III.*

16th-century portrait of Henry VI by François Clouet. Henry was a pious and well-intentioned man, easily swayed by his advisers.

Already early in his career, the playwright excels in portraying depravity. Queen Margaret, for instance, spills over with ruthless ambition, although she is allowed a moment of sadness when she embraces the severed head of her lover, Suffolk. Cardinal Beaufort of Winchester is unremittingly evil, a grotesque caricature of a Catholic prelate, who is even denied the right to repent on his deathbed. Gloucester is perhaps the only tragic character, anguishing as he wavers between his loyalty to the king and his love for his pernicious wife.

The brevity of the final battle scene at St. Albans indicates that Shakespeare fully understood the difficulties of depicting combat on stage. Thus, while the battles were important historical events, in the plays they become occasions for major speeches before and after brief moments of combat.

WHO'S WHO

Queen Margaret, wife of Henry VI, plots against the **Duke of Gloucester**, Henry's uncle and protector. Despite warning the king against the nobles who are plotting against him, Gloucester is murdered by Margaret and the **Duke of Suffolk**, Margaret's lover. Henry banishes Suffolk, who is killed by seamen loyal to Henry. Meanwhile, **Jack Cade** leads a commoners' rebellion, attacks London and is killed. At this point **Richard, Duke of York**, seizes his opportunity, rebels against the king and defeats Henry's force at the Battle of St. Albans.

SEEING THE PLAY

Cardinal Beaufort (Walker Jones) crowns Henry VI (Tom Nelis) in a production of the trilogy at the New York Shakespeare Festival.

WITH HENRY SEEMINGLY UNABLE to defend his own crown, the battle for power revolves around the competing ambitions of Queen Margaret and Richard of York. They are the play's pivotal characters and much depends on how they are interpreted. Surprisingly, perhaps, they need not be portrayed as one-dimensional monsters. Shakespeare presents Margaret as cynical and merciless, as ready to cuckold her husband as she is to murder her enemies, yet she works incessantly to keep the hapless Henry on the throne. Similarly, York may be no less devious and cruel, yet Shakespeare treats his claim to the crown seriously, accepting the validity of a royal succession passing through the female line. Still, if the *Henry VI* trilogy is seen as a three-act play (and, in a sense, this is the most rewarding way of enjoying the three plays), this is the act in which all the battle lines are drawn in preparation for *Part III*.

One novelty of *Part II* is Shakespeare's use of a crowd-pleasing comic interlude, something that would become a feature of many later plays. Here, it involves the Cade mutiny that, although violent, is portrayed as a revolt of clowns. Perhaps the play's most memorable line is also uttered by one of Jack Cade's followers: "The first thing we do, let's kill all the lawyers." In reality, Cade's revolt was more serious than that, but Shakespeare instead used it to provide some raucous entertainment for the "groundlings," a welcome respite in a bleak play.

Graham Crowden (Gloucester), Charles Dance (Buckingham), Alan Howard (Henry VI), John Rhys-Davies (Beaufort), Helen Mirren (Queen Margaret), and Peter McEnery (Suffolk) in the acclaimed 1978 RSC production of the *Henry VI* trilogy at the Aldwych Theatre, London.

ON STAGE

GLOUCESTER'S MURDER

The first quarto edition of the play included Shakespeare's stage direction for the murder of Humphrey, Duke of Gloucester. "Then the Curtaine being drawne, Duke Humphrey is discovered in his bed, and two men lying on his brest, and smothering him in his bed. And then enter the Duke of Suffolke to them." The direction was omitted in the *First Folio* of 1623, but the idea has been used in some productions.

HENRY VI PART III

*H*ENRY VI, PART III, WHICH COVERS THE MOST CHAOTIC PERIOD of the Wars of the Roses, completes the *Henry VI* trilogy and leads directly into *Richard III.* Thought to have been written in 1590–1591, immediately after Part II, it was initially named *The True Tragedie of Richard Duke of York and the death of good king Henrie the Sixt.* But after reworking and publication in 1595, it was identified as the third part of *Henry VI.* Addressing the instability that can flow from challenges to the legitimacy of the crown, this play rang a warning bell to an England ruled by an ageing Queen Elizabeth I, whose successor had not been determined. The portrayal of Edward as a womanizer and his brother Richard as a monster echoed the Tudors' disapproval of the Yorkist dynasty. Shakespeare courts the queen's favor by having Henry VI praise the Earl of Richmond, later Henry VII, Elizabeth's grandfather.

BEHIND THE PLAY

THE PLAY COVERS THE YEARS BETWEEN 1455 AND 1471, a period of extraordinary confusion from which Shakespeare somehow extracts a comprehensible drama. He follows the broad lines of history, but as always telescopes events. He ignores the five years following the Battle of St. Albans and creates the impression that it was in 1455, and not after a fresh rebellion in 1460, that Henry was forced to accept York as his successor. Margaret rejected her husband's capitulation and defeated the Yorkists at Wakefield where York was killed (and not murdered by Margaret, as the play has it). York's son Edward then took up the Yorkist banner, defeated the Lancastrians and was proclaimed king in February 1461. In the play's last three acts, Shakespeare focuses only on key moments that portray the chaotic passage of power from the Lancastrian to the Yorkist dynasty: Edward IV's marriage to Elizabeth Woodville in 1464 and the resulting revolt of Warwick and Clarence which restored Henry to the throne; Edward's defeat of the rebels a year later; the murder of Henry in 1471. Here, at least, Shakespeare invents nothing: historical records show that the assassin was indeed Richard of Gloucester.

Henry, your sovereign,/ Is prisoner to the foe; his state usurped,/ His realm a slaughter-house, his subjects slain… 5.4

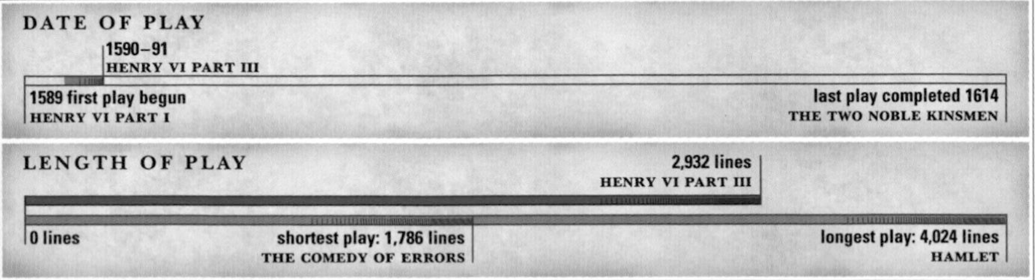

DRAMATIS PERSONAE

To the despair of his fierce wife, Queen Margaret (Penny Downie), gentle King Henry VI (Ralph Fiennes) fails to stand up for his rights.

KING HENRY VI
365 lines
The last Lancastrian king, a saintly man but a weak ruler, he worries about the legitimacy of his title; his French wife, Margaret, defends his crown on the battlefield, but Henry is murdered by Gloucester in the Tower of London.

EDWARD, PRINCE OF WALES
46 lines
Henry's son, he inherits his mother's courage, but is murdered at Tewkesbury by York's three sons.

LEWIS XI, KING OF FRANCE
67 lines
He supports Henry's restoration after Edward marries Lady Grey.

EARLS OF OXFORD, NORTHUMBERLAND, AND WESTMORELAND, DUKES OF SOMERSET AND EXETER, AND SIR JOHN SOMERVILLE
36; 30; 11; 39; 18; 0 lines
Nobles loyal to the royal House of Lancaster.

SIR WILLIAM STANLEY, DUKE OF NORFOLK, MARQUESS OF MONTAGUE, AND SIR JOHN MONTGOMERY
18; 3; 32; 14 lines
Nobles loyal to the Yorkist branch of the royal house.

LORD CLIFFORD
141 lines
He murders York to avenge his father's death at the Battle of St. Albans.

DUKE OF YORK
172 lines
He claims the throne and agrees to become Henry's successor, but later returns to arms; when captured at the Battle of Wakefield, he is murdered by Queen Margaret and Clifford.

EDWARD, EARL OF MARCH
436 lines
York's eldest son, he drives Henry out of office and becomes Edward IV; his most trusted ally, Warwick, ousts him from power, but he recovers the crown when Henry is murdered.

EDMUND PLANTAGENET
24 lines
York's second son, also the Earl of Rutland, he is murdered by Clifford.

GEORGE PLANTAGENET
112 lines
York's third son, named Duke of Clarence by Edward IV, he backs Warwick's rebellion, then rejoins Edward's forces.

RICHARD PLANTAGENET
404 lines
York's misshapen youngest son (also called Duke of Gloucester), he murders both Henry and the Prince of Wales, clearing his way to the throne.

EARL OF WARWICK
440 lines
Known as the "kingmaker," he brings Edward IV to the throne, then restores Henry VI to power, but dies in battle.

EARL OF PEMBROKE AND LORDS HASTINGS AND STAFFORD
0; 20; 0 lines
Nobles loyal to Edward IV.

SIR JOHN AND SIR HUGH MORTIMER
1; 0 lines
Uncles to the Duke of York.

HENRY, EARL OF RICHMOND
0 lines
The future Henry VII, he is praised by Henry VI.

EARL RIVERS
7 lines
The brother of Lady Grey.

A SON
22 lines
He has killed his father in battle.

A FATHER
27 lines
He has killed his son in battle.

QUEEN MARGARET
281 lines
The French-born queen of England, she emerges as an impressive military leader.

LADY ELIZABETH GREY
74 lines
Formerly Elizabeth Woodville, she becomes Edward IV's queen.

LADY BONA
9 lines
Sister-in-law to the French king, she agrees to marry Edward IV, but is rebuffed.

OTHER PLAYERS
Lords, Ladies, Mayors of York and Coventry, Tutor, Nurse, Infant Prince, Lieutenant of the Tower, Huntsman, Messengers, Soldiers, Watchmen, Keepers, Post, and other Attendants.

The Machiavellian Yorkist Richard (Wallace Acton) coldly plots his winding path to power.

PLOT SUMMARY

SIZE OF ACTS

ACT 1	ACT 2	ACT 3	ACT 4	ACT 5
585 lines	705 lines	581 lines	563 lines	498 lines

ACT ONE
585 lines

LONDON AND SANDAL CASTLE IN YORKSHIRE

After winning the Battle of St. Albans, the Duke of York prepares to assume power, when Henry VI arrives in London and orders him "to descend my throne." York refuses, claiming he is the rightful king, but Henry retorts that his own title comes through his grandfather, Henry IV, who "by conquest got the crown," though he admits to himself, "my title's weak." Then Henry proposes that York and his heirs succeed him. York agrees, outraging the queen, who accuses Henry of disinheriting his son, the Prince of Wales.

Who can be patient in such extremes?/Ah, wretched man! Would I had died a maid,/And never seen thee, never borne thee son… 1.1

In Sandal Castle, York's sons persuade him to "be king or die." As war resumes, York meets Margaret's 20,000-strong army near Wakefield where his son, Rutland, is slain by Clifford. When York, too, is captured, the queen mocks and reviles him. York retaliates with raging abuse and insults, before being stabbed to death, by Clifford and Margaret. The queen then orders York's head to be displayed on a stake in York.

Brave warriors, Clifford and Northumberland,/Come, make him stand upon this molehill here… 1.4

She-wolf of France, but worse than wolves of France,/Whose tongue more poisons than the adder's tooth!… 1.4

ACT TWO
705 lines

HEREFORDSHIRE AND YORKSHIRE

York's sons, Edward and Richard, learn of the deaths of both their father and brother. Warwick brings more bad news: when confronted by the queen's troops, his own forces fled. But he also reports that York's other son, George, has landed with soldiers from Burgundy.

In York, the queen shows Henry the head of his enemy. Upset, the king insists he did not break his word to York, but Clifford chastises him as "a most unloving father". York's sons, meanwhile, have mobilized 30,000 men to proclaim Edward, Earl of March, king. When the two sides meet, the Yorkists fear the day is lost, but Richard revives their spirits. Margaret orders Henry to leave the field. Alone, the king laments his fate, as he witnesses the horrors of civil war: a man carries in the body of his father, whom he has killed; another man drags in the body of his son, whom he has slain. Margaret tells

My gracious liege, this too much lenity/And harmful pity must be laid aside… 2.2

This battle fares like to the morning's war,/When dying clouds contend with growing light… 2.5

O tiger's heart wrapped in a woman's hide!/How couldst thou drain the lifeblood of the child… 1.1

the king to flee. Clifford, lying wounded, also predicts Henry's overthrow. As Edward, Richard, and Warwick arrive, Clifford dies, but they still insult him and order his head displayed in York. Edward names Richard Duke of Gloucester and George Duke of Clarence, while Warwick leaves to organize the king's coronation and negotiate his marriage to Lady Bona.

ACT THREE

581 lines

NORTH OF ENGLAND, LONDON, AND FRANCE

Henry, hiding in a forest, is overheard by two gamekeepers talking to himself about how Margaret has gone to Paris to seek help from the French king, while Warwick is also there requesting Lady Bona's hand for the king. On recognizing the fugitive king, the gamekeepers challenge and arrest him.

My Queen and son are gone to France for aid... 3.1

In London, Lady Grey petitions Edward for land confiscated after her husband died fighting alongside York. Edward's brothers, Gloucester and Clarence, notice that Lady Grey has charmed the new king. But the wooing is interrupted by word of Henry's imprisonment in the Tower of London. Alone, Gloucester reveals his own ambition to be king, imagining how he will eliminate those blocking his way, and dwelling obsessively on his deformities. In France, Margaret and her son beg King Lewis for help, and Warwick arrives to seek Lady Bona's hand for Edward. To Margaret's dismay, Lewis approves the match. But at the same moment, letters announce Edward's marriage to Lady Grey. Feeling betrayed, Warwick turns against Edward, and offers his daughter, Lady Anne, in marriage to the young Prince of Wales.

Ay, Edward will use women honourably./ Would he were wasted, marrow, bones, and all... 3.2

ACT FOUR

563 lines

LONDON, WARWICKSHIRE, AND YORKSHIRE

Edward's brothers warn that his marriage to Lady Grey will cause trouble. Before long, he hears that Lewis feels offended, Margaret has rebelled, and Warwick leads Henry's forces. When Clarence hears that Lady Anne is to marry the Prince of Wales, he decides to marry Warwick's other daughter and desert Edward. But Gloucester remains loyal.

On a battlefield in Warwickshire, Warwick leads a night raid on Edward's camp, capturing the king and recovering the crown. He then leaves for London to release Henry. In Yorkshire, Edward is held prisoner, but Gloucester frees him. In London, Henry, again king, cedes government to Warwick, and names Clarence as Protector. Henry heralds the young Earl of Richmond, the future Henry VII, as "likely in time to bless a regal throne" 66.

Come hither, England's hope. If secret powers/ Suggest but truth to my divining thoughts... 1.2

With Richmond safely in France, Warwick learns that Edward and Gloucester have returned to York. Edward at first decides to abandon his royal claim, but his followers dissuade him. As Warwick leaves to confront Edward at Coventry, Edward and his soldiers invade the royal palace in London and seize Henry.

ACT FIVE

498 lines

COVENTRY, BARNET, TEWKESBURY, AND LONDON

Outside Coventry, Edward promises to pardon Warwick if he surrenders. The noble rebuffs the offer, believing that reinforcements under Clarence are on their way. Instead, Clarence betrays Warwick and rejoins Edward's forces. Near Barnet, Warwick is badly wounded and knows the day is lost. Learning that his brother has also fallen, he dies.

With Margaret leading 30,000 men, Edward turns to meet them on the field of Tewkesbury. The queen addresses her officers like a true warrior 66, but she and her son are captured. The Prince of Wales is stabbed to death. Leaving Margaret mourning her son, Gloucester heads for London.

Great lords, wise men ne'er sit and wail their loss,/ But cheerly seek how to redress their harms... 5.4

As Gloucester enters King Henry's cell in the Tower, the doomed monarch prophesies that thousands will rue the day when the deformed Yorkist lord was born 66.

Hadst thou been kill'd when first thou didst presume,/ Thou hadst not lived to kill a son of mine... 5.6

Gloucester quickly stabs him, but cannot forget Henry's haunting insults. Back on the throne, Edward invites Clarence and Gloucester to show their love for his queen. Gloucester kisses her, whispering "so Judas kiss'd his master."

Clarence, thy turn is next, and then the rest,/ Counting myself but bad till I be best... 5.6

READING THE PLAY

COMPARISON OF PROSE TO VERSE

prose: 0% verse: 100%

"Lo, now my glory smeared in dust and blood!" (5.2). Warwick, once the "proud setter up and puller down of kings," resigns himself to defeat and death as his comrades Somerset and Oxford keep watch beside him. Engraving, *c.* 1850 by T. Browne after J. A. Houston.

THIS PLAY, WHICH COMPLETES the *Henry VI* trilogy, can be best understood if read after *Parts I* and *II* since both the sense of the narrative and some of the key characters are established in the earlier plays. As often in the history plays, there is also the problem of keeping up with changing names: here, George becomes Clarence, and Richard becomes Gloucester. The play is written in blank verse, including, unusually, the scene where a common soldier laments slaying his father and a father mourns the son he has killed in battle. Then, in one of the play's rare moments of poignancy, Henry meditates on the "piteous spectacle" of civil war. More prevalent is cruelty and abuse. Margaret's sadistic insults and crowning of York with paper before murdering him is matched by York's curses, calling her "she-wolf of France," before he dies.

Physical insults, though, are reserved for Gloucester: as each of his victims faces death, Clifford calls him "crook-back," the Prince of Wales abuses him as "thou mis-shapen Dick," and Henry describes him born as "an indigested and deformed lump." Yet Gloucester alone among the warring nobles is allowed an inner self, using his disfigured body to justify his twisted mind: "since the heavens have shaped my body so,/Let hell make crook'd my mind to answer it." Thus, having created in Gloucester his first memorable character, Shakespeare steadily prepares him in *Parts II* and *III* of *Henry VI* to dominate the final work of the tetralogy, *Richard III*. As Gloucester literally wipes Henry's blood off his hands at the play's end, the chronicle of death is not yet over: we are left waiting for the sequel.

WHO'S WHO

Henry VI, Lancastrian king of England, submits to the Yorkist revolt, and agrees to name the **Duke of York,** rather than his own son, as his successor. But Henry's wife, the tough and ruthless **Queen Margaret**, refuses to accept Henry's peace pact, and wages war on York, who is defeated and executed. York's son, **Edward, Earl of March**, defeats Henry and becomes King Edward IV. Edward's marriage to **Lady Grey** angers the loyal **Earl of Warwick**, who backs Henry and Margaret. Warwick defeats Edward, and reinstates Henry, but Edward returns and captures Henry. Edward kills Warwick in battle, while his youngest brother, the deformed **Richard, Duke of Gloucester**, murders Henry in the Tower. Edward is now undisputed king.

SEEING THE PLAY

IN THIS PLAY, SHAKESPEARE FOR THE FIRST TIME switches the focus from death on the battlefields to bloody murder. With the Yorkist offensive, ambition and revenge replace honor and patriotism as the driving forces of England's history. If produced as written, this is a grim and gory play; presented in any other way, it is meaningless. Yet endless changes of fortunes and loyalties also make it complicated to follow, above all if, as is likely given the huge cast of characters, actors must play several roles.

Henry VI can be portrayed simply as a weak, saintly, and unsuitable monarch, but he alone is remotely decent, even willing to acknowledge that his right to the throne is questionable. He is totally overshadowed, though, by Margaret and Gloucester, both personifications of ambition, courage and ruthlessness, who risk becoming caricatures in overheated productions. The play has no shortage of battle scenes, yet what propels the narrative is the spilling of individual blood. Thus, after York is stabbed to death by Margaret and Clifford, it follows that York's sons should murder Margaret's son and even mutilate Clifford's body after he dies in battle. It is on these occasions that Shakespeare dramatically conveys the senselessness of a nation tearing itself apart in fratricidal conflict.

A raging Margaret (Helen Carey) tries to knock some grit into her faint-hearted husband Henry VI (Philip Goodwin). Henry's light, flowing robes reflect his gentle moralizing nature in Michael Kahn's production at the Shakespeare Theatre, Washington D.C., in 1996.

"The owl shrieked at thy birth, an evil sign;/The night-crow cried, aboding luckless time" (5.6). Stripped of all, Henry (Alan Howard) still defies his executioner, Richard (Anton Lesser), with the power of his rhetoric, achieving heroic dignity in death, if not in life (RSC,1978).

ON STAGE

RICHARD'S INSTANT COMEBACK

Henry VI Part III slips seamlessly into its sequel *Richard III.* Richard's ambition bridges the gap, and Edward's closing lines, "For here, I hope, begins our lasting joy," lead naturally into the opening soliloquy of *Richard III,* "Now is the winter of our discontent...". Indeed, just before the curtain fell on *Henry VI* at the Birmingham Repertory, in 1952, a wry Richard slipped in the opening lines of *Richard III.*

RICHARD III

IN RICHARD III, the first of Shakespeare's great dramas, the playwright creates his most engagingly repellent character. Such has been the influence of the stage Richard III that the role has defined the king's image ever since. Written in 1592–93, the play follows the three parts of *Henry VI* and completes Shakespeare's first tetralogy. Its popularity in the playwright's lifetime can be gauged by the six quarto editions published before the *First Folio* of 1623. With Queen Elizabeth unmarried and childless, the Tudor era was nearing its end. Its place in history seemed assured, yet it was born with a blemish: the dynasty's founder and the queen's grandfather, Henry VII, seized power in 1485 through force of arms. Yet if the ousted Richard III was a recognized monster, Henry's usurpation could be justified. Thus, even before Shakespeare, plays were written presenting Richard as a depraved murderer.

BEHIND THE PLAY

SHAKESPEARE'S PRINCIPAL SOURCE is Holinshed's *Chronicles* but he also uses Sir Thomas More's *History of Richard III*, which reflected the Tudor caricature of Richard as an evil monster. In reality, while Richard killed Henry VI, he probably did not carry out the other murders attributed to him in *Richard III*—the verdict is still open on the murder of the princes in the Tower. He may not even have been deformed. This play is concerned primarily with events leading to Richard's seizure of power in 1483, his two-year reign and his violent end. As always, Shakespeare rearranges history to suit his purposes. For instance, he has Richard planning Clarence's murder and wooing Lady Anne almost simultaneously. In reality, Richard married Lady Anne in 1471, while Clarence was killed in 1478. Shakespeare takes other liberties in order to strengthen the play's dramatic structure. To recall past Yorkist crimes, Margaret, Henry VI's widow, is seen haunting the royal palace when in truth she disappeared from public view after her husband's murder. The account of the battle of Bosworth Field is broadly accurate: Richard really did lose his horse before he lost his crown.

But I am in/ So far in blood that sin will pluck on sin... 4.2

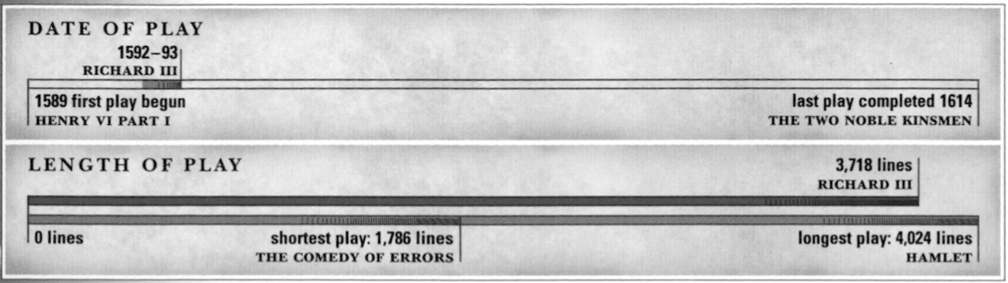

DATE OF PLAY

1592–93
RICHARD III

1589 first play begun
HENRY VI PART I

last play completed 1614
THE TWO NOBLE KINSMEN

LENGTH OF PLAY

3,718 lines
RICHARD III

0 lines

shortest play: 1,786 lines
THE COMEDY OF ERRORS

longest play: 4,024 lines
HAMLET

DRAMATIS PERSONAE

KING EDWARD IV
65 lines
He does not recognize the ambition of Gloucester.

EDWARD, PRINCE OF WALES
52 lines
Edward IV's heir, he is murdered on orders of his uncle, Gloucester.

RICHARD, DUKE OF YORK
49 lines
Edward IV's second son, he is murdered in the Tower.

GEORGE, DUKE OF CLARENCE
172 lines
King Edward's brother, he is murdered on orders of his brother, Gloucester.

RICHARD, DUKE OF GLOUCESTER
1171 lines
King Edward's brother, later Richard III, he orders the murders of his brother, Clarence, and nephews; he marries Lady Anne, then has her killed; he is killed at Bosworth Field by Richmond, the future Henry VII.

Warped in body and mind, the menacing Richard (Antony Sher) relishes his evil designs.

EDWARD PLANTAGENET
21 lines
Clarence's son, he believes Edward IV ordered his father's death.

HENRY TUDOR, EARL OF RICHMOND
136 lines
He gathers forces in France before defeating Richard III at Bosworth Field; as Henry VII, he weds Edward IV's daughter and, by uniting the Lancastrian and Yorkist lines, ends the Wars of the Roses.

CARDINAL BOURCHIER
9 lines
Archbishop of Canterbury.

THOMAS ROTHERHAM
12 lines
Archbishop of York.

JOHN MORTON
7 lines
Bishop of Ely.

DUKE OF BUCKINGHAM
376 lines
A strong ally in Richard's bid for the crown, he feels betrayed by the new king and rebels; he is executed.

DUKE OF NORFOLK, EARL OF SURREY, LORD LOVEL, AND SIR RICHARD RATCLIFFE
10; 1; 3; 30 lines
Supporters of Richard III.

EARL RIVERS AND LORD GREY
57; 15 lines
Elizabeth's relatives, they oppose Richard and are captured and executed.

MARQUESS OF DORSET
20 lines
Elizabeth's son from her first marriage, he joins Richmond in France.

EARL OF OXFORD, SIR JAMES BLUNT, SIR WALTER HERBERT, AND SIR WILLIAM BRANDON
2; 8; 1; 0 lines
Supporters of Richmond.

LORD HASTINGS
150 lines
Lord Chamberlain, he is killed by Richard.

Furious and fearful by turns, the aggrieved widows Margaret (Nancy Price) and Anne (Nadje Compton) rail in vain at Richard.

LORD STANLEY
101 lines
Also known as Derby, he supports Richmond.

SIR THOMAS VAUGHAN
7 lines
He is executed with Earl Rivers and Lord Grey.

SIR WILLIAM CATESBY
64 lines
Loyal to Richard.

SIR JAMES TYRREL
38 lines
He murders the princes in the Tower.

SIR ROBERT BRACKENBURY
39 lines
Lieutenant of the Tower.

CHRISTOPHER URSWICK AND JOHN
8; 1 lines
Two priests.

TRESSEL AND BERKELEY
0 lines
Attendants to Lady Anne.

LORD MAYOR OF LONDON
17 lines
He leads citizens who acclaim Gloucester as Richard III.

QUEEN ELIZABETH
276 lines
Edward IV's widow, she cannot prevent Richard from murdering her sons and desiring her daughter.

QUEEN MARGARET
218 lines
Henry VI's French-born widow, she delights in seeing her curses come true as her husband's enemies fall victim to Richard III.

DUCHESS OF YORK
142 lines
The widow of the Duke of York, she is mother to Edward IV, Clarence, and Richard III, and grandmother to the murdered princes; she laments the day that Richard was born.

LADY ANNE
167 lines
She is wooed into marrying Richard, who killed her father and murdered her husband and father-in-law; she too is murdered.

MARGARET PLANTAGENET
9 lines
Clarence's daughter, she believes Edward IV ordered her father's death.

OTHER PLAYERS
Ghosts of those murdered by Richard III, Lords, Gentlemen, Bishops, Attendants, Aldermen, Pursuivant, Scrivener, Page, Councillors, Citizens, Keeper in the Tower, Sheriff of Wiltshire, Murderers, Messengers, and Soldiers.

PLOT SUMMARY

SIZE OF ACTS

ACT 1	ACT 2	ACT 3	ACT 4	ACT 5
1083 lines	428 lines	835 lines	879 lines	493 lines

ACT ONE

1,083 lines

LONDON

Richard, Duke of Gloucester, by now almost unbalanced in his yearning for the throne, has deceived his brother, Edward IV, into arresting their brother, Clarence. As Clarence is led to the Tower of London, Gloucester feigns shock and promises to intercede with the king, but his plan is to eliminate all competitors for the crown. No less obscenely, Gloucester wants to marry Lady Anne, having killed her father, Warwick, and murdered both her husband and her father-in-law, Henry VI. As Anne travels with the late king's corpse for burial, Gloucester sets out to woo her. Disgusted, she insults him as "dreadful minister of hell." But, after first inviting her to kill him, he persuades her that he is repentant. As she leaves, he gloats.

Now is the winter of our discontent/ Made glorious summer by this sun of York... 1.1

Set down, set down your honourable load – / If honour may be shrouded in a hearse... 1.2

Was ever woman in this humour wooed?/ Was ever woman in this humour won?... 1.2

In the palace, Queen Elizabeth worries about the king's health, but Buckingham reassures her that Edward is on the mend and is eager to end the squabbling within his family. Gloucester sends two murderers to Clarence's cell but, to cover up his role, he accuses Elizabeth of turning Edward against Clarence. Queen Margaret, Henry VI's widow, jumps at the chance to berate Gloucester, calling him "a poisonous hunch backed toad" and a "bottled spider." In the Tower, the Duke of Clarence relates a nightmare to his jailer, then falls into a troubled sleep. The jailer allows the murderers into the cell and, as one of them hesitates, Clarence awakens and begs their pity. But the second murderer swiftly ends his plea by stabbing the duke to death.

Are you drawn forth among a world of men/ To slay the innocent?... 1.4

Look when he fawns he bites; and when he bites/ His venom tooth will rankle to the death... 1.3

ACT TWO

428 lines

LONDON

Sick and close to death, Edward believes he has ended feuding in the court. Elizabeth begs him to free his brother from the Tower, but Gloucester brings word that Clarence is dead. The king insists that he canceled the death sentence, but Gloucester says the reprieve

arrived too late. Edward is despondent. Clarence's two children also hear of their father's death, but their grandmother, the Duchess of York, denies it; they insist that their uncle Gloucester told them that the king had jailed their father.

Elizabeth appears, disheveled and in tears, with news that the king has died. With the Duchess now mourning yet another son, Gloucester pretends to console her. Buckingham, Gloucester's ally, announces he will bring the king's son, Edward, Prince of Wales, to London to be crowned. While awaiting the prince, Elizabeth learns that Gloucester has ordered the arrest of her brother Lord Rivers, and her son from her first marriage, Lord Grey. Fearing the worst, she goes into sanctuary with her youngest son, the Duke of York.

ACT THREE

835 lines

LONDON AND BAYNARD'S CASTLE NEAR LONDON

When Prince Edward reaches London, he is alarmed to learn that his mother and brother have fled. Buckingham tells Cardinal Bourchier to persuade the queen to deliver young York; if she refuses, he adds, Lord Hastings will simply seize him. Thinking ahead, Gloucester suggests that Prince Edward move to the royal quarters of the Tower and, after York arrives, the two boys reluctantly go there.

With his goal now within reach, Gloucester orders his ally, Sir William Catesby, to sound out Hastings, the Lord Chamberlain, on the succession. Hastings is warned by Lord Derby to be wary of "the boar" Gloucester, but he is unconcerned. When Catesby arrives, Hastings welcomes the news that Elizabeth's brother and son, leaders of the enemy Woodville clan, are to be executed. But he refuses to support Richard against the prince.

Buckingham, Hastings, Derby, and other nobles are meeting at the Tower to plan the prince's coronation as Edward V when Gloucester arrives in foul mood and blames his withered arm on Elizabeth's witchcraft. When Hastings is slow to agree, Gloucester abruptly orders him beheaded. Gloucester and Buckingham are with the Lord Mayor of London when Hastings's head is brought in and Gloucester puts on a show of

So dear I loved the man that I must weep./ I took him for the plainest harmless creature… 3.5

sorrow. Alone with Buckingham, Gloucester spells out his plan. Buckingham must convince the mayor and citizens that Edward IV's sons are bastards and that even King Edward was illegitimate, conceived when old York was warring in France. Buckingham should then lead a delegation of citizens to Baynard's Castle to beg Gloucester to become king.

When Buckingham arrives at the castle, Catesby announces solemnly that Gloucester is at prayer. But with Buckingham insisting that the mayor and citizens await him, Gloucester finally emerges. Buckingham begs him in the name of the people to take on "kingly government," but Gloucester affects humility and refuses the crown. When the citizens start to leave, however, they are called back and, with theatrical diffidence, Gloucester accepts the throne, and returns to London to be crowned.

Would you enforce me to a world of cares?/ Call them again. I am not made of stone… 3.7

ACT FOUR

879 lines

LONDON

Queen Elizabeth, the Duchess of York and Lady Anne, Gloucester's new wife, arrive at the Tower to visit Prince Edward, but they are refused entry. Derby summons Anne to Westminster to be crowned queen and even she is shocked. The Duchess, still hoping to block Gloucester, urges Dorset, another son from Elizabeth's first marriage, to join the Earl of Richmond in France.

No! Why? When he that is my husband now/ Came to me as I followed Henry's corse… 4.1

In the palace, Gloucester finally becomes Richard III, but he still wants the young princes killed. When Buckingham hesitates, Richard is told of Sir James Tyrrel who, for "corrupting gold," will do the job. He quickly orders Tyrrel to kill "those bastards in the Tower," and tells Catesby to spread the word that Lady Anne is dying: his new plan is to marry Edward IV's daughter, Elizabeth. When Buckingham reminds him of his promise to grant him an earldom, the new king dismisses him scornfully.

Richard exults that "my wife hath bid the world good night" as Tyrrel kills the two boys. But Catesby brings word that Buckingham has rebelled and plans to join forces with Richmond. In the palace, Henry VI's widow Margaret is celebrating the misfortunes befalling her enemies when Elizabeth and the Duchess of York arrive mourning the young princes. Each woman recites her woes, but Margaret is pleased that her darkest prophesies have come true.

The tyrannous and bloody act is done,/ The most arch deed of piteous massacre… 4.3

Bear with me! I am hungry for revenge,/And now I cloy with beholding it… 4.4

Richard ignores his mother's lament that "thou camest on earth to make the earth my hell." The new king tells Queen Elizabeth that he loves her daughter Elizabeth, and wants to marry her. The widowed queen is incredulous, asking how the girl could accept the man who killed her brothers and uncles and even his own wife. Richard persists, feigning remorse, but the queen stands her ground and resists him.

Look, what is done cannot be now amended./ Men shall deal unadvisedly sometimes… 4.4

I had an Edward, till a Richard killed him;/I had a Harry, till a Richard killed him:/Thou hadst an Edward, till a Richard killed him;/Thou hadst a Richard, till a Richard killed him… 4.4

Catesby reports that Richmond's "puissant navy" is approaching and Buckingham awaits him on shore. Richard mobilizes Salisbury and Norfolk for battle and orders Derby to bring his forces south. When Derby hesitates, Richard takes his son, George Stanley, as a hostage. Conflicting reports reach London: several nobles have joined the rebellion; Richmond's navy is dispersed; Buckingham is captured; Richmond has landed "with a mighty power."

ACT FIVE

493 lines

SALISBURY, TAMWORTH, AND BOSWORTH FIELD

Awaiting execution, Buckingham regrets betraying Edward IV's children and remembers Queen Margaret's curses. Richmond leads his troops to Bosworth Field where the king boasts an army three times larger than that of his enemy. As night falls, Richard orders Derby to join him at sunrise "lest George fall into the blind cave of eternal night." But Derby secretly visits Richmond, his stepson, and promises to help him against Richard.

Why, then All-Soul's Day is my body's doomsday... 5.1

In their sleep, Richard and Richmond are visited by the ghosts of Richard's many victims. Each ghost curses Richard and blesses Richmond's rebellion. Richard awakens with a start, alarmed by the spectral threats. Richmond, in contrast, is heartened by his "fairest-boding dreams" and confidently addresses his troops.

Give me another horse! Bind up my wounds!/ Have mercy, Jesu! – Soft! I did but dream... 5.3

Richard, recovering his aplomb, then urges his army to kill off "a scum of Bretons". Learning that Derby refuses to mobilize, Richard orders George Stanley beheaded, but Norfolk says the execution can wait. The battle erupts and Richard loses his horse, but fights on.

What shall I say more than I have inferred?/Remember whom you are to cope withal/A sort of vagabonds, rascals, and runaways... 5.3

Finally, Richard and Richmond meet in combat on Bosworth Field, and Richard is killed. Derby recovers the crown and presents it to Richmond, soon to become Henry VII. Richmond orders all nobles killed in the battle to be buried with honors. He then announces that he will marry Edward IV's daughter, Elizabeth, and thus "unite white rose and red". With that, the Wars of the Roses end and the Tudor dynasty begins.

Inter their bodies as becomes their births./ Proclaim a pardon to the soldiers fled... 5.5

A horse! A horse! My kingdom for a horse!... 5.4

READING THE PLAY

COMPARISON OF PROSE TO VERSE

prose: 2% verse: 98%

IN THIS HISTORY PLAY, Shakespeare for the first time creates a character who is larger than the narrative. The play is fairly easy to follow because the plot is controlled throughout by Richard, who, as the Duke of Gloucester, anticipates each step of his climb to power. The chief weapon of his ambition, however, is not violence, but language, language fed by his intelligence, cynicism, and total amorality. Except in his exchanges with the widowed Queen Margaret, Richard is the recipient of frequent insults, yet these only inflate his desire for revenge. Cold and calculating when others are angry and emotional, he retains the initiative. His soliloquies are shockingly honest, as he dwells on both his tortured body and twisted mind: "Deformed, unfinished, sent before my time/Into this breathing world, scarce half made up,/And that so lamely and unfashionable." He bides his time, but nothing can stop him, certainly not the weeping widows, Queens Margaret and Elizabeth and Lady Anne.

WHO'S WHO

Richard, Duke of Gloucester plots to become king. He kills his brother **Clarence** and seduces **Lady Anne**, daughter of the Earl of Warwick and briefly wife to Edward, Prince of Wales, son of the deposed and murdered Henry VI. When Richard's elder brother, **King Edward IV**, dies of natural causes, Richard plots to succeed him. He first has Edward's sons, **Edward, Prince of Wales** and **Richard, Duke of York**, imprisoned in the Tower, then declares them bastards and seizes the throne. Once crowned, he orders the murder of the princes. Alarmed at the growing bloodshed, **Henry Tudor, Earl of Richmond**, great great-grandson of John of Gaunt, Duke of Lancaster, prepares to invade England; Richard is killed at Bosworth Field and Richmond becomes Henry VII.

Indeed, Richard's treatment of women is cruel in the extreme, not only in his seduction of the pitiable Lady Anne (and his lust for his niece, Elizabeth of York), but also in his disdain for Margaret, Elizabeth, and the Duchess of York. Some scholars have interpreted Richard's misogyny as prototypical of the sexually insecure *macho*. But he is perhaps closer to the ageless figure of the absolute dictator: anyone perceived as a threat to him must be destroyed. Ultimately, Richard's destiny matches the outcome of the English morality play, in that his Vice is vanquished by Henry VII's Virtue. But the play itself, Shakespeare's first built around one character, belongs entirely to Richard.

PLAY HISTORY

CIBBER'S PLAY

From 1700 to the mid-19th century, it was not Shakespeare's play, but Colley Cibber's adaptation that was performed in England and the US. Cibber cut the play in half, eliminated Clarence's nightmare and Queen Margaret, added speeches from other Shakespearean dramas, and introduced a good deal of new text. Shakespeare's original was finally restored in 1854 by Samuel Phelps.

Edmund Kean's melodramatic performance in 1814 terrified and thrilled Victorian audiences. *Edmund Kean*, a painting by John James Halls, 1814.

SEEING THE PLAY

ON STAGE

SHORE'S WIFE
Because Edward IV was regarded in his day as a debauched womanizer, his beautiful married mistress, Jane Shore, sometimes appears on stage in a nonspeaking role. Richard refers to "that harlot, strumpet Shore" when he blames her for the sorcery that withered his arm. Historical records show she was indeed put on trial for witchcraft. Her punishment—to walk barefoot through London carrying a lighted candle—is also occasionally enacted.

EVERY PRODUCTION OF THIS PLAY raises the question: how grotesquely should Richard be portrayed? Shakespeare himself implicitly offers stage directions when he has the tyrant describe himself as "rudely stamped," "cheated of feature by dissembling Nature," and complain, "Behold mine arm/Is like a blasted sapling, wither'd up." Since the link between his physical and moral deformity is also spelled out, rare is the Richard who does not appear on stage with hunchback, heavy limp, shrunken left arm, or clawlike hand. Yet too hideous a Richard can also distract from the disturbing power of his mind, which he uses to charm, seduce, and manipulate. Indeed, through his soliloquies and asides, he turns the audience into his accomplice. And this adds to the powerful experience of seeing, rather than just reading, this play.

A deceptively avuncular Richard III (Simon Russell Beale) plays piggyback with the doomed princes (Kate Duchene, Annabelle Apsion) while plotting their end in the RSC's 1993 production, directed by Sam Mendes.

Compared to Richard, Edward IV and the future Henry VII are bland, while Buckingham's switch from sycophant to rebel is hard to believe. At least the play's widows stand up to the villain. Queen Margaret veers toward the long-winded, but she is also closest to Richard in character as she delights in seeing her curses come true. But to convey the immensity of Richard's crimes, Shakespeare opts for the theatrical standby of parading the ghosts of the king's victims before him on the eve of the Battle of Bosworth Field. Then, with Richard's final words, Shakespeare links the outcome of the muddy battle to the destiny of England: "A horse! A horse! My kingdom for a horse!"

In the climactic battle, Richard (Jasper Britton) seems to have the upper hand over Richmond (Steve Treves) in a production at the Open Air Theatre, Regent's Park, London, in 1995.

BEYOND THE PLAY

SHAKESPEARE WENT BEYOND TUDOR PROPAGANDA by presenting a Richard who is as seductive and intelligent as he is violent and evil. In the process, he created one of the finest villains of the English theater. It may seem puzzling that a figure as cruel and violent as Richard III should have a charmed stage life. The secret lies in the character's physical deformity, so belabored by Shakespeare and so enjoyed by generations of actors. No matter how foul his intentions, Richard must exploit his charm and intelligence in order to triumph over his misshapen body. In that sense, he is a more disturbing character than, say, *Othello*'s no less evil Iago: Richard recognizes his unsightliness as the engine of his ambition.

Although Shakespeare's history plays are understandably performed little outside England, *Richard III* is a good metaphor for political evil everywhere. As with *Hamlet, Othello,* and *King Lear,* productions of *Richard III* are generally remembered for the actor in the title role. In fact, it may have been the first written by Shakespeare for Richard Burbage, the leading actor of the Lord Chamberlain's Men. To this day, it is the actor's performance which determines whether the play is a terrifying melodrama or a black comedy. Most leading English actors have jumped at the chance of playing the role. But none, it seems, have matched the sinister power of Laurence Olivier's Richard at the New Theatre in London in 1944. Since then, acclaimed Richards have included Alec Guinness, Ian Holm, Antony Sher, Ian McKellen, Simon Russell Beale, and Kenneth Branagh.

ON SCREEN

FILM VERSIONS OF RICHARD III

Movie directors have been drawn to *Richard III* since the silent era. The first full-length American feature, made in 1912, starred Frederick Warde. But Laurence Olivier's 1955 *Richard III* remains the screen classic. By contrast, Richard Loncraine updated his 1995 version to a chilling Fascist state, while Al Pacino's *Looking for Richard* in 1996 documented actors rehearsing and performing the play.

Richard (Ian McKellen) is cast as a corrupt dictator in Loncraine's 1930s Fascist Britain.

"Go, gentlemen, every man unto his charge" (5.3). Richard (Laurence Olivier, center) mobilizes his forces, Norfolk (John Phillips, left), and Catesby (Norman Wooland) in the boldly theatrical movie *Richard III*, 1955.

KING JOHN

King

KING JOHN IS A NEGLECTED PLAY about a flawed king. It was popular in the 18th and 19th centuries, but nothing is known about its fate during Shakespeare's lifetime. Most scholars believe that the play was actually written in 1595 or 1596, but no record survives of a performance or quarto edition before its inclusion in the *First Folio* of 1623. Shakespeare uses Holinshed's *Chronicles* as a source, but also borrows extensively from *The Troublesome Reign of King John*, an anonymous play owned by the Lord Chamberlain's Men and published in 1591. This play, like *King John*, portrays John as a cruel, corrupt, buffoonish monarch. Shakespeare then invents the character of Philip the Bastard to personify English decency and heroism. Shakespeare's depiction of France and the Roman Catholic Church as perennial threats to England's sovereignty made the play highly topical.

BEHIND THE PLAY

EVEN BEFORE USURPING THE THRONE IN 1199, John had proven his treachery, first by joining his older brother, Richard the Lionheart, against their own father, then by rebelling when Richard was king. After John stole the crown from the rightful heir, his nephew Arthur, the French king backed Arthur's claim, but the boy was captured in 1202 and believed murdered the following year. Shakespeare exercises considerable license, compressing John's entire 17-year reign into a succession of dramatic moments: John's invasion of France, his excommunication, his loss of most French territories, and his subsequent truce with Rome in 1213. To these historical events, however, Shakespeare adds a few variations. Specifically, Arthur is kept alive until Act 4 so that his death can explain a French invasion of England and a rebellion by nobles. In reality, Arthur's murder had long been forgotten when barons protesting high taxes and abusive rule forced John to sign the Magna Carta limiting royal power. Shakespeare is correct in noting that some barons offered the English crown to the French Dauphin. But when John died, it was his son, Henry III, who inherited a nation in chaos.

Your strong possession much more than your right,/ Or else it must go wrong with you and me... 1.1

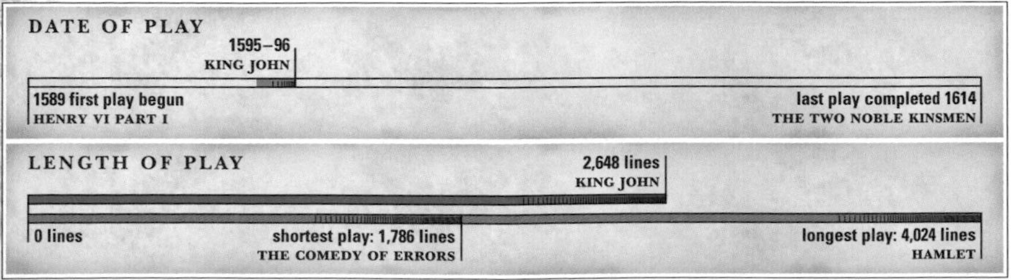

DRAMATIS PERSONAE

KING JOHN
441 lines
Vain, cruel, and indecisive, he surrenders French territories in exchange for a failed peace agreement, orders his nephew's murder and defies Rome, before bowing to papal power.

John (Herbert Beerbohm Tree) sits uneasily on the throne he took by might rather than right.

PRINCE HENRY
30 lines
The king's son, he becomes Henry III.

ARTHUR
120 lines
The king's nephew and rightful heir, he bravely tries to calm both his mother and Hubert, his designated murderer; he dies in a bid to escape.

EARL OF ESSEX
3 lines
A noble loyal to John.

EARLS OF SALISBURY AND PEMBROKE, LORD BIGOT
79; 158; 9 lines
They rebel against John, but repent upon learning Lewis plans to kill them.

HUBERT DE BURGH
205 lines
An Angiers politician, he is ordered by John to murder Arthur, but is moved by the boy's pleading and sends him into hiding.

ROBERT FAULCONBRIDGE
22 lines
He reveals that his brother, Philip, is his mother's illegitimate son.

PHILIP THE BASTARD
523 lines
The illegitimate son of Richard the Lionheart and Lady Faulconbridge, he is named Sir Richard and Plantagenet by King John; he dislikes the hypocrisy of court life, but displays courage in battle and loyalty to England.

JAMES GURNEY
1 line
The servant to Lady Faulconbridge.

PETER OF POMFRET
1 line
A soothsayer, he is hanged for predicting that John will surrender his crown.

KING PHILIP II
193 lines
The French king, he backs Arthur's claim to the English throne, but then makes peace with John, later breaking the truce under threat of excommunication.

The Bastard (Jo Stone-Fewings) is disgusted by the royal court's principles of "Commodity."

LEWIS THE DAUPHIN
154 lines
Philip's ambitious and self-possessed son, he marries John's niece, Blanche, and invades England.

LIMOGES
34 lines
He wears a lion's skin to boast that he killed Richard the Lionheart; the Bastard kills him in battle.

CARDINAL PANDULPH
164 lines
A scheming papal envoy, he urges Lewis to invade England, then orders his withdrawal after John bows to papal authority.

MELUN
39 lines
A French noble, he is wounded in battle.

CHATILLON
41 lines
A French envoy.

QUEEN ELEANOR
55 lines
King John's mother, she endorses John's right to be king and condones the murder of her grandson.

CONSTANCE
264 lines
Arthur's widowed mother, she becomes hysterical when she realizes her son will be killed.

BLANCHE
42 lines
The king's niece, she marries the Dauphin.

LADY FAULCONBRIDGE
15 lines
The Bastard's mother, she admits that Richard the Lionheart is his father.

OTHER PLAYERS
Lords, Citizens, Sheriff, Heralds, Officers, Soldiers, Executioners, Messengers, and Attendants.

Appalled by the duplicity of the French king, Constance (Kelly Hunter) rages long and poignantly against his high-handed injustice. Although she wavers on the hysterical, the reality of her grief and her heroic defiance remain compelling.

PLOT SUMMARY

SIZE OF ACTS

ACT 1	ACT 2	ACT 3	ACT 4	ACT 5
278 lines	609 lines	635 lines	589 lines	537 lines

ACT ONE
278 lines

ENGLAND: THE KING'S PALACE IN LONDON

Carrying a message from King Philip of France, Chatillon tells King John to step down in favor of Arthur, Duke of Brittany, who as son of John's older brother, Geoffrey, is the rightful heir. The French envoy warns that Philip will fight to install Arthur, but John promises to match "war for war and blood for blood." John's mother, Queen Eleanor, blames Arthur's widowed mother, Constance, for involving the French.

Robert Faulconbridge and his elder brother Philip ask John to settle a dispute over their inheritance. Robert claims his dying father revealed that Philip was a bastard, conceived while the noble was at war. Eleanor notices Philip's resemblance to her oldest son, Richard the Lionheart, John's predecessor on the throne, and she urges the young man to forget his dispute and follow her into battle. When Philip the Bastard agrees, John knights him "Sir Richard and Plantagenet." As the Bastard contemplates his new status ❟, his mother arrives, furious that her honor is in doubt. But she admits that the Bastard's true father was King Richard. "With all my heart I thank thee for my father," he tells her.

A foot of honour better than I was,/ But many a many foot of land the worse!... 1.1

Well then, to work! Our cannon shall be bent/ Against the brows of this resisting town... 2.1

ACT TWO
609 lines

FRANCE: NEAR ANGIERS

Assembled outside Angiers with his son, Lewis the Dauphin, and Limoges, Duke of Austria, King Philip vows that, once Angiers has recognized Arthur as England's king, he will give the boy John's crown. Chatillon warns that John is approaching, accompanied by Queen Eleanor, his niece Blanche, and Richard's bastard son. When John appears, the French king pledges peace if John surrenders the throne to Arthur. Constance speaks up for her son, but she is silenced by Eleanor. Austria intervenes and is denounced by the Bastard as Richard's killer. Finally King Philip asks Angiers to choose between Arthur and John.

John reminds Angiers that he stopped the French attack, while Philip warns that he will defend Arthur's claim to the English throne. The citizens promise to open their gates to the proven

king. As the English and French fight, Philip and John both claim victory, but Angiers is unconvinced. Impatient, the Bastard suggests the two armies join forces to punish the city. A citizens' spokesperson, Hubert de Burgh, hurriedly proposes a compromise—that John's niece, Blanche, marry Philip's son, Lewis, the Dauphin. If Lewis agrees, John says, Blanche's dowry will include English territories in France.

By heaven, these scroyles of Angiers flout you, Kings,/ And stand securely on their battlements... 2.1

That daughter there of Spain, the Lady Blanche,/ Is niece to England... 2.1

Declaring his love for Blanche, the Dauphin observes pompously that he had never loved himself until he saw himself "drawn in the flattering table of her eye." Disgusted, the Bastard deplores that "there should be/In such a love so vile a lout as he." With the marriage agreed to, John promises to compensate Arthur by making him Earl of Richmond and Duke of Anjou. Alone, the Bastard is shocked at how easily the two kings have betrayed their principles to "Commodity"—John by giving up his French territories, Philip by abandoning Arthur.

Mad world! Mad kings! Mad composition!... 2.1

ACT THREE 635 lines

FRANCE: NEAR ANGIERS

Outraged to learn of the French king's betrayal of her son, Constance turns her wrath on him. Philip's ally, the Duke of Austria, tries to calm her, but she mocks the lion's skin that he wears as a symbol of his defeat of King Richard. When Austria says he would punish such words if spoken by a man, the Bastard repeats them aggressively, eager for a chance to avenge his father's death.

Gone to be married? Gone to swear a peace?/False blood to false blood joined! Gone to be friends?... 3.1

War! War! No peace! Peace is to me a war... 3.1

Cardinal Pandulph brings instructions from Pope Innocent for King John to name Stephen Langton as Archbishop of Canterbury, but John replies that he takes orders from "no Italian priest". Pandulph excommunicates him and tells Philip to break his pact with John. The Dauphin begs his father to measure "purchase of a heavy curse from Rome,/Or the light loss of England for a friend." When Pandulph warns that Philip too will be excommunicated, the French king abandons his truce with John, leaving Blanche weeping that "Whoever wins, on that side shall I lose."

What earthy name to interrogatories/ Can task the free breath of a sacred king?... 3.1

All form is formless, order orderless,/ Save what is opposite to England's love... 3.1

The English take Angiers and seize Arthur, while the Bastard arrives triumphant, carrying Austria's head. John summons Hubert de Burgh, the Angiers politician, and tells him that Arthur is "a very serpent in my way." Hubert promises to hide the boy, but the king bursts out: "Death." At the French king's camp, Constance is hysterical over her son's capture. Philip and Pandulph promise to rescue him, but she tears at her hair, convinced she will never see him again. As she leaves with Philip, Pandulph urges Lewis to invade England, telling him that, since Arthur's death is certain, he and Blanche can claim the English throne.

Grief fills the room up of my absent child,/ Lies in his bed, walks up and down with me... 3.4

ACT FOUR 589 lines

ENGLAND: A CASTLE AND THE KING'S PALACE IN LONDON

At a castle in England, Hubert de Burgh orders his henchmen to heat some irons, but he is disturbed by Arthur's innocent affection for him. He shows the boy the paper ordering his eyes to be burned out,

Have you the heart? When your head did but ache,/ I knit my handkercher about your brows... 4.1

but Arthur pleads to be spared. Finally, Hubert breaks down and tells Arthur to go into hiding.

At the king's palace, where John has been crowned a second time, Salisbury, Pembroke, and other lords deride his "wasteful and ridiculous excess" and urge him to free Arthur. When Hubert announces the boy's death, the nobles leave in fury to find his grave.

John feels suddenly alone. He learns that his beloved mother as well as Constance are dead and that French troops have landed in England. The Bastard brings a captured soothsayer who has prophesied that "ere the next Ascension Day at noon,/Your highness should deliver up your crown." Furious, the king orders the man hanged and tells the Bastard to recall the lords. When Hubert reports unrest over Arthur's death, John blames him for the crime, but Hubert reveals that the boy is in fact still alive.

Arthur tries to escape, but dies jumping from the castle wall. When summoned to the palace, Pembroke, Salisbury, and Bigot plan to join the Dauphin but, on seeing Arthur's body, they vow revenge. With the lords now backing the Dauphin, the Bastard is resigned once more to "doggèd war".

Go, bear him in thine arms./ I am amazed, methinks, and lose my way... 4.3

ACT FIVE

537 lines

ENGLAND: THE KING'S PALACE IN LONDON, THE DAUPHIN'S CAMP AT ST. EDMUNDSBURY, A BATTLEFIELD, AND SWINSTEAD ABBEY

Having surrendered his crown to Pandulph and received it back in the name of the Pope, John realizes that, as prophesied, he has delivered his crown on Ascension Day, but he tells himself that he did so voluntarily. He is puzzled that English lords are supporting the Dauphin's invasion of England until he too learns of Arthur's death. The Bastard tells him to prepare for battle, but John wavers, still believing Pandulph will end the French offensive. Unconvinced, the Bastard urges John to defend England against "a beardless boy".

O inglorious league!/ Shall we, upon the footing of our land,/ Send fair-play orders... 5.1

Salisbury tearfully laments that "two Christian armies" should fight, but the Dauphin consoles him with the promise of riches. Pandulph reports that John is now reconciled with Rome, but the Dauphin refuses to abandon his invasion, noting that England has accepted him as its new king. When the Bastard warns him that John is ready to fight, the Dauphin takes up the challenge.

By all the blood that ever fury breathed,/ The youth says well!... 5.2

Faint with fever, John withdraws to Swinstead Abbey. A wounded French lord tells Salisbury, Pembroke, and Bigot to rejoin John since the Dauphin plans to execute them. At the French camp, the Dauphin learns that his reinforcements have been shipwrecked. At the abbey, John is poisoned by a monk. After pardoning the rebel lords at the request of his son, Prince Henry, John dies in the abbey's orchard. The Bastard prepares to fight the French anew, until Salisbury reports they are withdrawing. As Henry leaves to bury his father, the Bastard proclaims that England will never be conquered so long as it remains united.

Poisoned – ill fare! Dead, forsook, cast off;/And none of you will bid the winter come/To thrust his icy fingers in my maw... 5.7

This England never did, nor never shall,/Lie at the proud foot of a conqueror... 5.7

READING THE PLAY

COMPARISON OF PROSE TO VERSE

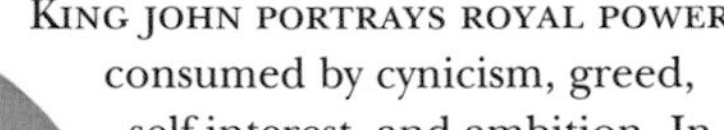

HISTORICAL SOURCES

MAGNA CARTA

In 1215, disaffected members of the nobility rebelled and forced King John to seal the Magna Carta, a document that guaranteed the nobles their feudal privileges and promised that the king would uphold the nation's laws. This episode, left out by Shakespeare, was included in Herbert Tree's 1899 production.

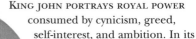

By the Thames at Runnymede, John seals the Magna Carta.

KING JOHN PORTRAYS ROYAL POWER consumed by cynicism, greed, self-interest, and ambition. In its structure, *King John* remains a complex play, with its three interwoven themes: John's usurpation of the English throne claimed by his nephew Arthur; John's stormy relations with the Vatican; and his troubles with rebellious barons. Caught in this whirlwind, John has little time for reflection. Thus, the best language in this all-verse play comes from outsiders.

Constance, for example, betrayed by both the English and French kings, speaks of the imminent loss of her son Arthur with deep poignancy. Yet it is a measure of how rotten things were in the days of "bad" King John that Shakespeare had to invent a figure of decency in Philip the Bastard. As someone raised outside the royal court, he can be objective about what he sees. Courageous among cowards, honest among liars, he supports John even knowing the king to be a usurper because his greater loyalty is to England. When the Bastard ends the play with his famous plea for English unity, he is of course speaking not to early 13th-century England, but to Elizabethan audiences.

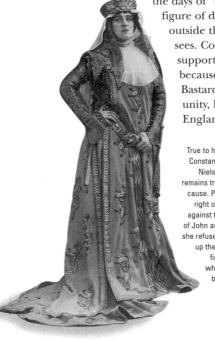

True to her name, Constance (Julia Nielson, 1868) remains true to her cause. Pitting the right of her son against the might of John and Philip, she refuses to give up the unequal fight, even when faced by certain defeat.

WHO'S WHO

King John is the brother of Richard the Lionheart. His nephew, **Arthur,** the rightful heir to the English crown, is backed by the French. But when the king's niece, **Blanche**, marries the **Dauphin**, son of the French king, **Philip II**, the English and French make peace. Richard the Lionheart's illegitimate son, **Philip the Bastard**, believes they have betrayed their causes. **Cardinal Pandulph** excommunicates John and war erupts. English nobles back a French invasion, but John makes peace with Rome and drives the French out before dying. He is succeeded by his son **Prince Henry**, who becomes Henry III.

SEEING THE PLAY

In the 18th century, during a wave of anti-Catholic hysteria, *King John* was rewritten in a tub-thumping style by Colley Cibber as *Papal Tyranny in the Reign of King John.* Then, during the Napoleonic wars, Shakespeare's anti-French tone again made it popular. Later in the 19th century, it was often presented as a richly costumed pageant, its main roles performed by leading actors of the day. Today, it is rarely staged. Nevertheless, *King John* is easier to enjoy on stage than on the page, not least because audiences readily identify with the invented hero, Philip the Bastard. Not only does he satirize the absurdities of the English and French courts, but he rises to the occasion when England is threatened. He often shares his thoughts with the audience in asides, and whenever he is on stage his ebullient presence ensures that the narrative gathers pace. John, in contrast, is vain, moody, and unprincipled, although the success of any production can depend on whether he is interpreted as a buffoon or as a man totally unsuited to be king.

John (Guy Henry) is recrowned by the papal legate Cardinal Pandulph (RSC, 2001). In a dramatic replay of medieval pageantry, the flickering backlight reflects the fiery rhetoric of the play.

While other roles—King Philip, the Dauphin, Queen Eleanor—are fairly two-dimensional, the character of Hubert de Burgh changes in an interesting way: he starts as an obsequious politician willing even to murder Arthur and ends up as the voice of the king's inert conscience. Constance poses a problem because, although right is on her side, her hysteria can become as tiresome to audiences as it is to the English and French courts.

The epic Battle of Angiers was staged at Her Majesty's Theatre, London, in 1899.

EDWARD III

EDWARD III HAS ONLY RECENTLY BEEN ADMITTED into the Shakespeare canon. The play was long thought to be the work of one or more anonymous actors or stage hands, but in the late 1990s leading scholars decided to add it to the Bard's complete works. Even so, it is highly unlikely that he penned the entire play. Probably written some time between 1590 and 1594, with Holinshed's *Chronicles* and Froissart's *Chronicles of France* as its main sources, it was first published in 1596. Shakespeare was possibly moved to write it by his purported jealousy of Christopher Marlowe who, at the time of his murder in 1593, was the better known playwright. But while Marlowe's *Edward II* caused a sensation in its day, Shakespeare's *Edward III* was ill-fated. With James VI of Scotland set to succeed Queen Elizabeth, it was soon banned because of its scornful treatment of the Scots.

BEHIND THE PLAY

EDWARD III, WHO RULED ENGLAND from 1327 to 1377, assumed the throne at the age of 14, replacing his father, Edward II, who had been deposed and would soon be murdered. Edward's claim to the French throne came through his mother, Isabella, whose father was King Philippe IV. Her three brothers left no heirs, prompting Edward to press his claim. However, because France's Salic law excluded women from dynastic succession, Philippe VI of Valois stepped into the void. In *Edward III,* Shakespeare alters dates and events to add drama to the narrative. The play also completely ignores Philippe VI, the French king defeated in 1340 at the Battle of Sluys, and in 1346 at Crécy; instead, in the play, it is Philippe's son, John, or Jean II "Le Bon," who loses these battles as well as the Battle of Poitiers in 1356. Historical chronology is further blurred when King David II of Scotland is captured in 1346, then brought before Edward as he awaits the outcome of the Battle of Poitiers 10 years later. But the play faithfully depicts an incident when wealthy citizens of Calais offered their lives to save their city from destruction. Edward's attempted seduction of the Countess of Salisbury may also have some basis in fact.

He will have vanquished, cheerful, death and fear,/And ever after dread their force no more... 3.4

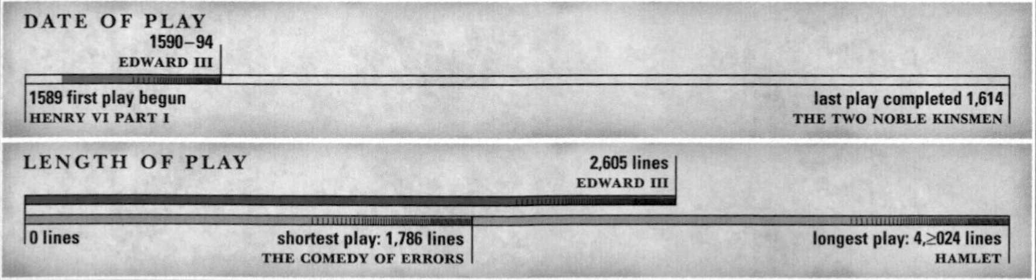

DRAMATIS PERSONAE

An autocratic but astute monarch, Edward III (David Rintoul) drew wise counselors around him, and successfully united his nobles.

THE ENGLISH PARTY

EDWARD III
749 lines
Claiming the French throne through his French mother, he sets off the Hundred Years' War; he adopts strong positions, then is persuaded to change his mind.

PRINCE EDWARD
281 lines
The legendary Black Prince, he proves his valor at the battles of Crécy and Poitiers.

EARL OF WARWICK
121 lines
Trapped between duty and love, he is ordered by the king to persuade his married daughter, the Countess of Salisbury, to become the royal mistress.

EARL OF SALISBURY
92 lines
An English military commander in France, his wife is wooed by the king while he fights for England in France.

EARL OF AUDLEY
103 lines
Elderly adviser to Edward III, he accompanies Prince Edward to France and is wounded at the Battle of Poitiers.

EARL OF DERBY AND LORD PERCY
45; 18 lines
English nobles.

LODWICK
46 lines
Edward III's secretary, he is summoned by the king to write a love poem to the Countess of Salisbury.

SIR WILLIAM MONTAGUE
14 lines
An English knight.

SIR JOHN COPLAND
17 lines
He captures King David of Scotland and delivers him to Edward III outside Calais.

ROBERT OF ARTOIS
58 lines
Banished to England, he backs Edward III's claim to the French throne and is named Earl of Richmond.

LORD MOUNTFORD
9 lines
A French noble loyal to Edward, he is named Duke of Brittany.

GOBIN DE GRAIE
1 line
Captured by the English, he serves as a loyal guide to Edward III.

PHILIPPA
17 lines
The English queen, she defeats the Scottish invaders and is deeply relieved when her son, Prince Edward, crushes the French at Poitiers.

COUNTESS OF SALISBURY
210 lines
Warwick's beautiful, married daughter, she cleverly rebuffs Edward's efforts to seduce her.

THE FRENCH PARTY

KING JOHN
269 lines
He is defeated by King Edward's forces at the battles of Sluys and Crécy, and is captured at Poitiers.

CHARLES OF NORMANDY
86 lines
John's oldest son, he fights at the Battle of Poitiers.

PHILIP
33 lines
John's second son, he is captured at Poitiers.

DUKE OF LORRAINE
39 lines
He is sent to England to demand English recognition for King John.

VILLIERS
31 lines
A captured French officer.

KING OF BOHEMIA
3 lines
He fights with the French and is killed in battle.

The lovely Countess of Salisbury (Caroline Faber) attracted, and artfully deflected, the royal lust.

THE SCOTTISH PARTY

KING DAVID
33 lines
He invades England and captures the Countess of Salisbury, but is driven back across the border; he again invades and is captured.

EARL OF DOUGLAS
4 lines
A loyal Scottish noble.

OTHER PLAYERS
Citizens of Calais, Squires, Captains, Frenchmen, Frenchwomen, Heralds, Mariner, Messengers, and other Attendants.

PLOT SUMMARY

SIZE OF ACTS

ACT 1	ACT 2	ACT 3	ACT 4	ACT 5
353 lines	708 lines	642 lines	646 lines	256 lines

ACT ONE 353 lines

LONDON AND ROXSBURGH CASTLE

King Edward receives Robert of Artois, a French noble loyal to him, who explains how Edward's claim to the throne of France has been rejected because it passes through his mother's line. The French King John dispatches the Duke of Lorraine to offer Edward a dukedom if he swears allegiance to him, but Edward responds angrily that he will soon have the entire kingdom, not merely a dukedom. Word reaches London that King David of Scotland has invaded England and is besieging the Countess of Salisbury in Roxsburgh Castle. The king announces that he will handle the Scots and tells his son, Prince Edward, and the Earl of Audley to raise an army to fight in France. The Earl of Derby is ordered to seek allies in Europe. At Roxsburgh Castle, having vowed never to make peace with England, David tries to woo the Countess of Salisbury but, learning of Edward's advance, he decides to flee north. When Edward arrives, the countess urges him to rest before pursuing David. The king hesitates because he is so disturbed by her beauty, but she persuades him to stay and rest.

See how occasion laughs me in the face!... 1.1

Let not thy presence, like the April sun,/ Flatter our earth, and suddenly be done... 1.2

ACT TWO 708 lines

ROXSBURGH CASTLE

Lodwick, the king's secretary, is alarmed by the king's growing infatuation with the Countess. The king seems lost in love and orders Lodwick to invoke "some golden Muse" to write a poem to one who deserves to learn "how

I might perceive his eye in her eye lost,/ His ear to drink her sweet tongue's utterance... 2.1

Tell him the crown that he usurps is mine,/ And where he sets his foot he ought to kneel... 1.1

passionate,/How heart-sick, and how full of languishment,/Her beauty makes me”. Is it a woman, Lodwick wonders. “What, thinkst thou I did bid thee praise a horse?” Edward snaps back before resuming his enraptured eulogy of the countess. Lodwick finally offers two lines: “More fair and chaste than is the queen of shades/More bold in constancy.” Wanting to hear nothing of chastity and constancy, the king decides to speak for himself because “love cannot sound well but in lovers’ tongues.” As he takes up pen and paper, the countess appears.

She is grown more fairer far since I came hither… 2.1

Of such estate, that hers is as a throne,/ And my estate the footstool where she treads… 2.1

Finding him gloomy, she promises to cheer him up. Having forced her to vow to make him happy, the king then proclaims his love for her. She replies that she will offer all the love “that I have power to give,” but adds that she cannot give her body without losing her soul. The king recalls her oath, but she admonishes him. Just as she owes her love to her husband, she says, the king is so bound to his queen. Still hopeful, Edward traps Warwick, the countess’s father, into swearing he will do as instructed. He then orders Warwick to command his daughter “to be my mistress and my secret love.” Distraught, Warwick reluctantly tells her that it is better “To pawn thine honour, rather than thy life,” as honour can be regained, but life has “no recovery.” When she reacts furiously, “Unnatural besiege, woe me unhappy,” refusing to be a part of the king’s “graceless lust,” Warwick is relieved and praises her. Derby, Audley, and Prince Edward report that an army is ready to invade France, but Edward, irritable and distracted, sends them away. The countess agrees to obey her father’s command “Provided that yourself remove those lets/That stand between your highness’ love and mine.” When the king agrees, she explains that “it is their lives, that stand between our love,” so their deaths must come first. Producing two knives, she offers one to the king, then points the other at her own heart and threatens to kill herself, unless Edward swears never again to solicit her. Returning to his senses, the king promises to respect the countess as a “true English lady”, then issues a summons to prepare for war.

But that your lips were sacred, my lord,/ You would profane the holy name of love… 2.1

Why now thou speak’st as I would have thee speak,/ And mark how I unsay my words again… 2.1

Even by that power I swear, that gives me now/ The power to be ashamed of myself… 2.2

ACT THREE

642 lines

FRANCE

King John learns that Edward has raised a powerful army in England and has won support in Holland, but he boasts that his

Resolute to be dissolv’d, and therefore this:/ Keep but thy word, great King, and I am thine… 2.2

allies include the Scots, the King of Bohemia, Poles, Danes, and Sicilians. As the English navy approaches, John orders his son, Charles, and Bohemia to secure the flanks; he and his other son, Philip, will defend the middle ground. Hearing the sound of naval warfare, John is confident of victory, but a sailor rushes in with news that the English have landed. As rumors of war spread, French citizens debate Edward's claim, one noting that "Edward is son unto our late king's sister/Where John Valois is three degrees removed." Prince Edward proudly announces that he has overrun several French towns, but he warns his father that John has assembled at least 100,000 troops at Crécy.

Before the new battle, the two kings meet, with John insulting Edward as "a false pernicious wretch" and mocking him for his thirst for gold. Edward responds that he has come "to skirmish not for pillage, but for the crown." King John calls on his soldiers to fight the "foreigner" 66, while the English king prepares his son for his first battle by giving him arms—a coat of armor, a helmet, a lance, and shield—adding that the honor of a knighthood can only be won on the field of battle.

Lords and my loving subjects, now's the time,/ That your intended force must bide the touch... 3.3

As the armies meet, Artois, Derby, and Audley successively bring word that Prince Edward's life is in danger, but the king refuses to rescue him, responding that "We have more sons/Than one, to comfort our declining age." He then explains that this is the prince's chance "to season his courage" 66. When Prince Edward returns from battle triumphant, his father knights him, then orders the prince to follow King John to Poitiers, while Edward will take Calais.

Exclaim no more, for none of you can tell/ Whether a borrow'd aid will serve, or no... 3.4

ACT FOUR

646 lines

FRANCE: BRITTANY, CALAIS, AND POITIERS

Having conquered Brittany, the Earl of Salisbury wants to join Edward in Calais, but he must first cross French territory. He summons a French prisoner, Villiers, and promises him freedom in exchange for safe conduct. Meanwhile, having laid siege to Calais, Edward hears that his queen, Philippa, has captured King David of Scotland. and that she is angry because John Copland, the English soldier who seized David, insists on delivering him personally to the king. As Edward awaits Philippa, a French captain reports that Calais has agreed to surrender if its citizens' lives and property are spared. The king responds that, before the city is spared, six wealthy merchants must first prostrate themselves before him.

Near Poitiers, when Prince Charles of Normandy refuses Salisbury safe conduct, Villiers insists on returning to captivity. Charles mocks him for keeping his word, but after Villiers insists that his honor is at stake, the prince issues Salisbury a passport. As John boasts that Prince Edward is trapped and outnumbered at Poitiers, Prince Charles reads a hermit's prophecy: when feathered fowl make his army tremble and flint stones rise, the French king will advance into England as far as Edward has invaded France 66. Puzzled, John remains confident of driving the English from the country.

I have a prophecy, my gracious lord,/Wherein is written what success is like/ To happen us in this outrageous war... 4.3

Audley warns Prince Edward that he faces a mighty army, but the prince is unimpressed 66. A messenger from the French king calls on the prince to surrender, another from Charles of Normandy offers him a horse on which to flee, a third from Philip delivers a

Death's name is much more mighty than his deeds... 4.4

book of prayers, but Prince Edward dismisses them all. Audley tells him there is no cause for fear since destiny alone will define the outcome.

To die is all as common as to live:/ The one in choice, the other holds in chase... 4.4

With battle looming, "ugly ravens" are frightening the French soldiers, but John insists that the ravens await the flesh of English soldiers. Salisbury is brought before John, who orders him hanged, but Charles and Villiers intervene to save him. The battle begins, and French soldiers are immediately distracted by the ravens and attacked by "fire-containing flint." As John recalls the prophecy, he and Philip are captured by the English.

ACT FIVE

256 lines

FRANCE: CALAIS

Six wealthy citizens of Calais are brought before Edward, who orders them executed. They beg him to spare the town and he agrees, but in exchange their bodies will be "dragged about these walls." Queen Philippa successfully intervenes, convincing her husband that, by showing mercy, the entire city will embrace him as its king.

Ah, be more mild unto these yielding men!/ It is a glorious thing to stablish peace... 5.1

Copland arrives with King David and, presenting the prisoner to Edward, is pardoned for his insubordination to Philippa. Salisbury also reaches Calais, but brings news from Poitiers that Prince Edward is surrounded and probably doomed. The king comforts Philippa by pledging that, if their son is killed, he will wreak such vengeance that the prince's knell will be "the groaning cries of dying men."

He was, my lord; and as my worthless self,/With forty other serviceable knights,/ Under safe-conduct of the Dolphin's seal... 5.1

Trumpets announce Prince Edward's arrival, with King John and Philip as his prisoners and the French crown in his hand. When Edward tells John that he will now be taken to England, the French king realizes the hermit's prophecy has come true. Excited by victory, Prince Edward vows to fight France, Spain, Turkey "and what countries else/That justly would provoke fair England's ire," but the king urges patience and prepares to return to England, "Where, in a happy hour I trust we shall/Arrive, three kings, two princes, and a queen."

Sheath up your swords, refresh your weary limbs,/ Peruse your spoils... 5.1

READING THE PLAY

COMPARISON OF PROSE TO VERSE

prose: 0% verse: 100%

WHO'S WHO

Edward III, the English king, defends England from the invading Scots and presses his claim—on his mother's side—to the French throne. He aggressively woos the **Countess of Salisbury**, daughter of the Earl of Warwick, but is cleverly rebuffed. Edward's son, **Prince Edward**, the legendary Black Prince, is victorious at the Battle of Crécy. Edward besieges Calais, where his wife **Queen Philippa**, persuades him to spare the lives of six wealthy citizens. Meanwhile, the Black Prince captures **King John**, the French monarch, at the Battle of Poitiers.

At Crécy, the English army vanquished the French, felling over 10,000, while losing less than 200 of their own. The heat of battle was captured at the time in *Les Chroniques de France,* a French manuscript.

FROM A HISTORICAL point of view, *Edward III* seeks to justify the Hundred Years' War by arguing Edward's case to become king of France. However, the play makes little effort to explain that, unlike England, 14th-century France was a land of competing dukedoms and had yet to become the nation-state of Shakespeare's day. The broad thrust of the play seems designed to boast England's military prowess and to endorse the myth of the Black Prince as a precursor to Henry V. Two military scenes stand out for their language: Edward's stubborn refusal to rescue his son at Crécy in the belief that, if the prince wins, "he will have vanquished, cheerful, death and fear"; and Audley's reflections on life and death before the Battle of Poitiers.

The mischief and wit of Act II, which portrays Edward's failed seduction of the Countess of Salisbury, offers the best poetry in the play, and is also the strongest evidence of Shakespeare's hand. Warwick's speech to his daughter (2.1) even repeats the final line of his Sonnet 94, "Lilies that fester smell far worse than weeds." But since a similar phrase already existed as a proverb, this is not definitive proof that Shakespeare wrote the play. This act also illustrates the limits of the king's power: he can conquer France, but not the countess. One parallel theme is the importance of oaths, notably the countess's oath of marriage contrasted with her promise to obey the king. This is later echoed in Villiers's refusal to break his oath to return to captivity if he fails to obtain the Earl of Salisbury's safe conduct. Thus, even the French are not without honor. Still, by devoting an entire act to the countess's witty rejection of the king, Shakespeare is also simply being true to his duty to entertain.

PLAY HISTORY

DATING THE PLAY

First published without attribution in 1596, *Edward III* may have been written between Shakespeare's two tetralogies devoted to the Wars of the Roses and the Hundred Years' War. *Edward III,* however, stands alone. Although the play was succeeded by *Richard II,* the final scene of *Edward III* takes place some 40 years before the opening scene of *Richard II.*

SEEING THE PLAY

ON STAGE

CHILLING EFFECTS
In the RSC's first-ever production of *Edward III* in 2002, the play's sound effects had cawing ravens circling above the audience in Stratford's small Swan Theatre. The flapping ravens served as a chilling harbinger of the fate awaiting French troops at the Battle of Poitiers.

NOW OCCASIONALLY PERFORMED as a curiosity, *Edward III* lacks the quality to become a favorite. It is therefore unlikely that even the director of a new production of this play will have seen it performed before. The temptation is to read it as a panegyric to Edward the Black Prince. Since the king participates in no battles, which all take place off stage, it is his son who personifies English valor. However, the Royal Shakespeare Company's first-ever production of *Edward III* in 2002 made the case that the king is the dominant figure. While the prince is battling the French, it is the king who gives the orders. Indeed, for all the Black Prince's heroism, he seems above all intent on pleasing his father.

Edward's character, though, is given shape by the scenes with the Countess of Salisbury and the citizens of Calais. Gruff and autocratic, he is also emotional and easily swayed: the countess brushes aside his efforts to bed her, while Queen Philippa appeals to his vanity to rescue the citizens of Calais from execution. The RSC production, directed by Anthony Clark, further highlighted the king's violent desire for the countess, a lust that, according to Jean Le Bel's 14th-century *Vrayes Chroniques*, in fact led Edward to rape her. Some respite from the play's solemnity is provided by two comic characters, Edward's secretary Lodwick, and Scotland's King David, whose portrayal as a buffoon led to the play's prohibition in Shakespeare's lifetime. In theatrical terms, though, *Edward III* is still very much a work in progress. Further productions could throw fresh light on the play.

Vibrant colors and deep shadows intensify the drama on the eve of battle as the Black Prince (Kyle Ingelman) receives his battle arms from King Edward III (Christopher Cappiello) and his knights (Jarad Scott, Robert Grindlinger, and Alec P. McNayr), in the National American Shakespeare Company production, 2003.

BEYOND THE PLAY

So did Shakespeare write *Edward III*? It was first published in 1596 with the note that "it has been sundry times played about the city of London," but with no mention of an author or a theater company. It was then banned from the stage for being anti-Scottish and was omitted from the *First Folio* in 1623. It was only in 1760 that an English scholar, Edward Capell, added it to Shakespeare's complete works, arguing that "there was no known writer equal to such a play." At the time, few scholars agreed.

In 1875, the German scholar Alexander Teetgen described neglect of this masterpiece by Shakespeare as "one of the most ridiculous, futile, humiliating things in literary history." But in 1908, believing it was written by an Elizabethan contemporary, George Peele, C.F. Tucker Brooke included it in his *Shakespeare Apocrypha.* There was no consensus among 20th-century scholars over Shakespeare's authorship of the play.

The case against Shakespeare's authorship rests on the absence of any documentary link to the playwright and on the play's varied quality. But it was computer analysis of the language that finally won *Edward III* its place in the canon. Along with resonances from Sonnets 29, 94, and 142, there are echoes of imagery found in *Love's Labour's Lost* and *Measure for Measure.* Resemblances with other works also include earthy puns, and such favorite topics as oaths (as in *Henry IV Part II*), prophesies (*Macbeth*), and the human frailties of "divinely anointed" kings (*Richard II*). Yet even now, while some scholars believe Shakespeare penned the entire play, others still prefer to specify which scenes, such as the Countess of Salisbury's rebuff of the king, seem convincingly Shakespearean.

HISTORICAL SOURCES

EDWARD III
Edward's determined bid for the French crown sparked off the 100 Years' War, while also plunging him into conflict with his subjects. Ultimately, he proved a popular king, reforming the law and uniting the nobility.

Edward's royal arms (top left) are quartered with the French fleur-de-lis and English lion, broadcasting his claim to the French throne. Engraving, *c.* 1650.

In *The Raigne of King Edward III*, staged in 1986 at The Globe Playhouse, Los Angeles, the director Dick Dotterer dressed the players in Elizabethan, rather than medieval, garb, in an effort to capture the spirit of Shakespeare's times.

RICHARD II

RICHARD II IS SHAKESPEARE'S MOST LYRICAL history play. With it, he inaugurates the second tetralogy, known as the "Henriad," which also includes *Henry IV Part I* and *Part II*, and *Henry V*. This new four-play cycle completes Shakespeare's unbroken account of English history between 1398 and 1485. Written in 1595, with Holinshed's *Chronicles* as its principal source, *Richard II* was published in four quartos before its inclusion in the *First Folio* in 1623. Perhaps because the play portrays usurpation of the throne, Richard's abdication does not appear in the two quartos published before Queen Elizabeth's death in 1603. The Restoration in 1660 brought several adaptations of *Richard II*, but Shakespeare's text has been used since the mid-18th century. Today, its reputation rests on its remarkable poetry and its poignant portrayal of personal downfall.

BEHIND THE PLAY

THE HISTORIC RICHARD II was just 10 in 1377 when he succeeded his grandfather, Edward III. His own father, Edward the Black Prince, had died a year earlier. Richard was a cultivated monarch who both supported Chaucer and renovated Westminster Hall. In 1396, after the death of his first wife, he made peace with France by marrying Isabel, the eight-year-old daughter of the king of France. But at home he faced frequent trouble from ambitious barons. *Richard II* begins after the scandalous murder of the Duke of Gloucester, the king's own uncle, in 1398. The play then neatly summarizes events leading to Richard's downfall: the banishment of Bolingbroke and seizure of his lands, John of Gaunt's death, Richard's Irish campaign, and Bolingbroke's revolt. Shakespeare also takes some liberties. He portrays Isabel as an adult when she was still a child. He also depicts Richard as being murdered, when in fact the king starved, or was starved, to death. Shakespeare wraps Richard in an aura of poetic resignation, although Holinshed suggests that the king never accepted being overthrown. Henry IV's accession to the throne was nonetheless a turning point in English history, since it led inexorably to the Wars of the Roses.

For God's sake let us sit upon the ground/ And tell sad stories of the death of kings...
3.2

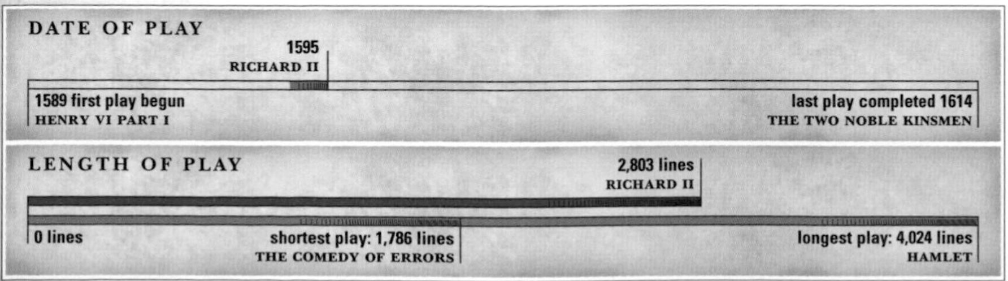

DATE OF PLAY

1595
RICHARD II

1589 first play begun
HENRY VI PART I

last play completed 1614
THE TWO NOBLE KINSMEN

LENGTH OF PLAY

2,803 lines
RICHARD II

0 lines

shortest play: 1,786 lines
THE COMEDY OF ERRORS

longest play: 4,024 lines
HAMLET

DRAMATIS PERSONAE

RICHARD II
758 lines

Grandson of Edward III, son of Edward the Black Prince, he grows despotic after the death of his uncle, John of Gaunt, Duke of Lancaster; by seizing Gaunt's properties, he provokes the duke's son, Henry Bolingbroke, to rebel; facing defeat, Richard gives way to introspection and self-pity; he is murdered after Bolingbroke's coronation as Henry IV.

JOHN OF GAUNT
191 lines

The king's uncle, Duke of Lancaster, he is broken-hearted when Richard banishes his son, Henry Bolingbroke; he accuses the king of destroying "this royal throne of kings."

EDMUND OF LANGLEY
290 lines

The king's uncle, Duke of York, he criticizes Richard for seizing John of Gaunt's property and becomes a reluctant supporter of Bolingbroke's rebellion; he later denounces his son's plot to kill the new Henry IV.

HENRY BOLINGBROKE
413 lines

John of Gaunt's son and the king's cousin, he is banished by Richard II; when the king seizes his family's properties, he organizes a rebellion that leads to his coronation as Henry IV.

Bolingbroke (David Troughton) seizes the crown.

DUKE OF AUMERLE
86 lines

York's son, he plots Bolingbroke's murder, but his mother's intercession saves him from death.

THOMAS MOWBRAY
135 lines

Duke of Norfolk, his quarrel with Bolingbroke leads Richard to banish them both from England; he dies in exile in Italy.

DUKE OF SURREY, EARL OF SALISBURY, AND LORD BERKELEY
10; 20; 8 lines

They are loyal to Richard.

BUSHY, BAGOT, AND GREEN
40; 23; 33 lines

Richard's favorites, they are blamed for the king's bad policies; Bushy and Green are executed, and Bagot is put on trial.

EARL OF NORTHUMBERLAND
142 lines

The first noble to back Bolingbroke.

HARRY PERCY
45 lines

Northumberland's son, he is also known as Hotspur.

LORDS ROSS, FITZWATER, AND WILLOUGHBY
22; 27; 12 lines

Supporters of Bolingbroke.

Dressed in all their majesty, Isabel (Peggy Ashcroft) and Richard II (John Gielgud) are blissfully unaware of the troubles to come.

BISHOP OF CARLISLE
63 lines

He warns Bolingbroke that his *coup d'etat* will bring bloodshed.

ABBOT OF WESTMINSTER
10 lines

He joins the plot against Henry IV, but dies before he is arrested.

LORD MARSHAL
25 lines

He presides over the duel between Bolingbroke and Mowbray.

SIR STEPHEN SCROOP
37 lines

He brings tidings of Bolingbroke's advance to Richard.

SIR PIERS OF EXTON
21 lines

He murders Richard in Pomfret Castle, believing it is Henry's will.

A WELSH CAPTAIN
15 lines

He reports that Richard's Welsh army has dispersed, believing him dead.

ISABEL
115 lines

Richard's French-born queen, she is dismayed by her husband's deposition.

DUCHESS OF YORK
94 lines

She persuades Henry IV to forgive her son for plotting his murder.

DUCHESS OF GLOUCESTER
58 lines

She seeks revenge for her husband's murder, but dies before Richard is deposed.

OTHER PLAYERS

Lords, Ladies, Heralds, Soldiers, Keeper, Groom, Gardeners, Messenger, and Attendants.

PLOT SUMMARY

SIZE OF ACTS

ACT 1	ACT 2	ACT 3	ACT 4	ACT 5
659 lines	649 lines	590 lines	340 lines	565 lines

ACT ONE
659 lines

LONDON AND COVENTRY

Alarmed by political unrest, Richard II summons two feuding nobles. The king's cousin, Henry Bolingbroke, accuses Thomas Mowbray of stealing royal funds and of murdering the Duke of Gloucester, the king's uncle. Mowbray denies the charges, but admits he once foolishly tried to kill John of Gaunt, Duke of Lancaster, another royal uncle, and Bolingbroke's own father. Annoyed to be reminded of his own role in Gloucester's death, the king tells the two men to "forget, forgive." When they ignore him, he orders them to decide their quarrel in a duel. The Duchess of Gloucester begs John of Gaunt to avenge her husband's death, but he says the crime was ordered by God's "deputy," the king himself.

Accompanied by his favorites, Bushy, Bagot, and Green, Richard wishes his cousin Bolingbroke "fortune in this royal fight." But when trumpets sound, Richard suddenly stops the duel and banishes Bolingbroke for 10 years and Mowbray for life. Mowbray accepts the verdict with sorrow. Richard then reduces Bolingbroke's exile to six years, but John of Gaunt laments he will never again see his son. As Richard imagines Bolingbroke returning to woo the people, he learns of an Irish rebellion and wonders how to pay for an army. Bushy reports that John of Gaunt is ailing, and Richard rushes to visit him, hoping to find him dead.

A heavy sentence, my most sovereign liege,/And all unlooked-for from your highness' mouth... 1.3

One vial full of Edward's sacred blood,/ One flourishing branch of his most royal root,/ Is cracked, and all the precious liquor spilt;/ Is hacked down... 1.2

ACT TWO
649 lines

LONDON, WINDSOR, AND GLOUCESTERSHIRE

While awaiting the king, John of Gaunt says he wants Richard to hear his dying words, but his brother notes that the king's ears are filled "with other, flattering sounds." Rehearsing his speech, John of Gaunt laments how once glorious England, "this royal throne of kings," has become a place of scandal. The king arrives to inquire after John of Gaunt's health. "Gaunt as a grave", the old man replies, adding that the king is still sicker for bringing shame to England. Richard says the "lunatic lean-witted fool" would die for his insolence were he not brother to the king's own father. John of Gaunt responds that blood ties did not save his brother, Gloucester.

Methinks I am a prophet new-inspired,/ And thus, expiring, do foretell of him... 2.1

O, how that name befits my composition!/ Old Gaunt indeed, and gaunt in being old... 2.1

Once John of Gaunt's death is confirmed, the king seizes his property. York reminds Richard that his father, Edward the Black Prince, warred against the French, not his friends. By confiscating Bolingbroke's inheritance, York prophesies, "you pluck a thousand dangers on your head".

O, my liege,/Pardon me if you please... 2.1

As Richard leaves for Ireland, Northumberland discloses that Bolingbroke is sailing toward England. At Windsor Castle, where Bushy is trying to cheer up the queen, Green reports that Bolingbroke has landed at Ravenspurgh in Yorkshire. When Bolingbroke reaches Gloucestershire, Northumberland and the other nobles swear loyalty to him. Only York, named Regent in Richard's absence, denounces Bolingbroke as a traitor to the throne.

ACT THREE
590 lines

BRISTOL, WALES, AND LANGLEY

In Bristol, Bolingbroke accuses Bushy and Green of misleading Richard and orders their execution. Richard lands in Wales, ready to defend his crown. York's son, the Duke of Aumerle, warns him of Bolingbroke's strength, while the Earl of Salisbury informs him that his Welsh followers have dispersed, thinking him dead.

Needs must I like it well. I weep for joy/To stand upon my kingdom once again... 3.2

The king still hopes for York's help, but more bad news arrives: citizens are flocking to Bolingbroke's cause, and Bushy and Green are dead. Richard suddenly resigns himself to defeat, his regal pride replaced by dark thoughts about "sad stories of the death of kings". The Bishop of Carlisle urges him not to give up, but when the king learns that the Duke of York

No matter where. Of comfort no man speak./ Let's talk of graves, of worms, and epitaphs... 3.2

A thousand flatterers sit within thy crown,/Whose compass is no bigger than thy head... 2.1

has joined Bolingbroke, he decides to await his fate at Flint Castle.

Outside the castle, Bolingbroke promises to lay down his arms if his banishment is repealed and his lands are returned. Richard, seemingly confident again, warns that Bolingbroke will have to stain the land with "faithful English blood" before he wins the crown.

We are amazed; and thus long have we stood/ To watch the fearful bending of thy knee... 3.3

Northumberland announces Bolingbroke's conditions of surrender and the king grants his "fair demands." But Richard again loses his nerve and imagines himself already deposed and buried. Seemingly ready to abdicate, he tells Bolingbroke that "what you will have, I'll give, and willing too." In York's palace at Langley, the queen overhears a gardener and two servants discussing how Richard would still be king if he had "dress'd his land as we this garden." When challenged, the gardener reports that Richard is now Bolingbroke's prisoner.

What must the King do now? Must he submit?/ The King shall do it. Must he be deposed?... 3.3

ACT FOUR

340 lines

LONDON

In London, Bolingbroke demands to know the truth about Gloucester's death. Bagot blames Aumerle, and several nobles confirm the charge. Bolingbroke postpones Aumerle's trial until Mowbray's return from exile, but he then learns that his old foe has died in Italy. When York reports that Richard has agreed to give up the throne, Carlisle denounces Bolingbroke as a traitor and predicts that "the blood of English shall manure the ground." With Carlisle under arrest, Bolingbroke summons Richard to confirm his abdication.

Marry, God forbid!/ Worst in this royal presence may I speak... 4.1

Richard, still convinced of his divine right to rule, compares his fate to that of Christ. When York asks him if he is stepping down, Richard invites Bolingbroke to seize the crown. Bolingbroke then repeats the question. This time, both mocking and hysterical, Richard replies, "Ay, no. No, ay," then adds bitterly, "God save King Henry, unking'd Richard says."

Alack, why am I sent for to a king/Before I have shook off the regal thoughts/ Wherewith I reigned?... 4.1

Ordered to read aloud the charges against him, Richard says he cannot see through his tears. He asks for a mirror and stares at himself, then smashes the glass on the ground to show "how soon my sorrow hath destroyed my face." When Bolingbroke orders Richard to the Tower, Carlisle, Aumerle, and the Abbot of Westminster start plotting the usurper's murder.

They shall be satisfied. I'll read enough/When I do see the very book indeed/Where all my sins are writ... 4.1

ACT FIVE

565 lines

LONDON, POMFRET CASTLE, AND WINDSOR

As Richard is led to the Tower, Queen Isabel protests that he is accepting his fate too mildly, but he tells her to return to France to mourn "the deposing of a rightful king." He is informed that he is now to go to Pomfret Castle.

At Langley, York tells his wife how, when they entered London, Bolingbroke was acclaimed by the crowds, while Richard was scorned. Their son, Aumerle, arrives wearing a seal in which York discovers the plot against the new king. The old man leaves to warn Henry; the duchess tells her son to hurry to seek Bolingbroke's pardon.

Then, as I said, the Duke, great Bolingbroke,/ Mounted upon a hot and fiery steed... 5.2

Bolingbroke is alone, worrying about the bad company kept by his "unthrifty son," Prince Henry, when Aumerle bursts in to beg his forgiveness. York then arrives, followed by his tearful wife, who extracts a pardon for her son. As Bolingbroke leaves, Exton claims he has heard the new king ask, "Have I no friend will rid me of this living fear?"

At Pomfret Castle, the deposed Richard compares his prison cell to a world peopled with his thoughts. He hears music and, instructing the musicians to keep time, he reflects gloomily on how "I wasted time, and now doth time waste me." A jailer brings him food and, when the man refuses to taste it, Richard beats him. As Exton enters with some henchmen, Richard seizes an ax and kills two of them before he is slain by Exton. At Windsor, Exton arrives with Richard's body in a coffin. Suddenly remorseful, Bolingbroke vows to travel to the Holy Land "to wash this blood off from my guilty hand."

I have been studying how I may compare/This prison where I live unto the world... 5.5

READING THE PLAY

COMPARISON OF PROSE TO VERSE

prose: 0% verse: 100%

SHAKESPEARE'S DRAMATIZATION of the phenomenon of "the King's Two Bodies" in *Richard II* is outstanding. Richard's return from Ireland starts the countdown to his deposition as a divinely anointed monarch, but it also initiates his lengthy meditation on his newly discovered humanity. The psychological struggle between these two Richards stands at the heart of this intensely lyrical, all-verse play. Shakespeare also dwells on the perils of absolute power when John of Gaunt excoriates Richard for sullying "this royal throne of kings," and when the Bishop of Carlisle prophesies that Bolingbroke's treachery will bring "disorder, horror, fear, and mutiny." Bolingbroke, in contrast, is allowed introspection only in the play's last lines, when he vows to do penance in the Holy Land for Richard's murder. His reference to his "unthrifty son" anticipates the drama of the two parts of *Henry IV* that follow.

This illustration from a medieval manuscript shows Richard II setting out on his invasion of Ireland. It is this departure which triggers the events that lead to the king's downfall.

But it is Richard who articulates his own downfall in a series of memorable speeches, starting with his sudden recognition of the inevitability of his defeat. He then soulfully anticipates exchanging "my large kingdom for a little grave." In Westminster Hall, he seems to accept his fate when, after studying his once-royal face in a mirror, he throws the glass to the ground. Finally, in Pomfret Castle, he embraces death in language both simple and moving: "I wasted time and now doth time waste me." The arrogant king who deserved no sympathy has become a solitary man worthy of pity. Thus, Richard's dignity is seen to triumph over Bolingbroke's ambition.

PLAY HISTORY

PATRIOTIC POETRY

In the 19th century, John of Gaunt's "royal throne of kings" speech (2.1) became a paean to patriotism, learned by heart by generations of English schoolchildren. During perilous moments for the nation, like the Battle of Britain and the Blitz in World War II, it was also frequently recited on the radio to raise public spirits. Of course, not all the speech could be used; John of Gaunt's stirring description of "this sceptred isle,/This earth of majesty, this seat of Mars,/This other Eden" is followed by his denunciation of Richard for destroying England through abuse of power.

Spitfires over the Forth Bridge, by Frank Wootton.

SEEING THE PLAY

Ted van Griethuysen (right) presented a passionate yet ailing John of Gaunt who stands up to a tyrannical Richard II (Richard Thomas) in Michael Kahn's production at the Shakespeare Theater, Washington D.C., 1993.

NINETEENTH-CENTURY STAGINGS of *Richard II* customarily used the duel between Bolingbroke and Mowbray and the abdication scene in Westminster Hall as excuses for parading legions of finely costumed extras. Today, the focus is more on Richard's struggle with himself. In theory, Bolingbroke is his foe, but the rebel is a one-dimensional character, subservient before his banishment, calculating and hypocritical once he seeks power.

The key to a good production therefore lies entirely with the actor playing Richard. Above all, he must offer a satisfactory answer to why the king so quickly resigns himself to defeat and takes refuge in self-pity. Some productions show Richard as a petty and arbitrary monarch who, like any bully, retreats when challenged. Others portray him as a Christlike figure who is as obsessed by his divine appointment as he is dismayed to be abandoned by God. A few have suggested that a homoerotic relationship between the warring cousins explains Bolingbroke's easy domination of Richard. Occasionally, Richard is seen to end up insane, although this does not explain his coincidental discovery of profound and self-revelatory poetry.

The play's other great role is, of course, John of Gaunt. He is sometimes presented as a doddering old fool, who is understandably mocked by Richard, but this does not do him justice. His final adieu to his son is touching, and, in daring to warn Richard of the perils of despotism, he delivers the play's most famously patriotic speech—"This blessèd plot, this earth, this realm, this England...".

Jeremy Irons portrayed Richard II as a lost, frightened king in this bleak RSC production at the Barbican in London in 1987.

BEYOND THE PLAY

SINCE SHAKESPEARE'S HISTORY PLAYS were built around juggling the lessons of the past, Elizabethan audiences would have understood *Richard II* as both a contemporary political statement and a chronicle of an earlier era. Thus, Shakespeare's company took an immense risk when it accepted 40 shillings to perform the play in full, including Richard's abdication scene, on the eve of Essex's failed uprising in February 1601. Queen Elizabeth evidently understood Essex's purpose and was understandably furious to be identified with Richard. An uncensored text of the play was published after her death, although it is not known whether it was then again staged. However, records show that *Richard II* and *Hamlet* were both performed by crew members on an East India Company ship, the *Dragon*, off the coast of Sierra Leone in 1607.

It is Richard, at first arbitrary, later defenseless, who should dominate the play. The pageantry of 19th-century productions buried the poignancy of the role, but, by the turn of the 20th century, leading actors were drawn by its very ambiguity. In 1899, for instance, the noted British actor Frank Benson's Richard won praise from one critic for portraying "the capable and faithful artist in the same skin as the incapable and faithless king." John Gielgud, who first played Richard in 1929 and frequently returned to the role, used his remarkable voice and diction to show language to be the king's best defense.

More recent productions have explained Richard's easy surrender to Bolingbroke by having actors portray him as weak and effeminate. In their different ways, for instance, David Warner, Ian McKellen, Jeremy Irons, and Ralph Fiennes all emphasized Richard's physical and emotional fragility. Some productions have played on the idea that Richard and Bolingbroke are two faces of the same character by having actors alternate in the roles. However, the very fact that no definitive Richard has yet appeared is proof enough of the character's enduring complexity.

PLAY HISTORY

CONSPIRACY AT THE GLOBE

On February 7, 1601, the eve of a revolt led by the Earl of Essex, Shakespeare's company was hired to perform *Richard II* at the Globe. The rebels believed the play justified ousting a monarch. After the revolt failed and Essex was executed, however, Shakespeare's company pleaded ignorance of the conspiracy. The incident nonetheless shook the aged and ailing queen. "I am Richard the Second, know ye not that," she later said.

Engraving of Robert Devereux, Earl of Essex.

PLAYER PROFILE

FIONA SHAW

In her National Theatre production in London in 1995, Deborah Warner cast an actress, Fiona Shaw, as Richard, saying she wanted to show "incredible intimacy" between the king and Bolingbroke which, she felt, would not be possible if two men were, as is usual, playing the roles. When Fiona Shaw's Richard II kissed David Threlfall's Bolingbroke on the lips, the interpretation added a new twist to the idea that the cousins are both bound and torn apart by homoerotic tensions.

Fiona Shaw in Deborah Warner's *Richard II*.

HENRY IV PART I

HENRY IV PART I, ARGUABLY SHAKESPEARE'S most sophisticated history play, introduces one of his greatest characters, Sir John Falstaff, the dissolute, witty, and calculating mentor to the young Prince Hal. *Henry IV Part I* also touches on darker subjects, such as Hotspur's challenge to Henry IV's legitimacy and the king's remorse over the murder of Richard II. Written around 1596–97 as the second episode of the "Henriad" tetralogy, the play was very popular in Elizabethan and Jacobean times; it was published in six quarto editions before its inclusion in the *First Folio* of 1623. Its main source is Holinshed's *Chronicles,* but it also borrows from *The Famous Victories of Henry V,* an anonymous play staged in 1595. Today, with *Henry IV Part I* frequently performed as part of the "Henriad," Prince Hal's gradual transformation into the heroic Henry V is viewed as the play's underlying theme.

BEHIND THE PLAY

HENRY BOLINGBROKE HAD LITTLE difficulty in wresting the crown from Richard II in 1399 but within months he faced revolt and, even after Richard's death, his claim to the throne was constantly challenged. This play is broadly true to history: it starts with the English victory over the Scots at Homildon Hill in 1402, includes the Welsh revolt led by Owen Glendower, and ends with Henry's victory over Hotspur and the rebellious Percys at the Battle of Shrewsbury in 1403. But, as always, Shakespeare bends the facts to suit his needs. Hotspur was 23 years older than Prince Henry, or Hal, but Shakespeare portrays them as contemporaries so that the king can wish his son to be the valiant Hotspur, rather than the profligate Hal. Then, to show how Hal replaces Hotspur in the king's affections, the play has the prince killing the rebel at Shrewsbury, although this incident was also invented. Records show that Hal was indeed a brave warrior who, during his visits to London, enjoyed the city's night life. But there is no evidence of a Falstaff-like figure leading him down the path of vice. These plot lines—Hotspur's rebellion, Falstaff's carousing, and the king's fretting about his son—all serve to forge Hal's character.

No more the thirsty entrance of this soil/ Shall daub her lips with her own children's blood,/No more shall trenching war channel her fields... 1.1

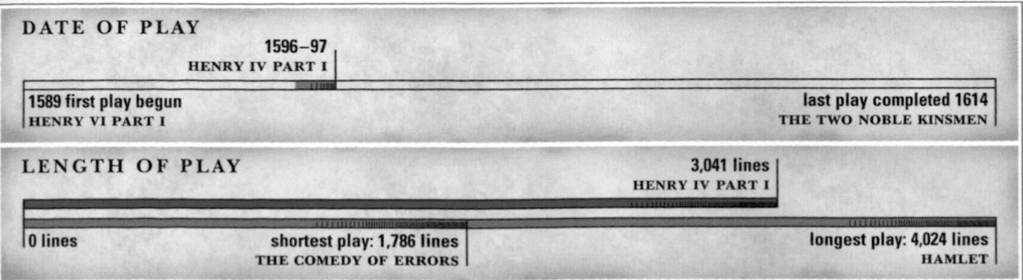

DRAMATIS PERSONAE

Henry IV (J.M. Rodero) is troubled by two concerns: the rebellion of the Percys and the dissolute character of his son.

KING HENRY IV
341 lines
Formerly Henry Bolingbroke, he is plagued by guilt over his deposition and murder of Richard II. He worries that his oldest son, Hal, has fallen in with disreputable company; he compares the prince unfavorably to Hotspur and is surprised when he is victorious against the Percys at the Battle of Shrewsbury.

HENRY, PRINCE OF WALES
551 lines
Henry's oldest son, a wild young man known to friends as Hal, he spends his time in taverns with Falstaff and lives up to his reputation of being irresponsible; but he shows his mettle by killing Hotspur in battle.

PRINCE JOHN
8 lines
Henry IV's third son, the Duke of Lancaster, he is brave in battle.

EARL OF WESTMORELAND
41 lines
Loyal to the king.

SIR WALTER BLUNT
41 lines
Loyal to the king, he dies fighting the Percys.

THOMAS PERCY, EARL OF WORCESTER
189 lines
Hotspur's uncle, he organizes a rebellion but is executed after the Battle of Shrewsbury.

HENRY PERCY, EARL OF NORTHUMBERLAND
26 lines
Hotspur's father who once backed Henry, he encourages the revolt against the king but fails to support Hotspur in battle.

EDMUND MORTIMER, EARL OF MARCH
60 lines
Richard II's rightful heir, he is captured by the rebel Owen Glendower and marries his daughter; he supports the rebellion.

HENRY PERCY, ALSO HOTSPUR
562 lines
A valiant warrior, he defeats the Scots at Holmedon but he rebels when the king refuses to help free his brother-in-law, Mortimer, from capture by Owen Glendower; he is killed by Prince Henry at Shrewsbury.

Hotspur (Laurence Olivier) is loyal and courageous, fighting for the release of Mortimer.

RICHARD SCROOP
34 lines
Archbishop of York, he backs the rebellion.

ARCHIBALD, EARL OF DOUGLAS
46 lines
A brave Scottish noble, he joins the revolt against Henry IV; although he is captured at the Battle of Shrewsbury, Prince Henry saves his life.

OWEN GLENDOWER
79 lines
Welsh rebel, he captures Mortimer and backs his claim to the throne.

SIR RICHARD VERNON
66 lines
Rebel executed after the Battle of Shrewsbury.

SIR JOHN FALSTAFF
616 lines
A decadent aristocrat whose appetite for wine, women, and song is matched only by his wit and intelligence, he leads Prince Hal toward a life of debauchery but also teaches him the ways of the world.

Falstaff (Timothy West) is one of Shakespeare's best-loved characters.

SIR MICHAEL
8 lines
Member of the household of the Archbishop of York.

POINS, GADSHILL, PETO AND BARDOLPH
79; 45; 15; 29 lines
Falstaff's companions.

FRANCIS
15 lines
A drawer (waiter) at the Boar's Head Tavern.

LADY PERCY
57 lines
Hotspur's wife, she scolds him for his secrecy.

LADY MORTIMER
0 lines
Mortimer's wife and Glendower's daughter, she speaks only Welsh.

MISTRESS QUICKLY
49 lines
Hostess of the Boar's Head Tavern, she tries in vain to maintain order when Prince Hal joins Falstaff and his collection of disreputable drinking cronies at her inn; she offers comic relief in times of war.

OTHER PLAYERS
Lords, Officers, Sheriffs, Soldiers, Messengers, Vintner, Chamberlain, Ostler, Waiters, Carriers, Travelers, and Attendants.

PLOT SUMMARY

SIZE OF ACTS

ACT 1	ACT 2	ACT 3	ACT 4	ACT 5
627 lines	854 lines	653 lines	387 lines	520 lines

ACT ONE
627 lines

LONDON

As Henry IV prepares to travel to the Holy Land to atone for the murder of Richard II, he learns that Mortimer, Earl of March, has been captured by the Welsh rebel, Owen Glendower. Better news comes from the north where Henry Percy, known as Hotspur, has defeated the Scots at Holmedon and captured several Scottish nobles. The king contrasts the valiant Hotspur with his own wastrel son, Henry, Prince of Wales, but he also summons Hotspur to explain why he has not surrendered his prisoners.

Yea, there thou makest me sad, and makest me sin/ In envy that my Lord Northumberland/ Should be the father to so blest a son... 1.1

Untouched by England's troubles, Prince Henry, or Hal, is drinking with Sir John Falstaff, mocking his old friend for his gluttony and girth. Falstaff takes it in good stride, worried more about how his meager funds can keep him in drink. Poins, another ne'er-do-well, suggests robbing pilgrims and the prince agrees just once to be "a madcap." When Falstaff leaves for his favorite inn, Poins suggests a practical joke. He and the prince should arrive too late for the assault, then appear in disguise and take the booty from Falstaff. Alone, the prince muses that his "loose behavior" will make him look better when he changes his ways.

Thou art so fat-witted with drinking of old sack... 1.2

I know you all, and will awhile uphold/ The unyoked humour of your idleness... 1.2

At the palace, Hotspur's uncle, Earl of Worcester, complains that the king has ignored his family's role in giving him the crown. Hotspur, at first deferential, explains that he kept his prisoners when "a certain lord, neat and trimly dressed,/Fresh as a bridegroom" came to fetch them. But the king protests that Hotspur still wants to exchange the prisoners for his brother-in-law, Mortimer, a man who has proven his treachery by marrying Glendower's daughter. As he leaves, the king warns Hotspur to hand over the prisoners "or you will hear of it." Hotspur angrily accuses his father, Northumberland, of installing Bolingbroke as king when Richard's rightful heir was Mortimer. Now determined to topple Henry, Hotspur joins forces with the Archbishop of York, Glendower, and Douglas, the Scottish leader.

My liege, I did deny no prisoners... 1.3

Nay then, I cannot blame his cousin King/That wished him on the barren mountains starve... 1.3

ACT TWO
854 lines

ROCHESTER, WARKWORTH CASTLE, AND LONDON

Near Rochester, as Falstaff prepares to rob some pilgrims, Prince Hal and Poins announce that they will wait in hiding in case the travelers escape. But as soon as Falstaff and his cronies, Gadshill, Bardolph, and Peto, seize their spoils, the prince and Poins attack them and they

While I by looking on the praise of him/See riot and dishonour stain the brow/ Of my young Harry... 1.2

flee in panic. At Warkworth Castle, Hotspur reacts angrily to a letter urging him to be cautious. His wife, Kate, is puzzled by his erratic behavior and asks if he still loves her. Yes, he says, but it is best that she not share his secrets.

At the Boar's Head Tavern in Eastcheap, the prince is teasing the pub's taciturn waiter when Falstaff arrives complaining of the prince's cowardice. Replenished with drink, Falstaff recounts his bogus version of the hold-up, with each breath inflating his bravery. Finally, the Prince reveals his own involvement but the old knight responds nimbly, pretending he was not fooled.

That ever this fellow should have fewer words than a parrot, and yet the son of a woman!... 2.4

By the Lord, I knew ye as well as he that made ye... 2.4

An envoy summons the prince to the palace, but the party continues. Falstaff suggests they rehearse Hal's audience. Falstaff, speaking as the king, bemoans the prince's bad company, except for "a good portly man" named Falstaff. The two switch roles and the prince, now playing his father, complains about, "That villainous abominable misleader of youth, Falstaff, that old white-bearded Satan." In the role of the prince, the old man jumps to his own defense, saying that the king should banish everyone but "sweet Jack Falstaff". This mordant game is interrupted by the Sheriff looking for money stolen by "A gross fat man," but Falstaff hides and promptly falls asleep. As the Sheriff leaves, Hal pledges to replace the missing money.

Peace, good pint-pot, peace, good tickle-brain... 2.4

Swearest thou, ungracious boy? Henceforth ne'er look on me... 2.4

But to say I know more harm in him than in myself were to say more than I know... 2.4

ACT THREE

653 lines

BANGOR, LONDON

Meeting with fellow plotters in Wales, Hotspur ridicules Glendower for claiming that the earth shook when he was born. When Glendower boasts that he can call spirits from the deep, Hotspur retorts: "But will they come when you do call for them?" The group divides the country into three areas to be ruled by Glendower, Mortimer, and Hotspur but Hotspur complains that his share is too small. Mortimer and Worcester rebuke him for his rudeness but to no avail. When Mortimer introduces his new wife who, he notes, "can speak no English, I no Welsh," Hotspur again teases them, only to be scolded by his own wife as a "giddy goose."

In London, the king sternly reminds Prince Henry how Richard II lost all dignity by mixing with "capering fools". Now he sees Hal behaving like Richard, while Hotspur, "Mars in swaddling clothes," displays the same courage that the king himself showed when he seized the crown. With his enemies in revolt, he asks, will Hal join them "to show how much thou art degenerate?" Remorseful, the prince promises to prove his worth by defeating Hotspur in combat. Reassured, the king orders him to join royal forces gathering near Shrewsbury.

God pardon thee! Yet let me wonder, Harry,/ At thy affections... 3.2

Do not think so, you shall not find it so;/And God forgive them that have so much swayed... 3.2

I was as virtuously given as a gentleman need to be. Virtuous enough. Swore little. Diced not above seven times a week. Went to a bawdy house not above once in a quarter—of an hour... 3.3

At the Boar's Head Tavern, convinced that his days are numbered, Falstaff begs Bardolph to entertain him with a bawdy song ❝. As Mistress Quickly, the inn-keeper, pesters Falstaff to pay his debts, the prince and Peto march in dressed as soldiers. Falstaff complains that he was pickpocketed of a small fortune while sleeping but no one believes him. The prince interrupts the banter to announce that Falstaff will lead a band of infantrymen into battle. Taken aback, the old man orders Mistress Quickly to bring him breakfast.

Why, there is it. Come, sing me a bawdy song, make me merry… 3.3

ACT FOUR

387 lines

NEAR SHREWSBURY, OUTSIDE COVENTRY, AND YORK

At the rebel camp near Shrewsbury, Hotspur learns that his father is unwell and cannot join them. Worcester fears that Northumberland's absence could be read as "dislike for our proceedings," but Hotspur is unworried. Sir John Vernon, a rebel knight, brings word that three columns are approaching: one is headed by the king himself; another by Westmoreland and the king's third son, John; and a third led by Prince Henry, who is riding his steed like "feathered Mercury." To add to the rebels' problems, Glendower's forces have been delayed, but Hotspur claims he is ready for battle.

On a road near Coventry, Falstaff dispatches Bardolph to find a bottle of sack and is left contemplating his ❝ motley followers. Prince Henry appears and remarks on the "pitiful rascals," but Falstaff boasts they will serve as "food for powder."

If I be not ashamed of my soldiers, I am a soused gurnet… 4.2

Outside Shrewsbury, Sir Walter Blunt assures the rebels that the king laments past offences and offers them a pardon, but Hotspur recalls that, as Bolingbroke, the king broke his promise to claim only his rights as Duke of Lancaster ❝. As Henry IV, he then murdered Richard, sent Mortimer into battle in Wales and turned against the Percy family. Hotspur asks for time to reflect.

The King is kind, and well we know the King/ Knows at what time to promise, when to pay… 4.3

ACT FIVE

520 lines

NEAR SHREWSBURY

Dispatched by Hotspur to the royal camp, Worcester now reminds the king himself how, having abandoned his vow not to seek the throne, he turned against his

It pleased your majesty to turn your looks/ Of favour from myself, and all our house… 5.1

former friends. Prince Henry proposes that, to avert a bloodbath, he and Hotspur should meet in combat, but the king prefers reconciliation, saying that "every man/Shall be my friend again." As Worcester leaves, the prince is persuaded that war is unavoidable and he teases Falstaff that "thou owest God a death." The old man is left wondering whether his honor is at stake but hurriedly dismisses the idea.

'Tis not due yet – I would be loath to pay him before his day… 5.1

At the rebel camp, Worcester ignores the king's peace offer and tells Hotspur to prepare for battle. Hotspur replies with a defiant message, but he also seeks news of Prince Henry. Vernon notes that the prince's offer of a duel was twinned with praise of Hotspur and he remarks on Hal's new-found dignity. If the prince survives the day, he says, "England did never owe so sweet a hope."

No, by my soul, I never in my life/ Did hear a challenge urged more modestly… 5.2

On the battlefield, Douglas slays Blunt, believing he is the king but then discovers that "The King hath many marching in his coats." As the fight rages, Prince Henry is wounded but he refuses to withdraw. The king is attacked by Douglas but he is saved by his son, who notes that he has given the lie to those who said he wanted his father dead. Finally, Prince Henry and Hotspur meet in combat and Hotspur is killed, dying in the middle of a sentence that Hal completes.

For worms, brave Percy. Fare thee well, great heart!… 5.4

In the middle of their fight, Falstaff is knocked over by Douglas and feigns death. Spotting Falstaff on the ground, the prince bids "Poor Jack, farewell!" But then Falstaff rises, sees Hotspur's body and carries it before the prince, hoping for reward. As trumpets sound the retreat, the king orders Worcester and Vernon executed, but Prince Henry seeks mercy for Douglas. With the battle won, the king prepares to fight Northumberland and Glendower.

Embowelled! If thou embowel me today, I'll give you leave to powder me and eat me too tomorrow… 5.4

What is that honour? Air. A trim reckoning! Who hath it? He that died a'Wednesday. Doth he feel it? No. Doth he hear it? No… 5.1

READING THE PLAY

COMPARISON OF PROSE TO VERSE

prose: 43% | verse: 57%

"Many a nobleman lies stark and stiff/Under the hoofs of vaunting enemies" (5.3). The death of Hotspur at the Battle of Shrewsbury, an illustration by James Doyle.

THANKS TO FALSTAFF, this play's finest language is written in prose. Falstaff provides both wit and philosophy, which are easier to appreciate in print than amid the turmoil of the stage. Falstaff has an insatiable appetite for food, drink, and women, but he never surrenders his intelligence. He is Prince Henry's guide to a debauched life, yet he never forgets that one day the young man will be king. He is above all a survivor, a man who demands respect, but refuses to risk his life in the name of honor. For the high politics of the realm, Shakespeare follows tradition by using verse. The prince's early soliloquy meditating on his "loose behavior" also establishes one of the play's key themes: Hal's awareness that sooner or later he must change his ways. Before the Battle of Shrewsbury, he is already described as "feathered Mercury" to Hotspur's Mars. For classical oratory in the spirit of medieval chivalry, though, Hotspur has the last word, both when he confronts the king and when he justifies his rebellion with reckless bravura, "Doomsday is near. Die all, die merrily."

PLAY HISTORY

FALSTAFF

Henry IV Part I has long been considered Falstaff's play—Queen Elizabeth herself requested a new play showing Falstaff in love. Shakespeare obliged and gave the fat knight his own comedy in *The Merry Wives of Windsor.* Shakespeare initially gave the fictitious Falstaff the name of a real person, Sir John Oldcastle, a brave knight who fought alongside Henry V. Oldcastle's descendants complained that he had been vilified, and Shakespeare quickly renamed the character.

SEEING THE PLAY

Prince Hal (Tom Donaldson, right) and Poins (Richard Allan Edwards, in doorway) tease Francis (Gregory Ward Schroeder, left) at The Boar's Head Tavern in an American Shakespeare Festival production, Stratford, Connecticut.

THE LARGER-THAN-LIFE CHARACTER of Falstaff fills the stage with his rambunctious disdain for civilized behavior. Queen Elizabeth I loved him and audiences are no less devoted today, while successive generations of leading actors continue to pad their waistlines for the chance to play the role. The principal peril is overacting: if Falstaff is portrayed as too much of a buffoon, his wisdom and wit can be lost in the commotion—and these are the qualities that truly distinguish him. Prince Henry is his pupil, not only in rabble-rousing, but also in understanding human nature. On stage, then, even during the scenes in Mistress Quickly's noisy tavern, the "other" prince—and future king—should somehow be visible.

The prototype for the conquering hero of *Henry V* is Hotspur—and Shakespeare's sympathy for him is apparent. Brave, principled, mischievous, and moody, Hotspur overshadows the passive figure of King Henry just as Henry V will overshadow his father in history. The play's final battle scene poses special challenges because, while the fury of war must be conveyed, it includes key psychological insights. Prince Henry's rescue of his father reveals the unresolved tensions in their relationship, a point that becomes central in *Henry IV Part II.* And when confronted with the inert body of Hotspur, the prince exorcises another dominant figure in his young life.

Hotspur (Adam Levy) seizes the opportunity to goad a troubled Henry IV (David Troughton).

BEYOND THE PLAY

THE MORALITY PLAYS performed across England between the 14th and 16th centuries are at the root of *Henry IV Part I.* This kind of play pitted Virtue against Vice. While Virtue triumphed in the end, comic entertainment was assured by Vice, whose antics were often borrowed from bawdy folk stories. By Shakespeare's day, the morality play had given way to more modern drama but Elizabethan audiences would have recognized Falstaff as akin to Vice. The public, fully conscious of Henry V's place in history, knew he would eventually reform. Furthermore, Shakespeare indirectly identifies Hal as Virtue when, albeit in jocular vein, the prince denounces Falstaff as "that reverend Vice, that grey Iniquity, that Father Ruffian, that Vanity in years" and finally as "that old white-bearded Satan."

Unsurprisingly, popular interest in this play has long centered on Falstaff. Will Kemp, one of Shakespeare's fellow actors at the Theatre, quickly made the role his own. In 1622, both parts of *Henry IV* were fused and presented simply as *Sir John Falstaff.* Thanks to Falstaff, *Henry IV Part I* quickly returned to the stage after the Restoration and has remained popular ever since. Actors with natural girth, from Orson Welles to John Goodman, have been drawn to Falstaff. Yet the most acclaimed Falstaff of recent decades, Ralph Richardson, who played the fat knight at the New Theatre in London in 1945, was anything but corpulent.

The recent practice of presenting the "Henriad" in sequence has given new stature to Prince Henry. Since the same actor usually plays the role in both parts of *Henry IV* as well as in *Henry V*, it becomes easier to track the maturing of the prince as duty calls.

ON SCREEN

CHIMES AT MIDNIGHT

Orson Welles's 1965 film, *Chimes at Midnight*, tracked Falstaff and Prince Henry from *Richard II* to *Henry V* in a telescoped version of the tetralogy. The cast included Welles as Falstaff, John Gielgud as Henry IV, Keith Baxter as Hal, Margaret Rutherford as Mistress Quickly, and Jeanne Moreau as Doll Tearsheet. While it has attracted some criticism for its hasty production values and poor synchronization, the *New Yorker* acclaimed it as "one of Welles's best and least seen movies... The film is a near-masterpiece."

Keanu Reeves (left) and River Phoenix in Gus van Sant's *My Own Private Idaho* (1991), based on Shakespeare's *Henry IV* plays. It features a Falstaffian figure, a male prostitute, with dangerous sexual appeal.

HENRY IV PART II

HENRY IV PART II IS DOMINATED BY the extravagant personality of Falstaff, but in it the fat knight gradually loses sway over Prince Henry and is finally rejected by the newly crowned Henry V. The play picks up the narrative where *Henry IV Part I* left off. Viewed by most scholars as a lesser play than *Part I,* it is saved by Falstaff's antics and language, but it lacks the spark of Hotspur's personality and a display of heroism by Prince Henry. Although *Part II* has never been as popular as *Part I,* it provides the crucial bridge to *Henry V* because the young prince is finally able to persuade his dying father than he is a worthy heir. This play was not immediately revived after the Restoration and was performed less frequently than *Part I* in later centuries. Only in the 1920s were the two parts finally performed consecutively. Today, they are regularly staged together as part of the "Henriad."

BEHIND THE PLAY

SET BETWEEN THE BATTLE OF SHREWSBURY in 1403 and Henry IV's death in 1413, the play covers a period in which the increasingly infirm monarch faced several revolts and threats of invasion. Shakespeare focuses on the 1405 uprising which, as the play recounts, was put down through duplicity: the Archbishop of York, Richard Le Scrope, and Thomas Mowbray disbanded their troops under a peace accord with Prince John, Duke of Lancaster, and were promptly beheaded. Northumberland finally revolted in 1408, but he was defeated and fled to Scotland. The Welsh insurrection was also put down in 1411 by Prince Henry, although Shakespeare gives him no credit for this. Indeed, Prince Henry, or Hal, is largely absent from the play until his final reconciliation with the dying king. Shakespeare is accurate in portraying King Henry's last years as dominated by illness and the play also correctly emphasizes the king's strained relations with his heir. While Prince Henry was forced to act when his father was incapacitated, he was accused of coveting the throne when the king recovered. Whether or not they made peace with each other, the king's death was probably welcomed by his son.

The commonwealth is sick of their own choice;/ Their over-greedy love hath surfeited... 1.3

DATE OF PLAY

1598
HENRY IV PART II

1589 first play begun
HENRY VI PART I

last play completed 1614
THE TWO NOBLE KINSMEN

LENGTH OF PLAY

3,255 lines
HENRY IV PART II

0 lines

shortest play: 1,786 lines
THE COMEDY OF ERRORS

longest play: 4,024 lines
HAMLET

DRAMATIS PERSONAE

RUMOUR
41 lines
He abjures false rumor.

KING HENRY IV
296 lines
Haunted by political unrest and deep distrust for his heir, he is gradually immobilized by illness; on his deathbed, he again believes the prince has betrayed him, but they are finally reconciled.

HENRY, PRINCE OF WALES
292 lines
Also Harry and Hal, after spending his youth reveling with Falstaff, he persuades his dying father that he is fit to be king and, as Henry V, rejects Falstaff.

Hal (Michael Maloney) leaves his wild days behind him.

THOMAS, DUKE OF CLARENCE
23 lines
The king's second son.

JOHN, DUKE OF LANCASTER
108 lines
The king's third son.

HUMPHREY, DUKE OF GLOUCESTER
17 lines
The king's youngest son.

EARL OF NORTHUMBERLAND
106 lines
He encourages the rebels, but withdraws upon hearing of his son's death.

SCROOP, ARCHBISHOP OF YORK
150 lines
He leads the rebellion.

LORD MOWBRAY
56 lines
A rebel who is executed.

LORD HASTINGS
57 lines
A rebel who is executed.

LORD BARDOLPH
87 lines
A companion of Northumberland.

TRAVERS AND MORTON
16; 78 lines
Servants.

SIR JOHN COLEVILLE
8 lines
A rebel knight.

EARLS OF WARWICK AND SURREY
78; 0 lines
Loyal to the king.

EARL OF WESTMORELAND
111 lines
He confronts the rebels.

GOWER
8 lines
Lord Chief Justice's assistant.

HARCOURT AND SIR JOHN BLUNT
8; 0 lines
Knights loyal to the king.

LORD CHIEF JUSTICE
147 lines
Falstaff's nemesis.

Mistress Quickly (Charlotte Rae) and Doll Tearsheet (Ray Allen) at the Boar's Head Tavern. Falstaff attempts to seduce Doll, in vain.

SIR JOHN FALSTAFF
637 lines
A fallen aristocrat who rejoices in his dissolute life; he hopes to prosper when the prince is king, but he is instead rejected and jailed.

BARDOLPH, PISTOL, POINS, PETO, AND FALSTAFF'S PAGE
51; 76; 68; 6; 27 lines
Falstaff's henchmen.

ROBERT SHALLOW
185 lines
A Justice of the Peace.

SILENCE
40 lines
Shallow's cousin.

DAVY
34 lines
Shallow's servant.

FANG AND SNARE
9; 3 lines
Sheriff's officers.

MOULDY, SHADOW, WART, FEEBLE, AND BULLCALF
12; 5; 2; 11; 14 lines
Falstaff's recruits.

FRANCIS AND WILL
10; 11 lines
Drawers (waiters) at the Boar's Head Tavern

LADY NORTHUMBERLAND
5 lines
She advises her husband.

LADY PERCY
46 lines
Hotspur's widow.

MISTRESS QUICKLY
169 lines
Innkeeper of the Boar's Head Tavern, she complains about Falstaff but still likes the old rascal.

DOLL TEARSHEET
80 lines
A rough-tongued prostitute.

A DANCER
34 lines
She delivers an Epilogue.

OTHER PLAYERS
Lords, Officers, Soldiers, Servants, Musicians, Porter, Drawers, Beadles, Grooms, and Attendants.

PLOT SUMMARY

SIZE OF ACTS

ACT 1	ACT 2	ACT 3	ACT 4	ACT 5
627 lines	789 lines	424 lines	878 lines	537 lines

ACT ONE 627 lines

WARKWORTH CASTLE, LONDON, AND YORK

Rumour, a character "painted full of tongues," recounts how false rumor has persuaded Northumberland that his son, Henry Percy, or Hotspur, has won the Battle of Shrewsbury and has even killed King Henry and Prince Hal. But soon a messenger tells of hearing that "Harry Percy's spur was cold" and a second confirms that Hotspur is dead. Heartbroken, Northumberland vows vengeance ❝. He is reminded how he encouraged Hotspur to confront King Henry, but news that the Archbishop of York is continuing the rebellion offers him some consolation.

For this I shall have time enough to mourn... 1.1

In London, Prince Henry's drinking pal, Sir John Falstaff, is tracked down by the Lord Chief Justice who complains of his bad influence over the prince. The old knight responds that the chief justice is too old to know pleasure, to which the judge lists all the signs of Falstaff's advanced age ❝. Falstaff responds that he is old only in wisdom. But the justice tells him his good times are over because the king has ordered him to join the campaign against the Archbishop of York.

Do you set down your name in the scroll of youth, that are written down old with all the characters of age?... 1.2

In York, the archbishop and Lords Hastings, Mowbray, and Bardolph are plotting their offensive, but they worry that Northumberland may let them down, just as he broke his word to help Hotspur at Shrewsbury. Hastings believes the king can still be defeated because his forces are also engaged in France and against the Welsh rebel, Owen Glendower. The archbishop bemoans the "over-greedy love" of those who turned against Richard II and helped install Henry as king but who now mourn Richard and wish Henry deposed ❝.

Let us on,/And publish the occasion of our arms./ The commonwealth is sick of their own choice... 1.3

ACT TWO 789 lines

LONDON AND WARKWORTH CASTLE

Summoned by Mistress Quickly of the Boar's Head Tavern in Eastcheap two sheriffs, Fang and Snare, try to arrest Falstaff for not paying his bills. As a noisy brawl ensues, the Lord Chief Justice arrives, wondering why the fat knight has not left with the troops. Mistress Quickly complains that Falstaff has eaten her "out

By this hand, thou thinkest me as far in the devil's book as you or Falstaff... 2.3

Can a weak empty vessel bear such a huge full hogshead? There's a whole merchant's venture of Bordeaux stuff in him... 2.4

of house and home" and, further, has broken a promise to marry her. Falstaff dismisses her, then just as swiftly flatters her and is invited to dine at the inn.

Prince Henry, or Hal, learning that his father is ill, tells his companion, Poins, that he "bleeds inwardly" but would not display sorrow in "such vile company." Bardolph, another low-life, reports that Falstaff is dining with Mistress Quickly and Mistress Doll Tearsheet, prompting the prince and Poins to decide to eavesdrop on their conversation.

At Warkworth Castle, Northumberland seems intent on joining the new rebellion, but Hotspur's widow begs him not to go to war, noting bitterly that, having betrayed her husband, he should not now consider his own honor more important. At his own wife's suggestion, Northumberland decides to withdraw to Scotland and await the progress of the uprising.

O, yet, for God's sake, go not to these wars!/ The time was, father, that you broke your word... 2.3

At the Boar's Head Tavern, Falstaff arrives excitedly for his dinner date with Mistress Quickly and Doll. Pistol, another local wastrel, appears, but Mistress Quickly wants no drunks in her inn. He is no drunk, says Falstaff, but a cheater. Pistol takes a shine to Doll, but she rebuffs him, proclaiming "I am meat for your master." As Falstaff runs out of patience and chases Pistol from the inn, the prince and Poins arrive in disguise and hear themselves being ridiculed by Falstaff. As they watch him trying to seduce Doll, Poins remarks: "Is it not strange that desire should so many years outlive performance?" Finally, they show themselves, but Falstaff, quick-witted as ever, explains that he spoke ill of the prince "before the wicked that the wicked might not fall in love with thee." The jesting ends when the prince is called to the palace and Falstaff is sent to fight.

ACT THREE
424 lines

LONDON AND GLOUCESTERSHIRE

At the palace, weighed down by worries and unable to sleep, Henry concludes that "uneasy lies the head that wears a crown". Lord Warwick insists that Northumberland will soon be defeated, but the king notes that the same Northumberland who turned against Richard has now betrayed him, just as Richard had foretold. Warwick again tries to offer him some comfort with the news that Glendower is dead.

How many thousand of my poorest subjects/ Are at this hour asleep... 3.1

In Gloucestershire, Shallow and his cousin Silence, both justices of the peace, are reminiscing when Falstaff arrives in search of recruits. As Mouldy, Shadow, Wart, Feeble, and Bullcalf are paraded as candidates, Shallow recalls the wild times that he and Falstaff spent together. As Falstaff leaves with his conscripts, he muses on Shallow's false memories, noting "how subject we old men are to this vice of lying!".

As I return, I will fetch off these justices... 3.2

ACT FOUR
878 lines

GAULTREE FOREST IN YORKSHIRE AND LONDON

Gathered with their troops in a Yorkshire forest, the Archbishop of York, Mowbray and Hastings learn that Northumberland has retreated to Scotland. Westmoreland arrives with the offer of a truce from King Henry's third son, Prince John, Duke of Lancaster. When the earl asks the archbishop why a man of peace opts for war, he hears complaints about the king's treatment of his former allies. Turning to Mowbray, Westmoreland notes that the king has restored his title of Duke of Norfolk. Mowbray responds that much evil would have been averted if King Richard had allowed his father to fight and defeat Henry Bolingbroke. Westmoreland insists that Prince John will satisfy their grievances and, although Mowbray remains sceptical, the archbishop believes the king weary of war "For he had found to end one doubt by death/Revives two greater in the heirs of life."

Wherefore do I this? So the question stands... 4.1

What thing, in honour, had my father lost/ That need to be revived and breathed in me... 4.1

When they meet in person, Prince John chastises the archbishop for turning against God's substitute, King Henry, but he also promises that the rebels' complaints "shall be with speed redressed." As the two sides toast their new-found peace, Hastings orders the rebel army to disperse, while John commands his troops to be discharged. But as soon as the rebel forces have disbanded, Westmoreland arrests Hastings, the archbishop, and Mowbray. The archbishop protests against the prince's bad faith, but John dismisses them as traitors and orders their execution. As the prince leaves for London, Falstaff presents him with a prisoner and asks him to speak well of his bravery. Alone, the old knight muses that "the sober-blooded" prince lacks wit because he drinks no wine, while Prince Hal is "very hot and valiant" thanks to his consumption of sack.

I would you had the wit; 'twere better than your dukedom... 4.3

In the Jerusalem chamber of the king's palace, the king is saddened to hear that Prince Henry is again reveling with his dissolute friends. As he bemoans his ill health, he suffers a fresh stroke and is taken to another chamber to rest. Prince Henry arrives and, believing his father dead, takes the

Why doth the crown lie there upon his pillow,/ Being so troublesome a bedfellow?... 4.5

crown. After he leaves, the king stirs and, noticing the missing crown, deplores "How quickly nature falls into revolt/When gold becomes her object." When the prince returns, the old man berates him for his impatience to become king and weeps at the thought of England under his rule. The prince begs his father's pardon, saying that he only took the crown to accuse it of bringing on his death. The king forgives him and, as his last counsel, tells him to keep the peace in England by engaging in "foreign quarrels." He then asks to be taken back to the Jerusalem chamber, thus fulfilling a prophesy that he would die in Jerusalem.

Thy wish was father, Harry, to that thought./I stay too long by thee, I weary thee... 4.5

ACT FIVE

537 lines

GLOUCESTERSHIRE AND LONDON

At Shallow's home in Gloucestershire, Falstaff is planning how to embezzle from his host, still unaware of King Henry's death. In London, though, the Lord Chief Justice is worried that, having once arrested Prince Hal for behaving dissolutely, he will now be punished. But instead the new king applauds his sense of duty and confirms him in his post, even appealing to him for guidance "as a father to my youth." Still reveling in Gloucestershire, Falstaff is entertained by Silence's song—"we shall/Do nothing but eat, and make good cheer"—when Pistol arrives to tell him "thou art now one of the greatest men in this realm." When the knight understands that Henry IV is dead, he hurries to London, convinced that "the laws of England are at my commandment" and "woe to my Lord Chief Justice!"

If I were sawed into quantities... 5.1

You are right justice, and you weigh this well./ Therefore still bear the balance and the sword... 5.2

Waiting on a London street as Henry V emerges from his coronation at Westminster Abbey, Falstaff shouts, "God save thee, my sweet boy!" The Lord Chief Justice tries to silence him but he cries out again. This time, the young monarch replies, adding "Presume not that I am the thing I was." Incredulous, Falstaff insists that "I shall be sent for in private to him," but instead the Lord Chief Justice orders Falstaff and his cronies to be held in a naval prison until they are reformed. Prince John reports that the king has summoned Parliament and he predicts that within the year England will be at war in France.

I know thee not, old man. Fall to thy prayers./ How ill white hairs become a fool and jester... 5.5

My father is gone wild into his grave,/ For in his tomb lie my affections;/ And with his spirits sadly I survive/ To mock the expectation of the world... 5.2

READING THE PLAY

COMPARISON OF PROSE TO VERSE

prose: 49% | verse: 51%

Jame's Gillray's hand-colored etching, "King Henry IV; the last scene," published by S.W. Fores in 1788, portrays Charles James Fox (1749–1806), Britain's first foreign secretary, as Sir John Falstaff.

FALSTAFF PROVIDES MUCH OF THE RICHEST LANGUAGE in this play. His verbal jousting with the Lord Chief Justice and the ladies of the Boar's Head Tavern is particularly adroit, while his attempts to swindle his old friend Shallow show him in his true colors. When alone, though, Falstaff is at his best, as in his mockery of Shallow's false memories and his celebration of the virtues of sack. Even when he is finally humiliated by Henry, the old knight cannot believe his roguish charm has failed him. Henry IV's gloom pervades the work. Its most famous verse speech is the king's reflection on his solitude and insomnia, with its memorable ending: "Uneasy lies the head that wears a crown." Then, on his deathbed, his bitterness toward his son bursts forth when he awakens to find his crown missing. In psychological terms, this scene—the king's sense of failure, his son's remorse, the king's forgiveness—stands at the heart of the play. It is also the scene in which Prince Henry finally embraces his new role. His subsequent rejection of Falstaff may be the cruelest moment in the play, yet Shakespeare uses it to underline Hal's transformation from wild prince to sober king.

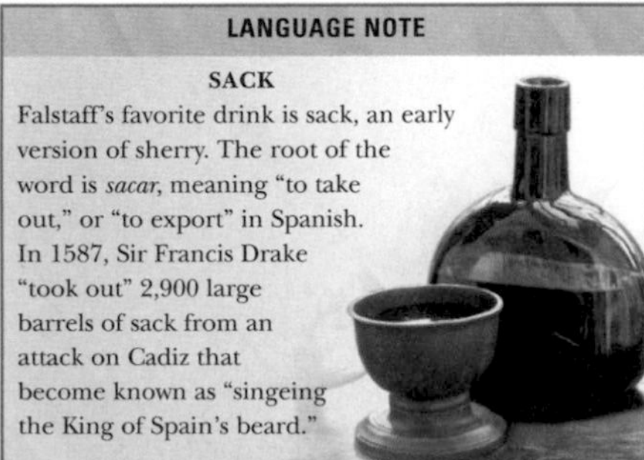

LANGUAGE NOTE

SACK

Falstaff's favorite drink is sack, an early version of sherry. The root of the word is *sacar*, meaning "to take out," or "to export" in Spanish. In 1587, Sir Francis Drake "took out" 2,900 large barrels of sack from an attack on Cadiz that become known as "singeing the King of Spain's beard."

SEEING THE PLAY

PLAYER PROFILE

LAURENCE OLIVIER
In 1947, Laurence Olivier *(right)* stole the show, playing Justice Shallow as an enfeebled and doddery old man, "like a man made after supper of a cheese-paring." His memories of roistering with Falstaff were made all the more poignant. He also played Hotspur in *Part I.*

IN THIS PLAY, confident of Falstaff's popularity, Shakespeare gives the old renegade a free reign. Falstaff finds a new enemy in the Lord Chief Justice, he chases women in the tavern and he revels at Shallow's house in Gloucestershire. Although Falstaff does his best to provide energy, wit, and mischief, the play is not only long but also laced with bitterness. Gone are the heroics of Hotspur and Prince Hal that enlivened *Part I.* The complaints of the northern rebels echo Hotspur in *Part I.* The scene in which Prince John uses deceit to disarm the rebels, then orders their execution is dramatic but hardly uplifting. The role of Prince Hal poses real difficulties. Between his charm in *Part I* and his boldness in *Henry V,* this play's Hal seems ambitious and ruthless. The power struggle between the king and his heir ends in reconciliation yet the prince can hardly wait to become king. In the final scene, when he humiliates Falstaff, the new Henry V seems heartless. The challenge is to show that Henry too is pained that the price of the throne includes the loss of old friends.

"Here's a goodly tumult!" (2.4). Jerome Kitty as Falstaff in the American Shakespeare Festival Theater's production of *Falstaff* at the Stratford Theater in Connecticut, 1966.

BEYOND THE PLAY

Roy Byford was an acclaimed Falstaff in 1932 when the Royal Shakespeare Theatre in Stratford-upon-Avon was inaugurated with both parts of *Henry IV*. The plays have often been performed together since.

LIKE HENRY IV PART I, this play evokes the morality plays that had been popular in England since the 14th century. But while in *Part I* Vice and Virtue battle without conclusion through the characters of Falstaff and Prince Henry, in this play Virtue triumphs when Henry repents his wild youth and Falstaff is rejected as the author of the prince's dissolution. Of course, in Elizabethan times no less than today, Vice is more entertaining than Virtue, so Shakespeare allows Falstaff to dominate this play just as he does *Part I* and *The Merry Wives of Windsor*. Further, since Falstaff was Queen Elizabeth's favorite character, the playwright was eager to please his monarch. The old reprobate was also popular with Jacobean audiences: in 1622, the two parts of *Henry IV* were compressed into one play called *Sir John Falstaff*.

However, unlike *Part I*, which returned to the stage soon after the Restoration, *Part II* was not revived until the 18th century. Even then, without the heroic figure of Hotspur and the climactic battle-scene at Shrewsbury, it was performed less frequently than *Part I*. In the 19th century, there were also moral objections to the bawdy tavern scene in which Falstaff prepares to seduce the local whore, Doll Tearsheet. Shakespeare himself was doubtlessly inspired by the antics of prostitutes and their clients in the inns of London, but it was nevertheless a spectacle that some Victorian theatergoers found shocking.

Still, Falstaff's very outrageousness explains his popularity with audiences and actors. For heavily built older actors, Falstaff is quite simply Shakespeares's best role.

ON STAGE

MAKEUP

Henry IV's long illness, which was both an historical fact and a metaphor for an ailing nation, is often portrayed through grotesque makeup showing the king's face covered in sores. In his day, it was thought he suffered from leprosy, although it is now believed that he contracted a different disfiguring disease.

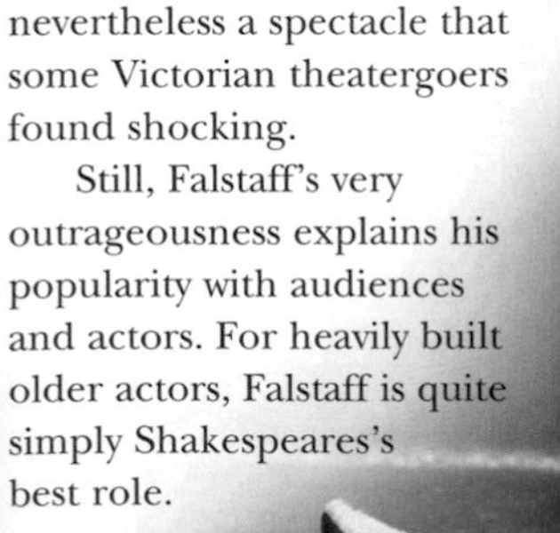

"O foolish youth! Thou seekest the greatness that will overwhelm thee" (4.5). Henry IV (David Troughton) bids farewell to Prince Henry (William Houston) in an RSC production.

HENRY V

HENRY V, THE EPIC FINALE OF THE 'HENRIAD', is Shakespeare's most patriotic play. Written in 1598, it is a less lyrical work than either *Richard II* or *Henry IV Part I*, but it may explain Shakespeare's decision to take on a new four-play cycle: in the 87 years covered by his two tetralogies, Henry V's reign was the only moment of national glory. Even then, given Queen Elizabeth's distaste for usurpers, Shakespeare does not allow Henry V to forget that his own father seized the throne by force. As with the other history plays, *Henry V* takes Holinshed's *Chronicles* as its main source, although it also makes use of an anonymous play, *The Famous Victories of Henry the Fifth*, as well as of Samuel Daniel's history of the period. *Henry V* was popular in Shakespeare's lifetime and, while it suffered mediocre adaptations in the early 18th century, it has been consistently performed in England since the 1730s.

BEHIND THE PLAY

THE PLAY COVERS THE PERIOD from Henry's accession to the throne in 1413 to his marriage to Princess Katherine of France in 1420, two years before his death. Although Shakespeare endorses Henry's dubious claim to the French throne through his great-great-grandmother, his account of key events is largely accurate. Shakespeare's main interest is the Battle of Agincourt in 1415, where he portrays Henry as a military leader who rose to the occasion. More daringly, Shakespeare hints strongly at the cruelty that accompanied Henry's warfare in France by having the king threaten horrific reprisals against Harfleur's inhabitants (in reality, the town was razed) and order the killing of French prisoners on the battlefield. However, the play creates a false impression when it implies that Henry conquered France at Agincourt: several English expeditionary forces pursued the war until 1420 when the Treaty of Troyes finally recognized Henry as heir to the French throne. Shakespeare also chooses to overlook the fact that France's Charles VI was probably insane at the time. Henry's wooing of Katherine is invented, but there is evidence that he was genuinely attached to his French bride.

The poor condemnèd English,/Like sacrifices, by their watchful fires/ Sit patiently, and inly ruminate/ The morning's danger...
4.CHORUS

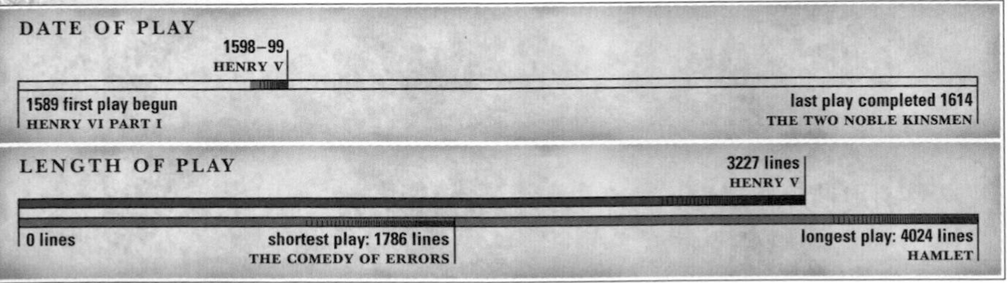

DRAMATIS PERSONAE

CHORUS
223 lines
A commentator in five Prologues and an Epilogue.

THE ENGLISH

KING HENRY V
1028 lines
Also known as Harry, once a wild young man, he becomes a brave warrior, skilled strategist, and fine orator; he defeats a larger French force at Agincourt, then marries the French king's daughter, Katherine, and succeeds to the French throne.

Ralph Richardson as Henry V, 1931.

DUKES OF GLOUCESTER, BEDFORD, AND CLARENCE
5; 7; 0 lines
The king's brothers, they also fight in France.

DUKE OF EXETER
130 lines
The king's cousin.

DUKE OF YORK
2 lines
The king's cousin; he is killed at Agincourt.

EARLS OF SALISBURY, WESTMORLAND, AND WARWICK
9; 27; 1 lines
English nobles.

ARCHBISHOP OF CANTERBURY
223 lines
He urges the king to claim the French throne.

BISHOP OF ELY
27 lines
He admires the king.

EARL OF CAMBRIDGE, LORD SCROOP, AND SIR THOMAS GREY
15; 13; 13 lines
They are bribed by the French to kill Henry.

Katherine (Emma Thompson) and her attendant, Alice (Geraldine McEwan), who teaches the French princess to speak English.

SIR THOMAS ERPINGHAM, GOWER, MACMORRIS, AND JAMY
7; 65; 20; 11 lines
Officers in Henry's army.

FLUELLEN
281 lines
A Welsh officer.

BATES, COURT, AND WILLIAMS
17; 2; 70 lines
English soldiers.

PISTOL, NYM, AND BARDOLPH
159; 46; 29 lines
Reluctant army recruits.

A BOY
72 lines
He joins the army in France.

HOSTESS
41 lines
Nell Quickly of the Boar's Head Tavern.

The comic trio Nym (Jeff Mayer), Pistol (Jess Weiss), and Bardolph (Jarlath Conroy) are unenthusiastic participants in the siege of Harfleur.

THE FRENCH

KING CHARLES VI
94 lines
King of France, he eventually recognizes the English king as his heir.

LEWIS THE DAUPHIN
115 lines
Son of King Charles and heir to the French throne.

DUKE OF BURGUNDY
68 lines
He sues for peace.

DUKES OF ORLEANS, BOURBON, BRITAINE, AND BERRI
40; 9; 9; 0 lines
French nobles killed at Agincourt.

THE CONSTABLE OF FRANCE
115 lines
He is killed at Agincourt.

RAMBURES AND GRANDPRÉ
8; 18 lines
French lords.

GOVERNOR
7 lines
He surrenders Harfleur after Henry threatens it.

MONTJOY
53 lines
A French envoy.

AMBASSADOR TO THE KING OF ENGLAND
17 lines
He delivers a gift from the Dauphin to Henry.

ISABEL
24 lines
Queen of France.

KATHERINE
58 lines
The French king's daughter; she eventually marries Henry and struggles in broken English to understand Henry's pledges of love for her.

ALICE
27 lines
Katherine's attendant.

OTHER PLAYERS
Lords, Ladies, Officers, Soldiers, Messengers, Citizens, Heralds, and Attendants.

PLOT SUMMARY

SIZE OF ACTS

ACT 1	ACT 2	ACT 3	ACT 4	ACT 5
451 lines	566 lines	700 lines	997 lines	513 lines

ACT ONE
451 lines

LONDON

With a stirring Prologue, Chorus prepares the audience to imagine the great Battle of Agincourt taking place in the "wooden O" of the Elizabethan theater. The play itself opens at King Henry's palace, where the Archbishop of Canterbury and the Bishop of Ely are marveling at the wild young prince's transformation into a wise monarch. The king has his eye on the French throne and inquires about France's Salic law, which forbids dynastic succession through women. Brushing aside any such obstacle, the archbishop notes that even the present French king's title passes through a female line. He urges Henry to pursue his own claim to France, inherited from his French great-great-grandmother, Edward III's Queen Isabella.

O for a Muse of fire, that would ascend/ The brightest heaven of invention,/A kingdom for a stage... Prologue

Then hear me, gracious sovereign, and you peers,/ that owe yourselves, your lives, and services... 1.2

An ambassador from the Dauphin, the French king's heir, tells Henry that there is "naught in France" for him and instead offers him a gift as consolation. The gift, a barrel of tennis balls, does not amuse Henry. He warns that the Dauphin's mockery "hath turned his balls to gun-stones" and vows that generations of French "shall have cause to curse the Dauphin's scorn."

We are glad the Dauphin is so pleasant with us./ His present, and your pains, we thank you for... 1.2

ACT TWO
566 lines

LONDON, SOUTHAMPTON, AND THE FRENCH KING'S PALACE AT ROUEN

Chorus recounts that, while England mobilizes for war, France has bribed three English nobles—Richard Earl of Cambridge, Lord Scroop, and Sir Thomas Grey—to

I will rise there with so full a glory/ That I will dazzle all the eyes of France... 1.2

murder the king before he sets sail from Southampton to fight in France.

As some of Henry's old drinking cronies meet in London, Bardolph reports that Mistress Nell Quickly, the inn-keeper of the Boar's Head Tavern, who had promised to marry Nym, has married Pistol. Nell and Pistol arrive and a furious argument follows, with Pistol telling Nym to marry Doll Tearsheet instead. A boy brings word that their old friend, Sir John Falstaff, is seriously ill. Nell laments that, by rejecting Falstaff, "the King has killed his heart."

Arriving in Southampton with the conspirators, Henry feigns ignorance of the plot. When he pardons a drunk who has insulted the crown, the three plotters even protest his mercy. But, the king asks them, if little faults cannot be forgiven, how can more serious crimes be overlooked? He then hands them papers describing their treachery. They promptly admit their guilt. Dismayed at how easily they have sold their souls, the king orders their execution.

The mercy that was quick in us but late/By your own counsel is suppressed and killed... 2.2

Outside a London tavern, Pistol announces that Falstaff has died. Heartbroken, Nell describes trying to keep him warm until she realized that he was dead.

I felt to his knees, and so up'ard and up'ard, and all was as cold as any stone... 2.3

Falstaff's friends reminisce fondly about the fat rascal until they leave for France.

At the French king's palace, Charles VI prepares to face the English invaders, but the Dauphin scoffs at a country led by "a vain, giddy, shallow, humorous youth." The Constable of France retorts that Henry is a changed man, while Charles recalls that Henry descends from Edward the Black Prince, who crushed the French at Crécy. Exeter delivers Henry's message ordering Charles to surrender his throne, and he warns the Dauphin to expect punishment for his gift of tennis balls.

ACT THREE

700 lines

HARFLEUR, THE FRENCH KING'S PALACE AT ROUEN, PICARDY, AND NEAR AGINCOURT

Chorus asks the audience to imagine not only the English forces landing in France and laying siege to Harfleur, but also Henry's response to the offer of the French king's daughter in marriage and "some petty and unprofitable dukedoms" as consolation.

To the cry "God for Harry, England, and Saint George!" Henry orders the attack outside Harfleur. Nearby, Bardolph is ready to fight, but Nym and Pistol hesitate until a Welsh officer, Fluellen, drives them on. The boy accompanying the three ne'er-do-wells decides to seek out employment with less cowardly soldiers.

Once more unto the breach, dear friends, once more,/ Or close the wall up with our English dead!... 3.1

As young as I am, I have observed these three swashers. I am boy to them all three... 3.2

After a ceasefire, Henry warns that Harfleur will be reduced to ashes if resistance continues, its "pure maidens" raped, its "naked infants spitted upon pikes". Since the Dauphin has not come to the rescue, Harfleur surrenders. As Exeter enters the town, Henry leads his forces towards Calais.

How yet resolves the Governor of the town?/ This is the latest parle we will admit... 3.3

In the French king's palace, his daughter Katherine is struggling to learn English from Alice, her attendant. Charles is furious that Henry has crossed the River Somme, while the Dauphin complains that French women are giving themselves to English soldiers "to new-store France with bastard warriors." Charles orders his nobles to capture

Henry, while the Constable predicts that the "sick, and famished" English army will be crushed.

At the English camp in Picardy, Bardolph is caught robbing a church and Henry orders his execution, adding that the French should be treated with respect. Through an envoy, Montjoy, the French king invites Henry to withdraw. Henry responds that he hopes to march unimpeded to Calais with his "weak and sickly guard," but will do battle if he is stopped.

Thou dost thy office fairly. Turn thee back,/ And tell thy King I do not seek him now... 3.6

ACT FOUR

997 lines

THE ENGLISH AND FRENCH CAMPS AND THE BATTLEFIELD AT AGINCOURT

Chorus describes the hours before the battle when the king stirs the courage of his outnumbered and exhausted soldiers with "a little touch of Harry in the night."

At the English camp, Pistol does not recognize the king in disguise. Identifying himself as a Welshman called Harry Le Roy, Henry tells three soldiers that he is an officer in Sir Thomas Erpingham's company, yet he speaks as if he knows the king's mind. Every soldier owes his duty to the king, he says, but must answer for his own soul. Williams suggests that, if caught, Henry will pay a ransom, but the king hotly denies this. Left alone, Henry wonders what, apart from ceremony, distinguishes him from his soldiers. Erpingham urges him to rejoin his commanders, but first Henry prays, begging God to forgive his father's usurpation of the throne.

Every subject's duty is the King's, but every subject's soul is his own... 4.1

O God of battles, steel my soldiers' hearts;/Possess them not with fear; take from them now... 4.1

With the French army's 60,000 soldiers outnumbering the English by five to one, the Earl of Westmorland wishes for another 10,000 men, but the king retorts that "the fewer men, the greater share of honour". Noting that it is Saint Crispian's Day, he promises that "we few, we happy few, we band of brothers" will always be remembered on this day.

What's he that wishes so?/ My cousin Westmoreland? No, my fair cousin./ If we are marked to die... 4.3

As the battle begins, the French are quickly dispersed, but Bourbon orders a fresh attack. Lacking men to guard French prisoners, Henry orders his soldiers to kill them. Gower reports that the French have slain the English boys. Furious, the king again swears that no French prisoner "shall taste our mercy". When Montjoy asks permission to collect the French dead, Henry realizes he has won the day. While 1,500 lords, barons, knights, and squires are among 10,000 slain French, only three English lords and 25 soldiers lie dead. Henry gives thanks to God and prepares to return to England.

ACT FIVE

513 lines

THE ENGLISH CAMP AT AGINCOURT AND THE FRENCH KING'S PALACE

Chorus describes how Henry, acclaimed by jubilant crowds on his return to England, modestly refuses to display his "bruisèd helmet and his bended sword."

O God of battles, steel my soldiers' hearts;/ Possess them not with fear; take from them now/ The sense of reckoning, if th'opposèd numbers/ Pluck their hearts from them... 4.1

After the Holy Roman Emperor visits London to seek peace between England and France, several years pass before Henry returns to France.

At the English camp, Fluellen complains to Gower that Pistol has insulted him for carrying a leek as a symbol of Wales. When Pistol arrives, he is cudgelled by Fluellen into eating the leek. Alone, Pistol mourns Nell's death and decides to blame the French wars for the wounds inflicted on him by Fluellen.

In the French palace, where Charles receives Henry and his lords, the Duke of Burgundy laments French suffering and prays for permanent peace between the two countries. Henry agrees to peace if France accepts all his demands. As nobles leave to work out the details, Henry asks Princess Katherine to stay behind since "she is our capital demand."

My duty to you both, on equal love,/Great Kings of France and England! That I have laboured/With all my wits, my pains... 5.2

Henry sets out to woo the young woman and, while barely understanding her French and broken English, he is undeterred, declaring his love for her and even testing his own rudimentary French. Henry begs her to proclaim "Harry of England, I am thine", but Katherine responds warily. When he asks her for a kiss, she protests that maidens do not kiss before their wedding day, but Henry says this does not apply to kings.

The princess is the better Englishwoman. I'faith, Kate, my wooing is fit for thy understanding... 5.2

O Kate, nice customs curtsy to great kings... 5.2

The French king accepts England's peace conditions and offers his daughter as Henry's bride so that "never war advance/His bleeding sword 'twixt England and fair France". Henry kisses the princess again and swears they will be true to each other.

In an Epilogue, Chorus recalls that "our bending author" has previously recounted how destiny had other plans. The couple's infant son, Henry VI, was indeed crowned king of France and England, but his courtiers so mismanaged things that "they lost France, and made his England bleed."

Small time, but in that small most greatly lived/ This star of England./ Fortune made his sword/ By which the world's best garden he achieved...

EPILOGUE

READING THE PLAY

COMPARISON OF PROSE TO VERSE

prose: 40% | verse: 60%

THIS PLAY, NOT one of Shakespeare's literary masterpieces, is built around a fast-paced linear narrative. Henry V has evidently quite forgotten the excesses of his youth, including his old drinking pal, Sir John Falstaff, who dies quietly off stage. Henry V is now the idealized English hero: firm, courageous, articulate, humorous, even romantic. Indeed, in his famous Saint Crispian's Day speech on the eve of battle, he personifies England itself, the small island nation that valiantly overcomes powerful enemies. At this point, all of Shakespeare's English heroes—Talbot, Edward the Black Prince, and Hotspur—come together in Henry.

Only in the solitude of his pre-battle prayer does Henry show doubt as he tries to convince God that he has made amends for his father's murder of Richard II. But Chorus, speaking for history, is all-forgiving, portraying the king as modest and devout.

Shakespeare switches from verse to prose when he gives voice to rascals and soldiers. More unusually, he has Henry speak in prose while wooing Katherine. The effect is to show that the orator-warrior has lost his gift for verse when faced with a beautiful woman. Henry is even forced to speak some French.

HISTORICAL SOURCES

AGINCOURT

The Hundred Years' War began when Edward III of England claimed the French crown. A protracted and sporadic conflict followed. The English won a series of victories, but were unable to defeat France because they lacked the troops and funds to dominate such a large territory. The Battle of Agincourt in 1415 was a famous victory, but from the 1430s the French began systematically to eject their English occupiers.

A French book illustration, c.1484, depicting the Battle of Agincourt. Although the English were outnumbered, their superior longbow technology ensured their victory.

SEEING THE PLAY

> **ON STAGE**
>
> **HECKLING**
>
> The Elizabethan tradition of heckling the French king and court was revived when the new Shakespeare's Globe in London encouraged 'groundlings' to behave as they might have done four centuries earlier. An early performance of *Henry V* at the new Globe was disrupted when a middle-aged Englishwoman began bombarding the actor playing Charles VI with old cabbages.

CHORUS, WHO OFFERS A PROLOGUE to every act as well as an epilogue, adds enormously to the theatricality of this play. Even in a building that bears no resemblance to the Globe's "wooden O," Chorus captures the essence of theater with the question: "Can this cockpit hold/The vasty fields of France?" Once the illusion is accepted, the siege of Harfleur and the Battle of Agincourt are less excuses for staged warfare than devices for glorifying "Harry, England, and Saint George." Indeed, just as Henry's call to arms at Harfleur is more important than the town's surrender, so is his preparation for Agincourt given more space than the battle itself. Since the public knows the outcome, what is on display is Henry's oratory—and Shakespeare's virtuosity.

As ever, though, the playwright is wary of trying his audience with too much solemnity. He brings back some of Falstaff's cronies from *Henry IV Part II* and adds other earthy characters, notably a garrulous trio of Irish, Scottish, and Welsh captains. He also exploits every chance to make fun of the French.

The play's dual themes—a magnificent monarch and a man in touch with his feelings—come together in the final act when Henry sets out to win Princess Katherine as his bride. When played well on stage, this scene is a delightful portrayal of robust passion meeting feminine wiles.

"And gentlemen in England now abed/Shall think themselves accursed they were not here,/And hold their manhoods cheap" (4.3). Michael Sheen plays Henry V in a RSC production (1997) that used World War II uniforms to reinforce the universality of conflict.

BEYOND THE PLAY

ELIZABETHAN AUDIENCES needed little encouragement to embrace *Henry V*. Henry V was already an icon of English heroism, and patriotism was in vogue. Barely a decade before the play's first performance in 1599, the English navy had destroyed the mighty Spanish Armada in the English Channel in what, like the Battle of Agincourt, was a triumph over all odds. Indeed, the exploits of Henry V had been celebrated in at least two plays before Shakespeare completed his.

Laurence Olivier's stirring 1944 film version of *Henry V*, starring himself as the heroic king and Renée Asherson as his French bride Katherine, dramatized wartime England's mood of defiant isolation.

Throughout the Victorian era, the play served as a paean to imperial power, frequently presented as a grandiose spectacle, with 200 extras hired for the battle scenes in Charles Kean's 1859 production. It was again performed as a patriotic anthem in World War I, while famous productions in the 1930s—Ralph Richardson played Henry in 1931 and Laurence Olivier in 1937—kept it in the public eye.

Unsurprisingly, the rest of the world does not regard *Henry V* as one of Shakespeare's great plays. While, say, *Richard II* and *Richard III* deal with the poison of political power in a universal manner, *Henry V* seems inexorably rooted in England. The French, otherwise unwavering fans of Shakespeare, ignored the play that ridicules them so cruelly. *Henry V* was not presented in France until Philippe Torreton played the English king at the Avignon Theatre Festival in 1999. The applause was muted.

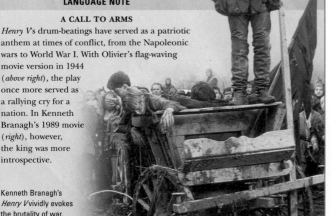

LANGUAGE NOTE

A CALL TO ARMS

Henry V's drum-beatings have served as a patriotic anthem at times of conflict, from the Napoleonic wars to World War I. With Olivier's flag-waving movie version in 1944 (*above right*), the play once more served as a rallying cry for a nation. In Kenneth Branagh's 1989 movie (*right*), however, the king was more introspective.

Kenneth Branagh's *Henry V* vividly evokes the brutality of war.

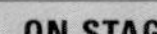

ON STAGE

A PLAY FOR THE GLOBE

Henry V's Prologue, with its reference to the "wooden O," reinforces the legend that it was the first play presented at the new Globe Theatre in Southwark in 1599. Indeed, Shakespeare himself may well have spoken the opening lines in the role of Chorus. In the prologue to Act 5, Shakespeare refers indirectly to the Earl of Essex's ongoing military campaign in Ireland, hoping that Essex would attain similar glory.

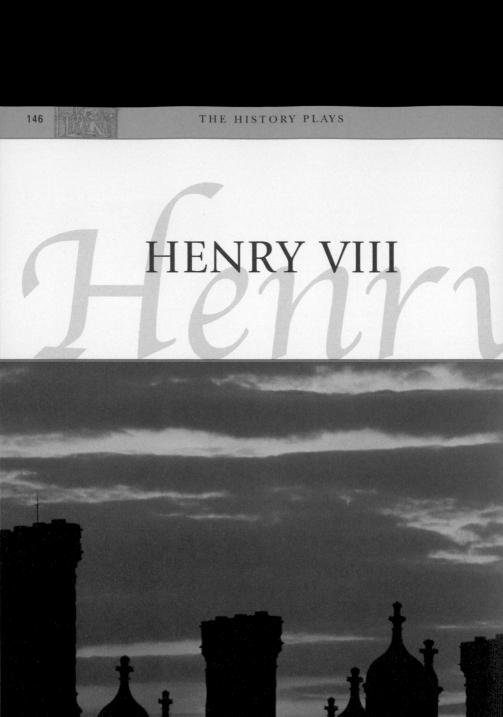

HENRY VIII

HENRY VIII, SHAKESPEARE'S LAST HISTORY PLAY, was written in 1612–1613, less than a century after the events it describes and barely a decade after the death of King Henry's daughter, Queen Elizabeth. Although it was included in the *First Folio* of 1623, Shakespeare's sole authorship of the play has long been questioned. A 1634 edition of the play attributed it to both Shakespeare and his young colleague, John Fletcher. Today, most scholars see Fletcher's hand in many scenes. More puzzling is why, 15 years after *Henry V*, Shakespeare returned to the historical theme and ceremonial style of his early plays. One explanation may be that new books and plays about Henry and the powerful Cardinal Wolsey had made the topic fashionable. Today, the play is rarely performed—many directors believe it presents history as a dry ritual and offers little insight into its main character.

BEHIND THE PLAY

HENRY VIII PORTRAYS THE MIDDLE YEARS of Henry's long reign, between 1521 and 1536, but Shakespeare is concerned only with key moments and he presents them in rapid succession: the rise and fall of Cardinal Wolsey; Henry's divorce from his Spanish-born wife, Katherine of Aragon, also his brother's widow; his marriage to Anne Boleyn (called Anne Bullen in the play); and the birth of Elizabeth I. As in his earlier history plays, Shakespeare displays little interest in dates. Yet in this play, also called *All is True*, he is careful to provide accurate accounts of the trials of Buckingham, Katherine, and Archbishop Cranmer. He also seems aware that mid-16th-century religious disputes were still not fully settled by the early 17th century. Indeed, James I was more tolerant of the Roman Catholic Church than the firmly Protestant Elizabeth. Thus, even though Henry's divorce from Katherine led to England's break with Rome, the play makes no mention of the rupture. And while Shakespeare portrays Henry as a distant and despotic monarch, he wisely protects himself by ending the play with a stirring paean to both Elizabeth and her Stuart successor, James, his two most prestigious patrons.

Would I had never trod this English earth,/Or felt the flatteries that grow upon it!... 3.1

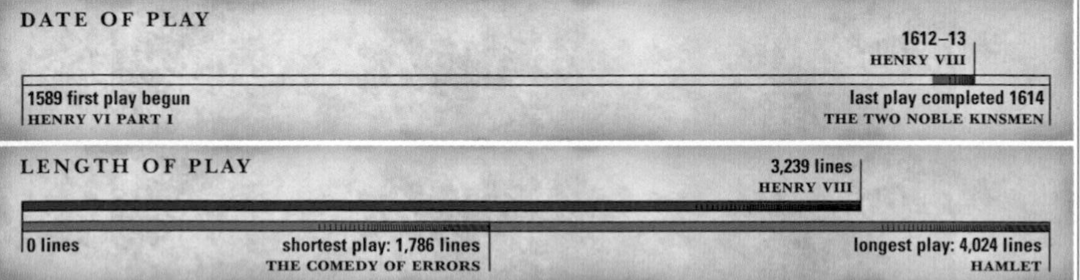

DRAMATIS PERSONAE

HENRY VIII
461 lines
An autocratic monarch, he breaks with Rome when the pope refuses to approve his divorce from Katherine of Aragon; he ousts Cardinal Wolsey as Lord Chancellor, paving the way for his marriage to Anne Bullen.

EARL OF SURREY
82 lines
Buckingham's son-in-law, he is a fierce opponent of Wolsey.

LORD CHAMBERLAIN
151 lines
A senior official, he presides at the King's court.

CARDINAL WOLSEY
439 lines
The all-powerful Lord Chancellor, he justifies the king's divorce from Katherine, but foolishly tries to block Henry's marriage to Anne Bullen, a move that leads to his downfall.

Wolsey (Henry Irving) is the king's confidante and adviser.

Henry VIII (Paul Jesson) revels in the pageantry of kingship, flanked by Katherine (Jane Lapotaire) and Wolsey (Ian Hogg).

CARDINAL CAMPEIUS
53 lines
A Papal envoy sent to support Wolsey.

CAPUCHIUS
11 lines
An ambassador sent to Katherine by her nephew, Emperor Charles V.

THOMAS CRANMER
136 lines
He becomes Archbishop of Canterbury and approves Henry's divorce.

DUKE OF NORFOLK
212 lines
A powerful noble, he presides over Buckingham's trial.

DUKE OF BUCKINGHAM
192 lines
A manipulative noble whose father was executed by Richard III, he tries to undermine Wolsey's power and is executed for treason.

DUKE OF SUFFOLK
93 lines
A powerful noble who turns against Wolsey.

LORD CHANCELLOR
32 lines
Sir Thomas More, he replaces Wolsey as senior legal officer in the land.

GARDINER, BISHOP OF WINCHESTER
92 lines
He tries to send Cranmer to the Tower of London.

BISHOP OF LINCOLN
8 lines
A member of the court.

LORD ABERGAVENNY
18 lines
An opponent of Wolsey.

LORD SANDS
48 lines
He flirts with Anne Bullen.

SIR HENRY GUILFORD
9 lines
A follower of Wolsey.

SIR THOMAS LOVELL
68 lines
An influential knight.

SIR ANTHONY DENNY, SIR NICHOLAS VAUX
4; 4 lines
Members of Henry's court.

THOMAS CROMWELL
49 lines
A close aide to Wolsey, he switches allegiance to Henry.

GRIFFITH
59 lines
An aide to Katherine, he accompanies her to her final refuge.

DOCTOR BUTTS
9 lines
The king's physician.

A SURVEYOR
61 lines
He betrays Buckingham and testifies against him.

BRANDON
14 lines
He arrests Buckingham and Abergavenny.

QUEEN KATHERINE
391 lines
She cannot stop Henry from divorcing her, but she courageously attacks Wolsey and retains her dignity even as she is discarded.

ANNE BULLEN
58 lines
A lady-in-waiting, she catches the king's eye and is chosen as his new queen.

AN OLD LADY
68 lines
She mocks Anne Bullen's claim to have no ambition to be queen.

PATIENCE
6 lines
Katherine's lady-in-waiting.

OTHER PLAYERS
Chorus, Lords, Ladies, Gentlemen, Gentlewomen, Bishops, Secretaries, Door-Keepers, Porter and his Man, Officers, Musicians, Dancers, Choristers, Guards, Criers, Pages, Messengers, Servants, Attendants, and Spirits.

Katherine of Aragon (Eva la Gallienne) is dignified and stoic.

PLOT SUMMARY

SIZE OF ACTS

ACT 1	ACT 2	ACT 3	ACT 4	ACT 5
764 lines	752 lines	737 lines	335 lines	651 lines

ACT ONE
764 lines

LONDON: THE KING'S PALACE AND A HALL IN YORK PLACE

A prologue cautions that this is not a happy tale for nobles whose "mightiness meets misery." One such noble, Buckingham, learning of the exaggerated splendor of Henry's recent meeting with the French monarch at the Field of the Cloth of Gold, complains of Cardinal Wolsey's sway over the king. He denounces Wolsey as "corrupt and treasonous" and promises to accuse "this holy fox" before the king. Norfolk warns him that Wolsey's power as Lord Chancellor makes him a dangerous foe, but too late: Buckingham is arrested and sent to the Tower of London.

Henry prepares to receive Buckingham's confession, but instead hears from Queen Katherine that unrest is mounting over a new tax imposed by Wolsey. The king knows of no such tax and the cardinal denies responsibility, blaming "ignorant tongues". When ordered by the king to cancel the tax, Wolsey cynically tries to take credit for its revocation. Katherine suspects trumped-up charges against Buckingham, but Henry nonetheless orders his trial.

And for me,/I have no further gone in this than by/ A single voice... 1.2

At York Place, the cardinal hosts a masked ball attended by lords and ladies, including Anne Bullen, the queen's lady-in-waiting. Henry arrives in disguise and invites Anne to dance. Removing his mask, he proclaims her "a dainty one."

ACT TWO
752 lines

LONDON: WESTMINSTER, THE KING'S PALACE, AND A HALL IN BLACKFRIARS

As Buckingham prepares to be beheaded in a moving speech asking for the prayers of his friends, word spreads of the king's separation from Katherine. Henry claims that in good conscience he cannot remain married to his brother's widow, but whom shall he marry? Wolsey would have him marry the French king's sister, but one noble notes that the royal conscience "has crept too near another lady." Henry orders Wolsey to allow Katherine to defend herself, but he also gives Anne the title of Marchioness of Pembroke as proof of his favor.

All good people,/ You that thus far have come to pity me... 2.1

At Blackfriars, Katherine defends herself poignantly and at length. When Wolsey intervenes, she vents her fury on "my most malicious foe" and rejects him as her judge. As Katherine leaves the court, Henry praises her nobility, but again justifies his divorce, noting her failure to give him a male heir. Annoyed by delays in Rome's approval of his divorce, he recalls Sir Thomas Cranmer, who had been sent into exile by Wolsey.

Sir, I desire you do me right and justice,/And to bestow your pity on me... 2.4

I may perceive/These Cardinals trifle with me. I abhor/This dilatory sloth and tricks of Rome... 2.4

ACT THREE

737 lines

LONDON: THE KING'S PALACE

Plunged in gloom, Katherine asks a gentlewoman to play the lute and sing to her. The queen then receives Wolsey, who advises her to surrender to the king's protection, but she mocks his counsel to "put my sick cause into his hands that hates me?". In the royal palace, Suffolk recounts that the king has intercepted a letter from Wolsey urging the Pope to withhold approval of the divorce since Henry is "tangled in affection" with Anne. Another lord reports that the king has already married Anne with Cranmer's blessing.

Orpheus with his lute made trees,/And the mountain tops that freeze... 3.1

Would I had never trod this English earth,/ Or felt the flatteries that grow upon it!... 3.1

Unaware of the marriage, Wolsey vows that Henry will still wed the French king's sister, and not Anne, "a spleeny Lutheran". But when Henry arrives, the king reveals that an inventory of Wolsey's wealth was sent to him mistakenly among state papers. Addressing the cardinal, the king extracts new pledges of loyalty from him and then hands him the incriminating papers. Wolsey realizes that he is doomed.

The late Queen's gentlewoman, a knight's daughter,/To be her mistress' mistress?... 3.2

What should this mean?/ What sudden anger's this? How have I reaped it?... 3.2

Lords arrive to confiscate his great seal and, while he objects, they insult him as "scarlet sin" and announce that all his property has been seized. When they leave, Wolsey confronts the suddenness

I have touched the highest point of all my greatness,/ And from that full meridian of my glory/I haste now to my setting... 3.2

So farewell – to the little good you bear me./ Farewell, a long farewell, to all my greatness!... 3.2

of his fall from grace ❝. Sir Thomas More has replaced him as Lord Chancellor, Cranmer is the new Archbishop of Canterbury, and Anne's coronation is being prepared.

ACT FOUR

335 lines

WESTMINSTER AND KIMBLETON

As crowds watch the procession through London following Anne's coronation, one gentleman bystander recounts the emotional scenes inside Westminster Abbey. He also points to Gardiner, Bishop of Winchester, as a sworn enemy of Cranmer.

In her refuge at Kimbleton, Katherine, now reduced to the rank of Princess Dowager, is informed of Wolsey's death in an abbey at Leicester. Katherine, herself ailing, shows him no pity, but her gentleman usher, Griffith, speaks up for the cardinal, saying that in the end he found "the blessèdness of being little" and died fearing God. Katherine is touched, telling Griffith that his words made her honor the ashes of "Whom I most hated living" ❝. She asks for music and, falling asleep, is visited by "spirits of peace".

After my death I wish no other herald,/ No other speaker of my living actions... 4.2

When she awakes, she recounts that the spirits "promised me eternal happiness and brought me garlands." Now ready for death, she tells an envoy from the king that she has written to Henry, begging him to care for their daughter and her servants. She asks the envoy to "tell him, in death, I blessed him" ❝ and she expresses the hope that she will be buried "although unqueened, yet like/A queen."

I thank you, honest lord. Remember me/ In all humility unto his highness... 4.2

ACT FIVE

651 lines

LONDON: THE KING'S PALACE

Hearing that Anne is in labor and her life is in danger, Gardiner responds that England would be well rid of both her and Archbishop Cranmer. An aide warns him that Cranmer is "the King's hand and tongue," but Gardiner says he must be rooted out ❝. The king receives Cranmer and warns him of plotting against him. Cranmer laments that he has few friends, but Henry encourages him to stand firm, even giving him a ring which he can show to his enemies as proof of the king's friendship. An old lady of the court informs Henry that Anne has given birth and, while the king asks hopefully if it is boy, she replies that the baby is a girl.

Yes, yes, Sir Thomas,/ There are that dare, and I myself have ventured/To speak my mind of him... 5.1

Arriving at the council chamber, Henry is angered to discover that Cranmer has been kept waiting outside. Cranmer is then informed he is to be sent to the Tower because no one dares testify against him while he is still in his post. As guards prepare to lead him away, Cranmer displays the king's ring and the lords realize their mistake. Henry chastises them and orders the lords and bishops to embrace the archbishop. He then invites Cranmer to baptize his daughter and serve as her godfather.

The court gathers for the christening of the baby Elizabeth and, with his power now restored, Cranmer gives flight to prophesies of the "thousand thousand blessings" that the royal baby will bring to Britain ❝. And when she dies, "yet a virgin," her successor will also have "peace, plenty, love, truth, terror" as his servants. Delighted, Henry promises that "when I am in heaven I shall desire/ To see what this child does."

Let me speak, sir,/ For heaven now bids me, and the words I utter/ Let none think flattery... 5.5

READING THE PLAY

COMPARISON OF PROSE TO VERSE

prose: 2% verse: 98%

LITERARY SOURCES

SOURCES FOR HENRY VIII

Shakespeare's literary sources for *Henry VIII* are Holinshed's *Chronicles*, which informed his earlier histories, as well as George Cavendish's *Life of Wolsey* and John Foxe's *Book of Martyrs*. Cavendish, an usher to Wolsey, offered an eyewitness account of the Cardinal's downfall, while Foxe wrote about Cranmer's rise to power. Shakespeare also probably knew Samuel Rowley's 1605 play about Henry VIII, *You See Me You Know Me.*

WHILE LISTED AMONG THE HISTORY PLAYS in the *First Folio* , *Henry VIII* lacks many signature features of Shakespeare's earlier epics. At the same time, the playwright includes some elements of his late romances, such as music, spirits, and pageantry. Further, compared with, say, *Richard II* or *Henry V*, who are allowed inner lives, Henry VIII is not portrayed in any complexity. Rather, he is a distant autocrat whose word is never questioned. In much of the play, he simply presides over the story that is being told: he only advances the narrative when he courts Anne, expels Wolsey, and saves Cranmer from the Tower. The lavish court scenes and processions add further to the feeling that Shakespeare is merely reenacting a glorious past for the delight of Jacobean audiences. Indeed, for the scholar Harold Bloom, *Henry VIII* is closer to a dramatic poem.

As in the romances, though, the play represents a cycle of life: just as Catholicism is being replaced by Protestantism, so the fall from power and demise of Buckingham, Wolsey, and Katherine are followed by the arrival of a new queen, a new archbishop, and a new baby. For dramatic purposes, Shakespeare lingers on the melancholic fates of Buckingham, Wolsey, and Katherine, who find poetry as they face death, giving poignant "farewell" speeches. Again, as in the romances, the playwright leaves the joy to the final act, although he does so with a twist. Never shy to praise his patrons, he has Cranmer prophesy that the real end of the play lies in the glorious reigns of Elizabeth and James.

HISTORICAL SOURCES

HENRY VIII (1491–1547)

When Henry VIII, already fearful of disputes over the succession, became infatuated with Anne Boleyn, he requested a papal annulment of his marriage to Katherine of Aragon. The pope was unresponsive, so Henry bullied the English clergy into recognizing him as head of the church. Henry married a total of six times. He had two of his wives, Anne Boleyn and Catherine Howard, executed and one wife survived him.

Hans Holbein's famous portrait of Henry VIII has served as a model for generations of actors who play this role.

SEEING THE PLAY

Violet Vanbrugh as Anne Bullen, at the Lyceum Theatre, London, in 1892.

AT THE HEIGHT OF ITS POPULARITY, *Henry VIII* was presented on an operatic scale, comparable perhaps to a lavish *Aida* today. Shakespeare provided ample ingredients: six scenes call for a vast assembly of lords and ladies, cardinals and bishops; two scenes are set in crowded streets; and one requires a flight of dancing "spirits of peace" to appear before Katherine in a dream. In the 19th century, directors embraced the challenge, often adding horses and coaches and hundreds of extras to the large cast of speaking roles.

Today, on the rare occasions that the play is presented, directors must work with more modest resources, focusing instead on the drama unfolding beyond the pageantry. Henry stands at the center of the play, but it is difficult for actors to portray him as anything other than an immobile and impassive figurehead. Similarly, while Anne Bullen is a popular part for young actresses, there is no hint of the tragedy that awaits her a mere three years into her marriage to Henry. Far more interesting roles are those of Katherine and Wolsey, both when they are still confident of their power and, more touchingly, after they are stripped of their titles. They also provide the keys to modern productions that cannot afford the excesses of trumpet-packed pageantry. Katherine above all, with her love of music, her introspection, and her devotion to her daughter and aides, can give the play a spiritual core absent from *Henry VIII*'s power politics.

ON STAGE

FIRE AT THE GLOBE
Henry VIII's stage life began badly: during a performance at the Globe on June 29, 1613, a cannon shot announcing Wolsey's masked ball sparked a fire in the thatched roof that destroyed the theater in less than two hours. Despite the ill omen, the play was a public favorite well into the 19th century.

In a production at the Bridewell Theatre, London, the confrontation between Lord Suffolk (Eugene Washington) and Cardinal Wolsey (James Horne) is literally pugilistic.

The COMEDIES

SHAKESPEARE'S THIRTEEN COMEDIES FORM AN ASTONISHING VARIETY OF PLAYS RANGING FROM THE FARCICAL TO THE MAGICAL AND EVEN TRAGICAL.

A COMMON ASSUMPTION is that comedies are funny plays with happy endings. But Shakespeare's comedies are not so easily categorized. For one, comical action and characters are hardly exclusive to the comedies. Sir John Falstaff, Shakespeare's most grandiose comic creation, stars in the comedy *The Merry Wives of Windsor,* but first appears in the history plays *Henry IV Part I* and *Henry IV Part II.* The tragedies also feature comic roles, from the gravediggers of *Hamlet* and drunken porter of *Macbeth* to the slapstick servants of *Romeo and Juliet* and *Coriolanus.* A happy ending is also an inadequate measure of the Shakespearean comedy. Many history plays conclude optimistically, while romances—some are listed in the *First Folio* under "Comedies"—also conclude joyously. Shakespeare's comedies generally do offer a happy ending but their conclusions are frequently characterized by only conditional happiness. Rather, these plays generally present life as ongoing, renewed through love, marriage, and the promise of a new generation to come.

ORIGINS OF THE COMEDY

The word "comedy" derives from the Ancient Greek *kōmos,* a Dionysian springtime ritual of music and dancing to celebrate cyclical rebirth attributed to the vegetal life cycle. Unlike animals, who mature and die, plants were seen to flourish, die, and be reborn in seasons of regeneration. Applied to humans, this view of the life cycle favors continuation over termination and rebirth over death. In contrast, tragic drama is centrally preoccupied with the mortality of the individual: in the tragedies, spectators confront death as an inescapable aspect of human existence. But set in a different aesthetic landscape, the comedies view life as hopeful and cyclical. Thus, within this tradition, Shakespearean comedies focus on larger frames of reference: the family, community, or society. They dwell on the fact that individuals enjoy a form of regeneration through the perpetuation of families and their communities. In this sense, then, the comedies do present happy endings: they direct attention away from the tragic sphere of death and toward the comic one of life, renewal, and forms of immortality.

SHAKESPEARE'S COMEDIES

Shakespeare explores comic terrain freely and widely. Indeed, for every generalization about Shakespeare's comedies, there is a handy exception. For instance, comedies generally steer clear of death and dying. But heartfelt mourning pervades scenes in *Love's Labour's Lost* and *Twelfth Night*. In fact, dark preoccupations with mortality haunt many Shakespearean comedies.

Another classic definition of a comedy is that it presents at least one romantic couple who marry by the end of the play. Following the Dionysian principle that the life cycle continues eternally, romantic couples in Shakespeare's comedies reassure audiences that love yields fertility, procreation, and the perpetuation of life beyond the fate of any individual. But again, Shakespeare does not always deliver this conventional feature of the genre. *The Comedy of Errors* concludes with no marriage and *Love's Labour's Lost* only suggests five marriages to come following a period of bereavement. Three "problem plays" often classified as comedies also challenge this definition, with none of these plays offering an unsullied portrayal of love or an unproblematic promise of marriage: *Troilus and Cressida*, *All's Well That Ends Well*, and *Measure for Measure*.

Love and the Search for Identity

If romantic characters are to compel audiences to rejoice in their union and celebrate the continuity of life, they must do more than simply meet, fall in love, and marry or promise to marry. Indeed, a central thread of action in the comedies explores lovers overcoming tests and gaining awareness, as much of themselves as of their chosen loves. One device Shakespeare employs frequently to develop romantic characters is disguise or mistaken identity. Four comedies—*Two Gentlemen of Verona*, *The Merchant of Venice*, *As You Like It* and *Twelfth Night*—go one step further: females disguise themselves as males. In these plays, young women cross-dressing as young men gain insights into hidden aspects of their beloveds.

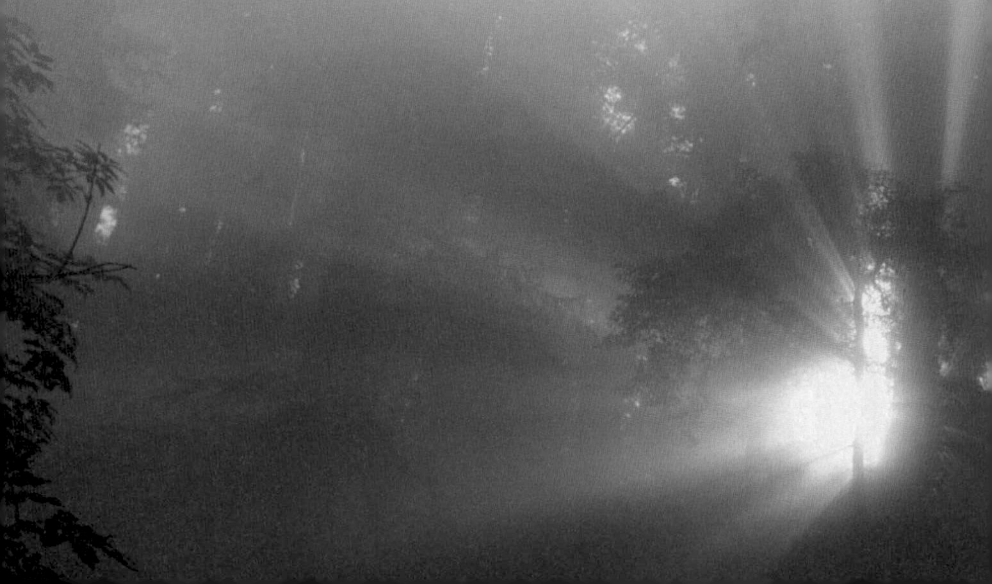

The romantic leads in Shakespearean comedies usually reveal and then heal problems between their own generation and that of their parents. Often, parents either intentionally or unintentionally drive their children to set out and discover who they are. For instance, in *The Two Gentlemen of Verona*, a father requires a son

to travel and broaden his mind; in *A Midsummer Night's Dream,* young lovers defy a father's will and run away from home; and in *As You Like It,* a young woman is sent into exile. The children generally return from real or symbolic journeys ready to marry and settle down. In this light, Shakespeare's comedies are conservative: continuity is assured from one generation to the next and no fundamental social order is rejected or overturned. Parents are often initially outraged by the unexpected departures of their children or their independent romantic lives, as in *The Merry Wives of Windsor,* but ultimately accept the inherent virtue of true love by the time children return home and marry.

Rebellion in the Comedies

Some argue that Shakespeare's comedies are in fact revolutionary because the younger generation overturns the status quo. The case is made that the comedies usually begin under the sign of a harsh law, whether familial or judicial. The law's validity is then undermined when defiant youth finally triumphs. Indeed, many of the opening acts of Shakespeare's comedies establish an authoritative figure (a rigid king, duke, or strict parent) who imposes a law or rule which, by the end of the play, is overturned or retracted to allow life to go on in a changed world. Thus, concluding scenes in the comedies have also been interpreted as celebrations of the dismantling of former and too-brittle social or judicial orders. In such cases, newly formed couples may well capture the radical values of a new generation.

Clearly, Shakespeare's comedies generate as much disagreement among specialists off stage as they represent between generations on stage. While they generally conclude with celebration, the rejoicing can easily be seen to reinforce the established social order as to topple it. Even if lovers in the comedies teach parents and rulers to accept true love, they never shatter social or familial authority.

Comic Resolutions

Concluding celebrations in the comedies are different from those of Shakespeare's history plays or romances. Optimistic

THE COMEDIES AT A GLANCE

Play	Setting	Source Author
The Comedy of Errors	Greece	Plautus
Love's Labour's Lost	Navarre	Original
The Taming of the Shrew	Italy	Ariosto
The Two Gentlemen of Verona	Italy	Giovanni Boccaccio
A Midsummer Night's Dream	Greece	Original
The Merchant of Venice	Italy	Giovanni Fiorentino
Much Ado About Nothing	Italy	Giraldus Cinthio
As You Like It	Unspecified	Thomas Lodge
Twelfth Night	Greece	Mateo Bandello
The Merry Wives of Windsor	England	Original
Troilus and Cressida	Troy	Chaucer, Homer
All's Well That Ends Well	Italy and France	Giovanni Boccaccio
Measure for Measure	Vienna	Giraldus Cinthio

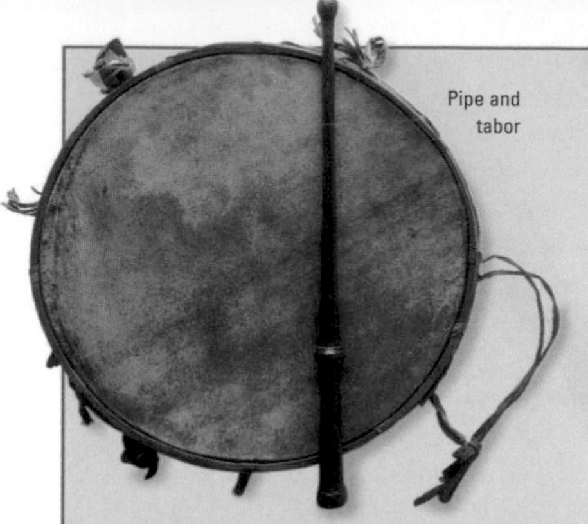
Pipe and tabor

MUSICAL INSTRUMENTS

During the "Golden Age" of English music, string instruments in particular conveyed the perfection of God's universe, the "music of the spheres." *Twelfth Night* opens with Duke Orsino's plea to musicians, probably string players: "If music be the food of love, play on." Shakespeare's plays include much instrumental music, and around 100 songs. Directors usually update the music, but Renaissance audiences responded passionately to favored instruments of the day.

Lute. With its pear-shaped body of pine or cedar and catgut strings plucked with the fingers, the lute enthralled audiences with its deep, warm tones and delicate resonances. Madrigals and folk songs were sung to accompaniment on the lute.

Viol. The viol's flat-backed body featured shoulders curving upward and its neck was broad but thin. Played with a bow, the strings produced elegant, bittersweet tones raising strong emotions.

Oboe. The oboe, which produced a screechier sound that today's oboe, served mainly to create disturbing off-stage effects in tragedies.

Trumpet. The trumpet was employed mainly to mark diplomatic or military engagement in the history plays. The horn was preferred to sound themes of warfare and patriotism.

Pipe and tabor. A recorderlike pipe, played with the left hand, accompanied rhythms tapped out with the right on the tabor, a drum attached to the musician by a string. The pipe and tabor invariably announced revelry or bold dancing and would have been heard for wedding festivities in the comedies.

conclusions in some history plays result from the successful overthrow of unwanted reigns or the defeat of enemies. Joy marks final scenes of the romances when family members or lovers separated by misfortune have been reunited against all odds. But in the comedies, celebration generally acknowledges the integrity of familial and social bonds able to withstand rebellious-minded young lovers or antisocial individuals. Certain figures, including Jaques in *As You Like It* and Malvolio in *Twelfth Night*, are so strong-willed or distressed that they refuse to join the happy ending. These figures take things a step further than Petruchio, who rejects the idea of attending his own wedding feast in the central act of *The Taming of the Shrew*. But by the end of the play, Petruchio and his formerly shrewish wife Kate merrily join the wedding feasts of others. As a rule, all central characters appear at the final celebration.

The inclusive atmosphere of the comedy's conclusion extends as well to the audience, whose final applause and reactions become part and parcel of any communal revelry. Some of the comedies feature an epilogue in which a character from the play speaks directly to the audience, encouraging its engagement with staged events. In *A Midsummer Night's Dream*, Puck suggests to his audience that the play just witnessed may only have been

Lute

a dream and requests applause: "Give me your hands." Today, with comedies usually given on rigidly territorial proscenium stages, some directors have players invite audiences to join the onstage merrymaking. While breaking traditional barriers separating players from their audiences, such approaches are faithful to those community values promoted by the comedies.

As a group, Shakespeare's comedies are in many ways his most complicated plays. Their plots are often convoluted; the multiple identities of many of their characters can be confusing; and the emotions they produce range freely from delight and wonder to anxiety and grief. But the comedies also include many of Shakespeare's most satisfying, spectacular, and popular plays. At one level, there is the sheer humor: the comedies are rife with extravagant characters given to outrageous behavior. At another, there is romance galore, although love can be unrequited or frustrated. But audiences also accompany characters into fantastic or seemingly ungoverned realms, where personalities can suddenly change, for better or for worse. Characters and audiences alike also discover that intrepid exploration of new territories, whether out in the world or within themselves, can alter and improve reality for the better. It is hardly surprising, then, that the comedies continue to give new generations good cause for celebration.

THE PROBLEM PLAYS

Three plays frequently included among Shakespeare's comedies are also known as "problem plays": *Troilus and Cressida, All's Well That Ends Well,* and *Measure for Measure.* Each brings unique challenges to any classification. *Troilus and Cressida,* while published as a tragedy in the *First Folio,* concludes with a comic epilogue and was published in quarto as a comedy. The play's tone is often playful, but the final scene, set on a battlefield, is riddled with slain bodies. *All's Well That Ends Well* is a play full of mourning, loss, desertion, and betrayal. *Measure for Measure* concludes with an ordered execution and an enforced marriage. Much ink has been spilled in efforts to grapple with these plays. Experts have asked which genres they belong to, or whether they constitute a distinct kind of drama. Perhaps unsurprisingly, all three plays date from around 1603, just as the English crown passed from Queen Elizabeth to King James. The problem plays are perhaps best understood as closely tied to the problems of the unsettling time in which they were written, a moment of uncertainty, reflection, and no little anxiety about what lay ahead for England.

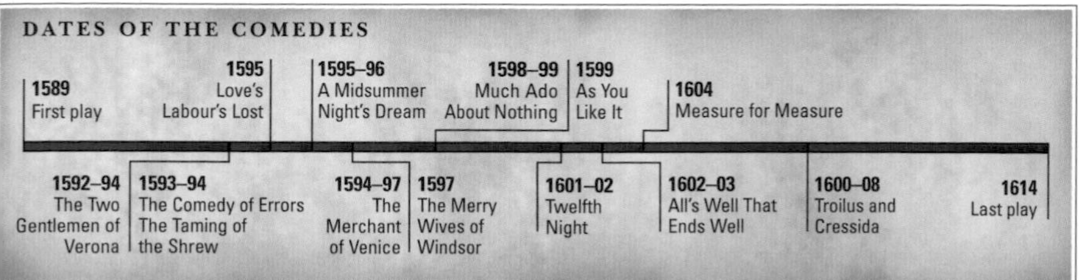

The COMEDY OF ERRORS

THE COMEDY OF ERRORS is Shakespeare's earliest comedy and, at 1,786 lines, the shortest of all his surviving plays. The play was given in 1594 at Gray's Inn for an audience of lawyers to conclude a night of revels. Referring to *The Comedy of Errors,* the records of Gray's Inn report that the "Night was begun, and continued to the end, in nothing but confusion and Errors; whereupon, it was ever afterward called *The Night of Errors.*" The play was given at court in 1604 and, in the centuries that followed, it has been produced in both unaltered and adapted forms. Shakespeare's immediate source for the plot was the Latin *Menaechmi,* by the Roman playwright Plautus. But Shakespeare made the play sublimely farcical by introducing a second pair of identical twins. It is his only play apart from *The Tempest* to observe the classical convention of setting action in a single location over a single day.

BEHIND THE PLAY

THE ACTION IS SET IN EPHESUS, today located in Turkey but in antiquity a center of Greek civilization. While Shakespeare took this setting from his Latin source, the Ephesus of *The Comedy of Errors* resembles Elizabethan England rather than any historical site. The conceit of the play is that merchants from Syracuse are not allowed to conduct business in Ephesus without paying a fine of 1,000 marks (the same applies for merchants of Ephesus working in Syracuse). If a merchant of Syracuse is unable to pay the fine, he must be put to death. As the play opens, Solinus, Duke of Ephesus, upholds this harsh law. He becomes more flexible when he hears why Egeon, a merchant of Syracuse who relates his sad life story, has come to Ephesus. In the final scene of the play, Egeon's lost wife Aemilia fills in a missing part of the family's story when she tells how her son and adopted son were stolen from her by fishermen in Corinth. Thus by the end of the play, Ephesus, with its unbending law and even the threat of death, becomes a site of multiple joys: a severed family is reunited, a man's life is saved, a marriage bond is strengthened, and a new romantic couple is formed.

...the one so like the other/ As could not be distinguished but by names... 1.1

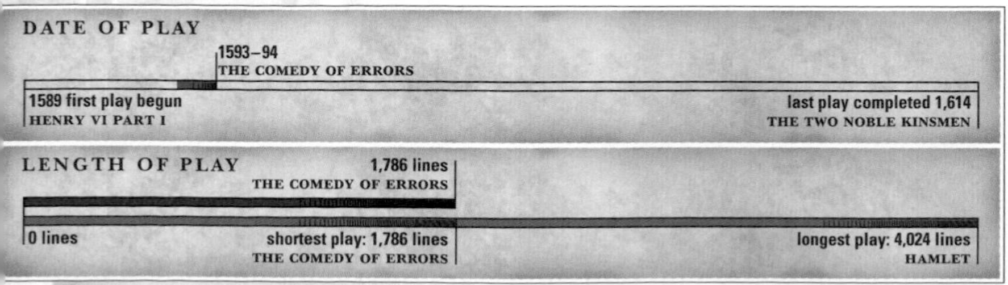

DATE OF PLAY

1593–94
THE COMEDY OF ERRORS

1589 first play begun
HENRY VI PART I

last play completed 1,614
THE TWO NOBLE KINSMEN

LENGTH OF PLAY

1,786 lines
THE COMEDY OF ERRORS

0 lines

shortest play: 1,786 lines
THE COMEDY OF ERRORS

longest play: 4,024 lines
HAMLET

DRAMATIS PERSONAE

SOLINUS

90 lines

Duke of Ephesus, he is required by law to fine Egeon 1,000 marks on pain of death, although he is moved by Egeon's story to grant the merchant one day to raise the sum.

EGEON

143 lines

An unlucky merchant of Syracuse, he manages to find words to relate "griefs unspeakable."

ANTIPHOLUS OF EPHESUS

210 lines

Son to Egeon and Aemilia and the twin brother of Antipholus of Syracuse, he commissioned a gold chain for his wife, Adriana, but when she locks him out of their home, he plans to give it to a prostitute instead.

ANTIPHOLUS OF SYRACUSE

269 lines

Son to Egeon and Aemilia and twin brother of Antipholus of Ephesus, he asks "Am I on earth, in Heaven, or in hell?" when the people of Ephesus take him for his twin.

Mistaking Antipholus of Syracuse (Richard Kerr-Carey) for her husband, Antipholus of Ephesus (Robert Eddison), Adriana (Margaretta Scott) is angered by her "husband's" behavior.

DROMIO OF EPHESUS

156 lines

Attendant on Antipholus of Ephesus and twin brother of Dromio of Syracuse, he remembers being beaten by his master since his birth.

DROMIO OF SYRACUSE

246 lines

Attendant on Antipholus of Syracuse and twin brother of Dromio of Ephesus, he is terrified when Luce, the wife of his twin brother, makes sexual advances on him at Adriana's house.

The long-lost twins Dromio of Syracuse (Ian Hughes) and Dromio of Ephesus (Tom Smith) are confused and bewildered by the events of a single day.

BALTHASAR

27 lines

A merchant, he advises Antipholus not to break down the door when he is locked out of his own home by Adriana.

ANGELO

78 lines

A goldsmith, he is shocked when Antipholus refuses to pay for the gold chain he just delivered to him.

FIRST MERCHANT

15 lines

He reminds his friend Antipholus of Syracuse that Syracusians are not allowed to do business in Ephesus.

SECOND MERCHANT

34 lines

He urgently needs the money Angelo owes him and thus helps the goldsmith recover the sum Antipholus is to pay for the gold chain.

PINCH

12 lines

A schoolmaster, he performs a ludicrous exorcism on the abused Antipholus of Ephesus, noting that "The fiend is strong within him."

AEMILIA

73 lines

Abbess of Ephesus and wife to Egeon, she is reunited with her family.

ADRIANA

264 lines

Wife to Antipholus of Ephesus, she is sure she is "being strumpeted" when her husband behaves oddly.

LUCIANA

95 lines

Sister to Adriana, she is a single woman for now, but would marry if she were able to "learn love."

LUCE ("NELL")

10 lines

Servant to Adriana, she helps Dromio of Syracuse guard the door to her lady's home.

A COURTESAN

35 lines

She entertains Antipholus of Ephesus when he is locked out of his house and later accuses him of stealing her diamond ring.

OTHER PLAYERS

Jailer, Headsman, Messenger, Officers, and other Attendants.

PLOT SUMMARY

SIZE OF ACTS

ACT 1	ACT 2	ACT 3	ACT 4	ACT 5
262 lines	330 lines	328 lines	437 lines	429 lines

ACT ONE

262 lines

PALACE OF THE DUKE AND THE MARKETPLACE OF EPHESUS

Duke Solinus spells out the dilemma to Egeon: laws in Syracuse and Ephesus forbid commerce between the two towns. As a merchant of Syracuse illegally in Ephesus, Egeon must therefore pay the fine of 1,000 marks or die. But the duke asks Egeon to "say in brief" why he came to Ephesus. Egeon explains that he was a merchant who traveled to Epidamnum on business. There, his wife gave birth to identical twin boys in the same hour that a servant woman also gave birth to identical twin boys. Egeon purchased the poor servants' sons to attend on his own. When their ship foundered in a storm on their return home, Egeon's wife tied one son to the mast along with one of the servant twins. Egeon did the same with the two other boys. But the family was separated when the boat hit rocks. Eighteen years later, the son with Egeon, accompanied by the servant twin, left home to search for his lost family. For five years Egeon has traveled throughout Greece looking for the missing boys. He accepts the death sentence, his life too unhappy to continue living. But Solinus, moved by his story, grants Egeon until sunset to raise the 1,000 marks.

Five summers have I spent in farthest Greece,/ Roaming clean through the bounds of Asia... 1.1

Antipholus of Syracuse, the son looking for his lost family, happens to be in Ephesus. In the marketplace, Antipholus sends Dromio, his servant, back to the inn where they lodge. Alone, the visiting Antipholus laments his situation ❝. Then Dromio of Ephesus, twin brother of Antipholus's servant, suddenly appears in search of his

He that commends me to mine own content/ Commends me to the thing I cannot get... 1.2

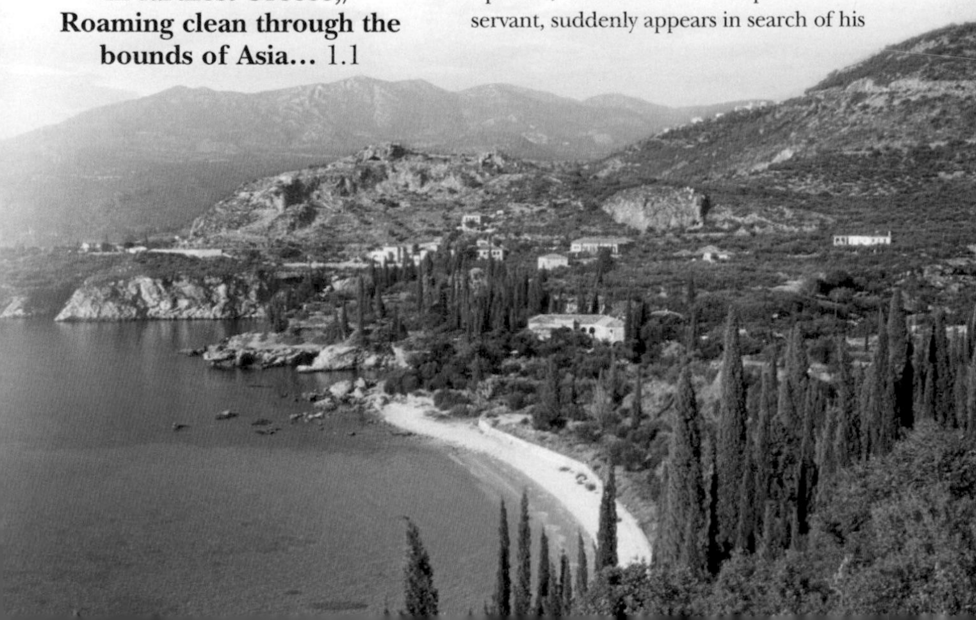

own master, Antipholus of Syracuse's twin brother, whose wife awaits him for lunch at their home, called the Phoenix. The visiting Antipholus asks "his" servant about the 1,000 marks of gold entrusted to him earlier. The local Dromio, having no clue what "Antipholus" is talking about, runs off to avoid a beating. Recalling that Ephesus is reportedly full of trickery, Antipholus heads back to the Centaur, the inn where he is staying.

ACT TWO

330 lines

THE PHOENIX—HOME OF ANTIPHOLUS OF EPHESUS—AND A PUBLIC SQUARE

Adriana, awaiting her husband for lunch, converses with her sister, Luciana, who says she will marry only when she learns to love. Dromio reports that his master has gone "stark mad," raving about gold marks and even denying he has a wife. When Adriana tells Dromio to go right back to the marketplace and fetch Antipholus, Dromio complains of being treated "like a football." Adriana believes her husband is having an affair: he promised her a gold chain, but now apparently has other interests.

Dromio of Syracuse finds his master in a public square. Antipholus is furious with his servant for pretending not to have the 1,000 marks of gold and for inventing a story about lunch and a wife. But Dromio cannot fathom his master's meaning. Adriana and Luciana arrive to chastise the men ❝. Antipholus wonders if he is dreaming: "What error drives our eyes and ears amiss?" He decides to go along with the illusion. Adriana and Luciana insist he return home for lunch and instruct Dromio to guard the gate. Antipholus, now thoroughly confused, goes along with the plan.

Ay, ay, Antipholus, look strange and frown./ Some other mistress hath thy sweet aspects... 2.2

ACT THREE

328 lines

BEFORE THE PHOENIX—HOME OF ANTIPHOLUS OF EPHESUS

Antipholus of Ephesus is accompanied by Angelo, a goldsmith making a chain for Adriana, and Balthasar, a merchant he looks forward to receiving at home. Antipholus is surprised to discover his door locked, and the voice of a porter refusing entry. When the porter, Dromio of Syracuse, announces himself as "Dromio," Dromio of Ephesus cries out, "O, villain, thou has stolen both mine office and my name." Antipholus is about to break his door down when Balthasar recommends they simply lunch elsewhere. Antipholus instructs Angelo to bring the gold chain to the Porpentine, where he offers to take Balthasar for lunch. If only to spite his wife, Antipholus decides he will offer the chain to a courtesan instead.

Luciana lectures "Antipholus" that he must at least pretend to love his wife “. But Antipholus of Syracuse has fallen in love with Luciana. She asks, "What, are you mad?" Dromio arrives to tell of "the kitchen wench" claiming to be his wife: Nell "is spherical, like a globe. I could find out countries in her." Dromio believes she is a witch. Antipholus agrees, and sends Dromio to the market to search for a ship sailing out of town. Although in love with Luciana, Antipholus is eager to sail to safer harbors ”. Angelo runs into "Antipholus" in the street and gives him the gold chain. While delighted to receive an unexpected gift, Antipholus is eager to find Dromio and ship out.

> **And may it be that you have quite forgot/ A husband's office?...** 3.2

> **'here's none but witches do ıhabit here,/And therefore 'tis high time that I were hence...** 3.2

ACT FOUR

437 lines

IN PUBLIC PLACES OF EPHESUS AND AT THE PHOENIX—HOME OF ANTIPHOLUS OF EPHESUS

A merchant tells Angelo he urgently needs the money he is owed. Antipholus of Ephesus appears, instructing Dromio of Ephesus to buy a rope, which he will use to beat his wife. Angelo insists on being paid for the chain and, when Antipholus swears he never received it, Angelo has an officer arrest him for theft. On his way to jail, Antipholus runs into Dromio of Syracuse, who reports that a boat departs that night. Antipholus asks about the rope, but Dromio knows nothing. As he is carted off to jail, the exasperated Antipholus instructs "Dromio" to return home for bail money.

Adriana learns that 'Antipholus' has been flirting with Luciana. When Dromio of Syracuse arrives to collect bail money for her husband, Adriana is further dismayed.

Antipholus of Syracuse wonders why he is so familiar to the townsfolk of Ephesus ”, when "Dromio" presents him with the purse full of gold. Antipholus fails to understand why Dromio thinks bail is required and why the courtesan asks him for a chain promised in exchange for a diamond ring. When the Syracusians flee, the courtesan understands why Adriana locked her crazy husband out of their house ” but, unwilling to lose her diamond ring, she plans to accuse Antipholus of theft.

> **There's not a man I meet but doth salute me/ As if I were their well-acquainted friend...** 4.3

> **Now, out of doubt, Antipholus is mad,/ Else would he never so demean himself...** 4.3

> **Belike you thought our love would last too long/ If it were chained together, and therefore came not...** 4.1

Happy to see Dromio, Antipholus of Ephesus asks his servant for "the money," but when Dromio of Ephesus says that "the money" was spent on "the rope," he receives a beating from his master. Adriana appears with Luciana, the courtesan and Pinch (the schoolmaster), who, confirming that Antipholus is possessed by Satan, performs a humiliating and ludicrous exorcism. Further provoked by Dromio's talk of a rope, Antipholus grows wild. Once he and his servant have been dispatched—deemed madmen, they will be restrained at home—Adriana learns from the courtesan that Antipholus stole a ring. But the Syracusian twins suddenly appear, rapiers drawn. Assuming that the lunatic pair has escaped, everyone else scatters. Antipholus thinks the inhabitants witches, and wants to flee Ephesus. Dromio would stay were it not for "the mountain of mad flesh that claims marriage of me." However, Antipholus will not hear of remaining.

I am an ass, indeed. You may prove it by my long ears… 4.4

ACT FIVE

429 lines

A STREET BEFORE A PRIORY

Angelo and the merchant see the Syracusians, with Antipholus wearing the gold chain. The merchant challenges "Antipholus" for lying to Angelo. But when Adriana arrives, the Syracusians run away, taking refuge in a priory. Adriana attempts to recover her husband, but the Abbess refuses to turn him over. When Duke Solinus arrives with Egeon's executioner, Adriana tries to explain the situation. The Ephesian twins suddenly appear, with Antipholus begging the duke for justice. Solinus believes everyone must be bewitched and calls for the abbess.

My liege, I am advisèd wha[t] I say,/Neither disturbed with effect of wine/ Nor heady-rash provoked with raging ire… 5.1

Egeon, meanwhile, is disappointed that "Antipholus" and "Dromio" do not recognize him, too changed by his travels and grief. When the abbess emerges with the Syracusian twins, all are amazed. The abbess reveals herself as Aemilia, Egeon's lost wife. After the shipwreck, her son and the servant twin were taken by "rude fishermen of Corinth" and she ended up in Ephesus. All confusion about the missing chain and ducats is sorted out and the abbess delights at the "nativity" of her sons after 33 years. She invites all to feast. They follow her, but the twins remain for a moment to get acquainted.

Not know my voice? O time's extremity… 5.1

Methinks you are my glass, and not my brother./ I see by you I am a sweet-faced youth… 5.1

READING THE PLAY

COMPARISON OF PROSE TO VERSE

prose: 13% | verse: 87%

WHILE THIS PLAY does not end with marriage as is customary in Shakespearean comedies, it does develop from discord and harsh law to concord and joyous feasting, and concludes with at least the promise of marriage (of Luciana to Antipholus of Syracuse). Curiously, *The Comedy of Errors* is the only Shakespearean play containing the word "comedy" in its title.

Aemilia and the infants Antipholus and Dromio are saved from the sea by "men of Epidamnum" in a painting by Francis Wheatley, engraved by J. Neagle, 1796.

The most common problem encountered in reading the play is that of keeping track of the identities of the pairs of twins. This problem is accentuated by the fact that most editions of the play identify the twins as in the *First Folio* edition: Antipholus of Syracuse is merely given as "S Ant," Dromio of Syracuse is "S Dro," and so on. Consequently, readers often find it helpful to recall that Antipholus of Ephesus, the local twin, husband of Adriana, does not appear until Act 3. His servant, Dromio of Ephesus, appears as early as Act 1, however, and is immediately mistaken for his twin brother. Efforts to keep track of the roles do pay off in the end since the play makes for entertaining and sometimes even moving reading. With its combination of poignant lyricism and hilarious prose, *The Comedy of Errors* already shows signs of what was to come in Shakespeare's later comedies.

LANGUAGE NOTE

ELIZABETHAN COURTESANS

"Courtesan" was among the Elizabethan words for a prostitute. The word came into English from the Italian *cortigiana*, meaning a woman of the court. Initially, such women served noblemen or men of wealth, but the word was later applied in English to prostitutes in general.

A 16th-century French painting of *The Prodigal Son with Courtesans*.

SEEING THE PLAY

The Comedy of Errors continues to inspire adaptation. *Bomb-itty of Errors*, a rap version of Shakespeare's classic, opened in London in 2003. With a cast of just four men, ingenious visual and verbal jokes conjure up an entire manic world.

AUDIENCES ENJOY THE SITUATIONAL HUMOR and physical comedy of *The Comedy of Errors* even when the Elizabethan verbal jokes fall flat. The success of the play on stage relies heavily on the comic talents of actors in the lead roles. But no less important is the dire solemnity of the opening scene: audiences must be moved by Egeon's story and believe that his life is at stake. If the gravity of these circumstances is unconvincing, the comic thrust of the central three acts loses purpose and momentum.

Adriana loses her temper in the final scene of a colorful production of the play by the RSC, 1990.

The final act requires ensembles to shift dramatic registers yet again. When the abbess of Ephesus turns out to be none other than Aemilia, long-lost mother of the twins and wife of the man about to be executed, the play suddenly abandons farcical humor to present a moving family reunion. Unless the play as a whole is given thoughtful treatment, and this sudden transition in particular is given some underlying motivation, the final scene can appear merely gratuitous.

Since the main plot is built on silly gags surrounding the double twins, the lead roles tend to attract actors who win audiences over with physical comedy, making the final scene all the more tricky to carry off. Strongly characterized secondary roles—Angelo, Balthasar, Pinch, and the Courtesan—also help to anchor the inane action of the play.

BEYOND THE PLAY

"After a play by William Shakespeare... long, long after!" is the writing credit for the 1940 film, *The Boys from Syracuse*, based on a 1938 Broadway musical hit by Rodgers and Hart.

EVER SINCE Samuel Coleridge read *The Comedy of Errors* as the epitome of farce, readers have debated whether the play is more of a farce than a comedy. *The Comedy of Errors* contains very serious story threads, especially in Acts 1 and 5, but its three central acts—with their violent physical humor and the absurdity of dual twins—are indeed ridiculous.

The word farce derives from the French for "stuffing," or "filler." Earlier, medieval farces were short, slapstick interludes given between segments of a play treating serious, religious themes. In Shakespeare's classical source, the Latin *Menaechmi* by Plautus, ridiculous situations and slapstick violence lie at the heart of the comedy. Decades before Shakespeare began working in the theater, English playwrights had already begun to employ elements of the medieval farce as they reset the Roman comedies of Terence and Plautus.

The Russian director Fyodor Komisarjevsky's landmark 1938 production of *The Comedy of Errors* at Stratford-upon-Avon used an idiom of surrealist modernism to show that even the most ludicrous elements of the play may not be dismissed as mere stage silliness. Instead, slapstick Shakespeare was seen to be rooted in timeless human experiences of a disturbing world.

ON STAGE

KYOGEN

Drawing on the 600-year-old comic tradition known as *Kyogen*, Japan's Mansaku Company performed its own version of the play *(below)* at Shakespeare's Globe, London, in 2001, entitling it *The Kyogen of Errors*. Performing in Japanese with supertitles, actors used their voices and bodies in a highly stylized manner.

In a 1938 production for the RSC, Fyodor Komisarjevsky employed nightmarish comic booklike sets and a mixture of period references. His production was hailed as "hallucinogenic."

The TAMING OF THE SHREW

THE TAMING OF THE SHREW was a farcical comedy for Elizabethan audiences. Today, it is Shakespeare's most controversial comedy about the sexual politics of marriage. Little is known about its earliest performances. A play entitled *The Taming of A Shrew* was staged, probably by Shakespeare's company, the Lord Chamberlain's Men, on June 11, 1594, at the Newington Butts Theatre in London. But it is not known whether this is the same play, or even a version of Shakespeare's *The Taming of the Shrew*. Although it was published in the *First Folio*, the earliest documented performance of *The Taming of the Shrew* is not until 1633, when it was well received at the royal court. Sources for the play include *The Arabian Nights* for the Induction scene and Gascoigne's 1566 translation of Ariosto's Italian *I Suppositi* for the main story of the shrew tamed by her husband.

BEHIND THE PLAY

WHEN SHAKESPEARE CREATED KATE, a warring sister and daughter transformed into a servile wife, he may have found inspiration in the feminine yet militaristic Elizabeth I. In 1588, a few years before Shakespeare wrote *The Taming of the Shrew*, Queen Elizabeth said as she reviewed her troops: "I know I have the body of a weak and feeble woman, but I have the heart and stomach of a king, and a King of England, too… I myself will take up arms, I myself will be your general, judge, and rewarder of every one of your virtues in the field." But the Bard's direct sources were literary rather than historical. The strongly antifeminist themes of this play were traditional dramatic fare, as was the slapstick violence of the shrew Kate and her husband Petruchio. Violence had also been used as a comic device by Roman playwrights whose works inspired Shakespeare. But the feminist movements of the 1970s gave new meaning to this play. Its portrayal of marital dominance and subservience, like its unromantic depictions of family strife, have made it difficult to read the play uncritically. Directors now rarely approach *The Taming of the Shrew* without paying close heed to current views on household politics.

Say that she frown, I'll say she looks as clear/ As morning roses newly washed with dew… 2.1

DATE OF PLAY

1593–94 THE TAMING OF THE SHREW

1589 first play begun HENRY VI PART I

last play completed 1614 THE TWO NOBLE KINSMEN

LENGTH OF PLAY

2,641 lines THE TAMING OF THE SHREW

0 lines

shortest play: 1,786 lines THE COMEDY OF ERRORS

longest play: 3,929 lines HAMLET

DRAMATIS PERSONAE

The romantic fop Hortensio (Victor Spinetti) has eyes only for "beautiful Bianca."

INDUCTION

A LORD
146 lines
He plays a trick on Sly, persuading him that he is a lord attending a play.

CHRISTOPHER SLY
63 lines
A tinker, he awakens from a drunken slumber to hear that he is a lord who has been asleep for 15 years.

ALEHOUSE HOSTESS
4 lines
She is not happy when Sly drinks but refuses to pay.

BARTHOLOMEW
16 lines
A page, his lord instructs him to pretend to be the wife of Sly.

TRAVELING PLAYERS
5 lines
They perform a play for Sly about the taming of the shrewish Kate.

HUNTSMEN
9; 3 lines
They accompany the lord.

SERVINGMEN
17; 13; 13; 5 lines
They help their master carry out his prank.

PLAY-WITHIN-THE-PLAY

BAPTISTA MINOLA
175 lines
A lord of Padua, he is the father of the shrewish Kate and Bianca.

VINCENTIO
47 lines
Father of Lucentio, he comes unexpectedly to Padua from Pisa to visit his son and is outraged to discover that he is being impersonated by an old schoolteacher.

LUCENTIO
190 lines
Suitor of Bianca, he disguises himself as "Cambio," a poetry tutor, so that he may gain access to Baptista's sequestered daughter, Bianca.

PETRUCHIO
586 lines
A flamboyant adventurer from Verona, he comes to "wive it wealthily in Padua"; he wins Kate's hand, but behaves outrageously until he is able to subdue his tempestuous bride.

Enterprising Petruchio (Jack Cannon) plans a seductive strategy to tame his feisty wife.

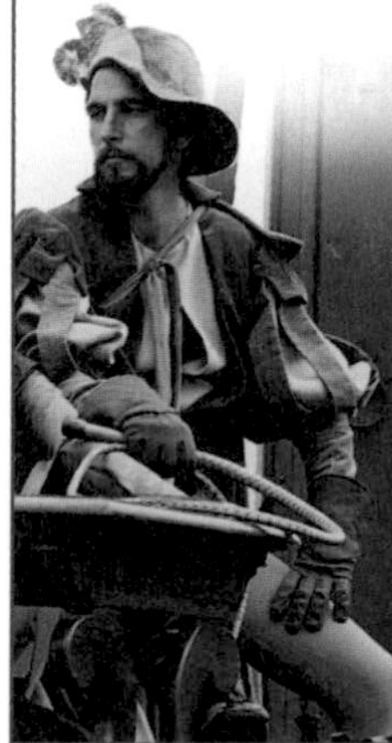

GREMIO
170 lines
A "pantaloon," or capering fool, and veteran suitor of Bianca, he is wealthy, old, and eager to include the pretty girl among his exotic treasures.

HORTENSIO
207 lines
Suitor of Bianca, and old friend of Petruchio, he warns the suitor that Kate "is intolerable curst"; he disguises himself as the music tutor "Litio" to gain access to Bianca, but a widow who has long loved him will eventually become his bride.

TRANIO
293 lines
A witty servant of Lucentio, he pretends to be his master so that Lucentio may, for his part, pose as Bianca's poetry tutor "Cambio."

BIONDELLO
102 lines
Second servant of Lucentio, he is not thrilled about having to pretend that his fellow servant, Tranio, is his master "Lucentio."

GRUMIO
171 lines
Servant of Petruchio, his irreverence gives Petruchio plenty of practice in the art of taming those of spirited disposition.

CURTIS
25 lines
Servant of Petruchio, he has a knack for obscene double-entendres.

A PEDANT
50 lines
A pedant or schoolteacher visiting Padua from Mantua, he is persuaded to impersonate Vincentio, but is discovered.

A TAILOR
17 lines
Petruchio orders him to make clothes, which he then rejects.

A HABERDASHER
1 line
He makes hats for Kate.

NATHANIEL, JOSEPH, NICHOLAS, PHILIP, AND PETER
5; 1; 2; 2; 2 lines
Servants of Petruchio.

KATHERINA (KATE)
219 lines
The shrew is "renowned in Padua for her scolding tongue"; Petruchio's unconventional methods change her to the point that she even argues that women are "bound to serve, love, and obey."

Unruly Kate (Josie Lawrence) throws a temper tantrum.

BIANCA
71 lines
Kate's younger sister, she is the victim of Kate's violent temper and the love-interest of three suitors; she marries Lucentio, to whom she is "the wishèd haven of my bliss."

A WIDOW
11 lines
She finally wins Hortensio for a husband.

PLOT SUMMARY

SIZE OF ACTS

Induction	ACT 1	ACT 2	ACT 3	ACT 4	ACT 5
284 lines	542 lines	423 lines	349 lines	710 lines	333 lines

INDUCTION 284 lines

OUTSIDE AN ALEHOUSE AND IN THE LORD'S CHAMBER IN WARWICK, ENGLAND

A lord returns from hunting to discover a drunken slumberer. For amusement, the lord decides to play a trick on the sleeper. Upon awakening, Christopher Sly is persuaded he is a lord who has been comatose for 15 years. His "wife"—the real lord's page in disguise—weeps to see the "lord" revived. When players arrive, Sly is told that his doctor advised he take in a comedy because it "lengthens life." Sly instructs his "wife" to sit by him and attend the play.

ACT ONE 542 lines

IN A STREET OF PADUA AND BEFORE THE HOUSE OF HORTENSIO

With his obliging servant Tranio, Lucentio comes to Padua to study philosophy. But when he sees Bianca, Lucentio falls in love. Lucentio eavesdrops on Baptista, who explains to suitors Gremio and Hortensio that Bianca will not marry until a husband is found for his other daughter, Kate. The daughters shall be confined at home to study music and poetry under tutors. Gremio and Hortensio decide to apply themselves to the considerable task of finding a husband for Kate so that they

Think'st thou, Hortensio, though her father be very rich, any man is so very a fool to be married to hell?... 1.1

may woo Bianca. Lucentio schemes to gain access to the sequestered Bianca by posing as a tutor. He asks his servant Tranio to assume his identity and the two exchange clothes.

Sly, watching the play, appears to be falling asleep again. Asked if he is paying attention, he wishes the play were over.

Accompanied by his surly servant Gremio, Petruchio has come to win a rich wife in Padua. His old friend Hortensio tells Petruchio about Kate, warning that she is intolerably shrewish. But Petruchio is only interested in her wealth. Hortensio explains that he will disguise himself as a tutor to woo Bianca. Gremio arrives with the poetry tutor "Cambio," who is Lucentio in disguise. Gremio and Hortensio are both upset to meet "Lucentio" (Tranio disguised as his master), who also intends to woo Bianca. But 'Lucentio' lightens the mood by proposing that he and the other suitors get along as lawyers do: "Strive mightily, but eat and drink as friends."

ACT TWO

423 lines

IN BAPTISTA MINOLA'S HOUSE

Kate interrogates Bianca, who swears she loves neither Hortensio nor Gremio. When Kate strikes Bianca, their father accuses Kate of having a "devilish spirit." Guests arrive. Petruchio introduces "Litio" the music tutor, who is Hortensio in disguise, and announces himself Kate's suitor. Gremio introduces the poetry tutor, "Cambio," and "Lucentio," who announces himself as Bianca's new suitor and offers gifts for the daughters' lessons: a lute and books. The tutors are sent to give the girls lessons, but "Cambio" soon returns because Kate smashed her new lute on his head. Petruchio is all the more eager to seduce Kate.

I pray you do. I'll attend he here,/And woo her with some spirit when she comes... 2.1

When Kate arrives, as rough and rude as ever, Petruchio, unfazed, informs her he is "born to tame you, Kate." Insisting to Baptista that Kate is only wild in the company of others, Petruchio announces

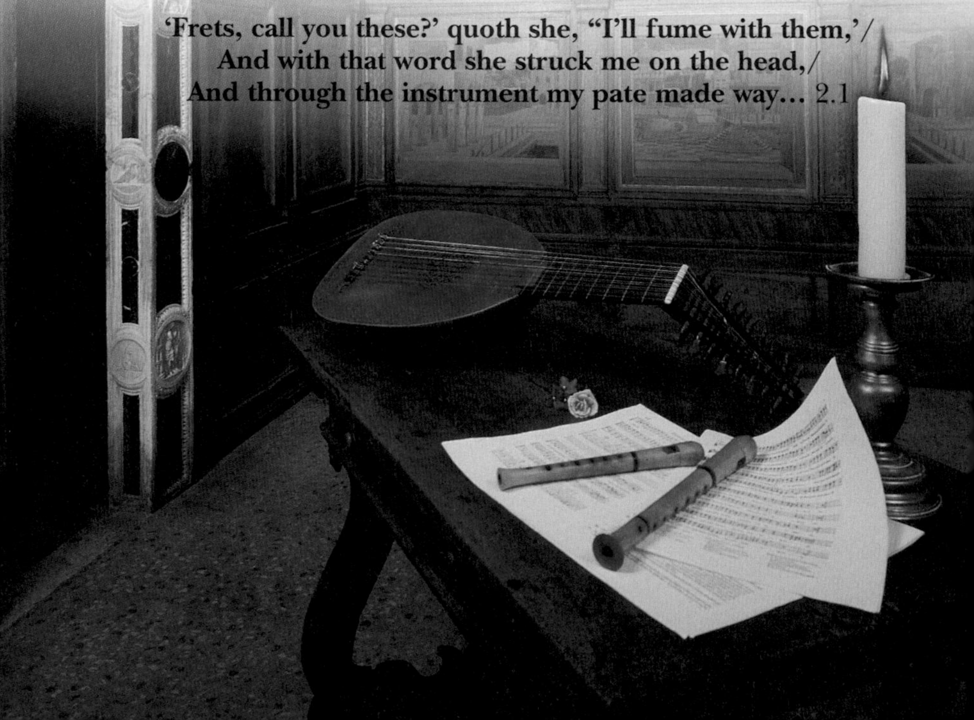

'Frets, call you these?' quoth she, "I'll fume with them,'/ And with that word she struck me on the head,/ And through the instrument my pate made way... 2.1

his departure for Venice to buy wedding clothes while others prepare the ceremony. The delighted Baptista informs Gremio and "Lucentio" that Bianca's hand is now available to the wealthiest suitor. When it appears that "Lucentio" is the richer man, Baptista promises Bianca to him… so long as guarantees for the promised gifts arrive from his father, Vincentio.

ACT THREE

349 lines

IN AND BEFORE THE HOUSE OF BAPTISTA MINOLA

"Cambio" and "Litio" bicker over the order of Bianca's lessons. Reminding them that the choice is hers, Bianca instructs "Litio" to tune his instrument while "Cambio" tutors her in poetry. Lucentio reveals to Bianca his true identity while pretending to translate a passage of Ovid ❝. Hortensio tries a similar trick with a musical scale, but Bianca is less charmed.

'*Hic ibat*', as I told you before… 3.1

Kate is reduced to tears when her groom does not show for the wedding. But Biondello reports that Petruchio indeed arrives, only he sports outrageous clothing and rides an unsightly nag ❝. When Baptista insists he change into appropriate clothing, Petruchio justifies his dress in terms of his bond with Kate, "To me she's married, not unto my clothes," and departs for the church. In an aside, Tranio plans to find an impersonator of Vincentio, needed to seal the marriage of "Lucentio" to Bianca. Gremio returns from the church to tell of the "mad marriage." Petruchio behaved wildly, striking the priest and throwing cake and wine in the sexton's face. And Kate "trembled and shook" until Petruchio kissed her loudly on the lips. The wedding feast finally commences, but Petruchio shockingly refuses to attend ❝. Instead, he leaves for his home in Verona with Kate in tow—"Be mad and merry, or go hang yourselves./But for my bonny Kate, she must with me."

Why, Petruchio is coming in a new hat and an old jerkin… 3.2

They shall go forward, Kate, at thy command… 3.2

ACT FOUR

710 lines

IN PETRUCHIO'S COUNTRY HOUSE IN VERONA, BEFORE BAPTISTA'S HOUSE IN PADUA, AND ON THE ROAD FROM VERONA TO PADUA

Gremio arrives home ahead of his master to tell fellow servant Curtis about the horrendous journey: Petruchio abandoned Kate in mud under her horse ❝. Curtis notes that Petruchio seems more shrewish than Kate. When the newlyweds arrive, Petruchio disturbs Kate by cursing and striking his servants. Alone, Petruchio refines his strategy: to tame the shrew, he will deprive her of food and sleep ❞.

Tell thou the tale. But hadst thou not crossed me… 4.1

Thus have I politicly begun my reign,/And 'tis my hope to end successfully… 4.1

In Padua, where he observes the romantic success of "Cambio" with Bianca, Hortensio decides to drop his suit and instead marry a widow who loves him. When a schoolmaster happens into town from Mantua, "Lucentio" persuades him to impersonate Vincentio of Pisa.

In Verona, Kate starves as Gremio tortures her with talk of meats and mustard. Petruchio finally offers food. A tailor and a hatmaker display items Petruchio ordered but, to Kate's disturbance, he lashes out at them. He says that the couple shall return to Padua in humble attire, "For 'tis the mind that makes the body rich" ❝. When Kate disagrees with her husband about the hour of the day, Petruchio remains stern: "It shall be what o'clock I say it is." At Baptista's house, "Vincentio"

Well, come my Kate, we will unto your father's/Even in these honest mean habiliments… 4.3

guarantees the dowry. "Lucentio" offers his lodging for the ceremony and "Cambio" sets out to tell Bianca she must prepare hastily for the wedding.

On the road to Padua, Petruchio torments Kate with impossible commands: she must call the sun the moon. When she follows instructions, he corrects her again. Petruchio addresses a man on the road, instructing Kate to embrace the "maid." When Kate obeys him, he corrects her anew: "This is a man, old, wrinkled, faded, withered." But the man introduces himself as Vincentio, father of Lucentio, on his way to Padua to see his son. Petruchio embraces Vincentio as his new kinsman and the group travels to Padua.

ACT FIVE

333 lines

IN PADUA, BEFORE AND WITHIN THE HOUSE OF LUCENTIO

Petruchio brings the real Vincentio before the home of Lucentio who, in his guise as "Cambio" the poetry tutor, is in the church marrying Bianca. When the Pedant refuses entry and claims to be the father of Lucentio, Vincentio is furious. Baptista is outraged when "Cambio" returns with Bianca as his bride. Lucentio asks his father, Vincentio, to forgive him and Tranio, explaining that "Love wrought these miracles." But Vincentio departs to take revenge on Tranio for "this villainy," and Baptista also leaves to get to the bottom of all "this knavery." Gremio, meanwhile, is sorry his suit failed, but will join the others at the feast in any event.

At Lucentio's house, witty remarks and jokes are bandied about during the wedding feast. The widow, Hortensio's new wife, joins the married sisters. When the women leave to chat on their own, Petruchio proposes a wager to the other new husbands: "Let's each one send unto his wife,/And he whose wife is most obedient/To come at first when he doth send for her/Shall win the wager which we will propose." Each bets 100 crowns. Lucentio calls for Bianca, but she "is busy and she cannot come." For her part, Hortensio's wife simply "will not come." But Kate arrives at once. Petruchio commands Kate to tell the other wives "What duty they do owe their lords and husbands." Kate passionately argues that women are "bound to serve, love, and obey" ❝. Petruchio is delighted. "Come on, and kiss me, Kate," Petruchio commands finally, taking his obedient bride off to bed. The other husbands are left to wonder how he tamed the shrew.

Fie, fie, unknit that threatening unkind brow,/ And dart not scornful glances from those eyes... 5.2

Thy husband is thy lord, thy life, thy keeper,/ Thy head, thy sovereign; one that cares for thee,/ And for thy maintenance... 5.2

READING THE PLAY

COMPARISON OF PROSE TO VERSE

prose: 22% | verse: 78%

"What, did he marry me to famish me?" (4.3). Starved and "giddy for sleep," Kate broods on her miserable lot. *The Shrew Katherina,* 1896, oil by Edward Robert Hughes.

NO PLAY BETTER DEMONSTRATES that Shakespeare wrote plays for theater audiences rather than readers. As with other comedies in which action is built around mistaken identity and physical, even farcical, humor, *The Taming of the Shrew* may initially strike readers as a two-dimensional play at best, and a confusing one at worst. Readers must keep track of disguised characters, especially the switch between Lucentio and Tranio.

The play contains many animal metaphors, similes, and allusions. Petruchio's strategy for taming Kate is described in terms of falconry. Kate, "my falcon," must learn "her keeper's call." Like a falconer his falcon, Petruchio tames his wife with food deprivation. Until she obeys, "she must not be full-gorged."

At the same time, *The Taming of the Shrew* features opaque and dated verbal humor. Many of the puns and jokes that captivated Elizabethan audiences no longer sound funny or even make much sense, although a well-annotated edition can help the reader tease out the humor of such lines as Bianca's "An hasty-witted body/Would say your head and butt were head and horn." However, the densest passages of joking and punning occur in exchanges of dialogue, that do not advance the action significantly. As a result, readers may take what they like from these exchanges and continue without missing the plot or becoming too enmeshed in word-for-word details. Fortunately, the fresh and strident voices of Petruchio and Kate are never far away. And when either of them is speaking, readers can enjoy sparkling dialogues and bold speeches.

WHO'S WHO

Characters impersonated by others:
Lucentio is played by his servant **Tranio** (by mutual consent).
Vincentio is played by a **Pedant** of Mantua (without Vincentio's knowledge).

Roles invented by suitors to gain access to **Bianca**:
Lucentio plays the poetry tutor "**Cambio**."
Hortensio plays the music tutor "**Litio**."

LITERARY SOURCES

MYSTERY PLAYS

Medieval mystery plays dramatizing the story of Noah's ark often portrayed comical knockabout relations between Noah and his stubborn wife. Such farcical conduct set a trend of verbal and physical humor that colored Shakespeare's earlier comedies, including *The Taming of the Shrew.* The figure of hard-headed Mrs. Noah, who refused to board the ark, left her mark on the portrayal of feisty Kate.

SEEING THE PLAY

ON STAGE

BREAKING DOWN ILLUSIONS

In Michael Bogdanov's Stratford production of *The Taming of the Shrew* (1978), a "drunk" man, in fact planted in the audience, made his way on to the stage to destroy a traditional theatrical set representing Padua and to reveal the innards of the theater itself to a bewildered audience. Later, the "drunk"—Michael Bogdanov's updating of Christopher Sly—returned to the stage as Petruchio on a motorcycle, his behavior as spirited and unruly as ever.

THE TAMING OF THE SHREW has become a director's play about power and gender. Directors must come to terms with delicate, ideologically-charged relationships on several domestic fronts: between a father and his daughters, and women and their suitors. Directors must also tackle the question of how to handle the play-within-the-play and the role of Christopher Sly, which Shakespeare unsatisfyingly amputated from the action following Act 1. Ever since the contours of the stage and its relationship to reality were thrown into question by such 20th-century manifestos as Antonin Artaud's *Theatre of Cruelty*, directors have found ingenious ways to turn Sly into a figure of anti-theatricality. Some have planted him in the audience or even outside the theater altogether so that his entrance dismantles boundaries between stage and audience, or between the theater and the world beyond. Most directors simply present the comedy without the framing Induction. But even the action set in Italy calls for directors to explore the limits of theatricality.

Petruchio's role as tamer, for instance, raises troubling questions about impersonation, play-acting, and its potentially violent implications. Relationships throughout the play, including that of Baptista and his daughters, are defined by fierce power struggles and displays of authority. With strong casts and solid interpretations, directors continue to prove that *The Taming of the Shrew* cannot be reduced to a period farce. Instead, the play invites audiences into a world of domestic politics, as pressing in our own time as in the Elizabethan era. Some recent productions have sought to mine the play's social relevance by setting it in contemporary dress, or using an all-female cas

Petruchio (Ralph Clanton) shows Kate (Claire Luce) who's boss in a 1951 New York City Theater Co. production.

BEYOND THE PLAY

MODERN REACTIONS TO KATE have been as temperamental as Kate herself, but are less predictable than one may expect. George Bernard Shaw said in 1897 that "The last scene is altogether disgusting to modern sensibility." But during the women's rights movement, the offensive scene was, according to feminist Germaine Greer, a triumph for women's causes. In *The Female Eunuch* (1971), Greer argued that "Kate's speech at the close of the play is the greatest defense of Christian monogamy ever written." In the end, *The Taming of the Shrew* is neither simple reflection nor parody of the social conditions of women, or even attitudes toward them during Shakespeare's era. The subject of woman's power in the household, however, was as fair game for comic entertainment in Shakespeare's time as it remains today.

Actors are drawn to the unique challenges of leading roles in *The Taming of the Shrew*. Kate has been interpreted by top stage actresses, including the memorable Victorian shrew Ada Rehan and the 20th-century stars Peggy Ashcroft, Lynn Fontanne, Claire Booth Luce, Katharine Hepburn, Elizabeth Taylor, Vanessa Redgrave, Fiona Shaw, and Meryl Streep. Even Laurence Olivier, as a 14-year-old choirboy, tackled Kate in an all-male production. Notable Petruchios include Ralph Richardson, Peter O'Toole, Timothy Dalton, and John Cleese in Jonathan Miller's BBC television production.

ON SCREEN

HUSBAND AND WIFE

Fascinated by the volatile dynamic between Petruchio and Kate, directors have enjoyed casting husband-and-wife teams in the lead roles. In a riotous film version of the play, Franco Zeffirelli directed the tempestuous husband-and-wife-team Richard Burton and Elizabeth Taylor *(above)* in 1966. The earliest movie version of *The Taming of the Shrew*, from 1929, matched Douglas Fairbanks Jr. with his spouse Mary Pickford *(below)*.

A poster for the blockbuster feature film *Kiss Me Kate* (1953), in turn based on Cole Porter's Broadway hit of 1948. With its brilliant score and lyrics by Cole Porter, the original musical won five Tony awards before closing in 1951 after 1,070 performances. The Broadway stars Alfred Drake and Patricia Morison led an equally tempestuous life on and off stage.

The TWO GENTLEMEN OF VERONA

ONE GENTLEMAN OF VERONA IS BETRAYED by another, his best friend, in the central love triangle of *The Two Gentlemen of Verona*, Shakespeare's earliest romantic comedy. The play's lyrical language, along with its themes of friendship and romantic betrayal, has been linked to Shakespeare's sonnets. This has led to speculation that Shakespeare drew from his own personal joys and disappointments of love and friendship while writing the play. No record attests to a performance during Shakespeare's lifetime, but a reference to it by Francis Meres in 1598 suggests that the play had been a success. The first record of a production of *The Two Gentlemen of Verona* is dated 1762, when it was given in a heavily adapted form at London's Drury Lane Theatre. It was also the first play to be tested on the boards of the reconstructed Shakespeare's Globe theatre in London in 1996.

BEHIND THE PLAY

ALTHOUGH THE PLAY IS set in Verona and Milan, it is clear from *The Two Gentlemen of Verona* that Shakespeare had absolutely no interest in the actual location of these land-locked towns. Valentine, for instance, departs from Verona to Milan by boat. Indeed, much of the geography of *The Two Gentlemen of Verona* is unreliable. Even the Duke of Milan seems uncertain of the territory of his dukedom, which he refers to as Verona in Act 3. Valentine's servant, Speed, also appears confused. Act 2, Scene 5 is set in Milan, but in the *First Folio* Speed greets fellow servant Launce in the opening line with the words "Welcome to Padua!" These detailed technical errors are dwarfed, however, by the more general disaster of the play's final scene, which strikes nearly every reader and director as unthinkable or slapdash: Proteus, who nearly rapes Silvia, is barely remorseful for his gross betrayals, yet immediately reverts his affection to his initial beloved, Julia, when she unmasks herself. For his part, Valentine instantly forgives his false and cruel friend. On the whole, *The Two Gentlemen of Verona* must not be read with great concern for consistency either of location or character motivation.

At first I did adore a twinkling star,/ But now I worship a celestial sun…
2.6

DATE OF PLAY

1592–94
THE TWO GENTLEMEN OF VERONA

1589 first play begun
HENRY VI PART I

last play completed 1614
THE TWO NOBLE KINSMEN

LENGTH OF PLAY

2,233 lines
THE TWO GENTLEMEN OF VERONA

0 lines

shortest play: 1,786 lines
THE COMEDY OF ERRORS

longest play: 4,024 lines
HAMLET

DRAMATIS PERSONAE

DUKE OF MILAN
200 lines
He hopes his daughter, Silvia, will marry Thurio and so banishes Valentine.

VALENTINE
383 lines
Initially in love with the idea of improving himself through travel, he woos his true love, Silvia, in Milan, but is banished from the city by her father, the duke.

PROTEUS
442 lines
Initially in love with Julia, he changes his mind the moment he lays eyes on Silvia, his best friend's girlfriend; when she refuses him, he argues he must love her "like a soldier," against her will.

ANTONIO
35 lines
Father of Proteus, when he hears it would be best for his son to broaden his mind rather than stay at home and do nothing, he insists that Proteus follow Valentine to Milan.

Julia (disguised as Sebastian) admires a picture of Sylvia, her rival in Proteus's affections.

THURIO
56 lines
A foolish suitor for Silvia's hand, he is not thought a serious rival by either Proteus or Valentine.

EGLAMOUR
28 lines
Silvia's accomplice in her flight from Milan.

HOST OF THE INN
37 lines
He offers to divert the sad "Sebastian" with some entertainment, but the music set to a bad poem praising Julia's rival Silvia only makes "Sebastian" even more unhappy.

OUTLAWS
22; 15; 25 lines
Led by Valentine during his banishment, they are learned and high-bred but have grown savage in the wilderness until Valentine restores their sense of morality; Valentine gallantly arranges for them to be pardoned by the duke in the last scene.

SPEED
194 lines
Servant to Valentine, he is far more intelligent than his slightly dense master, but is often late for meetings.

PANTHINO
43 lines
Servant to Antonio, he speaks freely to his master about ways to enrich Proteus's upbringing.

JULIA
322 lines
The beloved of Proteus, she disguises herself as "Sebastian," a page, in order to follow Proteus to Milan, where she is shocked to find him in love with Silvia.

SILVIA
155 lines
The duke's daughter and the beloved of Valentine; she remains true to Valentine, despite the machinations of Proteus.

LUCETTA
73 lines
Waiting-woman to Julia, she fashions the breeches and codpiece Julia wears to disguise herself as a boy.

OTHER PLAYERS
Servants, Musicians, and Attendants.

LAUNCE
203 lines
Servant to Proteus, and the most popular role in *The Two Gentlemen of Verona*, he delivers moving monologues to his pet dog, Crab, who remains unmoved by his emotions; Launce's affection for Crab seems to run deeper than his master's deceitful love for either Julia or Silvia.

Launce (Jay Laurier) and Crab the dog invariably win the hearts of audiences.

Proteus (Barry Lynch) and Julia (Clare Holman) bid a reluctant farewell when Proteus must go to Milan.

PLOT SUMMARY

SIZE OF ACTS

ACT 1	ACT 2	ACT 3	ACT 4	ACT 5
381 lines	640 lines	470 lines	473 lines	269 lines

ACT ONE

381 lines

A STREET IN VERONA, THE GARDEN OF JULIA'S HOUSE AND INSIDE ANTONIO'S HOUSE

Valentine wishes his friend Proteus would join him "To see the wonders of the world," instead of lazing about at home. But Proteus is too in love with Julia to think of leaving Verona.

He after honour hunts, I after love... 1.1

Valentine departs for Milan to be a guest of the duke at his palace.

Proteus asks Speed, Valentine's servant, about Julia's reaction to his love letter. There was none, Speed reports. Alone, Proteus hopes to find a better messenger.

Julia pretends to be uninterested in Proteus's love letter when her attendant, Lucetta, presents it. But, once alone, Julia admits that she loves Proteus. She recalls Lucetta and rips up the letter before her. Alone again, Julia pieces the letter together, torturing herself in her search for signs of Proteus's love.

But, since thou lovest, love still, and thrive therein,/ Even as I would when I to love begin... 1.3

Panthino advises Antonio that it would be best if his son, Proteus, joined his friend Valentine in Milan.

He wondered that your lordship/Would suffer him to spend his youth at home... 1.3

Proteus is reading a letter from Julia when his father suddenly appears. Proteus says the letter is from Valentine, wishing he were also in Milan. The delighted Antonio instructs his son to depart at once for Milan. Alone, Proteus is upset to see how changeable his love is.

ACT TWO

640 lines

IN THE DUKE'S PALACE AND IN A STREET OF MILAN, AND IN JULIA'S HOUSE AND A STREET IN VERONA

Speed notes that his master, Valentine, is lovesick. Silvia, the duke's daughter, has asked Valentine "to write some lines to one she loves." But when Valentine presents the fruits of his labor, Silvia says the poetry is for him to keep. Speed understands that Silvia has Valentine composing on her behalf a letter destined to none other than himself. But Valentine, too dim to fathom the ruse, leaves Speed unimpressed. About to separate in Verona, Proteus vows fidelity to Julia and they exchange rings. Launce, Proteus's servant, wonders why Crab, his pet dog, shows no sign of grief at Launce's departure for Milan.

Nay, 'twill be this hour ere I have done weeping... 2.3

In Milan, Valentine recommends Proteus to the duke. Valentine and Thurio, elderly suitor to Silvia, quarrel about love. When Proteus arrives,

Valentine confesses that he is in love with Silvia. Valentine and Proteus compare their loves, each sure that his lady is the finest ❝. Proteus agrees to help Valentine and Silvia elope. Alone, Proteus admits he is also smitten with Silvia ❝. Speed and Launce exchange rude jokes about their masters' love affairs before heading off to carouse at an alehouse.

Not for the world! Why, man, she is mine own;/And I as rich in having such a jewel/As twenty seas… 2.4

Even as one heat another heat expels,/Or as one nail by strength drives out another… 2.4

Proteus confronts his dilemma: if he loves Silvia, he loses Valentine and Julia. But if he does not love Silvia, he loses himself, more valuable than anyone else. Proteus schemes: once the duke learns of the secret elopement plan, he will banish Valentine.

In Verona, Julia wants to follow her beloved ❝. Julia asks Lucetta to make her breeches and a codpiece so that she can travel to Milan disguised as a boy.

The more thou dammest it up, the more it burns… 2.7

ACT THREE

470 lines

IN THE DUKE OF MILAN'S PALACE

Proteus slyly reveals Valentine's elopement plan to the duke, who is not worried: he locks his daughter up in a tower every night. But Proteus explains that the lovers aim to use a ladder to flee.

Testing Valentine, the duke says he intends to remarry and has his eye on a lady locked away at night. Valentine recommends the use of a rope-ladder concealed under a cloak. When the duke reaches for Valentine's own cloak, a rope-ladder and letter fall from its folds. Outraged to read in the letter, "Silvia, this night I will enfranchise thee," the duke banishes Valentine. Alone, Valentine laments ❞.

And why not death, rather than living torment?/To die is to be banished from myself… 3.1

Proteus pretends to be aghast at his friend's news. Launce contemplates his master's knavery before reading a letter about a milkmaid he adores.

I am but a fool, look you, and yet I have the wit to think my master is a kind of a knave... 3.1

The duke assures Thurio: with Valentine exiled, Silvia may be won, although for now she is grief-stricken by her beloved's departure. When Proteus suggests wooing Silvia with music and poetry, Thurio is delighted. He has already composed a poem for Silvia. Proteus and Thurio depart for town to hire musicians who may set Thurio's poetry to music.

ACT FOUR

473 lines

A FOREST NEAR MANTUA AND IN FRONT OF THE WINDOW OF SILVIA'S ROOM IN MILAN

Banished, Valentine and Speed take refuge in a forest inhabited by outlaws.

Disguised as "Sebastian", Julia has arrived in Milan, where musicians gather below Silvia's window to praise her in song.

Who is Silvia? What is she,/ That all our swains commend her?... 4.2

Julia observes from afar as Silvia, from her upstairs window, rejects the scheming Proteus, who insists that his former love, Julia, is dead. Finally, Silvia promises to give Proteus her portrait in the morning if he will leave her alone.

You have your wish; my will is even this,/ That presently you hie you home to bed... 4.2

Launce lovingly chastises Crab for wetting Silvia's dress. Proteus takes "Sebastian" into his service, instructing 'him' to deliver a ring to Silvia and retrieve the portrait. Julia is outraged: the ring is the one she gave to Proteus back in Verona. Silvia turns the portrait over as promised, but refuses to accept the ring, given to Proteus by a former lover. As "Sebastian" describes Julia, Silvia is moved to learn how Proteus has wronged her. Alone, Julia praises Silvia's virtues.

When a man's servant shall play the cur with him, look you, it goes hard... 4.4

And she shall thank you for't, if e'er you know her... 4.4

ACT FIVE

269 lines

IN AN ABBEY OF MILAN, IN THE DUKE'S PALACE AND IN THE FOREST

Silvia flees Milan with Eglamour. When the duke finds his daughter missing, all agree to go in search of her.

The outlaws have captured Silvia and promise her that their captain will not harm her. Valentine hides while Proteus, accompanied by "Sebastian," tells Silvia that, in exchange for rescuing her from the outlaws, all he asks is "but one fair look." Repeatedly rejected by Silvia, Proteus says he will love her "like a soldier," and take her by force. Valentine steps forward to challenge Proteus. But Proteus begs pardon and Valentine forgives him, prompting a stunned "Sebastian" to faint. When "Sebastian" accidentally produces the ring Proteus gave to Julia in Verona, she must reveal her identity. Although Proteus is mortified to be exposed as a false friend, he is overjoyed to see his love, Julia.

Thou common friend that's without faith or love – /For such is a friend now... 5.4

Behold her that gave aim to all thy oaths,/ And entertained 'em deeply in her heart... 5.4

The outlaws arrive with prisoners: the Duke of Milan and the suitor Thurio. The duke now finds Valentine deserving of Silvia's hand and grants his request that the outlaws be pardoned. As everyone leaves the forest, Valentine tells Proteus he looks forward to their marriages.

I am so far from granting thy request/That I despise thee for thy wrongful suit;/And by and by intend to chide myself/ Even for this time I spend in talking to thee... 4.2

READING THE PLAY

COMPARISON OF PROSE TO VERSE

prose: 25% | verse: 75%

WHO'S WHO

Before the action of the play begins, **Thurio**, a wealthy Milanese man, has already been selected by the **Duke of Milan** to marry his daughter, **Silvia**. When **Valentine** arrives from Verona, Silvia falls in love with him. **Proteus**, despite his betrothal to **Julia**, also falls in love with Silvia and strives to eliminate the competition, beginning with his best friend Valentine. But Silvia remains true to Valentine.
Silvia is in love with Valentine.
Valentine, young and naive, is in love with Silvia.
Thurio, older and wealthy, expects to marry Silvia.
Proteus, young and manipulative, loves Julia, then falls passionately in love with Silvia.

"TITUS AND GISIPPUS," a tale in Giovanni Boccaccio's *The Decameron*, may have served as one source for the main plot of this light comedy in the Italian style. The chivalric romance *Diana Enamorada*, written in Spanish by the Portuguese Jorge de Montemayor, was also consulted, either in the original or an English translation. But the play is not a simple transcription of narrative into drama. Instead, *The Two Gentlemen of Verona*, an early play, already displays Shakespeare's own dramatic style.

Few readers apart from scholars and dramaturgists are today drawn to *The Two Gentlemen of Verona*, even though the play is not devoid of lyrical language and its own breezy, yet thoroughly Shakespearean, comic ambience. *The Two Gentlemen of Verona* also offers telling evidence of Shakespeare's emerging interests and skills as a playwright. The play contains early crystallizations of what were to become strong thematic, structural, and lyrical signatures of Shakespeare's works, the comedies in particular. Silvia's cross-dressing scheme is one example; the strategy was to be employed again in *The Merchant of Venice, As You Like It,* and *Twelfth Night.* The balancing of romantic and comical threads, while often abrupt and crude in *The Two Gentlemen of Verona*, was to be refined in future comedies, most astonishingly in *A Midsummer Night's Dream.*

Characters in the play rarely hold the fascination of readers: Proteus is indeed a great scoundrel but his sudden changes of heart seem incredible and remain unexplored. Valentine, too, disappoints as a romantic hero, especially when he cannot muster the intelligence to realize that Silvia is in love with him. Proteus's servant Launce, however, stands out as a great comic character.

Musicians serenade Silvia in a lithograph by John Gilbert, *c.*1860. This scene has inspired many musical adaptations of the play.

SEEING THE PLAY

Produced by Joseph Papp, the New York Shakespeare Festival's free-swinging musical adaptation of *The Two Gentleman of Verona* was named Musical of the Year in 1971.

PRODUCTIONS OF *The Two Gentlemen of Verona* are rare today, although directors have shown that the play still holds audiences with its freely comical treatment of young lovers. The juiciest roles in the play are Proteus, Silvia, Julia, and Launce. The parts of the lovers include some fine Shakespearean verse language, but the most captivating lines belong to Launce and are in prose.

Following Shakespeare's lifetime, *The Two Gentlemen of Verona* was not revived until the late 18th century. Even then, it was little performed throughout the 19th century, although an operatic rendition by Frederick Reynolds in 1821 proved hugely popular. In 1904, a young Granville-Barker directed the play and even performed in the role of Speed at the Royal Court. In 1898 and 1910, William Poel's productions claimed to offer strictly Elizabethan stagings. Today, *The Two Gentlemen of Verona* remains very much a curiosity, dependent on good direction to be entertaining. In 1970 in Stratford-upon-Avon, Robin Phillips set action around a swimming pool on a college campus with a cast including Helen Mirren as Julia, Ian Richardson as Proteus, and Patrick Stewart as Launce.

Many directors, influenced by Joseph Papp's success with his 1971 musical adaptation in New York, have integrated existing compositions into productions of the play. In 1993, David Thacker used music by composers of the American 1930s.

n his 1988 production at the Swan Theatre, Stratford, Edward Hall staged the action in an updated Italy. The romantic leads were vain and materialistic. The servants, Launce (Mark Hadfield, left) and Speed (John Dougall, right), pictured here with Cassie as Crab, mocked their master's pretensions.

LOVE'S LABOUR'S LOST

Love's Labour's Lost is the playwright's most mannered and profoundly Elizabethan comedy, replete with witty debates, dazzling wordplay, and strongly drawn comic characters. With England's victory over the invading Spanish Armada so recent (1588), early audiences would have found the Spanish braggart Armado a delightful target of comical lambasting. Written around 1595, *Love's Labour's Lost* is an extraordinarily self-conscious play, at once respecting and undermining the comic form. Many see it as an anticomedy, for it ends not in joy but under a cloud of mourning. Nevertheless, it also concludes with the suggestion of marriages to come. Indeed, Shakespeare conceived this play as the first in a sequence of two. The second play, *Love's Labour's Won,* has not survived, but may well have brought separated couples back together to marry and celebrate their unions.

BEHIND THE PLAY

The action takes place in Navarre, a former kingdom situated between present-day France and Spain. In this play Navarre evokes a utopia inspired by the 16th-century literary vogue in France for restricted societies devoted to self-improvement through study. Shakespeare may have chosen to set his play in this French-speaking country after reading the 1586 translation of Pierre de la Primaudaye's *L'Académie Française,* published in 1577. However, the play's setting, in King Ferdinand's castle park, is more pastoral enclosure than historical landscape. Ferdinand's self-imposed rule bars women from approaching the court, which he has converted into a quasi-monastic site devoted to academic pursuits. When the Princess of France and her ladies arrive, however, the men who vowed to avoid women immediately fall in love with them, igniting a plot about the power of love over learning and affairs of state. But the real world intrudes on the revelry and romantic tension of play-acting in the final act, when news of the death of the princess's father forces the play to shift gears. This reminder of mortality introduces the play's final theme: the seasonal cycle of death and rebirth.

Navarre hath made a vow,/ Till painful study shall outwear three years,/ No woman may approach his silent court… 2.1

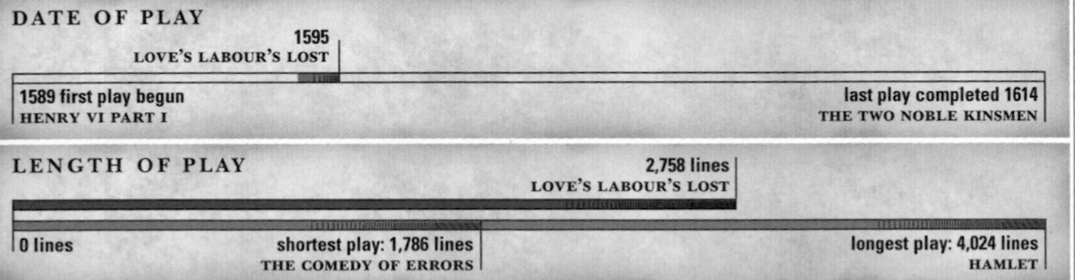

DRAMATIS PERSONAE

The entrance of the King of Navarre and his attendant lords in disguise. They retreat after courting the wrong ladies.

KING FERDINAND OF NAVARRE
314 lines
He turns his court into a pastoral-monastic academy, but its peace is disrupted by the arrival of ladies.

BEROWNE
613 lines
A lord attending the king, he turns everything he sees into "a mirth-moving jest"; he is surprised to fall in love with Rosaline, who he says is the least appealing of the ladies.

LONGAVILLE
68 lines
A lord attending the king, he is "Well fitted in arts, glorious in arms."

DUMAINE
87 lines
A "well-accomplished youth," he is a lord attending the king.

BOYET
232 lines
A French lord, he acts as a go-between.

MARCADE
4 lines
A messenger.

DON ADRIANO DE ARMADO
263 lines
A bombastic Spanish braggart, when he falls in love with Jaquenetta, he calls on the muse of poetry "for I am sure I shall turn sonnet."

Don Armado (John Wood) becomes ludicrous when overtaken by lovesickness.

HOLOFERNES
174 lines
A schoolmaster, he peppers his speech with Latin, or what passes for Latin, and admires the eloquence of Armado.

NATHANIEL
67 lines
A curate, he thanks God for the learning and wit of Holofernes.

DULL
28 lines
A simple constable, he understands very little.

COSTARD
189 lines
A swain, he initially courts Jaquenetta the dairymaid.

MOTE
144 lines
Don Armado's page, a clever boy, he is called "Moth" in some editions.

A FORESTER
5 lines
He receives recompense from the princess.

THE PRINCESS OF FRANCE
285 lines
A fine diplomat, skilled huntress, and great beauty, she discovers that the King of Navarre plans a practical joke, and she devises a trick of her own.

ROSALINE
177 lines
A lady attending the princess, she has "two pitch-balls stuck in her face for eyes," says Berowne, who falls in love with her.

MARIA
43 lines
A lady attending the princess, she falls in love with Longaville.

KATHARINE
46 lines
A lady attending the princess, she falls in love with Dumaine.

JAQUENETTA
17 lines
A dairymaid who is wooed by Armado.

OTHER PLAYERS
Lords and Attendants.

The princess and her ladies mock the lovesick lords by wearing masks and by bestowing attentions on each other's admirers instead of on their own.

PLOT SUMMARY

SIZE OF ACTS

ACT 1	ACT 2	ACT 3	ACT 4	ACT 5
469 lines	268 lines	195 lines	728 lines	1098 lines

ACT ONE

469 lines

IN NAVARRE: THE KING'S CASTLE AND THE SURROUNDING PARK

King Ferdinand is convinced that "Navarre shall be the wonder of the world," if his lords vow to study, fast, sleep little, and see no ladies for three years. Noting that "The mind shall banquet though the body pine," Longaville signs the king's contract. Dumaine also signs, but Berowne hesitates ❝. He notes that the king decreed "no woman shall come within a mile of my court… on pain of losing her tongue" and that any man caught talking with a woman will be shamed. Berowne reminds the king that the Princess of France is expected soon on a diplomatic mission. But the king, who had forgotten this, insists that the princess is an exception since she comes to court by "necessity." Believing that "necessity" will permit the king's rules to be broken freely, Berowne finally signs the oath. When he asks the king if any recreation is planned for them, he is assured that Armado, a visiting Spanish knight who "hath a mint of phrases in his brain," will, with the clown Costard, provide entertainment. As soon as the king has spoken, Costard delivers a florid letter from Armado detailing how he spied Costard speaking with "a child of our grandmother Eve, a female" in the garden. With the company of women forbidden, the king decrees punishment: Costard is to fast for one week, and Armado is to be his "keeper."

Why, all delights are vain, but that most vain/ Which, with pain purchased, doth inherit pain… 1.1

Armado asks Jaquenetta, a dairymaid, to meet him later and confesses his love for her. He orders Costard detained and punished. Alone, he reasons that if Cupid's arrow is too hard for Hercules's club, then his own Spanish rapier barely stands a chance; he is in love ❞.

I do affect the very ground, which is base, where her shoe, which is baser, guided by her foot, which is basest, doth tread… 1.2

Our court shall be a little academe,/Still and contemplative in living art… 1.1

ACT TWO

268 lines

VARIOUS LOCATIONS IN THE PARK SURROUNDING THE KING'S CASTLE

Boyet urges his princess to recall that the purpose of her visit is to discuss the status of the Aquitaine region. While Boyet announces the arrival of the Princess of France, her female attendants discuss the lords of Navarre. Maria once saw the witty Longaville in Normandy; Katharine admired the handsome Dumaine; and Rosaline passed an unforgettable evening in the company of Berowne. The princess concludes that her ladies are in love. The king arrives, apologizing for making them sleep in tents a mile from the court and recalling the oath he and his lords have taken. But the princess would rather discuss politics. The king reads the letter from her father, King of France, and notes a problem: France still owes Navarre 100,000 crowns and, until the sum is paid, Navarre will not give up the Aquitaine. The princess insists that proof of payment will arrive tomorrow. As they depart, each lord asks Boyet for information about his favorite lady: Dumaine asks after Katharine, Longaville after Maria, and Berowne after Rosaline. When they have gone, Boyet notes that the king was also smitten by the princess.

ACT THREE

195 lines

VARIOUS LOCATIONS IN THE PARK SURROUNDING THE KING'S CASTLE

Armado and his page, Mote, discuss love ❝. When Costard arrives, the three experiment with turning the refrain, *l'envoy*, for silly rhymes. Finally, Armado tells Costard

No, my complete master; but to jig off a tune at the tongue's end, canary to it with your feet… 3.1

Beauty is bought by judgement of the eye,/ Not uttered by base sale of chapmen's tongues… 2.1

"I give thee thy liberty, set thee from durance" in exchange for his delivering a love letter to Jaquenetta. Berowne bumps into Costard and also asks him to deliver a letter, but to Rosaline. Alone, Berowne is revolted with himself for having fallen in love with a woman, who he describes as unpleasant as "a German clock."

And I, forsooth, in love!/ I, that have been love's whip... 3.1

ACT FOUR

728 lines

STILL IN THE PARK

The princess is hunting with bow and arrow when Costard delivers the wrong love letter to the ladies. To their amusement, Boyet reads aloud the letter from Armado to Jaquenetta.

By heaven, that thou art fair is most infallible... 4.1

Observing the hunt, Nathaniel and Holofernes, both "book-men," endure the slow wit of Dull, a constable. Jaquenetta arrives with Costard and the letter "from Don Armado." She asks Holofernes, the literate schoolmaster, to read it for her. He and Nathaniel then read aloud Berowne's sonnet to Rosaline. Holofernes advises Jaquenetta to deliver the letter to the king, for "it may concern much."

Nervous but happy at the thought that Rosaline has received his sonnet, Berowne climbs a tree to spy on the king, who is reading aloud his own sonnet to the princess. The king in turn eavesdrops on Longaville reading his sonnet to Maria, while Longaville then observes Dumaine reading his to Katharine. Longaville confronts Dumaine, exposing the fellow lord's forbidden love for the French lady. But the king then steps forward to expose Longaville, adding that Berowne will mock them both for breaking their oaths. With that, Berowne himself descends from the tree to accuse all three men of foolery. Suddenly, Jaquenetta arrives with the important letter. Asked to look over it, Berowne immediately recognizes his own letter to Rosaline and rips it up. When Dumaine pieces the letter back together, though, Berowne finally confesses—they are all four in love. The king asks Berowne to "prove/Our loving lawful, and our faith not torn." Berowne obliges the king by defending love as a greater teacher than books. "A lover's eyes will gaze an eagle blind./A lover's ear will hear the lowest sound." The time has come for them to "lose our oaths to find ourselves," as Berowne puts it. The king proposes they entertain the women in their tents. Berowne agrees, "For revels, dances, masques, and merry hours/Forerun fair Love, strewing her way with flowers."

'Tis more than need./Have at you then, affection's men-at-arms!... 4.3

ACT FIVE

1,098 lines

IN THE KING'S PARK AND THE PRINCESS'S PAVILION

Holofernes and Nathaniel meet up with Armado. Following the king's request, the Spaniard is organizing entertainments for "the Princess at her pavilion in the posteriors of this day, which the rude multitude call the afternoon". Holofernes, impressed by Armado's way with words, recommends that they perform the Nine Worthies, a pageant of great historical conquerors.

Sir, the King is a noble gentleman, and my familiar, I do assure ye... 5.1

In the royal tent, the ladies marvel at the gifts sent to each of them by the lords of Navarre. Boyet reports that the lords are about to arrive disguised as Muscovites. The princess says that each lady, masked, should refuse to dance, and display a gift sent to a different lady, so that each man from Navarre will court the wrong French woman.

The "Muscovites" arrive with African musicians. With the ladies masked and displaying misleading gifts, the king courts Rosaline, thinking she is the princess. Berowne courts the princess, taken for Rosaline. Dumaine and Longaville also mix up their beloveds. Making no headway, the men leave and return without their Russian disguises to invite the ladies to court, but the princess, realizing this means the king breaks his oath, tells him "Nor God nor I delights in perjured men." Rosaline upsets Berowne with her hints of the lords' recent capers.

Thus pour the stars down plagues for perjury./ Can any face of brass hold longer out?... 5.2

Learning that he and the others were, furthermore, tricked to woo the wrong ladies, Berowne directs his anger at Boyet for telling the ladies in advance about the Russian disguises. Just as Boyet prepares to assault Berowne, Costard enters to announce the pageant of the Nine Worthies. The king would rather not see the performance, fearing it will only shame his court further, but Berowne argues for its presentation.

Neither of either; I remit both twain./ I see the trick on't... 5.2

Costard introduces himself as Pompey, Nathaniel follows as Alexander, Holofernes then enters as Judas, and Mote as Hercules. Armado plays Hector. Throughout the pageant, Berowne and the others comment on the play and mock the players. The pageant is halted by Marcade, who arrives from France to report to the princess that her father has died. The princess thanks the king for agreeing to give the Aquitaine to France and prepares to leave. When Berowne insists the lords are in love, the princess explains the ladies thought it was "like a merriment." But the men were serious. Nevertheless, the princess will mourn her father for one year. During that time, she says, the king should live in a hermitage "Remote from all the pleasures of the world." If he is still in love with her following this time, she will be his. Rosaline promises herself to Berowne if, after one year entertaining "the speechless sick," he is able to cure himself of his wounding tongue and wit.

A time, methinks, too short/ To make a world-without-end bargain in... 5.2

The return of the ladies to France disappoints the men. Armado will undergo his own testing phase with Jaquenetta: for three years he plans to farm with her. Finally, Armado introduces singers: a cuckoo, or spring, and an owl, or winter. The seasonal frame of their concluding song captures the play's basic themes: falling in love and mourning.

When daisies pied and violets blue/And lady-smocks all silver white... 5

Our wooing doth not end like an old play;/Jack hath not Jill. These ladies' courtesy/ Might well have made our sport a comedy... 5.2

READING THE PLAY

COMPARISON OF PROSE TO VERSE

prose: 35% | verse: 65%

Readers new to Shakespeare rarely begin with this play, mainly because so many other plays in the Bard's canon are more familiar. *Love's Labour's Lost* features a strong dose of quibbling—brief mock-debates filled with wordplay—and a structure that can seem rigid or repetitive. But these Elizabethan elements eventually grow on readers who initially appreciate the play for its strong comic characters; its masterful blank verse; or its embedded sonnets.

HISTORICAL SOURCES

HENRY OF NAVARRE

In 1589, Henry III of France was murdered and civil wars rocked the country for five years. In 1594, Henry of Navarre, one of three contenders for the French throne, was crowned Henry IV, King of France. News of these events may have influenced Shakespeare, who wrote *Love's Labour's Lost* in 1595, to set the action for this play in the kingdom of Navarre.

Students rarely miss the irresistible parallels between their own campuses or academic settings and the King of Navarre's court: intending to spend three years perusing books in a kind of academic gated community, the lords discover that love offers a greater education than formal learning. But the ladies they love ultimately require them to spend a year proving themselves—either by performing something akin to community services or by living in isolation. Even if the men would not endure such tasks in their own rights, they are motivated to try for the sake of love.

The play's language sometimes shifts suddenly from lofty, umptuous iambic pentameters (as when Berowne discourses n love) to wildly comical prose xchanges, often making fun of peakers who use language as a means f social advancement. When the ompous knight Armado meets the edantic schoolteacher Holofernes, hey spark fireworks of linguistic retension. Much of it is patently omical, but some is exquisitely ubtle, as when Armado wears "by the salt wave of the lediterraneum," meaning ea surrounded by land," a eliberately affected Latinism.

Lovesick Dumaine is observed by Longaville reading his sonnet to Katharine in a 19th-century engraving by J. Thompson, after a painting by S. Woodforde.

SEEING THE PLAY

"None are so surely caught when they are catched,/As wit turned fool..." (5.2). Love is revealed in an idyllic pastoral setting in Bridges-Adams's 1934 production at the Memorial Theatre, Stratford, England.

LOVE'S LABOUR'S LOST gained little attention as a stage production before the modern era. But the very deliberate theatricality that made the play once seem unperformable on stage is now viewed as a deeply modernist subject, ideal for modern drama. Effective productions require actors to work outside the traditional hierarchies of leading, secondary and minor characters. Strong ensemble work is also required to successfully carry off the two squadrons of male and female romantic leads. But even outstanding stage talents cannot give *Love's Labour's Lost* shape unless its director has found a current voice for its most stylized Elizabethan qualities.

In spite of the box-like nature of the four leading male and four leading female parts, the play also offers outstanding roles for character actors. Armado and Holofernes are among the great verbal clowns of Shakespearean drama, and their comic scenes often hold audiences spellbound. Modern directors and designers often feel free to experiment with this play. With the action set exclusively in the park of Navarre's castle, productions may either emphasize the timelessness of the natural setting, or place action in period gardens such as those of an Edwardian manor house. Whatever the setting, though, *Love's Labour's Lost* leads audiences into the exuberant physical and verbal cosmos of Elizabethan comedy.

A dim-witted Nathaniel (Paul Webster, left) and pedantic Holofernes (David Troughton, right) bandy wordplay in a modern-dress production by the Royal Shakespeare Company at the Barbican Theatre, London, 1991.

BEYOND THE PLAY

The Pageant of the Nine Worthies is performed at the princess's pavilion in a production by John Barton at the Royal Shakespeare Theatre, London, 1965.

Never one to mince words, William Hazlitt said of *Love's Labour's Lost* in 1817: "If we were to part with any of the author's comedies, it should be this." Following Shakespeare's time, the play was not staged until 1837. Its lack of clear leading roles made it unattractive to those theaters, such as David Garrick's Drury Lane in London, which built productions around charismatic actors, not least Garrick himself. In addition, the blatantly theatrical aspects of the comedy seemed to welcome neither realistic nor fantastical stagings. The fate of *Love's Labour's Lost* changed when its overall structure was seen to parallel the geometry of period dance. When characters enter in groupings or speak in mannered sequences, they echo patterned repetitions and variations of Elizabethan dance forms. This approach inspired Kenneth Branagh's song and dance screen version in 2000.

Over the last hundred years, *Love's Labour's Lost* has also become a favorite of other directors attuned to the choreographic qualities of the play: William Bridges-Adams, Peter Hall, John Barton, David Jones, Barry Kyle, and Terry Hands are among them. In turn, top actors have been drawn to the roles: Paul Scofield and John Wood have played the role of Don Armado, Ian Richardson and Roger Rees have interpreted Berowne, and Glenda Jackson and Josette Simon have portrayed Rosaline.

The most intrepid production remains Peter Brook's 1946 *Love's Labour's Lost*, in Stratford, England, modeled on the paintings of Watteau. Lighting effects brought the Pageant of the Nine Worthies into a realm of darkness so that news of the King of France's death extended from, rather than broke, the ambience of the play's concluding scene. Many directors have taken the cue from Brook to explore Navarre's castle park as a landscape composed of formal and linked variations on themes of language, love, and death.

Love "is a plague/That Cupid will impose for my neglect/Of his almighty dreadful little might" (3.1). Berowne (Roger Rees), suddenly in love, embraces "Dan Cupid," RSC, 1984.

LITERARY SOURCES

STOCK CHARACTERS
Although the play is based on no single source, its plot and cast list show the imprint of Italian comedies and, in particular, the tradition of the *commedia dell'arte.* Stock characters include the comic servant, the braggart, the pedant, and the harlequin, or fool *(below).* It is possible that Christmas revels of lawyers at Gray's Inn also provided real-life situations that Shakespeare integrated into this play.

A MIDSUMMER NIGHT'S DREAM

NO SHAKESPEAREAN COMEDY OFFERS SUCH A FEAST of magic, humor, music, and spectacle as *A Midsummer Night's Dream.* The title refers to the arrival of summer, which the Elizabethans observed with revels of enchantment, witchcraft, and even madness. The play is accordingly rich in otherworldly transgressions. Boundaries between reality and illusion are blurred in a nocturnal forest, where magic swirls through the dreams of lovers, and charms are cast on actors rehearsing a play. No performance of the play, usually dated 1595–96, was recorded during Shakespeare's lifetime. Yet the play's elaborate framing subject, the marriage of Theseus and Hippolyta, is among the reasons *A Midsummer Night's Dream* is thought to have been commissioned for an important wedding celebration and therefore performed for a court audience.

BEHIND THE PLAY

THIS IS ONE OF FEW SHAKESPEAREAN PLAYS not based on a single source story. The playwright drew freely from Latin (Ovid's *Metamorphoses,* and *The Golden Ass* by Apuleius) as well as English sources (Chaucer's *The Canterbury Tales*), but Shakespeare also recycled superstitions and folk beliefs he knew from his upbringing in Warwickshire. *A Midsummer Night's Dream* is set in ancient Athens, although this Athens closely resembles Shakespeare's England—Elizabethans did not view the past through a strict historical lens. The play's action does not actually unfold on midsummer night. Instead, action is set over four days leading up to May 1. May Day was a traditional wedding date, suitable for the marriage festivities closing this play. However, the heart of the play, set in nocturnal woods of magic and mischief, finds inspiration in the Elizabethan midsummer revels that provide the title. In the opening act of *A Midsummer Night's Dream,* the harsh law of Athens prevents young lovers from marrying. In the central three acts of the play, the lovers and others are changed by magical events in woods near Athens. In the last act, the action returns to Athens, where weddings of the lovers can at last be celebrated.

And as imagination bodies forth/ The forms of things unknown, the poet's pen/ Turns them to shapes, and gives to airy nothing/ A local habitation and a name… 5.1

DRAMATIS PERSONAE

Once Oberon has cast his spell, Titania (Nicola Redmond) wakes from her sleep and is bewitched by the first creature she sees—Bottom (Paul Bradley), who has been "translated" into an ass.

THESEUS
233 lines
Duke of Athens, he upholds ancient Athenian law and tells Hermia: "To you your father should be as a god."

Puck (Mary Honer) is a good-hearted mischief-maker who relishes administering the magic potions to the lovers.

EGEUS
41 lines
Father to Hermia, he insists she marry Demetrius.

LYSANDER
178 lines
In love with Hermia, he remains faithful until Puck accidentally causes him to dote on Helena instead.

DEMETRIUS
134 lines
Suitor to Hermia, he is pursued by Helena and eventually, having been bewitched by Oberon, falls in love with her.

PHILOSTRATE
24 lines
Master of the Revels to Theseus.

HIPPOLYTA
34 lines
Queen of the Amazons, she has recently been conquered by Theseus, to whom she is betrothed.

HERMIA
166 lines
In love with Lysander, she cannot believe her eyes when Lysander suddenly dotes on Helena.

HELENA
229 lines
She is in love with Demetrius, no matter how much he tries to discourage her.

ARTISANS OR "RUDE MECHANICALS"

PETER QUINCE
118 lines
A carpenter (who plays the "Prologue" in the artisans' play), he proposes that the cast of *Pyramus and Thisbe* rehearse at night in the woods to avoid detection.

NICK BOTTOM
261 lines
A weaver (playing "Pyramus"), he becomes Titania's unlikely lover when Oberon casts a spell on her.

FRANCIS FLUTE
57 lines
A bellows mender (playing "Thisbe").

SNUG
20 lines
A joiner (playing "Lion"), he is "slow of study," and finds his part hard to learn.

TOM SNOUT
16 lines
A tinker (playing "Wall"), he worries that the lion will scare the audience.

ROBIN STARVELING
12 lines
A tailor (in the artisans' play "Moonshine"), he confesses that he, for one, is afraid of the lion.

SUPERNATURALS

OBERON
226 lines
King of the fairies, he uses magic to take revenge on his queen, Titania, when she refuses to turn over to him the Indian boy she has recently adopted.

TITANIA
158 lines
Queen of the fairies, she is led to dote on Bottom by magic. She provides him with exotic luxuries, as when she commands her fairies: "And pluck the wings from painted butterflies,/To fan the moonbeams from his sleeping eyes."

The leafy robes of Titania (Jemma Redgrave) evoke the woodland setting of the play.

PUCK
209 lines
Also known as Robin Goodfellow, or Hobgoblin, he is a trickster figure who pulls pranks and brings good luck as "that merry wanderer of the night." He serves Oberon, king of the fairies.

PEASEBLOSSOM, COBWEB, MOTH, AND MUSTARDSEED
5; 5; 3; 6 lines
Fairies attending on Titania, they sing, dance, and serve the whims of their queen.

OTHER PLAYERS
Other fairies attending on Oberon and Titania. Attendants of Theseus and Hippolyta.

PLOT SUMMARY

SIZE OF ACTS

ACT 1	ACT 2	ACT 3	ACT 4	ACT 5
359 lines	429 lines	684 lines	265 lines	428 lines

ACT ONE 359 lines

THE PALACE OF THESEUS AND THE HOME OF PETER QUINCE

Duke Theseus and Hippolyta discuss their wedding, only four days away. The mood shifts as Athenians arrive to present their problems. Egeus wants his daughter, Hermia, to marry Demetrius, but she is in love with Lysander. Theseus reminds Hermia that Athenian law requires her to marry the man of her father's choosing. Punishment for disobedience is severe: "Either to die the death, or to abjure/For ever the society of men." Hermia has until Theseus's wedding day to decide which it shall be. But Hermia and Lysander prefer to reject the law altogether by running away 66. Hermia's best friend, Helena, complains that she loves Demetrius, but he only has eyes for Hermia. Hermia explains that everything will be fine once she and Lysander have left Athens for the woods. Alone, Helena reflects on the blindness of love 99.

Or if there were a sympathy in choice,/ War, death, or sickness did lay siege to it... 1.1

How happy some o'er other some can be!/ Through Athens I am thought as fair as she... 1.1

Common laborers gather to plan rehearsals of their play, *Pyramus and Thisbe*. It shall be given for Theseus "on his wedding day at night," as Peter Quince explains. Nick Bottom plays Pyramus, "A lover that kills himself, most gallant, for love." Bottom is sure he can play the role well 66. He is also eager to play a tyrant, however, even though there is no tyrant in the play. Peter Quince informs the cast that they will rehearse in the woods to avoid the prying of Athenians.

That will ask some tears in the true performing of it... 1.1

ACT TWO 429 lines

A WOOD NEAR ATHENS

Puck remembers that Oberon, the fairy king, is to hold revels in the woods tonight. But the king is angry at his queen, Titania, who keeps for herself a boy Oberon would like for his own entourage. Oberon and Titania arrive, quarreling about past lovers and the Indian boy she has adopted 66. When Titania leaves, Oberon remembers a herb for love charms. He sends Puck to fetch it. With the juice of this magic flower,

These are the forgeries of jealousy... 2.1

I must go seek some dewdrops here,/And hang a pearl in every cowslip's ear... 2.1

Oberon may enchant Titania. Invisible to the humans, Oberon hears Demetrius insist he is revolted by the sight of Helena. But Helena says she would rather die than not follow him. When Puck returns with the magic flower, Oberon prepares to trick Titania, and he also instructs Puck to use some magic juice on a young Athenian who rejects the love of a sweet lady. But Oberon offers scant information: "Thou shalt know the man/By the Athenian garments he hath on." Meanwhile, Titania listens to fairy music. As she slumbers, Oberon casts a spell so that Titania will fall in love with the first creature she beholds upon waking.

And even for that do I love you the more./ I am your spaniel... 2.1

You spotted snakes with double tongue,/ Thorny hedgehogs, be not seen... 2.2

Puck happens on the happy couple, Lysander and Hermia, sleeping chastely near one another. He is delighted to discover a youth in "Athenian garments," in Oberon's words, and applies the magic liquid to Lysander's eyelids. At this point, Demetrius rushes through, chased by an exhausted Helena. Pausing to rest, she awakens Lysander. Due to the magic juice, Lysander falls madly in love with Helena, who departs in confusion. But Lysander, absolutely sincere, pursues her eagerly. When Hermia is awakened by a nightmare to discover herself alone, she anxiously begins to search for her missing Lysander.

O, I am out of breath in this fond chase./ The more my prayer, the lesser is my grace... 2.2

ACT THREE

684 lines

STILL IN THE WOOD NEAR ATHENS

The artisans admire their wooded rehearsal space, but Bottom worries that the ladies of Theseus's wedding audience will not accept the suicide of Pyramus, whom he plays. Puck discovers the rehearsal and, when Bottom is alone in the bushes, Puck transforms the actor's head into that of an ass. Bottom consequently rejoins the rehearsal to terrify his fellow actors, who scatter. To console himself, Bottom begins to sing. Awakening, Titania falls instantly and passionately in love with the ass-headed Bottom. Titania commands her fairy attendants to serve the bemused man.

I pray thee, gentle mortal, sing again!/Mine ear is much enamoured of thy note... 3.1

Puck reports to Oberon on Titania's new lover. Puck also says there are "rude mechanicals" rehearsing in the wood. He confirms, too, that the Athenian youth has been enchanted as instructed. But just then, Demetrius and Hermia appear. Hermia accuses Demetrius of harming her beloved Lysander. Oberon sees that Puck has enchanted the wrong Athenian youth, Lysander, not Demetrius. Oberon therefore applies magic onto the eyes of sleeping Demetrius so that he will awake in love with Helena, who still loves him. Helena arrives with Lysander still in hot pursuit, but she is sure she is being mocked. Hermia appears, looking for an explanation from Lysander. But Helena is convinced that even Hermia is part of the conspiracy to trick her. Instead, Hermia is much dismayed to see both men now doting on Helena. She accuses Helena of seducing Lysander. The men leave to fight a duel over Helena, who runs off. Hermia remains alone, amazed.

My mistress with a monster is in love... 3.2

Out, dog! Out, cur! Thou drivest me past the bounds/Of maiden's patience... 3.2

O Helen, goddess, nymph, perfect, divine –/ To what, my love, shall I compare thine eyne?... 3.2

Lo, she is one of this confederacy./Now I perceive they have conjoined all three/To fashion this false sport in spite of me... 3.2

Thou seest these lovers seek a place to fight./ Hie therefore, Robin, overcast the night... 3.2

King Oberon commands Puck to prevent the men from fighting. Also, Puck should remove the spell from Lysander so that he thinks all has been merely a dream. Oberon shall attend to Titania and "all things will be peace." When Lysander and Demetrius begin to fight, Puck tricks them by impersonating their voices. When they fall asleep, Puck squeezes magic juice on the eyes of Lysander to remove the spell cast by accident.

ACT FOUR

265 lines

THE WOOD NEAR ATHENS AND THE HOUSE OF PETER QUINCE

Bottom, still ass-headed, enjoys the luxurious attention of the fairies, and Titania entwines herself around his body as "female ivy so/Enrings the barky fingers of the elm." Oberon triumphantly reports to Puck that he has finally won the coveted Indian boy from the bewitched Titania. When Oberon removes the spell from Titania's eyes, she remarks: "My Oberon, what visions have I seen! Methought I was enamoured of an ass." The fairy rulers dance and make amends.

Welcome, good Robin. Seest thou this sweet sight?/ Her dotage now I do begin to pity... 4.1

Theseus and others enter the wood on a May Day hunt and awaken the lovers. Theseus wonders how the young Athenians came there. "I cannot truly say how I came here," Lysander replies.

How comes this gentle concord in the world,/That hatred is so far from jealousy/To sleep by hate, and fear no enmity?... 4.1

Demetrius explains that he himself followed Hermia, and Helena came after him. But then his love for Hermia "melted as the snow."

My lord, fair Helen told me of their stealth,/ Of this their purpose hither to this wood... 4.1

Announcing that both couples shall be married, Theseus departs. The lovers remain mystified. "It seems to me/ That yet we sleep, we dream" Demetrius remarks. Elsewhere, Bottom is also confused: "Methought I was—there is no man can tell what."

Back at Quince's house, the "rude mechanicals" wonder where Bottom could be, for "the play is marred" without his participation. When Bottom shows up, the actors are delighted and prepare to go to the palace of Theseus.

ACT FIVE

428 lines

THE PALACE OF THESEUS

More strange than true. I never may believe/These antique fables, nor these fairy toys... 5.1

Theseus marvels at the story of the lovers. For the wedding festivities, Theseus chooses from a list of available diversions. Against the advice of Philostrate, Theseus selects the "tedious brief scene" of *Pyramus and Thisbe.* Quince sets the tone of the performance in his prologue: "If we offend, it is with our good will." He goes on to introduce in mime the characters and plot of the play. Pyramus and Thisbe are in love, but separated by Wall, through whom they whisper. With help from Moonshine, the lovers arrange to meet at a tomb. Thisbe arrives first, but is frightened off by Lion, leaving her mantle stained with blood. Snug, playing Lion, reassures his audience that he is not really a lion. Pyramus finds the mantle, assumes Thisbe dead, then kills himself with a blade. Thisbe returns and, seeing her beloved dead, kills herself with his dagger. Thisbe delivers the last line as she prepares suicide: "Asleep, my love?/What, dead, my dove?"

Bottom offers to perform an epilogue, but Theseus would rather dance. At midnight, Theseus announces it is "fairy time" and the revelers go to bed. Puck then enters to initiate the magic "time of night" and to "sweep the dust behind the door". Titania and Oberon reenter to bless the house of Theseus. Puck then offers that the play may have been "but a dream".

If we shadows have offended,/Think but this, and all is mended... 5.1

Now until the break of day/ Through this house each fairy stray... 5.1

READING THE PLAY

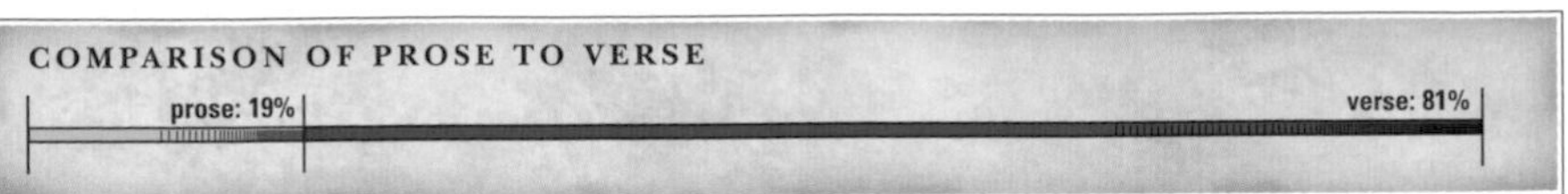

EVERYTHING ABOUT *A Midsummer Night's Dream* seems to be designed for the staging of spectacle, and yet the poetic language of the play makes for excellent reading. In fact, the play is so strong as literature that its lyrical speeches were, for many generations, deemed better suited to reading than staging. In 1818, William Hazlitt argued that *A Midsummer Night's Dream* was a "closet drama," that it was not written for the stage.

WHO'S WHO

Demetrius has been chosen as the husband of **Hermia**, but she is in love with **Lysander**, who is made—by Puck's magic—to fall in love with **Helena**, who is in love with **Demetrius**, who is eventually bewitched into returning her love.

For this play, Shakespeare employed a wide variety of poetic effects. The scintillating verbal palette of the play includes not only the prose exchanges of the "rude mechanicals," but also spells and charms, songs, rhyming couplets of iambic pentameter and enchanting blank verse. Many of the longer speeches are so beautiful that they are read for their poetry alone.

It is relatively easy to keep track of the characters in *A Midsummer Night's Dream.* Artisans, fairies, and members of the court of Theseus appear in clear clusters. The four Athenian lovers, however, are sometimes as difficult for readers as for Puck to sort out. Hermia needs to be distinguished from the similarly-named Helena. Although the language of the play dazzles, disquieting matters are not far below the surface of the festival themes associated with weddings. Here, violence, lust, jealousy, madness, nightmares, banishment, and even death haunt the Athenian woods.

LANGUAGE NOTE

DOTING ON DOTING

Much of the action in this play revolves around real or illusory love. Appearing more frequently in *A Midsummer Night's Dream* than in any other play by Shakespeare is the word "dote," which came to English from the early German *dotten,* meaning "to be foolish, imbecilic, or deranged." The same root appears in the English adjective "dotty", used today to describe a harmlessly foolish person.

The fairy retinue of Titania and Oberon that lies at the heart of *A Midsummer Night's Dream* has inspired generations of artists and stage designers. Paul Gustave Doré's *Les Fées,* 1873.

SEEING THE PLAY

ON STAGE

PETER BROOK

Born in 1925, Peter Brook is a theatrical innovator. His daring and imaginative productions have shaped understanding of Shakespeare since the 1950s. He has contended that the director is the main creative force in any production. Long associated with the RSC, he later set up a theater company in Paris, France.

Peter Brook's production of *A Midsummer Night's Dream* in 1970 used circus acts, trapezes, catwalks, and feats of balance and juggling to inject a feeling of danger into the world of the play.

FOR A LONG TIME, *A Midsummer Night's Dream* was a pretext to show off dazzling costumes and create a magical on-stage atmosphere. But for the last century, productions of *A Midsummer Night's Dream* have rarely allowed the masque components of the play to overwhelm its dramatic core and comical threads.

"Well roared, Lion!" (5.1). Jonathan McGuinness played Snug/Lion with Jules Werner as Flute/Thisbe at The Watermill, Berkshire, in 2003.

The evolution of the roles of Oberon and Titania perhaps offers the best measure of the play's transformation in theaters. Before World War I, the fairy king and queen were static creatures parading about the stage in lavish, stunning costumes with their exotic entourages. But from the early 20th century, directors have preferred to cast talented actors in these roles, and have paid due attention to the rich poetic language of their speaking parts. The Athenian lovers are among the most challenging romantic leads in the comedies of Shakespeare. Many actors struggle to give the parts independent characterization. A sure source of pleasure remains the "rude mechanicals" and their engrossing preoccupation with the tasks of presenting a play. Actors continue to show that these are among Shakespeare's most indestructibly comic scenes.

Max Reinhardt's 1935 Hollywood movie, based on a Broadway production of the play, was a regal and glamorous spectacle. James Cagney starred as Bottom, with Olivia de Havilland as Titania.

BEYOND THE PLAY

Cyril Guei played Bottom to Sophie Duez's Titania in *Le Songe d'Une Nuit d'Été,* at Le Théâtre de Nice, France, in 2003.

EVEN AS EARLY AS 1662, following the reopening of English theaters shut down by Parliament in 1642, *A Midsummer Night's Dream* was performed not as a drama but as a music spectacle. Samuel Pepys, who attended the 1662 production, noted with his signature intolerance that it was "the most insipid ridiculous play that ever I saw in my life." The 1692 opera version, *The Fairy Queen,* by Henry Purcell, and Felix Mendelssohn's 1826 "Overture to A Midsummer Night's Dream," along with many other musical compositions, including Benjamin Britten's opera and John Neumeier's 1977 ballet, have contributed to the play's reputation for inspiring leading composers.

In the early 20th century, directors began to turn their attention to the play as drama, attracting outstanding actors to lead roles. John Gielgud appeared as Oberon, Vivien Leigh, Peggy Ashcroft, and Judi Dench as Titania, and Charles Laughton as Bottom. Numerous directors have since found themes of violence and sex central to the play, and most now stage the Athenian woods as a place of danger, where some real thing, if not reality itself, is at stake.

Some directors have sought to preserve the otherworldly magic of the play by employing the naive visual idiom of children's picture stories, puppet theater or even comic books. As early as 1932, director William Bridges-Adam employed deliberately childlike "special effects" such as tinsel for the fairy scenes. A related approach was taken by director Christine Edzard, whose 2001 film, *Children's Midsummer Night's Dream,* is played exclusively by youngsters. But Shakespearean magic may lie closer to home. The Brunton Youth Theatre Company of Musselburgh retitled their 2002 adaptation *Not Exactly a Midsummer Night's Dream* and set the action in woods off a highway near their own town of Musselburgh, Scotland.

A program cover for a 1957 production at The Royal Opera House, Covent Garden, London, of the ballet *The Fairy Queen.* The music used, composed by Henry Purcell in 1692 was based on *A Midsummer Night's Dream.*

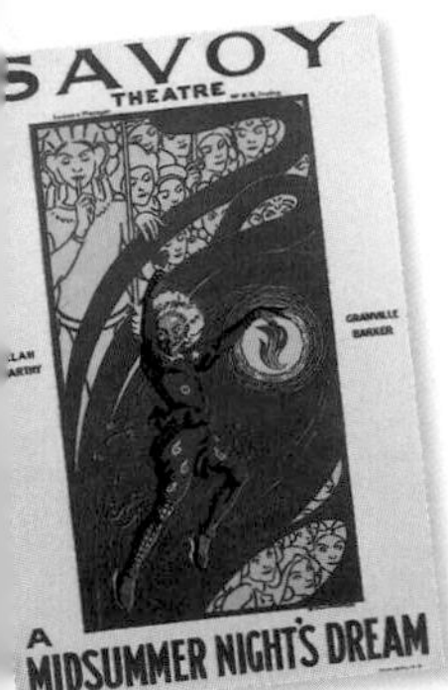

Harley Granville Barker's production at the Savoy Theatre, London, 1914, used the full text for the first time in centuries.

The MERCHANT OF VENICE

IN SHAKESPEARE'S MOST SUSPENSEFUL COMEDY, *The Merchant of Venice,* life and love can only be won by risking their loss. The play was written in 1594–97, but there is no trace of a performance during the reign of Elizabeth I. Records do show that the play was given twice at the court of James I, in 1604 and 1605. Shakespeare's sources for *The Merchant of Venice* included a story found in Giovanni Fiorentino's *The Simpleton* and Marlowe's 1589 play, *The Jew of Malta,* in which Barabas epitomizes the stock character of the evil Jew. Anti-Semitism was rife in Shakespeare's London; audiences of the day, primed to view Shylock as a natural-born villain, would therefore have been surprised to find any of his speeches moving. Since the Holocaust, however, productions of *The Merchant of Venice* have challenged the age-old caricature of the Jew.

BEHIND THE PLAY

BEFORE THE ACTION OF THE PLAY begins, two worlds have been established: one in Venice and the other in Belmont. In Venice, resentment and mistrust divide Jewish and Christian inhabitants. Shylock, a Jew and moneylender, carries an old grudge against the Christian merchant Antonio, who has abused him repeatedly in the Rialto. One of the islands comprising the city of Venice, the Rialto was the location of business transactions and commerce. Shylock despises Antonio not only for treating him as a subhuman "cur," but also for lending money at no interest to his business associates, thereby reducing Shylock's profits. When Shylock sees a legalistic opportunity to exact revenge early in the play, he seizes it without hesitation. In nearby Belmont, another kind of law must be observed. Portia, a wealthy heiress, is morally bound to respect the wishes of her late father, who fashioned an elaborate test for her potential suitors. Those who fail the test must renounce the right to marry. In both Belmont and Venice, characters are in search of justice, revenge, marriage, wealth, or happiness. But in order to achieve any goal, they must negotiate inflexible laws and take high risks.

> **If you prick us, do we not bleed? If you tickle us, do we not laugh? If you poison us, do we not die? And if you wrong us, shall we not revenge?...** 3.1

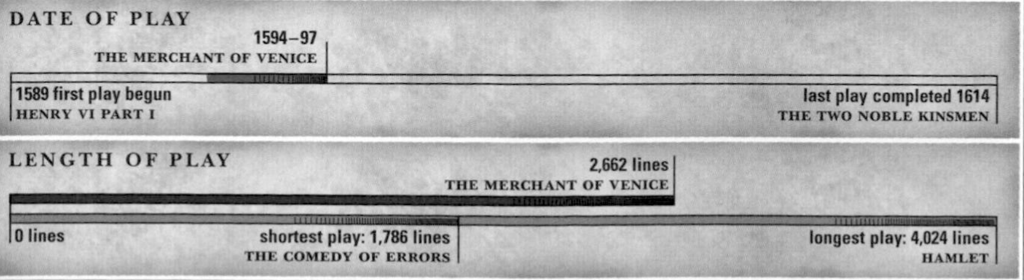

DRAMATIS PERSONAE

DUKE OF VENICE
57 lines
He must uphold the letter of Venetian law, lest "there is no force in the decrees of Venice."

DUKE OF MOROCCO
103 lines
Suitor to Portia, he makes the mistake of choosing the gold casket.

PRINCE OF ARRAGON
65 lines
Suitor to Portia, he makes the mistake of choosing the silver casket.

ANTONIO
188 lines
A merchant of Venice, he is initially depressed—"in sooth I know not why I am so sad"—but after he has guaranteed "with a pound of flesh" a loan for his best friend, Bassanio, he has something tangible to occupy his mind.

BASSANIO
336 lines
Suitor to Portia, he loves his friend Antonio unconditionally.

SOLANIO
56 lines
Friend to Antonio and Bassanio.

GRATIANO
175 lines
Friend to Antonio and Bassanio; "too wild, too rude, and too bold of voice" for some, he is a good husband for Nerissa.

SALERIO
128 lines
Another friend to Antonio and Bassanio.

LORENZO
179 lines
In love with Jessica, he anticipates inheriting Shylock's estate.

SHYLOCK
355 lines
A rich Jew and money-lender, he is, according to the duke, "an inhuman wretch,/Uncapable of pity, void and empty/From any dram of mercy." He has been mocked and scorned by Antonio, against whom he seeks revenge.

Shylock (Alec Guinness) looks to the law to exact the penalty and forfeit of his bond: a pound of flesh from Antonio.

Portia (Katharine Hepburn), as "Balthasar," demands Shylock shed not a drop of Christian blood and cut exactly one pound of flesh.

TUBAL
12 lines
A Jew, he supplies Shylock with ducats to be lent at no interest to Antonio.

LAUNCELOT GOBBO
168 lines
A clown, servant to Shylock, he fears he will become "a Jew if I serve the Jew any longer."

OLD GOBBO
37 lines
Father to Launcelot, he is a blind, "honest, exceeding poor man."

LEONARDO
2 lines
Servant to Bassanio.

BALTHASAR
1 line
Servant to Portia, she trusts him to carry a secret message to her cousin, Doctor Bellario of Padua.

STEPHANO
8 lines
Servant to Portia.

PORTIA
588 lines
A rich heiress of Belmont, she resents the test of the caskets devised for her suitors. When she realizes that her beloved Bassanio is devoted to Antonio, she disguises herself as a doctor of law, "Balthasar," to save Antonio's life.

NERISSA
84 lines
She focuses on helping Portia manage her suitors until she discovers she has one herself in the person of Gratiano.

JESSICA
86 lines
Daughter to Shylock, she may be of his blood but claims she is not of "his manners"; she elopes with the Christian Lorenzo.

OTHER PLAYERS
Nobles of Venice, Officer of the Court of Justice, Gaoler, Servants, and other Attendants.

PLOT SUMMARY

SIZE OF ACTS

ACT 1	ACT 2	ACT 3	ACT 4	ACT 5
499 lines	677 lines	665 lines	495 lines	326 lines

ACT ONE

499 lines

IN PUBLIC AREAS OF VENICE AND IN THE BELMONT HOME OF PORTIA

Antonio asks "why I am so sad." Solanio and Salerio suspect he frets about his merchandise, but Gratiano distracts the group with a confused endorsement of mirth. By asking Antonio for help, Bassanio begins to cure his sad friend. Bassanio urgently needs to borrow more funds from Antonio to woo Portia. Antonio has no money, but will help Bassanio borrow the funds.

Let me play the fool;/ With mirth and laughter let old wrinkles come... 1.1

Portia is also sad. She finds her suitors unsatisfactory: the Neapolitan prince is obsessed with horses; the English baron speaks nothing but English; and the German candidate appears to be alcoholic. Portia's late father left a will in which he devised a contest for her suitors, and she is required to respect his wishes. Suitors must stand before her and choose one of three chests in gold, silver, and lead. Attending Portia, Nerissa reminds her that no suitor will choose rightly "but one who you shall rightly love."

If to do were as easy as to know what were good to do, chapels had been churches... 1.2

"Shylock the Jew" is sure that Antonio hates "our sacred nation". When Antonio offers to guarantee a loan to Bassanio, Shylock sees a chance to get even with Antonio, who has long insulted him. Shylock echoes Antonio's old taunts: "Is it possible/A cur can lend three thousand ducats?" Shylock finally agrees in "a merry sport" to lend ducats at no interest save a "pound/Of your fair flesh, to be cut off and taken/In what part of your body pleaseth me." Bassanio objects, but Antonio sees no threat—his ships are coming in well before the appointed date of repayment. "I will seal unto this bond," Antonio tells Shylock.

How like a fawning publican he looks./I hate him for he is a Christian... 1.3

In Belmont is a lady richly left,/And she is fair, and, fairer than that word,/Of wondrous virtues... 1.1

ACT TWO

677 lines

THE HOUSE OF PORTIA, STREETS OF VENICE AND THE HOUSE OF SHYLOCK

In Belmont, the Prince of Morocco presents himself as another suitor to Portia, who explains the risks: if he should choose the wrong casket, he must agree never to marry.

Mislike me not for my complexion,/The shadowed livery of the burnished sun... 2.1

Launcelot, a Christian, debates whether he should run away from his Jewish master, Shylock. Bassanio arrives to answer two requests. First, he accepts Launcelot as his own servant. Next, he agrees to let Gratiano accompany him to Belmont, but on the condition that he tone down his wild behavior. At Shylock's house, his daughter Jessica is sorry to learn that Launcelot will leave, for "Our house is hell, and thou a merry devil." But she, too, plans to escape soon, to convert to Christianity and marry Lorenzo.

Certainly my conscience will serve me to run from this Jew my master... 2.2

Lorenzo wants Gratiano and Salerio, who are disguised as torch-bearers of a masque, to join him before Shylock's home. While Shylock dines reluctantly at Bassanio's house, Jessica, disguised as a boy, takes Shylock's ducats and the family jewels and elopes with Lorenzo.

The Prince of Morocco must choose one of the three caskets. He rereads the inscriptions, and is drawn to the gold casket: "Who chooseth me shall gain what many men desire." But inside it is a scroll reminding: "All that glisters is not gold." Back in Venice, rumors circulate that Shylock has discovered both his daughter and ducats missing, and has called on the duke for justice. In Belmont, Portia receives an unexpected suitor, the Prince of Arragon. He is seduced by the inscription of the silver casket: "Who chooseth me shall get as much as he deserves." But the scroll within the casket says his choice was foolish. Portia is about to retire when a messenger reports that a Venetian suitor now sails to her.

Some god direct my judgement! Let me see:/ I will survey th'inscriptions back again... 2.7

ACT THREE

665 lines

IN A STREET OF VENICE AND IN BELMONT, IN THE HOME AND GARDEN OF PORTIA

Salerio and Solanio cross paths with Shylock, who warns that Antonio should "look to his bond." The Christians wonder why Shylock cares about the bond, since a pound of human flesh has no value. But Shylock disagrees: "it will feed my revenge." Shylock asks them to consider that Jews are as human as Christians: "If you prick us, do we not bleed? If you tickle us, do we not laugh?". When his friend Tubal arrives, Shylock is first devastated to learn that his daughter has disappeared with his money and heirlooms, then delighted to receive confirmation of Antonio's financial demise.

To bait fish withal. If it wil feed nothing else, it will feed my revenge... 3.1

Portia would be happy for Bassanio to stay awhile before choosing a casket, but he is eager to be done with the contest. Portia requests music offering her favorite suitor crucial clues. Using his wits, Bassanio selects the lead casket. He cannot believe his good fortune: the casket contains Portia's portrait. While Bassanio has gained a bride, Gratiano has fallen in love with Nerissa. Venetian friends suddenly arrive with a letter from Antonio. His ships have all "miscarried" and Shylock will have his pound of

I pray you tarry, pause a d or two/Before you hazard for in choosing wrong/ I lose your company... 3.2

So may the outward show be least themselves./ The world is still deceive with ornament... 3.2

O sweet Portia,/Here are a few of the unpleasant'st words/That ever blotted paper!... 3.2

flesh. Portia swiftly organizes the immediate weddings of both couples before Bassanio departs to help Antonio. Portia gives Bassanio a ring, warning him never to part with it.

In Venice, Shylock informs Antonio: "I'll have my bond." But in Belmont, Portia secretly arranges to help Antonio, dear to her because Bassanio loves him. She appoints Lorenzo and Jessica to oversee her household, claiming she and Nerissa will live in a monastery until their husbands return. Portia sends her servant Balthasar to Padua, where her cousin, a doctor of law named Bellario, is to provide certain needed items urgently. She and Nerissa are to disguise themselves as men of law.

ACT FOUR

495 lines

IN VENICE, AT A COURT OF JUSTICE AND IN THE STREET

The duke invites Shylock to show mercy. But Shylock says that he has reasons for hating Antonio. The duke is about to close the case when Nerissa, disguised as a clerk, presents a letter from Bellario, the learned legal expert whose opinion the duke requested. The duke reads the letter aloud: Bellario, fallen ill, recommends in his stead a young legal doctor of Rome named Balthasar. Portia arrives, disguised as "Balthasar", to argue that mercy is higher than justice, higher than kings, "an attribute to God himself". But Shylock cares nothing for such arguments: "I crave the law," he says. "Balthasar" says Shylock is within his rights to carry out

I have possessed your grace of what I purpose,/And by our holy Sabbath have I sworn/To have the due and forfeit of my bond... 4.1

The quality of mercy is not strained,/It droppeth as the gentle rain from heaven/Upon the place beneath... 4.1

Hath not a Jew eyes?
Hath not a Jew hands, organs, dimensions, senses... 3.1

the letter of the law. Antonio bids Bassanio goodbye, and readies for death. Shylock is eager to take his revenge. But "Balthasar" warns he must only take flesh, and not a "drop of Christian blood." Realizing the task impossible, Shylock agrees to settle instead for three times the money due. But "Balthasar," examining the bond carefully in order to apply the law to the letter, argues that it must be exactly one pound of flesh. If the scales tip even a hair, Shylock will be condemned to death. Shylock proposes to take merely the principal money instead, but "Balthasar" continues: for attempting to take the life of a citizen, Shylock must by law forfeit his property. "Nay, take my life and all!" says Shylock.

Antonio demands that Shylock's property be passed on to Lorenzo and Jessica, and insists that the Jew "presently become a Christian." A subdued Shylock accepts the conditions and, "not well," leaves the court. In gratitude, Bassanio offers "Balthasar" anything he desires. Alarmingly, "Balthasar" desires the ring that Bassanio vowed would never leave his finger. Nerissa boasts that she too can recover the ring that she gave her husband and Portia urges her to try.

ACT FIVE

326 lines

BEFORE THE HOUSE OF PORTIA IN BELMONT

On a beautiful moonlit night, Jessica and Lorenzo enjoy Belmont. Musicians sweeten the atmosphere, prompting Lorenzo to observe that music has the power to change a person's nature ❝. On her return home, Portia also reflects on the mystery of music and moonlight. Finally, Bassanio introduces Portia to Antonio, "To whom I am so infinitely bound."

The reason is your spirits are attentive... 5.1

However, Belmont is not a utopia: Gratiano and Nerissa quarrel about the missing ring. And Bassanio confesses that he, too, gave away his ring to "Balthasar" ❝. Antonio admits that he is the "unhappy subject of these quarrels," and he offers his soul as collateral so that Bassanio will never again break a vow to Portia. The new husbands are amazed when their wives produce the missing rings and rejoice to learn that "Portia was the doctor" and Nerissa "her clerk." Portia gives Antonio a letter proving that three of his ships were not in fact wrecked. Antonio thanks her for having given him "life and living." The last lines belong to Gratiano, who is thinking about "couching with the doctor's clerk."

Sweet Portia,/If you did know to whom I gave the ring,/If you did know for whom I gave the ring... 5.1

Here will we sit and let the sounds of music/Creep in our ears; soft stillness and the night/Become the touches of sweet harmony... 5.1

READING THE PLAY

COMPARISON OF PROSE TO VERSE

prose: 21% | verse: 79%

WITH THE HIGH DRAMA of its courtroom scene, the fairytale world of Belmont, the intense enmity between Christians and Jews, and a number of outstanding speeches, comical and sentimental, *The Merchant of Venice* makes for captivating reading. Shylock alternately moves and revolts his readers, shifting as he does from a fully rounded character to a two-dimensional villain. Portia also presents a mixed persona, initially the morose rich daughter, later the brilliant wife disguised as a male doctor of law.

"You call me misbeliever, cut-throat dog,/And spit upon my Jewish gaberdine" (1.3). Shylock meets Antonio and Bassanio on the streets of Venice. Illustration, c.1900 by Sir James D. Linton.

Marxist interpretations of the play have shown the Christians of Venice to be as obsessed with wealth as Shylock. Conversations among Salerio, Solanio, Gratiano, and Lorenzo in particular reveal the dehumanizing centrality of commerce, jewelry, gold, and profit in Christian Venice. Even in the first scene of the play, it is possible to read Antonio's depressive state as an aspect of his overwhelmingly material existence.

Confusingly, the play features two characters named Balthasar. One is the trusted servant sent by Portia to Padua to fetch props and disguises at the home of her cousin, the legal expert Bellario. But "Balthasar" is also the alias Portia uses when she disguises herself as a male judge from Rome. Finally, the "merchant" in the title of the play refers not to Shylock, as many readers initially assume, but rather to Antonio. In Venice, Shylock is definitely not a merchant, but a moneylender.

A supplicant farmer negotiates with a Jewish moneylender in an unattributed engraving, 1531.

HISTORICAL SOURCES

JEWISH LONDON

The earliest Jewish settlers came to England with the Normans in the 1060s. In 1189, the fledgling community fell victim to the first of London's anti-Semitic pogroms culminating in their expulsion in 1290. Over the next 400 years, some Jews returned. When a Portuguese Jew, Dr. Roderigo Lopez, was executed in London in 1594 charged with trying to poison his patient, none other than Queen Elizabeth, a fresh wave of anti-Semitism followed.

SEEING THE PLAY

Shylock (Dustin Hoffman) prepares to cut the allotted one pound of flesh from Antonio (Leigh Lawson) in a production at the Phoenix Theatre, London, in 1989.

CURIOUSLY, THERE IS NO RECORD of a performance of *The Merchant of Venice* between Shakespeare's day and the mid-18th century. Once the play was revived, however, it remained a favorite among actors and audiences. Shylock and Portia have consistently attracted leading stage talents. And with the Shakespearean text accommodating varied interpretations, Shylock has been played as everything from a stock villain to a sympathetic man. Portia has also been given with great range, from a quasi-divine heroine to a spoiled rich girl transformed by love.

Following the Holocaust, the role of Shylock the Jew was reassessed, changing the course of the play's production history. Postwar directors have presented many roles, including secondary roles such as the Prince of Morocco—as invitations to audiences to examine their religious and racial prejudices. With scholarship also identifying love between Antonio and Bassanio, today directors often explore the play's intricate affective landscape, suggesting a love triangle encompassing Bassanio, Antonio, and Portia.

Some productions of the play have focused not on characters but on mercantile Venice, where ducats and bonds rule the lives of Christians and Jews alike, ultimately dividing them. Whatever the director's interpretation of Venice, Belmont is invariably treated as a world apart. One of the pleasures of attending the play is to see how Belmont is staged. In his 1999 production for Rome's Piccolo Teatro, director Stéphane Braunschweig set Belmont as an Elizabethan realm, reserving modern dress for scenes set in Venice.

"You must prepare your bosom for his knife..." (4.1). Blood red lighting emphasizes the violent threat posed by Shylock's demands in a production by the RSC in 1997.

BEYOND THE PLAY

Actor Ernst Deutsch (right) played Shylock at the Freie Volksbühne in Berlin in 1963. The set designs were created by Hans-Ulrich Schmückle.

IN THE MERCHANT OF VENICE, Shakespeare broke with Elizabethan conventions of portraying Jews as figures of absolute evil. But while moving passages were written for Shylock as a Jew, the play remains resolutely Christian. Prior to World War II, actors usually performed Shylock as an evil or comical figure akin to the Jewish protagonists of Renaissance drama. These portrayals echoed medieval Christian dramas in which the Jew was represented in the same manner as Satan: clever and calculating, a master of negotiation and deal-doing, at once physically and verbally comical.

Since World War II, critical readings and theatrical productions of the play have viewed Shylock in the context of the Holocaust. Morris Carnovsky was praised for his Shylock of 1957 in Stratford, Connecticut, where he interpreted Shylock's no-interest bond as a genuine effort to establish a less antagonistic relationship with Antonio and the Christian community. Another groundbreaking postwar interpretation was given in West Berlin by Jewish actor Ernst Deutsch at the Freie Volkbühne in 1963. Deutsch played Shylock as a man alienated as much by the commercialism as by the Christians of Venice. Even secondary roles, often used to establish the atmosphere of Venice, have been reexamined since World War II. In Bill Alexander's Royal Shakespeare Company production of 1987, Christians not only excluded Shylock from their society but were also actively hostile, pelting him with stones as they chased him onto the stage.

Early filmmakers turned frequently to this play. The Shylock of silent films could menace spectators with his gnarled features and fearsome facial expressions, as in J. Stuart Blackton's 1908 *The Merchant of Venice.* An Italian-language film sympathetic to Shylock was released in 1952 by French director Pierre Billon. Since then, other films have broadened the palette of directors presenting a more dimensional and, indeed, international Shylock. Pei Te Hurinui Jones translated Shakespeare's play into the Maori tongue for the 2002 New Zealand film *Maori Merchant of Venice,* demonstrating that the play engages audiences no matter what their religion or race. From Europe to the South Seas, *Merchant* remains above all a play asking whether love may heal a divided community.

ON STAGE

YIDDISH

For John Caird's 1984 London production, actor Ian McDiarmud prepared his role in Jerusalem, where the Yiddish of Mea She'arim Jews inspired him to play Shylock with a Yiddish accent. In Trevor Nunn's London production of the play in 1999, Yiddish itself was used in exchanges between Shylock and Jessica.

The MERRY WIVES OF WINDSOR

THE MERRY WIVES OF WINDSOR is Shakespeare's most enduringly popular comedy, yet also his most eccentric. It is the only comedy set entirely in England and there is no single source for the play. Tradition holds that Queen Elizabeth asked Shakespeare for a play showing Falstaff in love. She may have commissioned at least the finale if not all of *The Merry Wives of Windsor* for the Garter Feast celebrating her knights at Westminster on April 23, 1597. The reappearance of Falstaff and friends, who emerged in the "Henriad," invites comparisons between *The Merry Wives of Windsor* and both parts of *Henry IV*. In those plays, no space—from the tavern to the theater of war—is large enough to contain Falstaff's appetite and language. Transplanted to the town of Windsor, where the wives are chaste and the husbands outsmarted, Falstaff is another man.

BEHIND THE PLAY

THE MERRY WIVES OF WINDSOR is the first notable play in the English language to celebrate characters drawn from the middle classes. Two hundred years earlier, Geoffrey Chaucer captured voices of middle-class English speakers in his narrative *The Canterbury Tales*. However, until *The Merry Wives of Windsor*, most English plays presented lower-born characters as secondary to nobles and aristocrats, whose fates were conventionally held to be worthier of dramatic treatment. Settings in this comedy are unusually realistic, even readily identifiable: the Garter Inn existed, as did Windsor Park and Frogmore. Characters and action may also appear to be drawn from the real Elizabethan Windsor, but drama must not be mistaken for history. The play is set in a Windsor at once farcical and moral. While the bourgeois residents of Windsor appear as barely grown-up schoolchildren, their outrageous schemes are justified in a neat moral conclusion to the play. As Mistress Page says, summing up this dual world, "wives may be merry, and yet honest too." But with Falstaff never fully domesticated, the moral punchline hardly remains the point of this delightful romp through Windsor.

Have I laid my brain in the sun and dried it, that it wants matter to prevent so gross o'erreaching as this?... 5.5

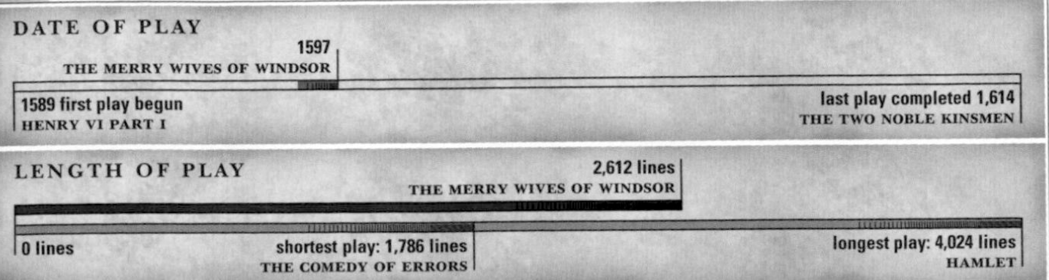

DRAMATIS PERSONAE

SIR JOHN FALSTAFF
433 lines
Known to audiences from the Bard's "Henriad," the big lover-of-life sets out on the path of finding a rich mistress to pay his debts.

Clutching a pair of identical love letters, Falstaff (Leslie Phillips) hopes to press his suit on two rich Windsor wives.

FENTON
94 lines
A young gentleman, he woos Anne Page.

ROBERT SHALLOW
114 lines
A country justice, he refuses to continue suffering Falstaff's abuses.

ABRAHAM SLENDER
141 lines
Shallow's kinsman, he is Anne's unlikely suitor.

FRANK FORD
305 lines
A citizen of Windsor, when he learns Falstaff is in love with his wife, he takes the alias "Brook" and adopts a scheme because "A man may not be too confident."

GEORGE PAGE
144 lines
A citizen of Windsor, when he learns Falstaff is in love with his wife, he is sure that the only thing the fat knight will get from Mistress Page is some harsh language.

WILLIAM PAGE
12 lines
Son of George Page and Mistress Page.

SIR HUGH EVANS
222 lines
A Welsh parson, he appoints himself the umpire in everyone else's disputes.

DOCTOR CAIUS
94 lines
A French physician and suitor to Anne Page, he unwittingly marries a boy.

A HOST
107 lines
Host of the Garter Inn, where Falstaff lodges.

BARDOLPH
23 lines
A follower of Falstaff, he finds work at the Garter Inn serving beer.

PISTOL
57 lines
A follower of Falstaff, fired for refusing to deliver love letters, he later disguises himself as "Hobgoblin."

NYM
28 lines
A follower of Falstaff, he is no mincer of words.

ROBIN
13 lines
Falstaff's page.

PETER SIMPLE
49 lines
Slender's servant.

The French Dr. Caius (Paul Mullins) and his servant, Mistress Quickly (Franchelle Stewart Dorn), add to the humor of the play with their colorful distortions of the English language.

JOHN RUGBY
10 lines
Dr. Caius's servant.

JOHN AND ROBERT
2; 1 lines
Frank Ford's servants.

MISTRESS FORD (ALICE)
167 lines
She decides to teach the "greasy knight" and her jealous husband a lesson.

MISTRESS PAGE (MARGARET)
306 lines
Also known as "Meg," she helps Mistress Ford make a mockery of Falstaff.

Two of Shakespeare's most spirited female characters, Mistresses Page and Ford (played by actress sisters Irene and Violet Vanbrugh), conspire to mock Falstaff.

ANNE PAGE
28 lines
Daughter of George Page and Mistress Page, she intends to marry Fenton, whatever her parents think.

MISTRESS QUICKLY
261 lines
Dr. Caius's servant, she acts as go-between for all the courting lovers.

SEVERAL CHILDREN OF WINDSOR
10 lines
They torment and torture Falstaff with pinches as they pretend to be fairies.

PLOT SUMMARY

SIZE OF ACTS

ACT 1	ACT 2	ACT 3	ACT 4	ACT 5
528 lines	592 lines	643 lines	544 lines	305 lines

ACT ONE

528 lines

BEFORE AND WITHIN THE HOUSE OF THE PAGE FAMILY, THE GARTER INN AND DR. CAIUS'S HOUSE

Justice Shallow can no longer abide the antics of Sir John Falstaff, who has "beaten my men, killed my deer, and broke open my lodge." Shallow decides to present the matter to the city council, but Sir Hugh Evans, the parson, would prefer to take the dispute to God. He also prays that his kinsman Slender will marry Anne Page. When Shallow agrees to enter the Page home to discuss the matter, he is not surprised to learn that Falstaff is there for a meal. Evans hopes to resolve the dispute, but Falstaff asserts his accusers will hear "all these matters denied." Slender would be happy to marry Anne, but he is so timid that when she invites him to join the others at table for dinner, he claims he is not hungry. Evans, unable to meddle to his satisfaction in the Shallow–Falstaff dispute, sends Simple to Dr. Caius's home with a letter requesting that his servant, Mistress Quickly, support Slender's bid for the hand of Anne Page.

At the Garter Inn, Falstaff announces that Ford's wife gave him "the leer of invitation" and Page's wife examined his "parts." He plans to make love to both of them. He also looks forward to spending their money. When Pistol and Nym refuse to deliver his love letters to the ladies, he fires them. They plan to seek revenge by telling Ford and Page of Falstaff's scandalous designs on their wives and purses. Simple reaches Caius's house with his letter, but Mistress Quickly hides him in a closet when her master, Caius, returns suddenly, as he is himself intent on marrying Anne. When Caius discovers Simple and learns that Evans is brokering Slender's suit for Anne, he is furious. Dr. Caius pens a letter to the meddling Evans, challenging the Welsh parson to a duel.

O, she did so course o'er my exteriors with such a greedy intention... 1.3

Briefly, I do mean to make love to Ford's wife. I spy entertainment in her... 1.3

As if two suitors for the hand of Anne Page were not enough, a third arrives: Fenton hopes Mistress Quickly will put in a good word for him as well.

ACT TWO

592 lines

BEFORE THE PAGE HOME, AT THE GARTER INN AND IN A FIELD NEAR WINDSOR

Mistress Page is shocked to receive a love letter from Falstaff. She is still more shocked when Mistress Ford arrives to show an exact replica of the letter, with only the name of the addressee changed. The wives agree to "consult together against this greasy knight," and involve Mistress Quickly in a plan of revenge.

We burn daylight. Here, read, read. Perceive how I might be knighted... 2.1

Pistol is the one to tell Ford, as Nym is to tell Page, that their wives are hotly pursued by Falstaff. Page is not bothered. But the jealous Ford arranges with the Host to go by the alias "Brook" at the Garter Inn in order to entrap Falstaff. Meanwhile, Evans and Caius, slated to duel, have each been told of a different meeting place.

On orders from the wives, Quickly tells Falstaff that Mrs Ford's husband will be away between 10 and 11 o'clock, when Falstaff is welcome to visit her. Mrs. Page is also in love with him, she says. "Brook" offers Falstaff money to make love to Mrs Ford, whose "purity" and "reputation" would then be broken down so that "Brook" himself could make headway in his own romantic pursuit of her. Pleased, Falstaff tells "Brook" of the secret meeting he just arranged with Ford's wife. Alone, Ford is outraged. Meanwhile, since Evans fails to appear for the scheduled duel, Caius assumes his opponent is a coward. The Host offers to take Caius to meet Anne.

Marry, this is the short and the long of it... 2.2

What a damned Epicurean rascal is this! My heart is ready to crack with impatience... 2.2

ACT THREE

643 lines

A FIELD NEAR FROGMORE AND VARIOUS LOCATIONS IN WINDSOR

Sir Hugh Evans, ready to fight, is convinced that Dr. Caius is not man enough to duel. When Caius and others arrive, the

To shallow rivers, to whose falls/Melodious birds sing madrigals... 3.1

And you may know by my size that I have a kind of alacrity in sinking. If the bottom were as deep as hell, I should down... 3.5

Host prevents the doctor and parson from dueling: "Peace, I say, Gallia and Gaul, French and Welsh, soul-curer and body-curer." The Host confesses he sent them to two locations so that Windsor would lose neither its doctor nor its parson.

Ford invites Page, Caius, and Evans home to behold "a monster." At the Ford house, the wives instruct servants one last time: when called, they are to take the laundry basket from the house and drop its contents in a muddy ditch by the Thames River. Falstaff arrives, quoting verse by Sidney: "Have I caught thee, my heavenly jewel?" But Falstaff instantly hides when Mrs. Page appears. According to the ladies' plan, Mrs. Page says Mr. Ford is on his way home "with half Windsor at his heels." Any lover must be hidden at once. Falstaff rushes out in a panic to hide in the laundry basket. Ford arrives and searches for Falstaff. But the knight has already disappeared in the basket carried out by the servants. The wives decide they are not done with Falstaff yet.

Tomorrow Mistress Quickly will help arrange a new prank. Meanwhile, finding no hidden lover, Ford asks the wives to pardon him. Fenton confesses to Anne that he first wooed her for money, but now has fallen in love with her.

Falstaff has survived being dumped in mud. Mistress Quickly invites Falstaff to come to Mrs Ford between 8 and 9 o'clock, while her husband is off bird hunting. Falstaff tells "Brook" in detail of being put in the basket, and of "the rankest… smell that ever offended nostril", but Falstaff also promises "Brook" he has an appointment to cuckold Ford this very morning. Alone, Ford boils with jealousy.

Go fetch me a quart of sack—put a toast in't… 3.5

Nay, you shall hear, Master Brook, what I have suffered… 3.5

ACT FOUR

544 lines

IN A STREET OF WINDSOR, AT FORD'S HOUSE AND AT THE GARTER INN

Falstaff arrives at the Ford home for his meeting. As before, Mrs. Page warns that Ford returns home unexpectedly. Falstaff is disguised in clothes of Mrs. Ford's "maid's aunt". When Ford discovers the "aunt" he despises and takes for a witch, he beats "her" out of the house.

The wives reveal all to their husbands, and Ford promises never to be suspicious again. The couples conspire together to play one last trick on Falstaff. A local legend tells of Herne the Hunter, who drags a heavy chain and haunts an oak tree in "a most hideous and dreadful manner." The wives will invite Falstaff to come to the oak disguised as Herne. There, Anne and other children portraying fairies will pinch him until he tells the truth.

Falstaff, still shaken by his beating, finds himself a changed man: he may even repent. Quickly follows Falstaff up to his room at the

I would all the world might be cozened, for I have been cozened and beaten too… 4.5

Garter Inn to extend the new invitation from the wives. Fenton requests that the Host arrange for a vicar to await him and Anne at the church between midnight and one, when they plan to elope.

ACT FIVE

305 lines

AT THE GARTER INN AND IN WINDSOR PARK

Mistress Quickly promises Falstaff she will procure the chain and horns he needs to portray Herne in Windsor Park according to the new secret arrangements. In turn, Falstaff invites "Brook" to come to the oak at midnight, when he may have his way with Ford's wife.

George Page tells Slender to lead Anne out of the park at midnight. She will be dressed in white. Mistress Page tells Caius that at midnight he will find Anne dressed in green. Evans meanwhile rehearses the schoolchildren in their roles as pinching fairies.

Falstaff enters the park at the appointed hour, adjusting to his role as Herne the Hunter by delivering quasi-heroic speeches to himself: "Remember, Jove, thou wast a bull for thy Europa. Love set on thy horns". He finally spies the wives and greets them lustily, but when he sees "fairies" arrive, he lies down and covers his face, convinced "he that speaks to them shall die." Quickly instructs the "fairies" to use flowers to spell out the credo of the knights of the Garter: *Honi soit qui mal y pense* (Evil to him who evil thinks). Evans, disguised as a satyr, smells "a man of middle-earth," a mortal. Pistol and Nym join in the playful torture, terrorizing Falstaff and burning him with tapers.

The "fairies" sing, pinching to the tempo and warning against "sinful fantasy," "lust and luxury". Caius leaves with a boy dressed in green, and Slender with a boy in white. Fenton departs with his beloved Anne. The wives and Ford reveal their pranks to Falstaff, who concedes: "I do begin to perceive that I am made an ass." Evans moralizes: Falstaff must serve God instead of base desires, and Ford must cease being jealous. Yet Falstaff is not the only fool: Slender and Caius return to report they had accidentally stolen off with boys. Caius was even married to the boy he erroneously took for Anne. When Fenton arrives, married to Anne, the Pages accept the new member of the family with joy.

Pinch him, and burn him, and turn him about... 5.5

Good husband, let us go home,/And laugh this sport o'er by a country fire... 5.5

READING THE PLAY

COMPARISON OF PROSE TO VERSE

prose: 87% | verse: 13%

HE MERRY WIVES OF WINDSOR initially ives the impression of being a history lay rather than a comedy. As early as the pening scene, the language is heavy with eferences to locations, persons, and offices f Windsor. Shakespeare may have written his play for an audience familiar with Vindsor, and these references may have erved as pleasing tributes. After the first ct, however, the wild plots of the wives nd the voice of Falstaff take over.

The Star and Garter in the Old Woolwich Road, London, SE1.

HISTORICAL SOURCES

THE ORDER OF THE GARTER

Knighthood was brought to England from France following the Norman invasion in 1066. The Garter Inn in Windsor, named after the Knights of the Garter, really existed, and many English pubs still bear the sign of the Garter and echo its chivalrous motto.

The English used in this play can be uzzling. The role of Sir Hugh Evans, the Velsh parson, is set in a dialect not easy to ecipher. Evans says "seese" for *cheese* and "putter" for *butter*. ven Falstaff notes that Evans "makes fritters of English." When r. Caius, the Frenchman, becomes excited, he switches into rench, as when he discovers he has married "oon garson." listress Quickly's English is virtually a tongue of its own. Striving show her wide-ranging vocabulary, Quickly is eager to use ultisyllabic words of Latin origin, but she is also satisfied to ronounce them however she may. When she says "fartuous" e actually means *virtuous*; she confuses "infection" for *affection*; nd she even uses the word "erection" for *detection*.

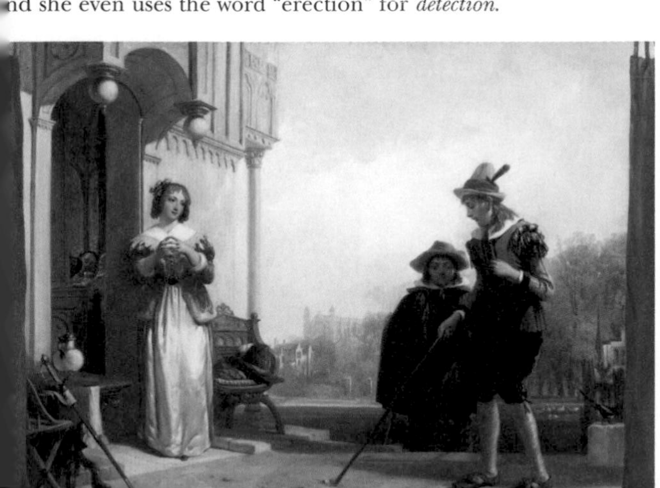

"I pray you, sir, walk in" (1.1). Anne Page invites her timid suitor Slender to come inside for supper, but he declines, preferring to wander outside. "I had rather walk here, I thank you" (1.1). Engraving, *c.*1850 by A. W. Calcott.

SEEING THE PLAY

ON STAGE

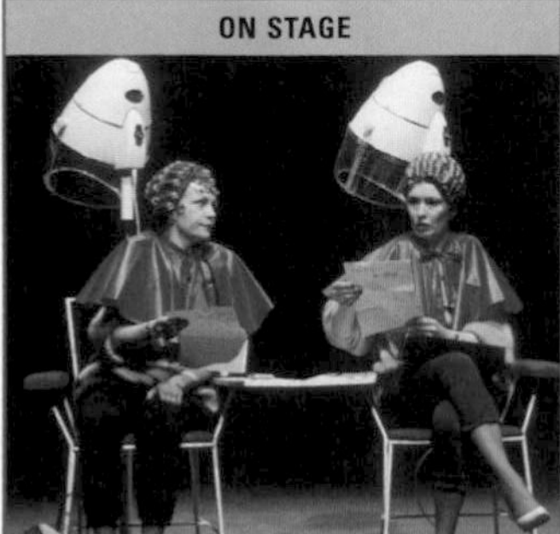

A POST-WAR ADAPTATION

For the Royal Shakespeare Company's 1985 production, action was set in the 1950s, when middle-class values of moral conformity espoused in the play found postwar urgency. Dialogues between the bourgeois Windsor wives were conducted at the hairdresser's. Anne Page, who insists on rejecting her parents' favorite suitors, was played as a rebellious teenager who overcomes boredom by tuning into rock and roll music.

"I warrant he hath a thousand of these letters" (2.1). Mistresses Page (Janet Dale, left) and Ford (Lindsay Duncan) compare love letters under the hair dryer.

WHILE IT HAS LONG BEEN DISMISSED as frothy entertainment, *The Merry Wives of Windsor* has remained one of Shakespeare's most popular plays since the day theaters reopened under Charles II in 1660. Apart from the leading romantic couple, Anne and Fenton, whose on-stage roles are not central, the play abounds in characters who bubble with mischief. The setting of the action in England, too, brings an earthiness and immediacy unique to the Shakespearean comedies. Many directors have updated the play, to say, Eisenhower's suburban America or Margaret Thatcher's northern England, to invite audiences into comic versions of environments they recognize as their own.

The ridiculous trials and tribulations of Falstaff as he attempts with stunning lack of success to woo two middle-aged, middle-class wives in the heart of England makes for an irresistible comic plot. Consequently, successful productions allow actors room to develop their timing and ensemble work, building on the play's inherent humor and perfectly shaped momentum. No stout leading actor in the English-speaking theater ends his career without at least one portrayal of Falstaff and, since *The Merry Wives of Windsor* is his play, it attracts fine Falstaffs. The play can also throw into relief new comic acting talents. Secondary and minor roles are so strongly drawn that audiences often find them every bit as unforgettable as the merry wives, their duped husbands, and the singular Falstaff.

For a fee, Mistress Quickly (Sada Thompson) happily agrees to help Falstaff (Larry Gates) win a wife in the 1959 production at the American Shakespeare Festival, Stratford, Connecticut.

BEYOND THE PLAY

No known source exists for *The Merry Wives of Windsor*, but Shakespeare clearly drew plots and settings from short and often rude stories called *fabliaux* (pronounced *fab-lee-OH*). Peopled with jealous spouses, surprised lovers, and outrageous sexual exploits, this form of comic tale arose in 13th-century France. Later, the form gained popularity in Italy, where the tales were anthologized in such works as Boccaccio's *Decameron* and Ser Giovanni's *Il Percone*, which Shakespeare perhaps tapped for the plot of this play. *The Merry Wives of Windsor* employs the wild love triangles and shocking humor of the *fabliaux*, and even includes a *fabliau*-like Frenchman in the explosive person of Dr. Caius.

However, Shakespeare's wives are not equipped with the limitless sexual appetites and guilt-free consciences of their Gallic counterparts. The Windsor wives remain chaste to the cheerful end in spite of abundant opportunities to cuckold their spouses. Thus, Shakespeare appears to have been more committed to respecting the courtly French motto of the Knights of the Garter—*Honi soit qui mal y pense*—than to portraying the *bourgeois* lust that marked saucy French tales. The uninhibited sex drives of the *fabliaux* protagonists, whose antics were enjoyed by medieval readers in privacy, were surely too much for a staged performance in honor of knights serving the queen, if this play was indeed initially written for such a noble audience. In Shakespeare's Windsor, "honesty" in the end is valued above all else.

Such is the play's popularity with audiences that it has never been neglected. With communities the world over recognizing themselves in Elizabethan Windsor, updated versions of the play are legion. A 2003 American production even set action in post-Civil War North Carolina, with Falstaff brandishing a Confederate saber. The play has been adapted for film, including two silent pictures, and television, but has been particularly successful in the hands of opera composers.

ON STAGE

MUSICAL ADAPTATIONS

Librettists have adapted Shakespeare's lyrical play to make it worthy of full-throttled operatic humor and emotion. As early as 1798, Antonio Salieri, Mozart's Italian contemporary, had scored a *Falstaff* based on the play. Arrigo Boito set a libretto for Verdi's stupendous final opera, *Falstaff*, which in 1893 took Milan's La Scala opera house by storm. Verdi's masterpiece in turn left its mark on theater directors. In a Stratford production of 1935, Komisarjevsky even staged *The Merry Wives of Windsor* as a Viennese operetta.

Top: A scene from Verdi's opera *Falstaff*. Left: Six broadsheet illustrations, *c.* 1890, of scenes from Otto Nicolai's immensely popular German opera *Die Lustigen Weiber von Windsor*, premiered in Berlin in 1849.

MUCH ADO ABOUT NOTHING

NO SHAKESPEAREAN LOVERS ENJOY QUARRELLING more than Beatrice and Benedick in *Much Ado About Nothing.* Indeed, even though Hero and Claudio are the principal characters, Beatrice and Benedick have become so central to productions of the play that their names have served as alternative titles. Very probably staged at the Globe before it was officially registered on 2 August 1600, the play is not known to have been performed before May 1613. *Much Ado About Nothing* was then staged twice at court (for Princess Elizabeth's betrothal and marriage to the Elector Palatine) under the title *Benedicke and Betteris.* Even Hector Berlioz made the secondary couple the central focus of attention in his 1861 opera, *Béatrice et Bénédicte.* Filled with music and mischief, *Much Ado About Nothing* is today among Shakespeare's most lively comedies.

BEHIND THE PLAY

THE PLAY IS SET EXCLUSIVELY IN MESSINA in Sicily , where Leonato is governor. Most of the action unfolds in Leonato's household but, as the plot thickens, scenes also spill out into the streets of the town, a prison-house, a church, and a graveyard. In the play's opening scene, Don Pedro, Prince of Arragon, has just emerged victorious in a military campaign against his illegitimate half-brother, the villainous Don John. Now that Don John has been reconciled with the prince, almost everyone is in a mood to celebrate. Those who distinguished themselves in battle are suddenly free to socialize in Leonato's home, but the postwar atmosphere in Messina is rather prickly. For one, Leonato's adopted "niece," Beatrice, enjoys a playfully caustic relationship with Lord Benedick of Padua, who had caught her attention even before the military campaign. And Don John is too inherently villainous to keep from plotting something wicked. Motivated by his jealousy of Claudio, a war hero of Don Pedro's court, Don John plots to destroy Claudio's social advancement. Claudio hopes to marry Hero, sole heir of the wealthy Leonato, but Don John will trick Claudio into rejecting his bride.

Let every eye negotiate for itself/And trust no agent… 2.1

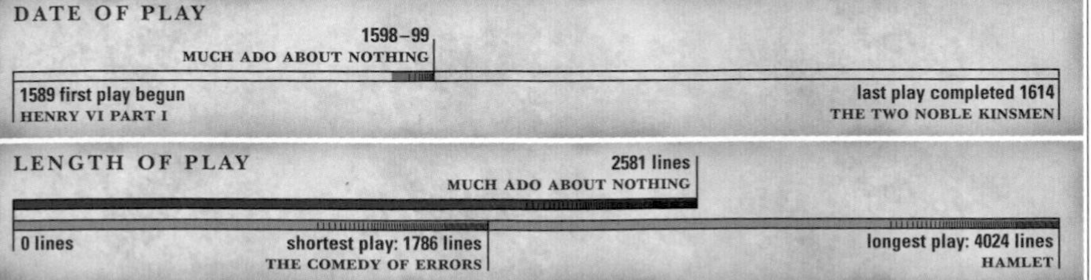

DRAMATIS PERSONAE

Claudio (Rashan Stone) is a romantic and earnest youth.

DON PEDRO
313 lines
Prince of Arragon, recently victorious in battle against his half-brother, Don John, he accepts Leonato's invitation to sojourn for a month in Messina.

DON JOHN
107 lines
The bastard brother of Don Pedro, he is jealous of the war hero Claudio, and schemes to destroy Claudio's wedding plans.

CLAUDIO
286 lines
A young lord of Florence, he falls in love with Leonato's daughter, Hero, and marries her by the end of the play.

BENEDICK
432 lines
A young lord of Padua, he initially claims he will never fall in love or marry, although he does fall for Leonato's adopted niece, Beatrice.

LEONATO
328 lines
Governor of Messina, he has adopted Beatrice as his "niece," but hints that she may be his illegitimate daughter; he is overcome with rage when Claudio suddenly refuses to marry his daughter, Hero, on the grounds of infidelity.

ANTONIO
55 lines
He tries to comfort Leonato, his brother.

BALTHASAR
28 lines
Attendant on Don Pedro.

CONRADE
35 lines
Follower of Don John, he and Borachio are arrested and forced to confess.

BORACHIO
123 lines
Follower of Don John, he tells Leonato: "If you would know your wronger, look on me."

FRIAR FRANCIS
82 lines
When Hero is accused of infidelity, he arranges for her to appear to have died so that Claudio will realize his false accusation.

DOGBERRY
175 lines
A constable, he manages to uncover Don John's dastardly plot.

VERGES
25 lines
He helps Dogberry interrogate Borachio and Conrade.

A SEXTON
15 lines
He joins Dogberry and Verges in the interrogation.

A BOY
2 lines
He serves Benedick.

HERO
131 lines
Daughter to Leonato, she is wrongly accused of "savage sensuality" and disloyalty thanks to the machinations of Don John, but in the end she marries Claudio.

BEATRICE
270 lines
An orphan and niece to Leonato, who says: "There is a kind of merry war betwixt Signor Benedick" and Beatrice. She is quick-witted and likes to banter.

MARGARET
62 lines
Gentlewoman attending on Hero, she is wrongly accused of helping Don John dupe Claudio.

Hero (Mlle Mastico) is virtuous and faithful, despite Don John's ploys to prove otherwise.

URSULA
48 lines
Gentlewoman attending on Hero, she helps to trick Beatrice into admitting her love for Benedick.

OTHER PLAYERS
Messengers, Watch, Lord, Musicians, and Attendants

Beatrice (Diana Wynard) and Benedick (John Gielgud), Phoenix Theatre, London, 1952. The couple's persistent verbal sparring suggests a strong, mutual interest and attraction.

PLOT SUMMARY

SIZE OF ACTS

ACT 1	ACT 2	ACT 3	ACT 4	ACT 5
384 lines	644 lines	547 lines	416 lines	590 lines

ACT ONE 384 lines

MESSINA: BEFORE AND WITHIN LEONATO'S HOUSE

A messenger reports to Leonato, Governor of Messina: Don Pedro, Prince of Arragon, is about to arrive in Messina, his army recently victorious in battle. Leonato is eager to play host to the prince and the valiant Count Claudio, who has distinguished himself in battle. Beatrice coolly asks after another soldier, Signor Benedick of Padua. When she learns that Benedick also served well in the war, Beatrice pretends to be unimpressed.

Don Pedro and his entourage receive a warm welcome. But as soon as they see each other, Beatrice and Benedick begin quibbling aggressively, each swearing never to fall in love. Don Pedro accepts Leonato's invitation to stay in Messina for a month. Even the bastard Don John is welcome to stay now that he has been vanquished by, and reconciled with, his legitimate half-brother, Don Pedro.

Claudio has fallen in love with Leonato's beautiful daughter, Hero, but Benedick vows to remain a lifelong bachelor. When Don Pedro adds that Hero is Leonato's only heir, Claudio is even more interested in wooing her. Don Pedro offers to disguise himself as Claudio during the evening's revelry, and to woo Hero on Claudio's behalf.

That a woman conceived me, I thank her... 1.1

But now I am returned and that war-thoughts/Have left their places vacant, in their rooms/ Come thronging soft and delicate desires... 1.1

Leonato learns from his brother, Antonio, that a servant overheard Claudio and the prince. It appears that the prince is in love with Hero and plans to woo her. Thinking the report reliable, Leonato prepares to inform Hero of this favorable situation.

Don John confesses to his follower, Conrade, that he is still a "plain-dealing villain". When Borachio, another follower, reports that he overheard the prince offering to woo Hero on behalf of Claudio, Don John sees an opportunity to get even with the "young start-up" Claudio.

I had rather be a canker in a hedge than a rose in his grace... 1.3

ACT TWO 644 lines

IN LEONATO'S HOUSE AND GARDEN

Beatrice reminds Leonato that she has no intention of marrying. Disapproving of Beatrice's disposition, Antonio urges Hero to "be ruled by" her father,

Leonato. But Beatrice gives her cousin very different advice, likening the state of being in love to an exhausting Scottish jig.

> **The fault will be in the music, cousin, if you be not wooed in good time…** 2.1

Guests arrive in masks for the evening's revels. Don Pedro pretends to be Claudio, and woos Hero on the count's behalf; Balthasar pursues Hero's attendant, Margaret; and Antonio insists he is not Antonio even though Ursula, another attendant of Hero's, is sure he is. Not recognizing Benedick, Beatrice confides to the masked man that Benedick is "the Prince's jester, a very dull fool." Don John, recognizing Claudio through his disguise, tells him that Don Pedro is in love with Hero. Alone, Claudio believes he has been deceived by Don Pedro.

> **Thus answer I in name of Benedick,/ But hear these ill news with the ears of Claudio…** 2.1

Benedick, also alone, cannot believe Beatrice called him "The Prince's fool!"

The prince has been successful in his match-making plan: Leonato promises Hero to Claudio, and all confusion about Don Pedro's intention vanishes. Don Pedro even persuades Hero to assist him in further match-making: he believes Benedick could make a fine husband for Beatrice.

Don John is revolted to hear that Claudio is to marry Hero, but Borachio comes up with a satisfyingly fiendish plan: Borachio himself will impersonate a lover and Margaret will be tricked into playing the role of Hero. The night before the wedding, Claudio will observe them and think another man is having an affair with his betrothed. Don John promises Borachio 1,000 ducats for carrying off his scheme.

Alone, Benedick wonders how Claudio changed from a soldier into a lover. Seeing Claudio and the prince approach, Benedick hides to observe them, but the men know that Benedick is nearby, and instead play a trick on him.

> **I do much wonder that on man, seeing how much another man is a fool whe he dedicates his behaviou to love…** 2.3

First, Balthasar practises the love music he will use to serenade Hero for Claudio the next night, softening the mood. Then, Leonato, Claudio, and Don Pedro say that Beatrice is so in love with Benedick that she has become suicidal. Alone, Benedick realizes that he is in love with Beatrice. When Beatrice arrives to call him to dinner, Benedick interprets her every word as a secret love message.

> **Sigh no more, ladies, sigh no more,/Men were deceivers ever…** 2.3

> **This can be no trick. The conference was sadly borr They have the truth of thi from Hero…** 2.3

ACT THREE
547 lines

IN LEONATO'S GARDEN AND HOUSE, IN A STREET OF MESSINA AND HERO'S APARTMENT WITHIN LEONATO'S HOUSE

Joining in the match-making plot, Hero also stages a conversation with Margaret and Ursula. Beatrice overhears Hero praise Benedick but complain that Beatrice is too in love with herself to be in love with someone else. Horrified to discover herself "condemned for pride and scorn," Beatrice is now ready to return Benedick's love.

> **O god of love! I know he doth deserve/ As much as may be yielde to a man…** 3.1

Don Pedro and Claudio are overjoyed to discover that Benedick is in love. But the mood darkens when Don John claims that Hero is disloyal and invites the men to observe Hero that night.

With dubious authority, constable Dogberry and his partner, Verges, round up some men to serve as guards at Leonato's house. The watchmen then spy on Conrade and Borachio, who discuss

> **You have; I knew it would be your answer…** 3.3

the trick just played on Claudio: falling for their trap, he mistook Margaret and Borachio for Hero and a mysterious lover. Seizing the culprits, the guards haul them off to jail.

In Hero's room, the ladies help her dress for her wedding and tease Beatrice for being in love. Dogberry tries to inform Leonato of the recent arrests, but the governor, busy with his daughter's wedding, tells Dogberry to examine the suspects himself. Leonato departs for the church and Dogberry returns to the prison.

Moral? No, by my troth, I have no moral meaning; I meant plain holy-thistle... 3.4

ACT FOUR

416 lines

A CHURCH AND A PRISON

In church, Claudio rejects his bride, accusing Hero of disloyalty and calling her "this rotten orange". At first Leonato cannot believe his ears. But when even Don Pedro supports Claudio's claim, Leonato suspects his daughter of lying. Claudio says that Hero was conversing with a man between midnight and one last night. Don Pedro adds that the man seen with Hero "Confessed the vile encounters they have had/A thousand times in secret." Claudio, Don Pedro and Don John storm out of the church as Hero faints.

Sweet Prince, you learn me noble thankfulness./ There, Leonato, take her back again... 4.1

When Hero revives, Leonato wishes his daughter would die, arguing that "Death is the fairest cover for her shame". But Friar Francis believes Hero is innocent when she tells her side of the story. Benedick suspects Don John lies behind the confusion, but Leonato remains angry. Finally, the friar proposes a solution: Hero appeared dead when the men left the church; if Hero were said to be truly dead, then Claudio would realize her innocence, and regret his own accusation. Hero is led off to feign death while Beatrice and Benedick cautiously confess love for one another. When Beatrice says she wishes she were a man so that she could avenge Hero's disgrace, Benedick promises to challenge Claudio as a token of his love for Beatrice.

Wherefore! Why, doth not every earthly thing/Cry shame upon her?... 4.1

I know not. If they speak but truth of her,/These hands shall tear her... 4.1

Farewell,/Thou pure impiety and impious purity!/ For thee I'll lock up all the gates of love... 4.1

Marry, this, well carried, shall on her behalf/Change slander to remorse... 4.1

In the jail, Dogberry and Verges extract full confessions from Borachio and Conrade.

ACT FIVE

590 lines

NEAR LEONATO'S HOUSE, IN HIS ORCHARD AND IN THE CHURCHYARD

Leonato finds philosophy useless in he face of real suffering and challenges Claudio to a duel for wronging "mine innocent child and me." Antonio agrees that Hero has been "slandered to death by villains."

Benedick crosses the paths of Don Pedro and Claudio, who tease him about his romance with Beatrice. When Benedick cuts relations with Don Pedro and challenges Claudio for having killed the innocent Hero, the men are shocked. When Benedick departs, Claudio believes his former friend has been changed by his love for Beatrice. But the prince is distracted by something Benedick said: Don John has fled Messina.

Dogberry and Verges present Conrade and Borachio, who reveals Don John's treachery to all. When Claudio and Don Pedro seek penance for their part in Hero's death, Leonato tells them to sing to Hero's bones in the churchyard. And tomorrow, Claudio must marry Hero's cousin, Antonio's daughter. Dogberry asks Leonato to punish the villain Borachio, too, for calling him an ass.

Moreover, sir, which indeed is not under white and black, this plaintiff here, the offender, did call me ass… 5.1

Benedick prepares to meet Beatrice in the orchard. When Beatrice refuses to kiss her lover until Claudio has been duly punished, Benedick says: "Thou and I are too wise to woo peaceably." Ursula interrupts the lovers with news that "the author of all" abuses is none other than Don John.

As instructed, Claudio reads an epitaph over the tomb where Hero is meant to have been buried, and Balthasar sings.

Pardon, goddess of the night,/Those that slew thy virgin knight… 5.3

After Leonato sends the ladies off to disguise themselves, Benedick asks him for Beatrice's hand in marriage. Claudio arrives suddenly and vows to marry the mysterious, veiled woman no matter what her appearance. Hero unveils to reveal herself to all. The guests are amazed but the friar promises to explain everything later.

Beatrice, also masked, reveals herself to Benedick for a final round of verbal sparring: each claims never to have been in love with the other. But revealing love sonnets written in their own hands are produced by their friends. Before she can say more, Benedick kisses Beatrice's mouth. Finally, making peace with Claudio, Benedick insists that everyone dance before the dual wedding. Even when a messenger reports that Don John has been captured, Benedick refuses to be distracted. "Think not on him till tomorrow," he urges, and dancing brings the play to an end.

I'll tell thee what, Prince; a college of wit-crackers cannot flout me out of my humour… 5.4

Let's have a dance ere we are married, that we may lighten our own hearts and our wives' heels… 5.4

READING THE PLAY

COMPARISON OF PROSE TO VERSE

prose: 72% | verse: 28%

IN MUCH ADO ABOUT NOTHING, two plots are carefully interwoven to form the volcanic fourth act, where the apparent destruction of one marriage (of Claudio and Hero) helps to bring about another (that of Benedick and Beatrice). Shakespeare is especially careful to balance serious and light layers of action, preventing the false death of Hero and the rage of her father Leonato from turning the comedy into a more disturbing kind of play. Much of the intrigue in *Much Ado About Nothing* is skillfully built as characters overhear conversations, often laden with misinformation to trick the eavesdropper.

"Sigh no more, ladies, sigh no more,/Men were deceivers ever" (Balthasar's song, 2.3). Illustration by John Gilbert from *The Library Shakespeare,* 1856.

Most of Acts 1 to 3 are written in prose, but the lyrical language of Acts 4 and 5 yields moving, passionate speeches. Throughout, comical prose exchanges advance the action while keeping it light: the more they quibble and pretend to mock one another, the more Benedick and Beatrice fall in love; Don John and Borachio are deliciously transparent villains who enjoy spinning their dastardly plot; and Dogberry and Verges are among Shakespeare's most charmingly comical law enforcement officers.

The plot is not without its unfortunate dead ends. For example, in Act One Leonato believes that Don Pedro is in love with his daughter, Hero. And then Claudio believes that Don Pedro is wooing Hero for himself, rather than as his spokesman. A grand romantic subplot involving Don Pedro appears to be in the making, but it fizzles out. In Act Two Don Pedro, no longer a source of concern, celebrates the betrothal of Claudio to Hero. But the few dead ends hardly detract from the plot-driven pleasures of reading this play.

WHO'S WHO

Leonato is the governor of Messina. His daughter, **Hero**, is wooed by, rejected by, and eventually reconciled with **Claudio**, a young lord of Florence, whom she marries in the end. Leonato's adopted niece, **Beatrice**, despite protesting the contrary, falls in love with **Benedick**, a young lord of Padua, who returns her love and asks for her hand in marriage.

LITERARY SOURCES

BEATRICE AND BENEDICK

Shakespeare invented Beatrice and Benedick, but took the story of the plot about Hero and Claudio from various sources: a novella by the Italian Matteo Bandello; a canto from Ariosto's *Orlando Furioso*; and another canto from Spenser's 1590 *Faerie Queene*. This popular story about a lady wrongly accused of infidelity, rejected by her lover and, following trials and tribulations, finally restored to him, was used for the plot of an English play, *Fedele and Fortunio* (c.1584), which Shakespeare possibly read or attended.

SEEING THE PLAY

MUCH ADO ABOUT NOTHING CAN BE a difficult play to stage today. The greatest problem is that audiences tend to gravitate much more toward the subplot featuring Beatrice and Benedick than the main plot and its principal characters, Hero and Claudio. Even though the verbal sparring between Beatrice and Benedick is often difficult for audiences to decipher precisely (much of the wordplay has worn so thin as to be incomprehensible in current English), spectators readily understand that Beatrice and Benedick mock one another because they are too tough-minded to speak comfortably about love. One of the text's central enigmas – whether Beatrice and Benedick are in love from the outset, or whether they gradually fall in love – is usually settled in rehearsals or solved by directors of new productions.

"Let's have a dance ere we are married" (5.4). Katharine Hepburn (second from left) played a vibrant Beatrice at Stratford, Connecticut, in 1957.

Directors must find ways to balance the plots and subplots in production, and to give the action – set in a socially frivolous and wealthy postwar household – comical meaning. Many directors have opted to update the action. Among the inventive period settings to which the play has been reassigned are: the American Wild West; the Italian *risorgimento*; the antebellum South of the United States; 1890s Sicily; 1930s Cuba; Edwardian England; post-Mutiny India; and even a 20th-century tourist cruise ship. Updating the play gives it fresh relevance, but some of the most effective productions, relying more heavily on outstanding actors, have given prominence to the text, by sudden turns absurdly funny, witty, and moving.

The masked revels at Leonato's mansion were colourfully staged in *Beaucoup de Bruit Pour Rien*, a French production at Theatre 13 in Paris, starring Xavier Gallais as Benedict and Tamara Krcunovic as Beatrice.

BEYOND THE PLAY

Hot on the trail of Don John, the comic sleuth Dogberry (Newton Blick, right) instructs his sidekick Verges (Clifford Rose) in an atmospheric period-dress production at the Royal Shakespeare Theatre in 1961, directed by Michael Langham and designed by Desmond Heeley.

In the 1623 first folio version of *Much Ado About Nothing*, the name 'Kemp' appears at the end of Act 4 in lieu of "Const" for the constable Dogberry, revealing that the company actor who created Dogberry was William Kemp. A player with the Lord Chamberlain's Men until 1599, Kemp was the leading Elizabethan comedian. As playwright for the Lord Chamberlain's Men, Shakespeare created roles specifically suited to Kemp's comic talents. Apart from Dogberry, the roles of Peter in *Romeo and Juliet* and Bottom in *A Midsummer Night's Dream* are also thought to have been created for him.

Many comic talents have stolen the show in the Kempian role of Dogberry since Shakespeare's text was revived by David Garrick at Drury Lane in 1748, but leading romantic actors are also drawn to the saucy verbal jousting and emotional development of Benedick and Beatrice. Garrick himself played Benedick to Mrs Pritchard's Beatrice, and they were succeeded by scores of exceptional acting teams, including: John Philip Kemble and Mrs Jordan; ohn Gielgud and Peggy Ashcroft; Michael Redgrave and Googie Withers; Donald Sinden and Judi Dench; Robert Stephens and Maggie Smith; Kevin Kline and Blythe Danner. In the star-studded 1993 film by Kenneth Branagh, Branagh and Emma Thompson played the couple and Michael Keaton interpreted Dogberry.

In any production, there must be a delicate balance between the light and serious scenes of he play. In his New York roduction, director Robert ichmond established the nock-serious tone in the pening moments of the play, vith bowler-hatted males, arrying suitcases and guns, osed in freeze-frames recalling he opening sequences of ames bond films.

nma Thompson starred as Beatrice, ft, and Kate Beckinsale as Hero, enter, in Kenneth Branagh's lush and sty movie version of the play (1993).

AS YOU LIKE IT

As you like it is a self-consciously theatrical comedy. Characters in the play often see themselves as actors, and in the end audience members are invited to think of themselves as actors too. *As You Like It* may have been the first play performed in the new Globe Theatre in 1599, and it was officially registered by the Lord Chamberlain's Men on August 4, 1600. Shakespeare's source was Thomas Lodge's 1590 *Rosalynde*, a prose tale based on a medieval narrative poem, but the playwright also drew on tales and plays about Robin Hood, whose merry outlaws live in woods resembling the Forest of Arden in *As You Like It*. Inhabited by shepherds, the forest becomes a rural counter-court for a group of exiles from the duke's palace. In this natural setting, the exiles make peace with the world they have left behind, and discover themselves anew.

BEHIND THE PLAY

The forest of Arden evokes a pastoral paradise crossed with a university campus, where one may find "books in the running brooks," and "sermons in stones." It is also a place of suffering; in the forest, travelers are hungry, cold, fatigued, and disturbed by violence. Yet everything seems staged. *As You Like It* is set in a folktale world, where characters come in symmetrical groupings, and injustices often lack motivation. Characters like Oliver, the mean-spirited son of a recently-deceased nobleman, and the usurper Duke Frederick, who has banished his older brother, are never fully *evil* in the manner of, say, Iago in *Othello*. Instead, they are more like stock characters of folktale, who are simply programmed to be wicked. Yet, by the end of the play, both Oliver and Duke Frederick are converted by Christian ideals of love into good men. In the Epilogue, the boy actor who would have played Rosalind on a Shakespearean stage speaks directly to his audience, dismantling boundaries between fantasy and reality. The ultimate context of *As You Like It*, therefore, is nothing less than the social world beyond the theater, where members of the audience, like actors, play roles.

All the world's a stage,/And all the men and women merely players... 2.7

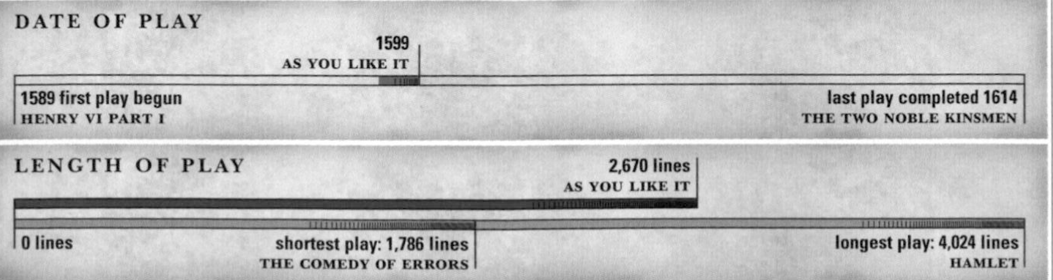

DRAMATIS PERSONAE

The court fool Touchstone (David Fielder) at first disdains the rustics of Arden, then falls for the simple goatherd Audrey.

DUKE SENIOR
109 lines
He is banished to the Forest of Arden.

DUKE FREDERICK
69 lines
The younger brother of Duke Senior, he usurps the dukedom.

AMIENS
37 lines
A lord attending on Duke Senior, he is a gifted singer.

JAQUES
225 lines
A melancholy lord attending on Duke Senior, he likes "to rail against our mistress the world."

LE BEAU
46 lines
A courtier, he always arrives "with his mouth full of news."

CHARLES
41 lines
A successful wrestler who has broken many bones, he is beaten by Orlando.

OLIVER
147 lines
Eldest son of Sir Rowland de Boys, he plots to kill his younger brother, Orlando, as he sleeps.

JAQUES DE BOYS
17 lines
Son of Sir Rowland, his brother Oliver has funded his education and protects him.

ORLANDO
297 lines
Youngest son of Sir Rowland, he falls in love with Rosalind; and even his wicked brother, Oliver, says that he is "enchantingly beloved."

ADAM
65 lines
Servant to Oliver until he asks to serve Orlando, who recognizes in the old man "The constant service of the antique world."

DENNIS
3 lines
Servant to Oliver.

TOUCHSTONE
275 lines
A clown in the court of Duke Frederick, he finds life in the Forest of Arden both pleasing and tedious; he makes his peace with rustic life when he courts, and marries, Audrey.

SIR OLIVER MARTEXT
4 lines
A vicar, he is called upon to officiate the marriage of Touchstone and Audrey.

CORIN
68 lines
A shepherd, he is "a true laborer: I earn that I eat, get that I wear...envy no man's happiness."

SILVIUS
75 lines
A shepherd, he is in love with Phebe.

WILLIAM
11 lines
A country fellow, he is also in love with Phebe, but is scared off by Touchstone.

HYMEN
30 lines
The god of marriage.

ROSALIND
677 lines
Daughter of the exiled Duke Senior, she disguises herself as a youth named Ganymede and poses as the brother of Aliena, the name taken by her dear cousin, Celia.

A testing role and the longest speaking part in the play, Rosalind (Maggie Smith) has always attracted top actors.

CELIA
276 lines
Daughter to Duke Frederick, she disguises herself as Aliena in order to accompany Rosalind into the Forest of Arden.

PHEBE
86 lines
A shepherdess, she falls in love with "Ganymede" but ultimately marries Silvius.

AUDREY
18 lines
A country girl, she may become Touchstone's bride, as long as she is not a "foul slut"; She assures him: "I am not a slut, though I thank the gods I am foul."

OTHER PLAYERS
Lords, Pages, Foresters, and Attendants.

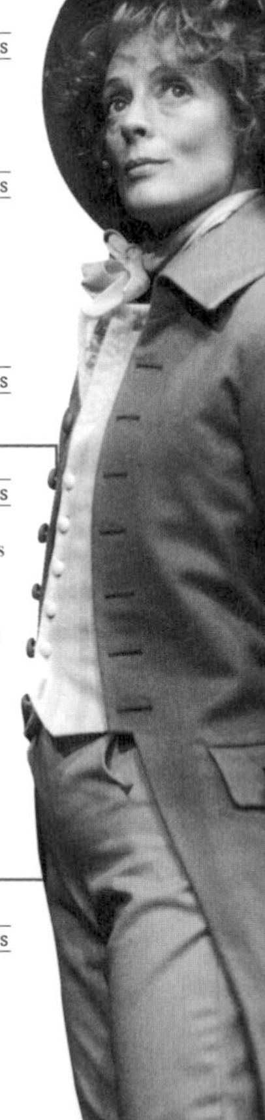

PLOT SUMMARY

SIZE OF ACTS

ACT 1	ACT 2	ACT 3	ACT 4	ACT 5
568 lines	548 lines	720 lines	403 lines	431 lines

ACT ONE
568 lines

ORCHARD OF OLIVER'S HOUSE AND DUKE FREDERICK'S PALACE

Cut out of his inheritance by his older brother, Orlando will seek his fortune. Charles the wrestler arrives from court with news: old Duke Senior has been banished and now lives in the Forest of Arden, like "Robin Hood of England." The old duke's daughter, Rosalind, has stayed to live with Celia, daughter of the usurping Duke Frederick. Charles is to wrestle on the following day, and hopes his opponent is not Orlando in disguise, as rumored, because Charles will compete as viciously as usual. Oliver, Orlando's wicked brother, pretending he will prevent Orlando from being so foolish as to wrestle Charles, secretly hopes Charles will kill Orlando.

In the duke's palace, Rosalind and Celia talk about the sport of love as the wrestlers arrive. The girls are smitten with the disguised Orlando, whom they fear Charles will injure. When Orlando triumphs, Duke Frederick is upset to discover the boy is the son of Sir Roland de Boys, his old enemy. Rosalind, whose father loved Sir Rowland, gives her chain to Orlando, who falls in love with her. Rosalind is in love too.

When Duke Frederick banishes Rosalind on pain of death because he suspects her of treachery, Celia proposes that both girls hide together in the Forest of Arden. Rosalind will disguise herself as the youth Ganymede, and Celia will be Aliena, Ganymede's sister. With Duke Frederick's tyranny growing, both as ruler and father, Celia proclaims the friends depart "To liberty, and not to banishment."

I did not then entreat to have her stay;/It was your pleasure and your own remorse... 1.3

What passion hangs these weights upon my tongue?/ I cannot speak to her, yet she urged conference... 1.2

ACT TWO

548 lines

THE FOREST OF ARDEN, THE PALACE AND OLIVER'S HOUSE

Duke Senior praises his exile in the Forest of Arden, noting how "Sweet are the uses of adversity" . He hears that his melancholy attendant Jaques, grieving over a hunted stag, has likened all humans to tyrants.

Now my co-mates and brothers in exile,/Hath not old custom made this life more sweet/Than that of painted pomp?... 2.1

Duke Frederick is incensed to discover his daughter has run away with Rosalind and Touchstone, the clown. When he hears the girls were admiring Orlando's body and may have left with him, the duke sends for Oliver, Orlando's eldest brother. Household servant Adam then warns Orlando not to return home, as Oliver plans to burn him in his bed. Orlando accepts Adam as his loyal servant . Disguised as "Ganymede" and "Aliena" , Rosalind and Celia observe Silvius telling an older shepherd, Corin, of his love for Phebe. Hungry, the visitors leave with Corin to purchase food from the shepherd in his cottage.

O good old man, how well in thee appears/ The constant service of the antique world... 2.3

Amiens, a lord attending Duke Senior, sings for the appreciative Jaques . Then they sing together. Jaques tells Duke Senior that he met a fool in the forest and conversed with him on the subject of time . As the duke's entourage prepares to sup, a starving Orlando arrives, sword drawn. The duke welcomes him and, as Orlando leaves to fetch Adam, Jaques reflects on life as theater. Orlando returns with Adam to eat while Amiens sings a bitter song .

Under the greenwood tree,/ Who loves to lie with me... 2.5

A fool, a fool, I met a fool i'th'forest,/ A motley fool... 2.7

Blow, blow, thou winter wind/Thou art not so unkind... 2.7

ACT THREE

720 lines

MAINLY IN THE FOREST OF ARDEN

Duke Frederick warns Oliver: find Orlando or lose the de Boys fortune. Meanwhile, as Orlando hangs love poems to Rosalind on trees in the forest, Corin and Touchstone debate the relative merits of the shepherd's and courtier's life. Rosalind reads a poem found on a tree. When Celia reveals the author to be Orlando, the love-struck Rosalind suddenly laments her disguise: "Alas the day, what shall I do with my doublet and hose?" When Orlando appears, "Ganymede" proposes to cure him of lovesickness: each day he must pretend to woo "her" as "Rosalind." Elsewhere, Touchstone, planning to wed Audrey, has called for a vicar. But marriage is delayed when Jaques counsels against marrying "under a bush like a beggar."

Rosalind is in a foul mood because Orlando has not returned as promised. She and Celia observe Silvius's hopeless wooing of Phebe . When "Ganymede" instructs Phebe to thank heaven "for a good man's love," the shepherdess is smitten with "him." Phebe reassures Silvius by proposing he deliver her "very taunting letter" to "Ganymede" .

I would not be thy executioner./ I fly thee, for I would not injure thee... 3.5

Think not I love him, though I ask for him./'Tis but a peevish boy. Yet he talks well... 3.5

O wonderful, wonderful, and most wonderful wonderful, and yet again wonderful, and after that out of all whooping!... 3.2

ACT FOUR

403 lines

THE FOREST OF ARDEN

Late for his session with "Ganymede," whom he now calls "Rosalind," Orlando receives a scolding lecture on time and the lover. When Orlando claims he would die for love of Rosalind, "Rosalind" says no one ever died for love. "Aliena" plays vicar to the lovers in a mock marriage.

Say 'a day' without the 'ever'. No, no, Orlando, men are April when they woo, December when they wed… 4.1

Orlando promises to return at two in the afternoon. Following a hunt, Jaques asks Amiens for a song that could be used to present the slain deer to the duke as if he were "a Roman conqueror". Rosalind is upset when Orlando is again late, but she is diverted by the tortured love letter from Phebe to "Ganymede." Suddenly, Oliver arrives bearing a bloodied cloth. No one recognizes him as Orlando's brother. He says Orlando found him under a tree, about to be attacked by wild animals. Instead of taking revenge, Orlando saved his brother, and in doing so was injured by a lioness. Oliver, converted to kindness by his brother's act, was asked by Orlando to present the bloody cloth to the boy pretending to be Rosalind. Seeing the cloth, "Ganymede" faints, then explains "he" was just pretending. But Oliver suspects the genuine swooning.

What shall he have that killed the deer?/His leather skin and horns to wear… 4.2

When last the young Orlando parted from you,/ He left a promise to return again/Within an hour… 4.3

ACT FIVE

431 lines

THE FOREST OF ARDEN

Touchstone mocks the country lad William, a rival suitor of Audrey, and sends him packing. Elsewhere, Oliver wants to give Orlando the family fortune, and adds that he loves "Aliena." "Rosalind" later consoles the injured Orlando, who tells her that Oliver and "Aliena" shall marry. For his part, Orlando "can live no longer by thinking." Claiming to know magical arts, 'Ganymede' says that if Orlando truly loves Rosalind, he shall marry her tomorrow.

I will weary you then no longer with idle talking… 5.2

Still in love with "Ganymede," Phebe arrives, followed by Silvius. "Ganymede" promises to fulfil the wishes of each, including Orlando, "tomorrow." If ever she would wed any woman, she says, she promises to marry Phebe. Meanwhile, Touchstone and Audrey, happy that they too will marry, are entertained by two page boys.

It was a lover and his lass,/ With a hey, and a ho, and hey nonino… 5.3

On the wedding day, Jaques thinks Audrey and Touchstone look like a pair of beasts boarding the ark of a second flood. But Touchstone gives Jaques a lesson in rhetoric.

If any man doubt that, let him put me to my purgation… 5.4

Hymen, the god of marriage, arrives with Celia and Rosalind, who gives herself to Orlando. Hymen officiates the four marriages, sealed in song.

Wedding is great Juno's crown,/O blessèd bond of board and bed… 5.4

Suddenly, Jaques de Boys, second son of Sir Rowland, brings news that Duke Frederick had prepared an army against Duke Senior. But, converted by a religious man, he instead passes his crown to his banished brother and returns all lands to those in exile. Duke Senior is pleased, but insists everyone enjoy "rustic revelry" before leaving the forest. Jaques, eager to converse with the new convert, leaves the wedding party.

Rosalind speaks to her audience, at first as herself, then, in the final lines, as a boy actor of the Elizabethan theater: "If I were a woman, I would kiss as many of you as had beards that pleased me".

It is not the fashion to see the lady the epilogue, but is no more unhandsome than to see the lord the prologue… 5.4

Play, music, and you brides and bridegrooms all,/ With measure heaped in joy, to th'measures fall… 5.4

READING THE PLAY

COMPARISON OF PROSE TO VERSE

prose: 54% | verse: 46%

As you like it is rich in lively prose exchanges, especially when characters are debating subjects such as love, time, or nature. But there are also outstanding verse passages, and speakers from all social strata employ both verse and prose. In other Shakespearean plays, prose is often reserved for characters of the lower classes, while courtly speakers sound more at home in verse. Here, in the special pastoral setting of the Forest of Arden, shepherds are given license to produce beautiful poetry. Equally, the nobles, liberated from the more measured world of the court, are freer in the forest to speak in relatively colloquial prose. Scholar Frank Kermode has called attention to the play's subtle and sophisticated Elizabethan language, as when fondness for pastoral poetry and other "fashions of the court and city are paralleled and mocked by inhabitants of the forest."

"Truly, the tree yields bad fruit." (3.2). Touchstone and Rosalind ridicule the "tedious" poems hanging on the trees. A print from *c.*1870.

As You Like It curiously doubles two sets of names: Jaques and Oliver. In the last scene, the two characters named Jaques add to the confusion when they converse with one another. The central Jaques is the melancholy attendant of Duke Senior, while the other, the middle son of Sir Rowland de Boys, only appears as a messenger figure in the play's last scene. One of the Olivers is the eldest son of Sir Rowland, but the other is a vicar appearing in a comical exchange between Touchstone and Audrey. Elsewhere, identity confusion is among the play's deliberate and most enjoyable themes. Few scenes are more engrossing than those in which Rosalind is disguised as a boy named Ganymede who in turn impersonates "Rosalind" in order to cure Orlando of lovesickness.

"Aliena," as the vicar, weds Orlando to "Rosalind" in *The Mock Marriage of Orlando and Rosalind*, an oil painting by Walter H. Deverell, 1853.

LANGUAGE NOTE

THE FOREST OF ARDEN

The Forest of Arden, which does not appear in the sources used for *As You Like It*, was Shakespeare's own invention. He may well have been thinking of his mother's maiden name, *Arden*, for the forest, or of the real Forest of Arden which can be found in the playwright's native Warwickshire. Records show that Shakespeare himself was cast in the role of Adam, the kind old servant who follows Orlando into the Forest of Arden to serve him faithfully.

SEEING THE PLAY

"I would I were invisible, to catch the strong fellow by the leg." (1.2). Celia (Nancy Carroll, far left) and Rosalind (Alexandra Gilbreath) are partisan observers of a pugilistic match between Charles (Joshua Richards) and Orlando (Anthony Howell) in a production by the RSC at The Pit in 2001.

AS YOU LIKE IT AFFORDS DIRECTORS great license to explore the world of the Forest of Arden. Early productions emphasized the pastoral forest as a counter-urban utopia. In the post-Freudian era, directors have staged the Forest of Arden as a sphere of the unconscious, where characters evolve by acting out fantasies. Some directors have distinguished the woods from the initial court setting by moving the stage into an entirely different location, requiring audiences to literally follow actors as they move into the new space. For his design of the play, Spanish painter Salvador Dalí created a disturbingly surreal Forest of Arden. However staged, the force of the play lies with its actors, especially the player of Rosalind. Gifted comic actors are drawn to Phebe, Silvius, Touchstone, and Charles. Principal roles bring their own challenges: the romantic Orlando can be overpowered by Rosalind, while the enigmatic Jaques must be at once engaged in and detached from the play's action. The dramatic diversity of scenes—wrestling, hunting, clowning, and musical interludes—adds to every audience's enjoyment of this play.

"Ganymede" (Lena Breban), Touchstone (Thomas Blanchard) and Audrey (Julie Pilod) in a 2003 French production of *Comme Il Vous Plaira* at the Chat Borgne Theater, Paris.

BEYOND THE PLAY

SINCE 1740, WHEN the Shakespearean text of *As You Like* It returned to theaters, leading actresses have been attracted by the mercurial intellect and physical stamina required to play Rosalind, the Bard's greatest comic heroine. Peggy Ashcroft, Katharine Hepburn, Vanessa Redgrave, and Maggie Smith are among them. Indeed, the heart of *As You Like It* belongs to Rosalind. In the English-speaking world today, ambitious actresses understandably view the role as a rite of passage. Rosalind's purpose is to forge her own identity, but also to embrace role-playing itself as a mode of survival. In the forest realm of exile and freedom, Rosalind experiments with the theatrical limits of social engagement. Her orchestration of disguised identities and her love lessons to Orlando in many ways liken her to a theater director. Jaques observes that "All the world's a stage," but Rosalind goes further: she welcomes her fate as a player on this stage, and even fashions roles for others.

An attractive theory holds that Shakespeare built the role around a talented boy actor who probably also played similar female roles in other late Shakespearean comedies, including Portia in *The Merchant of Venice* and Viola in *Twelfth Night.* Since 1920, directors have staged all-male productions of the play highlighting the impact of a male Rosalind. Like the Elizabethan boy actor, the male player of Rosalind is a male playing a female playing a male playing a female. Whatever the actor's gender, Rosalind beguiles audiences with her peerless investigation of the very human phenomenon of acting.

Film versions of the play have attracted top talent since the silent picture era. Director Paul Czinner's 1936 movie starred Elisabeth Bergner as Rosalind.

In Christine Edzard's 1992 film version of the play, Arden is set in an urban wasteland inhabited by the homeless. At a mobile café, Touchstone (Griff Rhys Jones) woos his sweetheart, Audrey (Miriam Margolyes).

STAGE NOTE

IMPROVISATION

For his 1999 production of *As You Like It* at the Williamstown Theater Festival in Massachusetts, director Barry Edelstein integrated a four-piece jazz band and singer to suggest through improvisational music the characters' searches for identities in the Forest of Arden. Gwyneth Paltrow's Rosalind accordingly experimented with different selves in the forest before settling comfortably into a wedding dress for the final scene, in which she marries Orlando.

Handsome wrestler Orlando (Alessandro Nivola) is "overthrown" by Rosalind (Gwyneth Paltrow).

TWELFTH NIGHT *or* WHAT YOU WILL

TWELFTH NIGHT OR WHAT YOU WILL, Shakespeare's only play to receive a double title, also displays a split personality. Commonly referred to as *Twelfth Night,* the play stirs moods of mournful sorrow and gleeful humor. The only known performance during Shakespeare's lifetime was for lawyers belonging to the Middle Temple in the Inns of Court, a professional society, on February 2, 1602. Today it is one of the playwright's most popular comedies, receiving inventive productions which explore bereavement and revelry as aspects of a single vision. The play examines varieties of human desire, from baser urges for food, drink, sex, and revenge to loftier longings for justice and love. And although the play offers comic resolution in the final scene, Malvolio's last words warn of unfinished business: "I'll be revenged on the whole pack of you!"

BEHIND THE PLAY

AS IN THE COMEDY OF ERRORS, Roman comedy again provides Shakespeare's main plot device: twins separated by misfortune. But here the twins are brother and sister, requiring the audience to accept the improbable premise that Viola and Sebastian could be mistaken for one another. Barnabe Rich's tale "Of Apolonius and Silla" (1581) provides the theme of a woman dressed as a man serving the ruler she loves. But Shakespeare's improvisations on his sources push *Twelfth Night* almost beyond the boundaries of comedy. The play is set in Illyria, a fictional kingdom on the Adriatic Sea. As the play opens, two deaths shape the plot: Olivia grieves over the loss of her brother, whom she has sworn to mourn for seven years before laying eyes on another man; and Viola fears that her twin brother, Sebastian, has perished in the same storm that wrecked her on the shore of Illyria. The main action of the play resolves this dual loss. A subplot focuses on Malvolio, the prudish steward to Olivia, who is tricked into thinking that the lady he serves is secretly in love with him. His situation is never fully resolved, and the play ends with the suggestion of a less comical story to come.

If this were played upon a stage now, I could condemn it as an improbable fiction… 3.4

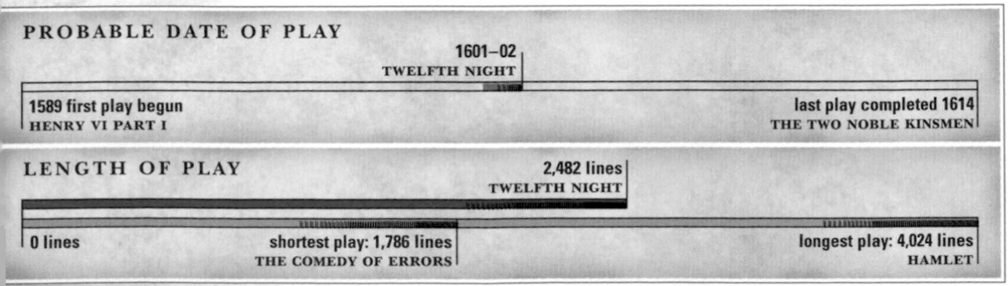

PROBABLE DATE OF PLAY

1601–02
TWELFTH NIGHT

1589 first play begun
HENRY VI PART I

last play completed 1614
THE TWO NOBLE KINSMEN

LENGTH OF PLAY

2,482 lines
TWELFTH NIGHT

0 lines

shortest play: 1,786 lines
THE COMEDY OF ERRORS

longest play: 4,024 lines
HAMLET

DRAMATIS PERSONAE

ORSINO
219 lines
Duke of Illyria , he woos Olivia even as she mourns her dead brother, but he finally returns Viola's love with a promise of marriage.

SIR ANDREW AGUECHEEK
147 lines
A wealthy and inane guest in Olivia's home, where, at the impish prompting of Sir Toby, he makes sloppy attempts to woo Olivia.

MALVOLIO
275 lines
Steward to Olivia, peevish and servile, he is accused of believing "that all that look on him love him"; fed up with his pomposity, certain members of Olivia's household set out to humble him and take their pranks too far.

The pride of Malvolio (Laurence Olivier) provokes a plot to mock and belittle him.

FESTE
308 lines
Clown in the home of Olivia, he is a brilliant wit and impersonator who finds himself sparring verbally with everyone in his own household and even in the palace of his neighbor, Duke Orsino; he captures the bittersweet tone of the comedy when he sings: "Present mirth hath present laughter;/ What's to come is still unsure"; he acts as a commentator on events.

VIOLA
337 lines
Twin sister to Sebastian, she disguises herself as "Cesario", a male page, in order to win the favor of Duke Orsino, with whom she falls in love.

MARIA
141 lines
Olivia's gentlewoman, she is fondly described by Sir Toby as "my little villain"; she is the witty author of the plot to humiliate Malvolio.

Olivia (Helen McCory) is a striking figure in mourning. She breaks her vow to grieve for seven years when she meets "Cesario."

SEBASTIAN
124 lines
Brother of Viola, his twin, he is initially feared to have perished in a storm at sea.

FABIAN
109 lines
A servant to Olivia, he joins in the mockery of Malvolio.

ANTONIO
106 lines
A sea captain and friend to Sebastian, his concern that Duke Orsino still takes him for a "pirate and saltwater thief" links the action in Illyria to a grittier past marked by naval war; he is arrested and eventually forgiven.

VALENTINE AND CURIO
13; 5 lines
Gentlemen attending on Duke Orsino.

SIR TOBY BELCH
332 lines
Uncle to Olivia, a lover of drink and merry-making, he plays countless pranks on the dim-witted Sir Andrew and irritates Malvolio, who finds him uncivil; he is eager to bring the unpopular Malvolio "some notable shame."

OLIVIA
308 lines
A rich countess, having vowed to mourn her dead brother for seven years, she rejects the advances of Duke Orsino, who calls her a "marble-breasted tyrant," but she finds time to woo "Cesario" and later marries Sebastian.

OTHER PLAYERS
Lords, Priests, Sea Captain, Sailors, Officers, Musicians, Servant, and other Attendants.

Viola (Lillah McCarthy) as the loyal "Cesario." In love with Orsino, "Cesario" earns his trust and respect and acts as the duke's envoy to Olivia.

PLOT SUMMARY

SIZE OF ACTS

ACT 1	ACT 2	ACT 3	ACT 4	ACT 5
578 lines	590 lines	675 lines	223 lines	416 lines

ACT ONE
578 lines

DUKE ORSINO'S PALACE, THE SEACOAST, AND OLIVIA'S HOME

Duke Orsino of Illyria, an incurable romantic, is in love with the countess Olivia. When he learns that Olivia refuses male company for seven years to mourn her deceased brother, Orsino is not put off: he loves her all the more for her sentimental devotion.

If music be the food of love, play on,/Give me excess of it, that, surfeiting,/The appetite may sicken, and so die... 1.1

Meanwhile, Viola and her twin brother, Sebastian, are separated when a storm wrecks their ship. Viola reaches shore, fearing the worst for her brother. Discovering she is in Illyria, she recalls her late father's praise of its unmarried ruler, Duke Orsino. Determined to win his favor, Viola prepares to gain access to the duke by disguising herself as a male page named Cesario. Orsino grows fond of the page, whom he commissions to "unfold the passion of my love" to Olivia. "Cesario" promises to try, although Viola has already fallen in love with Orsino.

Maria and Sir Toby Belch encourage the most unlikely of suitors, Sir Andrew Aguecheek, to court the grieving Olivia. But she is in no mood for love. As it is, her patience is tested by the irreverent wit of her clown, Feste, and members of her household, who carouse against her wishes. When "Cesario" arrives to woo her on behalf of Orsino, Olivia succumbs to the irresistible page. Pretending the youth left a ring as a gift from Orsino, Olivia instructs Malvolio to find "Cesario," return the ring, and tell him she rejects the duke's love. But she will explain the rejection if the page returns tomorrow.

Thy tongue, thy face, thy limbs, actions, and spirit/ Do give thee fivefold blazon... 1.5

And what should I do in Illyria?/My brother, he is in Elysium./Perchance he is not drowned... 1.2

ACT TWO

590 lines

THE SEACOAST OF ILLYRIA, IN AND AROUND OLIVIA'S HOME, AND DUKE ORSINO'S PALACE

Sebastian, Viola's twin brother, has reached the shore of Illyria. He insists to his friend, Antonio, that the two should separate so "I may bear my evils alone." Sebastian leaves for Orsino's palace and Antonio, who says he has enemies in Orsino's court, goes his own way.

Malvolio finds "Cesario" and attempts to return the ring. Alone, Viola realizes that Olivia has fallen in love with her in her male disguise.

I left no ring with her; what means this lady?/ Fortune forbid my outside have not charmed her!... 2.2

Malvolio discovers Maria, Sir Toby, Feste, and Sir Andrew making merry late at night at Olivia's house, and vows to tell Olivia of their "uncivil rule." When he threatens to accuse Maria falsely of encouraging the noisy revels, Maria plans revenge: she will pen a love letter, forged in her lady's hand; when Malvolio finds it, he will believe Olivia loves him. The group is ecstatic over this scheme. Concluding it is far too late to sleep, Sir Toby settles in for more drinking.

Feste provides entertainment in the Duke's palace as Orsino and "Cesario" converse about love. Viola suggests her own feelings for the Duke without revealing her identity. Duke Orsino produces a ring for "Cesario" to present to Olivia.

Come away, come away, death/And in sad cypress let me be laid... 2.4

In Olivia's garden, Maria and the others hide, joined by the servant Fabian. They spy on Malvolio, who, thinking he is alone, fantasizes he is *Count* Malvolio. Malvolio finally discovers the forged letter, in which Olivia requests her unnamed beloved to wear cross-gartered yellow stockings and to smile as often as possible. Convinced that the letter was written to him, Malvolio thrills at the prospect of his new social status.

By my life, this is my lady's hand. These be her very C her U's and her T's... 2.5

To be Count Malvolio... calling my officers about me, in my branched velvet gown, having come from a day-bed, where I left Olivia sleeping... 2.5

ACT THREE 675 lines

IN AND AROUND OLIVIA'S HOME

Viola as "Cesario" banters with the clown Feste, who seems too wise to be a fool. In the garden, Olivia reveals to "Cesario" her love for "him." Viola chooses her words carefully to maneuver through the exchange. Eavesdropping on the conversation, Sir Andrew concludes that his pursuit of Olivia is now pointless. But Sir Toby persuades him that Olivia is merely testing his affection. Sir Toby advises Sir Andrew to challenge "Cesario" in a letter, one written in "a martial hand." Maria confirms that Malvolio observes "every point of the letter" she forged. "He does smile his face into more lines than is in the new map with the augmentation of the Indies."

This fellow is wise enough to play the fool;/ And to do that well craves a kind of wit... 3.1

Antonio joins Sebastian to explain that, in a former battle against Orsino's warships, he offended the duke. If Antonio were recognized in Illyria, there would be bloodshed. Antonio gives Sebastian a purse of money to use for sightseeing and trinket-shopping in Illyria. They arrange to meet at an inn.

Olivia calls for Malvolio, believing his "sad and civil" manner will do her good. She is shocked to discover him wearing cross-gartered yellow stockings. When Olivia leaves to join "Cesario," Malvolio interprets everything in his own favor. But Sir Toby and Maria resolve to bind Malvolio and place him in a dark room to treat his madness.

O ho! Do you come near me now? No worse man than Sir Toby to look to me!... 3.4

Sir Andrew arrives with his letter to "Cesario," a confused declaration of war. Sir Toby offers to deliver it, encouraging Sir Andrew to fight "Cesario" at the earliest convenience. Sir Toby then informs "Cesario" that his rival, Sir Andrew, is a great fighter. But Viola is unaware of any such rival. Sir Toby goes on to frighten Sir Andrew by claiming "Cesario" a deadly foe. But just as "Cesario" and Sir Andrew nervously draw swords, Antonio rescues Viola, mistaking her for Sebastian. On orders of the duke, law officers arrest Antonio. As he is being led away, he calls Viola "Sebastian." Viola now wonders if her brother is alive.

ACT FOUR 223 lines

IN AND NEAR OLIVIA'S HOME

Feste mistakes Sebastian for "Cesario" and the two argue. Sir Andrew arrives to fight Sebastian, whom he, too, mistakes for "Cesario." Sir Toby seizes Sebastian and a battle ensues just as Olivia chases off the household ruffians. Olivia, also mistaking Sebastian for "Cesario," invites him into her home. Sebastian, delighted, has fallen in love with Olivia.

Feste disguises himself as the curate "Sir Topas" to visit Malvolio the "lunatic," now in the dark cell where the group has bound him. But Malvolio fails the test of madness administered by "Sir Topas." When Sir Toby worries that the pranks have gone too far, Feste sings. Malvolio complains to the clown, "Fool, there was never a man so notoriously abused," and requests a candle, paper, pen, and ink so that he may describe his predicament to Olivia in writing.

Hey Robin, jolly Robin!/Tell me how thy lady does... 4.2

Alone, the ecstatic Sebastian revels in his wonderful situation. His beloved Olivia presents a priest and the three of them head to a chapel for the marriage ceremony.

This is the air; that is the glorious sun;/This pearl she gave me, I do feel't and see't... 4.3

ACT FIVE 416 lines

BEFORE OLIVIA'S HOME

Duke Orsino arrives as Feste and Fabian spar verbally. Antonio and the police officers follow. "Cesario" points out her rescuer: Antonio. Duke Orsino recognizes him as an enemy, but Antonio explains that he entered Illyria only for love of Sebastian. When Olivia arrives, Orsino suggests that he may harm her beloved "Cesario" to punish her for not returning his love. Olivia ia upset. Convinced she is betrayed by her husband when "Cesario" prepares to leave with Orsino, she asks the priest to confirm that she and "Cesario" were just married. Now Orsino is perplexed. And confusion soars when Sir Andrew arrives to report that "Cesario" wounded him and Sir Toby in a sword fight.

And thus the whirligig of time brings in his revenges... 5.1

To everyone's amazement, Sebastian arrives to apologize to Olivia for harming her kinsmen. Orsino is dismayed by the sight of Sebastian and Viola together, until the twins reveal their stories. Viola explains her "Cesario" disguise, and tells how her own clothes were left with a sea captain arrested by Malvolio. Olivia, prompted to remember her mad steward, calls for Malvolio. Feste reads Malvolio's protest letter, impersonating the voice of a madman. Puzzled, Olivia asks Fabian to read it in a normal voice. Orsino proposes marriage to Viola, and Malvolio arrives to inform Olivia: "Madam, you have done me wrong;/Notorious wrong." He shows her the letter Maria forged. Fabian reports that Sir Toby has married Maria. But Malvolio departs with angry words: "I'll be revenged on the whole pack of you!" Orsino pursues him, entreating peace and hoping to find Viola's real clothes. Feste has the last word in a sad song, sung to the refrain: "For the rain it raineth every day." ♫.

But that's all one, our play done,/And we'll strive to please you every day... 5.1

READING THE PLAY

COMPARISON OF PROSE TO VERSE

prose: 61% | verse: 39%

THIS IS NOT A PLAY rich in great speeches touching on universal human themes. Instead of a soliloquy on folly, or a protracted exchange about the meaning of love, the play offers comments on life by steeping the reader in action, in the immediacy of the story's details. As a result, tempo is crucial to any reading of the play. In order to appreciate the recurring displays of wit and repartee as well as the finely tuned timing of prose and verse exchanges, it can be helpful for two or more to read this play aloud.

But, reading *Twelfth Night* cannot take account of music, which guides the play's moods and rhythms. The play opens with the romantic music to which the lovesick Orsino has become hopelessly addicted: "If music be the food of love, play on" is difficult to appreciate without accompanying sound. Feste's songs, too, go beyond mere entertainment to reflect on the drama as a whole. While imagination is required to follow action based on purely theatrical effects, as when Sebastian is mistaken for Viola disguised as "Cesario," readers can nevertheless enjoy the play's rollicking humor and pace. Feste's crisp philosophical wit and wordplay also offer entertaining food for thought.

WHO'S WHO

Viola, a survivor of a shipwreck, comes ashore in Illyria, where she disguises herself as a page boy named "Cesario" to serve the ruler of Illyria, **Duke Orsino**, with whom she falls in love. He dispatches her to woo, on his behalf, **Olivia**, a rich countess who immediately falls in love with "Cesario." Viola learns that her twin brother, **Sebastian**, whom she had believed was drowned, is alive and in Illyria. When Olivia meets him, she marries him, thinking he is none other than "Cesario." When the true identity of "Cesario" is revealed to all, Duke Orsino proposes marriage to Viola.

LANGUAGE NOTE

EVIL DESIRE

Colorful insults abound in the play, and most are directed at Malvolio. His very name suggests he may deserve to be lambasted. "Malvolio" is a compound of *mal*, "evil," and *volio*, meaning "I desire" in Italian. But whether Malvolio harbors improper intentions, including that of becoming "Count" Malvolio, some believe he is treated too harshly.

Malvolio poses in cross-gartered yellow stockings before Olivia, believing she is secretly in love with him, in a painting by Johann Ramberg, 1789.

SEEING THE PLAY

"I will be strange, stout, in yellow stockings and cross-gartered, even with the swiftness of putting on" (2.5). A pompous and be-suited Malvolio (Philip Voss) falls prey to the plot, gleefully observed by Fabian (Malcolm Seates), Aguecheek (John Quayle), and Belch (David Calder), RSC, 1997.

TWELFTH NIGHT has been a star magnet ever since Richard Burbage interpreted Malvolio and Robert Armin the clown Feste in 1602. With Malvolio as the comic lead, the play remained a perennial favorite, but was often staged in adapted versions with songs. In 1823, a London performance came to leave its mark on the play's production history. Actor Robert Bensley interpreted Malvolio in a new way. Critic Charles Lamb wrote: "He was starch, spruce, opinionated, but his superstructure of pride seemed bottomed on a sense of worth. It was big and swelling, but you could not be sure that it was hollow." Since then, others have explored Malvolio as a tragic figure who transcends mere clowning. This has had the effect of darkening the entire play, challenging actors and directors alike to capture its mixed currents of playful wit and troubled longing.

Viola is one of the most demanding of Shakespearean female leads. She is in love with Orsino, yet clear-headed enough to serve him while disguised as a male. Sir Toby Belch, Sir Andrew Aguecheek, and Maria call on actors to engage in hilarious ensemble work. But gifted clowns often steal the show in the role of Feste. His razor-sharp wit, deadpan humor, and stirring songs are frequently hard acts to follow.

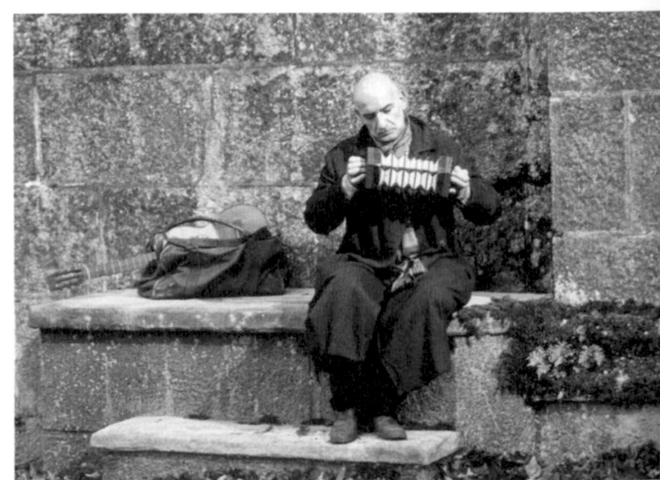

The renowned theater director Trevor Nunn turned his hand to a screen version of *Twelfth Night* in 1996, with Ben Kingsley in the role of Feste.

BEYOND THE PLAY

THE TITLE TWELFTH NIGHT REFERS to the twelfth night of Christmas, when the so-called Feast of Fools, a pagan rite, continued to be observed during Shakespeare's era. Celebrations briefly inverted standard hierarchies, overturned social orders, and praised human folly. In this spirit, some productions of *Twelfth Night* have exploited the play's special license to overstep boundaries. Others have sought to avoid offense. Director William Poel, while devoted to the idea of playing Shakespeare as authentically as possible, cut 30 lines on the basis of obscenity alone, and struggled to make the play at once "Elizabethan" and respectable for his London audiences of 1895.

More recent productions have embraced the "anything goes" sense of the play's alternative title: *What You Will*. For a 1998 New York production, set designer Bob Crowley created Illyria as a water realm. Lovers splashed playfully and clowns received rude dunkings in an on-stage pool, while Orsino, puffing an opium pipe, used the water to gaze at his own reflection. In London, director Lindsay Posner surprised audiences when Olivia stole one last kiss from Viola, the unmasked "Cesario."

Some directors prefer to warn audiences that life's cruelties encroach even on Illyria. In John Barton's influential 1969 RSC production, the set included a half-dead garden and a graveyard. Zoë Wanamaker played a Viola grieving the twin brother she presumes dead. *Twelfth Night* remains a nimble play, as able to examine harsh realities as it is to offer theatrical refuge from them.

Kyra Sedgwick (Olivia) and Rick Stear (Sebastian) in Nicholas Hytner's inventive interpretation at the Vivian Beaumont Theater, New York, in 1998, which dazzled audiences by transforming the stage into a water paradise.

ON STAGE

MALVOLIO

Well before Malvolio came to be perceived as a quasi-tragic figure, he was the comic star of *Twelfth Night*. In 1623, shortly after Shakespeare's death, the play was given at court under the title *Malvolio*. And a poem of 1640 by Leonard Digges attests to the character's popularity: "The Cockpit galleries, boxes, are all full/To hear Malvolio, that cross-gartered gull."

Olivia (Matilda Ziegler) steals a last erotic kiss from the lips of Viola (Zoe Walters) in the final scene of Lindsey Posner's RSC production in London, 2002.

TROILUS AND CRESSIDA

TROILUS AND CRESSIDA, AT ONCE COMICAL, FARCICAL, satirical, heroic, and even tragic, is Shakespeare's least classifiable play. A 1609 quarto identifies it as a comedy, but no Jacobean performance of this "problem play" is documented. It is set amidst the Trojan war immortalized in Homer's epic, *The Iliad.* During the Middle Ages, poets changed the story, recasting Homeric heroes as chivalric knights. Among the popular medieval additions was the story of *Troilus and Cressida,* which Geoffrey Chaucer rendered in prose as *Troilus and Criseyde* in the 14th century. Shakespeare, who studied Chaucer, was probably familiar with this work. The first recorded production of Shakespeare's text was before Ludwig II of Bavaria in 1898. The play was also given in Hungary, Austria, and France before receiving its first modern production in London in 1912.

BEHIND THE PLAY

TROILUS AND CRESSIDA IS SET IN TROY during classical antiquity. As in the *The Iliad*—the Ancient Greek epic attributed to Homer—Shakespeare's play begins with the action of the story under way. The Greeks and Trojans have been warring for seven years. The queen of Sparta, Helen, has been abducted by a prince of Troy, Paris. Helen's husband, King Menelaus, has joined his brother, Agamemnon, to lead heroic Greek warriors against Troy in order to rescue her. Shakespeare, however, is only sporadically and tangentially concerned with events of the Trojan War. *Troilus and Cressida* focuses on the young lovers of its title, both Trojans. Troilus is the brother of Paris, who has abducted the beautiful Helen. Cressida is the daughter of Calchas, a Trojan prophet who has defected to the Greeks, believing they will win the Trojan War. Much of the action of the play is set in the Greek camp. One Greek warrior, Ajax, is more brawn than brains, but Achilles is a proud and moody knight. The two grand subjects of the play are war and love, but by using inflated rhetoric and finely-tuned registers of speech, Shakespeare satirizes both warriors and lovers in *Troilus and Cressida.*

Take but degree away, untune that string,/And hark what discord follows! Each thing meets/ In mere oppugnancy... 1.3

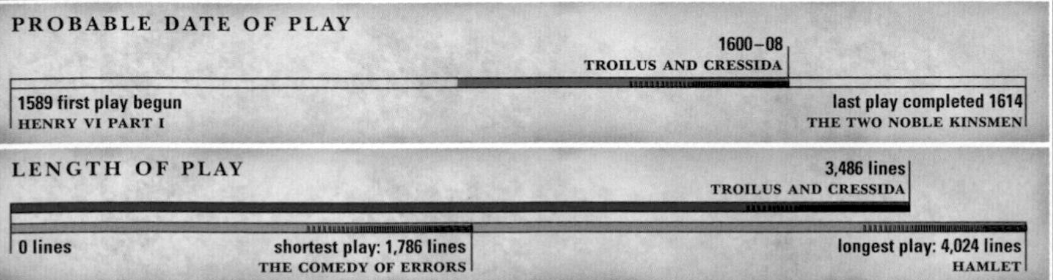

DRAMATIS PERSONAE

THE TROJANS

PRIAM
20 lines
King of Troy.

HECTOR
213 lines
Eldest son of Priam, he challenges the Greeks.

TROILUS
537 lines
Son of Priam, he falls deeply in love with the shy Trojan beauty, Cressida; but when betrayed by her, he turns bitter and vengeful.

The "matchless knight" Troilus (Ralph Fiennes) finds himself quite disarmed by "sweet Cressid".

PARIS
98 lines
Son of Priam, he refuses to give up Helen, the abducted queen of Sparta.

DEIPHOBUS AND HELENUS
2; 0 lines
Other sons of Priam.

MARGARELON
3 lines
A bastard son of Priam.

AENEAS
146 lines
A Trojan commander.

ANTENOR
0 lines
A Trojan prisoner of war.

CALCHAS
31 lines
Cressida's father, a Trojan priest, he defected to the Greek side when he foresaw that the Greeks would win the war.

PANDARUS
394 lines
Uncle to Cressida.

The bitter clown Thersites (Simon Russell Beale) bemoans the absurdity of war and warriors, hurling rancid insults all around.

ALEXANDER
33 lines
Servant to Cressida.

SERVANT
1 line
He serves Paris.

ANDROMACHE
15 lines
Wife to Hector, she foresees her husband's death.

CASSANDRA
37 lines
Priam's mad daughter.

CRESSIDA
295 lines
Beloved by Troilus, she pledges her fidelity, but proves false, falling for Diomedes; a human heroine, she is flawed, like Helen, and fated to fall, like Troy.

Cressida (Helen Mirren) plays "hard to win," knowing that "Men prize the thing ungained more than it is" (1.2).

THE GREEKS

AGAMEMNON
195 lines
The Greek general.

MENELAUS
12 lines
Husband of Helen.

NESTOR
158 lines
An elderly sage.

ULYSSES
488 lines
He cleverly manipulates Ajax and Achilles for the Greek cause.

ACHILLES
190 lines
The greatest of the Greek knights, he is too proud.

AJAX
84 lines
A blockheaded warrior, he also has Trojan blood.

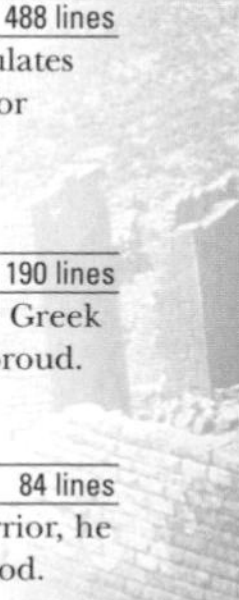

DIOMEDES
104 lines
Charged with escorting Cressida to the Greek camp, he falls for her.

PATROCLUS
65 lines
He entertains Achilles with his impersonations of the Greek commanders.

THERSITES
284 lines
A deformed and scurrilous commentator.

HELEN
24 lines
Abducted wife to King Menelaus of Sparta.

OTHER PLAYERS
Chorus, Trojan and Greek Soldiers, Servants, and Attendants.

PLOT SUMMARY

SIZE OF ACTS

PROLOGUE & ACT 1	ACT 2	ACT 3	ACT 4	ACT 5 & EPILOGUE
828 lines	612 lines	676 lines	690 lines	680 lines

PROLOGUE
31 lines

A Prologue welcomes the audience to Troy, where Greeks battle Trojans. Helen, wife of the Greek king of Sparta, is the lover of Paris, a Trojan prince, and the Greeks wage war to take her back.

ACT ONE
797 lines

IN TROY AT THE PALACE OF KING PRIAM AND IN CRESSIDA'S HOME; THE GREEK CAMP

Troilus is too much in love with fellow Trojan Cressida to wage war against the Greeks. He praises Cressida's virtues to Pandarus, her kinsman. Alone, Troilus says Pandarus will help him win Cressida ❞. Aeneas escorts Troilus to the battlefield. Cressida learns that Hector is angry for receiving a battle wound ❝. But Pandarus insists that Troilus is superior to Hector. As the Trojans return from battle, Pandarus comments on each warrior for Cressida's benefit, saving highest praise for Troilus. Alone, Cressida determine to prolong the courtship.

Peace, you ungracious clamours! Peace, rude sounds!/Fools on both sides!... 1.1

his man, lady, hath robbed many beasts of their particular additions... 1.2

The Greeks gather in a council of war and Agamemnon notes the greatness of their army ❝. Nestor agrees, but Ulysses argues that they are weak, the army's order and hierarchy unrespected. Patroclus has taken to imitating Greek commanders for the amusement of Achilles, who lounges in his tent, laughing at the impersonations and refusing to battle. Trojan Aeneas delivers a message: tomorrow, Hector proposes to challenge any Greek who thinks his lady love greater than Hector's ❝. Nestor, the sage, believes that Achilles should answer Hector's challenge. Ulysses has a craftier plan: to offer "the dull brainless Ajax" as the best Greek warrior, thus provoking "proud" Achilles to take action.

Princes,/What grief hath set the jaundice on your cheeks?... 1.3

Trumpet, blow loud;/Send thy brass voice through all these lazy tents... 1.3

Women are angels, wooing;/Things won are done; joy's soul lies in the doing... 1.2

ACT TWO

612 lines

IN THE GREEK CAMP AND IN THE TROJAN PALACE OF KING PRIAM

The Greek servant Thersites accuses Ajax of being moronic and jealous of Achilles. Haughty Achilles informs Ajax that a Greek knight is to meet Hector in single combat tomorrow.

Ay, do do! Thou sodden-witted lord, thou hast no more brain than I have in mine elbows... 2.1

Priam holds a council of war in Troy. He notes the Greeks' latest offer: "Deliver Helen," and all will be settled. Priam's son Hector sees no reason to fight over valueless Helen. But Troilus says Helen's worth "hath launched above a thousand ships." Priam's prophetic daughter, Cassandra, warns him to deliver Helen to the Greeks. But Paris insists that Helen is worth keeping. Hector finally supports his brothers, if only to preserve Trojan dignity. Delighted, Troilus is sure Helen will bring glory.

Virgins and boys, mid-age and wrinkled old,/Soft infancy, that nothing can but cry,/ Add to my clamour!... 2.2

In the Greek camp, Thersites bemoans the stupidity of warriors. The commanders arrive, driving Achilles into his tent to mope. Agamemnon, annoyed by Achilles's conduct, says the warrior is too self-important. Ajax asks the meaning of "pride"; everyone is talking about Achilles's "pride." When Agamemnon explains that it is a very bad thing, Ajax devotes himself to abolishing "pride." To make Achilles jealous, Ulysses flatters the block-headed Ajax, telling him that he is brilliant.

Thank the heavens, lord, thou art of sweet composure; /Praise him that got thee, she that gave thee suck... 2.3

ACT THREE

676 lines

IN TROY AND IN THE GREEK CAMP

At Helen's request, Paris takes a day off from warring to make love. Pandarus arrives with a simple message for Paris, but the atmosphere of the couple's love-nest makes plain speaking impossible. Indeed, Helen even insists Pandarus sing to them. Finally, Pandarus makes his point: when Priam calls Troilus to supper, Paris is to make excuses for his brother's absence. Pandarus leaves the couple to their "hot thoughts, and hot deeds." Pandarus conveys Troilus to an orchard to meet Cressida. Alone, Troilus is overwhelmed by love. Pandarus presents the shy, veiled Cressida, and Troilus praises boundless love. Once Cressida confesses her love for him, Troilus kisses her and believes their love is pure. He even foresees future lovers swearing themselves "As true as Troilus." Ominously, Cressida vows that if she is untrue to Troilus, false maids will in future be called "As false as Cressid." Pandarus shoos the

Love, love, nothing but lov still love, still more!... 3.1

I am giddy; expectation whirls me round./ Th'imaginary relish is so sweet/That it enchants my sense... 3.2

Hard to seem won; but I was won, my lord,/ With the first glance that ever – pardon me... 3.2

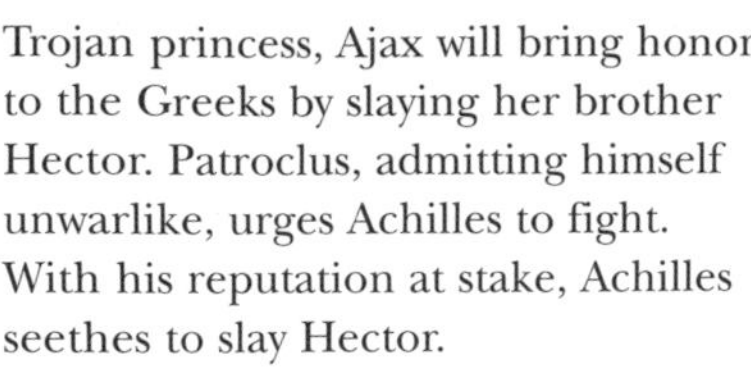

Love, friendship, charity, are subjects all/To envious and calumniating time... 3.3

couple off to bed in Calchas's house, where Cressida lives.

In the Greek camp, Calchas seeks recompense for his defection: he asks the Greeks to exchange their Trojan prisoner, Antenor, for his daughter, Cressida. Agamemnon orders Diomedes to carry out the plan. The Greek commanders alarm Achilles by treating him disrespectfully. When Achilles asks what he is reading, Ulysses says it is a work about human virtue lying dormant unless expressed to, and then reflected in, others. Tomorrow, he says, Ajax will surpass all Greeks for this very reason: he is a true hero, not self-absorbed. Since Achilles remains in his tent, his greatness is forgotten ❝. Ulysses also needles Achilles for being in love with Polyxena, Priam's daughter. While Achilles dotes on a Trojan princess, Ajax will bring honor to the Greeks by slaying her brother Hector. Patroclus, admitting himself unwarlike, urges Achilles to fight. With his reputation at stake, Achilles seethes to slay Hector.

'ime hath, my lord, a wallet at his back,/Wherein he ›uts alms for oblivion... 3.3

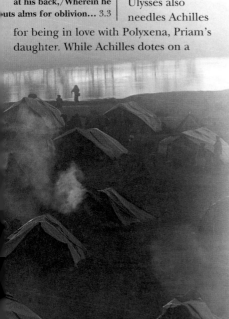

ACT FOUR 690 lines

IN TROY AND THE GREEK CAMP

Diomedes delivers Antenor to the Trojans and demands Cressida in exchange. While Aeneas fetches Cressida, Paris asks Diomedes who deserves Helen more: King Menelaus or himself? Diomedes reasons that Helen is a whore in both men's beds ❝. Aeneas rouses Troilus from Cressida's bed. When Pandarus explains the situation to Cressida, she says she loves Troilus more than her own father. Pandarus urges her to "be moderate," but Cressida says love cannot accommodate moderation ❝. Pandarus participates in the lovers' intimate parting. Troilus laments the separation and tokens are exchanged. Cressida receives a sleeve and offers a glove to her beloved Troilus, who warns her not to be tempted by Greek men. Troilus then cautiously delivers Cressida to Diomedes.

Both alike:/He merits well to have her, that doth seek her... 4.1

Why tell you me of moderation?/The grief is fine, full perfect, that I taste... 4.4

The Greeks welcome Cressida with flirtatious kisses. But Ulysses notes the girl's dangerous charms ❝. When the Trojans arrive to attend Hector's single combat, Achilles admires Troilus. Hector refuses to battle Ajax, his kinsman. Instead, Hector embraces Ajax and is invited to Achilles's tent. There, Achilles boasts he will slay Hector: they are friends tonight, but tomorrow, back on the battlefield, they shall be enemies. Troilus asks Ulysses for directions to Calchas's tent. There,

Fie, fie upon her!/There's a language in her eye, her cheek, her lip... 4.5

Ulysses says, Diomedes gazes at Troilus's beloved Cressida. Ulysses asks if Cressida had a lover in Troy. "She was beloved, she loved, she is, and doth," Troilus replies.

ACT FIVE

658 lines

IN AND NEAR THE GREEK CAMP

Achilles confides to Patroclus that he is in love with Polyxena, Priam's daughter. Alone, Thersites considers Agamemnon an "ass and ox". Diomedes sneaks off to Calchas's tent, where Troilus and Ulysses, and then Thersites, secretly observe Cressida as she receives Diomedes. Reluctantly, Cressida gives Troilus's sleeve to Diomedes, who vows to display it in battle and slay the Trojan who gave it to her. Cressida is torn by her dual love. Observing, Troilus is also tortured: "This is, and is not, Cressid!" Troilus vows to slay Diomedes and decries Cressida's infidelity: "O Cressid! O false Cressid! False, false, false!"

With too much blood and too little brain, these two may run mad… 5.1

Troilus, farewell! One eye yet looks on thee,/ But with my heart the other eye doth see… 5.2

Thersites reels at the latest developments: "Lechery, lechery, still wars and lechery."

In Troy, signs foretell Hector's death. But, rejecting family pleas, Hector insists on keeping his vow. In turn, Hector tries to dissuade Troilus from arming, but Troilus, also vengeful, determines to fight. When Pandarus delivers a letter from Cressida, Troilus rips it up angrily.

Thersites prepares to observe combat between the "Trojan ass" who "loves the whore" and "that Greekish whore-masterly villain". Agamemnon discovers only havoc on the battlefield, with Patroclus among the slain. Ulysses notes that Achilles and Ajax burn for revenge. Ajax teams up with Diomedes to battle Troilus while Hector fights a Greek in glorious armor. Trojan Margarelon, bastard son of Priam, encounters the unwarlike Thersites, who says: "I am a bastard, too; I love bastards." But, accusing Thersites of cowardice, Margarelon pursues him. When Achilles discovers Hector unarmed, he slays the Trojan and drags his corpse through the battlefield.

Now they are clapper-clawing one another; I'll go look on… 5.4

Stand, stand, thou Greek; thou art a goodly mark… 5.[illegible]

The dragon wing of night o'erspreads the earth,/ And stickler-like, the armies separates… 5.8

With Hector slain, the Greeks hope the war has ended. Troilus laments the death of his brother, but adds: "Hope of revenge shall hide our inward woe."

EPILOGUE

22 lines

Pandarus arrives with news, but Troilus, who will hear none of it, departs. Turning to the audience, Pandarus promises that, when he writes his will, he shall "bequeath you my diseases."

I like thy armour well;/ I'll frush it, and unlock the rivets all,/But I'll be master of it… 5.6

READING THE PLAY

COMPARISON OF PROSE TO VERSE

prose: 31% | verse: 69%

LITTLE ATTENTION WAS PAID to the literary value of *Troilus and Cressida* until George Bernard Shaw read it as a missing piece in the puzzle of Shakespeare's canon. Shaw argued in 1884 that the play, written between *Henry V* and *Hamlet*, bridged a gap between those plays "with its cynical history at one end and pessimistic tragedy at the other." With Shaw's reassessment of the play as a masterpiece heralding the naturalistic modern dramas of Ibsen, the play began to interest scholars and critics. *Troilus and Cressida* presents numerous passionate, albeit suspiciously inflated, verse speeches about love and war. Trojan lover, Troilus, and Greek commander, Ulysses, deliver especially potent language. But the play is also rich in naturalistic prose, most of it comical and bitingly farcical, as when Thersites outrageously mocks Ajax. Pandarus's match-making is fussy but charming, and his voyeurism offensive but delightful. For its naturalism, pacing, economy of language, and theatricality, nothing in Shakespeare's works matches the opening scene of Act 3, where Pandarus struggles through the lust fogs of Helen and Paris's chamber to clear the way for Troilus's first meeting with Cressida.

WHO'S WHO

Cressida is the daughter of the Trojan Calchas, who defects to the Greek side during the Trojan War. With the help of her interfering uncle, **Pandarus**, she is wooed by the Trojan, **Troilus**, son of **Priam**, king of Troy. One of Priam's other sons, **Paris**, has abducted the Greek princess, **Helen**, wife of **Menelaus**, king of Sparta. When the Greek, **Diomedes**, is charged with the responsibility of exchanging a Trojan prisoner for Cressida, he falls in love with her.

LITERARY SOURCES

CHAPMAN'S ILIAD

Before writing *Troilus and Cressida*, Shakespeare read *Seven Books of the Iliad*, published in 1598 by George Chapman (*c.*1560–1634). It was to be the first installment of Chapman's historic translation of Homer's *Iliad*, completed in 1611. Shakespeare was not the only playwright to be inspired by Chapman's work. Henry Chettle and Thomas Dekker also wrote a *Troilus and Cressida* in 1599, now lost.

"As I kiss thee – Nay, do not snatch it from me" (5.2). Diomedes and Cressida steal a clandestine kiss, and wrestle with Troilus's love token, overseen by an anguished Troilus. Engraving by J. Thompson, *c.*1850.

SEEING THE PLAY

At the Greek camp the two Trojan princes, Troilus (John Christopher) and Hector (Beeson Carroll), parley with the Greeks, Patroclus (Richard Kline) and the aged Nestor (Ron Faber), realistically frail, in Joseph Papp's modern-dress production at the New York Shakespeare Festival, Lincoln Center, 1973.

SINCE TROILUS AND CRESSIDA SATIRIZES romantic love and military might alike, the play is rarely given in wartime. Between World Wars I and II, the play received almost 50 major productions, over half in Germany and Austria. Then, during World War II, it received virtually no attention. But after the war, the play again became popular, with productions in England, the US, Italy, and Germany.

Troilus and Cressida features an unusually broad range of strongly-characterized male roles: proud Achilles, love-struck Troilus, decadent Paris, crafty Ulysses, and cynical Thersites. Female roles are fewer but no less sharply drawn: inconstant Cressida, mad Cassandra, lustful Helen. Actors greatly enjoy the license this play gives them to explore degrees of earnestness and satire in their lines. But in most respects, *Troilus and Cressida* remains a director's work. Since Shakespearean texts of the play have reached theaters only fairly recently, directors find that audiences come to *Troilus and Cressida* with unformed expectations and refreshingly open minds. Directors are able to explore *Troilus and Cressida* on their own terms as there are few established norms weighing on interpretation of the play.

ON STAGE

THE PITY OF WAR

On the eve of World War II, in 1938, *Troilus and Cressida* was played in modern dress at London's Westminster Theatre. Reading the play as a bold critique of warfare as well as war rhetoric, director Michael Macowan had actor Stephen Murray play Thersites as an intellectual left-wing journalist. Heroes were dressed in up-to-date uniforms, Greeks in khaki, Trojans in blue.

"Strike, fellows, strike" (5.8). Achilles (Timothy Stickney) closes in for the kill as Hector (Daniel Southern) rests from battle (Royal Shakespeare Theatre, 1992).

BEYOND THE PLAY

TROILUS AND CRESSIDA HAS BEEN classified as one of three "problem plays." But unlike *All's Well That Ends Well* and *Measure for Measure*, *Troilus and Cressida* pushes beyond the boundaries of comedy fully to incorporate tragic elements. Confusion surrounding the play's generic status has been attributed to textual problems. Both the quarto and *First Folio* versions of *Troilus and Cressida* conclude with the comical (albeit sour) final address of Pandarus. But textual evidence suggests that Shakespeare may have intended to end the play on a tragic note with Troilus's closing line: "Hope of revenge shall hide our inward woe."

Whatever the correct ending, *Troilus and Cressida* remains an unusual work. While the subject of the Trojan war brims with heroism, here the lofty rhetoric of battle speeches and love confessions casts doubt on speakers' sincerity. The action of the play, too, tilts toward irony and away from authentic tragedy. There is no single figure to admire apart from Thersites, who notes the stupidity and shamefulness of warriors and lovers in both camps. But for all of his moral outrage, Thersites is hardly a hero. Instead, he is more like a foul-mouthed provocateur who sees all too clearly that others occupy a world not of epic grandeur, but of bogus values, rancid priorities, and bloated self-importance.

With its irreverence towards sex and politics, *Troilus and Cressida* is a favorite Shakespeare play on college and university stages. Pacifists conjecture that the play captures Shakespeare's personal views about the pointlessness of war. More plausibly, *Troilus and Cressida* suggests that classical ideals and chivalric codes of honor are no longer at home in a severely transitional London, as the English crown was passing from Elizabeth to James.

ON STAGE

ALLEGORY OF WAR AND REVOLUTION

Troilus and Cressida has been staged in Central and Western Europe and in North America as an anti-war statement. For his landmark Stratford production in 1960, Peter Hall staged the play as a dual allegory of the Cold War and the sexual revolution. Designer Leslie Hurry covered the stage in sand, so that it resembled both a wasteland and a playground sandbox, adaptable for both war and sex scenes.

Troilus (Ian Holm, center) and his brother Hector (Derek Godfrey) plan tactics at the Trojan war council called by their father, King Priam of Troy (Donald Layne-Smith, enthroned rear right).

ALL'S WELL THAT ENDS WELL

IN ALL'S WELL THAT ENDS WELL, one of Shakespeare's "problem plays," women of all generations conspire to prevent a foolish young count from ruining his life. They do so by using a ploy known as the "bed-trick," by which a lady tricks a man who rejects her into becoming her husband. Shakespeare borrowed this story from a folk tale retold in the 14th century by Giovanni Boccaccio in his *Decameron.* Written in 1602–03, *All's Well That Ends Well* received no recorded performance in Shakespeare's lifetime. The play has fared little better since then, in part because its dramatic charms remain elusive. A lukewarm reception also stems from textual problems. The 1623 *First Folio* version of the play, the sole "original" version, was based on an uncorrected manuscript draft. Nonetheless, *All's Well That Ends Well* is an engrossing play, a mature work about immaturity.

BEHIND THE PLAY

ALL'S WELL THAT ENDS WELL is set mainly in palaces, those of the Countess of Rossillion (today Roussillon), in France; the King of France in Paris; and the Duke of Florence in Italy. In Florence, settings also include a battle camp and a widow's home. One brief scene is even set in a street of Marcellus (Marseille). Before the action of the play begins, the Count of Rossillion has been dead for six months. His widow is grieving her husband's death and her son Bertram's imminent departure to become the charge of the King of France. Also living in the palace is another young person, Helena, who has also recently lost her father, a brilliant medical doctor. Like the countess, Helena is grieving, but not for her father, as the countess initially suspects. Instead, Helena, in love with Bertram, cannot bear the thought that he is moving to Paris. While Rossillion is filled with mourning, the king's palace in Paris is hardly better: there, the king is gravely ill. Motivated by unwavering love for Bertram and using her formidable intelligence, Helena follows him to Paris. The play ends in Rossillion, where death and mourning are finally converted into promises of birth and joy.

...great floods have flown/ From simple sources... 2.1

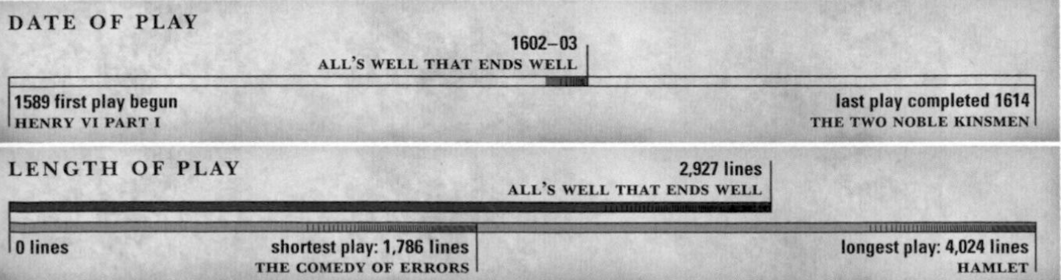

DRAMATIS PERSONAE

KING OF FRANCE
386 lines
He is about to die when Helena brings him a remedy; she asks that he allow her to marry the lord of her choosing.

DUKE OF FLORENCE
19 lines
At war with Sienna, he welcomes the French lords who support him.

BERTRAM
273 lines
Count of Rossillion, he is a ward of the King of France; when the king insists he marry Helena, he flees to Florence.

LAFEW
275 lines
An old lord, he does not understand the new generation, and he especially fails to appreciate Bertram's hanger-on Parolles, who calls Lafew an "old, filthy, scurvy lord."

THE BROTHERS DUMAINE
115; 148 lines
French lords, disguised as foreign troops, they ambush and interrogate Parolles near Florence.

RYNALDO
43 lines
A steward, he prepares a letter from the countess to her son in Paris.

LAVATCH
193 lines
A gloomy clown, "foul-mouthed" and bad-tempered, he darkens every conversation with his cynical calumny but, paradoxically, evokes patience in others.

A GENTLEMAN
22 lines
An astringer or "hawk-keeper" to the French court, he crosses paths with Helena and Diana and carries a letter from them to the king.

Lavatch (Floyd King), a pessimistic court jester of sardonic humor, fears and exaggerates the worst in everything.

COUNTESS OF ROSSILLION
281 lines
Mother to Bertram, she initially mourns both her husband's death and the departure of her son; she later grieves over the reported death of Helena and cuts ties with her son.

Although a stern grande dame, the countess (Peggy Ashcroft) loves Helena like a daughter.

PAROLLES
366 lines
A parasitical follower of Bertram, he proves himself a hollow trickster, "a most notable coward, an infinite and endless liar." Ambushed by his fellow Frenchmen near the Florentine camp, he betrays everyone, from his master Bertram to the people of Florence, in order to avoid torture.

HELENA
473 lines
A young girl brought up by the countess, she loves the higher-born Bertram; with the king's help, she cleverly wins him as her husband.

Gifted and determined, Helena (Sophie Thompson) overcomes all obstacles.

A WIDOW
66 line
A Capilet of Florence, she is old and eager to help Helena, whom she pities.

DIANA
136 line
Daughter to the widow, she remains a chaste maid throughout the play, even though Bertram is sure he had sex with her.

MARIANA
21 line
A neighbor of the widow and Diana.

OTHER PLAYERS
Lords, Officers, Page Gentlemen, French Soldiers, Florentine and French Citizens, Messenger, Attendants, and Servant.

PLOT SUMMARY

SIZE OF ACTS

ACT 1	ACT 2	ACT 3	ACT 4	ACT 5
570 lines	742 lines	503 lines	637 lines	475 lines

ACT ONE 570 lines

THE COUNT'S PALACE IN ROSSILLION AND THE KING'S PALACE IN PARIS

The Count of Rossillion has died and Bertram, his son, is to become ward of the King of France, himself dying. Bertram's mother, the countess, wishes her physician could help the king. But he has also recently died, leaving his poor daughter, Helena, to be adopted by the countess. As the countess bids her son farewell 🙶, Helena speaks in solitude of her love for Bertram, a noble beyond her reach. Parolles, who is accompanying Bertram to Paris, advises Helena not to remain a virgin. But Helena plans to follow Bertram ❟.

Be thou blessed, Bertram, and succeed thy father/In manners as in shape!… 1.1

Our remedies oft in ourselves do lie,/Which we ascribe to heaven… 1.1

Bertram arrives in Paris, causing the king to remember his late father fondly. In Rossillion, the clown Lavatch has impregnated Isabel, a serving woman, and seeks to marry her. The clown sings irreverently of Helen of Troy ♫.

'as this fair face the cause, quoth she,/Why the recians sackèd Troy?… 1.3

Rynaldo, the countess's steward, informs his lady that he overheard Helena expressing love for Bertram. The countess recalls that she herself was once a slave to "love's strong passion," and she tells Helena that she is as a daughter. But Helena, worried about the unromantic implications of being Bertram's sister, confesses her love for him 🙶. When Helena says she has a remedy for the king's ailment and may cure him, the countess encourages her to go to Paris.

Then I confess,/Here on my knee, before high heaven and you… 1.3

ACT TWO 742 lines

THE KING'S PALACE IN PARIS AND THE COUNT'S PALACE IN ROSSILLION

The king is sending lords to fight in Italy, but Bertram is told he is too young to join them. Lafew, a lord accompanying Bertram, announces Helena's arrival. The king sees no hope for recovery, but Helena, as daughter of the great physician Gerard de Narbon, argues that

I am undone: there is no living, none,/If Bertram be away. 'Twere all one/That I should love a bright particular star/And think to wed it, he is so above me… 1.1

What I can do can do no hurt to try,/ Since you set up your rest 'gainst remedy… 2.1

expectations are often fulfilled when they are least expected. When she says she would venture her life on the remedy, the king accepts the wager. If she cures him, the king promises that Helena may choose a husband from among his lords.

Methinks in thee some blessèd spirit doth speak/ His powerful sound within an organ weak… 2.1

The countess dispatches Lavatch to Paris with a letter for Helena. In Paris, all marvel that the king has been cured. When Helena chooses Bertram as her husband, he resists marrying a poor girl. But the king promises to add titles and wealth to Helena's inherent virtues. Bertram accepts and the wedding is prepared.

My honour's at the stake, which to defeat,/I must produce my power… 2.3

When Lafew brings news to Parolles that Bertram, "your lord and master," is married, Parolles claims to serve only God. Lafew is outraged. Bertram confides that he refuses to consummate his marriage and Parolles proposes they join the wars in Italy. Lafew warns Bertram not to trust Parolles: "The soul of this man is his clothes." Bertram dispatches Helena with a letter for his mother, and claims he will rejoin her later. Privately, Bertram swears he will never return home so long as Helena lives.

ACT THREE

503 lines

VARIOUS LOCATIONS IN FLORENCE: IN AND NEAR THE DUKE'S PALACE, IN A BATTLE CAMP AND IN THE HOUSE OF THE WIDOW CAPILET; ALSO IN THE COUNT'S PALACE OF ROSSILLION

In Florence, the duke is happy to receive young lords of France for his war effort, but in Rossillion, the countess receives a disturbing letter from her son: Bertram rejects Helena and refuses to return to France. Lavatch, meanwhile, has fallen out of love with the lady he impregnated and will not marry her either. Helena notes that Bertram's letter says he will not marry until Helena removes the ancestral ring from his finger and bears a child he has fathered. Alone, Helena reasons that she is responsible for putting Bertram in danger and resolves to steal away to Florence come nightfall.

'Till I have no wife I have nothing in France.'/ Nothing in France until he has no wife!… 3.2

While Bertram throws himself into the Florentine wars, the countess discovers Helena's goodbye note: she has become a pilgrim and has left to embrace death. The countess prepares a letter to Bertram: she hopes that, when he hears Helena has left, Bertram will return home and that Helena will follow him. Now a pilgrim, Helena arrives in Florence, where she learns from a widow that Bertram has been courting her daughter, Diana.

ACT FOUR

637 lines

IN THE WIDOW'S HOUSE AND BATTLE CAMP OF FLORENCE; THE COUNT'S PALACE IN ROSSILLION

French lords say Parolles is unworthy of Bertram's company. One lord proposes to ambush and interrogate Parolles so that Bertram can witness his treachery. Bertram, accepting the plan, sends Parolles on a phoney mission.

Helena reveals to the widow that she is Bertram's wife and offers a scheme: Diana should agree to meet Bertram, take his ring, and then, during a secret sexual encounter, allow Helena to replace her. The widow accepts the plan.

On his mission, Parolles schemes to make himself appear heroic with false wounds. The Frenchmen seize and blindfold him, speaking a nonsense language so that they will pass for foreign troops.

What the devil should move me to undertake the recovery of this drum…

When you have conquered my yet maiden bed,/ Remain there but an hour, nor speak to me./ My reasons are most strong and you shall know them... 4.2

Persuaded by such indecipherable phrases as "boskos vauvado" that his captors mean business, Parolles promises to reveal all secrets to the enemy troops.

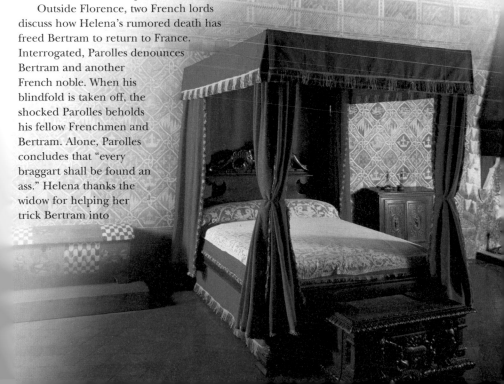

Diana tells Bertram that his vows to Helena are holy, but Bertram says that love itself is holy and asks Diana to succumb "unto my sick desires" to cure him. When Diana requests his ring, Bertram claims it an heirloom. But Diana says her virginity is no less valuable. Diana wins the ring and instructs Bertram to come to her at midnight, when she will place a ring on his finger and become his wife. Alone, Diana marvels that Bertram wooed her exactly as her mother predicted.

'Tis not the many oaths that makes the truth,/ But the plain single vow that is vowed true... 4.2

...or which live long to thank both heaven and me!/You may so in the end... 4.2

Outside Florence, two French lords discuss how Helena's rumored death has freed Bertram to return to France. Interrogated, Parolles denounces Bertram and another French noble. When his blindfold is taken off, the shocked Parolles beholds his fellow Frenchmen and Bertram. Alone, Parolles concludes that "every braggart shall be found an ass." Helena thanks the widow for helping her trick Bertram into consummating their marriage. The widow and her daughter will now accompany Helena on her return home to Rossillion.

Nor you, mistress,/Ever a friend whose thoughts more truly labour/To recompense your love... 4.4

In Rossillion, where Helena is presumed dead, Lafew arranges for Bertram to marry his own daughter and be reconciled to the king. The king and Bertram are both due to arrive this night.

ACT FIVE

475 lines

IN A STREET OF MARCELLUS AND IN THE COUNT'S PALACE IN ROSSILLION

Traveling to Rossillion, Helena and the other women cross paths with the king's hawk-keeper, riding swiftly to rejoin the king. Helena gives him a letter to deliver to the king, who is already in Rossillion.

A repentant Parolles returns home to Rossillion, where Lafew treats him kindly. The king has forgiven Bertram for his foolishness. Bertram claims he always loved Helena. The king encourages Bertram to marry Lafew's daughter, Maudlin. When Lafew asks Bertram for a token for his daughter, Bertram produces the ring "Diana" had placed on his finger during their sexual encounter. But the king, recognizing it as the ring he gave Helena, puts it on his own finger. Disgusted by Bertram's lying, the king sends him away.

Praising what is lost/Makes the remembrance dear... 5.3

The king's hawk-keeper delivers Helena's letter, in fact signed by Diana. In it, she tells how Bertram dishonored her and that she comes to Rossillion to seek justice. Lafew, horrified by Bertram, retracts the offer of his daughter's hand. Bertram returns on the king's orders to see Diana, who insists they are husband and wife. Bertram calls Diana "a common gamester to the camp," but when Diana produces his heirloom ring, everyone is persuaded that she is his wife. The king calls for Parolles to serve as witness, while Bertram explains that he "boarded" Diana "i' th' wanton way of youth." When Diana recognizes "her" ring on the king's finger, Bertram confesses that she gave it to him in bed and Parolles testifies that Bertram promised to marry Diana. But when Diana says that she never gave the ring to Bertram, the king orders her to prison. To the amazement of all, Helena suddenly appears, pregnant with Bertram's child. Bertram begs forgiveness and promises to love her "dearly, ever, ever dearly." The king is eager to hear the whole story, but first invites Diana to choose a husband.

If you shall marry/ You give away this hand, and that is mine... 5.3

Yes, so please your majesty/ I did go between them... 5

All's well that ends well yet,/ Though time seems so adverse and means unfit... 5.1

READING THE PLAY

COMPARISON OF PROSE TO VERSE

prose: 46% | verse: 54%

"A poor physician's daughter my wife! Disdain/Rather corrupt me ever!" (2.3). The young Count of Rossillion rails against the very idea of marrying low-born Helena, despite her virtue and beauty.

WITH THE ONLY SURVIVING TEXT based on the draft of a work-in-progress, *All's Well That Ends Well* is no literary masterpiece. At first glance, the play may resemble a traditional folktale comedy, set in a fantasy world: parents send young lovers into the world to undergo trials, and the action resolves in happy unions. But *All's Well That Ends Well* is also an unusual and sophisticated work, keenly aware of social realities. The play's plot turns on challenging issues such as the conflicting values of love and money, virtue and social status.

Themes of death and dying occupy the entire first act: "In delivering my son from me, I bury a second husband" laments the widowed countess. Older characters are forgiving and understanding, and while younger characters can be outrageously insolent, even their roles are written with sensitivity. No romantic hero in Shakespeare's comedies is more offensive than Bertram, but even he has good reasons for being odious: his mother clings to him, and just as he begins to live independently, the King of France forces him to marry against his will. Determined to forge his liberty, Bertram escapes from France as soon as he has obliged the king by marrying Helena. One is tempted to see Bertram as a villain but he is ultimately just a foolish youth making mistakes he will later regret. Helena, too, initially seems merely determined to have her way. But her love for Bertram, genuine and self-sacrificing, explains her campaign to secure him as her husband.

While it contains exceptionally strong passages in verse as well as prose, *All's Well That Ends Well* as a whole should be read as the older generation reads the younger in the play: with open-minded acceptance of even the most improbable developments, and with faith in the unexpected good in human nature: "briars shall have leaves as well as thorns/And to us sweet as sharp."

PLAY HISTORY

BITTERSWEET

Some believe that *All's Well That Ends Well* should be viewed as one of a group of plays (*Hamlet, Twelfth Night, Troilus and Cressida,* and *Measure for Measure*) written around the same time, when Shakespeare must have been deeply troubled. But there is no real evidence for such a view. Rather, in a way typical of the darker comedies, Shakespeare highlights the bittersweet realities of life and human nature.

SEEING THE PLAY

"My art is not past power, nor you past cure" (2.1). Helena (Irene Worth) tends to the invalid King of France (Alec Guinness) in the 1953 production in Stratford, Ontario, Canada.

RARE IS THE OPPORTUNITY TO ATTEND *All's Well That Ends Well* in the theater. During Shakespeare's lifetime, a play called *Monsieur Paroles* appears to have paid tribute to the popularity of the Shakespearean Parolles in the Jacobean theater. For nearly 200 years following Shakespeare's death, the play was frothed up with songs and dances, altered in the extreme to satisfy the popular preference for diverting showiness or fairytale romance. Parolles consistently stole the show in these revised versions of the play. But from the late 18th century, the Shakespearean text began to receive more attention.

The extraordinary lead roles in the play also began to attract the interest of prominent actors. Perhaps unsurprisingly, the lovable braggart Parolles remained a sought-after role; a young Laurence Olivier portrayed Parolles in 1927. But the emotional complexity of the older characters also attracted major actors: Alec Guinness interpreted the curious *gravitas* of the King of France in 1953, and Peggy Ashcroft played the grieving Countess of Rossillion in 1981. Today, the play may be presented as it has been since the early 20th century: as a fantasy romance drawing on the folktale tradition. More intrepid directors, however, reject the temptation to deliver the play as a Cinderella-like set piece. Instead, they explore *All's Well That Ends Well* as a naturalistic drama in which social realities are clearly observed, with an emphasis on the power of parental and romantic love to accept even the greatest follies of youth.

At once a "light Italian" romantic comedy and a dark Shakespearean play, *All's Well That Ends Well* is one of the playwright's most challenging works to stage. Most directors leave the play alone, or approach it only once they have considerable experience with other Shakespearean plays.

"I'll love her dearly, ever, ever dearly." (5.3). Bertram (Martin Walker) and Helena (Eileen Beldon) clasp hands in the innovative modern-dress production designed by Paul Shelving and directed by H. K. Ayliff at the UK's Birmingham Repertory Theatre in 1927. Watching from the sidelines, Parolles (Laurence Olivier, second from left) wears a gaudy three-piece suit.

BEYOND THE PLAY

IN ACT FOUR OF ALL'S WELL THAT ENDS WELL, a French lord notes: "The web of our life is of a mingled yarn, good and ill together." Indeed, *All's Well That Ends Well* is itself a mingled yarn. The play begins with mourning, loss, illness, and despair, and things get a lot worse before they end well. All eventually seems to conclude happily when Bertram and Helena are reunited and expecting a baby. But just as the play achieves comic resolution, the King of France repeats a mistake he made at the outset, when he invited the low-born Helena to choose any lord in his court as her husband. In the final passage of the play, the king offers the poor Diana any husband she desires and promises to pay her dowry. Thus, while the king brings the action full circle, Shakespeare plants the suggestion that the follies of youth, just like the errors of old age, will be repeated generation after generation.

Along with the perpetual generation gap of the comedies, *All's Well That Ends Well* also represents a gap between rich men and poor women. Helena and Diana are both impoverished women socially barred from marrying wealthy, titled nobles. Both are virtuous women: Helena is a gifted healer and devoted lover; Diana is chaste and inherently virtuous. But in the social world of *All's Well That Ends Well*, goodness alone is not enough for lowly women. Skill, wealth, and power are needed to realize social advancement; but even the king's nearly magical power is called into question: in the Epilogue, the actor playing the king proclaims himself a beggar and pleads for audience applause.

Many characters in the play believe in upward social mobility. The Countess of Rossillion's clown, Lavatch, has impregnated Isabel, a serving girl, and early in the play requests leave to marry her. But once he has had a taste of the king's court in Paris, Lavatch changes his plans: "The brains of my Cupid's knocked out, and I begin to love as an old man loves money, with no tomach." In *All's Well That Ends Well*, male preoccupations with ex and status are finally onquered by love.

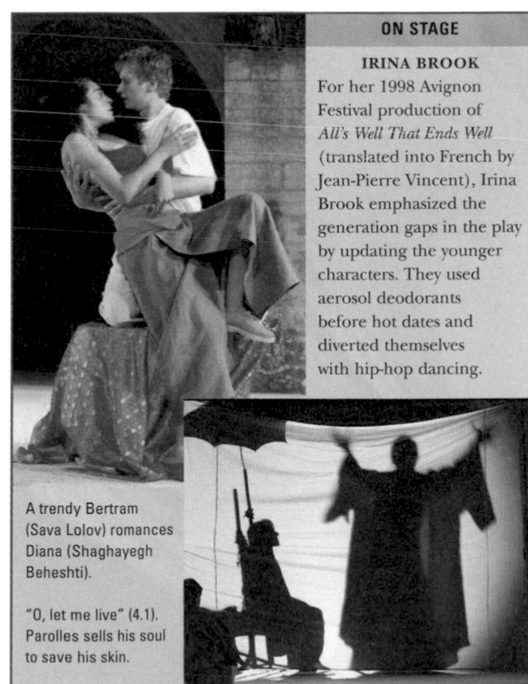

ON STAGE

IRINA BROOK

For her 1998 Avignon Festival production of *All's Well That Ends Well* (translated into French by Jean-Pierre Vincent), Irina Brook emphasized the generation gaps in the play by updating the younger characters. They used aerosol deodorants before hot dates and diverted themselves with hip-hop dancing.

A trendy Bertram (Sava Lolov) romances Diana (Shaghayegh Beheshti).

"O, let me live" (4.1). Parolles sells his soul to save his skin.

MEASURE FOR MEASURE

A POWERFULLY INTELLECTUAL DRAMA, *Measure for Measure* is one of three "problem plays" that fit uncomfortably into the genre of comedy. Its unconventional characters, themes, and conclusion led it to be neglected for centuries. Today, *Measure for Measure* has found new life on modern stages, partly because it weighs personal moral values against theological doctrine and social justice. Topically, it also asks whether and how human behavior should be regulated by the state. The only Jacobean reference to the play is the record of court revels, which suggests a performance before King James I on December 26, 1604. However, *Measure for Measure* was probably given at the Globe earlier the same year. Shakespeare integrated into the basic plot a traditional story motif, known as the "bed-trick," by which a man is tricked into having sex with a woman he has rejected.

BEHIND THE PLAY

AS THE THREE-DAY ACTION of *Measure for Measure* begins, Vincentio has been Duke of Vienna for 14 years, and his lax governance has begun to bear ugly fruit. With moral and social corruption rife, Vincentio has lost the credibility needed to enforce laws himself. He deputizes Lord Angelo to govern in his place. Then, disguised as a friar, Vincentio not only observes the extent of corruption and depravity in his dukedom, but also intervenes in the troubled lives of his subjects. He cunningly orchestrates two schemes designed to correct rampant moral and judicial imbalances. One, the "bed-trick," exposes Angelo's monstrousness and forces him to take responsibility for his lack of moral rectitude. Another, which could be called the "head-trick," involves passing off the head of another prisoner for that of Claudio, whom Angelo ordered decapitated. But despite these drastic solutions to sex-and-death dilemmas, the morality of everyone in Vienna is not only called into question as the action unfolds, but it also remains in question even as the play comes to an end. This unresolved conclusion is among the reasons *Measure for Measure* is often designated a "problem play."

Hence shall we see/If power change purpose, what our seemers be... 1.3

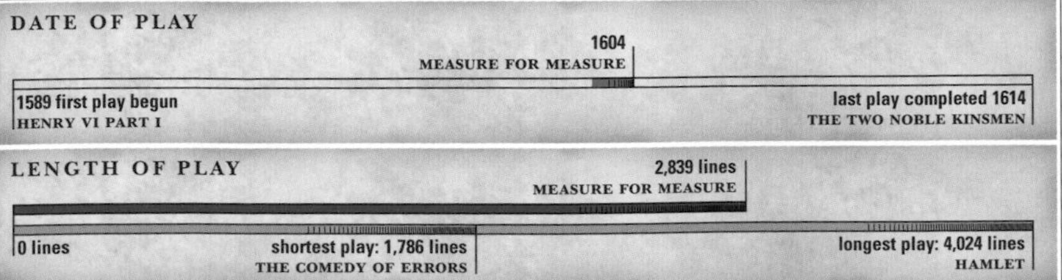

DRAMATIS PERSONAE

VINCENTIO
852 lines
The Duke of Vienna, he disguises himself as "Friar Ludowick" in order to walk unnoticed among the citizens of his corrupt dukedom.

ANGELO
322 lines
The duke's cold and authoritarian deputy, he falls violently in love with Isabella, but finally marries Mariana.

ESCALUS
188 lines
A lord, he urges a more lenient government.

CLAUDIO
113 lines
A young gentleman, he is condemned to death for impregnating his lover.

LUCIO
302 lines
Claudio's indiscreet and "fantastic" friend, he tells "Friar Ludowick" all about Duke Vincentio.

TWO GENTLEMEN
22; 10 lines
They appear with Lucio.

A PROVOST
163 lines
He knows the secret of Friar Lodowick's true identity.

FRIAR THOMAS
6 lines
He disguises the duke.

FRIAR PETER
36 lines
He officiates the marriage of Angelo and Mariana.

A JUSTICE
3 lines
He notes that "Lord Angelo is too severe."

VARRIUS
0 lines
He is a friend of the duke.

ELBOW
68 lines
A simple constable, he hauls pimps and prostitutes off to prison.

A headstrong youth, unjustly condemned to death, Claudio (Toby Stephens) confronts his human frailty.

FROTH
10 lines
A foolish gentleman.

POMPEY
158 lines
A clown, he is jailed for pimping, but accepts a reduced sentence in exchange for a prison job.

ISABELLA
420 lines
Chaste and religious sister to Claudio, Isabella refuses to have sex with Angelo to save her brother's life; at the end, when the duke asks for her hand in marriage, she doesn't reply.

A merciful Isabella (Josette Simon) helps save Angelo's life in the final scene.

ABHORSON
19 lines
An executioner, he has more work than he can handle when Angelo comes to power.

BARNARDINE
14 lines
A dissolute prisoner.

MARIANA
68 lines
Betrothed to but rejected by Angelo, she is disguised as "Isabella" for a sexual rendezvous with Angelo.

JULIET
10 lines
Beloved of Claudio, she is not his wife, but is pregnant with his child.

FRANCISCA
9 lines
A nun in the Catholic order of Saint Clare.

MISTRESS OVERDONE
29 lines
A bawd, or brothel-keeper she worries about the new clampdown on sex crime offenders, until jailed by the authorities herself.

OTHER PLAYERS
Lords, Officers, Citizens, Boy, Prisoner, Messenger, Servant, and Attendants.

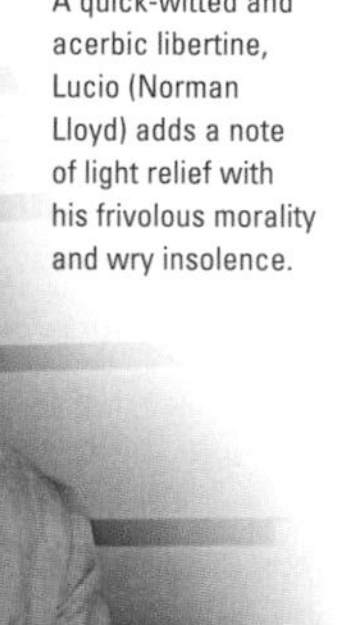

A quick-witted and acerbic libertine, Lucio (Norman Lloyd) adds a note of light relief with his frivolous morality and wry insolence.

PLOT SUMMARY

SIZE OF ACTS

ACT 1	ACT 2	ACT 3	ACT 4	ACT 5
429 lines	739 lines	553 lines	539 lines	579 lines

ACT ONE 429 lines

IN VIENNA: THE DUKE'S PALACE, A STREET, A FRIARY, AND A NUNNERY

Vienna has become too corrupt for Duke Vincentio to enforce the law. He deputizes Angelo as governor. Angelo's harsh rule is quickly felt. Mistress Overdone reports that Claudio is to be executed in three days for "fornication." His lover, Juliet, is pregnant. Overdone's servant Pompey delivers fresher news: suburban brothels are being torn down. Overdone, who runs a brothel, frets about the clampdown. Claudio explains to his friend, Lucio, that Angelo is using him to set an example. Claudio says that his virtuous sister, Isabella, is about to enter a convent. Lucio could ask her to appeal to the "strict deputy."

Angelo,/There is a kind of character in thy life/ hat to th'observer doth thy history/Fully unfold... 1.1

Unhappily, even so./ And the new deputy now for the Duke – / Whether it be the fault and glimpse of newness... 1.2

The duke tells Friar Thomas that Vienna's social order has collapsed because he failed to enforce "biting laws" over the last 14 years. The duke asks to be disguised as a friar so that he may secretly observe strict Angelo. Isabella is also strict. About to take vows with the sisterhood of Saint Clare, she wishes the order were stricter. Lucio explains her brother's life-threatening predicament, urging Isabella to seek Angelo's pardon.

We have strict statutes and most biting laws,/ The needful bits and curbs to headstrong weeds... 1.3

Therefore, I prithee,/ Supply me with the habit, and instruct/How I may formally in person bear me/ Like a true friar... 1.3

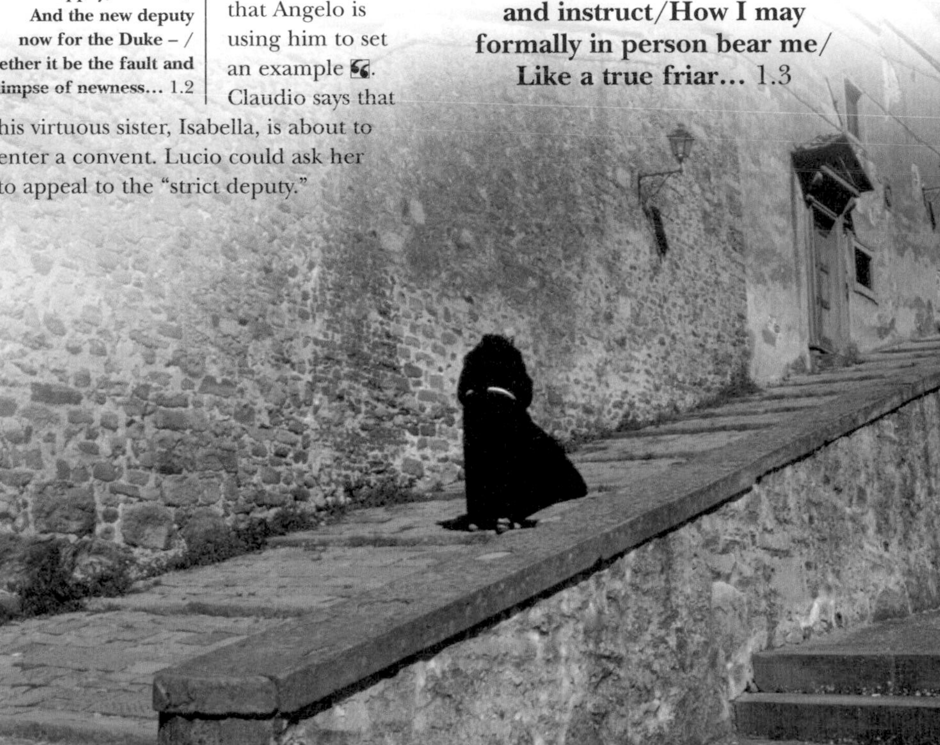

ACT TWO

739 lines

IN ANGELO'S HOUSE, IN A COURT OF JUSTICE AND IN A PRISON

Lord Escalus argues that Claudio does not deserve to die. But Angelo reasons that, were he himself found guilty, he too should be put to death. Angelo calmly prepares for Claudio's execution in the morning. In the law courts of Vienna, Angelo is at pains to extract information from suspects, and leaves Escalus to mete out justice. Froth is accused of fornicating with Elbow's wife; Escalus urges Froth to stay out of trouble, then dismisses him. Pompey is found guilty of pimping; Escalus excuses him as well.

'Tis one thing to be tempted, Escalus,/ Another thing to fall... 2.1

Isabella pleads to Angelo to spare her brother Claudio, but Angelo's will is unbending. When Isabella speaks passionately of "proud man,/ Dressed in a little brief authority," Angelo invites her to return the next day. Alone, Angelo is tortured to discover himself in love for the first time. The duke, disguised as "Friar Ludowick", ministers to the condemned in prison, where the pregnant Juliet is horrified to learn that her lover Claudio is to be executed.

The law hath not been dead, though it hath slept... 2.2

What's this? What's this? Is this her fault or mine?/ The tempter, or the tempted, who sins most? 2.2

Angelo is no longer interested in matters of state; he is in love. He receives Isabella and asks her hypothetically if she would exchange her virginity for Claudio's life. Isabella says no: better her brother die once than that she "die for ever" in the eternal flames of hell. Angelo makes a more concrete offer: if Isabella will have sex with him, he will pardon Claudio. Isabella has a counteroffer: if Angelo will not pardon her brother, she will publicize "What man thou art." He says no one would ever believe her. Alone, Isabella reasons that her brother will submit to death to preserve her honor.

To whom should I complain? Did I tell this,/ Who would believe me?... 2.4

ACT THREE

553 lines

THE PRISON

Claudio hopes to live but the "friar" says that life is more deathlike than death itself. The duke listens in disguise as Isabella tells her brother how Angelo asked her to exchange her virginity for his freedom. But Claudio fears death, and argues that her sin becomes a virtue if it saves her brother's life. Isabella departs with harsh words: "Die, perish."

Be absolute for death: either death or life/Shall thereby be the sweeter... 3

Ay, but to die, and go we know not where,/ To lie in cold obstruction and to rot... 3.1

"Friar Ludowick" proposes a solution to Isabella: Angelo was once betrothed to Mariana, whom he dishonored by retracting his marriage offer on false pretenses. Isabella could accept Angelo's offer, but then allow Mariana, disguised, to replace her. Isabella accepts the plan.

Elbow jails Pompey for pimping. Lucio tells the "friar" that Vincentio is a "very superficial, ignorant, unweighing fellow." When the "friar" asks his name, Lucio happily supplies full information and further insults the duke's reputation before departing. Mistress Overdone is also hauled into prison. She complains that Lucio, who informed on her, is a hypocrite: he impregnated Kate Keepdown and promised to marry her. Alone, Duke Vincentio determines to expose Angelo's "inner vice."

Thou art not thyself,/ For thou exists on many a thousand grains/ That issue out of dust... 3.1

ACT FOUR

539 lines

A GRANGE AT ST. LUKE'S, THE PRISON AND ANGELO'S HOUSE

Take, O take those lips away/That so sweetly were forsworn... 4.1

Mariana listens to a bittersweet song while Isabella gives the "friar" news: Angelo expects her in the middle of the night. Mariana worries about having sex with Angelo in Isabella's stead. But "Friar Ludowick" assures Mariana she is Angelo's wife "on a pre-contract."

The Provost offers Pompey a reduced prison sentence in exchange for serving as assistant executioner. Tomorrow, Claudio and the murderer Barnardine are to die.

Not so, not so; his life is paralleled/Even with the stroke and line of his great justice... 4.2

When dawn approaches, a message arrives. The duke believes it will be Angelo's pardon, but instead it is an order to execute Claudio and send his head to Angelo by 5 am. To save Claudio, the duke reveals his identity to the Provost and instructs him to send Barnardine's head for Claudio's.

Pompey notes that the prison house resembles the brothel where he used to work; many of the people are even the same.

I am as well acquainted here as I was in our house of profession... 4.3

Abhorson and Pompey prepare Barnardine for execution but, with the prisoner determined to live, the Provost instead offers the head of Ragozine, a pirate who just expired of fever and, happily, resembled Claudio. Alone, the duke plots his official return to Vienna.

When Isabella hears the false report that Claudio was executed, she becomes vengeful. But the "friar" says she will be able to sue for justice when the duke returns. Lucio insults Duke Vincentio, then brags to the "friar": "Thou knowest not the duke so well as I do."

Escalus and Angelo receive instructions about the duke's return to Vienna. The Viennese may petition for "redress of injustice" one hour before the duke's return, and then they are to meet Duke Vincentio at the city gates. Alone, Angelo believes he had no choice but to kill Claudio, lest he seek revenge. As for Isabella, Angelo thinks she would never dare to complain.

This deed unshapes me quite, makes me unpregnant/And dull to all proceedings... 4.4

ACT FIVE

579 lines

BEFORE THE CITY GATES

At the city gates, Isabella calls out for "justice, justice, justice, justice!" But when Duke Vincentio gives Angelo the honor of meting out justice, Isabella protests: "O worthy Duke,/You bid me seek redemption from the devil." Angelo says she is crazy, and Isabella accuses him of being an "archvillain". Isabella explains that she yielded to Angelo's outrageous demands in the vain hope of purchasing the life of her brother, Claudio, who was nevertheless executed.

O prince, I conjure thee, as thou believ'st/ There is another comfort than this world... 5.1

In brief, to set the needless process by,/ How I persuaded... 5.1

Isabella names "Friar Ludowick" her witness. As Isabella is led off, Mariana, veiled, is presented to Angelo, who is to judge his own case. Unveiling, Mariana claims she is Angelo's wife: she, not Isabella, knew him carnally. The duke sends for "Friar Ludowick," then leaves Angelo and Escalus to exact justice.

Accompanied by the Provost and Isabella, the duke returns as "Friar Ludowick". Escalus threatens to torture the "friar" for suborning the women. Lucio, boldly declaring that the "friar" must show his "sheep-biting face," yanks off Ludowick's hood to reveal Duke Vincentio to all. Lucio is instantly arrested. Escalus is pardoned and Angelo confesses, saying he should be put to death, but the duke orders him to marry Mariana. When Mariana and Angelo return married, the duke orders that Angelo suffer the same fate as Claudio. Isabella tries to prevent the execution, arguing that Angelo's intentions were evil but his acts were not. The duke rejects this and asks the Provost why Claudio was executed. The Provost presents Juliet, Barnardine, and a masked Claudio. Barnardine is pardoned and Claudio unmasked. The duke tells Isabella that, if this man resembles Claudio, he is pardoned. The duke then asks for her hand in marriage. He orders Lucio to marry Kate Keepdown, after which he will be hanged. The duke endorses bonds between Claudio and Juliet and Angelo and Mariana. His final words are for Isabella: "What's mine is yours, and what is yours is mine."

O my dread lord,/ I should be guiltier than my guiltiness... 5.1

Most bounteous sir,/ Look, if it please you, on this man condemned/ As if my brother lived... 5

They say best men are moulded out of faults... 5.1

READING THE PLAY

COMPARISON OF PROSE TO VERSE

prose: 38%
verse: 62%

Measure for measure was for centuries read as a strange and dated play. But since the 20th century, readers have been captivated as much by the high stakes of its characters' fates as by the play's unconventional approach to moral and political problems.

More than any other comedy by Shakespeare, *Measure for Measure* places unusual demands on its readers. The play frames numerous questions about the nature of good and evil, and the rights and responsibilities of subjects and rulers. With the action of the play never fully resolved, however, most of these questions remain unanswered. Readers are left to contemplate whether Isabella will accept the duke's offer of marriage and, perhaps more importantly, to evaluate the conduct and claims of each of the Viennese characters. In the end, the reader is placed in the position of both judge and arbiter, perhaps to succeed where the duke and Angelo failed.

"To be imprisoned in the viewless winds... 'tis too horrible." (3.1).
In his prison cell, a despondent Claudio confides in his sister, confessing his horror of death. Illustration from *The Works of William Shakespeare*, 1850.

Unsurprisingly, *Measure for Measure* is often classified as a "play of ideas" because it offers as much food for thought as it does entertainment. Yet many of the longer speeches are as poetically engaging as they are intellectually stimulating. The prose exchanges of the comical characters, the outlandish discoveries, the juxtapositions of the silly and the serious, and the neat resolution of the final act, are all masterfully built.

WHO'S WHO

Duke Vincentio, appalled at the corruption and depravity of his state, deputizes **Angelo** to act as proxy ruler. Angelo condemns **Claudio** to death for fornication with **Juliet,** who is carrying his child. But he will spare Claudio's life in exchange for sex with **Isabella**, Claudio's chaste sister. The duke plots for **Mariana**, disguised as Isabella, to have sex with Angelo, to whom she was once betrothed. Ultimately, the duke brings about marriages between Angelo and Mariana, and Claudio and Juliet. He hopes to keep Isabella for himself.

LITERARY SOURCES

POWER PLAY

Shakespeare's main source was a 1582 narrative fiction that George Whetstone had adapted from his own play of 1578: *The History of Promos and Cassandra.* But the same plot, about a proxy ruler pardoned for gross abuse of power, also appears in another work that the Bard consulted: a story from the 1565 collection by Italian Giraldi Cinthio, *Gli Hecathommithi.*

SEEING THE PLAY

ON STAGE

AUDIENCE PARTICIPATION

In 1999, the Expanded Arts Company of New York offered *Measure for Measure* in its free "Shakespeare in the Park(ing Lot)" series. The director Jerry McAllister updated the action to the present, and set the play where it was performed: in a municipal parking lot between Ludlow and Essex streets in Lower East Side Manhattan. Unwittingly, New Yorkers strolling through the parking lot became extras in the play.

Isabella (Clare Holman, right) "lends a knee" to plead for the life of Angelo (Stephen Boxer, rear right) with Vincentio (Robert Glenister, rear left), RSC, 1998. The dark-lit stage, with dark robes and menacing shadows, reflects the shifting disguises, dark passions, and moral uncertainties of the play.

MORE THAN ANY OTHER SHAKESPEAREAN COMEDY, *Measure for Measure* is one thing on the page, and something altogether different as theater. The play requires exceptional contributions from both directors and actors to be effective on stage. Directors must adopt a stance on the relationship between justice and human lapses, and actors must give intrinsic credibility and human warmth to characters, especially Angelo and Isabella, who often strike audiences as absurdly rigid. But the role of Vincentio is even more demanding. His is one of the largest parts in the Shakespearean repertoire and particularly difficult to interpret convincingly. If played as a Machiavellian duke, Vincentio appears to know from the start that Angelo is a villain. But Vincentio is also the author of disturbing speeches and vexing decisions, as when he lets Isabella believe her brother has been executed.

For their parts, Mistress Overdone and Froth are only ever charmingly corrupt, and Elbow is delightfully inept as the constable. Pompey is among the great comic roles of Shakespeare's later comedies. His job interview with Abhorson, the overworked executioner, offers one of the play's many exquisite comic sketches. But even at their most hilarious, Pompey and Abhorson can be unsettling: audiences find themselves laughing at a conversation about the relative merits of pimping and serving as prison executioner.

Isabella (Flora Robson), dressed in virginal—or is it matrimonial?—attire prepares to commit herself to a celibate life in a 1933 production in London.

BEYOND THE PLAY

"I have begun and now I give my sensual race the rein." (2.4). In a 1994 Cheek by Jowl production in the UK, Angelo (Adam Kotz) assaults Isabella (Anastasia Hille), raising moral issues for modern audiences.

MEASURE FOR MEASURE is a boldly philosophical play. It investigates new ideas and time-honored Catholic doctrine alike and examines the concrete experiences of individuals through the problematic moral lens of their leader, the duke. The play would have given its earliest audiences much to think about. James I, tolerant of Catholics, had only just been crowned; Puritan-led wrangling continued about the moral and judicial problems of the so-called Liberties in London's suburbs (whose brothels, prisons, and theaters are evoked by *Measure for Measure*); and moralizing was in vogue. In 1597, under Elizabeth I, Francis Bacon had published his *Essays,* which examined moral as well as political issues. During Elizabeth's reign, Bacon's work was not well received. As Shakespeare was writing *Measure for Measure,* however, Bacon's *Essays* earned new attention, and it appears that James's court enjoyed debating moral issues raised by the philosopher.

Shakespeare's play was not revived until 1738, when it was given at London's Drury Lane Theatre. Outstanding productions benefited from actors who incarnated the strong-principled characters persuasively, but it was not until the 20th century that this so-called problem play came into its own. Tyrone Guthrie directed the work in 1933, with Charles Laughton taking London's Old Vic Theatre by storm in the role of Angelo.

In England, *Measure for Measure* was among the most frequently produced Shakespeare plays between 1979 and 1990, when Margaret Thatcher was Prime Minister. Six major productions were mounted in London and Stratford during her tenure, and many were seen as urgent invitations to reflect on politics.

PLAY HISTORY

THE POLITICS OF POWER

In the US, *Measure for Measure* enjoyed fresh relevance during the troubled Clinton administration of the 1990s. When the Monica Lewinsky affair led to impeachment proceedings in 1997, directors extracted topical moral-political issues from the play, relocating it to a US troubled by sexual harassment and abuse of the death penalty.

The duke (William Hutt) persuades Mariana (Jackie Burroughs) to impersonate Isabella. In his 1976 Ontario production, director Robin Phillips set the action in 1912 Vienna, where Freud conducted his famous experiments in psycho-analysis. Characters were dressed in constricting garments to suggest a society plagued by sexual repression.

The TRAGEDIES

IN HIS TEN TRAGEDIES, SHAKESPEARE CONFRONTS THE DRIVING FORCES OF HUMAN NATURE, FROM HUNGER FOR ROMANTIC LOVE TO GREED FOR POLITICAL POWER.

MOST OF SHAKESPEARE'S tragic heroes are based on historical figures. Plutarch's *The Lives of Noble Greeks and Latins* is the principal source for his Roman plays, *Titus Andronicus, Julius Caesar, Antony and Cleopatra,* and *Coriolanus,* while *Timon of Athens* is set in ancient Greece. *King Lear* and *Macbeth* are set in early Britain, with protagonists modeled on monarchs documented in Holinshed's *Chronicles*: Lear was an English king, Macbeth a Scottish one. The Danish prince Amleth, also recorded in chronicles, became the subject of *Hamlet,* set in Denmark. The two remaining tragedies, *Romeo and Juliet* and *Othello,* which unfold in households of Verona and Venice, are based on Italian narrative fictions by Giraldi Cinthio. As a group, the tragedies range in style and structure, from the stricter, Senecan progress of *Titus Andronicus,* the playwright's earliest surviving tragedy, through the lyrical *Romeo and Juliet* and soliloquy-rich masterpieces *Hamlet* and *Macbeth,* to the pathos of *Timon of Athens.*

THE "GOLDEN PERIOD"

Tragedies figure among Shakespeare's very earliest and latest works, with four written during the reign of Queen Elizabeth and six under King James. Nevertheless, Shakespeare's most productive years, known as the "Golden Period," were between 1600 and 1608, covering the end of Elizabeth's reign and the first five years of James's rule. He then wrote 10 great plays, six of which are major tragedies: *Hamlet, Othello, King Lear, Macbeth, Antony and Cleopatra,* and *Coriolanus.* To explain this exceptional output, some historians have argued that uncertainty accompanying the transition between monarchs prompted the playwright to wrestle with tragic subjects; others point to the changed mood of England, from optimism in Elizabeth's reign to philosophical enquiry under James. Ultimately, Shakespeare's achievement resists all explanation.

Despite their variety, these plays may be viewed as a group. Tragedies are often contrasted with comedies. While comedies generally resolve conflicts happily, tragedies pursue conflicts to the point where they destroy individuals, families, and social orders. Where comedies focus confidently on familial and social continuity, tragedies acknowledge the deaths of individuals and the ruination of their worlds. And just as comedies represent the flexibility of communities adjusting to new values and practices, tragedies portray society as rigid, unable to accommodate its most assertive individuals.

Origins of the Tragedy

As a Western dramatic form, the roots of tragedy reach back to Ancient Greece. The word "tragedy" is built on the Ancient Greek *tragos*, "goat." Strictly speaking, the *tragōidia* was a work "singing about" a goat. While the comedy represents life in terms of seasonal renewal and rebirth, the tragedy confronts the animal existence of the human being and the inevitability of death. It has been conjectured that the tragedy originated in prehistoric rituals in which mammals (such as the goat) served a symbolic role, allowing spectators to identify their own mortality with that of the sacrificial animal. By the 5th century BC, the tragic outcome of individual action was represented not only in ritual form but also in dramas. Since the tragic hero was an exceptional person with no option but to die, the dramatic outcome aroused feelings of pity and terror in spectators. These Ancient Greek elements remain central to Shakespeare's tragedies.

The Christian Middle Ages

For a thousand years leading up to Shakespeare's lifetime, the most pressing questions about life and death were addressed in religious terms. Throughout Europe, the life, death, and resurrection of Jesus Christ came to incarnate and explain the tragic aspect of human existence. Early medieval dramas, played in churches, were integral to Christian ritual. Central moments of the Passion of Christ, often symbolized by a lamb, a descendent of the Ancient Greek *tragos* and Hebraic *scapegoat* were initially represented by church clerics speaking Latin. One of the earliest church dramas was the *Quem Quaeritis*—Latin for "Whom do you seek?"—in which male clerics played the roles of three Marys in a brief exchange drawn from *Luke 24*. Even in its earliest guises, liturgical drama invited Christians to embrace mortality as a tragedy ultimately redeemed by the promise of a spiritual afterlife.

At the end of the English Middle Ages, the liturgical drama moved initially into churchyards and later into squares, inn-yards, and even the streets of towns. At Easter, 15th-century English towns witnessed the development of whole cycles of plays, known as mysteries, in public spaces. These were performed in English, often on wagons serving as mobile stages, by amateur actors from trade guilds (hence "mysteries," from the French word *métiers*, "trades"). Reenacting Biblical scenes, mystery plays represented humanity's redemption in the death of Christ.

TRAGEDIES AT A GLANCE

Play	Setting	Method of tragic death
Titus Andronicus	Ancient Rome	Titus is slain by sword.
Romeo and Juliet	Verona	Romeo drinks poison; Juliet stabs herself.
Julius Caesar	Ancient Rome	Caesar is stabbed by conspirators.
Hamlet	Denmark	Hamlet is slain by poisoned sword; Ophelia drowns herself.
Othello	Venice	Othello stabs himself with blade; Desdemona is strangled.
King Lear	Ancient Britain	Lear dies from a surfeit of emotion; Cordelia is hanged.
Macbeth	Scotland	Macbeth is slain in battle; Lady Macbeth commits suicide.
Antony and Cleopatra	Ancient Egypt/Rome	Antony stabs himself; Cleopatra is bitten by a snake.
Coriolanus	Ancient Rome	Coriolanus is stabbed by enemies.
Timon of Athens	Ancient Athens	Timon: unknown.

During the same period, morality plays dramatized the struggle between good and evil, represented on stage by one area called "heaven" and another designated "the jaws of hell." As with the mystery plays, the central story of morality plays was the tragic lot of all Christians. In these Christian dramas, all human beings sin, suffer, and die. But salvation in the afterlife, secured by Christ's death and covenant with God, assured a special kind of happy ending. The ultimate generic character of human existence was, therefore, comic rather than tragic.

Shakespearean Tragedy

In Elizabethan and Jacobean theaters, tragedy became a secular form of drama responding to new questions about human existence, those that could not be answered by Christian doctrine or drama from the liturgical tradition. Not surprisingly, Shakespeare set most of his tragedies in pre-Christian periods: without a Christian framework, protagonists are given no ready explanations for their trials. The classical settings of the four Roman plays and *Timon of Athens* achieve this since it was believed that Ancient Greeks and Romans had no recourse to a redemptive cosmos explaining human action and death. Even *King Lear* is set in pre-Christian Britain, with no ready explanations given for Lear's sufferings. Thus, the secular tragedies of the English Renaissance led authors and spectators into uncharted waters, forcing them to look outward for new ideas and alternative explanations or to look inward toward a self rife with questions which Christianity could not answer.

The Soliloquy

Nowhere is the secular human quest for understanding so stark in Shakespeare's plays as in the tragic masterpieces: *Hamlet, Othello, King Lear,* and *Macbeth.* Aptly, these tragedies employ sophisticated soliloquies, which present characters exploring their actions in speech delivered directly to the audience. From the Latin *soli-* "alone" + *loqui* "to speak," a soliloquy in the strictest sense is a speech delivered by an actor alone on the stage. In late medieval and early Tudor drama, the soliloquy was typically spoken by an evil character, such as a demon or Satan himself. In the morality plays, it was the figure of Vice, the ancestor of Shakespeare's Iago in *Othello,* who most often spoke in soliloquy to divulge dastardly plots intended to snare innocent Christians. Over time, the soliloquy evolved to capture the more refined reflections and intentions, eventually suiting speakers beyond good or evil. In Shakespeare's hands, the soliloquy allowed tragic speakers to probe unsettling human doubts and longings. Hamlet, for instance, examines destiny itself in a soliloquy beginning "To be or not to be—that is the question." In Shakespeare's tragedies, up to 10 percent of the staged speech occurs in soliloquy. Densest in soliloquy are *Hamlet* and *Macbeth,* where the action of the entire play progresses in relation to the protagonist's evolving state of mind. The soliloquy in Shakespeare's tragedies often serves as a portal, drawing readers and audiences further into the world of a tragic figure progressing inevitably toward death.

Death and the Theater

In Shakespeare's time, amphitheaters like the Globe prompted audiences to recall the precariousness of life. Large and

THE TRAGIC STAGE

Shakespeare's tragedies represent human action in a secular world. But the tragedies also address broader, ultimately cosmic implications of the tragic protagonist's progress and death. Shakespeare's tragedies, whether performed at the Globe or the Blackfriars Theatre, therefore employed the stage from top to bottom.

The "heavens" or the "shadow." A roof projected over the stage and supported by pillars captured upper limits of the theater's expansive symbolic scope. At the Globe, the ceiling was decorated with zodiac signs, as in the new Shakespeare's Globe *(right).* Characters could descend from or be lifted up into "the heavens" with suspension gear.

Aloft or above. A space above the "tiring room" or dressing room at the back of the stage, it probably served as Juliet's balcony in *Romeo and Juliet.*

Hell. A trap door, probably placed in the middle of the stage and used as a variety of settings: a pit in *Titus Andronicus* or Ophelia's tomb in *Hamlet.*

Discovery space. An area at the back of the stage concealed by a curtain or "arras," (black for tragedies and multicolored for comedies) that could be pulled aside to reveal a surprising sight, such as the slain body of Polonius in *Hamlet.*

Stage. The platform on which the main action was played. At the Globe, it was around 27 by 43 feet wide and raised five feet off the ground. Emphasis on horizontal action favored audience interaction and allowed tragic figures to explore the breadth of their existence, as when Lear discovers his humanity in the storm scene of *King Lear.* "Here I stand," he says on the stage.

crowded theaters, natural breeding grounds for deadly diseases, were routinely shut during the plague epidemics that swept through London. The design of the public theaters also recalled both bull- and bear-baiting arenas, where animals battled to their deaths, or the inn-yard, where spectators attended plays but also sword fights. The tragedies themselves were steeped in violence. Animal blood, particularly pig's blood, was employed to lend realism to messy death scenes. Gorier tragedies, such as *Titus Andronicus* and *Macbeth,* left the stage of the Globe awash with the sight and smell of blood.

In modern playhouses, the stamina required to interpret Shakespeare's tragic heroes has reputedly taken the lives of leading tragedians. One was John Philip Kemble, who left the London stage in mid-performance of *Othello* only to perish soon after. Macbeth too is a play with pagan undertones which has left casualties. Since the mid-20th century, directors have brought spectators closer to death in staging Shakespeare's tragedies. Some have aimed to reintroduce ancient ritual energies into modern playhouses, even to the point of placing animal corpses on stage. Others have underlined the tragic through references to painful events within recent memory. Death, that tragic fact of life, became a subject of vigorous secular examination in Shakespeare's tragedies. But with death as mysterious today as then, Shakespeare's tragedies remain the playwright's most urgently probing plays.

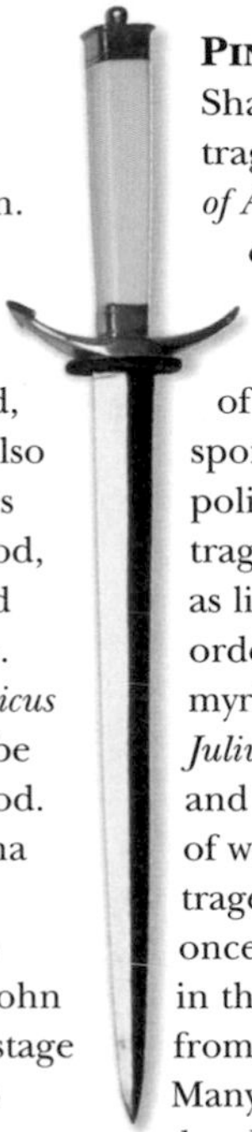

Pinnacles of Dramatic Art

Shakespeare's earliest and latest tragedies, *Titus Andronicus* and *Timon of Athens,* are rarely performed. Two of his greatest tragedies, *Antony and Cleopatra* and *Coriolanus,* have captured the enthusiasm of directors and audiences only sporadically, often depending on political climates. The remaining tragedies have been widely recognized as literary achievements of the highest order. In the original English and myriad translations, *Romeo and Juliet, Julius Caesar, Hamlet, Othello, King Lear,* and *Macbeth* have entered the pantheon of world literature. Each of these tragedies has secured its own place at once in the imaginations of readers and in the repertoires of theater companies from nearly every region of the globe. Many scholars and stage directors agree that *Hamlet, Othello, King Lear,* and *Macbeth* are the four finest tragedies to have been written in English and among the greatest dramatic masterpieces of any language or era. To read or attend them amounts to nothing less than to participate in their bold journeys into the deepest human fears and desires. For 400 years, these plays have engaged questions about the nature and meaning of universal experiences. For just as long, they have also been subjected to unceasing critical enquiry and commentary. But no amount of analytical investigation or staged interpretation has diminished Shakespeare's monumental tragedies.

DATES OF THE TRAGEDIES

- **1589** First play
- **1593–94** Titus Andronicus
- **1594–96** Romeo and Juliet
- **1599** Julius Caesar
- **1600–1601** Hamlet
- **1604** Othello
- **1605** King Lear
- **1605–06** Macbeth
- **1607–08** Antony and Cleopatra, Coriolanus, Timon of Athens
- **1614** Last play

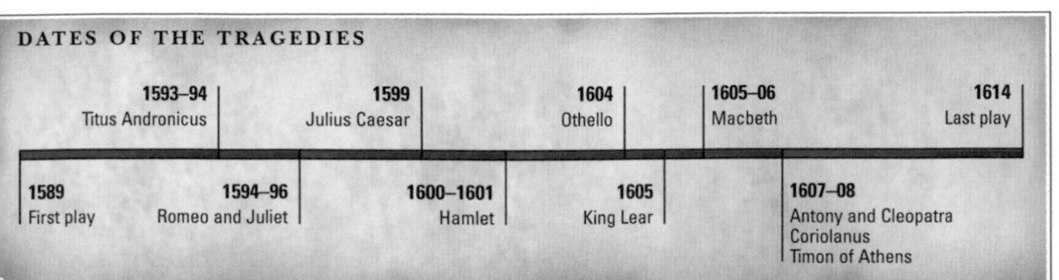

TITUS ANDRONICUS

TITUS ANDRONICUS, SHAKESPEARE'S FIRST TRAGEDY, is quite the bloodiest play he ever wrote. Indeed, it is so gory that for centuries many scholars were reluctant to accept it as his work. But Shakespeare almost certainly wrote this "revenge tragedy," probably in 1593–1594, and it was an immediate hit. Its earliest recorded performance was at the Rose theater on 24 January 1594; it was his first play to be published in a quarto edition, also in 1594 (albeit without his name); and it was still being performed 20 years later. Shakespeare took two pivotal plot elements—the rape and mutilation of Titus's daughter, and cannibalism—from Ovid's *Metamorphoses VI*. He may also have consulted an Italian prose narrative, *The History of Titus Andronicus*. From the mid-17th century, considered too violent for audiences, *Titus Andronicus* was abandoned, returning to the stage only in 1923.

BEHIND THE PLAY

THE PLAY IS SET IN NO SPECIFIC PERIOD of Roman history, although the presence of the Goths as "barbarous" threats to Rome suggests that it takes place somewhere around the 3rd century AD. While the story is fictitious, it conveys an accurate picture of Roman power divided among the competing forces of the emperor, the tribunes and senators, and the military. It also captures the early stages of Goth influence over Rome. The play is dominated by Titus's desire to avenge the rape and mutilation of his daughter, Lavinia, but other revenge variables are also at work. The Goth queen Tamora has good reason for retribution after Titus orders the execution of her eldest son. The emperor is also offended when, having been promised Titus's daughter, she refuses him. But Titus never identifies his most dangerous foe, Aaron the Moor. Aaron's power is that of Iago in *Othello*: he sets in motion a scenario of horror without showing his hand; and when unmasked, he displays no remorse. Yet in the tradition of the history plays that Shakespeare was also writing in the 1590s, *Titus Andronicus* ends on an upbeat note: the stage is covered with corpses, but the new emperor, Lucius, promises to unite Rome.

Vengeance is in my heart, death in my hand,/Blood and revenge are hammering in my head... 2.3

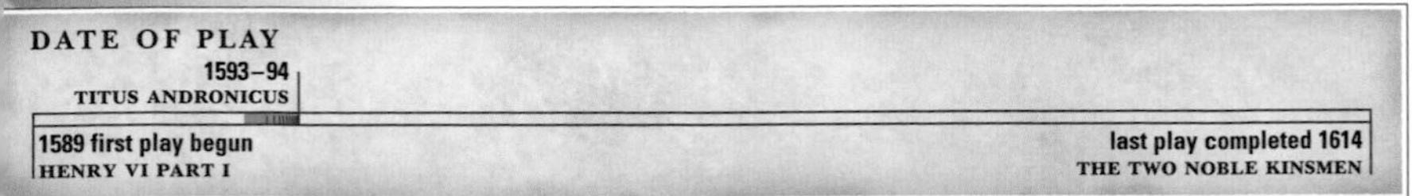

DATE OF PLAY

1593–94
TITUS ANDRONICUS

1589 first play begun
HENRY VI PART I

last play completed 1614
THE TWO NOBLE KINSMEN

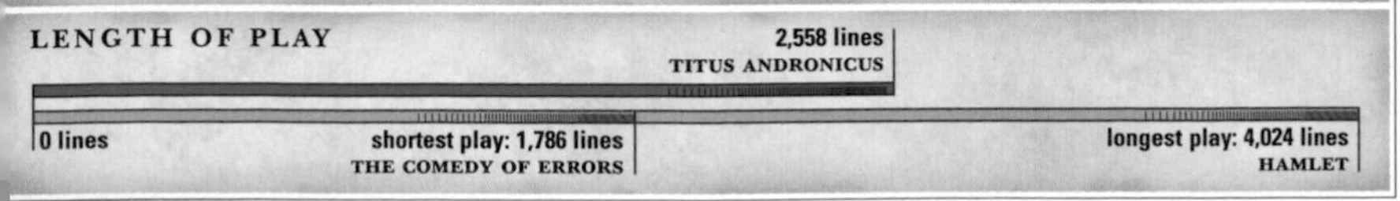

LENGTH OF PLAY

2,558 lines
TITUS ANDRONICUS

0 lines

shortest play: 1,786 lines
THE COMEDY OF ERRORS

longest play: 4,024 lines
HAMLET

DRAMATIS PERSONAE

SATURNINUS
211 lines
The Roman emperor, he marries Tamora, queen of Goths; when Titus kills Tamora, Saturninus kills Titus and is himself murdered by Lucius.

BASSIANUS
63 lines
Saturninus's brother, he marries Lavinia and is killed by Tamora's sons.

YOUNG LUCIUS
45 lines
Lucius's son, he delivers a threatening message to Chiron and Demetrius from an enraged Titus.

AEMILIUS
21 lines
A noble Roman, he acts as herald and messenger, and, at the end of the action, proclaims Lucius to be the new emperor.

AARON THE MOOR
356 lines
Tamora's unrepentantly evil lover, he encourages her sons, Demetrius and Chiron, to kill Bassianus and to ravish his wife, Lavinia; he frames Titus's sons for the murder, then organises their deaths and the amputation of Titus's hand. At the end, he is sentenced to death by Lucius, the new emperor.

A CLOWN
21 lines
He delivers a message for Titus to Saturninus, and is hanged for his trouble.

TAMORA
260 lines
Queen of Goths, captured by Titus, she marries Saturninus, but keeps Aaron the Moor as her lover and has his baby; she sets out to avenge the killing of her son Alarbus by destroying the family of Titus Andronicus.

TITUS ANDRONICUS
723 lines
A Roman war hero, he turns into a machine of revenge after his daughter is raped and mutilated, his son-in-law murdered, and two of his sons executed; he wavers on madness, but coldly plots his revenge, killing five people before he is himself slain.

A tireless warlord, Titus (Anthony Hopkins), faces his enemies with courage and cold-blooded cunning.

LAVINIA
60 lines
Titus's daughter, she is raped and has her hands and tongue amputated by Chiron and Demetrius; after Titus kills them, he murders Lavinia to end her shame and his sorrow.

A NURSE
19 lines
She delivers the child of Tamora and Aaron, but is then killed by Aaron.

MARCUS ANDRONICUS
312 lines
Titus's younger brother, a voice of reason, he is devastated when he discovers that his niece, Lavinia, has been raped and mutilated.

LUCIUS
190 lines
Titus's oldest son, exiled from Rome, he joins forces with the Goths and becomes emperor after he kills Saturninus.

QUINTUS AND MARTIUS
29; 33 lines
Titus's sons, they are wrongly accused of murdering Bassianus and are executed.

MUTIUS
4 lines
Titus's son, he tries to protect Lavinia from Titus, who kills him in fury.

PUBLIUS
14 lines
The son of Marcus Andronicus.

SEMPRONIUS, CAIUS AND VALENTINE
0 lines
Followers of Titus.

ALARBUS
0 lines
Tamora's oldest son, he is killed by Titus's sons as a sacrifice to the gods.

DEMETRIUS AND CHIRON
94; 52 lines
Tamora's sons, they murder Bassianus, rape and mutilate his wife, Lavinia, and, with Aaron, orchestrate the wrongful arrest and execution of Titus's sons, Quintus and Martius; in revenge, Titus kills them and serves their bones and blood to Tamora as pasties.

Though maimed and silenced, "gentle Lavinia" (Jennifer Woodburne) finds a way to name her rapists.

OTHER PLAYERS
Senators, Tribunes, Soldiers, Messengers, Attendants, and Goths.

PLOT SUMMARY

SIZE OF ACTS

ACT 1	ACT 2	ACT 3	ACT 4	ACT 5
508 lines	538 lines	389 lines	547 lines	576 lines

ACT ONE
508 lines

ROME: NEAR THE CAPITOL AND THE FORUM

As Saturninus and his brother Bassianus seek election as emperor of Rome, Marcus Andronicus announces that his own brother, Titus Andronicus, is returning victorious from "weary wars against the barbarous Goths". Titus arrives before his family's tomb, accompanied by four sons, two of them carrying a coffin. Among his prisoners are Tamora, queen of Goths, her three sons, and her dark-skinned lover, Aaron the Moor. Titus buries his twenty-first son to die in battle. Lucius asks for the proudest prisoner to be sacrificed, and Titus picks Alarbus, Tamora's first-born. As Tamora begs for mercy, Alarbus is led away and killed.

Princes that strive by factions and by friends/ Ambitiously for rule and empery… 1.1

Hail, Rome, victorious in thy mourning weeds!… 1.1

Titus learns from Marcus that he is Rome's choice to become emperor, but he refuses the honor and urges the tribunes to pick Saturninus. The new emperor chooses Titus's daughter, Lavinia, as his wife, but when Titus hands over the captured Goths, Saturninus is smitten by their queen. Suddenly Bassianus claims Lavinia as his own, angering Titus, who tries to seize her. When Titus's son Mutius blocks his way, he kills the young man and orders Lavinia restored to Saturninus. But the emperor now prefers to marry Tamora instead.

And therefore, lovely Tamora, Queen of Goths,/ That like the stately Phoebe 'mongst her nymphs/Dost overshine the gallant'st dames of Rome… 1.1

When Titus refuses to bury Mutius in the family tomb, his sons beg him to relent. Finally he yields: "bury him, and bury me the next." The court reassembles and, as Titus kneels before Saturninus, Tamora defends him publicly. She then whispers to the emperor "I'll find a day to massacre them all".

Not so, my lord. The gods of Rome forfend/ I should be author to dishonour you… 1.1

A nobler man, a braver warrior,/Lives not this day within the city walls… 1.1

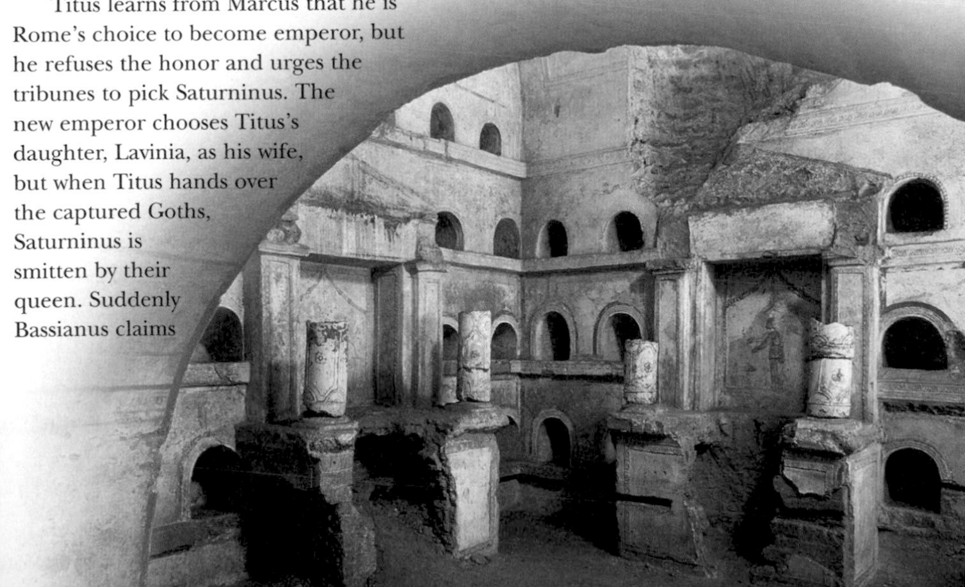

ACT TWO
538 lines

ROME, AND A ROYAL FOREST NEAR ROME

Alone, Aaron celebrates Tamora's swift rise to power knowing that she still loves him. Her sons, Demetrius and Chiron, yearn for Lavinia, but Aaron warns them against courting a Roman woman. When Demetrius claims to be fearless, Aaron unveils a plan. During the emperor's hunt, when "the lovely Roman ladies" stroll in the woods, they can take Lavinia "by force, if not by words."

Now climbeth Tamora Olympus' top,/ Safe out of fortune's shot, and sits aloft... 2.1

Aaron is busy burying gold when Tamora, in a seductive mood, invites him to lie with her, but he declines, too distracted by his plan for her sons. As they appear, Aaron slips Tamora a letter for Saturninus and tells her to provoke a fight with Bassianus.

My lovely Aaron, wherefore look'st thou sad,/ When everything doth make a gleeful boast?... 2.3

Tamora tells Bassianus that he will soon be cuckolded, but Lavinia mocks Tamora's own "goodly gift in horning" with the Moor. When Tamora's sons appear, she complains that Bassianus and Lavinia called her a "foul adulteress" and demands revenge. Chiron and Demetrius promptly murder Bassianus. Tamora orders Lavinia's death, but her sons first want to ravish her. Lavinia pleads for mercy, but she is mocked and dragged away. Bassianus's body is thrown into a pit.

When did the tiger's young ones teach the dam?/O, do not learn her wrath... 2.3

Aaron pretends to lead Titus's sons, Quintus and Martius, to a panther in a pit. Martius promptly falls into the pit and stumbles on Bassianus's body. As Aaron leaves for the emperor, Quintus also falls into the pit. Tamora shows Saturninus a letter ordering Bassianus's murder. Displaying his gold as the killers' reward, Aaron persuades Saturninus that Titus's sons are guilty. Titus is distraught, but Tamora promises to help them.

After Lavinia has been raped, her hands amputated, and her tongue cut out, Chiron and Demetrius abandon her to "her silent walks." Marcus finds the blood-drenched young woman alone and is shaken when he first sees her arms "lopped and hewed," then notices blood flowing from her mouth. He leads her gently to her father.

Who is this? My niece, that flies away so fast?/ Cousin, a word. Where is your husband?... 2.4

The milk thou sucked'st from her did turn to marble,/ Even at thy teat thou hadst thy tyranny... 2.3

ACT THREE
389 lines

ROME: A STREET AND TITUS'S HOUSE

Titus begs the tribunes and senators to pardon Martius and Quintus, but he is ignored. As Lucius reports that he has been banished, Marcus arrives with Lavinia. Titus is overwhelmed by her plight. Noticing tears in her eyes when he reports the likely loss of her brothers, he too breaks down.

Hear me, grave fathers; noble tribunes, stay! For pity of mine age... 3.1

If they did kill thy husband, then be joyful,/ Because the law hath ta'en revenge on them... 3.1

Aaron reports that Martius and Quintus will be saved if Titus, Marcus or Lucius sends a hand to the emperor. Marcus and Lucius volunteer, but Titus instead orders Aaron to cut off his left hand. Aaron promises to return with Titus's sons, "Their heads, I mean," he murmurs. Moments later, a messenger brings their heads, along with the hand of Titus. His mood darkens. Now

Why? I have not another tear to shed... 3.1

intent on revenge, Titus dispatches Lucius to raise an army. He and Marcus carry out the heads of the brothers, while Lavinia takes Titus's hand between her teeth.

At a family dinner, Titus behaves oddly. He claims to understand Lavinia's signs to mean "she drinks no other drink but tears." When Marcus kills a fly, Titus asks angrily, what "if that fly had a father and mother?" Marcus replies that it was "a black ill-favoured fly,/Like to the Empress's Moor." Somewhat appeased, Titus leaves with Young Lucius to read to Lavinia.

ACT FOUR

547 lines

ROME: TITUS'S HOUSE, AND INSIDE AND OUTSIDE THE ROYAL PALACE

To identify her attackers, Lavinia raises her amputated arms to indicate there were two. From Young Lucius's books, she picks out Ovid's *Metamorphoses* and turns to the story of Philomel, who was raped by Tereus. Taking a staff in his mouth, Marcus shows her how to write in the sand. Lavinia understands and quickly writes, "Stuprum," meaning rape in Latin, "Chiron—Demetrius". Titus has the words engraved on brass, then sends Young Lucius with presents and a message for Chiron and Demetrius.

At the palace, the boy delivers Titus's gifts. Chiron mocks the message written in Latin, but Aaron understands that Titus "hath found their guilt," After trumpets announce the birth of a son to the emperor, Tamora's nurse brings Aaron a dark-skinned baby from her mistress with orders to kill the infant. Recognizing his own, Aaron calls it "a beauteous blossom" and declares it shall not die. Instead, he kills the nurse and has a newly born fair-headed baby sent to the palace. Finally, he leaves to rejoin the Goths where he can raise his son "to be a warrior".

A joyless, dismal, black, and sorrowful issue./ Here is the babe, as loathsome as a toad... 4.2

Titus gathers his family and friends for an archery shoot in which each arrow bears a letter to a god. While Marcus fears for his brother's sanity, his son Publius assures Titus that Pluto approves revenge. As arrows fly into the emperor's court, a Clown appears with a basket of pigeons. Identifying him as an emissary from the gods, Titus tells him to give the birds to Saturninus, along with a message wrapped around a knife. Finding letters attached to arrows, the emperor wonders if Titus is mad. When the Clown brings two pigeons and a note, Saturninus reads it, then orders the Clown hanged. But he is alarmed by reports that Lucius is marching on Rome,

Come, Marcus, come; kinsmen, this is the way./ Sir boy, let me see your archery... 4.3

but Tamora promises to "enchant" Titus. She sends Aemilius to invite Lucius to his father's house, then visits Titus herself.

ACT FIVE

576 lines

THE COUNTRYSIDE OUTSIDE ROME, AND TITUS'S HOUSE IN ROME

Aaron is captured by Lucius's army who orders the Moor hanged "And by his side his fruit of bastardy." But Aaron offers to disclose dark secrets if Lucius swears "To save my boy, to nurse and bring him up." He then reveals that the baby's mother is Tamora, that her sons killed Bassianus, and then raped and mutilated Lavinia. He also boasts his own role in all the tragedies befalling the Andronici.

Indeed, I was their tutor to instruct them... 5.1

When Lucius asks if he regrets any of his "heinous deeds," Aaron scoffs at the idea.

Outside Titus's house, Tamora is disguised as Revenge, Chiron as Rape, and Demetrius as Murder. Titus tells Tamora as Revenge to kill Rape and Murder, but she refuses. Titus then asks Demetrius to stab a murderer, Chiron to knife a rapist, and Tamora to kill the empress and her Moor. Tamora says she will deliver the empress and her sons, but Titus insists that Rape and Murder stay behind. Once she has left, her sons are bound and gagged. With Lavinia holding a basin, Titus announces he will feed pasties made with their blood and bones to their mother. He then cuts their throats.

Come, come, Lavinia; look, thy foes are bound./ Sirs, stop their mouths... 5.2

Lucius arrives at his father's house with Aaron, but hides the Moor. As Saturninus and Tamora take their seats, Lavinia's face is hidden by a veil. Dressed as a cook, Titus says his food should "fill your stomachs." He then asks if Virginius was right to kill his daughter after she was raped. When Saturninus agrees, Titus unveils Lavinia and kills her, proclaiming, "with thy shame thy father's sorrow die." Saturninus summons the culprits. "Why, there they are, both baked in this piece," responds Titus before killing Tamora. The emperor instantly kills Titus and is in turn slain by Lucius. Amid the uproar, Marcus addresses the crowd. Lucius justifies murdering the emperor by recalling the horrors that followed Bassianus's death. Finally, Aemilius proclaims Lucius the new emperor. Promising "to heal Rome's harms," Lucius orders Aaron to be buried up to his neck and starved. He then decrees official funerals for all but "that ravenous tiger, Tamora," whose body is thrown to beasts and birds of prey.

You sad-faced men, people and sons of Rome,/By uproars severed, as a flight of fowl/Scattered by winds and high tempestuous gusts... 5.3

O, let me teach you how to knit again/This scattered corn into one mutual sheaf,/These broken limbs again into one body... 5.3

READING THE PLAY

COMPARISON OF PROSE TO VERSE

prose: 2% verse: 98%

TITUS ANDRONICUS IS CERTAINLY easier to read than to see. On the page, a stage direction such as, "He kills her," or "Enter a messenger with two heads and a hand," is tolerable; in performance, it is another occasion for pots of blood to be spilled.

"Thy hand once more; I will not loose again" (2.4). Quintus struggles in vain to pull Martius out of the "detested, dark, blood-drinking pit". Frontispiece to a 19th-century edition of the play.

Through the text, it is also clearer to the reader that this play is the work of a young author trying his hand at his first tragedy. Shakespeare frequently introduces Latin words and expressions, an affectation abandoned in his later Roman plays. As if wanting to impress, he also packs *Titus Andronicus* with more classical allusions than any other play, many of them echoing *The Rape of Lucrece* and *Venus and Adonis*, the two narrative poems that he wrote around the same time.

Still, Shakespeare pointedly goes beyond Ovid's *Metamorphoses VI*, in which Tereus rapes and cuts out the tongue of Philomela: in *Titus Andronicus*, Lavinia is often referred to as Philomela, but, in fact, she suffers more: her hands are also amputated. The play's revenge cycle leaves little room for introspection. Titus's early murder of his son Mutius goes unexplained. And even when Titus demonstrates he is in control of events in Act 5, he gives every impression of being unbalanced, as when he vows: "I will grind your bones to dust,/And with your blood and it I'll make a paste." More surprising is Aaron the Moor, who turns the reader (or audience) into his accomplice by sharing his macabre plans. He also evokes sympathy with his fatherly response to the dark-skinned baby Tamora has borne him. And, while unapologetically evil from start to finish, he goes to his death with his pride intact.

WHO'S WHO

Titus Andronicus kills his son, Mutius; Tamora, queen of the Goths; her sons, Chiron and Demetrius; and, finally, his daughter, Lavinia, to end her shame. **Titus's sons** sacrifice Alarbus, first-born son of Tamora, to appease their dead brothers. **Chiron** and **Demetrius** murder Bassianus, the emperor's brother, and rape and mutilate his wife, Lavinia, to avenge the death of their brother Alarbus. **Saturninus**, the Roman emperor, orders the deaths of Titus's sons Martius and Quintus, as well as the Clown, and, finally, kills Titus. **Lucius**, eldest son of Titus, murders Saturninus to avenge his father and, once emperor, orders the death of Aaron, Tamora's Moorish lover. **Aaron** kills the Nurse who delivers his and Tamora's child.

SEEING THE PLAY

ON STAGE

SYMBOLIC VENGEANCE

In his 1955 production of *Titus Andronicus,* Peter Brook avoided provoking unwanted laughter at the play's sensational violence by representing it symbolically. Instead of using stage make-up to turn Lavinia's hands into hewed stumps, he tied long red velvet ribbons to her wrists to suggest the "crimson river of blood" flowing over her body.

Titus Andronicus was evidently written to be seen, at least by Elizabethan audiences who had a taste for bloody melodrama. But contemporary critics sniffed at it: in 1614, Ben Jonson said that anyone who believed Kyd's *Spanish Tragedie* or *Titus Andronicus* were great plays must be someone "whose judgment has stood still these five and twenty, or thirty years." In the 18th century, Samuel Johnson wrote, with some prescience, "The barbarity of the spectacles, and the general massacre which are here exhibited, can scarcely be conceived tolerable to any audience." In modern times, the play's violence and cruelty have provoked more theater walk-outs than any other Shakespearean drama. Indeed, *Titus Andronicus* probably holds the record for the number of people fainting during a Shakespearean performance. On the other hand, such is the play's devotion to serial killing that many audiences find it absurd to the point of being humorous.

The challenge for today's director, then, is to track the emotional heart of the play—revenge—without sliding into black comedy. This is no easy task. Lavinia, the heroine-victim who is raped and mutilated, is an immensely tragic figure, yet risks ridicule if her grunting and weeping are overplayed. The audience must also witness the gory sights of Lavinia carrying Titus's amputated hand between her teeth, and Chiron and Demetrius having their throats cut. Then there is Titus "the cook" serving up baked body parts. Little wonder that Aaron the Moor, one of Shakespeare's first great villains, seems nuanced in contrast. He delights principally in his own power to manipulate others to make them carry out the depravities that he imagines. In the end, though, it is the actor playing Titus who must prove convincing, a man who cannot live without enacting revenge, even though he, too, becomes its victim.

Lavinia (Miriam Healy-Louie) rails against the wanton evil of Demetrius (Sebastian Roche, middle) and Chiron (Jean Loup Wolfman) in Julie Taymor's stark 1994 production.

BEYOND THE PLAY

AFTER THE RESTORATION of 1660, *Titus Andronicus* was no longer performed. Even in the 18th century, when Shakespeare assumed his place as England's greatest playwright, the play was ignored by all but the most dedicated scholars. Finally, in 1923, Robert Atkins directed Shakespeare's text at the Old Vic to mark the third centenary of publication of the *First Folio.* But it was only in 1955, with Peter Brook's landmark production at Stratford-upon-Avon, with Laurence Olivier as Titus and Antony Quayle as Aaron, that the play began to win acceptance.

PLAY HISTORY

RAVENSCROFT'S TITUS

When Edward Ravenscroft adapted *Titus Andronicus* in 1678, he speculated that Shakespeare merely gave the play "some master-touches". His version, which eliminated some violent scenes, was occasionally revived as late as the 1850s, when a black American actor, Ira Aldridge *(left),* portrayed Aaron the Moor as a figure of nobility.

Since then, it has been performed with some regularity, although audiences still approach it with trepidation. Some feminist scholars have interpreted Lavinia's mutilation as an allegory for the silencing of women by men. At Johannesburg's Market Theatre in 1995, Gregory Donan directed Antony Sher as Titus in a production that drew parallels with the cycles of violence and revenge that convulsed apartheid-era South Africa. There were also modern-day echoes in Deborah Warner's acclaimed production in Stratford-upon-Avon in 1987, with Brian Cox as Titus. *Titus Andronicus* may have become more acceptable thanks to screen violence, from Sam Peckinpah's *Straw Dogs* to Quentin Tarantino's *Pulp Fiction.* Certainly, Julie Taymor did not shy away from the gore in her 1999 screen adaptation, *Titus,* with Anthony Hopkins as Titus, Henry Lennix as Aaron and Jessica Lange as Tamora.

"Give me a sword, I'll chop off my hands too. (3.1).
Titus (Brian Cox) struggles to contain his boundless grief at the sight of his mutilated daughter, Lavinia (Sonia Ritter), in Deborah Warner's RSC production, 1987.

itus (Wilfrid Walter, right) confronts the malicious threesome, Tamora lorence Saunders, top), Demetrius (Rayner Barton, left) and Chiron ohn Laurie, centre), masquerading as Revenge, Murder and Rape, the landmark Old Vic production, directed by Robert Atkins in 1923.

ROMEO AND JULIET

ROMEO AND JULIET, SHAKESPEARE's first great tragedy, has long been among his most beloved plays. Shakespeare was around 30 years old when he wrote this work about passionate young lovers who defy the ancient enmity between their families. While no production was officially documented before 1662, quarto editions published in 1597 and 1599 suggest that *Romeo and Juliet* was well-received by Elizabethan audiences. The title page of the earliest quarto notes that the play "hath been often (with great applause) plaid publiquely". The story of Romeo and Juliet was popular in Italy well before Shakespeare adapted it for his play. His direct source was *The Tragicall Historye of Romeus and Juliet*, a narrative poem by Arthur Brooke. But it is Shakespeare's version that has survived and inspired movies, ballets, and operas.

BEHIND THE PLAY

SHAKESPEARE FOLLOWED HIS SOURCE MATERIAL by setting the main action of *Romeo and Juliet* in Verona. But while he retained the basic plot, he changed and added details to sharpen and expand the story. He also turned flat, functional characters into poignant roles and romantic icons who have influenced lovers the world over. The raging feud between the families of the lovers, the Montagues and the Capulets, is never explained. At the very start of the play, Chorus simply introduces the "ancient grudge" as a fact. Indeed, many aspects of the play contribute to an impression that the entire story, including the lovers' suicides, is pre-written in some grand cosmic scheme which no one may escape. Romeo's dreams repeatedly predict his disastrous fate and the keenly sensitive Juliet finds forbidding omens even in her beloved Romeo's complexion. Just as the family feud appears to have existed forever, so do the lovers seem destined to sacrifice their lives for a cause larger than their own love. The play focuses on passionate emotions, whether suicidal love or murderous hatred. The oppositions explored throughout the play are finally supplanted by quiet resignation to tragic events.

For stony limits cannot hold love out,/And what love can do, that dares love attempt... 2.2

DATE OF PLAY

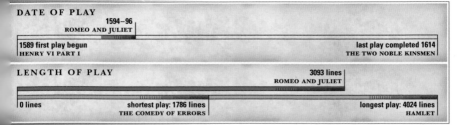

1594–96
ROMEO AND JULIET

1589 first play begun
HENRY VI PART I

last play completed 1614
THE TWO NOBLE KINSMEN

LENGTH OF PLAY

3093 lines
ROMEO AND JULIET

0 lines

shortest play: 1786 lines
THE COMEDY OF ERRORS

longest play: 4024 lines
HAMLET

DRAMATIS PERSONAE

ESCALUS
76 lines
Prince of Verona, he forbids the Montagues and Capulets from brawling in the street on pain of death.

PARIS
70 lines
A young nobleman, kinsman to the prince, he expects to marry Juliet.

MONTAGUE
41 lines
He is head of the Montague household.

CAPULET
273 lines
He is head of the Capulet household.

AN OLD MAN
000 lines
An old man of the Capulet family.

ROMEO
612 lines
Son to Montague, he is accused of effeminacy by his friends, the friar, and even himself, but in fact he is a man of extreme passion; he loves Juliet more than his kinsmen hate her family, the Capulets.

MERCUTIO
261 lines
Kinsman to the prince and friend to Romeo, he wields words more deftly than weapons.

BENVOLIO
160 lines
Nephew to Montague, and friend to Romeo.

TYBALT
36 lines
Nephew to Lady Capulet, he detests the Montagues.

PETRUCHIO
0 lines
A mute follower of Tybalt.

FRIAR LAURENCE
351 lines
A Franciscan, he marries Romeo and Juliet.

FRIAR JOHN
13 lines
A Franciscan friar.

BALTHASAR
32 lines
Servant to Romeo, he carries his suicide note.

Romeo (Leonard Whiting) and Juliet (Olivia Hussey) are symbols of romantic love.

Juliet (Nora Kerin) trusts and confides in her Nurse (Blanche Stanley) who acts as her go-between and advisor.

ABRAM
5 lines
Servant to Montague.

SAMPSON, GREGORY AND CLOWN
31; 20; 23 lines
Servants to Capulet.

PETER
33 lines
Servant to Juliet's nurse.

A PAGE
9 lines
Page to Paris.

AN APOTHECARY
7 lines
He sells Romeo poison.

SIMON CATLING, HUGH REBECK, AND JAMES SOUNDPOST
9; 4; 1 lines
Three musicians, they play at Juliet's wedding.

LADY MONTAGUE
3 lines
Wife to Montague, she dies of grief when Romeo is banished from Verona.

LADY CAPULET
115lines
Wife to Capulet, she finds it difficult to communicate with her teenage daughter, Juliet.

JULIET
544 lines
Daughter to Capulet, she is uninterested in marriage until she sets eyes on Romeo at the Capulets' ball.

NURSE
281 lines
Nurse to Juliet, she is adored and trusted; but when she encourages Juliet to forget Romeo and marry Paris, she finally loses Juliet's confidence.

OTHER PLAYERS
Chorus, Citizens of Verona, Gentlemen and Gentlewomen of both houses, Maskers, Torchbearers, Pages, Guards, Watchmen, Servants, and Attendants.

Mercutio (Eric Mayne) is cynical about romantic love and Romeo's lovesickness.

PLOT SUMMARY

SIZE OF ACTS

PROLOGUE & ACT 1	ACT 2	ACT 3	ACT 4	ACT 5
739 lines	685 lines	821 lines	407 lines	441 lines

PROLOGUE
14 lines

CHORUS SPEAKS DIRECTLY TO THE AUDIENCE

The subject of this play is an "ancient grudge" between families whose children fell in love and took their own lives, putting an end to the feud.

ACT ONE
725 lines

IN THE STREETS OF VERONA AND WITHIN THE HOUSE OF CAPULET

Capulets exchange insults with Montagues in the street. When the Capulet Tybalt joins, the conflict escalates to brawling. But the Prince of Verona halts the fight and forbids public disturbance on pain of death. Old Montague finds Romeo's conduct worrying. But Benvolio discovers that his cousin is merely in love, with Rosaline. Old Capulet invites Paris to a feast and encourages him to woo Juliet. An illiterate Capulet servant happens on Benvolio and Romeo, who help him decipher a list of guests he is to invite to the feast. When Romeo learns that Rosaline will attend, he is persuaded by Benvolio that, although Montagues, they should join in the festivities.

ebellious subjects, enemies to peace,/Profaners of this eighbour-stainèd steel... 1.1

Alas that love, whose view is muffled, still/ Should without eyes see pathways to his will!... 1.1

Juliet's nurse tires Lady Capulet with recollections of Juliet's infancy. Romeo and others arrive before the Capulet home. But Romeo, disturbed by a recent dream, hesitates. His friend Mercutio, familiar with dreams, discourages superstition. When the masked Montagues join the Capulet feast, Romeo marvels at Juliet's beauty. Juliet's cousin Tybalt, recognizing Romeo's voice, prepares to fight. But old Capulet forbids him from stirring up trouble. Tybalt departs, incensed, while Romeo gives Juliet worshipful kisses. When the nurse calls for Juliet, Romeo realizes that he has fallen in love with a Capulet. And Juliet discovers that her beloved Romeo is a hated Montague.

Even or odd, of all days in the year,/Come Lammas Eve at night shall she be fourteen... 1.3

O, then I see Queen Mab hath been with you./She is the fairies' midwife... 1.4

O, she doth teach the torches to burn bright!/ It seems she hangs upon the cheek of night/ As a rich jewel in an Ethiop's ear... 1.5

Tell me, daughter Juliet,/How stands your dispositions to be married?... 1.3

ACT TWO

685 lines

NEAR AND WITHIN THE CAPULET'S ORCHARD, IN A STREET OF VERONA, AND IN FRIAR LAWRENCE'S CELL

At the Capulet home, friends searching for Romeo finally depart. Within the orchard, Romeo is dazzled by the sight of Juliet on her balcony. He eavesdrops as Juliet reasons that "Montague" is only a name. Romeo reveals himself and the lovers vow loyalty. Juliet says that, if Romeo intends to marry, he should send word tomorrow. As they separate, Juliet finds parting "sweet sorrow."

> **But soft! What light through yonder window breaks?...** 2.2

> **Thou knowest the mask of night is on my face,/ Else would a maiden blush bepaint my cheek...** 2.2

Romeo must find the friar. Friar Lawrence is tending medicinal plants, remarking on admixtures of virtue and vice in nature and mankind. Romeo persuades the friar to help him marry Juliet.

Mercutio and Benvolio discuss alarming news: Tybalt challenges Romeo. When Romeo appears, Mercutio teases him about being out all night. Juliet's nurse arrives, and Mercutio mocks her too. But Romeo tells the nurse that Juliet should come to the friar's cell to be married. Alone, Juliet wonders why her nurse delays. Finally, the nurse brings news and Juliet joins Romeo to be married.

> **Now, afore God, I am so vexed that every part about me quivers...** 2.4

ACT THREE

821 lines

IN STREETS OF VERONA, IN THE CAPULET HOME, AND ORCHARD AND IN THE FRIAR'S CELL

In the heat of the day, Mercutio accuses his friend and kinsman Benvolio of being

O, be some other name!/ What's in a name? That which we call a rose/ By any other word would smell as sweet... 2.2

ay, an there were two such, we should have none shortly, for one would kill the other... 3.1

hot-headed, and then spars verbally with Tybalt. Romeo, now married to a Capulet, tries to prevent a fight. But Mercutio cannot resist provoking Tybalt, who strikes him and flees. The wounded Mercutio also leaves. Benvolio soon reports that Mercutio has died. When Tybalt returns to fight, he is slain by the newly vengeful Romeo. As punishment, the prince exiles Romeo.

No, 'tis not so deep as a well, nor so wide as a church door... 3.1

Juliet is impatient for night time and Romeo's arrival. But news that her husband has murdered her cousin horrifies her. And she is even more distressed by Romeo's banishment. Romeo laments his exile. When the nurse reports Juliet's misery, Romeo tries to stab himself. But the friar persuades Romeo to flee to Mantua. Meanwhile, Old Capulet and Paris set Thursday as the young noble and Juliet's wedding day.

Gallop apace, you fiery-footed steeds,/Towards Phoebus' lodging!... 3.2

Shall I speak ill of him that is my husband?/Ah, poor my lord, what tongue shall smooth thy name... 3.2

Hold thy desperate hand./ Art thou a man? hy form cries out thou art./ Thy tears are womanish... 3.3

Having spent his wedding night with Juliet, Romeo prepares to leave at daybreak. Juliet at first prevents his departure but then, realizing the danger of any delay, urges him to leave.

Vilt thou be gone? It is not yet near day... 3.5

Lady Capulet tries to lift Juliet's spirits by recalling that Paris will marry her on Thursday, but old Capulet is saddened to see his daughter grieving. When Juliet refuses to marry Paris, Capulet grows wrathful and even Juliet's nurse supports Paris. Juliet claims she will go to confession to be absolved. If the friar offers no remedy, Juliet reasons privately, suicide remains an option.

hen the sun sets the earth doth drizzle dew,/But for he sunset of my brother's ı/It rains downright... 3.5

ACT FOUR

407 lines

WITHIN THE FRIAR'S CELL AND THE CAPULET HOME

Juliet is stunned when Paris greets her as "wife" in the friar's cell. Alone with the friar, Juliet says she is prepared to kill herself. But the friar proposes that instead she drink a potion making her appear dead. She will then be laid to rest in the Capulet tomb. Romeo, informed by letter, will take her from the tomb to Mantua.

Tell me not, Friar, that thou hearest of this,/ Unless thou tell me how I may prevent it... 4.1

The Capulets, delighted that Juliet now accepts Paris, plan the wedding feast. Alone, Juliet imagines the horror of awakening in the Capulet tomb beside Tybalt's corpse. Finally, she drinks the vial and falls onto her bed. Lady Capulet, having been up all night preparing for the wedding, instructs the nurse to awaken Juliet. But the nurse instead discovers Juliet's inert body. Old Capulet notes that the wedding music will be supplanted by funeral music. A servant and the musicians remain to quibble farcically.

I have a faint cold fear thrills through my veins/That almost freezes up the heat of life... 4.3

Mistress! What, mistress! Juliet! Fast, I warrant her, she./Why, lamb! Why, lady! Fie, you slug-abed!... 4.5

ACT FIVE

441 lines

A STREET IN MANTUA, FRIAR LAURENCE'S CELL, AND A CHURCHYARD INCLUDING THE CAPULET FAMILY VAULT

In Mantua, Romeo has dreamed sweetly of Juliet, but his friend Balthasar brings news that Juliet is dead. Romeo persuades an

If I may trust the flattering truth of sleep, my dreams presage some joyful... 5.1

Well, Juliet, I will lie with the tonight./Let's see for means. O mischief, thou art swift/To enter... 5.1

apothecary to sell him poison, and plans to kill himself.

In Verona, Friar Lawrence learns that Romeo never received the letter explaining Juliet's false death. With Juliet soon to reawaken, the friar departs for the vault.

Paris creeps into the churchyard to visit Juliet's tomb, but hides as Romeo and Balthasar approach. After agreeing to deliver a letter for Romeo, Balthasar also hides nearby. Paris suddenly challenges Romeo as Tybalt's murderer, but is slain. Finally recognizing his adversary, Romeo determines to bury Paris near Juliet. Within the tomb,

For here lies Juliet, and her beauty makes/ This vault a feasting presence full of light... 5.3

Romeo marvels at Juliet's beauty. And, spying Tybalt's corpse, he begs forgiveness for killing him. Finally, he drinks poison and falls to his death.

Just as Juliet stirs, the friar reports the deaths of Romeo and Paris. Refusing to depart with the friar, Juliet tries to take poison in kisses from Romeo's lips.

What's here? A cup, closed in my true love's hand?/ Poison, I see, hath been his timeless end... 5.3

But with the night watch arriving, she seizes Romeo's dagger and stabs herself. Discovering carnage in the Capulet vault, watchmen send for the prince and parents, and hold the friar. All arrive save Lady Montague, who died of grief over her son's exile. The friar explains: he joined the couple in marriage but his scheme failed. Balthasar produces Romeo's letter, which the prince reads: Romeo poisoned himself to "lie with Juliet". The prince calls for the fathers to witness the outcome of their childrens' love. Capulet and Montague embrace. The prince will later pardon and punish but for now notes that these sad events bring a muted peace.

I will be brief, for my short date of breath/ Is not so long as is a tedious tale... 5.3

For never was a story of more woe/Than this of Juliet and her Romeo... 5.3

READING THE PLAY

COMPARISON OF PROSE TO VERSE

prose: 12% | verse: 88%

Painting by Edwin A. Abbey of the death of Mercutio in *Harper's Monthly Magazine*, July 1903.

ROMEO AND JULIET, one of the playwright's most lyrical plays, contains some of Shakespeare's best poetry. Romeo and Juliet entrance readers as readily as they do one another. "She speaks", says Romeo, "O, speak again, bright angel". They find words for the mysteries of romantic love, as when Juliet says: "The more I give to thee,/The more I have, for both are infinite." The lovers' mesmerizing poetry is framed by the nitty-gritty world that surrounds and ultimately destroys them. The opening scene sets the fast pace for combative, decidedly unromantic action in Verona: the dialogue is rapid-fire and hard words segue into violent physical exchanges. The action jumps from Veronese streets to interior spaces, building a city-wide web of warring tensions. When action places Romeo and Juliet in the Capulet orchard or in Juliet's chamber, the impression of romantic bliss is heightened by real dangers—angry parents or hostile kinsmen—encroaching on the lovers. Love talk in *Romeo and Juliet* is also counter-balanced by the mercurial wit of Mercutio, whose frankness brings Romeo down to earth in poetry as well as prose. An anti-lover of sorts, Mercutio challenges Romeo to ask if there is more to life than romance: "Why, is not this better now than groaning for love? Now art thou sociable. Now art thou Romeo. Now art thou what thou art." While the Italian story of Romeo and Juliet forms its own tradition of poems, tales, ballads, and plays, it is loosely analogous to earlier stories of passionate lovers who die tragically. Ancient literary cousins of Romeo and Juliet include Pyramus and Thisbe, Hero and Leander, and Aneas and Dido. Other tragic lovers of antiquity whose stories form the bases of Shakespearean plays are Troilus and Cressida, and Antony and Cleopatra.

How silver-sweet sound lovers' tongues by night" 2.2). A 19th-century art nouveau postcard after the riginal painting by Jennie Harbour.

LANGUAGE NOTE

ALL IN THE STARS

Romeo and Juliet, often set in nocturnal secrecy, explores cosmic orders of tragic fate. Accordingly, the play is rich in poetic references to stars. A few examples include the opening verses, in which the lovers are called "star-crossed"; Romeo compares Juliet's eyes to the stars (2.2); and Juliet imagines Romeo's body cut out "in little stars" so flattering to the sky that "all the world will be in love with the night" (3.2).

SEEING THE PLAY

ON STAGE

INTERPRETING ROMEO

Romeo and Juliet has been inventively cast. In 1744, Theophilus Cibber performed Romeo with his daughter, Jenny, as Juliet. David Garrick directed Cibber's wife as Juliet in 1750 and later played Romeo at age 44. Women have also played Romeo. Ellen Tree delivered the part in London in 1829 and was followed by Priscilla Horton in 1834. In 1845, the American Charlotte Cushman performed Romeo in London across from her sister, Susan.

Charlotte and Susan Cushman at the Theatre Royal, Haymarket, London, in 1845.

DIRECTORS FREQUENTLY CUT ROMEO AND JULIET to suit interpretations and time constraints. But no matter how the relationship between socially-riven Verona and the lovers is construed, the clash of generations, and the sacrifice of life for ideals of love continue to play as great tragedy. The actors playing Romeo and Juliet face a major challenge. To be at all convincing, they must be young—probably in their teens, as in Shakespeare's day, when a boy would also play Juliet—and attractive. They, after all, are asked to personify the purity and innocence of love through the ages. At the same time, their roles are physically and emotionally exhausting, and their speaking parts enormous.

Juliet's parents, Capulet ,and Lady Capulet, in contrast, represent the older generation whose inflexibility brings on the tragedy. Tybalt, in turn, illustrates how the Capulet–Montague feud has also poisoned the younger generation; brash and aggressive, he is ready to kill and to die. Friar Laurence is a difficult role that requires an experienced actor. He speaks for an older generation that does understand the lovers' dilemma, even though his attempt to help them sets in motion the misunderstanding that leads to their deaths.

For many actors, though, the most attractive and lovingly written roles in the play are Juliet's fussy nurse and the sharp-tongued Mercutio. Each is strongly characterized and sure to engross audiences with their distinct yet highly complementary brands of comic language. The real clowns of the play, however, are the servants and entertainers in the household of the Capulets, who perform comic interludes between scenes of private romance and public violence.

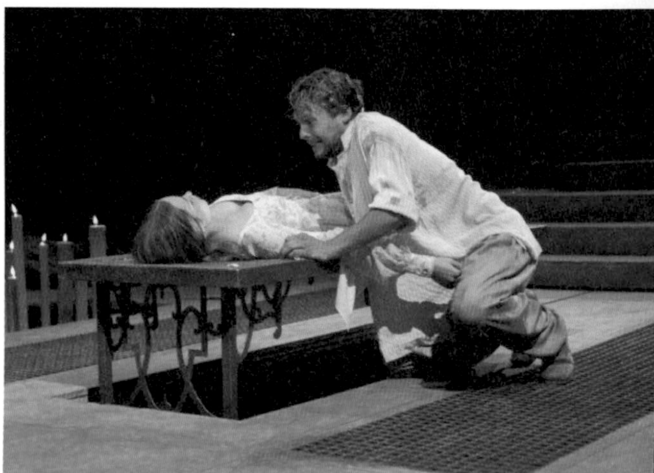

Romeo (Lex Shrapnel) and Juliet (Emily Blunt) in the Capulet tomb, in a production at the Chichester Festival Theatre, England, August 2002.

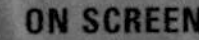

BEYOND THE PLAY

FOR ALL ITS POPULARITY, *Romeo and Juliet* is a challenging play to produce. In Elizabethan England, the role of 13-year-old Juliet would have been given to a boy trained to play females. Surviving documents suggest that the professional boy actors were extraordinarily capable, even in tragic leads. But after 1660, when women began performing on re-opened English stages, casting curiously became more challenging. Samuel Pepys noted in 1662 that of all plays, *Romeo and Juliet* "was the worst acted that ever I saw these people do". Today, directors try to strike a balance between age and experience when casting *Romeo and Juliet*. Actors are often deemed either too mature or too inexperienced to play the leads. At age 19 in 1924, John Gielgud was found to be too old for Romeo. For his 1968 film, Franco Zeffirelli cast a 17-year-old Romeo and a 16-year-old Juliet, whose youth was applauded but whose teenage delivery of the Shakespearean English was not.

Recent productions of the play have shown bold directorial visions. The 1961 film version of Leonard Bernstein's musical, *West Side Story*, showed that Romeo and Juliet could remain passionately moving even when re-written as a musical about Hispanic and white gangs in New York. In 1968, Washington D.C. saw a *Romeo and Juliet* about racial war set in 19th-century Louisiana. The Capulets were a black family hosting a mardi gras masked ball and the intruding Romeo was of the white Montague clan. In Birmingham in 2001, director Nick Fogg controversially turned the play into a lesbian love story. Among outstanding adaptations in other art forms, there are two operas, Bellini's *Capuleti e i Montecchi* and Gounod's *Roméo et Juliette*, as well as Prokofiev's ballet, *Romeo and Juliet.*

ON SCREEN

FILM ADAPTATIONS

Starting with Ernst Lubitsch's 1920 silent version, *Romeo and Juliet* has been filmed many times, including the Egyptian Kamal Selim's Arabic *Shuhaddaa el-gharam* and Mexican Miguel M Delgado's *Romeo y Julieta*, both made in the 1940s. More recent movies include Peter Perry's 1968 soft porn version, *The Secret Sex Lives of Romeo and Juliet*, and Baz Luhrmann's critically acclaimed 1996 film with Leonardo DiCaprio as Romeo and Claire Danes as Juliet.

Baz Luhrmann's *Romeo + Juliet* was set in a fictional Californian 'Verona Beach' plagued by gang violence.

Octavio Cervantes as Romeo and Lesvi Vasquez as Juliet in a production by Mexico's Laboratorio de Teatro Campesino in Central Park, NY.

JULIUS CAESAR

Julius

JULIUS CAESAR, SHAKESPEARE'S MOST POPULAR ROMAN PLAY, recounts the plot to kill the legendary military leader and the violent power struggle that followed his death. The play leaves open the possibility that Rome may have been well served by Caesar's murder. In this, Shakespeare's ambiguity may simply have been politic: the Tudor dynasty emerged from the deposition of the despotic Richard III, but Queen Elizabeth also famously disapproved of challenges to any sitting monarch. Further, by 1599, when *Julius Caesar* was written and first performed at the new Globe Theatre, the aged and childless queen, much like Caesar, was facing threats to her absolute rule. First published in the *First Folio* of 1623, *Julius Caesar* returned to the stage soon after the Restoration in 1660 and by the 19th century had become one of Shakespeare's most studied and performed plays.

BEHIND THE PLAY

JULIUS CAESAR offers a remarkably accurate account of what actually occurred. The play is set in 44 BC, the year of Caesar's murder and two years after he was proclaimed perpetual dictator. As the conqueror of Gaul and the victor in a civil war against Pompey, his power was close to absolute. But the Senate, with its squabbling nobles, survived as a symbol of what remained of the once mighty Roman Republic. It was in the name of this republic that the plot against Caesar was hatched. However, while Caesar was murdered, the republic's defenders, Brutus and Cassius, were in turn soon defeated by Mark Antony and Octavius Caesar. In that sense, Caesar's influence lived on. In *Julius Caesar*, Shakespeare conveys this by parading Caesar's ghost and having Brutus and Cassius die by the very swords that killed Caesar. Although the playwright telescopes some dates and events, he closely follows the description of scenes and the tenor of speeches in Plutarch's *Lives of the Noble Grecians and Romans*. Shakespeare then adds ambiguity to the main characters, portraying Caesar as both demigod and mortal, Mark Antony as both loyal and opportunistic, and Brutus as both idealistic and vain.

The evil that men do lives after them,/The good is oft interrèd with their bones... 3.2

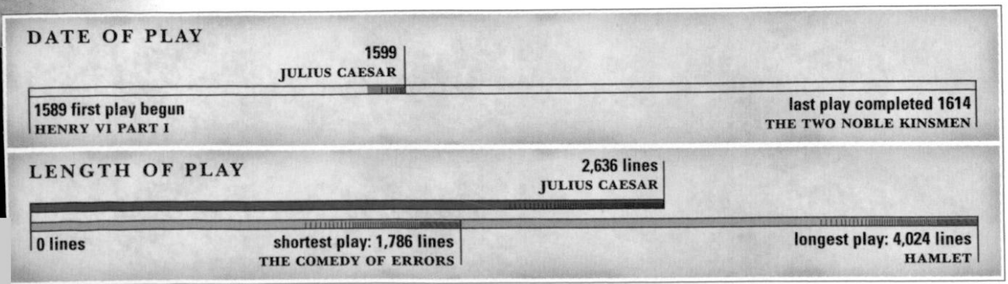

DATE OF PLAY

1599
JULIUS CAESAR

1589 first play begun
HENRY VI PART I

last play completed 1614
THE TWO NOBLE KINSMEN

LENGTH OF PLAY

2,636 lines
JULIUS CAESAR

0 lines

shortest play: 1,786 lines
THE COMEDY OF ERRORS

longest play: 4,024 lines
HAMLET

DRAMATIS PERSONAE

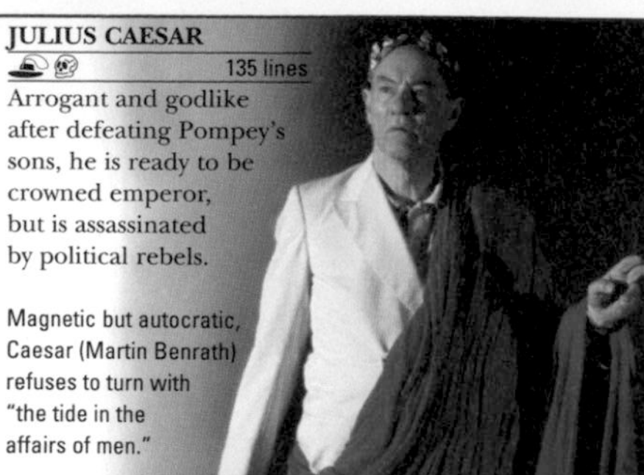

JULIUS CAESAR

135 lines

Arrogant and godlike after defeating Pompey's sons, he is ready to be crowned emperor, but is assassinated by political rebels.

Magnetic but autocratic, Caesar (Martin Benrath) refuses to turn with "the tide in the affairs of men."

OCTAVIUS CAESAR

46 lines

Julius Caesar's great-nephew and adopted son, he claims to be Caesar's heir, bringing tensions to his relations with Mark Antony.

MARK ANTONY

329 lines

Caesar's most loyal follower, he quickly shows himself to be duplicitous, manipulative, and eager for wealth and power; his oration at Caesar's funeral turns the mob against Cassius and Brutus.

AEMILIUS LEPIDUS

4 lines

The third member of the triumvirate, he enjoys little power and is dismissed by Mark Antony as "a slight unmeritable man."

CICERO

9 lines

A renowned orator and respected senator, he is executed by Mark Antony.

PUBLIUS AND POPILIUS LENA

2; 2 lines

Roman senators.

MARCUS BRUTUS

728 lines

An honorable and idealistic republican, he reluctantly joins the plot against Caesar when he sees Rome falling under his tyranny; after Caesar's murder, still convinced that he acted morally in slaying Caesar, Brutus fights Mark Antony for power; rather than be captured, he kills himself.

CAIUS CASSIUS

525 lines

Consumed by envy for Caesar's power and success, he manipulates Brutus into joining the conspiracy to kill Caesar; after the murder, he is distraught when Brutus accuses him of corruption; he commits suicide.

DECIUS BRUTUS

44 lines

One of the conspirators, he persuades Caesar to ignore various warnings not to visit the Senate.

CASCA, TREBONIUS, CAIUS LIGARIUS, METELLUS CIMBER, AND CINNA

133; 9; 15; 17; 18 lines

Other conspirators against Julius Caesar.

FLAVIUS AND MARULLUS

26; 31 lines

Roman tribunes who are opposed to Caesar.

ARTEMIDORUS

19 lines

He names the conspirators but Caesar ignores him.

A SOOTHSAYER

18 lines

He warns Caesar, "Beware the ides of March."

CINNA THE POET

14 lines

He is killed by a mob avenging Caesar's death.

A POET, A CARPENTER, AND A COBBLER

7; 1; 16 lines

They celebrate Caesar's military victories.

TITINIUS

32 lines

He kills himself with the sword of Cassius.

YOUNG CATO

8 lines

A follower of Brutus, he is killed by Messala.

LUCILIUS, MESSALA, AND VOLUMNIUS

26; 39; 3 lines

Followers and friends of Brutus and Cassius.

VARRO, CLITUS, CLAUDIUS, STRATO, LUCIUS, AND DARDANIUS

6; 10; 4; 7; 33; 3 lines

Servants to Brutus.

PINDARUS

17 lines

Cassius's servant, he helps his master kill himself.

CALPHURNIA

27 lines

Caesar's wife, she pleads in vain for him not to attend the Senate.

PORTIA

92 lines

Brutus's loyal wife, she is worried by her husband's troubled behavior and finally kills herself.

OTHER PLAYERS

Senators, Citizens, Guards, Soldiers, Messenger, Attendants, Servants, and the Ghost of Caesar.

"Hungry" for power and status, Cassius (Tim Piggott-Smith, left), persuades the liberal idealist Brutus (Greg Hicks) to topple Caesar.

PLOT SUMMARY

SIZE OF ACTS

ACT 1	ACT 2	ACT 3	ACT 4	ACT 5
574 lines	552 lines	670 lines	461 lines	379 lines

ACT ONE
574 lines

ROME: A STREET AND A PUBLIC PLACE

Two tribunes are lamenting Julius Caesar's victory over Pompey's sons when Caesar himself arrives in the company of his wife, Calphurnia, and prominent senators. His favorite, Mark Antony, joins him after running in a race. Caesar hears a voice in the crowd cry, "Beware the ides of March." A Soothsayer steps forward and repeats the warning, but Caesar dismisses him and leaves for the Capitol.

As Caius Cassius complains of Marcus Brutus's aloofness, they hear cheering. "I do fear the people/ Choose Caesar for their king," Brutus says gloomily. Cassius now feels free to speak openly against Caesar ❛❛. "I was born free as Caesar," he says, adding bitterly: "And this man/Is now become a god, and Cassius is/A wretched creature."

I know that virtue to be in you, Brutus,/ As well as I do know your outward favour... 1.2

Caesar sees Brutus and Cassius whispering and remarks on Cassius's "lean and hungry look." Caesar adds that he fears no one ❛❛, but distrusts Cassius. Casca reports how three times Caesar refused the crown before falling to the ground, foaming at the mouth. Cassius observes Brutus's ambivalence ❜❜ and decides to encourage him with forged letters.

Would he were fatter!/ But I fear him not... 1.2

Well, Brutus, thou art noble; yet I see/ Thy honourable mettle may be wrought/From that it is disposed... 1.2

Cicero the orator wonders if strange omens refer to Caesar's planned visit to the Capitol the next day. Cassius is sure that "the strange impatience of the heavens" is a warning to a man "most like this dreadful night" ❛❛, meaning Caesar. Now confident his plot is taking shape, Cassius gives Cinna a letter to toss through Brutus's window.

You are dull, Casca, and those sparks of life/ That should be in a Roman you do want/ Or else you use not... 1.3

Why, man, he doth bestride the narrow world/Like a Colossus, and we petty men/ Walk under his huge legs... 1.2

ACT TWO

552 lines

ROME: BRUTUS'S ORCHARD, CAESAR'S HOUSE, AND A STREET NEAR THE CAPITOL

Early on the ides of March, Brutus concludes that, once crowned, Caesar will become a tyrant. His servant, Lucius, brings an anonymous letter urging Brutus to "Speak, strike, redress." Cassius arrives with five conspirators and proposes an oath, but Brutus says that their word is enough. Cassius then suggests that Mark Antony also be killed, but Brutus overrules him: "Let us be sacrificers, but not butchers."

> **It must be by his death; and for my part,/ I know no personal cause to spurn at him...** 2.1

> **Our course will seem too bloody, Caius Cassius,/ To cut the head off and then hack the limbs...** 2.1

Cassius fears Caesar may cancel his visit to the Capitol, but Decius says he will persuade the general to attend. As the visitors leave, Brutus's wife, Portia, finding her husband awake, chastises him for not sharing his troubles. Still wanting to know his secret, she displays a wound she made in her thigh as "strong proof of my constancy."

> **Not for yours neither. Y' have urgently, Brutus,/ Stole from my bed...** 1.2

Amid thunder and lightning, Caesar hears the cries of his sleeping wife, Calphurnia: "Help, ho! They murder Caesar!" When she awakes, Calphurnia forbids Caesar from leaving the house, pointing to a night of dire signs. Caesar is fatalistic, noting that death "Will come when it will come". When priests also warn him, Caesar retorts "Danger knows full well/That Caesar is more dangerous than he." Finally, after Calphurnia appeals to him on her knees, he agrees to send word that he is unwell.

> **Cowards die many times before their deaths;/ The valiant never taste of death but once...** 2.2

Decius asks for a reason, "Lest I be laughed at when I tell them so." Caesar recounts that, in a dream, Calphurnia saw his statue, "Which, like a fountain with an hundred spouts,/Did run pure blood." Decius says it is an allegory for how Caesar will revive Rome, adding that the Senate will be puzzled to learn that "mighty Caesar" is afraid. Suddenly, Caesar changes his mind.

> **This dream is all amiss interpreted;/It was a vision fair and fortunate...** 2.2

Artemidorus, supporter of Caesar, has written to him warning of the plotters: "If thou beest not immortal, look about you." At Brutus's house, the Soothsayer

> **Let's kill him boldly, but not wrathfully;/Let's carve his as a dish fit for gods,/Not hew him as a carcass fit for hounds...** 2.1

says he will renew his warnings. Alarmed, Portia sends Lucius to the Senate for news.

ACT THREE
670 lines

ROME: BEFORE THE CAPITOL, THE FORUM, AND A STREET

"The ides of March are come," Caesar mocks the Soothsayer. "Ay, Caesar, but not gone," the man replies. Artemidorus offers his letter, but Caesar ignores him. Inside the Capitol, Metellus begs Caesar to lift his brother's banishment, but he is rebuffed. Casca then stabs Caesar and others quickly join the slaughter. As Brutus turns on him, Caesar exclaims in disbelief, "Et tu, Brute? Then fall Caesar!". Brutus orders the murderers to bathe their hands in Caesar's blood. As they smear themselves, Mark Antony's servant is assured of his master's safety.

I could be well moved, if I were as you;/If I could pray to move, prayers would move me;/But I am constant as the northern star... 3.1

Standing by Caesar's body, Mark Antony says he would feel honored to die like Caesar. He then shakes each killer by the hand, and asks if he may speak at Caesar's funeral. Brutus agrees over Cassius's protests. Left alone with Caesar's body, Antony sheds his mask and vows revenge. Octavius Caesar, Caesar's great-nephew and adopted son, sends word that he is near Rome.

O mighty Caesar! Dost thou lie so low?/Are all thy conquests, glories, triumphs, spoils/Shrunk to this little measure?... 3.1

O, pardon me, thou bleeding piece of earth,/That I am meek and gentle with these butchers... 3.1

Before a crowd, Brutus explains that under Caesar Romans would have become slaves. "There is tears for his love; joy for his fortune; honour for his valour; and death for his ambition." As Caesar's body is carried inside, Brutus introduces Mark Antony and leaves.

Be patient till the last./Romans, countrymen, and lovers, hear me for my cause... 3.2

Mark Antony begins cautiously, noting that Brutus said Caesar was ambitious—"And Brutus is an honourable man." He recalls that Caesar shared his victories with the people, that three times he refused the crown, yet Brutus claims he was ambitious. Sensing the crowd's changing mood, Mark Antony says: "It is not meet you know how Caesar loved you." As public anger mounts, he then identifies each hole in Caesar's bloody mantle, and points to Brutus's "most unkindest cut of all." Finally, uncovering Caesar's body, he says that, in his place, the orator Brutus would move "The stones of Rome to rise and mutiny."

Friends, Romans, countrymen, lend me your ears;/I come to bury Caesar, not to praise him... 3.2

If you have tears, prepare to shed them now... 3.2

Good friends, sweet friends, let me not stir you up/To such a sudden flood of mutiny... 3.2

As the angry crowd carries off Caesar's body, Mark Antony gloats: "Now let it work. Mischief, thou art afoot." A servant reports that Octavius waits at Caesar's house and that Brutus and Cassius have fled Rome. When the commoners leave, they come across Cinna the Poet and, misidentifying him as Cinna the conspirator, they kill him.

ACT FOUR
461 lines

A HOUSE IN ROME, BRUTUS'S CAMP NEAR SARDIS, AND BRUTUS'S TENT

The new triumvirate debates the fate of the plotters. As Lepidus leaves to collect Caesar's will, Mark Antony mocks him as "a slight unmeritable man," but Octavius protests that he is "a tried and valiant" soldier. Mark Antony reports that Brutus and Cassius are gathering an army.

At Brutus's camp, Cassius protests, "you have wronged me." Brutus retorts that Cassius has been dabbling in corruption, by selling offices, and recalls that Caesar was killed in the

Remember March, the ides of March remember./ Did not great Julius bleed for justice' sake?... 4.3

name of justice. Consumed by self-pity, Cassius draws his dagger and asks Brutus to strike him, "as thou didst at Caesar." Shocked, Brutus apologizes.

Brutus says he is grief-stricken because Portia has died swallowing burning coal. He has also learned that Octavius and Mark Antony are marching toward Philippi. Messala reports that the triumvirate has put to death 100 senators; Brutus says he heard that Cicero was among the victims. When Brutus proposes awaiting the enemy at Philippi, Cassius disagrees, but he is overruled.

Brutus asks Lucius to sing as he prepares to sleep, but Lucius falls asleep first. While Brutus is reading, he is visited by Caesar's ghost, who identifies himself as "Thy evil spirit, Brutus," and adds that "thou shalt see me at Philippi." Disturbed, Brutus decides to leave for Philippi early in the morning.

ACT FIVE

379 lines

THE PLAINS OF PHILIPPI

As the two armies face each other, Mark Antony and Octavius argue over tactics. Nearby, noting that the omens point to defeat, Cassius tells Brutus that this may be their last meeting. Yes, Brutus concedes, "But this same day/Must end that work the ides of March begun."

In the battle, Mark Antony gains advantage over Cassius, who sends Titinius to identify distant troops. When Pindarus reports that Titinius has been captured, Cassius is disconsolate. Ordering his servant to stab him, he cries, "Caesar, thou art revenged,/Even with the sword that killed thee". When Messala and Titinius bring word that Brutus has defeated Octavius, they find Cassius's body. Alone, Titinius places a victory wreath on Cassius's head, and kills himself.

Come down; behold no more./O, coward that I am to live so long... 5.3

Why didst thou send me forth, brave Cassius?... 5.3

Finding their bodies, Brutus praises Cassius, but his spirit is broken. Noting glumly that slaying "is a deed in fashion," he whispers to Clitus who recoils in shock. He next summons Dardanius who also refuses to kill him. Brutus then tells Volumnius that "I know my hour is come", and asks him to hold his sword, "whilst I run on it." As the battle comes closer, Brutus bids his friends farewell. Finally, ordering Strato to hold the sword, Brutus falls on it.

Nay, I am sure it is, Volumnius./Thou seest the world, Volumnius, how it goes... 5.5

Farewell to you; and you; and you, Volumnius... 5.5

Learning of his death, Mark Antony comments that Brutus alone acted honestly, for the common good. Octavius orders his body to be buried "With all respect and rites," and calls an end to the battle.

This was the noblest Roman of them all./ All the conspirators save only he/Did that they did envy of great Caesar... 5.5

'Our day is gone;/Clouds, dews, and dangers come; our deeds are done... 5.3

READING THE PLAY

COMPARISON OF PROSE TO VERSE

prose: 6% | verse: 94%

JULIUS CAESAR STANDS OUT for its strong and direct language, and its scant resort to metaphors, puns, and other lyrical flourishes. From the very first scene when the two tribunes announce their opposition to Caesar's mounting power, the play is largely plot-driven. Yet at each crucial moment, the action pauses so that the ambiguities of each character can be explored. One moment Caesar is playing god and referring to himself in the third person; the next moment he is accepting that death "Will come when it will come." The theme of fate versus free will is further developed in Brutus, who acts to halt Caesar's dictatorship, then commits suicide as an act of destiny predicted by Caesar's ghost. Both Mark Antony and Cassius are torn between public service and private interest: both plot in the name of Rome, but also look for personal advancement. Nowhere is this clearer than in Mark Antony's famous funeral oration, in which he skillfully turns the Roman mob against Caesar's killers and paves the way for his own rise to power. Thus, throughout the play, Shakespeare explores how Rome's fate is dependent on the vagaries of human will. It is Brutus's almost-Hamletian misgivings over his role in Caesar's death, though, that make him the play's most complex character. Brutus alone looks deeply into himself and battles with his conscience.

"I think it is the weakness of mine eyes/That shapes this monstrous apparition" (4.3). A guilt-stricken Brutus is tormented by Caesar's bloody ghost. Illustration by Edwin Austin Abbey for *Harper's Monthly* (1906).

LITERARY SOURCES

RENAISSANCE ICON

The subject of prose, poetry, and drama, Julius Caesar had been a Renaissance hero long before Shakespeare wrote his *Julius Caesar.* For his source material, Shakespeare leaned heavily on Sir Thomas North's 1579 translation of *Plutarch's Lives of the Noble Grecians and Romans,* which seven years later provided him with material for *Antony and Cleopatra* as well. Shakespeare may have also known the 1578 translation of Appian's *Civil Wars,* and the anonymous play *Caesar's Revenge.*

A man of arms and letters, Caesar embodied the Renaissance ideal of individual excellence. Roman bust, *c.* 50 BC.

SEEING THE PLAY

PLAY HISTORY

AN ACTOR'S PLOT

In a 1864 American production of *Julius Caesar*, three brothers—Edwin Booth, Junius Brutus Booth, and John Wilkes Booth *(left)*—played Brutus, Cassius, and Mark Antony. A year later, John Wilkes Booth assassinated President Abraham Lincoln at a performance at Ford's Theater, Washington, D.C.

The success of any production of *Julius Caesar* depends on whether the lead actors can convey the subtleties of the main characters. Caesar, Brutus, Cassius, and Mark Antony belong to history, yet their motivations remain human. If Caesar is interpreted as a bombastic tyrant (or, as was recently popular, as a 20th-century fascist dictator), his insecurity and fatalism risk being overlooked. But these flaws are important because they mirror the humanity that enables Mark Antony to turn the mob against Caesar's killers.

In this play, though, black and white quickly become gray. On the one hand, while Mark Antony's funeral oration enables him to pose as an unblemished hero, driven to fight Brutus and Cassius out of loyalty to his slain leader, he is in fact quickly corrupted by power. On the other hand, the conspirators against Caesar may claim to represent the republic's resistance to tyranny but, with the exception of Brutus, they are in fact defending the interests and privileges of their own class. It is for this reason that the mob briefly assumes a central role on stage. Even at the risk of a new civil war, it chooses the authoritarianism personified by the dead Caesar over the decadent republic represented by Brutus.

The two female roles, Calphurnia and Portia, serve as mirrors of male power politics. The truly tragic figure in a coherent production, though, is not Caesar, but Brutus, the flawed idealist who kills—and dies—for a republic that is no longer worth saving. Indeed, his very decency proves to be his undoing: by saving Mark Antony's life, he seals his own fate.

"Speak hands for me!" (3.2). With daggers drawn, the rebels rush Caesar (Christopher Benjamin) in the 1994 RSC production. Although audiences today may not share the Elizabethan fondness for gore on stage, Caesar's murder is inevitably bloody, especially as it is followed by the almost-religious ritual in which Brutus and his fellow assassins bathe their hands in Caesar's blood.

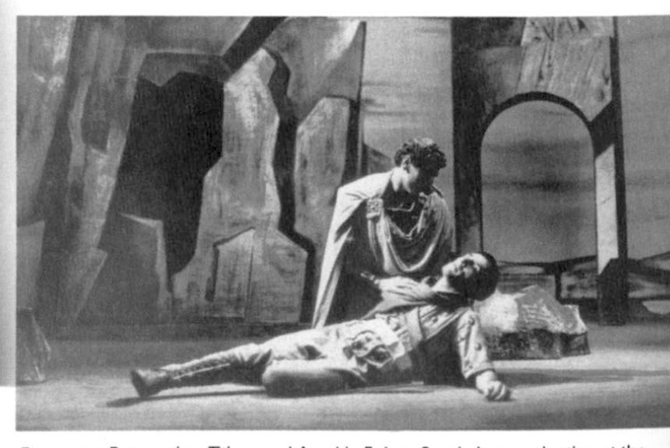

Francesco Pettenati as Titinus and Arnoldo Foà as Cassio in a production at the Piccolo Teatro di Milano, Italy, in 1953–54.

BEYOND THE PLAY

ON SCREEN

OSCAR-WINNER

The play's strong plot, high drama, and famous speeches have made it easily adaptable to the screen, even three times as a silent movie. Perhaps the best-known version is Joseph Mankiewicz's star-studded movie made in 1953, which won an Oscar for artistic direction. A 1969 English movie directed by Stuart Burge starred John Gielgud, Charlton Heston, and Jason Robards.

A poster for Mankiewicz's Hollywood extravaganza, *Julius Caesar,* starring Marlon Brando as Mark Antony, John Gielgud as Cassius, James Mason as Brutus, and Louis Calhern as Caesar.

THE FIRST RECORDED PERFORMANCE of *Julius Caesar* was at the Globe on September 21, 1599, when a Swiss traveler, Thomas Platter, reported having seen it. Although there is no known quarto edition of the play, there are indications that it remained popular after Shakespeare's death: the text published in the *First Folio* of 1623 is of unusually good quality and if, as seems likely, it was taken from a production text, this could mean that the play was still in the repertory of the King's Men.

When London's theaters reopened after the Restoration of 1660, *Julius Caesar* was quickly revived and, even in the 18th century, it escaped the fashion for adapting and rewriting Shakespearean works. By the 19th century, it was one of Shakespeare's most popular plays across Europe. In Victorian England, the parallel between the British and Roman empires was self-evident. The play was not, however, without its critics: George Bernard Shaw was prompted to write his own version, *Caesar and Cleopatra,* in 1898.

Nevertheless, generations of actors have disagreed with Shaw. One of the play's attractions for male actors is that it has four good roles and, interestingly, Caesar is not the most coveted part. Frequently, leading actors have tried their hand at more than one role over the course of their careers. Charles Mayne Young and Charles Macready at various times acted both Cassius and Brutus. But most famously, during his long career, John Gielgud not only played Antony and Caesar, but also returned frequently to Cassius, his favorite Roman role. Among noted productions are those directed by Orson Welles and John Houseman in 1937, and Minos Volanakis in 1962.

PLAYER PROFILE

ORSON WELLES

A youthful Orson Welles starred in the 1937 modern-dress *Julius Caesar,* played before blood-red walls. Welles acted Brutus as a "bewildered liberal, the man of character and principle in a world threatened by fascist destruction."

"Bear with me, good boy" (4.3). A sleepy Lucius (Arthur Anderson, left) attends his troubled master Brutus (Orson Welles, right).

HAMLET

HAMLET IS SHAKESPEARE'S FIRST masterpiece, arguably the greatest tragedy in the English language. Dissected and debated more than any other Shakespearean play, it leaves unsolved as many riddles about the human psyche as about Shakespeare's art. For centuries, coming to terms with *Hamlet* has been a rite of passage for leading directors, actors, and scholars. It may have been presented in Oxford in 1600, but there is no record of a London performance during Shakespeare's lifetime. However, the play was published in quarto editions while Shakespeare lived, and was included in the *First Folio*, suggesting that it was indeed popular. The story finds its origins in Old Norse legend with the folk-hero Amlothi, who feigned madness in order to exact revenge. The chronicler Saxo Grammaticus later assigned these traits to the historical Danish prince Amleth.

BEHIND THE PLAY

IN SHAKESPEARE'S HANDS, the story of *Hamlet* is changed from that of an eccentric folk-hero into one of a son struggling to find his place in a family disturbed as much by political events as by intimate relationships. Before the action begins, King Hamlet of Denmark, Prince Hamlet's father, had been challenged by King Fortinbras of Norway, whom he slew, gaining half of Norway's territory for Denmark. But now Prince Fortinbras, son of the slain Norwegian king, is preparing to regain what was lost. Hamlet's father has meanwhile died. The title of King of Denmark might have passed to Hamlet, but his mother, Gertrude, has married too quickly for the title to be transferred to her son. It has instead fallen to her new husband, Claudius, who is none other than the brother of Hamlet's father. The marriage, incestuous by Elizabethan standards, throws Hamlet into dual turmoil: it not only bars him from being king himself, but it also thrusts his uncle into the role of his surrogate father. When Hamlet's father appears as a ghost to explain that he was in fact murdered by Claudius, Hamlet is commanded to take revenge.

Remember thee?/ Ay, thou poor ghost, whiles memory holds a seat/In this distracted globe. Remember thee?... 1.5

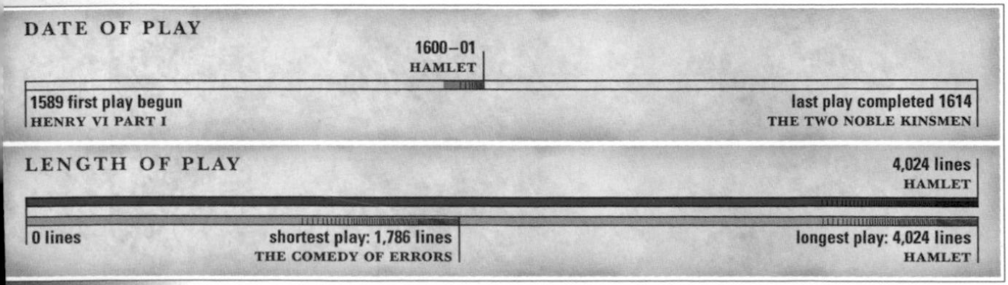

DATE OF PLAY

1600–01
HAMLET

1589 first play begun
HENRY VI PART I

last play completed 1614
THE TWO NOBLE KINSMEN

LENGTH OF PLAY

4,024 lines
HAMLET

0 lines

shortest play: 1,786 lines
THE COMEDY OF ERRORS

longest play: 4,024 lines
HAMLET

DRAMATIS PERSONAE

CLAUDIUS
550 lines
King of Denmark, he gains the title by murdering his brother and marrying his brother's widow; he is forced to confront his actions when visiting players perform.

LAERTES
206 lines
Son of Polonius, he comes from France to attend the coronation of Claudius, but immediately returns to France; he travels back to Elsinore to avenge his father by slaying Hamlet.

HAMLET
1495 lines
Son of the former king, and nephew to the usurper monarch, he returns to Elsinore to bury his father and is then drawn by his father's spirit into a plot of revenge; he is revolted by his mother's second marriage.

Hamlet (Jonathan Pryce), profoundly affected by his father's death, becomes deeply introspective.

POLONIUS
355 lines
Counselor to the king, he pays with his life for meddling in Hamlet's affairs.

HORATIO
291 lines
Friend to Hamlet and fellow student at Wittenberg, he comes to Elsinore to attend the funeral of King Hamlet.

Polonius (Michael Hordern) disapproves of Hamlet's affection for his daughter, Ophelia, and spies on Hamlet.

VOLTEMAND AND CORNELIUS
22; 1 lines
Danish ambassadors to Norway.

ROSENCRANTZ AND GUILDENSTERN
97; 53 lines
Childhood friends, they betray Hamlet, who orders their deaths.

OSRICK
48 lines
He invites Hamlet to challenge Laertes in swordplay.

MARCELLUS
68 lines
An officer, he notes "Something is rotten in the state of Denmark."

BERNARDO
39 lines
An officer, his "Who's there?" are the first words to the play.

FRANCISCO
10 lines
A soldier and sentinel.

REYNALDO
15 lines
Servant to Polonius, he spies on Laertes in Paris.

FORTINBRAS
27 lines
Prince of Norway, he goes to battle to honor the memory of his slain father and inspires Hamlet to avenge his own father's murder.

A NORWEGIAN CAPTAIN
12 lines
He informs Hamlet of Fortinbras's deployment of troops to Poland.

FOUR PLAYERS
96; 30; 6; 3 lines
They perform an interrupted adaptation by Hamlet of the play *The Murder of Gonzago.*

TWO CLOWNS
93; 18 lines
A gravedigger and his companion, they debate Christian doctrine and unearth Yorick's skull while digging.

ENGLISH AMBASSADORS
6 lines
They bring disturbing news from England.

GERTRUDE
157 lines
Queen of Denmark and mother of Hamlet, her hasty marriage to Hamlet's uncle prevents Hamlet from being named king.

OPHELIA
173 lines
Daughter of Polonius, in spite of her brother's warnings and her father's interdiction, she becomes the object of Hamlet's destructive affection.

THE GHOST OF HAMLET'S FATHER
95 lines
It orders Hamlet to avenge his father's death.

OTHER PLAYERS
Lords, Ladies, Officers, Soldiers, Sailors, Players, Messengers, and Attendants.

Queen Gertrude (Judith Anderson) tries to comfort Ophelia (Lillian Gish) who, overcome with grief at her father's death, sings melancholy, despairing songs.

PLOT SUMMARY

SIZE OF ACTS

ACT 1	ACT 2	ACT 3	ACT 4	ACT 5
922 lines	748 lines	929 lines	697 lines	728 lines

ACT ONE
922 lines

OUTSIDE AND WITHIN THE CASTLE OF ELSINORE IN DENMARK

Fortinbras of Norway has risen up against Denmark, placing Elsinore on high alert. At midnight, Horatio joins castle sentinels already twice alarmed by a Ghost. Horatio is amazed to behold the Ghost.

> **And then it started, like a guilty thing/Upon a fearful summons...** 1.1

King Claudius thanks his court for mirth in his marriage to the queen and for sorrow at the death of his brother, the former king. Now the court must address problems of state. Claudius dispatches ambassadors to inform the new King of Norway of his nephew Fortinbras's illegal warring. Noticing Hamlet's dejected appearance, the queen urges him to cease mourning his father. But Hamlet in turn warns his mother not to misjudge him. For his part, Claudius insists Hamlet accept him as a father.

> **Tis sweet and commendable in your nature, Hamlet,/ To give these mourning duties to your father...** 1.2

Alone, Hamlet considers suicide, revolted by the "incestuous sheets"of his mother and uncle. But when Horatio tells him about the Ghost, Hamlet sets aside thoughts of suicide; instead, he is eager to see the Ghost for himself.

> **O that this too too sullied lesh would melt/Thaw, and solve itself into a dew...** 1.2

Laertes bids his sister Ophelia farewell and begs her not to take Hamlet's wooing seriously. Polonius offers advice of his own to Laertes, who is about to return to Paris. When Ophelia reveals that Hamlet has expressed love for her, Polonius forbids her to speak to the prince.

On the guard platform, Hamlet condemns Claudius's habits. The Ghost appears and Hamlet showers it with questions. It beckons and Hamlet follows, dismissing his friends' warnings.

The Ghost commands Hamlet to avenge his murder. Claudius poisoned him, it says, while Gertrude, who would "prey on garbage," was easily seduced by Hamlet's uncle. Alone, Hamlet is outraged. Joining Horatio and Marcellus, Hamlet

> **There are more things in heaven and earth, Horatio,/ Than are dreamt of in your philosophy...** 1.5

says they must swear not to reveal what has happened. When they hesitate, the Ghost speaks from within the earth: "Swear". The terrified men vow silence.

ACT TWO

748 lines

WITHIN THE CASTLE

Polonius sends Reynaldo to Paris to spy on his son. But Polonius's daughter requires more urgent attention: Ophelia is distraught by Hamlet's unstable behavior. The king welcomes Rosencrantz and Guildenstern, childhood friends of Hamlet invited to investigate "Hamlet's transformation." Ambassadors report that Fortinbras will cease battling Denmark, but requests passage through the country en route to wage war on Poland. A bumbling Polonius argues that Hamlet has gone mad for love of Ophelia. When Claudius and Gertrude demand proof, Polonius proposes eavesdropping on the couple in conversation.

My lord, as I was sewing in my closet,/ Lord Hamlet, with his doublet all unbraced;/ No hat upon his head… 2.1

Madam, I swear I use no art at all./That he's mad, 'tis true. 'Tis true, 'tis pity,/ And pity 'tis 'tis true… 2.2

Hamlet answers strangely when Polonius asks him what he reads. But Polonius also finds Hamlet curiously insightful. Hamlet greets Rosencrantz and Guildenstern politely even though he senses mischief. Hamlet tells them he has "lost all mirth". Rosencrantz fears Hamlet will therefore find no joy in the tragedians who have just arrived in court. But Hamlet confides that he is a kind of player himself, for he only pretends to be mad. Polonius welcomes the actors. And Hamlet calls at once for a passionate speech, himself declaiming one by Aeneas. A Player delivers a tearful account of the story of Hecuba and Priam. Conversing secretly with the players, Hamlet arranges for them to perform *The Murder of Gonzago.*

I will tell you why. So shall my anticipation prevent your discovery… 2.2

I heard thee speak me a speech once, but it was never acted… 2.2

Alone, Hamlet praises the actor able to shed tears for the fictional Hecuba, and curses his own inability to express real emotions for real sufferings. But his spirits are lifted as he thinks of the tragedy to be performed: "The play's the thing/Wherein I'll catch the conscience of the King."

Now I am alone./ O, what a rogue and peasant slave am I… 2.2

ACT THREE

929 lines

WITHIN THE CASTLE AND IN THE QUEEN'S CLOSET

Polonius and the king spy on Hamlet and Ophelia. In his own world for a moment, Hamlet contemplates questions of existence. He then confuses Ophelia with mixed claims about his love for her. Ophelia is distressed to see him so changed. Having observed Hamlet and Ophelia together, Claudius is not convinced Hamlet is in love, no matter what Polonius thinks; nor does Claudius think Hamlet sounds like a madman.

To be, or not to be – that is the question;/Whether 'tis nobler in the mind to suffer/ The slings and arrows of outrageous fortune… 3.1

O, what a noble mind is here o'erthrown… 3.1

In preparation for the evening's entertainment, Hamlet instructs the players. He directs them to appear natural. Grateful for a friend he can trust, Hamlet asks Horatio to keep a keen eye on Claudius. If

Speak the speech, I pray you, as I pronounced it to you, trippingly on the tongue… 3.2

'Tis now the very witching time of night,/When churchyards yawn, and hell itself breathes out/Contagion to this world… 3.2

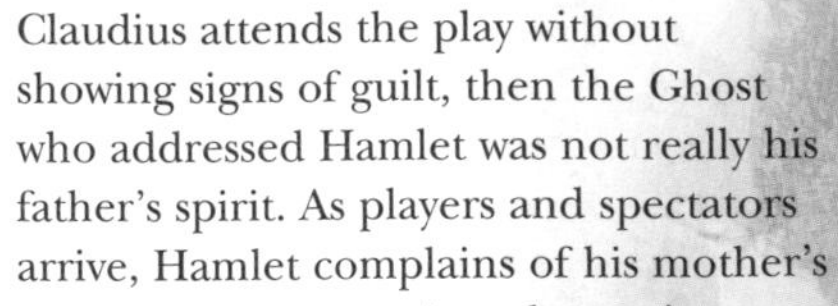

Claudius attends the play without showing signs of guilt, then the Ghost who addressed Hamlet was not really his father's spirit. As players and spectators arrive, Hamlet complains of his mother's unbecoming gaiety. Players portray the happily-married king and queen. But the Player King is ill, concerned about his wife's second husband. The Player Queen claims she will never remarry. A new player enters to poison the sleeping king. Hamlet says this man plots to win the love of the dead king's wife. With this, Claudius rises and departs, crying out for "Light!" Hamlet and Horatio agree that Claudius's reaction to the play was that of a guilty man. He must indeed have murdered Hamlet's father.

So long? Nay then, let the devil wear black, for I'll have a suit of sables… 3.2

When Rosencrantz and Guildenstern tell Hamlet that his mother has summoned him, Hamlet demonstrates to the former friends how they attempt to manipulate him, playing him as if he were a pipe. Alone, Hamlet discovers his growing thirst for revenge.

Alone, in a chapel, the king struggles with his desire to be absolved of his sins. As the king kneels to repent,

O, my offence is rank. It nells to heaven./It hath the rimal eldest curse upon't/ A brother's murder… 3.3

Hamlet enters. The opportunity to avenge the murder of his father is ideal. But Hamlet cannot bring himself to slay Claudius in prayer.

Now might I do it pat, now 'a is a-praying… 3.3

Polonius is behind the arras in Gertrude's closet as Hamlet threatens her. Frightened, she calls out, and Polonius responds, revealing his presence behind the divider. Hamlet stabs Polonius through the arras, asking his mother if he has slain the king. Inspecting the corpse, Hamlet mysteriously condemns "an act" of his mother's, but Gertrude does not understand his meaning. He explains that he is repulsed by her marriage. The queen, finally seeing her mistakes, begs for silence. But Hamlet bombards Gertrude with accusations as the Ghost, visible only to Hamlet, enters. The Queen notes her son's strange reaction and suspects Hamlet is hallucinating. But Hamlet insists he has not lost his senses. And he wishes his lustful mother would at least try to appear virtuous: if she were to avoid Claudius's bed, perhaps in time she might even become virtuous. Hamlet asks his mother to tell her husband that Hamlet knows his secret. For his part, Hamlet is due to leave for England soon. He reminds his mother that he will be accompanied by Rosencrantz and Guildenstern, whose

Alas, how is't with you,/ That you do bend your eye on vacancy,/ And with th'incorporal air do hold discourse… 3.4

O, throw away the worser part of it,/ And live the purer with the other half… 3.4

He is dead and gone, lady./He is dead and gone… 4.5

betrayal he plans to punish. Hamlet leaves, pulling Polonius's body after him.

ACT FOUR

697 lines

WITHIN THE CASTLE AND ON A PLAIN IN DENMARK

The king and queen discuss Hamlet's slaying of Polonius. Hamlet is summoned to explain where he has left Polonius's body, but he answers in riddles before disclosing its location. Hamlet must be sent to England for his own safety. Alone, Claudius rejoices to think that Hamlet will unwittingly carry to England sealed letters commanding he be put to death.

And, England, if my love thou holdest at aught… 4.3

On a plain in Denmark, Hamlet chances on a Captain of Fortinbras's army who explains that they march on Poland to fight for worthless territory. This news provokes Hamlet to reflect on his own inaction, and to give a concrete form to his burning desire for revenge.

How all occasions do inform against me/And spur my dull revenge!… 4.4

The queen receives a shattered Ophelia, who expresses herself in mournful songs. Claudius is alarmed that Laertes, who has returned from France, is being hailed king by the Danes. Laertes himself appears, enquiring about his murdered father. Laertes is devastated to behold his sister. Ophelia is lost in song and disconnected thoughts of flowers. Laertes seethes for revenge against Hamlet. Horatio receives a letter from Hamlet: pirates took him captive, and Rosencrantz and Guildenstern still make for England on their own.

, this is the poison of deep grief. It springs/ All from her father's death… 4.5

O heat, dry up my brains! Tears seven times salt/ Burn out the sense and virtue of mine eye!… 4.5

Horatio must join Hamlet at once, for he needs to impart some shocking news.

Claudius tells Laertes that Hamlet's crime went unpunished because he is adored. A letter arrives announcing Hamlet's return, prompting a shocked Claudius to ask Laertes if he loves his father enough to avenge his death. Laertes says he will fight Hamlet with a sword dipped in deadly poison. Claudius also offers to prepare a chalice to poison Hamlet in case Laertes fails to slay him. When Gertrude reports the death of Ophelia by drowning, Laertes's grief finds new depths.

Not that I think you did not love your father,/But that I know love is begun by time… 4.7

There is a willow grows askant the brook,/ That shows his hoar leaves in the glassy stream… 4.7

ACT FIVE

728 lines

IN A CHURCHYARD AND IN THE CASTLE

Gravediggers debate whether doctrine allows for Ophelia, who committed suicide, to receive a Christian burial. One gravedigger sings. Hamlet returns with Horatio to marvel at the gravedigger, who throws up bones as he works. Hamlet examines the skull of a former jester, and remarks how human beings can be reduced to dust. The court arrives, bearing the coffin of Ophelia, and a grief-stricken Laertes leaps into his sister's grave. Hamlet advances to tussle with Laertes, claiming his own grief greater: "Dost thou come here to whine?/To outface me with leaping in her grave?" But as Laertes's moment of revenge approaches, Horatio leads Hamlet away.

Let me see. Alas, poor Yorick! I knew him, Horatio. A fellow of infinite jest, of most excellent fancy… 5.1

Hamlet tells Horatio how he discovered the king's order that he be put to death in England. Hamlet replaced original commissions with a forged letter commanding instead that its bearers, Rosencrantz and Guildenstern, be killed. But Hamlet regrets the grief he has caused Laertes, and accepts Osrick's invitation to compete against Laertes in a sword-fighting game. The court arrives and Hamlet greets Laertes in a moving speech. Laertes accepts the words and swords are chosen. The king announces he will drink a cup of wine each time Hamlet wins a point. Hamlet wins a hit. And another. Gertrude raises a cup to honor her son, but it is the chalice intended for Hamlet and she is poisoned. Laertes and Hamlet wound one another, exchange swords in the confusion and continue to battle. Laertes falls, cut by his own poisoned weapon, now in Hamlet's hands. He warns Hamlet that he, too, shall soon expire and that all is the fault of Claudius. Hamlet uses the poisoned rapier to slay the king. Laertes exchanges forgiveness with Hamlet just before dying and Hamlet asks Horatio to tell his story to others.

Give me your pardon, sir. I have done you wrong./ But pardon't, as you are a gentleman... 5.2

It is here, Hamlet. Hamlet, thou art slain./ No medicine in the world can do thee good... 5.2

Heaven make thee free of it! I follow thee./ I am dead, Horatio... 5.2

With the sound of Fortinbras's victorious army approaching from Poland, Hamlet expresses his final wish: that Fortinbras rule Denmark. As ambassadors arrive from England to report Rosencrantz and Guildenstern slain, Horatio promises to explain the carnage to Fortinbras. Moved by the tragic demise of the Danish prince, Fortinbras commands a soldier's burial for Hamlet.

Not from his mouth,/ Had it th'ability of life to thank you... 5.2

Here hung the lips that I have kissed I know not how oft. Where be your gibes now? Your gambols, your songs, your flashes of merriment that were wont to set the table on a roar?... 5.1

READING THE PLAY

COMPARISON OF PROSE TO VERSE

prose: 28% | verse: 72%

SHAKESPEARE WAS PERHAPS DRAWN to the story of Hamlet for personal reasons. The death in 1596 of his eleven-year-old son, a twin named Hamnet, may have provided a deeply intimate basis for the writing of *Hamlet*, a play haunted as much by fathers and sons as by unfinished grieving and mortality.

Hamlet has been read as much for its unique literary insights into human nature as for its unsurpassed power as a drama of revenge. In his lectures of 1811–12, the poet Samuel Coleridge noted that in *Hamlet*, "Shakespeare wished to impress upon us the truth that action is the chief end of existence." Indeed, the momentous subjects raised in the play have made it a touchstone not only for scholars of literature but also for all manner of humanists, from psychologists to philosophers. For many, the figure of Hamlet gives peerless voice to universal dilemmas endured by human beings. Those new to Shakespeare usually find *Hamlet* one of the most satisfying plays to read. Threads of revenge are knotted up and unravelled with exquisite precision and pacing. Further, a great number of phrases born in this play have become part of today's language, most prominently perhaps those of Hamlet's famous soliloquies, such as "To be or not to be…" Others, too, are often repeated without reference to the play, such as when Gertrude notes of the Player Queen, "The lady doth protest too much, methinks," or when Hamlet urges Ophelia, "Get thee to a nunnery." Thus, the play is both familiar to new readers and yet constantly surprising. Electrifying, too, are the speeches and dialogues, by turns alarming and witty, in this, the most densely probing of Shakespeare's plays.

"Her clothes spread wide,/ And mermaid-like awhile they bore her up" (4.7). A painting of Ophelia drowned in the brook by John Everett Millais, 1851–52.

LITERARY SOURCES

REVENGE AND MELANCHOLY

A Revenge play about Hamlet, now lost, had already been set by 1589, possibly by Thomas Kyd. Shakespeare drew on this and other Revenge plays, but also turned to sources including the *Essays of Michel Montaigne,* and works about witchcraft and ghosts. Another source was *A Treatise of Melancholy* (1586) by Timothy Bright, in which Shakespeare must have been captivated to read "how melancholy altereth those actions which rise out of the brain.".

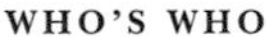

WHO'S WHO

Claudius has usurped the Danish throne by murdering his brother and marrying **Gertrude**, his brother's widow. **The Ghost** of the murdered king haunts his son, **Hamlet**, Prince of Denmark, ordering him to avenge the murder. Hamlet is tormented by his inability to act. He slays **Polonius**, the Lord Chamberlain, who is caught spying. His daughter, **Ophelia**, who is in love with Hamlet, slays herself. When Hamlet finally acts to avenge his father's death, he is slain by **Laertes**, the vengeful son of Polonius. **Fortinbras**, son of the slain King of Norway, leads an army into Denmark to avenge his father's death, gaining the Danish throne.

SEEING THE PLAY

ON STAGE

A STUDENT PRODUCTION

For a *Hamlet* given during student protests in 1965 at the Royal Shakespeare Company, director Peter Hall had actor David Warner play Hamlet as a working-class student, alienated as much from the political process as from society. Hall found that the play was about disillusionment and apathy so profound that "commitment to politics, to religion or to life is impossible."

No role in the Shakespearean corpus is more adaptable to the actor than Hamlet. Tragedians have variously interpreted Hamlet as a man driven to distraction by his love for Ophelia; as a son entranced by the commands of his father or repulsed by the impurity of his mother; as a prince deprived of the right to rule as king; or as a friend betrayed by those he has trusted since childhood. Some portray Hamlet as a sane person feigning madness to express grief or to test his entourage and himself. The play offers many other great roles and each requires careful study. Are the meandering speeches of Polonius to be considered annoying, pitiable, comical? Does Gertrude lust for Claudius in particular, or for all men, including her son, and is she ignorant of the offense she causes? Since action almost never moves outside the castle, secondary roles help to establish the dark magnetism of a Denmark ruled as much by family secrets, sworn silences, and suspicion, as by dynastic disorder. One of the main subjects of *Hamlet* is the power of acting to transform raw emotions into understanding of oneself and others, and to convert thought into action. Directors, challenged to generate intimate, disturbing self-reflection among spectators, use many techniques to attempt this. One simple and popular option is to cut scenes and characters. After all, *Hamlet* is Shakespeare's longest play; if performed uncut, it runs over four hours.

Gordon Craig used movable screens in his revolutionary designs for Stanislavsky's Moscow Art Theater production of 1911.

Peter Brook's 2001 multilingual *Hamlet*, developed at his Théâtre des Bouffes du Nord in Paris, featured leading international actors, including Adrian Lester as Hamlet (right), each delivering a role in his or her own tongue, including Ki-swahili, English, and Japanese. Audiences have so internalized the story of *Hamlet* that they were able to follow the action in spite of the different languages.

BEYOND THE PLAY

THE ENORMOUSLY ENIGMATIC ROLE of Hamlet has taken on an existence independent of Shakespeare's play. In 1900, Sigmund Freud, the founder of psychoanalysis, noted the universal relevance of Hamlet, whom he used to illustrate his theory of repression. "Hamlet is able to do anything – except take vengeance on... the man who shows him the repressed wishes of his own childhood."

About early performances of *Hamlet*, little survives. The play was probably given at Oxford in 1600. Richard Burbage is documented as the player of Hamlet and Shakespeare himself as the Ghost. Two amateur performances aboard the East India Company ship *Dragon* were recorded during Shakespeare's lifetime. On March 31, 1608, Captain Keeling noted: "I invited Captain Hawkins to a fish dinner, and had *Hamlet* acted aboard me, which I permit to keep my people from idleness and unlawful games or sleep."

The performance history of *Hamlet* is the richest of any of Shakespeare's plays. The role was taken by an array of major actors, from David Garrick (1742) and Henry Irving (1864) to John Gielgud (he played the role five times from 1929–44) and Laurence Olivier. But *Hamlet* has also moved audiences in foreign tongues and even in silent movies. Bolstering its nternational reputation, translations of he play have become classics in other anguages. A fine example is Boris Pasternak's 1941 Russian *Hamlet*. Audiences find that *Hamlet* responds as urgently to new dilemmas as it does to age-old concerns. Peter Zadek rejected reat German translations, including Schlegel's, to write a rough and rude cript for his 1977 *Hamlet*, played in n abandoned factory outside Berlin. There, Hamlet raged anarchically at xistence divided by The Wall. There ave also been English elaborations on he play, such as Tom Stoppard's *Rosencrantz and Guildenstern Are Dead*. So ong as audiences find that "something is otten" in the world, *Hamlet* is sure to emain one of the world's greatest plays.

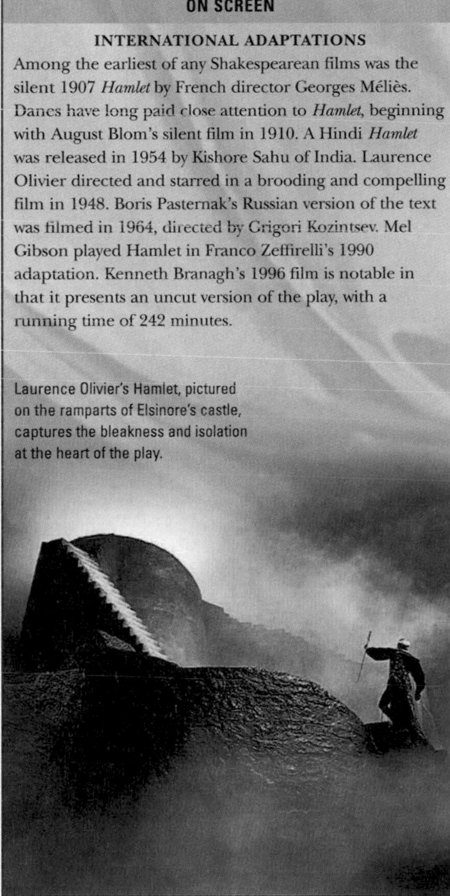

ON SCREEN

INTERNATIONAL ADAPTATIONS

Among the earliest of any Shakespearean films was the silent 1907 *Hamlet* by French director Georges Méliès. Danes have long paid close attention to *Hamlet*, beginning with August Blom's silent film in 1910. A Hindi *Hamlet* was released in 1954 by Kishore Sahu of India. Laurence Olivier directed and starred in a brooding and compelling film in 1948. Boris Pasternak's Russian version of the text was filmed in 1964, directed by Grigori Kozintsev. Mel Gibson played Hamlet in Franco Zeffirelli's 1990 adaptation. Kenneth Branagh's 1996 film is notable in that it presents an uncut version of the play, with a running time of 242 minutes.

Laurence Olivier's Hamlet, pictured on the ramparts of Elsinore's castle, captures the bleakness and isolation at the heart of the play.

OTHELLO

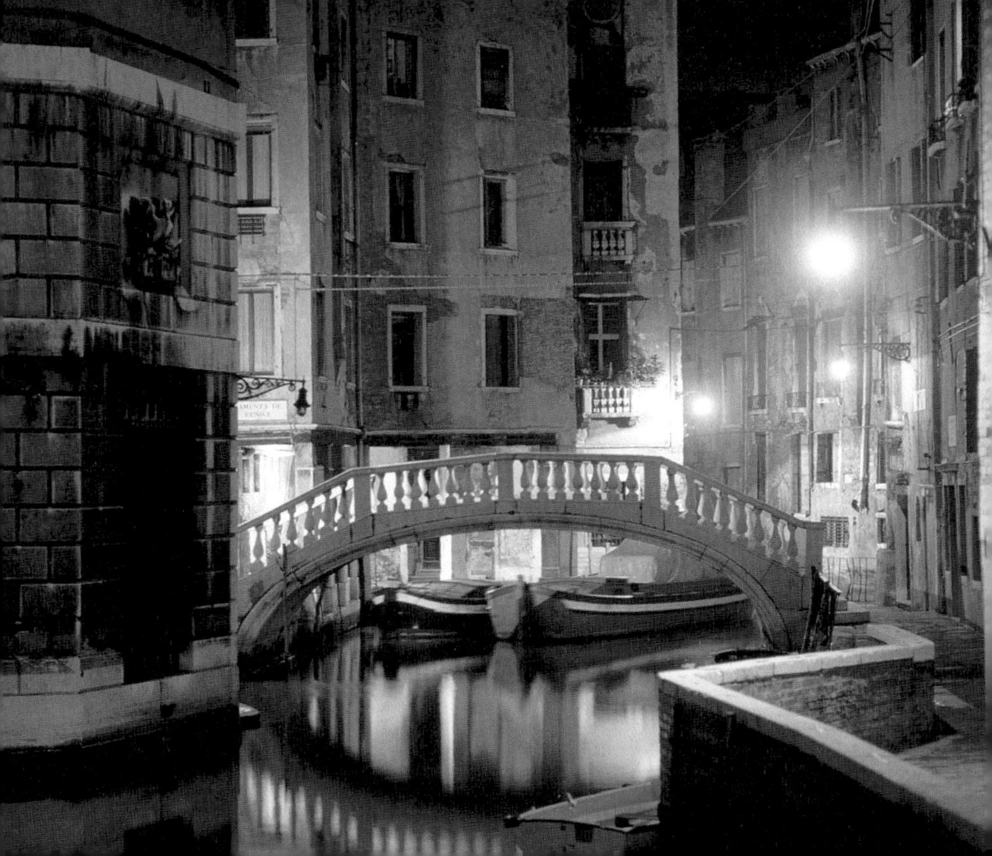

IN OTHELLO, SHAKESPEARE CREATES both his most hateful villain and his most poignant tragic hero. This masterpiece of revenge tracks the workings of a sick mind with breathtaking detail and explores the power of language to transform love into murderous jealousy. Three performances of *Othello* are recorded during Shakespeare's lifetime. The earliest was in 1604 at Whitehall Palace for King James. Other documented productions were at the Globe theater in April 1610 and in September that year in Oxford. Iago's pathological fiendishness has never been surpassed in dramatic literature, set against Othello's honesty, love, and purity of principle. Thus, with Othello the black Moor, Shakespeare subverts the racial stereotypes accepted by the audiences of his day to embrace the deception of appearances and the grave danger of assumptions.

BEHIND THE PLAY

OTHELLO, A MOOR AND AN IMMIGRANT TO VENICE, is the Venetian republic's most admired military commander. Enchanted by tales of his exotic past, Desdemona has fallen in love and eloped with him. As the action of the play begins, Venice is preparing to defend itself from a threatened naval attack by Ottoman Turks. As in the past, the leaders of Venice call upon Othello to lead their forces. But Brabantio, an influential senator, is also Desdemona's father. Enraged to discover that she has married Othello, he accuses the Moor of using witchcraft to steal his daughter. The other senators, more concerned with protecting Venice, take Othello's side in the dispute. The play's military context, however, is short-lived, serving mainly as a framework for the intense private wars that follow. And in this emotional arena, Othello is far less secure. His closest aide, Iago, who first sets out to entrap Cassio, soon understands that he has the power to undermine Othello himself. Othello then becomes his own chief antagonist as jealousy transforms him into a monster. Much of the action of the play is set in public spaces, but the final scene is situated in the tragic intimacy of Desdemona's bed chamber.

I must weep./ But they are cruel tears: this sorrow's heavenly – / It strikes where it doth love... 5.2

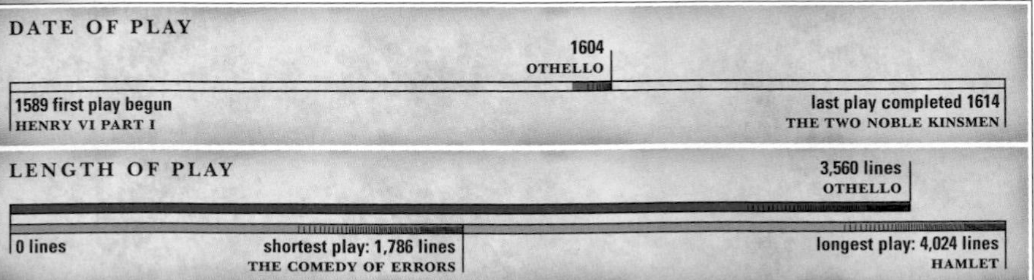

DRAMATIS PERSONAE

DUKE OF VENICE
73 lines
A great admirer of Othello's, he tells Brabantio "If virtue no delighted beauty lack,/ Your son-in-law is far more fair than black."

BRABANTIO
139 lines
Father to Desdemona, he tells Othello that his daughter would never "run from her guardage to the sooty bosom/Of such a thing as thou."

SENATORS
26; 5; 2 lines
They gather at night in their council chamber to plan for war.

GRATIANO
33 lines
A noble Venetian, he arrives in Cyprus with Lodovico.

LODOVICO
76 lines
A noble Venetian, as the play concludes, he promises to return to Venice and "This heavy act with heavy heart relate."

CASSIO
278 lines
An honorable lieutenant, he gains promotion to the very post Iago hoped to win, but Iago intends to correct this error.

IAGO
1098 lines
A villain, "ensign" or standard-bearer to Othello, by his own admission his methods are subtle: "I told him what I thought, and told no more/Than what he found himself was apt and true"; he sows and nurtures the seeds of jealousy and suspicion in Othello's mind.

Sinister, vengeful Iago (Ian McKellen)

RODERIGO
114 lines
A gullible gentleman, he aims to win Desdemona himself and is easily manipulated by Iago into seeking revenge; Iago uses him to discredit Cassio's name and then kills him.

MONTANO
63 lines
The governor of Cyprus, he is to decide the fate of Iago once the villain's infamy has been revealed to all.

A CLOWN
27 lines
A witty fool, he quibbles in the street with musicians and Cassio.

DESDEMONA
388 lines
Wife to Othello, she loves and honors him even when he begins to act strangely and suspect her of adultery; she says "guiltiness I know not; but yet I feel fear."

EMILIA
245 lines
Wife to Iago, she is called a "villainous whore" by her husband when she denounces him to Othello; she dies by her husband's hand while defending Desdemona's integrity.

BIANCA
34 lines
A courtesan, she adores Cassio, but he merely enjoys her company.

OTHER PLAYERS
Messenger, Herald, Officers, Gentlemen of Cyprus, Musicians, Sailors, and Attendants.

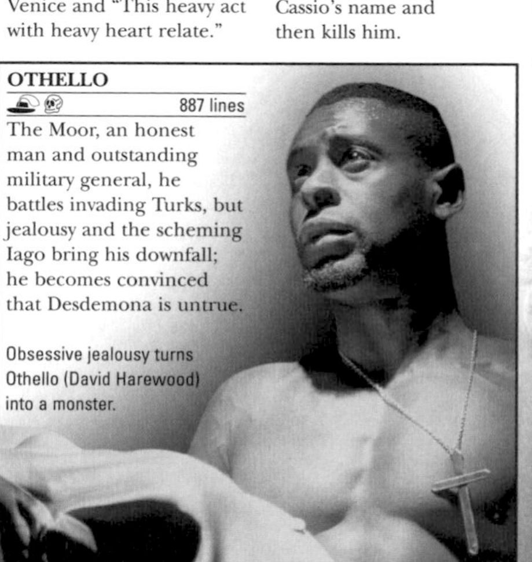

OTHELLO
887 lines
The Moor, an honest man and outstanding military general, he battles invading Turks, but jealousy and the scheming Iago bring his downfall; he becomes convinced that Desdemona is untrue.

Obsessive jealousy turns Othello (David Harewood) into a monster.

Tragic Desdemona (Uta Hagen) who embodies innocence, virtue, and fidelity, although Othello becomes blind to her qualities.

PLOT SUMMARY

SIZE OF ACTS

ACT 1	ACT 2	ACT 3	ACT 4	ACT 5
739 lines	736 lines	826 lines	691 lines	568 lines

ACT ONE
739 lines

IN STREETS AND A COUNCIL CHAMBER OF VENICE

Iago seeks revenge. Othello has promoted Cassio and Iago remains an under-officer in spite of his seniority.

O, sir, content you:/ I follow him to serve my turn upon him... 1.1

At night, Iago informs the Venetian noble Brabantio that his daughter and Othello are "making the beast with two backs." Iago's friend, Roderigo, puts it less crudely: Desdemona has eloped with Othello. Brabantio summons Othello.

Iago warns Othello that Brabantio will challenge the marriage. But Othello remains confident: "My parts, my title, and my perfect soul/Shall manifest me rightly." Cassio reports that Turks are putting a fleet into Cyprus, which means war, and the duke has called for Othello. But Brabantio accuses Othello of using magic to win Desdemona. The duke greets Othello and eventually recognizes Brabantio, who pleads for justice in the case of his daughter. Othello admits that he is married, but not due to witchcraft as accused. Sending for Desdemona to speak for herself, Othello says he won her by telling "the story of my life". Desdemona arrives to note "a divided duty." She owes her father respect, but her greater duty is to her husband. Finally, Brabantio admits defeat. Othello prepares to leave at once. Desdemona wants to travel with him, but Iago is to escort Desdemona separately to Cyprus.

O thou foul thief! Where hast thou stowed my daughter?/Damned as thou art, thou hast enchanted her... 1.2

Her father loved me, oft invited me,/Still questioned me the story of my life/ From year to year... 1.3

That I love the Moor to live with him,/My downright violence and storm of fortunes/May trumpet to the world... 1.3

Roderigo, who aims to win Desdemona for himself, is suicidal. Iago says he would rather "change my humanity with a baboon" than commit suicide for love and he lectures Roderigo on the will's relation to the body. Since they both detest Othello, Iago proposes that he and Roderigo join forces "in our revenge against him." Alone, Iago thinks about Othello, noting "it is thought abroad that 'twixt my sheets/H'as done my office." He reasons that he has a double pretext to hate the Moor and an excellent motive for revenge. Iago will persuade Othello that Cassio is Desdemona's lover. Iago delights in his evil scheme.

Thus do I ever make my fool my purse... 1.3

The Moor is of a free and open nature,/That thinks men honest that but seem to be so,/ And will as tenderly be led by th'nose/As asses are... 1.3

ACT TWO

736 lines

IN CYPRUS, ON THE COAST AND IN THE CITADEL

A storm has wrecked the Turkish fleet and prevented war, but Othello is still at sea. Iago disembarks with Desdemona in Cyprus, where Cassio greets her with kisses. Cassio asks Iago to forgive his higher breeding, which calls for such fancy gestures. Humiliated, Iago takes out his anger on his wife, Emilia, then satisfies himself that Cassio's upper-class behavior makes him look all the more like Desdemona's lover. Othello arrives, overjoyed to see his wife.

It gives me wonder great as my content/To see you here before me... 2.1

Iago shocks Roderigo by saying that Desdemona loves Cassio, then calms him. Iago plots: Roderigo will be on the watch and must find cause to provoke Cassio. Alone, Iago finds that he, too, is in love with Desdemona: she feeds his hunger for revenge.

Lay thy finger thus, and let thy soul be instructed... 2.1

That Cassio loves her, I do well believe 't:/ That she loves him, 'tis apt and of great credit... 2.1

Othello announces festivities to celebrate his marriage and the sinking of the Turkish fleet. Cassio has a problem with liquor and must not drink, but Iago persuades him to celebrate with the others. To encourage Cassio's drinking, Iago orders extra wine and sings.

And let me the canakin clink, clink... 2.3

Roderigo later provokes Cassio, who attacks as predicted. Othello asks "honest Iago" to explain what happened. Iago replies that he would rather not "do offense to Michael Cassio." But, he goes on, Cassio was offended by someone. Othello needs no further proof: "Cassio, I love thee:/But never more be officer of mine." Cassio's reputation is destroyed, but Iago persuades him all is not lost. Iago recommends Cassio plead his case through Desdemona. Alone, Iago plots: Othello must observe Cassio and Desdemona together.

And what's he then that says I play the villain,/ When this advice is free I give, and honest... 2.3

ACT THREE

826 lines

IN CYPRUS, ON THE STREETS AND IN THE CITADEL

Desdemona promises Cassio she will defend him. When Othello approaches, Cassio leaves urgently, allowing Iago to insinuate his guilt. Desdemona presses Cassio's case to her husband. Warning Othello against jealousy, Iago fuels his master's imagination. His suspicion complete, Othello sends Iago away. But Iago returns to request Othello "scan this thing no further." Othello notes Iago's honesty and Desdemona's betrayal. Desdemona arrives and tries to calm Othello's headache with her precious handkerchief. But Othello pushes it to the floor. Alone, Emilia steals the handkerchief as Iago requested.

O, beware, my lord, of jealousy!/ It is the green-eyed monster, which doth mock/ The meat it feeds on... 3.3

Delighted to receive the handkerchief, Iago plans to deposit it in Cassio's quarters. Othello returns, enraged by thoughts of Desdemona's infidelity. Othello believes his own name "is now begrimed and black/As mine own face." When Othello desires proof of Desdemona's wrongdoing, Iago tells of Cassio's behaviour while asleep, treating

I had been happy if the general camp,/Pioneers and all, had tasted her sweet body,/So I had nothing known... 3.3

My bloody thoughts with violent pace/Shall ne'er look back, ne'er ebb to humble love,/Till that a capable and wide revenge/Swallow them up... 3.3

Iago's body as if it were Desdemona's. Othello discounts this as mere dreaming. Iago says he saw Cassio wipe his beard with Desdemona's handkerchief. This, Othello can barely believe: "All my fond love thus do I blow to heaven." Othello kneels to vow revenge and Iago joins him, offering his services.

When Desdemona pressures Othello to meet Cassio, Othello asks to see her handkerchief. She cannot produce it, but Othello informs her of its magic and unusual history. He tells her to fetch the handkerchief at once.

That is a fault./ That handkerchief/ Did an Egyptian to my mother give... 3.4

Cassio asks Bianca to copy the embroidery onto his new handkerchief. Bianca is jealous, but Cassio reassures her: "I found it in my chamber."

ACT FOUR

691 lines

IN CYPRUS, IN THE STREETS AND IN THE CITADEL

Needled by Iago's disturbing suggestions about Desdemona, Othello falls into a trance. Iago offers Othello a chance to observe secretly as Cassio speaks of Desdemona. Cassio makes light of Bianca, mocking her. Thinking Cassio refers to Desdemona, Othello fumes: "How shall I murder him, Iago?" Othello vows also to murder his wife: "I will chop her into messes!" Iago recommends strangulation "in her bed, even the bed she hath contaminated". Othello welcomes the justice of this solution.

Lie with her? Lie on her? We say lie on her when they belie her... 4.1

Fresh from Venice, the nobleman, Lodovico, presents documents requesting Othello's immediate return and naming Cassio to Othello's post. Lodovico, however, also notes Othello's unusual behavior. Desdemona wonders if Othello is in a bad mood because he suspects her father of being "An instrument of this your calling back." But Othello says he is thinking about patience and then calls his wife a "cunning whore." Emilia is outraged. Desdemona is forced to turn to Iago for advice.

Ay! You did wish that I would make her turn./ Sir, she can turn, and turn, and yet go on,/ And turn again... 4.1

A halter pardon him and hell gnaw his bones!/ Why should he call her whore? Who keeps her company?... 4.2

Roderigo no longer trusts Iago, who promised to deliver gifts from him to Desdemona. But Iago flatters Roderigo, explaining that the "removing" of Cassio is the key to his happiness. When Roderigo asks what he means by "removing," Iago replies: "knocking out his brains." Iago suggests that he and Roderigo kill Cassio as he leaves Bianca's home that very night.

After dinner, Othello sends a fearful Desdemona to bed. Desdemona tells Emilia about her mother's maid, Barbary, who was in love with a man who proved mad. She died singing a song called "Willow" ♫.

The poor soul sat sighing by a sycamore tree,/ Sing all a green willow… 4.3

Desdemona asks Emilia if she would commit adultery. Emilia thinks she might, and believes other women would as well ❝.

Yes, a dozen: and as many to th'vantage as would store the world they played for… 4.3

ACT FIVE

568 lines

IN CYPRUS, IN A STREET AND IN DESDEMONA'S CHAMBER

Iago reasons it would be useful if he were rid of both Roderigo and Cassio. Roderigo attacks Cassio. In the scuffle, Roderigo is injured. Othello passes by, suspecting Iago is carrying out his earlier promise to murder Cassio. Hearing cries, Lodovico and Gratiano also arrive. Cassio reports that his attackers are nearby. Roderigo cries for help and Iago, going to him, takes the opportunity to slay him ☠. Cassio, for his part, suffers only a leg injury.

Othello observes Desdemona in her bed and thinks about murdering her ❝. Desdemona awakens, alarmed. He asks her to confess her sins but, when Desdemona pleads innocence, Othello smothers her. Emilia hears her lady's final words: "Commend me to my lord. O, farewell." Othello confesses murder and explains himself to Emilia: "Cassio did top her. Ask thy husband else." But Emilia now sees why Iago had her steal the handkerchief. Montano, Gratiano, Lodovico and others arrive. Gratiano is grateful Desdemona's father, now dead, need not endure his daughter's murder. When Emilia reveals that Iago ordered her to take the handkerchief, Iago kills her, and is at once taken prisoner ☠.

It is the cause, it is the cause, my soul:/ Let me not name it to you, you chaste stars!… 5.2

Othello is distraught, and thinks of killing himself ❝. He would kill Iago, but believes Iago is the devil, hence invincible. Othello is disarmed, then hears from Cassio of the deceptions schemed by Iago, whom Othello hopes will live to suffer. Othello then stabs himself with a concealed blade ❝. Othello falls over Desdemona and dies ☠. Lodovico asks Iago to "Look on the tragic loading of this bed./This is thy work..." Montano is to decide Iago's fate. And Lodovico announces he will report the events to Venice.

Behold, I have a weapon:/ A better never did itself sustain/Upon a soldier's thigh… 5.2

Soft you; a word or two before you go./ I have done the state some service and they know't:/ No more of that… 5.2

Yet I'll not shed her blood/Nor scar that whiter skin of hers than snow,/And smooth as monumental alabaster:/ Yet she must die, else she'll betray more men./ Put out the light, and then put out the light… 5.2

READING THE PLAY

COMPARISON OF PROSE TO VERSE

prose: 19% verse: 81%

OTHELLO IS FILLED WITH exquisite speeches and electric, even alarming exchanges. Readers will find a great variety of rhetorical language in this play, notably Desdemona's moving accounts of her love and admiration of Othello; Othello's frightening rages of jealousy when he believes she shares her body with Cassio; and Iago's deeply unnerving soliloquies, in which he brazenly exposes the audience to his evil genius. Cultural conventions of the day associated the colour black with the devil, but no figure in the works of Shakespeare is more diabolical than white Iago. When Iago is in dialogue, he manipulates language with such deception that a mere word or inflection suddenly changes his interlocutor's view of the world. Act 3 Scene 3 is a Shakespearean tour-de-force, where Iago fuels Othello's suspicion and jealousy by pretending to avoid saying anything controversial or upsetting, even warning Othello not to be jealous. Most of the play is in verse, and most of Iago's and Othello's key scenes are notable for their great verse language, but Iago proves himself just as stunning a scoundrel in prose. Still, reading falls short of seeing the play in scenes that must fully exploit the resources of the stage. One such scene occurs when Cassio is attacked at night by Iago and Roderigo in a street of Cyprus. But such moments are rare in *Othello* because Iago so relishes exposing the machinations of his mind. Othello's mind is less transparent. Some readers, notably T.S. Eliot, have criticized the character as too wooden, lacking insight or emotional depth. But, following Wordsworth, others have praised the hero's honesty and adherence to principles. Bloom has argued that Othello is perhaps "Shakespeare's most wounding representation of male vanity."

WHO'S WHO

Othello, the Moor, is an outstanding general, who has eloped with **Desdemona**, the daughter of a Venetian senator. His standard-bearer, **Iago**, eaten up with bitterness and jealousy, plots to bring down two superiors at once by persuading Othello that his lieutenant, the noble **Cassio**, is committing adultery with his wife. Iago embroils his own wife, **Emilia**, in his plots, persuading her to steal Desdemona's handkerchief. He even persuades **Roderigo**, Desdemona's rejected suitor, to attempt murder. Manipulated by Iago, Othello's jealousy escalates. When Othello smothers Desdemona, Iago is exposed as a villain and Othello kills himself.

"Then must you speak /Of one that loved not wisely, but too well" (5.2). A portrait of Othello by Anselm Feuerbach, 1829–80.

LITERARY SOURCES

GIRALDI CINTHIO

The source for *Othello*, an Italian story by Giraldi Cinthio, begins: "There once lived in Venice a Moor, who was very valiant and of a handsome person." Shakespeare may have read the tale in the original Italian, published in the 16th century in a collection entitled *Hecatommithi*.

SEEING THE PLAY

PLAYER PROFILE

EDMUND KEAN

The noted English actor (1789–1833) learned his craft as a strolling player, called upon to "play the whole round of tragedy, comedy, opera, farce." He excelled in tragic roles, playing both Iago and Othello. On 25 March 1833, playing Othello to his son Charles's Iago, he collapsed during the performance—his last.

OTHELLO EMPLOYS THEMES AS CAPTIVATING to modern theatergoers as they were to Jacobean audiences: racism, colonialism, domestic violence, substance abuse, and conflicts of seniority and power in the workplace. But the success of any production of *Othello* rests on the strengths of its actors. Shakespeare wrote strongly characterized language for nearly all roles in this play, but most parts require interpreters to reveal their inner selves in order to evolve persuasively. Othello, Iago and Desdemona are among the most challenging roles in the Shakespeare repertoire, but Cassio, Emilia and Roderigo also demand exceptional actors. There are no grand spectacles or special effects scenes to divert audience attention from the intensity of the human drama unfolding in this work. Consequently, effective productions of *Othello* allow actors to establish close bonds with their audiences. With Iago doing so most effectively in his soliloquies. Desdemona's death scene can also provoke acute audience reaction when performed effectively. A comment in Latin about a 1610 Oxford performance notes that the boy portraying Desdemona moved the spectators to pity with facial gestures during the death scene. When theatres reopened in London in 1660, Samuel Pepys remarked about *The Moor of Venice*, as *Othello* was then entitled, that a lady beside him in the audience at the Cockpit Theatre cried out when she saw Desdemona smothered. In the masterful hands of an 'actor's director,' no play of Shakespeare's is better set to take audiences on an unforgettable journey into the disturbing emotional world where envy yields to self-destruction, and love to homicidal jealousy.

Iago (Leo McKern) and Emilia (Catherine Lacey) in a production at the Old Vic in 1964. Emilia steals Desdemona's handkerchief on her husband's instructions

BEYOND THE PLAY

OTHELLO RAISES MORE QUESTIONS ABOUT race and racism than any of Shakespeare's plays. While Shakespeare designated Othello a Moor, any black Othello was for centuries unthinkable to white readers and audiences. Samuel Coleridge said it would have been "impossible for a girl to fall in love with a veritable negro." Othello was instead made a sun-burnished Arab. With make-up, generations of white actors passed for the tawny Moor. After David Garrick, Edmund Kean played the role from 1814 up until nearly the day of his death in 1833. Henry Irving gave a violent Othello in 1876 and 1881. One Othello of the late 19th century was neither black nor English-speaking: spectators including Henry James were beguiled by the unpredictable Othello of Tomasso Salvini, who performed in Italian while others in the cast spoke English on Italian stages. Orson Welles performed the lead in the film version he directed in 1952, as did Laurence Olivier in his 1964 film. Anthony Hopkins starred in a 1981 televised version for the BBC directed by Jonathan Miller, who said that a black actor would mislead the audience into thinking that the play was about blackness instead of jealousy.

In reality, black performers of many national origins have long taken on the role. In the 19th century, two African-Americans, James Hewlett and Ira Aldridge, were famous Othellos. (Aldridge, who worked mainly in London, also appeared in white make-up as Richard III, Shylock, Hamlet, Macbeth, and Lear.) Since then, with many directors now insisting on casting black actors in the role, there have been fine stage interpretations by Earle Hyman, Moses Gunn, Paul Winfield, William Marshall, James Earl Jones, Willard White, and Ray Fearson. In Oliver Parker's 1995 screen version, Laurence Fishburne also proved an electric Othello opposite Irène Jacob's Desdemona and Kenneth Branagh's Iago.

The play's intense drama has made it particularly suitable for operatic adaptation. In 1816, Rossini composed *Otello* for the Naples opera. Boito set a libretto for the magnificent music of Verdi's 1887 *Otello*, whose colossal title role is the most demanding and passionate tenor part in the Italian opera repertory.

ON STAGE

PAUL ROBESON
When the great singer-actor Paul Robeson played Othello in New York in 1943, it was considered a novelty, with the acclaimed production running for almost a year. Robeson himself described the play as "a tragedy of racial conflict, a tragedy of honor rather than jealousy".

Plácido Domingo interprets the role of Othello in Franco Zeffirelli's film version of Verdi's opera, *Otello*, November 1985, Crete.

KING LEAR

SHAKESPEARE'S MOST UNFORGIVING TRAGEDY, *King Lear* is a profound examination of the essence of human dignity. Shakespeare knew *The Chronicle History of King Leir*, a play staged around 1590, and he also drew from the *Chronicles of Holinshed* for some details about the historical king, an early ruler of England. The only recorded performance of Shakespeare's *King Lear* during his lifetime was on December 26, 1606, when it was given at court. But its publication in quarto editions as early as 1608 and its reprinting in the *First Folio* of 1623 suggest that the play was popular with theater audiences. Exploring the vulnerable grandeur of man when reduced to his elemental state, *King Lear* arguably represents Shakespeare's most fearless investigation of human nature. Today, it is celebrated as one of the greatest works of Western art in any period.

BEHIND THE PLAY

KING LEAR OPENS IN A FOLKTALE-LIKE WORLD, where Lear attempts to imbue objects, such as his own crown and a map of Britain, with simple meanings and values that can be neatly divided and parceled out to his three daughters. As the play progresses, though, this cozy picture of family, kingdom, and cosmos is lacerated by the forces of Nature, preparations for civil and foreign wars, and villainous individuals. The action of the play is situated entirely in Britain, with settings initially in various seats of power (palaces of Lear and Albany, the castle of Gloucester) and finally in and near battle camps by Dover, where the French army has crossed the channel to bring war to Britain. In the third act, the very heart of the play, action is mainly set on a heath and in modest shelters during a tremendous storm. This episode, in which Lear and others most intensely confront themselves as human beings, places the characters in a stark and unforgiving world dominated by Nature. Shakespeare deliberately wrote *King Lear* so that tragic outcomes may not be resolved by the intervention of a charitable Christian God but rather by and within human beings themselves.

As flies to wanton boys are we to the gods;/ They kill us for their sport... 4.1

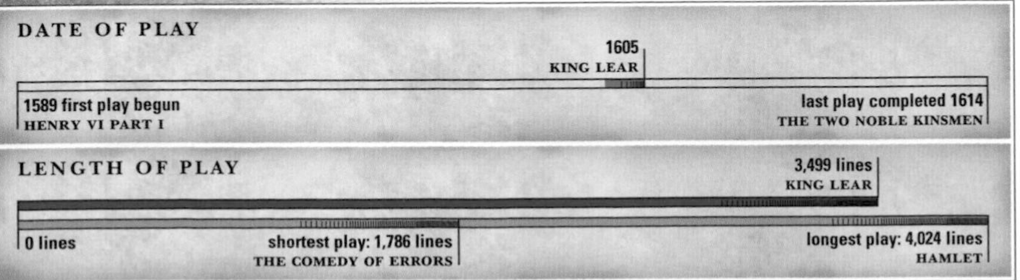

DRAMATIS PERSONAE

LEAR
758 lines

King of Britain, he surrenders his crown to enjoy old age in tranquility, but instead is thrust into a turbulent world to ask; "Who is it that can tell me who I am?"; he banishes his only true daughter, is abused by his other two, and is stripped of his retinue.

King Lear (Ian Holm) divides up his kingdom according to how much each daughter tells him she loves him. He mistakes hyperbole for sincerity.

KING OF FRANCE
32 lines

Suitor to Cordelia, he marries her even after Lear strips her of a dowry.

DUKE OF BURGUNDY
12 lines

Suitor to Cordelia until she is disowned.

DUKE OF CORNWALL
108 lines

Husband to Regan, he blinds Gloucester.

DUKE OF ALBANY
161 lines

Husband to Gonerill, he believes Lear has been wronged and opposes his wife's behavior.

EARL OF KENT
369 lines

Later disguised as "Caius," he remains loyal to Lear after he is banished from Lear's court for defending Cordelia; he serves Lear during his madness.

Gloucester (Kazunori Akitaya) is brutally blinded by power-hungry Cornwall and Regan as punishment for his loyalty to Lear.

EARL OF GLOUCESTER
342 lines

He adores his "natural son," Edmund, but is betrayed by him.

EDGAR
395 lines

Gloucester's legitimate son, he is later disguised as "Poor Tom."

EDMUND
315 lines

Bastard son of Gloucester, he vows himself a servant to the laws of Nature; he woos Gonerill and Regan.

OSWALD
76 lines

Gonerill's steward; he is insolent to Lear and provokes bad feeling.

FOOL
227 lines

Lear's Fool, he tells his master "I am a fool; thou art nothing"; he is devoutly loyal to Lear.

CURAN
9 lines

A gentleman of Gloucester's household.

Lear's fool (Antony Sher) is witty and diverting even as his humor touches the core of his master's bleak world.

AN OLD MAN
11 lines

A tenant of Gloucester.

A DOCTOR
18 lines

Attendant on Cordelia.

A HERALD
10 lines

He announces the charge of treason against Edmund.

GONERILL
202 lines

Lear's eldest daughter and Albany's wife, she lusts for Edmund and hopes he will eventually replace her husband.

REGAN
190 lines

Lear's second daughter and Cornwall's wife, she also lusts for Edmund and rejoices in her husband's death, making her available for remarriage.

CORDELIA
118 lines

Lear's youngest daughter, she says what she feels rather than what she ought to say, and is stripped of her dowry and banished; she returns with an army to defend and heal her father.

OTHER PLAYERS
Knights of Lear's Train, Gentlemen, Servants, Officers, Soldiers, Captain, and Attendants.

PLOT SUMMARY

SIZE OF ACTS

ACT 1	ACT 2	ACT 3	ACT 4	ACT 5
951 lines	678 lines	630 lines	763 lines	477 lines

ACT ONE
951 lines

KING LEAR'S PALACE, GLOUCESTER'S CASTLE, AND BEFORE ALBANY'S PALACE

The Earl of Gloucester introduces his bastard son to the Earl of Kent, who finds the young man handsome. Gloucester is not surprised, for "there was good sport at his making." Gloucester loves this boy, Edmund, as much as he does his elder, legitimate son, Edgar.

King Lear has divided his kingdom in three so that his daughters and their husbands may take on his former "cares and business." Lear questions his daughters: "Which of you shall we say doth love us most?" He will be most generous with the daughter whose love seems greatest. Gonerill says she loves him "more than word can wield the matter" and Lear shows her on a map the areas he distributes to her. Regan claims her only joy in life is to love her father and is rewarded her third of the kingdom. Cordelia, refusing to answer in the manner of her sisters and still unmarried, says she will divide her love between her husband and father. For her "truth," Lear disinherits and banishes his favorite child, and then divides her share of the kingdom between the older sisters.

Meantime we shall express our darker purpose./Give me the map there... 1.1

Let it be so! Thy truth then be thy dower!... 1.1

Accompanied by 100 knights, Lear expects to be hosted in turn by sons-in-law Albany and Cornwall and he passes his coronet to the men to share. When Kent accuses Lear of "hideous rashness," the king banishes him.

The Prince of Burgundy and the King of France, suitors to Cordelia, learn that she has been disowned. Burgundy withdraws his suit, but the French king finds that Cordelia "is herself a dowry" and proposes marriage. Departing for France, Cordelia asks her sisters to take care of their father. Alone, Regan and Gonerill find Lear infirm. "We must do something," Gonerill concludes.

Fairest Cordelia, that art most rich, being poor,/ Most choice, forsaken, and most loved, despised... 1.1

Sir, I love you more than word can wield the matter,/Dearer than eyesight, space, and liberty,/ Beyond what can be valued rich or rare,/No less than life... 1.1

The bastard Edmund believes himself as legitimate as his half-brother, Edgar, and has forged a letter to secure Edgar's downfall. Gloucester, shocked to read in the forged letter that Edgar plans to sieze the family estate, says that astrological events explain these "ruinous disorders." Alone, Edmund finds it repugnant that adulterers—such as his father—and other villains—such as himself—can be accounted for by planets and stars.

Thou, Nature, art my goddess; to thy law/My services are bound... 1.2

In Albany's palace, Gonerill complains that her father's "knights grow riotous." She instructs her servant Oswald to take the upper hand with the visiting Lear and his train.

Kent arrives disguised as "Caius", a poor man, to serve Lear. When Oswald insults Lear, "Caius" trips and pushes Oswald. The fool arrives to entertain Lear with insights into his situation.

Gonerill has had enough of her father's "insolent retinue". Lear asks "Are you our daughter?" but then turns to begin a painful process of self examination: "Does any here know me?" Gonerill is unamused, and says that Lear must reduce his entourage. Stunned by his child's ingratitude, Lear prays to Nature that Gonerill either become sterile or that she produce a child as cruel as herself.

Not only, sir, this your all-licensed fool/But other of your insolent retinue/Do hourly carp and quarrel... 1.4

Hear, Nature, hear! Dear goddess, hear!/Suspend thy purpose if thou didst intend/To make this creature fruitful... 1.4

When Gonerill requires Lear to reduce his train from 100 to 50 knights, he announces his departure. Gonerill dispatches Oswald to Regan's house with a letter warning her sister that Lear is on his way and hopes to take back his kingdom. Lear also sends the trusted servant "Caius" ahead with messages for Gloucester.

I'll tell thee – life and death I am ashamed/That thou hast power... 1.4

ACT TWO

678 lines

WITHIN AND NEAR GLOUCESTER'S CASTLE

Edmund tricks Edgar into fleeing, but puts out word that Edgar wanted his half-brother to murder their father. Hearing

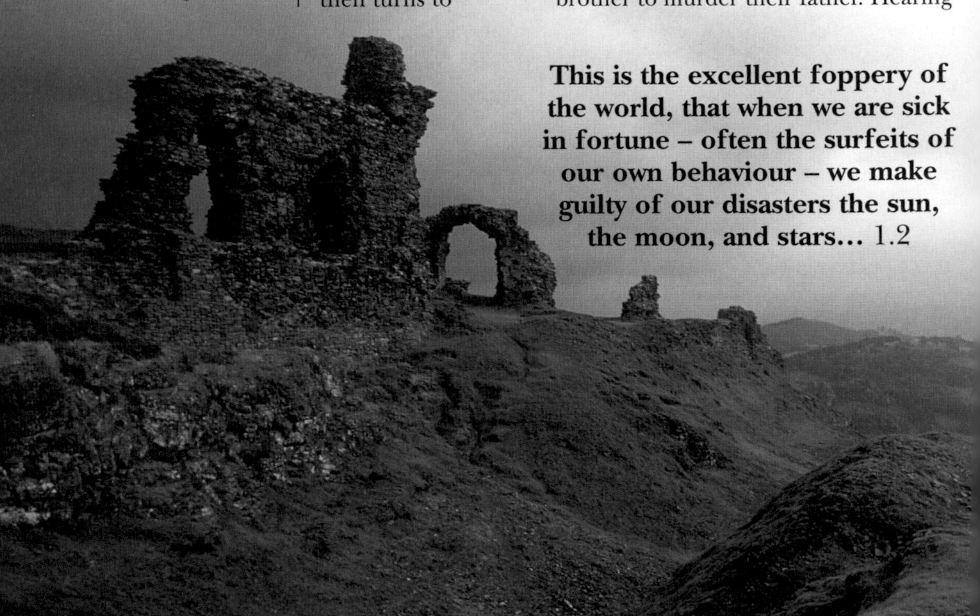

This is the excellent foppery of the world, that when we are sick in fortune – often the surfeits of our own behaviour – we make guilty of our disasters the sun, the moon, and stars... 1.2

this, Gloucester exiles Edgar and calls Edmund his "Loyal and natural boy." Regan and Cornwall arrive to tell Gloucester of the conflict between Lear and Gonerill.

Oswald, bringing messages from Gonerill, runs into "Caius," who attacks Oswald verbally and physically. Others arrive to hear "Caius" accuse Oswald of dishonesty. Cornwall condemns the disguised Kent's "plainness" and has him put in stocks. Alone, Kent finds consolation in a letter from Cordelia, who knows of Lear's predicament and intends to help him. Nearby, Edgar disguises himself as "Poor Tom," a lunatic beggar.

This is some fellow/Who, having been praised for bluntness, doth affect/A saucy roughness... 2.2

Having failed to find Regan at home, Lear arrives at Gloucester's castle and discovers "Caius" in stocks. Lear is outraged when Regan refuses to see him. Finally, Kent is released and Regan speaks to Lear, but only to insist he admit wrong-doing to Gonerill. Lear falls to his knees to deliver a sarcastic confession, but rises to curse Gonerill.

O sir, you are old./Nature in you stands on the very verge/Of his confine... 2.4

When Gonerill herself arrives, Lear cuts relations with her. Since Regan will now only tolerate 25 knights in Lear's train, Lear decides to go to Gonerill with the 50 she allowed. Gonerill, however, no longer sees why Lear needs 50 knights. And Regan finally asks "What need one?" Calling his daughters "unnatural hags," Lear promises revenge as a storm begins to rage.

O, reason not the need! Our basest beggars/Are in the poorest thing superfluous... 2.4

While the daughters agree to host no followers of Lear at all, Gloucester reports that Lear calls for his horse. "The King is in a high rage," the storm is severe and there is no shelter for miles.

But Regan thinks Lear deserves a lesson. She tells Gloucester to lock Lear out of the castle. Cornwall agrees: "Shut up your doors, my lord; 'tis a wild night."

ACT THREE

630 lines

WITHIN AND OUTSIDE GLOUCESTER'S CASTLE

Kent learns that Lear is outside enduring the bitter storm, and that King of France is preparing to wage war on England.

Contending with the fretful elements:/Bids the wind blow the earth into the sea... 3.1

In the heart of the storm, Lear calls on the elements to destroy him and describes himself as "a despised old man." "My wits begin to turn," he says. The fool then sings.

He that has and a little tiny wit,/With heigh-ho, the wind and the rain... 3.2

Gloucester confides in Edmund that he has received an alarming letter explaining how Lear was wronged and that France prepares war. The letter must be kept secret, Gloucester adds. Alone, Edmund plans to use the letter to destroy his father and further himself.

Lear believes he "will endure" but struggles to fight off encroaching madness. Helping his fool into the shelter, Lear realizes that the world is filled with "Poor naked wretches" and that he has taken "Too little care of this!" Edgar, disguised as "Poor Tom," is within the refuge. To the mad and naked "Poor Tom," Lear says: "Thou art the thing itself," and strips off his own clothing. Gloucester, looking for the king, is surprised to discover Lear in such lowly company. At home, Edmund shows Cornwall his father's secret letter.

Who gives anything to Poor Tom? whom the foul fiend hath led through fire and through flame... 3.4

Gloucester leads the king's group to a farmhouse. Lear, his fool and "Poor Tom" conduct an imaginary trial of Gonerill and Regan. Gloucester explains that the daughters are plotting Lear's death but safety awaits him in Dover.

When we our betters see bearing our woes,/We scarcely think our miseries our foes... 3.6

Edgar realizes that companions can lighten suffering.

Cornwall instructs Gonerill to return home and show her husband, Albany, Gloucester's incriminating letter. Gloucester will be punished. Gonerill recommends they "Pluck out his eyes!" and departs with Edmund. Regan and Cornwall bind and interrogate Gloucester.

Because I would not see thy cruel nails/Pluck out his poor old eyes... 3.7

Gloucester intends to see the king avenged. But Cornwall, assuring him he will never see it, presses out one of Gloucester's eyes. Gloucester's servants attempt to stop the proceedings and one badly wounds Cornwall, but is slain by Regan. Cornwall removes Gloucester's remaining eye, calling "Out, vile jelly!" Blinded, Gloucester suddenly sees that Edmund betrayed him and Edgar is innocent. Regan throws Gloucester out of his own home, saying "let him smell/His way to Dover." But Gloucester's surviving servants, morally outraged by the events, plan to help their master.

ACT FOUR

763 lines

A HEATH, BEFORE ALBANY'S PALACE, IN THE FRENCH CAMP BY DOVER, AND IN GLOUCESTER'S CASTLE

Edgar finds advantages in his lowly condition until he sees his blinded father. Keeping his disguise as "Poor Tom," Edgar learns how Gloucester has been changed by his ordeal. Intent on commiting suicide, Gloucester asks to be led to the brim of a Dover cliff.

There is a cliff whose high and bending head/ Looks fearfully in the confinèd deep... 4.1

Albany has also changed: he no longer tolerates Gonerill's schemes. Albany calls his wife "Most barbarous, most degenerate". But Gonerill finds her husband pathetic; the King of France invades yet he does nothing. A messenger delivers news: while putting out the eyes of Gloucester, Cornwall was slain by one of Gloucester's servants. Revolted by the blinding of Gloucester and by Edmund's treachery, Albany vows revenge.

O Gonerill,/You are not worth the dust which the rude wind/Blows in your face... 4.2

Cordelia's reaction to news of her father is reported to have been like "Sunshine and rain at once". But Lear is so ashamed of his "unkindness" toward his daughter that he will not see Cordelia.

Not to a rage; patience and sorrow strove/Who should express her goodliest... 4.

Cordelia is actively searching for her mad father, whom she hopes to restore to health. When a messenger reports that English troops advance, Cordelia notes that she goes to battle for love of her father.

Oswald, carrying an intimate letter from Gonerill to Edmund, is interrogated by Regan, who asks to "unseal the letter." Regan, who wants Edmund for herself, says Gonerill should leave Edmund alone.

As "Poor Tom," Edgar leads his father onto a heath and persuades him that they stand before the dizzying view from a Dover cliff. Gloucester prays to the gods in preparation for suicide and hurls himself forward. Edgar then

Come on, sir, here's the place. Stand still! how fearful/And dizzy 'tis to cast one's eyes so low!... 4

Blow, winds, and crack your cheeks! Rage! Blow!/ You cataracts and hurricanoes, spout/ Till you have drenched our steeples, drowned the cocks... 3.2

greets his father as if he survived falling from a cliff and says that the fellow with Gloucester up on the cliff's edge resembled a devil.

Hadst thou been aught but gossamer, feathers, air,/So many fathom down precipitating,/Thou'dst shivered like an egg... 4.6

"Fantastically dressed with wild flowers," Lear says: "They told me I was everything. 'tis a lie." Seeing Gloucester, the king forgives the earl for his sin of adultery and assures him that eyes are not needed to recognize injustices. Removing his coronet of flowers, Lear remembers passing his real coronet to his sons-in-laws and stomps on the flowers, crying "kill, kill, kill, kill, kill, kill!" Cordelia's attendants arrive to help, but Lear runs off, challenging them to chase him.

When Oswald accuses Edgar of helping the "traitor" Gloucester, Edgar slays Oswald. Among Oswald's belongings, Edgar finds the letter from Gonerill asking Edmund to kill Albany and become her husband.

Kent reveals his true identity to Cordelia and a doctor calls for music as Lear awakens to Cordelia kissing and comforting him. Falling to his knees, Lear recognizes his daughter and invites her to poison him, for she has cause. "No cause, no cause," Cordelia assures him. Lear asks her to "forget and forgive. I am old and foolish."

Pray do not mock me./ am a very foolish fond old man,/Four score and upward... 4.7

ACT FIVE

477 lines

NEAR DOVER, IN THE BRITISH CAMP AND IN A FIELD BETWEEN CAMPS OF BRITAIN AND FRANCE

As war between France and Britain breaks out, Edgar, still in disguise, gives Albany Gonerill's secret letter to Edmund. Albany promises to read it, but for the moment prepares with Edmund to confront the French in battle. Alone, Edmund decides to collaborate with Albany during the war, but then have Gonerill murder him.

To both these sisters have I sworn my love;/Each jealous of the other as the stung/Are of the adder... 5.1

Nearby, following a battle between the British and French, Edgar informs his father that Lear and Cordelia, whose titles remain King of England and Queen of France, are now prisoners of the English.

Lear tells Cordelia that, in prison, they will "pray, and sing, and tell old tales." But Edmund plans to have them both murdered, beginning with Cordelia. Surprised when Edmund refuses to release Cordelia and Lear to him, Albany arrests Edmund and Gonerill.

Stay yet; hear reason. Edmund, I arrest thee/ On capital treason, and, in thy attaint,/This gilded serpent... 5.3

Regan, suddenly feeling seriously ill, is taken to her tent. When a herald reads out the official charge, that Edmund has committed treason, Edgar steps forward in disguise to challenge his half-brother in single combat. Edgar is about to slay Edmund but Albany prevents him. Instead, Albany confronts Gonerill with her letter to Edmund. But she, now revolted by both Albany and Edmund, suddenly departs. Edmund and Edgar reveal concealed truths in succession: Edmund guiltily admits grave wrong-doing and Edgar exposes his true identity. When Edgar tells his story, which he says caused the heart of their father to "Burst smilingly", Albany and even Edmund are moved by Edgar's account.

Draw thy sword,/That if my speech offend a noble heart/Thy arm may do thee justice… 5.3

By nursing them, my lord. List a brief tale;/And when "tis told, O that my heart would burst!… 5.3

A gentleman reports that Gonerill poisoned Regan and then stabbed herself to death once her sister died. When Kent arrives, looking for his king, Edmund says there is no time to waste: by his own instructions, Lear and Cordelia are to be murdered. But it is too late: Lear enters with Cordelia's corpse in his arms. "Is this the promised end?" Kent asks. "Or image of that horror?" Edgar adds. Lear is optimistic: "This feather stirs – she lives!". Kent reveals his true identity to Lear, but Albany believes that Lear "knows not what he sees." It is pointless to speak to him now.

Howl, howl, howl! O, you are men of stones!… 5.3

A plague upon you, murderers, traitors all!/ I might have saved her; now she's gone for ever… 5.3

A messenger arrives to report Edmund dead. "That's but a trifle here," Albany responds, announcing that he restores all power to King Lear. But Lear the man is unable to bear Cordelia's death: "Thou'lt come no more;/Never, never, never, never, never." And then, just as Lear is sure his daughter is still alive, he expires. Albany asks Kent and Edgar to rule Britain with him. But the loyal Kent says he must follow his master, implying that he too will die. And Edgar invites the survivors to "Speak what we feel, and not what we ought to say."

No, no, no life!/Why should a dog, a horse, a rat have life,/ And thou no breath at all?… 5.3

READING THE PLAY

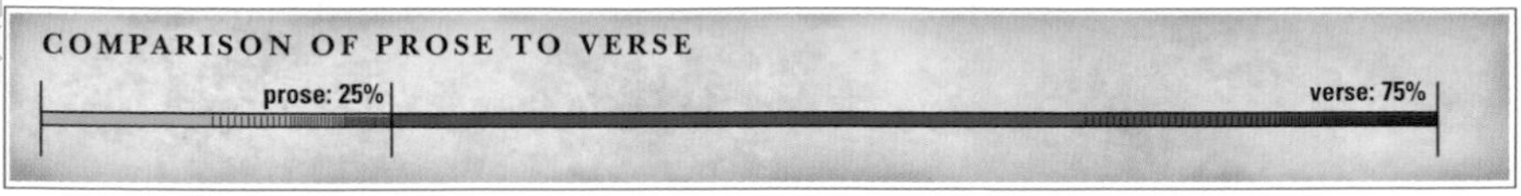
COMPARISON OF PROSE TO VERSE
prose: 25%
verse: 75%

WHO'S WHO

Lear, King of Britain, disowns his truthful daughter **Cordelia**, who marries the **King of France**. Instead, he favors his daughters **Gonerill**, who is married to the **Duke of Albany**, and **Regan**, who is married to the **Duke of Cornwall**. When the loyal **Earl of Kent** disputes Lear's decision, he is banished. Meanwhile **Edmund**, the illegitimate son of the **Duke of Gloucester**, dupes the old man into believing that his legitimate son, **Edgar**, is plotting against him. Edgar disguises himself as "the basest" man and Gloucester is driven from home. Lear, too, is turned out into the night by his daughters Gonerill and Regan and is forced to confront his own elemental self.

POETS AND SCHOLARS HAVE asserted over the centuries, and some still do, that *King Lear* is principally a literary achievement – one that ranks alongside Sophocles's *Antigone* and even the Biblical *Book of Job*. Thus it may be better suited to reading than performance; indeed, uncut productions are so rare that reading remains the surest way of taking in the entire play. Every aspect of *King Lear* offers readers tremendous satisfaction. The play abounds in daring philosophical ideas about the meaning of human existence, the place of individuals in the world and the frailty of lines demarcating madness from sanity, and chaos from order. Its language is lyrical in the extreme, ripe with astounding images and musical effects. The very construction of the play, with its vast breadth of action, is a matter of absorbing interest to readers familiar with other Shakespearean or Jacobean plays. Edmund, Gonerill, Regan, and Cornwall are among the most captivating villains ever characterized in English. By contrast, the loyalty shown by Cordelia, Edgar, and Kent is stirringly steadfast in spite of the moral disintegration of the sick world they occupy. The figure of Lear himself, whether intimately tied to his fool or majestically alone, overwhelms readers with the sheer scale of his emotional and physical journey as he is progressively stripped of his crown, his kingly power, his reason, all basic human comforts, and finally his children. *King Lear* has been called Shakespeare's best play because it is the most truthful. In it, the ugliest of human traits are examined: ingratitude, jealousy, meanness, hatred, deceit, lust, flattery, treachery. And no consoling explanation is found.

Cordelia Disinherited by John Rogers Herbert, 1850. All the pre-Shakespearean accounts of the Lear story offer happy endings – Lear and Cordelia are reunited and survive. Yet in Shakespeare's retelling, both Lear and his favorite daughter die tragically in the play's final scene.

SEEING THE PLAY

KING LEAR WAS LONG THOUGHT to be unplayable. Even today, many believe that *King Lear* is the most difficult Shakespearean play to stage effectively. Its intricate subplots and lyrical qualities, its length, and the physical demands of its roles and settings are among obstacles directors and critics frequently cite. Some directors address several problems at once by cutting the play for production. But by removing subplots and characters, or reducing dialogues and speeches, they risk diminishing the sense of cataclysm that gives the tragedy its exhaustive center of gravity.

Outstanding performers are drawn to *King Lear*. Lear himself is a gigantic role, which sets the mood of the play. The language of other key roles is equally lyrical; most characters undergo profound changes; and parts invite great freedom of interpretation. Effective productions of *King Lear* offer audiences an intrepid journey into a realm akin to the philosopher's, where humans who dare to ask basic questions are guaranteed no sure answers. For nearly two hundred years, this Shakespearean tragedy was only given in adapted versions featuring happy endings. The most enduring was Nahum Tate's 1680 *King Lear*, which eliminated Lear's fool and kept Cordelia alive so that she could marry Edgar. Since the early 19th century, however, Shakespeare's most astonishing and far-reaching work has been restored to the stage, initially in the form of passionate expressions of Romanticism and more recently as starker, modernist explorations of the human condition.

Rachael Kempson as Regan, Michael Redgrave as King Lear, Yvonne Mitchell as Cordelia and Joan Sanderson as Gonerill (left to right) in a 1953 production at Stratford-on-Avon.

BEYOND THE PLAY

The universality of Shakespeare's play is demonstrated in a Kathakali version of *King Lear* (Lear and the Fool), a South Indian classical drama form using stylized and elaborate costumes and make-up, performed at Shakespeare's Globe, London, July 1999.

KING LEAR IN MANY RESPECTS charts the immense pressures that new ideas brought to bear on previous understandings of the human condition. Thanks to the Renaissance, the place of the individual and indeed of mankind within the Judeo-Christian cosmos was challenged both in Britain and in Europe. In Italy, Niccolo Machiavelli's *The Prince* presented a revolutionary picture of the political leader as calculating statesman. The legacy of the Polish astronomer, Nicolaus Copernicus, who argued that the Earth orbited the sun, required poets and theologians to look anew at the place of humankind within the universe. In France, Michel de Montaigne's *Essays* showed that the self was an entity produced by the very process of using language to reflect on and investigate who is meant by "I."

With equally revolutionary implications, Shakespeare produced *King Lear*. The play presents an all-powerful king who, in choosing to divest himself of kingly powers, is made to come to terms with himself as a mere human, itself of questionable sense or value. In his search for the meaning of himself, Lear is made to confront the fragility of human existence. Lear is the only Shakespearean character to die on stage of a surfeit of emotions.

Shakespeare purposefully set *King Lear* in a pre-Christian world. A Christian setting would have allowed characters to attribute to their tragic searches and sufferings an ultimately redemptive spiritual meaning. Instead, characters in *King Lear* have nowhere to turn for answers but to themselves and their earthly world. Like Lear, audiences of Shakespeare's *King Lear* are denied any absolute cosmic design offering spiritual consolation or intelligible sense. Indeed, since 1838, when the Shakespearean play was finally preferred over "happy ending" adaptations, audiences have been made to confront their own sense of humanity in a play that is both terrifying and rewarding.

ON SCREEN

CINEMATIC LEAR

King Lear has inspired a huge variety of cinematic adaptations. In 1970, it was filmed by Peter Brook, starring Paul Scofield and Irene Worth. In 1983, the veteran Japanese director Akira Kurosawa made *Ran (left)*, an epic and stylish adaptation, in which sons were substituted for Lear's three daughters. Jean-Luc Godard's 1987 *King Lear* starred Peter Sellars as "Shakespeare junior the 5th," a character modeled on Lear. In 2001, *The King is Alive* was shot in English by Kristian Levring, the Danish Dogme '95 group director.

MACBETH

IN MACBETH, SHAKESPEARE'S SHORTEST but most unremittingly gruesome tragedy, a heroic and ambitious man murders his way to the Scottish throne, which he then holds with a reign of terror. The earliest recorded performance of *Macbeth* was at the Globe in 1611, but the play was very probably given before James I, the new Scottish-born King of England, at court on August 7, 1605. Shakespeare drew material from Holinshed's *Chronicles* to portray James's proclaimed ancestor, Banquo, in a favorable light. The play also celebrates the binding of Scotland and England under a single king— as James himself had done— in speeches filled with political propaganda. As with all Shakespearean tragedies, however, the main concern of *Macbeth* is not political, but rather the human flaws of its protagonist. Most engrossing is his transformation from a noble war hero into a tyrannical murderer.

BEHIND THE PLAY

BEFORE THE ACTION BEGINS, King Duncan of Scotland has relied on his lords to battle invading Norway. But one lord, the Thane of Cawdor, has joined traitors supporting Norway. As the play opens, Macbeth has proved his courage, leading Scottish troops to vanquish the enemy. Duncan determines to execute the current Thane of Cawdor for his treachery, and to transfer his title to the new battle hero, Macbeth. When Macbeth learns that this title has been bestowed upon him, just as predicted by three witches, he begins his tragic descent. For the witches have also predicted that Macbeth will be crowned King of Scotland, and to become king, Macbeth finally agrees with his wife that he must murder Duncan. Action is set mainly in Scotland, in and around battlefields and castles. Some scenes are loosely historical, such as the initial battle against Norway and the final siege at Dunsinane, but more often impressions of reality are quickly and profoundly disturbed. Scottish heaths become witches' haunts and castles teem with phantoms of the imagination. Hard and cold facts are readily reshaped by tormenting uncertainties. In *Macbeth*, appearance and reality blur to the point of no return.

By the pricking of my thumbs/ Something wicked this way comes./ Open, locks, whoever knocks!... 4.1

DATE OF PLAY

1605–06 MACBETH

1589 first play begun HENRY VI PART I

last play completed 1614 THE TWO NOBLE KINSMEN

LENGTH OF PLAY

2,477 lines MACBETH

0 lines

shortest play: 1,786 lines THE COMEDY OF ERRORS

longest play: 4,024 lines HAMLET

DRAMATIS PERSONAE

The three "weird sisters" (Katy Behean, Josette Simon and Lesley Sharp) grimly work their magic on Macbeth (Bob Peck).

DUNCAN
70 lines
King of Scotland, he is murdered by Macbeth.

MALCOLM
215 lines
Duncan's son, he finally seizes the Scottish crown.

DONALBAIN
12 lines
Duncan's second son, he flees to Ireland.

MACBETH
719 lines
Thane of Cawdor, he is pressured by his wife to murder Duncan and become King of Scotland; tormented by witches' prophesies, he is eventually slain in battle by Macduff.

Consumed by guilt, Macbeth (Rufus Sewell) is plagued by "daggers of the mind."

BANQUO
115 lines
Murdered by Macbeth, he reappears as a ghost.

MACDUFF
181 lines
He flees Scotland and returns to slay Macbeth.

LENNOX
79 lines
He joins the rebels.

ROSS
141 lines
He joins Macbeth's adversaries.

MENTETH
12 lines
He identifies the Wood of Birnam.

ANGUS
21 lines
He notes Macbeth's troops "move only in command,/ Nothing in love."

CATHNESS
11 lines
A rebel Scot.

FLEANCE
2 lines
Banquo's son, he flees from hired murderers.

SEYWARD
31 lines
Commander of the English force.

YOUNG SEYWARD
7 lines
His son, slain by Macbeth.

SEYTON
5 lines
An officer, he reports the queen's death to Macbeth.

SON OF MACDUFF
20 lines
A boy, he displays wisdom in a deeply moving exchange with his mother.

AN ENGLISH DOCTOR
5 lines
He reports that the English king cures his subjects by touch.

A SCOTTISH DOCTOR
40 lines
He admits that he cannot cure Lady Macbeth.

A PORTER
46 lines
He greets Macduff at Macbeth's castle with a discourse on drunkenness.

AN OLD MAN
11 lines
On the night of Duncan's murder, he cannot recall a more unnatural time.

THREE MURDERERS
32; 17; 8 lines
They are hired by Macbeth to kill Banquo and Fleance.

LADY MACBETH
265 lines
Wife to Macbeth, she eggs him on and questions his manliness when he hesitates to murder Duncan; once Macbeth is crowned, she is haunted by her role in the murder and kills herself.

Ruthless, and finally troubled, Lady Macbeth (Ellen Terry) remains one of the theater's most compelling villains.

WIFE OF MACDUFF
41 lines
She cannot understand why her husband has left his family in danger.

A GENTLEWOMAN ATTENDING ON LADY MACBETH
23 lines
She observes Lady Macbeth sleepwalking.

THREE WITCHES
83; 48; 48 lines
They predict Macbeth's and Banquo's futures.

HECATE
39 lines
The chief witch, she upbraids her sisters for revealing Macbeth's fate.

APPARITIONS
6; 8; 9 lines
Conjured by the witches, they speak to Macbeth.

OTHER PLAYERS
Lords, Officers, Soldiers, Sergeant, Gentlemen, Attendants, Messenger, and three other Witches.

PLOT SUMMARY

SIZE OF ACTS

ACT 1	ACT 2	ACT 3	ACT 4	ACT 5
551 lines	405 lines	514 lines	607 lines	400 lines

ACT ONE

551 lines

IN SCOTLAND: A HEATH AND A BATTLE CAMP, KING DUNCAN'S PALACE AT FORRES AND MACBETH'S CASTLE AT INVERNESS

Three witches gather in a storm and plot to meet Macbeth. In a battle camp, King Duncan learns that Macbeth's valor has brought victory against invading Norway. The Thane of Cawdor, turned traitor, will be executed and his title transferred to Macbeth.

Doubtful it stood,/ As two spent swimmers that do cling together/ And choke their art... 1.2

Banquo and Macbeth, returning from battle, are greeted by the witches, who predict Macbeth will be Thane of Cawdor, then King of Scotland, and that Banquo's sons will be kings. When Macbeth is hailed as the "Thane of Cawdor," he is consumed by the thought of becoming king.

Two truths are told/ As happy prologues to the swelling Act/ Of the imperial theme... 1.3

King Duncan welcomes him as a hero and even arranges to visit him in Inverness. But when Duncan names his own son Prince of Cumberland and his heir, "black and deep" feelings possess Macbeth. Lady Macbeth reads of the prophecies in a letter from her husband, but she is convinced he is "too full of the milk of human kindness" to seize the crown. She concludes that she will have to carry out the crimes necessary to make him king.

The raven himself is hoarse/That croaks the fatal entrance of Duncan/Under my battlements... 1.5

King Duncan arrives as a guest at Macbeth's castle. As supper is prepared, Macbeth confronts his own "vaulting ambition". He has second thoughts about harming Duncan, but Lady Macbeth urges him to be more manly. She will arrange for the king's chamberlains to fall into a drunken sleep and then be accused of the murder.

If it were done when 'tis done, then 'twere well/ It were done quickly... 1.7

Come, you spirits/ That tend on mortal thoughts, unsex me here/ And fill me from the crown to the toe top-full/ Of direst cruelty... 1.5

ACT TWO
405 lines

WITHIN AND OUTSIDE MACBETH'S CASTLE

While preparing to murder Duncan, Macbeth see visions and doubts his mind. As the bell rings midnight, Macbeth is resolved to act. When Macbeth reports that he has "done the deed" and murdered Duncan, Lady Macbeth sees that he has failed to leave the murder weapons within the chamber, where the chamberlains still doze. When he refuses to return to the scene of the crime, Lady Macbeth accuses him of cowardice: "The sleeping and the dead/Are but as pictures." As knocking is heard, Macbeth already regrets the murder. A porter, drunk, finally greets Macduff at the castle gate with thoughts on the effects of drink on sleep and sex. Macduff discovers the king's corpse and cries murder. Lady Macbeth feigns surprise, asking how the horror occurred "in our house?" Lennox suspects the chamberlains because their daggers are covered in blood. Macbeth adds that, in the confusion, he himself murdered the chamberlains for what was clearly their crime. Fearing for their lives, Duncan's sons flee: Malcolm to England, Donalbain to Ireland. Soon, Macduff suspects the king's sons of murdering their father and notes that Macbeth, already named Duncan's successor, is to be crowned King of Scotland.

Is this a dagger which I see before me,/The handle toward my hand?... 2.1

Here's a knocking indeed! If a man were porter of hell-gate he should have old turning the key... 2.3

ACT THREE
514 lines

IN AND NEAR THE PALACE OF FORRES, WHERE MACBETH IS NOW KING, AND IN A WITCHES' HAUNT

Banquo marvels at Macbeth's rise to the throne and recalls that his own sons were also predicted to become kings. Invited by Macbeth to supper, Banquo tells Macbeth that he must leave with his son, Fleance, but will return in time for the feast. Alone, Macbeth concludes that he has murdered the king only to wear "a fruitless crown," in future to be worn by Banquo's children. Macbeth gives instructions to the murderers he has hired to slay Banquo and Fleance. Lady Macbeth tries to console her distraught

To be thus is nothing;/ But to be safely thus!... 3.1

Or art thou but/A dagger of the mind, a false creation,/ Proceeding from the heat-oppressèd brain?... 2.1

husband— "what's done is done"—but Macbeth is consumed by maddening fear so long as Banquo's son remains alive. Macbeth tells his wife he has a scheme but will reveal it to her only when it has been accomplished.

We have scorched the snake, not killed it;/She'll close and be herself, whilst our poor malice/Remains in danger of her former tooth... 3.2

Banquo, traveling with his son Fleance, is slaughtered by one of Macbeth's hired murderers, but Fleance escapes.

On his way to supper, Macbeth agonizes over Fleance's escape. Lady Macbeth insists, however, that he host the supper with due ceremony. Macbeth is unnerved to see the ghost of Banquo in the king's seat.

When Macbeth talks as if Banquo were present, guests are puzzled. Lady Macbeth tells everyone that his strange behavior is an ailment suffered since childhood. But she warns Macbeth that he is hallucinating. While Macbeth is sure he saw Banquo, his wife finds him "unmanned in folly." To his guests, Macbeth backs up his wife's story about his "strange infirmity." But the ghost returns, and Macbeth addresses it aloud. The party breaks up with good wishes for Macbeth's better health. Privately, Macbeth tells his wife more blood must run and says Macduff was wrong to miss the supper. Tomorrow Macbeth will seek out the witches.

O proper stuff!/ This is the very painting of your fear... 3.4

What man dare, I dare... 3.4

Lennox thinks that Macbeth was right to slaughter the king's murderers. He also believes that Fleance, like the princes, fled after his own father's murder. Lennox learns that Macduff is disgraced for missing the supper, and has escaped to England. There, Duncan's son has been received by King Edward, while Macduff petitions the English king to attack Macbeth and return security to Scotland. Alarmed by developments, Macbeth also prepares for war.

ACT FOUR

607 lines

A WITCHES' HAUNT, MACDUFF'S CASTLE AND BEFORE THE CASTLE OF THE ENGLISH KING EDWARD

The three witches gather around a bubbling cauldron full of gruesome, foul ingredients. As they chant, Macbeth arrives with questions. The witches then conjure three apparitions to answer him. The first warns him against Macduff. The second encourages him to "scorn/The power of man, for none of woman born/Shall harm Macbeth." A third informs the king he shall never be vanquished "until/ Great Birnam Wood to high Dunsinane Hill/Shall come against him". Thrilled by the news, Macbeth also asks if Banquo's line will reign. A final apparition, of future kings descended from Banquo, terrifies Macbeth. When the witches vanish, he learns that Macduff has fled to England. He curses himself for hesitating; he had intended to murder Macduff. From now on, he will carry out his intentions, the first being to slay Macduff's family.

Round about the cauldron go;/In the poisoned entrails throw... 4.1

Thou art too like the spirit of Banquo. Down!/ Thy crown does sear mine eye-balls... 4.1

Lady Macduff asks the Scottish noble, Ross, why her husband has abandoned her and their children. Macduff is now branded a traitor, Ross explains, and whether out of wisdom or fear, he has left the country. Lady Macduff asks her son what he will do without a father. The child is responding when Macbeth's henchmen come to slay him and his mother.

In England at the king's castle, Duncan's son Malcolm tests Macduff's loyalty to Scotland. Malcolm says he is suspicious of Macduff for abandoning his

Be not offended;/ I speak not as in absolute fear of you... 4.3

wife and child so suddenly. Then he claims that, as he suffers from unmanageable vices, he would be a ruler worse than Macbeth.

Boundless intemperance/ In nature is a tyranny... 4.3

But Macduff reassures him. When Malcolm reveals that he is not speaking in earnest, but rather gauging Macduff's loyalty to Scotland, Macduff is disturbed by the strange method. A doctor reports that the English king is curing the sick with the touch of his hand. Ross arrives, at first withholding news from Scotland, then divulging that Macduff's entire family has been massacred. Macduff, by now fully unhinged, asks "All my pretty ones?/Did you say all?" Malcolm proposes he "Dispute it like a man". But Macduff says he "must also feel it as a man." Malcolm urges the lord to "Let grief/Convert to anger." With Macduff now primed to exact revenge on Macbeth, the "fiend of Scotland", Malcolm declares: "Our power is ready."

Macduff, this noble passion,/Child of integrity, hath from my soul/Wiped the black scruples... 4.3

ACT FIVE

400 lines

IN AND NEAR DUNSINANE, THE NEW CASTLE BUILT BY MACBETH

At Dunsinane, the doctor observes Lady Macbeth sleepwalking and imagining her hands covered in blood. Outside Dunsinane, rebel Scottish lords prepare to meet English soldiers near Birnam Wood. Troops are led by Malcolm, Macduff and Seyward, the English general. "Revenges burn in them," says Menteth, a Scottish rebel. Macbeth responds to unwelcome reports that troops have been mobilized against Scotland and that Lady Macbeth is incurable. Nearby, soldiers use boughs cut from Birnam Wood as camouflage. Macbeth receives more bad news: his wife has killed herself and Birnam Wood appears to be moving toward Dunsinane. Convinced he cannot be slain, Macbeth charges into battle and kills General Seyward's son, proclaiming "Thou wast born of woman". But Macbeth then confronts Macduff, who was "from his mother's womb/Untimely ripped," born by Caesarian section. As foretold, Macduff slays Macbeth.

Out, damned spot! Out, I say!... 5.1

Cure her of that./ Canst thou not minister to a mind diseased,/ Pluck from the memory a rooted sorrow... 5.3

She should have died hereafter./There would have been a time for such a word... 5.5

Carrying Macbeth's head, Macduff hails Malcolm as King of Scotland. With Scotland freed from "this dead butcher and his fiendlike queen," Malcolm invites all to attend his coronation.

Life's but a walking shadow, a poor player/ That struts and frets his hour upon the stage/ And then is heard no more... 5.5

READING THE PLAY

COMPARISON OF PROSE TO VERSE

prose: 8% verse: 92%

LONG CONSIDERED one of the great literary achievements of all time, *Macbeth* has accordingly been read with as much interest and enthusiasm as it has been attended in performances. As early as 1765, Samuel Johnson, suggesting the magnetic force of the play as literature, noted of Macbeth that "every reader rejoices at his fall." The play offers passages of such poetic power that they endure being read independently of the drama as a whole. Macbeth's own language is often riveting. Coiled with life, words spring from the pages to astonish readers. Lady Macbeth also captivates readers with her stark and terrifying imagery, as when she says of her own infant that she would have "plucked my nipple from his boneless gums,/And dashed the brains out." The witches, too, produce spell-binding effects with their ghastly lists of ingredients and inhuman-sounding trochaic meters. Shakespeare's audiences, of course, would have more readily believed in supernatural forces than anyone might today. For Jacobeans, the conjured visions and mysterious powers of the play recalled beliefs that marked their lives outside the theater.

However, it can be hard to keep track of the surprisingly large cast of characters, and confusion is compounded by the similarity among Scottish names. Editions providing full, rather than abbreviated, names are especially helpful. In any edition, though, *Macbeth* remains one of the most satisfying plays to read.

HISTORICAL SOURCES

THE GUNPOWDER PLOT

Angered by mounting oppression of Catholics in England, a band of zealots conspired to blow up Parliament on November 5, 1605. The plot backfired, but *Macbeth*, written in the same year, reflects the climate of conspiracy, fear, and show trials.

Guy Fawkes, one of the rebels who conspired in the Gunpowder Plot, was executed for treason.

"What are these,/So withered and so wild in their attire" (1.3). On a bleak and blasted Scottish heath Macbeth and Banquo stumble upon a witches' haunt. *Landscape with Macbeth and the Witches,* painting by Josef Anton Koch, (1829–30).

SEEING THE PLAY

ON STAGE

INGMAR BERGMAN
Swedish film-maker Ingmar Bergman directed three stage productions of *Macbeth*, the last in 1948 for the Gothenburg City Theater. Set designer Carl-Johan Ström designed a huge tree through which the witches clambered; bodies of hanged men swayed from its boughs, and carcasses of oxen hung from its branches during the banquet scene. The play was a disturbing examination of evil as an inescapable aspect of human experience.

Even though this play calls for inventive stagecraft and breathtaking special effects if directors choose to use them, nothing transfixes audiences more than the language and action of *Macbeth*. In the lead roles, great stage actors can conjure bloody daggers from thin air, and make spectators doubt their own sanity. Memorable bit parts, from the bleeding Captain to the Porter at Macbeth's castle, call upon actors to create strong characters in a matter of lines. Stage talents have found much to work with, and to excite audiences. Whether staging *Macbeth* as an abstract fable about human evil or as a play about patriotic military might, directors have found fresh ways of making it topical. However, in the most effective performances of *Macbeth*, theatrical illusion plays to the audience as a chilling uncertainty. No other Shakespearean play calls upon its cast as an ensemble to transform theaters, as *Macbeth* does, into realms of forbidding terror.

Lady Macbeth (Karin Pfammatter) strains to break Macbeth's (André Szymanski's) troubled, trance-like state, in Berlin's chic, dramatically-lit Schaubühne am Lehniner Platz production in 2002.

Macbeth (Raoul Bova) threatens Cawdor (Reza Azchirvani) in the Italian adaptation, *Macbeth Clan*, by Angelo Longoni at the Piccolo Teatro in Rome in 1998-99, in which the action was updated to a world of gun-toting street gangs.

BEYOND THE PLAY

SUPERNATURAL FORCES unlock terrifying human aspirations and fears in *Macbeth.* Attached to the Macbeth story even in Holinshed's *Chronicles,* the three witches were at first thought to be a "vain fantastical illusion," but Holinshed adds enigmatically that "everything came to pass as they had spoken." Shakespeare embellished the witches of chronicle by having them perform magic, utter spells, and conjure spirits with menacing realism.

Since Shakespeare's era, the witches have been presented in a wide range of modes. In his operatic adaptation of 1663, Sir William Davenant turned the witches into diverting dancers and singers. In 1744 David Garrick restored Shakespeare's text, but his witches were comical figures. Great liberties have been taken with the witches by directors seeking ways to make them speak to modern audiences unfazed by the idea of supernatural powers. In 1933, director Fyodor Komisarjevsky had the sisters speak with Scottish accents, and in 2001 at the replica Globe Theatre, the witches appeared as slapstick clowns.

Superstitions surrounding *Macbeth* endure in the theater world. Fearful of uttering its actual title, many professionals refer to *Macbeth* as "the Scottish play." Even today in Britain, some performers cast as the witches refuse to speak certain lines during rehearsal. The belief remains that some of the spells and charms Shakespeare used in the play are not only real, but also highly effective. Tradition also holds that the play may bring devastation to people as well as theaters. Fires in particular are thought to plague buildings in which "the Scottish play" is performed. Actors are also thought to be in danger of suffering physical or mental ailments while preparing or delivering their roles.

ON STAGE

THE VOODOO MACBETH

The Negro Theater Project of Harlem, New York, staged *Macbeth* in 1936, with Jack Carter leading an all-black cast *(below).* Director Orson Welles set the action atmospherically in 19th-century Haiti, where Voodoo replaced Jacobean witchcraft. The production got a bad review from *Herald Tribune* critic Percy Hammond. When he promptly caught pneumonia and died, it was rumored that angry priests had performed voodoo in revenge.

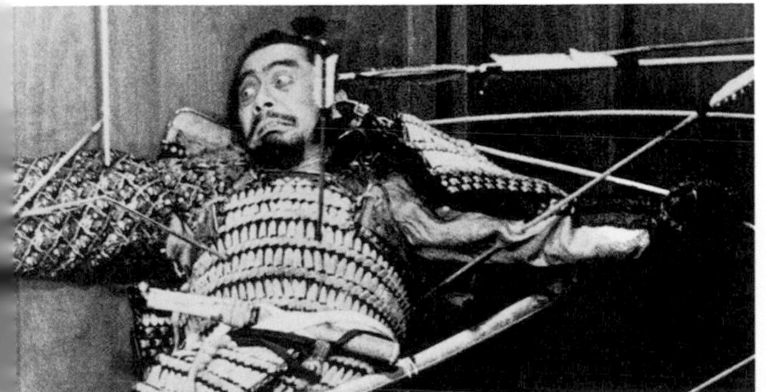

Perhaps the most gripping and successful movie adaptation of *Macbeth* remains the 1957 Japanese *Throne of Blood,* in which the director Akira Kurosawa, backdated the story to medieval Japan, borrowed from Noh drama and cast the heroes as *samurai* warriors to retrace the tragic fate of Macbeth.

ANTONY AND CLEOPATRA

ANTONY AND CLEOPATRA, a tragedy driven by politics and passion, is the story of a charismatic Roman warrior who sacrifices his immense power and prestige for the love of an exotic and seductive woman. The play's narrative focuses on Antony's gradual disintegration, but its mood is defined by the forceful and enigmatic personality of Cleopatra, arguably Shakespeare's most complex female character. Cleopatra represented the mystery and sensuality of the Orient and, more than Antony, was a fashionable subject for plays in 16th-century England, Italy, and France. Shakespeare may have known some of these dramas, although his main source is Sir Thomas North's 1579 translation of Plutarch's *Lives of Noble Greciens and Romanes*, principally the *Life of Marcus Antonius.* Popular in Shakespeare's lifetime, *Antony and Cleopatra* still captivates audiences.

BEHIND THE PLAY

WITH ITS ACTION STRETCHING over 10 years and covering a large area of the eastern Mediterranean, *Antony and Cleopatra* is a play of epic dimension. It opens in 40 BC, four years after Julius Caesar's death, with Antony sharing power in a triumvirate with Octavius Caesar and Aemilius Lepidus. By then, however, Antony was installed in Alexandria with Cleopatra, previously mistress to both Pompey the Great and Julius Caesar. The affair served the pair politically: Antony needed Egypt's wealth to finance his eastern campaigns; and Cleopatra used Antony's power to bolster her Ptolemaic kingdom. While staying close to Plutarch, Shakespeare provides dramatic coherence by telescoping events and altering historical details. He blames Cleopatra for Antony's defeat in the naval battle of Actium in 31 BC, although in reality she escaped with their treasuries, enabling them to survive another year. But, as the play suggests, Cleopatra's presence on the battlefield may have contributed to Antony's final defeat. The lovers' deaths marked a turning-point in ancient history: the end of the Roman Republic; the demise of the Ptolemaic dynasty; and the emergence of Octavius as unchallenged Roman emperor.

Egypt, thou knew'st too well/ My heart was to thy rudder tied by th'strings/ And thou shouldst tow me after…
3.11

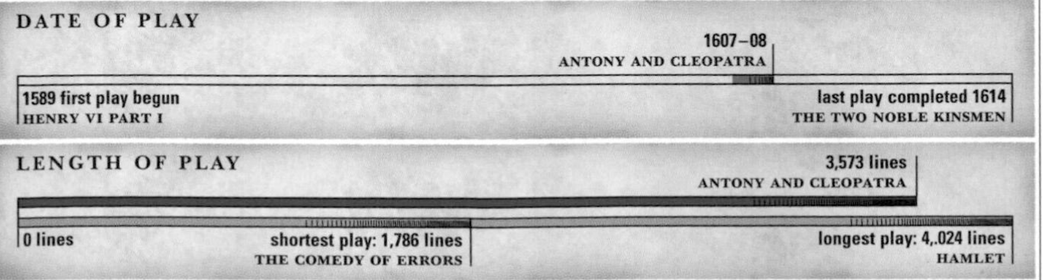

DRAMATIS PERSONAE

MARK ANTONY
851 lines
A brilliant warrior, he seizes power after Julius Caesar's murder, but then opts for a life of pleasure with Cleopatra, Queen of Egypt; he marries Octavius Caesar's sister, but soon returns to Cleopatra; twice defeated at sea by Caesar, he grows dejected; thinking Cleopatra has killed herself, he falls on his sword and dies in his lover's arms.

Beguiled by Cleopatra, Antony (Laurence Olivier) flouts the Roman code of duty.

A complex and charismatic character, Cleopatra (Tallulah Bankhead) plays a dangerous but thrilling game—seducing the world's most powerful men—until she is herself transformed by love.

OCTAVIUS CAESAR
421 lines
Julius Caesar's great-nephew and adopted son, he is Antony's competitor for power in the ruling triumvirate; young, cool-headed, ambitious, he finally defeats Antony.

AEMILIUS LEPIDUS
68 lines
The third and weakest triumvir, he tries to avert war between Antony and Caesar, but is accused of treachery and deposed and imprisoned by Caesar.

SEXTUS POMPEY
140 lines
Son of Pompey the Great, he rebels against the triumvirate and is killed on Antony's orders.

DOMITIUS ENOBARBUS
355 lines
Antony's chief lieutenant, he defects to Caesar's camp, then dies of guilt.

VENTIDIUS
30 lines
Antony sends him to fight the Parthians in Syria.

EROS
47 lines
He kills himself rather than having to kill Antony.

DEMETRIUS AND PHILO
5; 17 lines
Attendants to Antony, they worry that Cleopatra is distracting him from duty.

SCARUS, DECRETAS, CANIDIUS AND SILIUS
40; 21; 25; 12 lines
Attendants to Antony.

AGRIPPA
62 lines
Caesar's admiral, he suggests that Antony marry Caesar's sister.

DOLABELLA
48 lines
Caesar's attendant, he warns Cleopatra that she will be paraded through Rome as a war trophy.

PROCULEIUS
32 lines
Caesar's lieutenant, he orders Cleopatra's arrest.

MAECENAS, THIDIAS, GALLUS AND TAURUS
38; 31; 2; 1 lines
Attendants to Caesar.

EUPHRONIUS
16 lines
A schoolmaster sent to Caesar as Antony's envoy.

MENAS, MENECRATES AND VARRIUS
64; 6; 4 lines
Pirates allied to Pompey.

MARDIAN
19 lines
An Egyptian eunuch.

ALEXAS, SELEUCUS AND DIOMEDES
32; 5; 19 lines
Attendants to Cleopatra.

A SOOTHSAYER
31 lines
He predicts that Charmian will outlive Cleopatra and that Caesar will defeat Antony.

A CLOWN
28 lines
He brings Cleopatra a basket of figs with the deadly snakes that kill her.

CLEOPATRA
686 lines
Queen of Egypt, former mistress of Julius Caesar, she is fiery, passionate, self-admiring, mischievous, and capricious, but also politically astute; she and Antony enjoy a long and lusty affair, until Antony is recalled to Rome and duty; after Antony kills himself, Cleopatra also commits suicide to keep from being humiliated as Caesar's prisoner.

OCTAVIA
36 lines
Caesar's sister, she marries Antony, but he promptly leaves her for Cleopatra.

CHARMIAN
106 lines
Cleopatra's ever-loyal attendant, she also dies of a snake bite.

IRAS
26 lines
Cleopatra's attendant, she dies of sorrow when the queen bids her farewell.

OTHER PLAYERS
Ladies, Officers, Soldiers, Guards, Attendants, Messengers, Servants, Egyptians, and Romans.

PLOT SUMMARY

SIZE OF ACTS

ACT 1	ACT 2	ACT 3	ACT 4	ACT 5
582 lines	882 lines	886 lines	702 lines	521 lines

ACT ONE
582 lines

CLEOPATRA'S PALACE IN ALEXANDRIA AND CAESAR'S PALACE IN ROME

As two Roman officers lament that their leader has become "a strumpet's fool," Antony and Cleopatra flirt and speak of love. When a messenger arrives from Rome, Cleopatra teases Antony that perhaps his wife, Fulvia, or the "scarce-bearded Caesar" are sending him orders ❝. Antony ignores the messenger and leads Cleopatra away for "some pleasure now."

Nay, hear them, Antony./ Fulvia perchance is angry... 1.1

Charmian and Iras, Cleopatra's loyal attendants, joke about a Soothsayer's prediction that Charmian will outlive Cleopatra. On finally receiving the envoy, Antony learns that his wife Fulvia and his brother have challenged Caesar. Another envoy reports that Parthian forces have invaded Syria; Fulvia has died; and Sextus Pompey intends to avenge Julius Caesar's killing of his father, Pompey the Great. Antony decides to return to Rome ❝. In a sham of jealousy, Cleopatra asks how Antony could ever be true to her if he betrayed his wife. When Antony reveals that Fulvia has died, Cleopatra retorts: "Now I see, I see,/In Fulvia's death, how mine received shall be." But as Antony leaves, she wishes him "smooth success."

No more light answers. Let our officers/Have notice what we purpose... 1.2

In Rome, Caesar tells his fellow triumvir, Lepidus, that Antony is lost to decadence ❝. But, informed that Pompey's navy and pirates are roaming the seas, Caesar wishes once-brave Antony back in Rome ❝. In Alexandria, Cleopatra misses Antony. When he sends her a pearl, she pledges to write daily and boasts she loves him more than she ever loved Julius Caesar ❝.

You may see, Lepidus, and henceforth know/ It is not Caesar's natural vice to hate... 1.4

Antony,/Leave thy lascivious wassails... 1.4

My salad days, when I was green in judgement, cold in blood,/ To say as I said then... 1.5

ACT TWO
882 lines

POMPEY'S HOUSE IN MESSINA, LEPIDUS'S HOUSE AND CAESAR'S HOUSE IN ROME, CLEOPATRA'S PALACE, AND NEAR MISENUM

Pompey tells the pirates Menecrates and Menas that Caesar and Lepidus pose no threat. Learning that Antony has reached Rome, however, Pompey warns that Antony and Octavius may join forces.

These strong Egyptian fetters I must break,/Or lose myself in dotage... 1.2

Lepidus begs his fellow triumvirs not to quarrel. Enobarbus, Antony's chief lieutenant, suggests that they first fight Pompey. When Agrippa, Caesar's admiral, proposes that Antony marry Caesar's sister Octavia, Antony agrees and makes peace with Caesar.

When asked about Cleopatra, Enobarbus eagerly recounts her first appearance when she arrived in a splendid barge to meet Antony, comparing her to Venus. When Maecenas notes that, once remarried, Antony will have to leave her, Enobarbus scoffs: "Never; he will not."

I will tell you./ The barge she sat in, like a burnished throne,/ Burned on the water... 2.2

The Soothsayer warns Antony against confronting Caesar. Alone, Antony admits that the "very dice" obey Caesar, but decides that "I'th'East my pleasure lies." He sends Ventidius to fight the Parthians.

Cleopatra tells a messenger that good news will earn him gold. He reports that Antony is well and has made peace with Caesar. But when he discloses that Antony has married Octavia, a livid Cleopatra threatens him with a knife.

Pompey tells the triumvirate he must punish Rome for the death of his father, and mocks their peace offer, but he still invites Caesar, Antony, and Lepidus to his galley. At the banquet, Menas suggests murdering the triumvirs, but Pompey objects. As the party grows rowdy with song, Caesar observes disapprovingly, "Our graver business/Frowns on this levity."

Come, thou monarch of the vine,/Plumpy Bacchus with pink eyne!... 2.7

ACT THREE

886 lines

A PLAIN IN SYRIA, CAESAR'S HOUSE, CLEOPATRA'S PALACE, ANTONY'S HOUSE IN ATHENS, A CAMP NEAR ACTIUM, AND CAESAR'S CAMP IN EGYPT

Ventidius has defeated the Parthians, but he fears Antony's jealousy if he is thought too successful. In Rome, Caesar bids farewell to Antony and Octavia. In Alexandria, Cleopatra asks about Octavia, and persuades herself that her rival is "dull of tongue and dwarfish."

O Silius, Silius,/I have done enough. A lower place note well,/ May make too great an act... 3.1

In Athens, learning that Caesar has denounced him to the Senate, Antony orders Octavia to choose between her brother and her husband. Enobarbus recounts that, after defeating Pompey, Caesar accused Lepidus of treachery and imprisoned him, while one of Antony's officers murdered Pompey.

In Rome, Caesar is outraged: Antony has named Cleopatra "absolute queen" of Syria, Cyprus, and Lydia; he has given the title of king to Cleopatra's son by Julius Caesar; and has appointed his own children by Cleopatra to be "the kings of kings." Also, he has accused Caesar of keeping the wealth of Pompey and Lepidus. Just as Caesar agrees to share his bounty with Antony, Octavia arrives. Caesar informs his "most wronged sister" that her husband Antony has "given his empire/Up to a whore."

Contemning Rome, he has done all this and more/ In Alexandria... 3.6

Why have you stol'n upon us thus? You come not/ Like Caesar's sister... 3.6

With war imminent, Enobarbus urges Cleopatra not to join Antony on the battlefield for fear she will distract him. When Antony decides to fight Caesar at sea near Actium, Enobarbus warns him of Caesar's stronger navy, but Cleopatra quickly offers Antony 60 ships.

Your presence needs must puzzle Antony,/Take from his heart, take from his brain from's time,/What should not then be spared... 3.7

The next time I do fight./ I'll make death love me, for I will contend/Even with his pestilent scythe... 3.13

Enobarbus sees Cleopatra's fleet turn away and learns that Antony "flies after her." Back on shore, Antony is disconsolate.

Hark! The land bids me tread no more upon't;/It is ashamed to bear me... 3.11

When Cleopatra apologizes for her "fearful sails," Antony concedes that his fate is irrevocably tied to hers. Antony petitions Caesar to let him live in Egypt or Athens and to respect Cleopatra's dynasty. Caesar agrees to recognize Cleopatra's title if she will drive Antony from Egypt or kill him. Caesar then orders Thidias to separate the lovers. In Cleopatra's palace, Antony offers to fight Caesar "sword against sword." Thidias tells Cleopatra that Caesar wants her to leave Antony. When she offers Thidias her hand to kiss, Antony sees betrayal. "Not know me yet?" she asks. Antony suddenly decides to battle Caesar anew. Alarmed by the turn of events, Enobarbus resolves to defect to Caesar's camp.

I am satisfied./Caesar sits down in Alexandria, where/ I will oppose his fate... 3.13

ACT FOUR

702 lines

EGYPT: CAESAR'S CAMP AND CLEOPATRA'S PALACE

When Caesar refuses a duel, Antony vows "By sea and land I'll fight." But he tells his soldiers, "I look on you/As one that takes his leave". When Enobarbus protests his defeatist tone, Antony says he expects victory. Near Alexandria, soldiers hear music rising from the earth and fear it is an ill omen.

Tend me tonight./Maybe it is the period of your duty... 4.2

As Antony leaves Cleopatra with "a soldier's kiss," Enobarbus regrets his betrayal of Antony. Early success prompts Antony to expect victory on the morrow. On the battlefield, Enobarbus begs the soldiers to remember his remorse, and dies.

I am alone the villain of the earth,/ And feel I am so most... 4.6

Antony orders Cleopatra's ships to engage Caesar's navy, but is alarmed that no fighting follows. Seeing that his fleet has surrendered and again blaming Cleopatra, Antony orders his troops to flee. Alone, he rages against his mistress. When she appears, he chases her away with abuse. Fearing for her life, Cleopatra hides in her family tomb and sends word to Antony that she has killed herself. Still convinced of her betrayal, Antony is moved to learn of her final words: "Antony! Most noble Antony!" Stunned, he decides to follow

O sun, thy uprise shall I see no more./Fortune and Antony part here... 4.12

My good knave Eros, now thy captain is/ Even such a body... 4.14

Since Cleopatra died I have lived in such dishonour that the gods/ Detest my baseness… 4.14

her in death and orders his servant Eros to kill him. When Eros refuses and kills himself instead, Antony is inspired by his example and falls on his sword. As he lies bleeding, Antony learns that Cleopatra is still alive. He asks to be taken to her tomb, where she begs forgiveness. Asking to be remembered as "a Roman, by a Roman/ Valiantly vanquished," he dies in her arms. Cleopatra briefly faints, then decides to "make death proud to take us".

Thrice nobler than myself,/ Thou teachest me, O valiant Eros, what/I should, and thou couldst not… 4.14

No more but e'en a woman, and commanded/By such poor passion as the maid that milks/And does the meanest chares… 4.15

ACT FIVE

521 lines

Egypt: Caesar's camp and Cleopatra's monument

Caesar is paying tribute to Antony when Cleopatra's envoy arrives. Caesar sends his officer Proculeius to reassure her. Cleopatra says that, if her son rules Egypt, she will gladly kneel before Caesar. Suddenly soldiers seize Cleopatra and she vows to die in Egypt.

Sir, I will eat no meat, I'll not drink, sir – /If idle talk will once be necessary – / I'll not sleep neither… 5.2

When Caesar's officer, Dolabella, arrives, Cleopatra at first ignores him, dreaming instead of a triumphant Antony, until Dolabella discloses Caesar's plan to exhibit Cleopatra in Rome. Although Caesar promises to treat her well, Dolabella confirms that she will be paraded through Syria. Imagining her captivity in Rome, Cleopatra foresees her humiliation when she "shall see/Some squeaking Cleopatra boy my greatness/I'th'posture of a whore."

His legs bestrid the ocean; his reared arm/ Crested the world… 5.2

The Clown arrives with a basket of figs. "Hast thou the pretty worm of Nilus there,/That kills and pains not?" Cleopatra asks. The Clown confirms the snake is in the basket. Dressed in her finery, the queen prepares for death. As she kisses her attendants farewell, Iras dies of a broken heart. Putting one snake on her chest and another on her arm, Cleopatra also dies. Hearing guards, Charmian too is bitten by a poisonous snake and dies.

Give me my robe; put on my crown; I have/Immortal longings in me… 5.2

Caesar, moved by Cleopatra's death, orders her to be buried beside Antony, proclaiming "No grave upon the earth shall clip in it/A pair so famous."

Come, thou mortal wretch,/ With thy sharp teeth this knot intrinsicate/Of life at once untie… 5.2

READING THE PLAY

COMPARISON OF PROSE TO VERSE

prose: 8% | verse: 92%

A THOROUGHLY REWARDING PLAY to read, *Antony and Cleopatra* is profound in its analysis of the politics of personalities, exuberant in the sensuality of its poetry. Caesar fights Antony for power, but the real conflict is between Rome, personified by Caesar, and the East, represented by Cleopatra. This translates into parallel battles between man and woman, mind and heart, politics and passion, formal language and metaphoric verse. And in each conflict, it is Rome that wins.

At an emotional level, the play is complex. Scholars frequently remark on its ebbs and flows—the stop-start quality of the central love affair, in which passion is interrupted by jealousy and perceived betrayals. The magnificent language, almost entirely in verse, comes alive in this context. Antony seems constantly torn between pleasure and duty, between his sensual response to Cleopatra's Egypt and his responsibilities to the empire. In contrast, less self-absorbed than Antony, Cleopatra is the more astute commentator on life, never ceasing to view herself as a player on the global stage. Never is she more theatrical than when she prepares to die. Her clever repartee with the Clown about the nefarious qualities of "the worm"—the poisonous snake—suggests that she is still in full control of herself. She cries, "Husband, I come!" as the snake bites her, yet what prompts her to kill herself is pride—her refusal as Queen of Egypt to be humiliated before the Roman mobs as she is paraded in Caesar's triumphal march.

HISTORICAL SOURCES

KEY DATES IN THE PLOT

In *Antony and Cleopatra*, more than in any other tragedy, Shakespeare respects historical fact, but telescopes events.

51 BC Cleopatra is crowned Queen of Egypt.

48 BC Cleopatra seduces Julius Caesar.

46 BC Julius Caesar becomes dictator of Rome.

45 BC Cleopatra moves to Rome.

44 BC Julius Caesar is murdered; Cleopatra leaves Rome.

43 BC Antony, Octavius Caesar, and Lepidus form a triumvirate.

42 BC Antony and Caesar defeat Brutus and Cassius at the Battle of Philippi.

41 BC Antony rules eastern provinces and becomes Cleopatra's lover.

40 BC Antony marries Octavia, the sister of Octavius Caesar.

38 BC Ventidius defeats the Parthians.

36 BC Antony's Parthian expedition is unsuccessful.

34 BC Antony names Cleopatra queen of kings.

32 BC The triumvirate is dissolved.

31 BC Caesar defeats Antony at Actium.

30 BC Antony and Cleopatra both commit suicide.

27 BC Octavius Caesar becomes Emperor Augustus Caesar.

In the decisive sea battle at Actium, Antony and Caesar are evenly matched until Cleopatra takes flight. Oil by Neroccio de' Landi, *c.* 1485.

SEEING THE PLAY

Massive columns and dramatic lighting evoke the glory that was Egypt and the splendor of the Ptolemaic court where Cleopatra (Katherine Cornell) and Antony (Kent Smith) play out their tragic destinies.

WITH ITS 42 SCENES, this play is difficult to stage satisfactorily. To succeed, any production must above all be charged with erotic tension. Cleopatra, played by a succession of great actresses from Vivien Leigh and Tallulah Bankhead to Glenda Jackson and Vanessa Redgrave, is easily Shakespeare's most sensual invention, a woman who fully grasps that Antony is trapped by her sexual power. To convey this, many productions dress her in outfits evocative of Oriental belly-dancers, while some directors find occasion to display her naked. Obsessed by Cleopatra, Antony's physical and psychic dependence on her gradually overwhelm his sense of imperial responsibility. A shadow of the man who confronted Julius Caesar's murderers, Antony's decline, from macho warrior to emasculated failure, is often illustrated by heavy drinking, a weakness recorded by history but only hinted at by Shakespeare. On stage, Antony and Cleopatra are equally challenging roles because their moods and behavior constantly change. Opposing their volatility is the calm and calculating Octavius, a role written in formal political language which should be interpreted to project the grandeur of the future Emperor Augustus Caesar. He is a man of destiny, not a villain. Indeed, unusually, *Antony and Cleopatra* is a tragedy without a villain.

Several smaller roles have their appeal. Charmian is a delight, while the Soothsayer and Clown are pivotal to the story, but Enobarbus has more depth as a character. Although he enjoys the delights of Cleopatra's palace, he is ultimately so demoralized by Antony's military failure that he joins Caesar's camp and dies of guilt.

Erotic tension mounts as Antony (Stuart Wilson) and Cleopatra (Sinéad Cusack) explore their fatal attraction in the RSC's charged 2002 production.

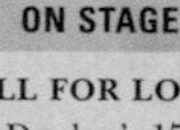

ON STAGE

ALL FOR LOVE

John Dryden's 17th-century adaptation, *All for Love*, and other blends of Dryden and Shakespeare, were popular in London's theaters until the mid-19th century. But it was not until the 20th century that the play won its just acclaim, attracting a succession of top actors: John Gielgud and Dorothy Green in 1930, Laurence Olivier and Vivien Leigh in 1951, Michael Redgrave and Peggy Ashcroft in 1953.

BEYOND THE PLAY

LISTED AMONG SHAKESPEARE'S TRAGEDIES, *Antony and Cleopatra* resists easy classification. Rich in humor and sex, with even its climax a self-inflicted tragedy, its very elusiveness adds to its appeal. The play recounts one of history's legendary love stories, yet its two main characters are hard to pin down. Except for one brief moment in Act 4 Scene 12, they are never alone together on stage, so their flirting and fighting can easily resemble play-acting. Their relationship remains a puzzle. Is it true love, or love of power and sex that unites them? Does Antony kill himself for love of Cleopatra or out of self-pity? Does Cleopatra sacrifice herself for love of Antony or out of pride? And would Cleopatra have even contemplated suicide if she believed she could seduce Octavius Caesar?

Shakespeare wrote this play at the height of his literary powers, the fourth in a remarkable sequence of tragedies that included *Othello*, *King Lear*, and *Macbeth*. Little is known about *Antony and Cleopatra* during Shakespeare's lifetime, except that Richard Burbage played Antony in its first production, almost certainly at the Globe. The first reliable text of *Antony and Cleopatra*, that of the *First Folio* of 1623, is thought to be a rare case where the editors could rely on Shakespeare's own manuscript, including detailed stage directions.

Cleopatra stands alongside Falstaff and Hamlet as among Shakespeare's most complex characters. The sheer unpredictability of her behavior gives the play the syncopated rhythm of a thriller. For some, such is her enduring mystique that even *Antony and Cleopatra* cannot fully accommodate Cleopatra. George Bernard Shaw so disliked Shakespeare's portrayal of her that in 1898 he wrote his own play, *Caesar and Cleopatra*. Cleopatra has also inspired myriad novels as well as several operas, including Handel's *Giulio Cesare*, the 18th-century German composer Johann Hasse's *Marc'Antonio e Cleopatra*, and Samuel Barber's 20th-century *Antony and Cleopatra*.

ON SCREEN

MOVIE QUEEN

Cleopatra is a movie favorite, with some 50 titles carrying her name, from a silent version in 1912 to the 2002 spoof, *Astérix & Obélix: Mission Cléopâtre*. The best known film—Joseph L. Mankiewicz's *Cleopatra* (1963), starring Elizabeth Taylor *(above)* and Richard Burton as the doomed lovers, with Rex Harrison as Julius Caesar—owed nothing to Shakespeare. At least in Charlton Heston's 1973 *Antony and Cleopatra (below)*, in which Heston played Antony to Hildegarde Neil's Cleopatra, Shakespeare shared writing credits. But the film failed to explore the human drama at the heart of the play. Television productions, directed by Trevor Nunn in 1974 and by Jonathan Miller in 1981, were more subtle and convincing.

CORIOLANUS

CORIOLANUS IS SHAKESPEARE'S MOST openly political play. It is thought to have been written in 1607–08, although there is no record that it was ever performed in the poet's lifetime. In essence, the play dissects democracy: it recognizes that ultimate power lies in the people, but demonstrates how swiftly the masses can be swayed; it endorses the need for strong leadership, but shows how easily leaders can become tyrants. The result is a theatrical but strangely unemotional play, a tragedy in which the victims evoke little sympathy. Indeed, through staging, interpretation, and astute cutting, *Coriolanus* has been used to justify either autocratic leadership or the will of the people. Today the play is infrequently performed, perhaps because Western democracies no longer feel threatened by class warfare or dictatorship. In many parts of the world, though, *Coriolanus* remains all too topical.

BEHIND THE PLAY

SET AROUND 490 BC, THE ACTION in *Coriolanus* takes place in and near Rome and in Corioli and Antium, the principal cities of the Volsces, Rome's enemies of the day. However, Shakespeare was never as interested in historical accuracy as he was in the dramatic potential of a story which, in this case, revolves around its tragic hero's three fated relationships: with the people of Rome, the Volscians, and his very own family. Caius Martius, who is given the title of Coriolanus to celebrate his ransacking of Corioli, serves the interests of the patricians who rule Rome from the Senate. At that time, the Senate was at loggerheads with the commoners, or plebeians, who elected two tribunes to serve as their spokesmen in the Popular Assembly. In this play, the Senate plans to advance Coriolanus to the high post of consul. A central part of the ritual requires any nominee to the post to wear a "gown of humility," literally a roughly hewn cloak of weeds, and to beg the approval of the plebeians at the meeting place known as the Forum. This is the procedure that provides the new consul with ultimate popular legitimacy. It is the people's rejection of Coriolanus that turns the drama into a political and personal tragedy.

In soothing them we nourish 'gainst our Senate/ The cockle of rebellion, insolence, sedition... 3.1

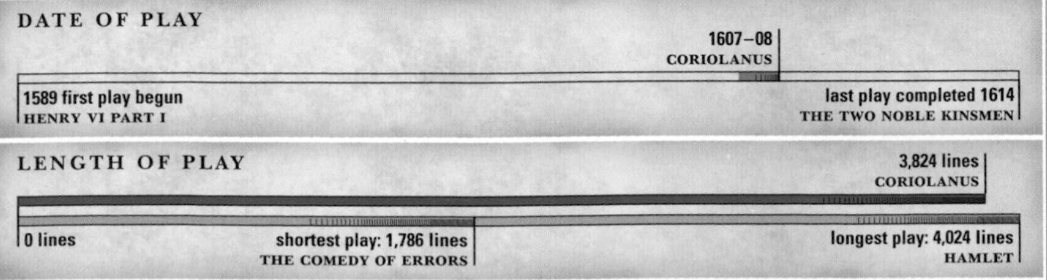

DRAMATIS PERSONAE

CAIUS MARTIUS, later CORIOLANUS
897 lines
A superb but deeply unpopular Roman warrior, he is given the title of Coriolanus after he conquers Corioli, but the Roman masses still reject him as consul; a man who can neither give nor accept flattery, he is thought "too absolute," even by his ambitious mother, Volumnia.

TITUS LARTIUS
60 lines
Roman general and admirer of Caius Martius.

COMINIUS
286 lines
Roman general and consul, he proposes rewarding Caius Martius with the title of Coriolanus for his victory at Corioli.

MENENIUS AGRIPPA
589 lines
A witty, verbal Roman patrician and friend of Caius Martius, his ability to speak both the formal language of the Senate and the livelier language of the street enables him to serve as a mediator between rulers and people.

SICINIUS VELUTUS AND JUNIUS BRUTUS
312; 254 lines
Tribunes who represent Roman plebeians in the Senate, they are adept at manipulating popular opinion through their speeches and at scheming against Caius Martius.

YOUNG MARTIUS
2 lines
The young son of Caius Martius, he already displays his strong martial stock; for fun, he tears butterflies to pieces with his teeth.

NICANOR
29 lines
A Roman, he is in the pay of the Volsces.

TULLUS AUFIDIUS
275 lines
The Volscian general who has long despised and battled with Caius Martius, he is nonetheless welcoming when Martius is banished from Rome; however, Aufidius grows envious of the Roman's popularity and orders his murder.

A LIEUTENANT TO AUFIDIUS
12 lines
He worries about Caius Martius's growing popularity among the Volsces and presses for action to be taken against the Roman.

Coriolanus (Kenneth Branagh), covered in blood after the battle at Corioli. A man of action rather than words, he is earnest, brave, and proud.

Tullus Aufidius (Keith Hamilton Cobb) ultimately deceives Coriolanus, driven by greed and envy.

CONSPIRATORS WITH AUFIDIUS
10; 9; 14 lines
They plan the murder of Caius Martius.

ADRIAN
20 lines
A Volsce.

SERVANTS TO AUFIDIUS
32; 36; 49 lines
A trio from Aufidius's household, they provide comic relief.

VIRGILIA
35 lines
Caius Martius's wife, she frets about her husband's well-being.

VALERIA
41 lines
Virgilia's confidante.

OTHER PLAYERS
Lords, Senators, Patricians, Gentlewoman, Officers, Soldiers, Citizens, Messengers, Heralds, and Guards.

VOLUMNIA
314 lines
Proud and power-hungry, cold-blooded and calculating, she raises her son, Caius Martius, to be a war machine, yet alone she succeeds in striking his most human chord when she persuades him not to destroy Rome.

Volumnia (Alison Fiske) is domineering and hard-hearted. She mocks Virgilia for her anxiety about Coriolanus's safety in battle.

PLOT SUMMARY

SIZE OF ACTS

ACT 1	ACT 2	ACT 3	ACT 4	ACT 5
842 lines	773 lines	802 lines	717 lines	690 lines

ACT ONE
842 lines

ROME AND THE BATTLEGROUNDS AROUND THE VOLSCIAN CITY OF CORIOLI

With food riots shaking Rome, Caius Martius, a haughty military hero who despises commoners, seems like a good scapegoat to the restless masses. But Menenius Agrippa, a respected elder, explains that the gods, not the patricians, are to blame for the famine. He also defends the nobility against charges of greed. If Romans regard the Senate as a fat belly, he says, they forget that it is nurturing all of society, down to "the great toe" of the commoners ❛❛. But hopes of calming the insurrection vanish when Martius arrives. Proclaiming that the mutineers should be hanged, he mocks their choice of Sicinius Velutus and Junius Brutus as tribunes.

There was a time when all the body's members/ Rebelled against the belly... 1.1

The Volsces have taken up arms against Rome and Martius is again called on to save the day. In Corioli, the Volscian general, Tullus Aufidius, believes he can avenge earlier defeats by Martius. As Martius heads off for battle, his wife, Virgilia, fears for his safety, but she is laughed at by his forceful mother, Volumnia, who recalls that he was raised to be fearless, his many wounds proof of his courage ❛❛.

I pray you, daughter, sing, or express yourself in a more comfortable sort... 1.3

Near Corioli, as the Roman offensive is weakening, Martius berates his tired troops ❛❛. Wounded and covered in blood, he then leads a fresh attack, even briefly fighting with Aufidius, who is saved by Volscian soldiers. With victory assured, the Roman generals Cominius and Titus Lartius hail Martius's courage and bestow on him the title of Coriolanus as a tribute to his conquest of Corioli. Aufidius, humiliated anew by his hated enemy, swears revenge.

All the contagion of the south light on you,/ You shames of Rome!... 1.4

Now put your shields before your hearts, and fight/With hearts more proof than shields... 1.4

ACT TWO

773 lines

ROME

As Martius, now known as Coriolanus, returns to Rome, his proud mother boasts that he has added two new war wounds to the 25 scars that he already carries. Word spreads that he is to be named consul, but Brutus and Sicinius conspire to prevent this. Roman custom dictates that Coriolanus must wear the "gown of humility" and display his wounds before a gathering of plebeians in the Forum. But the tribunes believe he is too arrogant to do so. When the Senate meets to hear Coriolanus's nomination, the tribunes remind him that he must seek the people's approval, which he admits he is reluctant to do.

I shall lack voice. The deeds of Coriolanus/Should not be uttered feebly... 2.2

Wearing the "gown of humility," Coriolanus visits the Forum before the plebian vote is held and persuades several groups of citizens that he should be judged by his actions, not his words. Pleased by the citizens' response and confident that he has done enough, he leaves to take off his gown. But immediately Sicinius and Brutus begin poisoning the commoners against him, recalling his "malice" toward the people and urging them to revoke their "ignorant election" of Coriolanus as consul. The two tribunes begin planning a popular revolt in the Forum.

Most sweet voices!/Better it is to die, better to starve,/Than crave the hire which first we do deserve... 2.3

ACT THREE

802 lines

ROME

Coriolanus learns that Aufidius has retreated to Antium and is again preparing war against Rome, but the Roman general has more immediate problems. Sicinius and Brutus confront him on a street and remind him that he is a servant of the people. Cominius and Menenius take his side, but Coriolanus erupts in anger, dismissing the "absolute power" of the people. Brutus summons citizens and orders guards to arrest Coriolanus. The general draws his sword and the crowd disperses.

Coriolanus returns home where, determined to see him named consul, his ever-ambitious mother urges him to display humility before the Forum. Volumnia tells him that, no less than when he confronts an enemy, he should lie to achieve his goal. Eventually, bowing to his mother, he promises to flatter the crowd as if possessed by "a harlot's spirit."

You are too absolute./Though therein you can never be too noble... 3.2

But by the time Coriolanus arrives at the Forum, Sicinius and Brutus have won over the citizens. When Coriolanus says he accepts the popular will, Sicinius accuses him of being a traitor and an aspiring tyrant. Furious, Coriolanus says he would now rather die than seek public approval. There are calls for his death, but the tribunes instead propose his banishment. Ever proud, Coriolanus curses the city that he has so often saved.

You common cry of curs, whose breath I hate/As reek o'th'rotten fens... 3.3

ACT FOUR

717 lines

ROME AND AUFIDIUS'S RESIDENCE IN THE VOLSCIAN CITY OF ANTIUM

At the gates of Rome, Coriolanus comforts his family and friends, but says little about his own plans. After he leaves, Volumnia insults Sicinius and Brutus, but they are pleased that the nobility is at last tasting the people's power.

Coriolanus arrives in Antium disguised as a beggar and seeks out Aufidius's house. Servants stop him from entering the main hall, but the commotion brings out Aufidius. Coriolanus reveals himself to his

O world, thy slippery turns!... 4.4

former foe. He admits the pain that he has inflicted on the Volsces and says he is ready to be punished but he also offers his "revengeful services" to help Aufidius conquer Rome. The Volscian leader embraces Coriolanus passionately and offers to share his command of the Volscian troops in a new war against Rome ❝.

O Martius, Martius!/Each word thou hast spoke hath weeded from my heart/ A root of ancient envy... 4.5

In Rome, Sicinius and Brutus are unnerved by reports that the Volsces have entered Roman territory and, worse, that Coriolanus has joined Aufidius. Cominius blames the tribunes for the disaster now threatening Rome. As citizens panic, Menenius tells them that they deserve the fate that awaits them.

At the Volscian camp near Rome, Aufidius is in dark mood, jealous that Coriolanus now commands not only the will of Rome, but also the loyalty of the Volscian troops. More than ever, he burns to avenge his own defeats by Coriolanus ❝.

All places yield to him ere he sits down,/ And the nobility of Rome are his... 4.7

ACT FIVE

690 lines

ROME, A VOLSCIAN CAMP NEAR ROME, AND ANTIUM

After Cominius has failed to dissuade Coriolanus from attacking Rome, he joins

For I will fight/Against my cankered country with the spleen/Of all the under fiends... 4.5

the remorseful Sicinius and Brutus in urging Menenius to lead a new peace mission. But when Menenius visits the enemy camp, his emotional appeals to "my son Coriolanus" are scornfully rebuffed. Coriolanus promises Aufidius that the Volsces will soon stand before the walls of Rome.

Coriolanus's mother, wife, and young son arrive unexpectedly at the camp and, while the Roman general at first ignores them, he is ultimately forced to hear them out. Assertive as always, Volumnia tells her son that to assault his own country would be like treading on his mother's womb. Coriolanus tries to leave, but Volumnia warns that his name will be forever abhorred if he destroys Rome. Finally, Coriolanus surrenders to her pleas, albeit knowing that he may have invited his own death. Aufidius falsely praises the warrior for allowing mercy to prevail over honor, but he recognizes it as a weakness that he can exploit.

Should we be silent and not speak, our raiment/ And state of bodies would bewray what life/We have led since thy exile... 5.3

O mother, mother!/What have you done? Behold, the heavens do ope,/The gods look down, and this unnatural scene/They laugh at... 5.3

As Volumnia is acclaimed by the Romans for saving the city, Coriolanus returns to Antium with Aufidius, who secretly plots Coriolanus's murder. The Volscian elders are not pleased that Rome has escaped destruction, but Coriolanus defends a truce that honors Volsces just as it shames Romans. Briefly, Coriolanus seems at peace with himself, but Aufidius's moment of revenge soon arrives. He accuses Coriolanus of breaking his oath and giving away victory "at his nurse's tears." Coriolanus returns the insults, but the conspirators call for his death and the crowd shouts its approval. Aufidius and his henchmen draw their swords and swiftly murder Coriolanus.

Hail, Lords! I am returned your soldier,/ No more infected with my country's love/Than when I parted hence... 5.6

The Volscian elders are stunned, but Aufidius tells them that their own lives were at risk. They order Coriolanus buried with full honors and chastise Aufidius for his impatience. But with his enemy slain, Aufidius's rage passes and he now claims to be "struck with sorrow." Even in the city where Coriolanus left so many widows and orphans, he declares, the Roman shall have a "noble memory."

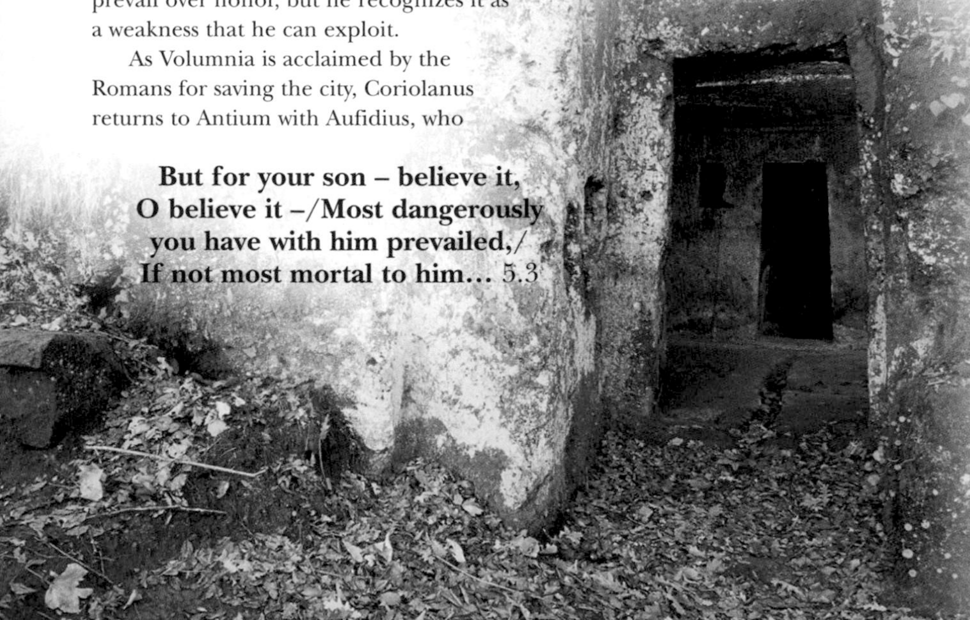

But for your son – believe it, O believe it –/Most dangerously you have with him prevailed,/ If not most mortal to him... 5.3

READING THE PLAY

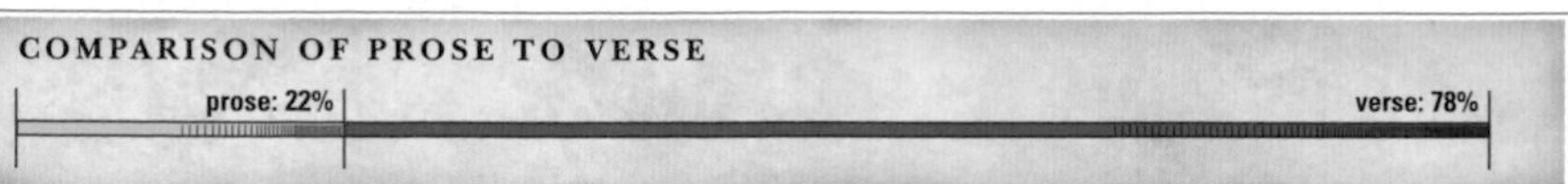

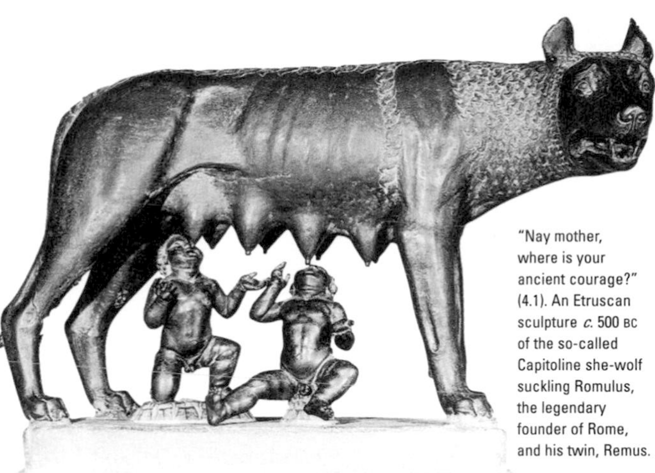

"Nay mother, where is your ancient courage?" (4.1). An Etruscan sculpture *c.* 500 BC of the so-called Capitoline she-wolf suckling Romulus, the legendary founder of Rome, and his twin, Remus.

HISTORICAL SOURCES

INFLUENCES

Like *Julius Caesar, Antony and Cleopatra,* and *Timon of Athens, Coriolanus* uses Plutarch's *Lives of Noble Greciens and Romanes* as its main source. But Shakespeare may also have been inspired by contemporary events, not least by food riots that erupted in northern England during the harsh winter of 1607–08, when the so-called "Diggers of Warwickshire" drew up a political manifesto for the local authorities.

CORIOLANUS IS OFTEN CRITICIZED for being a wooden play, while Coriolanus himself is considered inflexible, even by tragic hero standards. Yet alternations in the style and meter of the language reveal a play rich in dramatic shape and energy. Just as the tone of the language distinguishes private conversation from public speeches, so are the heroic verses of military chiefs balanced against the prose exchanges of the lower social classes. Menenius, the political go-between who personifies good sense, switches easily from comical prose to weighty verse, while Volumnia consistently manipulates language to suit her political ends. Indeed, in the scene preparing Coriolanus to address the Forum, Volumnia tries to teach him some of her rhetorical skills, noting that it is perfectly acceptable to lie when the goal is virtuous. In contrast, the servants of Aufidius bring welcome hilarity to an otherwise gloomy play, speaking in the raucous tongue of Shakespearean clowns. In a masterful transition, Shakespeare follows their inane prose with stirring verse exchanges between Coriolanus and his archenemy Aufidius. But the nobility of their reconciliation hides the hypocrisy of Aufidius's embrace of Coriolanus. Thus, the shadow of violence hangs over their every word.

"Down ladies! Let us shame him with our knees" (5.3). Volumnia begs Coriolanus to spare Rome.

SEEING THE PLAY

"Measureless liar, thou hast made my heart / Too great for what contains it" (5.6). Coriolanus and Aufidius (masked) in "One Act Coriolanus" performed by the Todd Theatre troupe (1996).

CORIOLANUS'S PRINCIPAL QUALITY is courage, amply on display at the Battle of Corioli, where he fights heroically. After that, he considers it below his dignity to boast of his courage before hostile crowds: he is a man of action, not of words. Being inarticulate himself, however, means he is vulnerable to words: he allows himself to be provoked by the tribunes, influenced by his mother, and deceived by Aufidius. Indeed, because he lacks sophistication, Coriolanus is a difficult character to portray sympathetically on stage. Is he a victim of his mother? Volumnia, one of Shakespeare's strongest female roles, is undoubtedly ruthless, proud of the killing-machine she has produced and almost alone in understanding how power works. As a woman, she wields influence indirectly through her son. Thus, it is her own ambition that Coriolanus become consul; and it is her own stature that grows when she saves Rome from destruction. But she has no love for Coriolanus. Some productions imply that, because he is rejected by his mother, Coriolanus accepts the love of Aufidius. If a homoerotic relationship is suggested, Coriolanus's murder takes on new meaning: he is killed because, by saving Rome, he chooses his mother over Aufidius. Either way, he is author of his own demise.

PLAY HISTORY

CORIOLANUS AND THE RESTORATION

After the Restoration, *Coriolanus* reappeared in adapted versions that were thought more relevant to contemporary concerns. Nahum Tate's 1682 *Ingratitude of a Common-Wealth* was set against Whig-Tory rivalry, while two other adaptations referred to the Jacobite Rebellions of 1715 and 1745. Thomas Sheridan's *Coriolanus, or The Roman Matron,* was widely preferred by London theaters until Shakespeare's original text was restored in the 19th century.

Toby Stephens as Coriolanus at the Royal Shakespeare Company at the Barbican, London, in 1995.

BEYOND THE PLAY

CORIOLANUS IS THE BEST KNOWN adaptation of the tragedy of the ill-fated Roman general, but the story's powerful political content inspired many other plays in Europe, both before and after Shakespeare's time. Most of these plays interpreted the story exclusively as a political drama, frequently focusing on events of the day. In the 15th century, for instance, it was presented as a pageant in Italy and as a tragi-comedy in Germany, while a dozen or more plays retold the story for French audiences between the 16th and 19th centuries. Beethoven's 1802 overture *Coriolan*, for instance, was not based on Shakespeare's play, but on a different *Coriolanus* by the Austrian playwright Heinrich Joseph von Collin.

ON STAGE

BERTOLT BRECHT

Banned by American occupation forces in Germany until 1953, *Coriolanus* returned in Brecht's Marxist version, which portrayed the masses as heroes. Günter Grass's *Plebeians Rehearse the Uprising* satirizes Brecht directing *Coriolanus* during East Germany's 1953 anti-Communist uprising.

Brecht's *Coriolanus*, performed at the Berliner Ensemble in 1964.

Shakespeare presents the story as an ideological power struggle, but he gives a human dimension to Coriolanus through his relationships with his mother and with Aufidius. Yet it was not until Peter Hall's 1959 production in Stratford-upon-Avon, with Laurence Olivier as Coriolanus, that the emphasis switched from militarism to personal tragedy. Then, in 1963, Tyrone Power set a precedent by exploring the possible homoerotic links between Coriolanus and Aufidius. In England and the United States, the play has continued to interest the theater world. The English playwright John Osborne reworked it as *A Place Called Rome* in 1970, while some leading English directors have been drawn to the tragedy.

Among celebrated actors who have taken on the earnest Roman general are Robert Ryan, Ian McKellen, Kenneth Branagh, and Ralph Fiennes. Today, though, audiences in Europe and North America rarely display great enthusiasm for *Coriolanus*. This is perhaps because debates about the "masses" seem outdated in a post-Cold War world. The play nonetheless addresses the core of political power.

"You souls of geese/That bear the shapes of men" (1.4). A martial Coriolanus (Ian McKellen) exhorts the unwilling Romans to battle, National Theatre, London, 1984.

PLAY HISTORY

A POLITICAL PLAY

Coriolanus's impact has been felt most in Europe. A production at the Comédie Française in Paris in 1934 provoked right-wing riots. In Germany, around the time of World War I, it was given an anti-militaristic focus. The Nazis, on the other hand, extolled the "heroism" of Coriolanus, who "as Adolf Hitler in our days wishes to lead our beloved German fatherland."

TIMON OF ATHENS

TIMON OF ATHENS IS IN MANY WAYS Shakespeare's most pessimistic tragedy because the Athenian noble's agony is entirely self-inflicted. Timon believes his generosity has earned him love, respect, and gratitude, but when his fortune runs out, his friends quickly abandon him. Dismayed, he devotes the rest of his life to hating humanity. The play has long troubled scholars because the only surviving text, that of the *First Folio* of 1623, appears to be unfinished or based on an unreliable manuscript. *Timon of Athens* was written in 1607–08 immediately after the great tragedies of *Othello, King Lear,* and *Macbeth,* although there is no record of a performance in Shakespeare's lifetime. The Shakespearean text was revived in 1851, but the play is rarely performed today. Peter Brook's minimalist *Timon of Athens* at the Théâtre des Bouffes du Nord in Paris in 1974 is among few memorable productions.

BEHIND THE PLAY

TIMON, AN ATHENIAN NOBLE, is much loved for hosting lavish banquets and handing out expensive gifts, but the play reveals little more about him. There is no mention of a wife or children and only a passing reference suggests he had once been an important military hero whose "sword and fortune" shielded Athens from its enemies. Otherwise, Timon remains a mystery, begging the questions of why he is so easily taken in by flattery and why he blames others for his misfortunes. In some ways, his madness is reminiscent of that of King Lear, although Timon's obsession with money is decidedly less dignified. Like Alcibiades, the Athenian general who sets out to avenge his banishment by the Senate, Timon is a victim of ingratitude. However, while Alcibiades punishes those who humiliated him, Timon tumbles into bitterness and self-pity. The cynical philosopher Apemantus warns Timon that he is being sucked dry by false friends and then returns at the end of the play to mock him. The hypocritical, self-serving Athenian lords who betray Timon may personify Athens sliding into decadence, but Shakespeare ends the play on a note of hope: Alcibiades seizes Athens and takes charge of its rebirth.

Lived loathed and long,/ Most smiling, smooth, detested parasites... 3.6

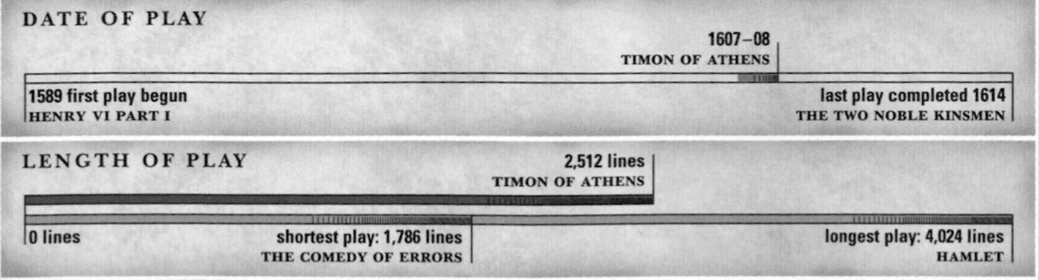

DRAMATIS PERSONAE

TIMON

865 lines

An Athenian noble, he responds to flattery by hosting banquets and giving gifts to his suitors; when his fortune runs out and his friends abandon him, he becomes an embittered recluse and finally withdraws to die.

Timon (Michael Pennington) brings about his own downfall.

LUCIUS, LUCULLUS AND SEMPRONIUS

0; 33; 27 lines

Flattering lords, they are happy to enjoy Timon's lavish hospitality but they refuse to help him pay off his debts.

VENTIDIUS

9 lines

Bailed out of debtors' prison by Timon, he then inherits a rich estate, but refuses to help Timon.

ALCIBIADES

163 lines

An Athenian general, he is banished after seeking the Senate's pardon for a friend sentenced to death; vowing revenge, he visits Timon in his retreat and is given gold to support his attack on Athens; he occupies Athens but only punishes his and Timon's enemies.

APEMANTUS

243 lines

A philosopher, professional cynic, and misanthrope who speaks unpleasant truths, he mocks Timon for his gullibility to flattery and scorns his suitors for their greed and obsequiousness.

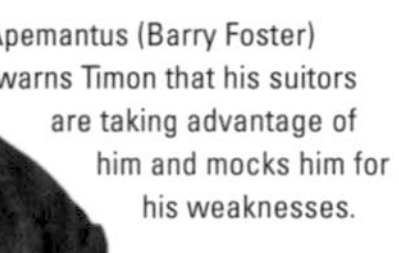

Apemantus (Barry Foster) warns Timon that his suitors are taking advantage of him and mocks him for his weaknesses.

FLAVIUS

207 lines

Timon's most loyal servant, he tells his master that his fortune is exhausted; he finds Timon's hideaway and again offers to be his servant; Timon sends him away with gold.

Flavius (John Woodvine) tries to protect his master from poverty but his warnings are ignored by Timon.

FLAMINIUS, LUCILIUS AND SERVILIUS

29; 45; 17 lines

Timon's servants, they are sent to borrow money for their master, but they return empty-handed.

HORTENSIUS, CAPHIS, PHILOTUS AND TITUS

11; 21; 6; 14 lines

Servants of a senator, flattering lords, and creditors, they are sent to collect Timon's debts.

A POET AND A PAINTER

111; 73 lines

They flatter Timon; later, learning that Timon has found gold, they visit him in hope of reward by denying their greed.

A JEWELLER AND A MERCHANT

12; 11 lines

The Jeweller boasts to the Merchant that he has a precious stone which he will sell to Timon at a good price.

AN OLD ATHENIAN

29 lines

He complains that Timon's servant is trying to seduce his daughter, but he is happy to take Timon's money.

THREE STRANGERS

31; 6; 1 lines

They report how Timon's former suitors refuse to lend him money.

A FOOL

22 lines

He exchanges witticisms with Athenian servants.

THREE SENATORS

91; 63; 35 lines

They order Alcibiades's banishment and then beg Timon to return to defend Athens.

THREE BANDITS

14; 7; 10 lines

They hear that Timon has found gold and are surprised when he gives some to them.

PHRYNIA AND TIMANDRA

3; 7 lines

Alcibiades's mistresses, they are insulted as whores when they beg for gold from Timon.

OTHER PLAYERS

Cupid and Amazons in the masque, Lords, Senators, Officers, Soldiers, Page, Messengers, Servants, and other Attendants.

PLOT SUMMARY

SIZE OF ACTS

ACT 1	ACT 2	ACT 3	ACT 4	ACT 5
578 lines	296 lines	571 lines	678 lines	389 lines

ACT ONE 578 lines

ATHENS

Outside the home of Timon, a rich Athenian, as visitors prepare to woo him with gifts, a Poet observes that, were the benevolent noble's fortunes to decline, his obsequious flatterers would soon fall away from him ❛❛.

When Fortune in her shift and change of mood/ Spurns down her late beloved… 1.1

Timon welcomes his suitors. Told that his friend Ventidius is in debtors' prison, he pays off the debt. An Old Athenian complains that Timon's servant, Lucilius, is courting his daughter; Timon promptly matches the girl's dowry. When a Poet and a Painter present their gifts to Timon, though, the philosopher-misanthrope Apemantus ridicules them. Alcibiades, an Athenian general, joins two lords hurrying to "taste Lord Timon's bounty."

Apemantus observes that "It grieves me to see so many men dip their meat in one man's blood" ❛❛. Timon toasts his guests as Cupid leads a masque of ladies dressed as Amazons ❛❛. When the banquet ends, Timon asks for his jewel casket with a view to distributing presents, but his servant Flavius knows that his master's wealth is exhausted. Apemantus mocks generous Timon for rewarding those who flatter him ❜.

I scorn thy meat. 'Twould choke me, for I should ne'er flatter thee… 1.2

O, no doubt, my good friends, but the gods themselves have provided that I shall have much help from you… 1.2

What will this come to?/ He commands us to provide and give great gifts,/And all out of an empty coffer… 1.2

ACT TWO 296 lines

ATHENS

A senator sends a servant to collect money owed to him by Timon, while Flavius waves unpaid bills as proof of Timon's penury. Returning from hunting, Timon is puzzled to find that other servants have come to collect debts. Flavius dismisses the servants, who exchange insults and witticisms with Apemantus and the Fool.

Realizing he is penniless, Timon berates Flavius for mismanaging his affairs, but his servant notes that Timon ignored his warnings ❛❛. Conceding that "unwisely, not ignobly, have I given," Timon still believes his friends will help him. But when he tells Flavius to borrow 1,000 talents from the senators, he learns that they have already

O my good lord,/At many times I brought in my accounts,/Laid them before you… 2.2

Thou givest so long, Timon, I fear thou wilt give away thyself in paper shortly… 1.2

They answer, in a joint and corporate voice,/ That now they are at fall, want treasure, cannot/ Do what they would... 2.2

refused. He sends Flavius to Ventidius, who has just inherited a rich estate, still unwilling to believe "That Timon's fortunes 'mong his friends can sink."

ACT THREE

571 lines

ATHENS

When one of Timon's servants, Flaminius, tries to borrow from Lucullus, he is told "this is no time to lend money." Lucius criticizes Lucullus for rebuffing the noble, but when Servilius, another of Timon's servants, requests a loan, Lucius too regrets he has "no power to be kind." Sempronius in turn complains that Timon did not seek him out first and retorts, "Who bates mine honour shall not know my coin".

How? Have they denied him?... 3.3

Servants of creditors return to Timon's house to demand payment, but he chases them away, telling Flavius to invite "all my friends" to one more feast.

At the Senate, Alcibiades seeks pardon for a friend condemned to death for killing a man who insulted his honor. When the sentence is confirmed, Alcibiades is furious, prompting the senators to banish him. Alone, Alcibiades vows revenge against Athens.

I am a humble suitor to your virtues;/For pity is the virtue of the law... 3.5

Now the gods keep you old enough, that you may live/ Only in bone, that none may look on you!... 3.5

Inviting his friends to take their places before covered dishes, Timon gives thanks to the gods but his speech quickly turns sour: "For these my present friends, as they are to me nothing, so in nothing bless them, and to nothing are they welcome". The dishes contain only warm water and stones, which Timon throws at his guests, proclaiming, "Henceforth hated be/ Of Timon man and all humanity."

You great benefactors, sprinkle our society with thankfulness... 3.6

ACT FOUR

678 lines

A BEACH OUTSIDE ATHENS

Alone on a deserted beach, Timon wallows in hatred for Athenians. Addressing "you good gods all", he begs: "And grant, as Timon grows, his hate may grow/ To the whole race of mankind, high and low. Amen".

Let me look back upon thee. O thou wall/ That girdles in those wolves, dive in the earth/ And fence not Athens... 4.1

As Timon's servants lament their master's fate, Flavius offers to share "the latest of my wealth." Alone, he considers how strange it is "When man's worst sin is he does too much good".

O the fierce wretchedness that glory brings us!/ Who would not wish to be from wealth exempt... 4.2

Timon is raging against flatterers and digging for roots when suddenly he strikes gold. "Why this? What, this, you gods?" he asks. Then, recalling the destructive power of gold, he vows: "I will make thee/Do thy right nature."

Alcibiades appears with two mistresses, Phrynia and Timandra, but he does not recognize Timon. "I am Misanthropos, and hate mankind," Timon says. When Alcibiades offers his friendship, Timon responds rudely. But hearing Alcibiades's plan to conquer Athens, Timon offers him gold and urges him to spare no one.

That by killing of villains/ Thou wast born to conquer my country... 4.3

Apemantus arrives next, warning Timon: "Do not assume my likeness." Timon responds: "Why shouldst thou hate men?/They never flattered thee". Impatient, Timon turns again to his gold. Apemantus leaves to spread word of Timon's wealth. When bandits appear, Timon offers gold

Not by this breath that is more miserable./Thou art a slave whom Fortune's tender arm/With favour never clasped... 4.3

Nor on the beasts themselves, the birds, and fishes;/ You must eat men... 4.3

to "do villainy", and "cut throats" and "break open shops" ❝. Surprised, one bandit remarks, "'Has almost charmed me from my profession by persuading me to it."

Flavius is shocked to find Timon "full of decay and failing". When Flavius identifies himself, Timon says he cannot remember anyone who was ever loyal to him. Flavius offers to serve him, but Timon sends him away with gold, telling him to "Hate all, curse all, show charity to none."

ACT FIVE

389 lines

A BEACH OUTSIDE ATHENS AND ATHENS
The Poet and the Painter also offer their services, admitting they know of Timon's gold, but insisting it is not what brought them. Timon mocks them as villains and sends them away with some gold.

Then, Timon, presently prepare thy grave./ Lie where the light foam of the sea may beat/ Thy grave-stone daily... 4.3

Accompanied by Flavius, two senators promise Timon "such heaps and sums of love and wealth" if he returns to defend Rome against Alcibiades. Timon rebuffs them. He has written his epitaph and is preparing to die. To forestall "wild Alcibiades' wrath," he suggests they hang themselves. He then tells them that he will soon lie "Upon the beachèd verge of the salt flood" ❝.

Come not to me again... 5.1

Near Timon's cave, a soldier finds a paper that reads: "Timon is dead, who hath outstretched his span./ Some beast read this; there does not live a man." He then sees a tomb with a strange engraving, which he copies. As Alcibiades reaches Athens, he promises that only his and Timon's enemies will be punished.

Learning of Timon's death, Alcibiades translates the mysterious epitaph ❝. The dead Athenian's final thoughts confirm his undiminished bitterness at life: "Here lie I Timon, who alive all living men did hate." Alcibiades enters Athens promising to "make war breed peace".

Here lies a wretched corse, of wretched soul bereft... 5.4

READING THE PLAY

COMPARISON OF PROSE TO VERSE

prose: 27% | verse: 73%

> **LITERARY SOURCES**
>
> **FARCE AND SATIRE**
> The play's sources are uncertain. An anonymous farce, *Timon,* was apparently performed in London around the same time as Shakespeare's play. A more likely source is *Timon, or The Misanthrope,* a Greek satire written by Lucian of Samosata in Greek in the 2nd century AD, which was available to Shakespeare in both Latin and French translations. There are also references to Timon in Plutarch's *Life of Alcibiades* and *Life of Antony.*

GIVEN ITS DARK AND CYNICAL portrayal of human nature, *Timon of Athens* is surprisingly uncomplicated to read. The text is unpolished: some speeches switch inexplicably between prose and blank verse, while an entire subplot involving Alcibiades's conflict with the Athenian Senate appears in Act 3 without prior notice. The play has no true villain, no comic characters, and no love interest. It is divided neatly into two parts: Timon's philanthropy and his misanthropy, and it remains focused on Timon. The subplot involving Alcibiades becomes relevant only when Timon sees him as an instrument for his own revenge.

Rather, it is Timon's ranting against humanity that dominates the play, from the moment of his "warm water and stones" banquet until his final epitaph. From Act 1, though, a central question is raised: does Timon deserve our compassion? The 18th-century view of Dr. Johnson and others was that Timon was justly punished for his vanity and ostentation: Apemantus may have been a cynic but he recognized the empty flattery that Timon so enjoyed. The favored views of 19th-century romantics, however, was that Timon was a noble Christ-like figure, who became a victim of his generosity of spirit and idealism. In either case, the moral issues raised here are open for debate. One contemporary view is that both of Timon's extreme postures reveal his blindness—first to sycophants and flatterers, then to any extenuating human qualities. In such a case, Timon's self-obsession and self-indulgence probably merit little sympathy. Certainly, in his epitaph, Timon asks for none. While Alcibiades searches for words of praise, his best effort is modest: "Dead/Is noble Timon, of whose memory/ Hereafter more."

"This is in thee a nature but infected" (4.3). Timon and Apemantus in a 19th-century engraving.

SEEING THE PLAY

Stephen Oliver's production of the play at the English National Opera in 1991 used a bare, unkempt stage to highlight Timon's loss of social respectability.

TIMON OF ATHENS IS RARELY PRODUCED, not least because its grinding pessimism can be off-putting to audiences. Yet, if staged successfully, the play can be moving and provocative. Peter Brook, whose 1974 production is considered a watershed of lucidity, once said that *Timon of Athens* is either about Timon or about Athens. If it is about Timon, the focus is on the noble's sudden, almost psychological leap from childlike innocence to despair. Today, such a Freudian approach can echo the dark existentialism of Samuel Beckett's plays. If a production dwells on Athens, it will show that, as slave of a corrupt, decadent and materialistic society, Timon believes first that money can buy love, and then that gold can promote hatred. This was the interpretation favoured by Karl Marx.

In either case, in the pivotal "warm water and stones" scene in Act 3, the actor playing Timon must switch convincingly from open-hearted philanthropist to close-minded misanthrope. Once alone on his deserted beach, Timon then commits himself to blinkered hatred, stubbornly resisting the friendship offered by Alcibiades and Flavius. The long scene in which Timon and Apemantus argue their justifications for misanthropy confronts the Freud-versus-Marx views of the play: Timon's emotional rejection of the world versus Apemantus's intellectual and cynical detachment. Timon may prove his sincerity by choosing death but Apemantus's mockery of death may ultimately prevail.

ON STAGE

TIMON IN NEW YORK

Michael Langham's production of *Timon of Athens* for the National Actors Theater in New York in 1994 *(left)* placed the play in Depression-era Europe. The first half was inspired by the partygoing 1920s (with music by Duke Ellington), while Timon's descent into misanthropy was set in the troubled prewar 1930s. Perhaps appropriately for an age when cynicism flourished, Apemantus was portrayed as a journalist.

The ROMANCES

DURING THE FINAL PHASE OF HIS CAREER, SHAKESPEARE WROTE OR COWROTE SIX ROMANCES—STORYBOOK ADVENTURES WHICH STIR FEELINGS OF GRIEF AND JOY.

SHAKESPEARE'S LAST seven plays date from between 1607 and 1614. Except for *Henry VIII*, all are romances. In Shakespeare's era, though, the term "romance" was not used to describe a play. Instead, plays now referred to as romances were simply made to fit into existing categories of drama. In the *First Folio* of 1623, two romances, *The Winter's Tale* and *The Tempest* were classified as comedies and one, *Cymbeline*, as tragedy. Of the three romances not printed in the *First Folio*, *Pericles* survives in only one questionable text; *Cardenio*, attributed to Shakespeare and coauthor John Fletcher is now lost; and *The Two Noble Kinsmen* is often viewed as predominantly Fletcher's work. None of these plays was appreciated as an example of a distinct dramatic genre until the late 18th century, when the term "romance" was coined to differentiate them as colorfully storied plays delving into bittersweet realms of the human soul.

Origins of the Romances

As applied to Shakespeare's plays, "romance" does not strictly refer to courtship or affairs of the heart. The word came into English from the medieval French *romanz*, longer narrative fictions in prose or verse first composed in the 12th century by Chrétien de Troyes, who interlaced the chivalric adventures of Arthurian knights with their amorous exploits. Similar fictions were favored in Italian, Spanish, and Portuguese. As a result, the term "romance" developed in connection with the literary form taken up by those writing in Romance languages. In fact, the literary ancestry of romance fiction can be traced back to the Hellenistic period, between 330–30 BC. In early Greek narrative romances reminiscent of Homer's *Odyssey*, protagonists separated from their families endure a rollicking sequence of astonishing perils, then discover lost loved ones just in time to live happily ever after.

Before the invention of paper, popular romances circulated throughout the Greek-speaking Mediterranean—from Asia Minor and Egypt to Sicily—in scrolled papyrus rolls. Action was broken down into episodic units so that artwork, accompanied by brief texts, could tell the story. Some of these romances were later translated into Latin. Surviving fragments from around 1000 AD show a comic-book-like approach employed to relate the story of Apollonius of Tyre, an illustrated romance narrative of high adventures set in the Mediterranean. The tale of Apollonius of Tyre was so popular as to be retold in vernacular languages throughout Western Europe. One English version appears in the writer John Gower's late medieval *Confessio Amantis*, which Shakespeare consulted for *Pericles*, his romance play based on the adventures of Apollonius of Tyre. In Shakespeare's case, romances are not determined by the form or even the themes of any source material he used; the playwright drew from the romance tradition for the plots of both comedies and romances alike. Instead, the signature feature of the Shakespearean romance is the mixture of emotions its action-packed plot elicits.

Blending Comedy and Tragedy

Like most Shakespearean comedies, the romances highlight young lovers. But the trials endured by lovers in the romances finally invite strong feelings of sympathy rather than lighter-hearted merrymaking. While the last scene of a romance resembles a comedy in that it ends happily, with the lovers finally joined to form a new couple, the heart of the romance is tragic. Death, loss, or catastrophe shape the main action of the play. And in its final scenes, the considerable turmoil suffered by its principal characters is never set aside, as it can be in the comedies. Instead, these difficulties establish the tone – both melancholic and joyful – in which Shakespeare's romances conclude.

Even the tragic core of the Bard's romance differs from the kind found in any of the playwright's tragedies. In the tragedies, a climate of realism governs the protagonist's progress. Quests for understanding or self-realization eventually meet up with immovable obstacles, such as social rigidity or individual destiny. In the romances, crises and disasters occur in settings taken from fiction, places safely removed from reality. Characters make discoveries through action rather than reflection. For instance, *Pericles*, a romance, explores the tragic implications of incest, as does the tragedy *Hamlet*. But *Hamlet* is set almost exclusively in broody Elsinore, where the hero stops to consider his situation in frequent soliloquies. The tragedy presents Hamlet's relationship to the world in part through the dilemmas occupying his mind. By contrast, *Pericles* is set in a typical romance landscape of

nonstop adventure, where Pericles is constantly propelled forward to another island or city. Thus, he has little occasion for probing reflection. Not surprisingly, soliloquies are rare in the romances.

Shakespeare's romance characters are less taken up with questioning than they are with searching. There is always a potential tragedy at the center of a romance but, instead of destroying protagonists and their families, these elements fuel their adventurous exploits and the sensations of wonder these produce. Eventually, the tragic thrust of a romance reunites separated family members, giving them cause to rejoice. Promises of marriage and social harmony in the final scenes of romances then bring their own variety of comic resolution.

Storybook Action

The romances are driven by intricate, fast-paced plots unfolding in clear, bracing episodes. Their plots are akin to those illustrated in Hellenistic romances or even their modern literary descendants: action hero comic books. Consequently, treatment of both space and time in the romances can seem highly unregulated. From one scene to the next, characters in *Cymbeline* travel from Rome to Britain and from Britain into the wilds of Wales. *The Winter's Tale* places action first in a folktale-like Sicilian court and later in a boisterously pastoral Bohemia. Years may pass in the gaps between scenes: 16 years famously fly by between two scenes of *The Winter's Tale* and 14 years suddenly elapse in *Pericles*. Indeed, the Shakespearean romance is called "a play of gaps" when it takes such liberties with the conventions of classical drama: unity of action and place. But with the romances, Shakespeare proved just as able to follow classical dramatic conventions as to break with them. *The Tempest*, held to be the last work Shakespeare was to author independently, observes classical rules to the letter: it is set in a single location over a single day. The only romance with no known single source, *The Tempest* nevertheless experiments with storytelling techniques in its own way. The characters' links to faraway settings frequently darken and condition their day on a magic isle, where anything can happen.

THE ROMANCES AT A GLANCE

Play	Miraculous event	Main source
Pericles	Goddess Diana appears	Gower, *Confessio Amantis*
Cymbeline	The God Jupiter appears	Holinshed, *Chronicles*; Boccaccio, *Decameron*
The Winter's Tale	A statue comes to life	Robert Greene, *Pandosto*
The Tempest	Prospero employs magical arts	Original
Cardenio	(The play is now lost)	Cervantes, *Don Quixote*
The Two Noble Kinsmen	Palamon miraculously spared execution	Chaucer, "The Knight's Tale," *Canterbury Tales*

COSTUMING THE ROMANCES

Audiences in Shakespeare's day were routinely dazzled by theatrical costumes. Some were originally garments of the rich, who sold them or gave them as forms of payment to theater companies. An inventory belonging to the Lord Admiral's Men testifies to the quality and range even of "antic suits," clown costumes. With their emphasis on spectacle for its own sake, the romances called for stunning costumes, giving Puritans more cause to complain of the theater's immorality. The list below is taken from the 1602 Lord Admiral's Men inventory of over 100 items.

Cloaks. A scarlet cloak laid down with silver lace and silver buttons; a short velvet cape cloak embroidered with gold and gold spangles; a purple satin welted with velvet and silver twist.

Gowns. The black velvet gown with white fur; a crimson robe striped with gold, faced with ermine; a cardinal's gown.

Antic Suits. A coat of crimson velvet cut in panes and embroidered in gold; a cloth of gold coat with orange-tawny bases; a silver coat with blue silk and tinsel bases.

Jerkins and Doublets. A crimson satin case laced with gold lace all over; a ginger-colored doublet; red velvet for a boy.

The storybook heritage of Shakespearean romance, with its freedom to represent improbable fictions, is most overt in the first of the playwright's romances, *Pericles*, where the plot of each act is advanced by a chorus representing John Gower, the author of Shakespeare's source narrative for the play. Gower's role emphasizes the notion that a fable is being reenacted, that an ancient story is being retold. The very title of *The Winter's Tale* captures the romance's debt to fictional narrative. Even Shakespeare's last romance, *The Two Noble Kinsmen*, opens with a prologue thanking Geoffrey Chaucer for the play's story, from *The Canterbury Tales*. Whether or not they are openly presented as stories recast for the stage, all of the Shakespearean romances convey the moods and rhythms of narratives from a venerable literary tradition linking love to adventure in picturesque settings.

Romances such as *The Winter's Tale* are often produced using colorful, elaborate costumes.

MIRACLES AND REUNIONS

At some point within the Shakespearean romance, a miraculous event offers protagonists and audiences a glorious cocktail of relief, tearful bliss, and awe. In *Pericles*, the goddess Diana appears in a dream to steer Pericles back to his adoring, lost family. In *Cymbeline*, Posthumus's vision of the god Jupiter leads him back to his beloved daughter Imogen and triggers the return of lost sons to the king of Britain. And in *The Winter's Tale*, Queen Hermione appears to return to life, restoring her to a husband and daughter amazed to behold her apparent rebirth. In *The Two Noble Kinsmen*, divine intervention takes the form of the accidental death of one cousin which saves the life of the other.

But while romance protagonists endure breathtaking tribulations, spectators need not worry much about their unfolding or ultimate fates. Suffering in the romances is usually a detached experience. Even unrelenting hardships occur under an umbrella of divine guidance that inevitably assures sensational rewards. The cruel separations of close kin or lovers is sure to result in incredible yet satisfying reunions. In *The Winter's Tale*, for instance, the baby Perdita is cast away on the stormy shore of Bohemia only to be reunited with her father as a young bride-to-be. Thus, the romances as a genre are often described as tragicomical and fantastical, melodramatic, and sentimental.

Rippling throughout Shakespeare's romances, too, are themes of incest, adultery, rape, jealousy, murder, and evil for evil's sake. But malevolent forces and unsound urges ultimately serve to sweeten the endurance of lovers and the survival of families. The final mood of celebration in the romances is consequently different from the playful revelry or wedding festivity concluding most Shakespearean comedies. Instead, the romances end on a note of rejoicing in the face of grave losses overcome. In sharp contrast to the comedies, too, the romances often include the death of a central character, whether wicked, as the stepmother queen of Cymbeline, or not, as the romantic hero Arcite in *The Two Noble Kinsmen.* These deaths partly serve to cast a weighty anchor of sacrifice into the joyful waters of concluding scenes. But even the death of a good person in the romances is never a fully tragic loss. For the romances finally celebrate the power of fantasy fiction, illusion, and the theater itself to turn death into an unexpected source of life.

DATES OF THE ROMANCES

1589
First play

1607–1608
Pericles

1609–10
Cymbeline

1610–1611
The Winter's Tale

1611
The Tempest

1613–1614
The Two Noble Kinsmen

PERICLES

PERICLES IS SHAKESPEARE'S FIRST EXPERIMENT with an entirely new approach to drama, blending tragedy and comedy, magic and allegory. This genre later became known as romance. The first recorded performance of *Pericles* was in 1607, yet it is the only one of the 37 plays attributed to Shakespeare at the time that was not published in the *First Folio* of 1623, probably because of doubts over the accuracy of available texts. *Pericles* was finally included in the *Third Folio* of 1663, along with six plays not written by Shakespeare. The play proved an immense hit with Jacobean audiences, but it never recovered its popularity after London's theaters were closed by Parliament from 1642 to 1660. Several adaptations were presented in the 18th and 19th centuries; Shakespeare's text was finally staged in London in 1939. The play, considered one of Shakespeare's lesser romances, is rarely performed today.

BEHIND THE PLAY

SHAKESPEARE PRESENTS HIS ROMANCES as if they were ancient tales being retold for the purpose of entertainment. This creates ample room for implausible accretions of events which, in *Pericles*, include incest, storms, jousting, pirates, a kidnapping, a magic potion, attempted murder, a drowning, two resuscitations, and one remarkable coincidence. To underline that this is only a tale, Shakespeare appoints a storyteller—John Gower, a 14th-century English writer and himself author of one of the play's sources—to accompany readers and audiences on Pericles's wanderings through the Aegean. The first three acts are largely devoted to Pericles's assorted adventures. The play then turns dark when a distraught Pericles concludes erroneously that both his wife and daughter are dead. Marina, Pericles's daughter, is kidnapped and forced into a brothel. Her purity reaffirmed, she then uses it to assuage Pericles's grief until, in a scene of exceptional beauty, they rediscover they are father and daughter. Only a touch of divine intervention is then needed for Pericles to be reunited with the wife he presumed dead. Thus, from misfortune comes rebirth.

Imagine Pericles arrived at Tyre,/ Welcomed and settled to his own desire...
4.CHORUS

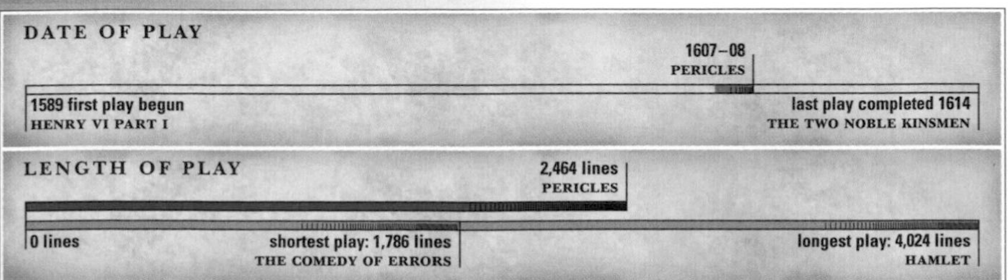

DRAMATIS PERSONAE

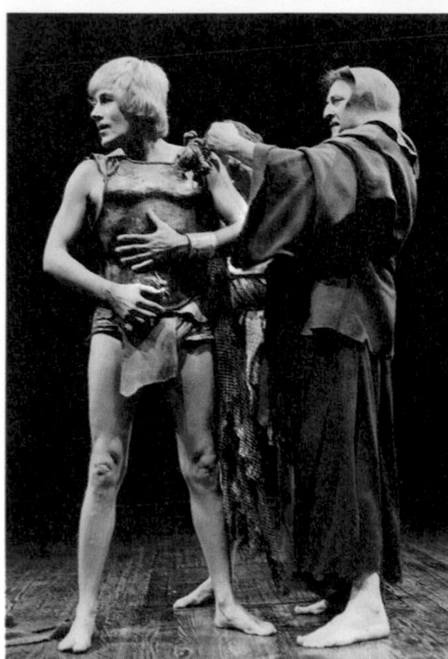
A shipwrecked Pericles (Nicholas Pennell) is rescued by a fisherman (Powys Thomas) on the coast of Pentapolis.

GOWER
308 lines
John Gower, a medieval poet, retells the ancient story of Pericles of Tyre as Chorus.

ANTIOCHUS
69 lines
The incestuous King of Antioch, he takes delight in killing his daughter's suitors.

PERICLES
609 lines
Prince of Tyre, a decent and innocent man, he confronts a series of misfortunes, including the apparent loss of his wife and daughter, but in the end good luck and the goddess Diana intervene to restore his joy.

HELICANUS
123 lines
A lord of Tyre who rules in Pericles's absence.

ESCANES
3 lines
A lord of Tyre.

SIMONIDES
157 lines
The "good" King of Pentapolis, he allows his daughter, Thaisa, to marry Pericles.

CLEON
112 lines
Governor of Tarsus, he is ruled by his wife, Dionyza.

LYSIMACHUS
103 lines
Governor of Mytilene, he meets Marina in a brothel and is persuaded to honor her virginity; he eventually marries her.

CERIMON
109 lines
A physician, he saves Thaisa's life after she is thrown into the sea inside a sealed casket.

THALIARD
27 lines
He is sent by Antiochus to murder Pericles.

PHILEMON
1 line
Cerimon's servant.

LEONINE
24 lines
A lord of Tarsus, he is ordered by Dionyza to kill Marina.

PANDER
28 lines
Bawd's husband, he runs the brothel that buys Marina.

BOULT
79 lines
A brothel servant, he helps Marina.

THE DAUGHTER OF ANTIOCHUS
2 lines
She revels in her incestuous relationship with her father.

DIONYZA
91 lines
Wife of Cleon, she conspires to have Marina murdered for overshadowing their daughter, Philoten.

THAISA
82 lines
Daughter of Simonides, she apparently dies on board ship, but is rescued in Ephesus.

MARINA
186 lines
Daughter of Pericles and Thaisa, she is kidnapped and sold to a brothel; she is eventually reunited with her parents.

Marina (Emily Pithon) acts as an angel of mercy to Pericles.

LYCHORIDA
11 lines
Marina's nurse.

BAWD
99 lines
Pander's wife, she also runs the brothel in Mytilene.

DIANA
10 lines
Goddess of chastity.

OTHER PLAYERS
A Marshal, Gentlemen, Lords, Knights, Sailors, Servants, Fishermen, Pirates, and Messengers.

The evil Dionyza (Rula Lenska) plans the murder of Marina.

PLOT SUMMARY

SIZE OF ACTS

ACT 1	ACT 2	ACT 3	ACT 4	ACT 5
503 lines	553 lines	340 lines	610 lines	458 lines

ACT ONE 503 lines

ANTIOCH AND TARSUS

Making his first appearance as Chorus, John Gower announces he will tell the story of Antiochus, the widowed King of Antioch, who has long engaged in incest with his daughter. Her beauty draws many suitors, but they must solve a riddle if they hope to marry her. Those who fail are condemned to die. Pericles, Prince of Tyre, the latest suitor, is impressed by the princess's entry. He is then given the riddle and, reading it aloud, is shocked to recognize an admission of incest. He responds indirectly, but the king realizes his secret has been discovered, and offers the prince more time to answer. Pericles fears for his life and flees. Back home, he gloomily predicts that Antiochus will now punish Tyre.

See where she comes, apparelled like the spring... 1.1

Great King,/ Few love to hear the sins they love to act... 1.1

Why should this change of thoughts,/The sad companion, dull-eyed melancholy,/Be my so used a guest... 1.2

He shares the incest secret with Helicanus, the acting governor, who urges him to sail to Tarsus. When Thaliard arrives from Antiochus to kill Pericles, the prince is already at sea.

In Tarsus, Cleon, the governor, and his wife Dionyza are bemoaning the severe famine afflicting their citizens. Learning that ships have been sighted, they fear enemies. But instead, Pericles brings much-needed food and is welcomed as a hero.

ACT TWO 553 lines

TARSUS, PENTAPOLIS, AND TYRE

Gower relates that Pericles, still in danger, sets sail again, but he is shipwrecked. As three fishermen discuss the storm, Pericles seeks their help. They

Wind, rain, and thunder, remember earthly man/ Is but a substance that must yield to you... 2.1

tell him he is in Pentapolis ruled by the "good" King Simonides, who has organized a royal tournament where knights will joust for the love of his daughter, Thaisa. Recovering his armor, Pericles joins the tournament. Thaisa is impressed by his performance and gives him the wreath of victory. Although Pericles says he is only "a gentleman of Tyre," Thaisa falls for him.

In Tyre, Helicanus learns that Antiochus and his daughter have been killed by "a fire from heaven" 66. Since Pericles has vanished, the lords of Tyre invite Helicanus to become their ruler, but he proposes that Pericles be given a year to return home.

No, Escanes, know this of me,/Antiochus from incest lived not free... 2.4

In Pentapolis, Simonides tells the other knights that Thaisa will wear "Diana's livery" of chastity for another 12 months. But once they leave, still unaware of Pericles's royal blood, he reveals his daughter's love for Pericles.

ACT THREE

340 lines

AT SEA, EPHESUS, AND TARSUS

Gower recounts that Pericles and Thaisa have had a festive wedding, and Thaisa is now pregnant. Pericles receives word that, unless he returns to Tyre within 12 months, Helicanus will replace him. In this way, the people of Pentapolis learn that Pericles is a king, and they urge him to leave with his new queen. But, Gower notes, when their ship is caught in a fierce storm, Thaisa goes into labor.

On board, Pericles is begging the gods to intercede 66 when Lychorida, a nurse, brings his newborn daughter. Handing him the baby, she reports that Thaisa has died. Grief-stricken, Pericles learns that maritime superstition requires her sealed casket to be buried at sea. He reluctantly bids farewell to his wife 66, then turns toward Tarsus. The baby Marina is left with Cleon and Dionyza.

The god of this great vast rebuke these surges,/Which wash both heaven and hell... 3.1

A terrible childbed has thou had, my dear;/No light, no fire; th'unfriendly elements/Forgot thee utterly... 3.1

At Ephesus, servants bring Cerimon a heavy chest that has washed ashore. When opened, it reveals an unblemished Thaisa, "shrouded in cloth of state, balmed and entreasured." In the coffin, Pericles has left a note requesting that she be given a burial worthy of "a daughter of a king." But seeing her "fresh," Cerimon, a skilled physician, calls for potions that soon revive her. Convinced that she will never again see Pericles, Thaisa devotes herself to Diana, goddess of chastity.

ACT FOUR

610 lines

TARSUS AND MYTILENE

Gower recounts how, with 14 years passed, Marina has grown into a clever and beautiful girl. But Dionyza is envious that her own daughter is overshadowed by Marina's grace. As Marina mourns her nurse's death, Dionyza suggests she walk along the shore with Leonine, who has orders to kill the girl. But as he prepares to murder Marina, pirates abduct her.

Why would she have me killed?/Now, as I can remember, by my troth,/ I never did her hurt in all my life... 4.1

At a brothel in Mytilene, Pander, Bawd, and Boult are complaining about the dismal state of their business. But when pirates sell them Marina, the brothel-keepers invite bids for the young virgin's honor.

In Tarsus, believing Marina dead, Cleon and Dionyza decide to tell Pericles that she expired "at night" and, as proof of their grief, they build her a fine tomb. Gower reports that when Pericles reaches Tarsus and is informed of Marina's death, he cannot be consoled. Vowing never to wash his face or cut his hair, he leaves again by sea.

In Mytilene, Marina has managed to remain a virgin, driving the brothel's owners and clients to distraction with her preaching. Bawd tells her to abandon her "virginal fencing," but the girl even persuades Lysimachus, the local governor, to respect her. Bawd orders Boult to "crack the glass of her virginity," but, charmed, he places her in an "honest house" where she can teach locals to "sing, weave, sew, and dance."

Fie, fie upon her! She's able to freeze the god Priapus and undo a whole generation... 4.6

ACT FIVE

458 lines

MYTILENE AND EPHESUS

Pericles has been blown off course to Mytilene, where Lysimachus learns he is paralyzed by grief. To lift his spirits, Lysimachus sends Marina to sing to him. Pericles ignores her, but she continues talking, even noting her royal parentage. Suddenly Pericles sees her resemblance to his dead wife Thaisa. He interrogates her until she discloses her name and Pericles is overcome with joy. That same night, the goddess Diana orders him to travel to Ephesus.

I am a maid,/ My lord, that ne'er before invited eyes... 5.1

Now blessing on thee! Rise; thou art my child... 5.1

Marina agrees to marry Lysimachus, but first Pericles must thank Diana for protecting her. In Ephesus, as Pericles addresses Diana, Thaisa hears his voice and faints. As she stirs, Pericles recognizes her voice. Now reunited with wife and daughter, Pericles decides that Marina and Lysimachus will rule Tyre, and that he and Thaisa will be crowned in Pentapolis. Gower concludes with word that Cleon and his wife have been burned to death by angry mobs.

This is the rarest dream/ That e'er dull sleep did mock sad fools withal./This cannot be my daughter, buried!... 5.1

READING THE PLAY

COMPARISON OF PROSE TO VERSE

prose: 18% | verse: 82%

WHAT SOME CRITICS REGARD as the patchy quality of *Pericles* is partly due to the lack of accurate sources for Shakespeare's original text, and partly because the playwright either did not write the first two acts or collaborated on them with George Wilkins, whose fictional narrative, *The Painful Adventures of Pericles, Prince of Tyre,* appeared in 1609. Some scholars believe *Pericles* is a play that can be better appreciated on stage, not least because the cleansing role of the sea becomes more apparent as it takes and transforms key characters. Yet, despite Ben Jonson's dismissal of *Pericles* as "a moldy tale," numerous passages merit attentive rereading.

The high point of the play comes in Act 5 in the long emotional build-up toward the reunion of Pericles and Marina. One scholar, Harold Bloom, has written that "the 150 lines of the recognition scene are one of the extraordinary sublimities of Shakespeare's art." Comparable perhaps to King Lear's reunion with Cordelia, it is a dialogue of an intensity that Shakespeare was not to recreate in later romances, even where they, too, include final act meetings between long-separated fathers and daughters. In *The Winter's Tale,* King Leontes finds the "lost" Perdita off stage, with the drama focused on his reunion with his "dead" queen. And in *Cymbeline,* King Cymbeline seems more touched by rediscovering his "lost" sons than his "dead" daughter, Imogen. But in *Pericles,* it is the rebirth of Marina that provides Pericles's redemption.

Thaisa's casket is washed ashore on the coast of Ephesus in an illustration from Charles Folkard's *The Children's Shakespeare,* 1911.

WHO'S WHO

Antiochus, King of Antioch, has an incestuous relationship with his daughter. When **Pericles**, Prince of Tyre, discovers this incest, he flees to Pentapolis, where he marries the local king's daughter, **Thaisa**, who apparently dies after giving birth at sea. She is washed ashore at Ephesus, alive. Their daughter, **Marina**, is left at Tarsus. Years later, pirates capture Marina and sell her to a brothel in Mytilene, where she is reunited with her grief-stricken father, Pericles. Together, they travel to Ephesus to find that Thaisa is alive. Marina, who against all odds has preserved her virginity, marries **Lysimachus**, Governor of Mytilene.

SEEING THE PLAY

The brothel-keepers cannot decide what to do with the stubbornly virginal Marina in a modern production by the Jean Cocteau Repertory Theater, New York, 1979.

THE FIRST HALF OF THE PLAY is so packed with nasty characters and harrowing action that directors often present *Pericles* as an overblown spectacle. Indeed, how can Antiochus and his daughter not be portrayed as diabolic, or Cleon and his wife not be painted as murderous hypocrites? How can jousting, a kidnapping, and two tremendous storms not be exciting? Shakespeare, of course, never shies from entertainment for its own sake, but his purpose in the romances is to build toward a climactic finale. Too much distraction can therefore weaken the audience's emotional attachment to Pericles and Marina, whose relationship provides the play's heartbeat. Certainly, by the time father and daughter are reunited, the audience should be ready to share the pair's rapture. However, it is the actor playing Pericles who must convey the miraculous joy of the moment.

When the scene begins, Marina, already reborn by her escape from the brothel, is happy to recount her life to an apparent stranger. In contrast, Pericles starts out as a broken man, who gradually returns to life as he realizes that he has found his lost daughter. Thus, this moment of re-birth is recorded principally by Pericles. In contrast, while Shakespeare idealizes his teenage heroines, he cannot resist poking fun at Marina's unwavering virginity when he has Bawd complain about "her quirks, her reasons, her master reasons, her prayers, her knees." When written, the role was played by a boy, although today Marina is a popular showcase for young actresses.

ON STAGE

CENSORSHIP

The opening scene of Pericles is shockingly direct in its treatment of incest, while Marina's verbal jousting to protect her virginity is also a jewel of repartee. In 1854, Samuel Phelps's production of *Pericles* at Sadler's Wells in London, mindful of Victorian sensibilities, eliminated the incest and brothel scenes, leaving no way of highlighting the play's theme of purity.

In the RSC production of *Pericles* at the Roundhouse, London, in 2002 the disembodied heads dangling over the stage provided a dark counterpoint to the play's drama of redemption.

CYMBELINE

CYMBELINE IS AN ACTION-PACKED DRAMA set in pre-Christian Britain. Listed as a tragedy in the *First Folio* of 1623, it is now considered a romance. It is thought to have been written in 1609, shortly after *Pericles*, although the only documented reference to the play in Shakespeare's lifetime is to a performance some time before 1611. Charles I is reported to have "well liked" the play when it was presented in court in 1634. In 1682 it was rewritten by Thomas d'Urfey, who renamed it *The Injured Princess*, or *The Fatal Wager*, and focused on Imogen's trials of love. David Garrick restored Shakespeare's text in the mid-18th century. Rarely performed, *Cymbeline*'s complex plot and melodrama have earned the disdain of some critics. The play nonetheless includes some of Shakespeare's most beautiful late verse and offers perhaps his purest romantic heroine.

BEHIND THE PLAY

CYMBELINE IS ONE OF SHAKESPEARE'S most plot-driven plays, its narrative advancing at the pace of a breathless action movie. It constantly switches locations between London, Wales, and Rome, and time periods between pre-Christian Britain, Ancient Rome and Renaissance Italy. The play's main sources are Holinshed's *Chronicles* for the life of King Cymbeline, and Boccacio's *Decameron* for the story of a wager over a woman's virtue. History provides the play's main characters, but almost nothing of the story. While Cymbeline did actually exist—he ruled Britain from from 33 BC to AD 2—in practise, history merely serves as a backdrop for the romantic ritual of jealousy, betrayal, courage, repentance, and redemption. Unusually, while Cymbeline gives the play its name, he has only a secondary role. He is browbeaten by his second wife and then largely vanishes until he presides over the happy ending. Such continuity as exists is provided by Imogen. And thanks to her goodness, Imogen overcomes the evil doings of the queen and her son Cloten, she exposes the deception of the wily Italian, Iachimo, and she forgives the violent jealousy of her husband, Posthumus.

The natural bravery of your isle, which stands/ As Neptune's park, ribbed and paled in/ With rocks unscaleable... 3.1

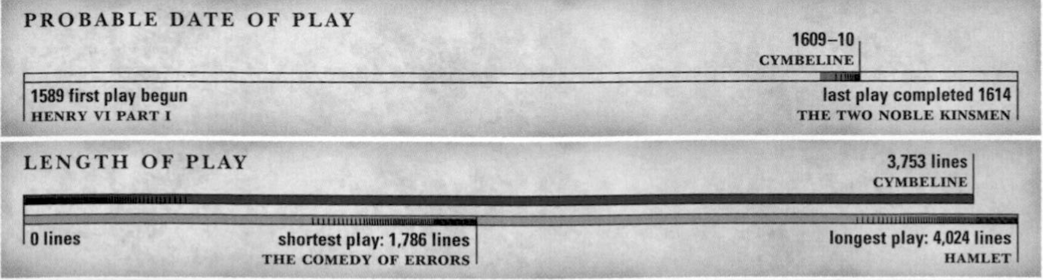

DRAMATIS PERSONAE

CYMBELINE
296 lines
A pre-Christian King of Britain, he is manipulated by his domineering second wife and rebels against Rome.

CLOTEN
269 lines
The oafish and vulgar son of the queen from an earlier marriage, he is rebuffed by Imogen and decides to take revenge.

POSTHUMUS LEONATUS
442 lines
Cymbeline's adopted son, he is banished for marrying Imogen; when Iachimo falsely claims to have seduced Imogen, Posthumus orders her murder.

BELARIUS
346 lines
Unfairly banished from Cymbeline's court 20 years earlier, he retaliated by abducting two of the king's infant sons; he took the name 'Morgan'.

GUIDERIUS
170 lines
The king's oldest son, he was abducted as a child by Belarius, who named him "Polydore."

Though King Cymbeline (Edward Petherbridge) is offstage for much of the play's action, he presides over the final happy ending.

ARVIRAGUS
145 lines
The king's second abducted son, now known as "Cadwal."

PHILARIO
42 lines
A friend of Posthumus in Rome.

IACHIMO
430 lines
A wily Italian, he tries unsuccessfully to seduce Imogen, but deceives Posthumus into believing he has done so.

CAIUS LUCIUS
105 lines
A Roman general sent to Cymbeline's court to demand tribute.

Iachimo (Paul Freeman) finds it difficult to overcome his lust for Imogen as she lies sleeping in her bedchamber.

PISANIO
218 lines
Posthumus's servant, he refuses to obey his master's order to murder Imogen.

CORNELIUS
74 lines
A physician in King Cymbeline's court.

TWO BRITISH CAPTAINS
4; 7 lines
They arrest Posthumus during the battle against the Romans.

A FRENCHMAN, A DUTCHMAN, AND A SPANIARD
22; 0; 0 lines
They argue the respective worth of their countries' women with Posthumus and Iachimo.

TWO LORDS OF CYMBELINE'S COURT
39; 45 lines
They mock Cloten for his stupidity.

TWO GENTLEMEN OF CYMBELINE'S COURT
67; 13 lines
They reveal Posthumus's marriage to Imogen.

TWO GAOLERS
45; 1 line
They hold Posthumus Leonatus prisoner.

QUEEN
170 lines
Cymbeline's vicious second wife, she wants her son Cloten to marry Imogen and plans to make him king.

IMOGEN
605 lines
Cymbeline's beautiful and pure daughter, she resists the advances of Iachimo and Cloten, yet is wrongly accused of adultery by her husband, Posthumus; she disguises herself as a boy called "Fidele."

The renowned actress Ellen Terry performed as a regal Imogen at the Lyceum in 1896.

HELEN
13 lines
Imogen's lady-in-waiting.

OTHER PLAYERS
Jupiter and the Spirits of Posthumus's Father, Mother and Two Brothers. Lords, Ladies, Roman Senators and Tribunes, Soothsayer, Musicians, Officers and Soldiers, Roman Prisoners, Messengers, and Attendants.

PLOT SUMMARY

SIZE OF ACTS

ACT 1	ACT 2	ACT 3	ACT 4	ACT 5
807 lines	522 lines	839 lines	634 lines	951 lines

ACT ONE

807 lines

BRITAIN AND ROME

King Cymbeline banishes his adopted son, Posthumus Leonatus, for marrying his daughter Imogen without his permission. He had pledged her to Cloten, the queen's son by an earlier marriage. Feigning sorrow, the queen promises Imogen to ask Cymbeline to revoke the order. After telling his servant Pisanio to care for his heartbroken wife, Posthumus gives Imogen a bracelet and receives a diamond ring in return.

In Rome, Posthumus meets Iachimo and a group of foreigners who are boasting the beauty of their countries' women. When Posthumus speaks of Imogen's grace and virtue, Iachimo questions her constancy, even betting gold against Imogen's ring that he can seduce her.

You may wear her in title yours, but, you know, strange fowl light upon neighbouring ponds… 1.4

In Britain, the queen persuades the court physician to give her poison to kill pests, but he suspects her intentions and supplies only a strong sleeping potion. She passes the "medicine" to Pisanio in the hope it will kill him.

Weeps she still, say'st thou? Dost thou think in time/ She will not quench, and let instructions enter/Where folly now possesses?… 1.5

Iachimo reports to Imogen that Posthumus is known in Rome as "The Briton reveller." Expressing pity for the lonely Imogen, he suggests she avenge the affront by giving herself to him. When Imogen rebuffs him angrily, Iachimo quickly apologizes, explaining he was merely testing her with "a false report." He then asks her to keep a trunk carrying presents for the Roman Emperor in the safety of her bedroom.

Away! I do condemn mine ears that have/ So long attended thee… 1.6

ACT TWO

522 lines

BRITAIN AND ROME

Cymbeline's lords are ridiculing Cloten, wondering how so crafty a mother could have borne so foolish a son. Inside the palace, where Imogen sleeps, Iachimo emerges from the trunk stored in her bedroom. He studies the room, then, seeing her half-naked, he yearns to touch her. Instead he takes Posthumus's bracelet off her arm and admires a mole on her left breast before hiding again. Cloten's musicians serenade Imogen, but she tells him that Posthumus's "meanest garment" is more dear to her than Cloten could ever be.

The crickets sing and man's o'er-labour'd sense/ Repairs itself by rest… 2.2

As news reaches Rome that Cymbeline refuses to pay tribute to the emperor, Iachimo returns to inform Posthumus that, "your lady being so easy," he has won their bet. When Posthumus demands proof, Iachimo describes her bedroom, shows off the bracelet and boasts that he has kissed the very mole on her left breast. Enraged by jealousy, Posthumus hands over Imogen's ring and vows vengeance upon her.

Is there no way for men to be, but women/ Must be half-workers?… 2.5

He sits 'mongst men like a descended god./He hath a kind of honour sets him off/ More than a mortal enemy… 1.6

ACT THREE
839 lines

BRITAIN AND ROME

Caius Lucius, a Roman general, demands that Cymbeline pay tribute to Rome, but the queen and Cloten insult him, saying Britain would rather face the emperor's fury. Two letters from Posthumus reach the palace, one ordering Pisanio to kill Imogen, the other telling Imogen to meet her husband in Milford-Haven in Wales. Accompanied by Pisanio, Imogen leaves hurriedly for the rendezvous with Posthumus.

That opportunity/ Which then they had to take from us, to resume/ We have again... 3.1

Outside a cave in the mountains of Wales, the elderly "Morgan" orders his sons to hunt for food. He then muses how, just as he is not 'Morgan' but Lord Belarius, his sons "Polydore" and "Cadwal" are really Guiderius and Arviragus, children of Cymbeline, whom he stole as infants to avenge his banishment from the court.

How hard it is to hide the sparks of nature!... 3.3

When Imogen and Pisanio arrive near Milford-Haven, Pisanio shows her Posthumus's letter accusing her of adultery and ordering her death. Shaken and disbelieving, Imogen challenges Pisanio to kill her, but he refuses, proposing instead that they send Posthumus a bloody handkerchief as proof of her death. Further, he says, she should dress as a boy and travel to Rome where she can observe Posthumus first-hand. Finally, to protect her from seasickness, Pisanio gives her the "medicine" he received from the queen.

False to his bed! What is it to be false?/ To lie in watch there and to think on him?... 3.4

At Cymbeline's palace, Cloten learns that Imogen is meeting Posthumus at Milford-Haven. Dressed in one of Posthumus's garments, Cloten rushes off, vowing to rape Imogen and kill Posthumus. Imogen, now dressed as a boy, is caught eating food in Belarius's cave, but she is welcomed and she gives her name as 'Fidele'.

I see a man's life is a tedious one... 3.6

ACT FOUR
634 lines

BRITAIN

Feeling unwell, Imogen takes Pisanio's "medicine," while Belarius and his "sons" go hunting. Cloten arrives outside the cave and is recognized by Belarius. After insults are exchanged, Cloten draws his sword and disappears in combat with Guiderius. Moments later, Guiderius returns with Cloten's head and then leaves again to drop it in a creek "to tell the fishes he's the queen's son." In the cave, Imogen appears to be dead. Grief-stricken, Guiderius and Arviragus bid their new friend farewell with a melancholy song. With Belarius insisting that Cloten be buried "as a prince." he and his sons leave to dig graves.

Fear no more the heat o' the sun,/Nor the furious winter's rages... 4.2

Imogen awakens to find a headless body beside her. She recognizes Posthumus's garments and faints. When Lucius and his officers arrive, they believe they have found two corpses, but Imogen comes alive. Impressed by the loyalty of the "boy" to "his" fallen master, Lucius invites Imogen to accompany him. In Cymbeline's palace, the queen has fallen ill worrying about Cloten's disappearance. As news arrives that Roman legions have landed, Belarius and his "sons" decide to fight the invaders.

ACT FIVE

951 lines

BRITAIN

Carrying Imogen's bloody handkerchief, a remorseful Posthumus has landed with Roman troops. Convinced they will triumph, he seeks death by dressing like a local peasant and fighting with the British. The two armies meet. At one point, Posthumus disarms Iachimo; at another, Belarius and his "sons" rescue Cymbeline. Nearby, Posthumus recounts the heroism of the trio, then gives himself up to the British armies of King Cymbeline.

Yea, bloody cloth, I'll keep thee, for I wish'd/ Thou shouldst be colour'd thus... 5.1

Close by the battle, ditch'd, and wall'd with turf... 5.3

Awaiting execution, Posthumus is visited by the spirits of his father, mother, and two brothers, who call on Jupiter to save him. Jupiter chastises his supplicants, but promises that Posthumus "shall be lord of lady Imogen." A prison guard comforts Posthumus, who is summoned to the king.

A heavy reckoning for you, sir; but the confort is, you shall be called to no more payments... 5.4

Although ignorant of their true identities, Cymbeline honours Belarius and his "sons" for their courage. The court physician reports that the queen has died after confessing her plan to kill the king and put Cloten on the throne. Lucius and other Roman prisoners are brought in, accompanied by Posthumus and Imogen, both still in disguise and unaware of each other. Belarius and his "sons" recognize "Fidele" while Pisanio sees through Imogen's disguise, but they say nothing. Imogen spots her ring on Iachimo's finger and challenges him. He admits his villainy and praises the nobility of Posthumus.

Upon a time – unhappy was the clock/ That struck the hour!... 5.5

Posthumus confesses his crime and Imogen reassures him that she is alive, but he strikes down the "scornful page." As Pisanio admits that he never killed Imogen, she recovers and is reunited with her husband. Finally, Belarius reveals that he abducted the king's two sons, whom he now returns to their father. Cymbeline forgives him just as Posthumus forgives Iachimo. And to ensure peace, the king announces that Britain will pay its tribute to Rome.

Jupiter descends in thunder and lightning, sitting upon an eagle: he throws a thunderbolt...

STAGE DIRECTION 5.4

READING THE PLAY

COMPARISON OF PROSE TO VERSE

prose: 14% | verse: 86%

WHO'S WHO

Cymbeline is king of Britain. His beautiful and innocent daughter, **Imogen,** has married, unbeknownst to him, his adopted son **Posthumus**, who is banished and flees to Rome. There he meets the evil and manipulative **Iachimo**, who falsely persuades Posthumus that he has seduced Imogen. When Cymbeline's loutish stepson **Cloten** is killed, she mistakenly believes it is Posthumus.

BECAUSE NO SINGLE CHARACTER dominates *Cymbeline*, the play can appear diffuse and confusing. Yet because every scene advances the story, it can be read like a thriller, with many "what next?" moments. The play is also carefully structured so that small incidents in opening scenes later become pivotal: Posthumus and Imogen exchange bracelet and ring; the queen gives Pisanio a "medicine" box; and Imogen tells Cloten he is worth less than Posthumus's "meanest garment".

Yet the narrative also allows room for enjoyment of the language. Shakespeare uses strong sexual metaphors to express the desire that Iachimo and Cloten feel for Imogen, but our heroine's purity is too strong: Iachimo could have raped Imogen, but he dares not; Cloten wants to rape Imogen, but he cannot. When her husband Posthumus doubts her innocence, Imogen is comforted by the simple love expressed by Guiderius and Arviragus. They do not know she is their sister and still believe her to be a boy, yet they respond to her apparent death with verse and song of great beauty.

In many ways, Imogen personifies the soul of Britain as it fights both to overcome the corruption of Cymbeline's court and to resist the foreign decadence represented by the Italian Iachimo. The turning-point comes when she finds the "good" Britain personified by Belarius and his adopted sons hidden in the hills of Wales. In the play's tumultuous final scene, while Shakespeare allows the foreigner Iachimo a fine confession, he gives short shrift to Posthumus's reunion with Imogen. By giving a reformed Cymbeline the last word, Shakespeare seems eager to demonstrate that, after endless trials and tribulations, the monarchy is secure and the country is at peace.

HISTORICAL SOURCES

THE REAL KING CYMBELINE

According to Holinshed, Cymbeline succeeded his father with the approval of Emperor Augustus Caesar and ruled Britain from 33 BC to 2 AD. Holinshed also notes that Cymbeline raised Posthumus Leonatus as his son. The real Cymbeline was succeeded by his sons, Guiderius and Arviragus; their kidnapping by a disgruntled lord is an invention.

The brothers Guiderius and Arviragus grieve over the apparently dead 'Fidele' in an Arthur Rackham illustration from Charles Lamb's *Tales from Shakespeare*, 1909.

SEEING THE PLAY

In a colorfully costumed RSC production of 1997, an elated Iachimo (left) shows a bracelet to Posthumus (right) to "prove" he has seduced Imogen. Posthumus, despondent, declares "Let there be no honour/Where there is beauty; truth where semblance" (2.4).

ON STAGE

IMOGEN

Originally spelled Innogen, echoing "innocent," the name Imogen was the result of a misprint in the *First Folio* of 1623. The role has long been coveted by talented young actresses. Sarah Siddons in the 18th century, Ellen Terry in 1896 at the Lyceum, and Sybil Thorndike, Peggy Ashcroft, Vanessa Redgrave and Judi Dench in the 20th century have all given interpretations of her.

DIRECTORS ARE CHALLENGED to strike a balance between *Cymbeline*'s formal absurdity and its underlying seriousness. George Bernard Shaw was so irritated by the play that, having mocked its ending as "a tedious string of unsurprising denouements with insincere sentimentality after a ludicrous stage battle," he rewrote Act 5 and called it *Cymbeline Refinished.* A more practical approach is to imbue the production with a dream-like atmosphere, turning the play's absurdities into romantic fantasies. This approach enables directors and designers to exploit magic, spectacle, and even technology. The mood of any production, however, depends on how key characters are interpreted. Iachimo, a figure reminiscent of Iago in *Othello,* is unavoidably wicked, but Posthumus, while eventually redeeming himself, is also a victim of his own foolish vanity when he accepts the wager over Imogen's virtue. Both Iachimo and Posthumus are roles sought out by leading actors, but the most popular part is that of Imogen. She can be shown as innocent, beautiful, and passive, but Shakespeare also allows for a stronger, assertive, and resolute Imogen, one who not only stands up to Cymbeline, the queen, Cloten and Iachimo, but who also takes the initiative to solve the puzzle of Posthumus's sudden and inexplicable change of heart.

Sybil Thorndike took on the role of Imogen at the New Theatre in 1923.

Mike Alfreds' production of Cymbeline at Shakespeare's Globe in London in 2001 used just four men and two women, who doubled up to play all the roles. This small cast even portrayed the British and Roman armies who, as Shakespeare instructed, "march over, and go out, then enter again in skirmish" (5.2).

The WINTER'S TALE

THE WINTER'S TALE IS THE ROMANCE PLAY which plunges most deeply into tragedy before veering toward joy and redemption. Although it borrows from Greek tragedies and Ovid's *Metamorphoses*, its principal source is *Pandosto: The Triumph of Time*, a prose pastoral by Robert Greene published in 1588 and reprinted in 1607. Written in 1610–11, its first recorded performance was on May 15, 1611, at the Globe Theatre. Later that year, *The Winter's Tale* was presented at Whitehall before King James I and in 1613 it formed part of celebrations of the marriage of James's daughter, Elizabeth, to the Elector Palatine. After the closure of London's theaters from 1642 to 1660, the play reappeared in adapted form, but since the 19th century, the original text has been regularly staged. Popular today, the play includes Shakespeare's most famous stage direction: "Exit, pursued by a bear."

BEHIND THE PLAY

CASUAL REFERENCES TO BOTH the Delphic oracle and the Russian empire signal the curiously atemporal atmosphere of *The Winter's Tale.* Mundane matters such as time and place have little importance. For instance, while in Greene's version, Pandosto, King of Bohemia, is the jealous tyrant, Shakespeare assigns the role of the paranoid monarch to Leontes, King of Sicily. His reason for doing so may have been political—perhaps Princess Elizabeth was already betrothed to the German prince, or perhaps he believed Sicilians to be more convincingly hot-headed than Bohemians. In any event, Shakespeare showed little concern for geography, allowing a baby princess to be abandoned on the shores of Bohemia, a landlocked country. Similarly, while setting a sheep-shearing feast in Bohemia, Shakespeare borrows its bucolic mood from country fairs in his own Warwickshire. But the main narrative is driven by passion, ignited by Leontes's belief that his wife has committed adultery with his best friend. The play's climax, with the "lost" daughter found and the "dead" spouse coming alive, conforms to the tradition that pastoral romances end with dispersed families reuniting in joy.

A sad tale's best for winter... 2.1

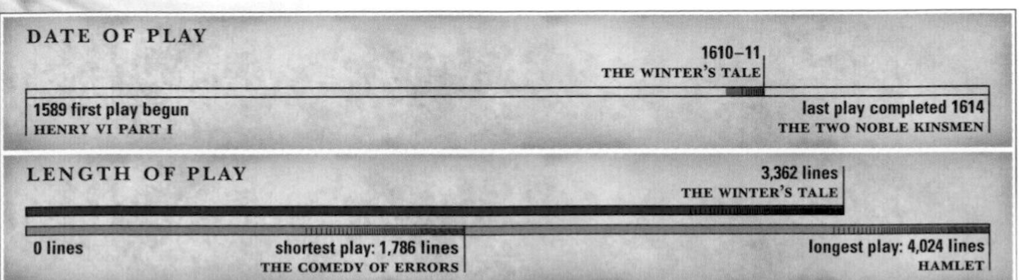

DRAMATIS PERSONAE

LEONTES

692 lines

King of Sicily, he is happily married to Hermione until he suspects that she is carrying the child of his best friend. Gripped by madness, he destroys those dearest to him before Hermione's innocence is asserted by the Delphic oracle.

Leontes (Antony Sher) is overcome with grief.

MAMILLIUS

22 lines

Leontes's young heir, the Prince of Sicily, he dies after his mother is imprisoned.

CAMILLO

299 lines

A Sicilian lord, he refuses Leontes's order to poison Polixenes and flees with him to Bohemia.

ANTIGONUS

112 lines

A loyal Sicilian lord, married to the outspoken Paulina, he is ordered by Leontes to abandon Hermione's baby daughter Perdita on a deserted shoreline; he is then eaten by a bear.

CLEOMENES AND DION

24; 28 lines

Two Sicilian lords, they are sent by Leontes to Apollo's Temple and return with the Delphic judgment that Hermione is innocent.

POLIXENES

273 lines

King of Bohemia, he flees Sicily after Leontes orders his murder for supposedly wooing Hermione; he later tries to stop his son's marriage to Perdita, believing her to be a lowly shepherdess.

FLORIZEL

206 lines

Prince of Bohemia, he adopts the name of Doricles and falls in love with the shepherdess Perdita; his father forbids him from marrying a commoner, but he is vindicated when she is revealed to be a princess.

ARCHIDAMUS

22 lines

Bohemian lord, he goes with Polixenes to Sicily.

AN OLD SHEPHERD

135 lines

A talkative and comic peasant, he finds the baby Perdita abandoned by Antigonus on the Bohemian shore and raises her as his daughter; he blesses her betrothal to Florizel and is rewarded by Leontes when she is found to be a princess.

CLOWN

184 lines

The shepherd's son, he witnesses the bear's attack on Antigonus and is later robbed by the roguish thief Autolycus.

AUTOLYCUS

294 lines

A charming rascal, he peddles what he steals and charms everyone with beautiful ballads.

HERMIONE

211 lines

Leontes's queen, a charming and loyal wife, her life seemingly ends when she is wrongly accused by her husband of adultery with Polixenes.

PERDITA

131 lines

Abandoned in Bohemia as a baby, the princess of Sicily is raised by the Old Shepherd and falls in love with Florizel.

PAULINA

340 lines

The wife of Antigonus, she bravely denounces Leontes as a tyrant and looks after the queen for 16 years; she then unveils the statue of Hermione and presides over her "return" to life.

EMILIA

21 lines

Attendant to Hermione.

The shepherdess Perdita (Inga Swenson) and the disguised prince Florizel (Richard Easton) fall in love.

MOPSA AND DORCAS

20; 12 lines

Shepherdesses who sing at the sheep-shearing fair.

OTHER PLAYERS

Chorus (as Time), Lords, Ladies, Gentlemen, Mariner, Jailer, Servants, Officers, Shepherds, and Shepherdesses.

Paulina (Jessie Royce Landis) presents the living statue of Hermione (Florence Reed) to an anxious Leontes (Henry Daniell).

PLOT SUMMARY

SIZE OF ACTS

ACT 1	ACT 2	ACT 3	ACT 4	ACT 5
584 lines	566 lines	434 lines	1142 lines	636 lines

ACT ONE
584 lines

THE ROYAL PALACE IN SICILY

Polixenes, King of Bohemia, is ending a nine-month visit to his childhood friend Leontes, King of Sicily. Leontes begs him not to leave and urges Hermione, his pregnant queen, to convince Polixenes to change his mind. When she good-naturedly orders the Bohemian to stay another week, he readily agrees. Leontes is disturbed that Polixenes ignored his appeal, yet heeded Hermione's words—words, he notes darkly, spoken as gracefully as when, many years earlier, she had told Leontes himself, "I am yours forever." Then, as Hermione affectionately offers her hand to Polixenes, Leontes is suddenly transformed by jealousy.

Too hot, too hot!/ To mingle friendship far is mingling bloods... 1.2

Mamillius, Leontes's young son, arrives, but Leontes's eyes are fixed on Hermione and Polixenes, their every smile and gesture further convincing him that he has been betrayed. Leontes reveals his wife's infidelity to Camillo, a trusted Sicilian lord, and orders him to poison Polixenes. Though Camillo doubts that Hermione has been unfaithful, he agrees to kill Polixenes on condition that the queen be forgiven. But when questioned by Polixenes about Leontes's strange behavior, Camillo confides that he has orders to murder the Bohemian for touching Hermione "forbiddenly." Shaken and offended, Polixenes insists on his innocence. Camillo urges him to leave Sicily immediately and begs his protection.

To your own bents dispose you: you'll be found,/ Be you beneath the sky... 1.2

Is whispering nothing?/ Is leaning cheek to cheek? Is meeting noses?... 1.2

ACT TWO
566 lines

THE ROYAL PALACE IN SICILY

As Mamillius prepares to tell his mother a story, noting that "a sad tale's best for winter," Leontes learns that Polixenes and Camillo have fled Sicily, thus confirming his suspicions. Ordering that

Sir, spare your threats!/ The bug which you would fright me with I seek... 3.2

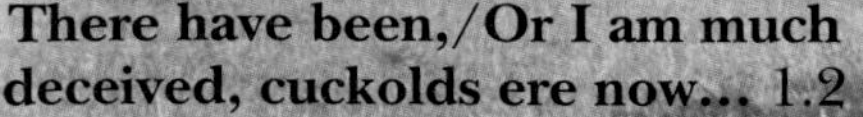

There have been,/Or I am much deceived, cuckolds ere now... 1.2

Mamillius be kept away from his mother, Leontes turns on Hermione, accusing her of carrying Polixenes's child. She swears this is not true, but Leontes, as if possessed, continues ranting, calling her an adulteress and traitor, then ordering her imprisonment. He brushes away protestations from Antigonus and other Sicilian lords, although he admits he has sent two envoys, Cleomenes and Dion, to consult the Delphic oracle at the temple of Apollo.

Paulina, Antigonus's strong-willed wife and Hermione's closest friend, hears that the queen has given birth to a daughter. Hoping to soften the king's heart, she seeks his blessing for the baby. Leontes, already alarmed that Mamillius has taken ill, is enraged by Paulina's visit and accuses her of baiting him with "the issue of Polixenes." Paulina responds courageously, telling the king that his behavior smacks of tyranny. Stunned, Leontes blames Antigonus for her outburst. The old man denies encouraging her, but vows to do everything to save the "innocent" child. Leontes orders him to abandon the baby in "some remote and desert place, quite out of our dominions." As Antigonus leaves with the child, Cleomenes and Dion bring word from the Temple of Apollo.

It is yours;/And, might we lay th'old proverb to your charge,/So like you... 2.3

ACT THREE

434 lines

A COURT OF JUSTICE IN SICILY AND THE COAST OF BOHEMIA

Leontes summons Hermione to hear the indictment accusing her of adultery. She proclaims her innocence and responds that her love for Polixenes was "as yourself commanded." Having lost her crown, her son and her baby daughter, she says, she does not fear death, but she swears that the oracle will vouch for her virtue. Cleomenes and Dion deliver the sealed letter from the Delphic oracle, which is read aloud: "Hermione is chaste; Polixenes blameless; Camillo a true subject; Leontes a jealous tyrant; his innocent babe truly begotten; and the king shall live without an heir, if that which is lost be not found."

Sir, spare your threats!/The bug which you would fright me with I seek... 3.2

Furious, Leontes denounces the oracle, but he is interrupted by word that Mamillius has died. Hermione faints and is carried away. Suddenly, Leontes becomes aware of Apollo's wrath as well as his own irrational folly. Paulina then brings word that Hermione is also dead. Distraught and repentant, Leontes vows to mourn his queen and their son for the rest of his days.

Apollo, pardon/My great profaneness 'gainst thine oracle!... 3.2

On the stormy shores of Bohemia, Antigonus has landed with his tiny charge and, as he prepares to desert her, he recalls a dream in which Hermione chastises him as the "thrower-out" of the baby Perdita and warns him that he will never again see his wife. Still believing

Perdita to be Polixenes's child, Antigonus thinks he has acted properly in leaving the baby "upon the earth of its right father." He hears the sound of a hunt and a bear chases him. The Old Shepherd discovers the baby, while his son, Clown, reports that the bear has "half-dined" on Antigonus. They celebrate the jewels found with the changeling as "fairy gold" and, in gratitude, they promise to bury what is left of Antigonus.

ACT FOUR

1142 lines

THE ROYAL PALACE IN BOHEMIA, THE COUNTRYSIDE, AND A SHEEP-SHEARING FEAST NEAR A SHEPHERD'S COTTAGE

Time, as played by Chorus, announces the passage of 16 years. Leontes is still grieving, but Perdita and Florizel, Polixenes's son, are now in love. In the palace, Polixenes and Camillo speculate about Florizel's fondness for the daughter of the Old Shepherd. On a country road, Autolycus, a peddler, rascal and minstrel, is singing the joys of spring and the delights of his profession, when Clown appears on his way to a sheep-shearing feast. Autolycus promptly pickpockets Clown's purse. Outside the shepherd's cottage, Perdita and Florizel appear in costumes, Perdita dressed as a goddess and Florizel as a peasant. Florizel, who has adopted the name "Doricles," recalls that his falcon's flight led him to Perdita, but she predicts that one day the king will separate them.

When daffodils begin to peer,/With heigh, the doxy over the dale... 4.1

The sheep-shearing feast draws a large crowd of locals as well as Polixenes and Camillo in disguise. Ordered to play hostess, Perdita gives flowers to Polixenes who, while charmed, warns that noblemen should not marry beneath their rank. The love-struck Florizel assures Perdita that her every act is that of a queen and even Polixenes senses that Perdita is "too noble for this place." As the young lovers join the dance, the king interrogates the Old Shepherd, who tells of the love of "Doricles"—in reality, Florizel—for his daughter. Autolycus arrives with more songs as well as trinkets and ballad sheets to sell. As the merriment grows, Florizel and

Perdita (Phyllida Hancock) hands out flowers at the sheep-shearing feast in an RSC production from 1992.

Say there be;/But Nature is made better by no mean/ But Nature makes that mean... 4.4

Lawn as white as driven snow;/Cypress black as e'er was crow... 4.4

Daffodils,/That come before the swallow dares, and take/ The winds of March with beauty; violets, dim,/ But sweeter than the lids of Juno's eyes... 4.4

Perdita ask the Old Shepherd to marry them. Still in disguise, Polixenes questions "Doricles" about his father. When Florizel brushes away the question, the king reveals himself and threatens to disinherit his son.

Mark your divorce, young sir,/Whom son I dare not call… 4.4

With Polixenes gone, Camillo urges Florizel to make peace with his father, but the young prince refuses. Even as Perdita recalls her fateful prediction, Florizel announces that he will renounce his succession and, together, they will leave Bohemia by ship. Camillo tells Florizel to go to Sicily and pretend he is sent by his father to make peace with Leontes. Florizel enthusiastically accepts Camillo's plan and exchanges his garments with Autolycus to disguise his flight with Perdita. The Old Shepherd, worried that the king will punish him, is persuaded by Clown to tell the king that Perdita is a changeling and to show her jewelry as proof. Autolycus meets the pair as they hike to the palace and fools them into giving him gold. The rascal then rushes off to join Florizel.

ACT FIVE

636 lines

THE ROYAL PALACE IN SICILY

Cleomenes and Dion tell the king that he has mourned enough and should now find a wife to ensure the succession, but Paulina warns him that no one can replace Hermione. Leontes pledges never to marry without Paulina's approval. Florizel and Perdita arrive at the palace and Leontes is deeply moved by Polixenes's message of love and forgiveness. Polixenes's own arrival in Sicily is then announced. Outside the palace, news quickly spreads that, after Perdita's true identity was revealed to Leontes, father and lost daughter have at last been reunited.

There is none worthy,/ Respecting her that's gone… 5.1

Leontes and his Bohemian guests gather at the chapel in Paulina's house to admire what they believe is the statue of Hermione. Paulina warns them that the queen looks lifelike and Leontes even sees wrinkles that did not exist 16 years earlier. He wants to kiss the figure, but Paulina stops him, preparing him instead for "more amazement." She then orders the "statue" to descend. In what appears to be a miracle, Hermione comes to life and embraces Leontes before learning with joy that Perdita is alive. Paulina celebrates "you precious winners all," but adds that she will forever lament her lost Antigonus. But Leontes steps forward and offers Camillo as her new husband-to-be.

Music, awake her, strike!/'Tis time: descend; be stone no more… 5.3

Still methinks/There is an air comes from her. What fine chisel/ Could ever yet cut breath? Let no man mock me,/ For I will kiss her… 5.3

READING THE PLAY

COMPARISON OF PROSE TO VERSE

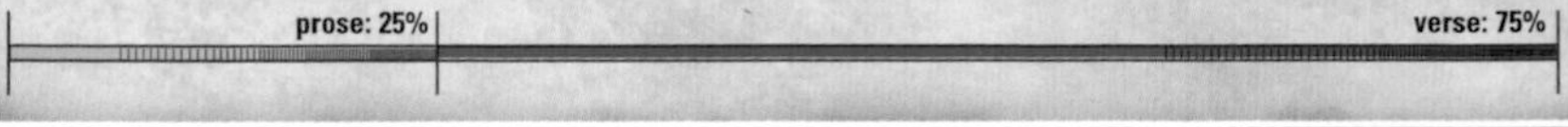

prose: 25% | verse: 75%

WHO'S WHO

Leontes is King of Sicily, and is married to **Hermione**. He believes, erroneously, that Hermione is carrying the child of **Polixenes,** his best friend, King of Bohemia, who flees Leontes's wrath. Polixenes's son, **Florizel**, falls in love some 16 years later with **Perdita**, Hermione's child, who was abandoned on a distant shore when her mother was accused of adultery.

Jealousy is the subject of *The Winter's Tale*. But unlike the Moor in *Othello* and Posthumus in *Cymbeline*, whose minds are manipulated by the evil schemers Iago and Iachimo, Leontes serves up his own poison. And from the moment he takes it, his language shows the venom at work, first as he misinterprets his wife's innocent warmth toward Polixenes, then as he persuades himself of her adultery, and finally as he steps toward murder. Paulina and Camillo are voices of reason, but they are drowned out by Leontes's manic tirades.

Once Leontes has done his worst and has become paralyzed by remorse, Shakespeare changes mood. In a gesture of theatrical bravura, at the beginning of Act 4 Time announces the passage of 16 years in 16 rhyming couplets. The break in time is further underlined by a medley of words contrasting present and past: joy/terror; good/bad; and fresh/stale. The entire second half of the play is suffused with humor, music, and young love. Winter is over and spring brings light (and the mischievous Autolycus). Of Leontes's two surviving victims, Shakespeare chooses to focus on Hermione, the source of Leontes's unfounded jealousy. By having Hermione appear to return to life and forgive Leontes, Shakespeare completes the circle of his tale and provides the family reunion typical of a romance.

PLAY HISTORY

FLORIZEL AND PERDITA

After a checkered post-Restoration history, John Philip Kemble restored most of Shakespeare's text in 1702. In the mid-18th century David Garrick shrunk the first three acts into a 150-line Prologue and presented the rest as the love story of *Florizel and Perdita*. Once *The Winter's Tale* had been renamed a romance, its life-death-resurrection cycle was better understood.

"Thou met'st with things dying, I with things new-born" (3.3). The famous rescue of baby Perdita on the "shores of Bohemia" has even been used to decorate a label for German meat extract.

SEEING THE PLAY

ON STAGE

FAMOUS PRODUCTIONS

There have been many memorable productions of *The Winter's Tale* since the 19th century. In the 1820s, William Charles Macready was a popular Leontes. In 1912, Harley Granville-Barker's staged a "post-impressionist" version of the play, which relied on the poetic language to achieve credibility. Acclaimed modern directors of the play include Peter Brook (1951) and Nicholas Hytner (2001).

AN EMOTIONAL ROLLER COASTER, *The Winter's Tale* dives into anger and bitterness before rising to love and redemption. Shakespeare displays his mastery of the stage when the jealousy, tyranny, and death of the first three acts give way to the love, music, and rebirth of the last two acts, complete with new characters and a pastoral scene. Such timeless emotions are encouraged by the play's purposefully vague setting in time or place. In fact, the only scene that requires definition is the sheep-shearing feast. Here, seemingly tired of portraying medieval English fairs, modern directors have variously turned the scene into a hippie jamboree, a rock festival, and a country-and-western gathering (each with appropriate music).

More crucial to a successful production, however, is casting. Leontes must seem credible when, almost inexplicably, he is unbalanced by jealousy. Unpleasant as he is as a tyrant, he must evoke sympathy when he later repents—"I have deserved/All tongues to talk their bitt'rest." The other pivotal roles are Paulina, the queen's lady-in-waiting who alone dares challenge Leontes, and Autolycus, whose mischief and songs enliven the sheep-shearing feast. Hermione and her daughter, Perdita, are popular roles for regal young actresses (on one occasion, the same actress played both parts). But they are not complex characters. Polixenes too is somewhat unidimensional, albeit something of a snob in vetoing his son's marriage to a mere commoner.

Finally, the staging of this play offers two famous challenges: how to depict the bear that chases Antigonus off stage and how to portray the "statue' of Hermione that comes alive. If handled badly, they provoke laughter rather than surprise.

ON STAGE

A LITERAL TRANSLATION

In a Swedish-language production of *The Winter's Tale* for Stockholm's Royal Dramaten Theater in 1995, the stage and screen director Ingmar Bergman interpreted the play's title literally. Inspired by Mamillius's remark that "a sad tale's best for winter," he set it in a 19th-century Swedish country mansion in the depth of winter and presented the play as after-dinner entertainment for bourgeois guests.

The Clown, Autolycus, Mopsa, and Dorcas lighten the mood of Bergman's Nordic production.

Though Hermione and Polixenes are faithful to their spouses in Bergman's production they seemed outrageous flirts.

BEYOND THE PLAY

Leontes (Alex Jennings) shares a moment with his short-lived son Mamillius (Thomas Brown-Lowe) in Nicholas Hytner's very modern version of Shakespeare's play staged by the Royal National Theatre, London, in 2001.

LONG HAUNTED BY its hybrid nature, *The Winter's Tale* is a tragic story that was listed in the *First Folio* as a comedy and was later labeled a romance. Its melodrama, music and magic ensured its popularity with Jacobean audiences and it was performed at the Globe long after Shakespeare's death. But by the 1660s the play was abandoned. In 1672, John Dryden said it was "so meanly written, that the Comedy neither caus'd your mirth, nor the serious part your concernment." Even after the original play's revival in the 19th century, the problem of defining the play was not settled. Writing in 1868, Victor Hugo said it was "one of the most serious and profound dramas of the poet." And he added: "*The Winter's Tale* is no comedy; it is a tragedy."

To this day, some theatergoers remain unconvinced by Leontes's irrational, almost psychotic jealousy. Others are still troubled by the play's split personality: half bitter, half sweet. Yet *The Winter's Tale* has gradually secured its place on the stage. Harley Granville-Barker's 1912 London production was hailed for emphasizing its poetic beauty. Peter Brook's 1951 London production, with John Gielgud as Leontes and Flora Robson as Paulina, was acclaimed for bringing clarity to a mongrel play, while Ian McKellen, Jeremy Irons, Antony Sher, and Alex Jennings have all been persuasive in the testing role of Leontes.

On the screen, starting with Barry O'Neil's silent *Winter's Tale* in 1910, the play has fared poorly. The intrinsic absurdity of the story clashes with the reality of film. The BBC adapted it for television in 1961, with Robert Shaw as Leontes, and in 1981, with Jeremy Kemp as the Sicilian king.

Miss Ellen Terry's first appearance in 1856.

PLAYER PROFILE

ELLEN TERRY

In 1856, Charles Kean set the play in 4th-century BC Syracuse with all the pageantry loved by Victorian audiences. Ellen Terry, just nine at the time, played Mamillius; 50 years later, she returned to the play as Hermione. That year, 1906, she celebrated her golden jubilee at the Theatre Royal, Drury Lane.

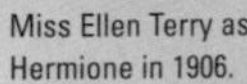

Miss Ellen Terry as Hermione in 1906.

The TEMPEST

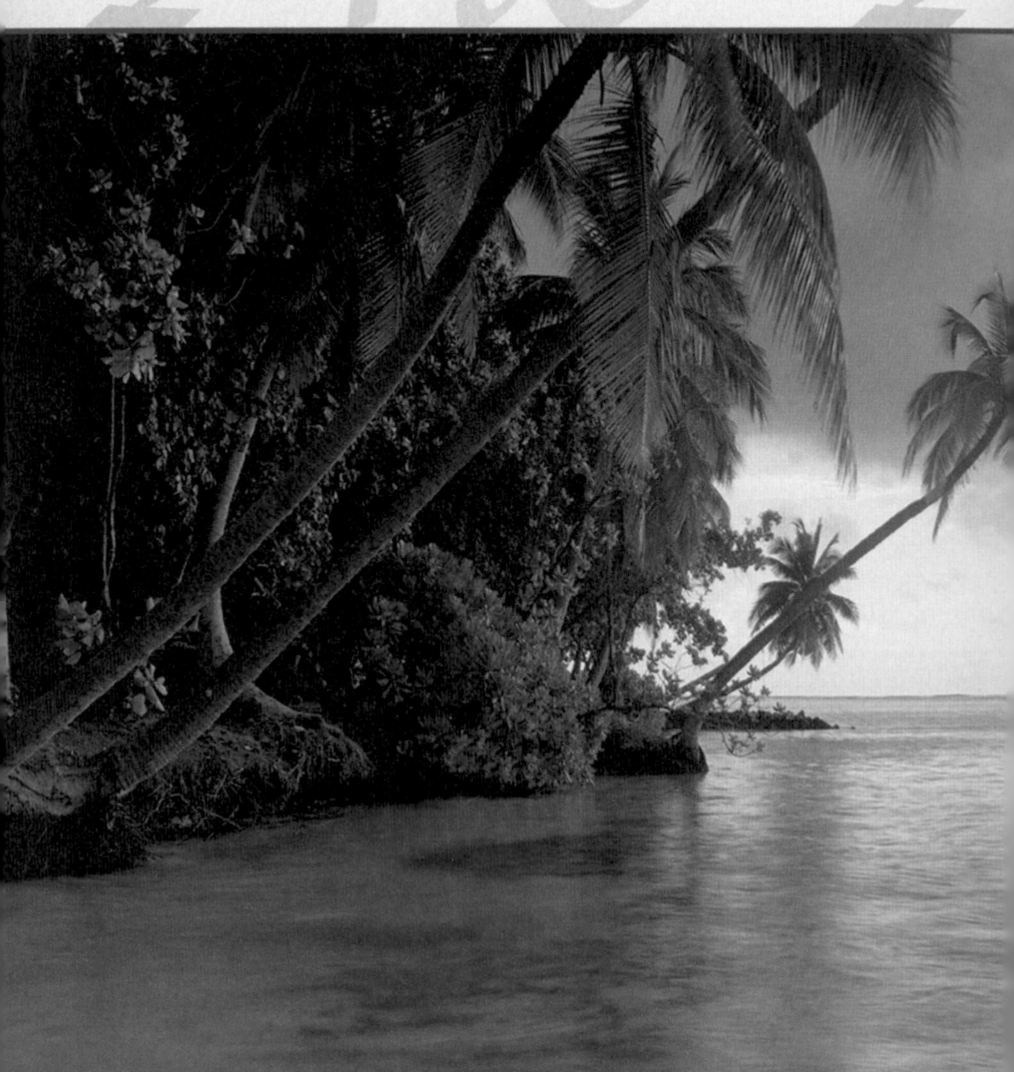

THE TEMPEST IS THE LAST PLAY attributed exclusively to Shakespeare. Written in 1611 and first performed in November that year before King James at Whitehall, it remains one of the playwright's most popular works. Often presented as a visual spectacular of magic, song, dance, and masque, it has also served as an allegory for every imaginable political and psychological situation. The sources for *The Tempest* are not known and what Shakespeare had in mind is an enigma. One view is that, about to retire, he uses the magician Prospero to reflect on his own life as a poet and playwright—in the Epilogue Prospero claims that his "art to enchant" has come to an end. But *The Tempest* speaks with fresh purpose to every age. In Shakespeare's day, it echoed popular belief in witchcraft, excitement at the discovery of exotic new lands, and disapproval of usurpation of power.

BEHIND THE PLAY

THE ACTION TAKES PLACE almost entirely on an island that evokes fantasies of paradise and political utopia. The island resembles an idealized New World colony of Shakespeare's era, a powerful realm of the imaginary, much like the theater itself. King Alonso, his heir Ferdinand, and members of the court of Naples are returning home by ship from Tunis, where they have attended the marriage of Alonso's daughter to the King of Tunis. Also on board is Antonio, the usurper Duke of Milan who 12 years earlier ousted his reclusive but popular brother, Prospero. Prospero and his baby daughter were left to die on a leaking boat, but instead ended up on a tiny tropical island. They found the island had been settled by Sycorax, a witch banished from Algiers who had already died but whose evil influence lived on. The spirit Ariel, who had been imprisoned for refusing to obey her, somehow remained her captive, while her monster-son, Caliban, still wandered the island, claiming to be her heir. When Prospero and Miranda land, the magician quickly asserts his power, turning Ariel and Caliban into his subjects. Now, learning that Alonso's fleet is sailing nearby, Prospero prepares his revenge.

We are such stuff/ As dreams are made on; and our little life/ Is rounded with a sleep... 4.1

DATE OF PLAY

1611 THE TEMPEST

1589 first play begun HENRY VI, PART I

last play completed 1614 THE TWO NOBLE KINSMEN

LENGTH OF PLAY

2,275 lines THE TEMPEST

0 lines

shortest play: 1,786 lines THE COMEDY OF ERRORS

longest play: 4,024 lines HAMLET

DRAMATIS PERSONAE

ALONSO

109 lines

King of Naples, he allowed Antonio to usurp the title of Duke of Milan, and presumes Prospero to have died at sea.

SEBASTIAN

120 lines

Brother of Alonso, lazy and suggestible, he is persuaded by Antonio to try to kill Alonso and become King of Naples.

PROSPERO

674 lines

The rightful Duke of Milan, put to sea in a tiny boat by his brother Antonio, he makes good use of his magic on the island where he and Miranda are shipwrecked; he grabs the chance to avenge his humiliation.

Prospero (Derek Jacobi) is a powerful magician who in the end gives up magic to regain his dukedom.

ANTONIO

148 lines

Usurper of Prospero's title as Duke of Milan, he hopes Sebastian will follow his example by killing his own brother, Alonso.

FERDINAND

140 lines

Son of Alonso and Prince of Naples, he falls in love with Prospero's daughter, Miranda, whom he gallantly woos while he is Prospero's prisoner; Prospero then approves their match.

GONZALO

161 lines

Honest old councilor in the court of King Alonso, he allowed Prospero to take his books into exile; Prospero remembers him with affection and does not take revenge on him.

ADRIAN AND FRANCISCO

12; 11 lines

Lords of Alonso's court.

CALIBAN

175 lines

Savage, deformed, but eloquent slave, he is the son of the dead witch Sycorax; taught to speak by Miranda, he is made captive on the island by Prospero after he attempts to rape the girl, but finds a new master in Alonso's alcoholic butler, Stephano.

TRINCULO

105 lines

Witty jester, he forms a clown-like trio with Caliban and Stephano to overthrow Prospero.

STEPHANO

163 lines

Alonso's butler, he introduces Caliban to the pleasures and pitfalls of liquor.

MIRANDA

142 lines

Daughter of Prospero, she falls in love with Ferdinand; she epitomizes Shakespearean Romantic heroines when she comments, "How beauteous mankind is!"

Miranda (Toyah Willcox) and Ferdinand (David Meyer) fall in love in Derek Jarman's highly stylized film version of 1980.

ARIEL

194 lines

Spirit once enslaved to Caliban's late mother, the "foul witch Sycorax," he is subsequently liberated by Prospero and becomes the "industrious servant" of his new master; he wins his freedom by helping Prospero to humiliate his enemies.

IRIS, CERES, AND JUNO

41; 24; 7 lines

They are characters in a masque, played by Ariel and other spirits.

OTHER PLAYERS

Master of a ship, Boatswain, Mariners, Nymphs, Reapers, and other Spirits in the service of Prospero.

Caliban (Robert Glenister) bitterly resents being a servant to Prospero.

PLOT SUMMARY

SIZE OF ACTS

ACT 1	ACT 2	ACT 3	ACT 4	ACT 5
659 lines	555 lines	393 lines	287 lines	381 lines

ACT ONE

659 lines

ON A SHIP IN A STORM AND ON AN ISLAND BEFORE PROSPERO'S CELL

A ship carrying King Alonso of Naples and his court is caught in a fierce storm and looks set to sink. On a nearby island, Prospero the magician is delighted, but his daughter, Miranda, is upset by his reaction. He finally reveals to her that he was once Duke of Milan and that, more interested in books than power, he allowed his greedy brother, Antonio, to govern in his name. But Antonio conspired with Alonso to replace him as Duke of Milan. Prospero was too popular to be murdered, so he and Miranda were set adrift on a leaking boat which brought them to the island. Now, Prospero explains, with Alonso's fleet nearby, he has ordered Ariel, his slave spirit, to conjure up a storm. His enemies are at last at his mercy.

'Tis time/I should inform thee farther. Lend thy hand,/And pluck my magic garment from me... 1.2

Ariel reports the ship is safe and its passengers alive, whilst the rest of the fleet returns to Naples, believing Alonso and his son, Ferdinand, to have perished. Having again proved his worth, Ariel reminds Prospero of his promise to free him, but the old sorcerer is in irritable mood. When he arrived on the island, he recalls, Ariel was still enslaved to Sycorax, even though the hag-witch had already died. But he will keep his word if Ariel follows orders. Sycorax's monster son, Caliban, curses the day he was turned into a slave on his own island, but Prospero notes that Caliban was treated "with human care" until he tried to rape Miranda.

I must eat my dinner./ This island's mine, by Sycorax my mother... 1.2

By accident most strange, bountiful Fortune,/Now my dear lady, hath mine enemies/Brought to this shore... 1.2

Eager to please, Ariel returns with Alonso's son Ferdinand in tow. Ariel is invisible to all but Prospero, but Ferdinand follows the spirit's song and is led to Miranda. It is love at first sight. Miranda cannot remember seeing a man other than her wizened father and the deformed Caliban. Ferdinand, no less infatuated, promises to make her Queen of Naples. But Prospero's game has only just begun. He declares Ferdinand his prisoner and, when the young prince resists, he uses magic to immobilize him. Miranda protests, but Ferdinand is consoled that he can see his new love.

Come unto these yellow sands,/And then take hands... 1.2

Elsewhere on the island, Trinculo, the court jester, meets Caliban and is horrified by his appearance. They are joined by Stephano, Alonso's drunken butler who boasts rescuing wine from the king's flagship. Caliban is fed some liquor, which immediately goes to his head. He proclaims Stephano to be a god and kisses his feet. Seeing a chance to be free of "the tyrant I serve," Caliban offers to show Stephano and Trinculo the island. Stephano, believing Alonso to be dead, imagines himself as King Stephano. The dissolute trio then set off to explore the magical island.

Here's neither bush nor shrub, to bear off any weather at all, and another storm brewing... 2.2

ACT TWO

555 lines

THREE DISPERSED LOCATIONS ON THE ISLAND

Having swum ashore with his courtiers, Alonso is distraught over the apparent loss of his son. A lord tells him that he saw Ferdinand swimming to safety, but Alonso is unconvinced. Sebastian, Alonso's brother, and Antonio, the usurper Duke of Milan, make light of the shipwreck. When Gonzalo, a decent old nobleman, imagines ruling a paradise island, they taunt him. Invisible to the group, Ariel plays music that puts all but Sebastian and Antonio to sleep. As the two men observe the sleeping king, Antonio encourages Sebastian to kill his brother so that he can assume the throne of Naples. But Ariel sings in Gonzalo's ear and the group awakes before the villains can act.

I'th'commonwealth I would by contraries/ Execute all things... 2.1

What have we here? A man or a fish? Dead or alive? A fish! He smells like a fish; a very ancient and fish-like smell... 2.2

ACT THREE

393 lines

TWO DISPERSED LOCATIONS ON THE ISLAND

Put to work by Prospero, Ferdinand is carrying logs and dreaming of Miranda. With Prospero watching secretly from afar, Miranda joins the young man, telling him to rest and offering to do his work. Thinking they are alone, they declare their love for each other and exchange vows of marriage. Seeing Miranda both happy and tearful, Prospero is touched by this "Fair encounter/of two most rare affections," but he still has much to do.

There be some sports are painful, and their labour/ Delight in them sets off... 3.1

As Stephano, Trinculo and Caliban stagger drunkenly around the island, the invisible Ariel adds to their confusion by imitating their voices and rousing them to blows. Caliban reveals that Prospero's magic power will vanish if his books are destroyed. Prospero could then be killed and the beautiful Miranda taken by Stephano as a wife and queen. The ever-alert Ariel has much to report back to his master, Prospero.

Be not afeard; the isle is full of noises,/Sounds, and sweet airs, that give delight and hurt not... 3.2

In another part of the island, Alonso, Sebastian, Antonio and the others are hungry and exhausted. To torture them, Prospero summons strange shapes who appear before them and invite them to a banquet. But Ariel, in the guise of a harpy, claps his wings and the banquet disappears. With Prospero present but invisible to the nobles, Ariel chastises the group for chasing Prospero from Milan and explains that the storm was Nature's punishment.

You are three men of sin, whom destiny – / That hath to instrument this lower world… 3.3

When Ariel vanishes, Alonso, Sebastian, and Antonio are so shaken that Gonzalo sees it as a measure of their "great guilt."

ACT FOUR

287 lines

BEFORE PROSPERO'S CELL

Prospero summons Ferdinand from his cell and offers him Miranda's hand, but insists they remain chaste until their wedding day. Ferdinand modestly agrees. Delighted by the love match, Prospero organizes a masque, or pageant, to celebrate, with an array of spirits acting out the roles of Iris, Ceres, Juno, nymphs and reapers, amid much song and dancing.

If I have too austerely punished you,/ Your compensation makes amends… 4.1

The festivities end abruptly when Prospero remembers Stephano, Trinculo and Caliban. Telling Ferdinand and Miranda to hide, he orders Ariel to bring the trio to him. Wet from falling into a horse pond and drunker than ever, they can see neither Prospero nor Ariel. Arguing among themselves, they notice lavish garments laid out by Ariel which they promptly put on. Prospero responds by releasing spirits in the form of snarling hounds, which give chase to the terrorized men.

You do look, my son, in a moved sort,/As if you were dismayed… 4.1

ACT FIVE

381 lines

BEFORE PROSPERO'S CELL

Prospero has now made all of the preparations necessary to complete his magician's turn. As he stands before his cell in his magic robes, Ariel reports that King Alonso and his court are full of remorse for their past actions. Moved by the spirit's gentle words, Prospero decides to favour virtue over vengeance. Sending for Alonso and the nobles, he draws a magic circle on the ground. Alonso and his followers enter the circle and find themselves trapped inside it. One by one, Prospero reproaches them for their

Now does my project gather to a head./My charms crack not, my spirits obey… 5.1

Ye elves of hills, brooks, standing lakes, and groves… 5.1

treachery and then forgives them. Only the good Gonzalo escapes his fury. But the king and nobles have still not recognized their captor. Finally Prospero casts off his magic robes and orders Ariel to dress him in the finery of the "wronged" Duke of Milan.

Alonso and his courtiers are amazed to find Prospero still alive. Realizing he now has a good reason to beg for forgiveness, Alonso hurriedly restores Prospero to his title of Duke of Milan. Savoring the moment, Prospero says that, just as Alonso has lost a son, he has lost a daughter. He then explains why. With a theatrical flourish, he reveals Ferdinand playing chess in the cell with Miranda. Alonso is joyfully reunited with his son, who announces that he is to marry Miranda. Gonzalo realizes excitedly that a descendant of the ousted Duke of Milan will one day become the King of Naples.

As the king's flagship is readied to sail, Ariel presents Stephano, Trinculo, and Caliban. Prospero mocks them for plotting to kill him, but pardons them. Suddenly repentant, Caliban pledges he will be "wise hereafter,/And seek for grace." Prospero invites the king and his court to spend the night in his cell before they all return to Naples to prepare the marriage of Ferdinand and Miranda. Prospero orders Ariel to provide calm seas and strong winds for the journey and then frees his ever-loyal slave spirit.

Left alone, having renounced his magic, Prospero turns to the audience and asks for the applause "of your good hands" to set him free, "or else my project fails/ Which was to please".

Now my charms are all o'erthrown,/And what strength I have's mine own... 5.1

How many goodly creatures are there here!/How beauteous mankind is! O brave new world,/That has such people in't!... 5.1

READING THE PLAY

COMPARISON OF PROSE TO VERSE

prose: 21% verse: 79%

Miranda and Prospero confront Caliban, observed by Ariel, in a 19th century engraving after a painting by Henry Fuseli.

THIS SHORT PLAY presents few problems for readers because plot developments are constantly anticipated by the main protagonists, Ariel and Prospero. Yet, below the cheerful spirits, comic silliness and sweet love talk, a dark disturbance underpins the play. Specifically, the half-hidden story of Caliban's mother, the witch Sycorax, haunts the action from the outset. Although now pleasingly enchanted, the island was once a terrifying place where unspeakably "abhorred" deeds were carried out. That former savagery is never far away from *The Tempest.* Indeed, the island's dark power is always greater than that of Prospero's enemies, who never understand that their every move is controlled by an outside force. The stereotype of Prospero as a sanitized Merlin-the-Magician figure is therefore misleading. He is much more than that, if only because he harbors a powerful need for revenge. Neither simple nor purely good, he is strongly linked to the themes of darkness, enslavement, and anger that initially seem associated exclusively with Caliban. Thus, while raw emotional power moves us and the island enchants us, the magic of *The Tempest* is that it also unsettles us. Little wonder that, at the end of the play, even Prospero begs release from the island.

HISTORICAL SOURCES

THE NEW WORLD

With Spain already colonising the Americas, England's own imperial ambitions were also stirring. In the 1580s, Sir Walter Raleigh had attempted to found an English colony at Roanoke in Virginia. Further excitement was fuelled by a 1610 account of sailors shipwrecked on the "enchanted" island of Bermuda. *The Tempest* evokes the mystery of this new period of exploration.

WHO'S WHO

Sycorax, a witch who ruled the island, is now dead. Her son **Caliban**, a deformed savage, has been imprisoned by the embittered **Prospero**, the rightful duke of Milan, whose position has been usurped by his brother Antonio. He has been exiled by **Alonso**, the King of Naples, who is shipwrecked on Prospero's island with his son **Ferdinand**, the prince of Naples, who falls in love with **Miranda**, Prospero's daughter. **Ariel**, a former slave of Sycorax, is Prospero's industrious servant.

SEEING THE PLAY

"I am subject to a tyrant, a sorcerer, that by his cunning hath cheated me of the island" (3.2). Caliban (Jasper Britton) rails against Prospero in a production at Shakespeare's Globe, London, in 2000.

ON STAGE

MAKING ARIEL FLY
Even the earliest productions made a point of putting Ariel to flight, precariously attached to an assortment of wires. But the great Italian director, Giorgio Strehler, turned this rustic technology into a pun to illustrate Ariel's fate. In his 1978 production of *The Tempest,* the cable that lifted Ariel was also the rope that imprisoned the spirit. Ariel could fly, but not fly away.

THIS PLAY SHOULD BE A DELIGHT to attend and, unsurprisingly, stage directors and actors usually enjoy it as much as audiences. The opening tempest and the cavorting spirits call for imaginative special effects. The large number of songs keeps the mood light. And the trio of Caliban, Stephano, and Trinculo provide constant humor. Prospero is usually played by older and experienced actors who can convey the full depth of the magician's desire for revenge and his eventual embrace of forgiveness. Ariel and Caliban, representing air and earth respectively, are also challenging roles (women often now play Ariel). But Shakespeare has more in mind than pure entertainment, weaving in other messages—about love, treachery, enslavement, freedom, and mercy—that make the play ever topical. In the post-colonial era, for instance, it has become fashionable to present Caliban not as a vile monster, but as a victim of oppression. More timelessly, Caliban can be portrayed as someone who is trapped by "original sin" inherited from his witch mother but who can nonetheless be saved when Prospero chooses forgiveness over revenge. In the romance tradition, the Epilogue serves as a reminder that we have been watching a tale unfold. Prospero's final words, though, are most significant because they seem to capture the voice of the playwright himself announcing his retirement as he begs the audience to "Let your indulgence set me free."

A Japanese production by the Nina Gawa Theatre Company at the Play House Theatre, Edinburgh, 1988.

BEYOND THE PLAY

AS WITH MANY OF SHAKESPEARE'S PLAYS, when theaters reopened after the Restoration in 1660, *The Tempest* reappeared in drastically altered adaptations. The most famous was *The Tempest, or The Enchanted Island* by John Dryden and Sir William Davenant (Shakespeare's godson). This version, written in 1667, ruled the London stage for over a century until David Garrick restored Shakespeare's text. Since then, leading actors have lined up to play Prospero. The role of Miranda, written for a boy actor in his early teens, also came to launch many a future female star, from Peggy Ashcroft to Lee Remick. The play has found life in a remarkable range of other genres, from silent movie to puppet show, opera, ballet, and television adaptation. In *Une Tempête* for example, an inventive post-colonial adaptation inspired by the life of Malcolm X, Aimé Césaire, a Martinique-born French writer, portrayed Caliban as a black slave, with Prospero his white master.

Thus *The Tempest* speaks with fresh purpose to every age. In Shakespeare's day, it echoed popular belief in witchcraft, excitement at the discovery of exotic new lands, and disapproval of usurpation of power. In post-imperial times, it was frequently used as a vehicle for denouncing the excesses of colonialism. Today, with psychological interpretations more in vogue, Prospero's form of revenge can seem perverse: he forces his enemies to beg his pardon and then boasts his own magnanimity. Yet if *The Tempest* presents a timeless allegory, it may simply be that of the playwright's magical sway over his public. Like Prospero, Shakespeare shows his mastery of the stage.

PLAYER PROFILE

JOHN GIELGUD
For much of the 20th century, it was hard to imagine Prospero without thinking of John Gielgud. The great English actor first played the role in 1940 and returned to it frequently, even at the age of 87 when he appeared in Peter Greenaway's 1991 raunchy and exuberant movie adaptation of the play, called *Prospero's Books.*

A scene from *The Forbidden Planet*, a science fiction movie made in 1956, which daringly attempted to transpose Shakespeare's play into a futuristic context.

The Tempest, a television adaptation directed by Jack Bender in 1998 and set in the Mississippi bayous after the civil war, with Peter Fonda (right) as Guideon Prosper.

The TWO NOBLE KINSMEN

THE TWO NOBLE KINSMEN is the last surviving play to which Shakespeare can be linked. Written in 1613–1614, it was initially attributed to John Fletcher, Shakespeare's likely collaborator for *Henry VIII.* Although the play was not included in the *First Folio* of 1623, a quarto edition published in 1634 identified it as a work by Shakespeare and Fletcher. Then, in 1679, it was listed in the *Second Folio* of works by Fletcher and Francis Beaumont. Yet the play's connection with Shakespeare somehow survived, and in the mid-1960s major publishers added it to Shakespeare's complete works as a romance co-authored with Fletcher. Perhaps performed at Blackfriars Theatre as early as 1614, *The Two Noble Kinsmen* was reworked by William Davenant in 1664 as *The Rivals,* but there was no recorded production of Shakespeare's text between 1642 and the early 20th century. It is rarely staged today.

BEHIND THE PLAY

TWO DISTINCT VOICES CAN be heard in the play: one, complex and poetic; the other, simple and linear. Scholars who have carefully studied this play believe Shakespeare wrote close to half of it: Act 1; Scene 1 of Act 3; and all of Act 5 except Scene 2. Fletcher contributes a country fair and the subplot involving the Gaoler's Daughter (whose madness echoes that of Ophelia in *Hamlet*). Shakespeare in turn provides the emotional drama as he follows the devoted cousins, Palamon and Arcite, who fight over their competing love for Emilia. By the code of chivalry, nothing ranked higher than a knight's adoration of his lady love; to have two nobles, in this case also best friends, fighting over the same damsel offered just the kind of complicated predicament that Shakespeare enjoyed exploring. The story, set in ancient Greece during Theseus's reign over Athens, closely follows Chaucer's *The Knight's Tale.* In both stories, Arcite triumphs, but is thrown from his horse and, before dying, cedes Emilia to Palamon. Arcite's accident may seem contrived in the extreme, but it offers the unexpected—even miraculous—twist of fate that always precedes the conclusion of Shakespeare's romances.

Here we are,/ And here the graces of our youths must wither/Like a too-timely spring... 2.2

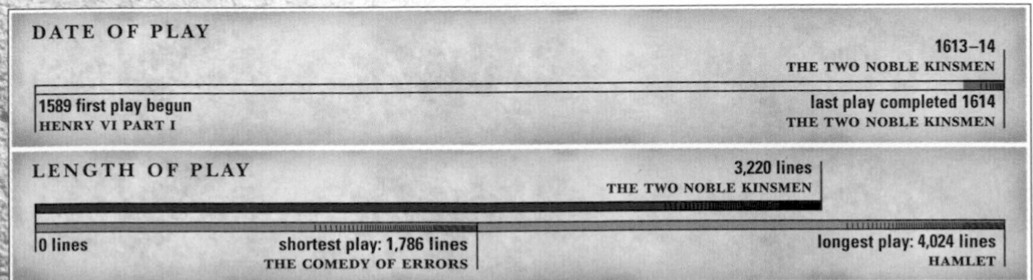

DRAMATIS PERSONAE

THESEUS
324 lines
Duke of Athens, he delays his marriage to Hippolyta in order to attack Thebes, where he captures the princes Palamon and Arcite. He orders a duel to resolve their dispute over Emilia.

PIRITHOUS
125 lines
Theseus's closest friend and comrade-in-arms.

ARTESIUS
0 lines
An Athenian soldier.

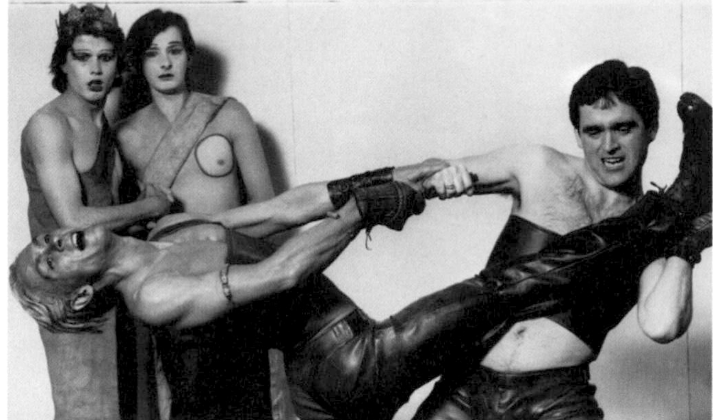

In this startling production by the Cherub Company at the Young Vic, London, 1979, the powerful intimacy between Palamon and Arcite survives even their dueling.

PALAMON
579 lines
A prince of Thebes, nephew of King Creon and cousin to Arcite, he falls in love with Emilia from afar while in prison and eventually wins her as his bride.

ARCITE
511 lines
A prince of Thebes, nephew of King Creon and cousin to Palamon, he too falls for Emilia. When released from prison and banished, he returns in disguise to pursue Emilia, defeating Palamon in a duel. He is thrown from his horse and, before dying, surrenders Emilia to his kinsman Palamon.

VALERIUS
12 lines
A Theban attendant.

SIX KNIGHTS
8; 7; 2; 0; 0; 0 lines
They accompany Palamon and Arcite during their duel and are forsworn to share their fate.

A GAOLER
114 lines
He guards the princes and is distraught over his daughter's madness.

A WOOER
104 lines
He disguises himself as Palamon to help restore the sanity of the Gaoler's Daughter, whom he loves.

Theseus, his betrothed Hippolyta, her sister Emilia, and Theseus's best friend Pirithous are key members of the high court in Athens.

A DOCTOR
81 lines
He is summoned to cure the Gaoler's Daughter.

A SCHOOLMASTER
98 lines
He organizes Morris dancing and songs to entertain Theseus and his courtiers.

HYMEN
0 lines
God of marriage.

HIPPOLYTA
102 lines
Queen of the Amazons and Theseus's bride-to-be.

EMILIA
370 lines
Hippolyta's younger sister, she is unable to decide between her suitors, Palamon and Arcite.

THREE QUEENS
64; 40; 39 lines
Three widowed queens, they persuade Theseus to postpone his marriage to Hippolyta in order to attack Thebes and rescue their husbands' bodies from the battlefield.

GAOLER'S DAUGHTER
312 lines
She is infatuated with Palamon, but goes mad when he ignores her.

A WOMAN
14 lines
Emilia's servant.

OTHER PLAYERS
A Chorus, Brother, and Friends of the Gaoler, Gentlemen, Messengers, Attendants, Nymphs, Countrymen, Garland-bearer, Countrywomen, Hunters, Maids, Herald, Executioner, Soldiers, Taborer, Boy, Servant.

The Gaoler's Daughter (Imogen Stubbs) is driven insane by Palamon's neglect.

PLOT SUMMARY

SIZE OF ACTS

ACT 1	ACT 2	ACT 3	ACT 4	ACT 5
605 lines	647 lines	819 lines	465 lines	684 lines

ACT ONE
605 lines

ATHENS AND THEBES

After a Prologue thanks Chaucer for the story, Theseus, Duke of Athens, and his bride, Hippolyta, Queen of the Amazons, arrive for their wedding ceremony, accompanied by a boy singing.

Roses, their sharp spines being gone,/Not royal in their smells alone,/ But in their hue... 1.1

Three queens kneel before Theseus, Hippolyta, and her unmarried sister, Emilia, to beg that their husbands' bodies be recovered from the battlefield where they were slain by Creon, King of Thebes.

We are three queens, whose sovereigns fell before/The wrath of cruel Creon... 1.1

Theseus insists that his wedding proceed, but Hippolyta and Emilia persuade him to rescue the bodies.

In Thebes, the princes Palamon and Arcite are planning to flee the court of their tyrannical uncle Creon. But when they hear that Theseus is approaching with an army, they decide to remain in Thebes and defend the city.

In Athens, Hippolyta remarks on the "knot of love" binding Theseus and Pirithous, the duke's closest friend.

Tied, weav'd, entangled, with so true, so long,/ And with a finger of so deep a cunning... 1.3

Emilia recalls her childhood love for Flavina, who died at the age of 11. After Flavina, she says, she shall never "love any that's called man." Theseus returns victorious from Thebes, where Palamon and Arcite were captured. He orders a state funeral for the three kings, who are buried with pomp.

Urns and odours bring away,/Vapours, sighs, darken the day... 1.5

ACT TWO
647 lines

ATHENS

The Gaoler's Daughter is chattering excitedly about the captured young princes, noting that "'Tis pity they are in prison, and 'twere pity they should be out." Palamon and Arcite lament their fate, but they are consoled by the strong

Dear Palamon, dearer in love than blood,/ And our prime cousin... 1.2

Let's think this prison holy sanctuary/ To keep us from corruption of worse men... 2.2

bonds that unite them, with Palamon saying, "I do not think it possible our friendship/Should ever leave us." At that moment, Palamon sees Emilia walking in a garden and is smitten. When Arcite sees her, he too is entranced. Palamon claims he saw her first, but Arcite says he also loves her. Suddenly, their friendship gives way to insults and they threaten to resolve the dispute with swords.

After Arcite is summoned by Theseus, Palamon learns that the duke has freed his cousin and banished him from Athens. But Arcite chooses not to return to "a heape of ruins" in Thebes. When he meets country folk going to a sports fair hosted by Theseus, he joins them in disguise.

As the Gaoler's Daughter ponders her love for Palamon, Arcite emerges the strongest and swiftest athlete at the sports fair. Theseus, Hippolyta and Emilia are impressed and, when Pirithous assigns him to Emilia's service, Arcite is ecstatic.

Let all the dukes and all the devils roar,/ He is at liberty!... 2.6

Meanwhile, the Gaoler's Daughter confides that she has freed Palamon and will soon meet him secretly.

ACT THREE

819 lines

ATHENS

As the sports fair continues, Arcite withdraws to celebrate his good fortune. Palamon, still wearing prison irons, emerges from a bush and insults his cousin. Arcite tries to calm him, but Palamon asks to be freed from his chains so he can fight for Emilia. The Gaoler's Daughter is wandering alone, deranged by Palamon's disappearance. Arcite brings his cousin a file, food, clothes and perfume, and promises to return for their duel. The Gaoler's Daughter again appears, now singing her woes. At the fair, a Latin-spouting schoolmaster is organizing some entertainment for Theseus and his entourage before the hunt resumes.

Traitor kinsman,/ Thou shouldst perceive my passion... 3.1

He has mistook the brake I meant, is gone/ After his fancy... 3.2

For I'll cut my green coat a foot above my knee/ And I'll clip my yellow locks... 3.4

Nearby, Arcite brings sword and armor for two, and seeks reassurance that Palamon is strong enough to fight. Behaving again like old friends, Palamon says that if he dies, he forgives his cousin. As soon as they clash, horns announce Theseus's hunting party. Arcite urges his cousin to hide, but Palamon refuses. When Theseus berates them for dueling without his permission, the cousins reveal their identities and announce that they are fighting for Emilia's love. Unimpressed, Theseus orders that they both be put to death.

Defy me in these fair terms, and you show/More than a mistress to me... 3.6

Hold thy word, Theseus./ We are certainly both traitors, both despisers/ Of thee and of thy goodness... 3.6

Hippolyta and Emilia beg him to rescind the order, with Emilia proposing that the cousins be banished. Instead, Theseus asks her to pick one of them, but she says "they are both too excellent." Finally, Theseus orders them to return in one month to duel for Emilia. The cousin who proves his greater strength "shall enjoy her; the other lose his head."

ACT FOUR

465 lines

ATHENS

The Gaoler is alarmed by his daughter's madness. Her suitor reports that he heard her sing her love for Palamon and that he saved her from drowning. The daughter arrives, raving unintelligibly, frequently naming Palamon.

I'll tell you quickly. As I late was angling/ In the great lake that lies behind the palace... 4.1

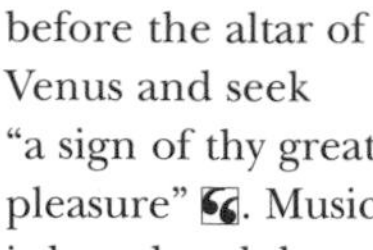

Alone in the palace, Emilia studies pictures of the princes, first praising Arcite's "sweet face," then dreamily contemplating Palamon's "brown manly face," but she cannot choose between them.

> **Yet I may bind those wounds up, that must open/ And bleed to death for my sake else...** 4.2

Theseus and his court arrive with news that the cousins have returned to Athens.

Summoned to treat the Gaoler's Daughter, a doctor decides he has no cure for her "perturbed mind." Instead, he tells the Wooer to pretend that he is Palamon. If he sings to her, and they eat and drink together, the doctor says, her sanity will return.

ACT FIVE

684 lines

ATHENS

Palamon and Arcite are left alone to pray. Arcite and his knights prostrate themselves before the altar of Mars and beg "some token of thy pleasure." A clanging of armor and the thunder of battle are heard. Palamon and his knights kneel before the altar of Venus and seek "a sign of thy great pleasure". Music is heard and doves flutter overhead. Finally, Emilia pledges to Diana that, if both princes die, "I a virgin flower must grow alone unplucked." Instruments are heard and a single rose falls from a tree.

> **Hail, sovereign queen of secrets, who hast power/ To call the fiercest tyrant from his rage...** 5.1

The Wooer, now dressed as Palamon, says the Gaoler's Daughter believes she has found her true love. As the duel between the princes begins, Emilia refuses to watch, but she hears the sound of trumpets and cries. When Palamon's name is shouted, she believes he is close to victory. Then Arcite is proclaimed the winner, and he presents himself before Emilia.

> **Arcite is gently visag'd, yet his eye/Is like an engine bent...** 5.3

> **Emilia,/To buy you, I have lost what's dearest to me...** 5.3

As Palamon and his knights prepare to die, Pirithous rushes in with news that Arcite has been thrown from his horse and fatally injured. Accompanied by Theseus, Hippolyta, and Emilia, Arcite is carried in and, as he dies, he tells his cousin to "take Emilia." Calling for two days of mourning to be followed by a wedding, Theseus reflects on what the "heavenly charmers"—Mars and Venus—have brought and concludes stoically, "Let's go off, and bear us like the time."

> **In this place first you fought: e'en very here/ I sund'red you...** 5.4

In an Epilogue, the playwright expresses hope that his tale—"For 'tis no other"—has pleased the audience.

> **Never fortune/Did play a subtler game. The conquer'd triumphs,/The victor has the loss; yet in the passage/ The gods have been most equal...** 5.4

READING THE PLAY

COMPARISON OF PROSE TO VERSE

prose: 5% verse: 95%

LITERARY SOURCES

CHAUCER AND SHAKESPEARE

The story is taken from *The Knight's Tale* of Chaucer's *The Canterbury Tales* and borrows a scene from a 1613 Beaumont masque. It also revives Theseus, Duke of Athens, and Hippolyta, Queen of the Amazons, who earlier presided over *A Midsummer Night's Dream*, although the pair are portrayed differently in this play.

An illumination from *The Canterbury Tales*.

Many features of Shakespeare's romances, including a family rupture, divine interventions, and a happy ending born of death, are found in *The Two Noble Kinsmen*. However, while Shakespeare's romances usually introduce a tragic development, such as the real death of Leontes's young son in *The Winter's Tale* and the presumed deaths of Thaisa and Marina in *Pericles*, here Arcite's death, coming in Act 5, unusually darkens the play's conclusion.

John Fletcher succeeded Shakespeare as the main playwright for the King's Men. The pair collaborated in the writing of *The Two Noble Kinsmen*, having previously worked together on Shakespeare's final history play, *Henry VIII*.

It is not known how Shakespeare and Fletcher collaborated on *The Two Noble Kinsmen*, although it is not hard to see the play as the work of two writers. By the time it was completed, Fletcher had probably already succeeded Shakespeare as chief playwright of the King's Men, but his limitations are apparent. He may have invented the subplot of the Gaoler's Daughter, which served to remind audiences that commoners should never aspire to marry aristocrats. He undoubtedly created the country fair as a nod to the pageantry, music, and dancing beloved of Jacobean audiences. But the prose in these episodes adds little to the quality of the play. Shakespeare, in contrast, kept closer to Chaucer's *The Knight's Tale*. Above all, he took charge of the central relationship between the noble kinsmen Palamon and Arcite, his penetrating verse exploring the pain implicit in the cousins' mutual betrayal. Along with Emilia's poignant evocation of her friend Flavina, it is at these moments that both poetry and drama are most effective.

Although Prospero's Epilogue in *The Tempest* is considered by many to be Shakespeare's farewell to theater life, his final words written for the stage may well be Theseus's last phrase in *The Two Noble Kinsmen*: "Let's go off, and bear us like the time." However, not too much should be read into this; many of Shakespeare's plays end on a valedictory note.

WHO'S WHO

Theseus, Duke of Athens, is to marry **Hippolyta**, Queen of the Amazons. Her younger sister, **Emilia**, is loved by both **Palamon**, a prince of Thebes and nephew of King Creon, and by his cousin **Arcite**, another prince of Thebes, both of whom have been imprisoned in Athens following their defeat in battle. The **Gaoler's Daughter** is responsible for helping Palamon to escape. Arcite, meanwhile, is released and banished.

SEEING THE PLAY

ONE PROBLEM WITH STAGING *The Two Noble Kinsmen* is that plot digressions slow the pace of the narrative. When Palamon, Arcite, or Emilia are on stage, it is hard not to be engaged. Yet most of Act 1 is irrelevant to the main story. The lengthy scene in which three widowed queens beg Theseus to recover their husbands' bodies is merely a device to capture Palamon and Arcite. Similarly, the Gaoler's mad daughter seemingly only exists to free Palamon from prison (although some actresses prefer this overblown role to that of the ever-solemn Emilia). The country fair, with its music and dancing, would have appealed to Jacobean audiences accustomed to an interlude of light entertainment.

In a rare production of *The Two Noble Kinsmen* in 2000, the new Shakespeare's Globe theater in London filled the center of the stage with the skull of a giant horse. Some critics felt it interfered with the acting, but others thought the skull cleverly reminded the audience of the links between chivalry, love, and death.

However, the real drama of the play is provided by the resolution of the love triangle, which is fraught with danger because two best friends are wooing the same woman. Early in the play, the stage is set for a bitter dispute in two scenes where Palamon and Arcite express their lifelong devotion and loyalty to each other. Thus, when they both fall for Emilia, it is apparent that their rivalry will be equally intense.

Although they become enemies, Arcite (Hugh Quarshie) and Palamon (Gerard Murphy) are still affectionately attached to each other.

If well acted, the scenes among these three characters can offer psychological insights. The warring Palamon and Arcite, for instance, should not simply go from being friends to enemies; even as they duel, they remain beloved cousins who have been trapped by fate. Emilia is also cornered; flattered to be loved by two men, she dare not choose between them. Appropriately, it is the gods who decide.

Non-dramatic POETRY

SHAKESPEARE'S NARRATIVE POEMS BROUGHT HIM FAME IN HIS OWN LIFETIME. TODAY HIS LYRICAL POEMS, THE SONNETS, ARE HELD TO BE AMONG HIS GREATEST WORKS.

By the time Shakespeare had reached the age of 28, he was already a popular playwright on the London theater scene. However, in that year, 1592, there was an outbreak of plague and public theaters in London were shut for nearly two years. While some theater companies toured the countryside, the theater talents remaining in the capital had to find new ways to earn a living. Shakespeare turned to writing poetry.

Perhaps Shakespeare felt the time was ripe to exploit his growing literary prestige. In Elizabethan England, writers like Marlowe, Nashe, Peele, and Greene gained their literary credentials not as playwrights but as poets; drama was not considered to be a gentleman's art. A lofty poem, employing classical themes and florid rhetoric, could win Shakespeare renown; and, if the poem were at once erotic, comical, and moving, it could also be popular, hence lucrative.

In 1593, Shakespeare published *Venus and Adonis* in an edition printed by his friend from Stratford, Richard Field. This, the playwright's earliest narrative poem, would prove more marketable than any other of his works printed during his lifetime: no less than nine quarto editions were issued before his death in 1616.

The following year, Field published Shakespeare's *The Rape of Lucrece*, a second narrative poem of mesmerizing themes and images. It, too, was a great success with London readers. By then, even the most envious of his competitors would have recognized that the young, middle-class writer with no university eduction was in fact a refined and inspired poet.

Shakespeare was also moved to write poetry as much by poetic thoughts as by social pressure and ambition. Over several years from 1593, he was probably writing his famous sonnets and circulating them among trusted readers. It is not known whether he approved the publication of *Shake-speare's Sonnets* in 1609. But by then, with his reputation secure, perhaps he no longer had reason to keep even intimate poems from public scrutiny.

Shakespeare may well have believed that his non-dramatic works would become his only enduring contribution to English literature. Time, the poet's favorite subject, would prove him wrong, for Shakespeare's plays would eventually rank among the greatest of literary achievements from any era in history. And while his narrative poems have earned new admiration in recent decades, Shakespeare's sonnets have indeed proved timeless.

The Narrative Poems

Measured by the number of editions published during his lifetime, two of Shakespeare's narrative poems, *Venus and Adonis* and *The Rape of Lucrece*, represent his greatest literary successes. Probably composed during 1592–94, both poems were dedicated to Henry Wriothesley, the Earl of Southampton. Reprinted in quarto editions and available through booksellers, they were immensely popular, as much for their erotic passages as for their elegant Elizabethan verses.

Although these long poems examine desire, they vary in theme, form, and tone. *Venus and Adonis* presents Venus alternately as sensual love goddess and sex-crazed buffoon. It concludes in an elegiac vein with the death of Adonis, its lovers safely removed from tragic human experience. By contrast, *The Rape of Lucrece* recounts in unsettling detail the story of a woman raped by her husband's friend, examining disturbing corners of human conscience.

These, and two other narrative poems, are presented by narrators suited to the stories they tell. In *Venus and Adonis* and *The Rape of Lucrece*, the narrators are omniscient, but in *The Phoenix and the Turtle*, the narrator resembles a solemn conjurer, drawing loquacious birds out of thin air to attend a funeral ceremony. And in *A Lover's Complaint*, the narrator speaks in the first person, claiming to have witnessed the events he recounts.

All of Shakespeare's narrative poems draw directly or indirectly on works by Ovid. The mythological *Metamorphoses*, published in an English translation by Arthur Golding in 1567, abounds in stories of magical encounters and miraculous transformations. Shakespeare drew from it for *Venus and Adonis*. Ovid's *Fasti* or "Chronicles" offered material for the *The Rape of Lucrece*. The complaint, fashionable in the Elizabethan era and employed with innovation in *A Lover's Complaint*, can be traced back to Ovid's heroic narratives. Even the bird mass revisited by *The Phoenix and the Turtle* was an Ovidian subject. Like Ovid, Shakespeare made even the oldest stories new by telling them as they had not been told before.

THE NARRATIVE POEMS AT A GLANCE

	First Publication	Main Source	Form
Venus and Adonis	1593 (9 eds. in WS's day)	Ovid, *Metamorphoses*	6-line stanzas
The Rape of Lucrece	1594 (6 eds. in WS's day)	Ovid, *Fasti* ("Chronicles")	"rhyme royal" 7-line stanzas
The Phoenix and the Turtle	1601 (reprinted 1611)	Ovidian tradition of the Bird Mass	quatrains +*threnos* in 3-line stanzas
A Lover's Complaint	1609	Ovidian heroic narrative	"rhyme royal" 7-line stanzas

VENUS *and* ADONIS

NO WORK OF SHAKESPEARE was more popular during the poet's lifetime than the erotic yet playful *Venus and Adonis*. Based on a story in Ovid's *Metamorphoses,* it was composed in 1592–93 and Shakespeare referred to it as the "first heir of my invention" in his dedication. In this context, he did not choose to acknowledge his plays, perhaps agreeing with his contemporaries that plays were lowly compared to poems. He seems to have viewed *Venus and Adonis* as his first truly literary work. The poem's elaborate language, precise formal features, and carefully-balanced structure would also suggest that Shakespeare composed it with a mind to gaining literary prestige. Its instant success confirmed that the new playwright was also a gifted poet.

SUMMARY OF THE POEM

Adonis sets out to hunt one afternoon, but Venus, ignited by his beauty, plucks him from his horse and pushes him to the ground, offering to release him only in exchange for "one sweet kiss." Adonis agrees but then refuses the promised kiss [1–90]. Venus attempts to seduce with flattery, then criticism, finally advocating "the law of nature" as she lays beside the beautiful youth on the grass in the afternoon sun. But Adonis, fearing sunburn, wants to leave [91–215]. When Venus is reduced to tears, Adonis's irresistible cheek dimples only torment her further [216–52].

Still intent on hunting, Adonis leaps up, but his stallion, sexually excited by the sight of a mare, flees into a wood [253–324]. Adonis sulks while Venus recommends the

example set by his horse: seize the opportunity to love. Adonis only likes boar-hunting, he says, and is too young for love [325–426].

Venus faints. Thinking her dead, Adonis attempts to revive her with a kiss [427–80]. "The night of sorrow now is turned to day" for the delighted Venus. Adonis sees night falling and consents to only one more kiss before departing [481–540]. Kissing, the couple falls back to the ground in a hot embrace, which inflames Venus with even more passion. Can they meet "to-morrow," she asks, but the answer is no. Adonis says he is going boar-hunting with friends [541–588].

Venus prophesies that, unless he hunts a less vicious beast, he will die, but night has fallen and Adonis intends to join his companions [589–720]. Venus argues that the moonless night invites him to remain and love her. But, Adonis protests, what she calls Love is in fact offensive Lust. He finally runs off, leaving Venus alone and upset [721–816].

Wandering in the wilderness, Venus first hears, then sings with the echoes of her lamenting voice. Finally, a lark's song announces daybreak, releasing Venus from her anguish. Alarming yelps of hunting dogs send her rushing to their source [817–900]. Seeing a boar, its mouth stained with blood, Venus rails against Death until

'Venus and Adonis' (1553–54) by Titian captures the tumbling, desperate movement of the poem's verse language.

the distant voice of a hunter persuades her that Adonis is alive [901–1,026]. Flying to greet him, Venus is crushed to discover Adonis's bloodied corpse. In an elegy spoken over his body, Venus sees that his groin was pierced by the beast. Even the boar must have been in love with Adonis, she reasons. She confesses that she may even have killed her beloved first had she had tusks, so passionately did she desire to kiss him [1,027–1,122]. Staining her face with Adonis's blood, Venus prophesies that sorrows will forever accompany love [1,123–1,164]. Adonis's body then melts "like a vapour from her sight" and from his blood on the ground a purple flower appears. Venus plucks the blossom and, vowing to kiss the flower forever, mounts her chariot to return home and mourn [1,165–1,194].

A Stanza from the Poem

In lines 547–552, the narrator describes Venus's aggressive sexual appetite for Adonis:

Now quick desire hath caught the yielding prey,
And glutton-like she feeds, yet never filleth,
Her lips are conquerors, his lips obey,
Paying what ransom the insulter willeth;
Whose vulture thought doth pitch the price so high
That she will draw his lips' rich treasure dry

Reading the Poem

Hugely popular in Shakespeare's day and reprinted in quarto editions through to 1675, *Venus and Adonis* suddenly fell out of favor in the late 17th century. Its 1,194 lines, in stanzas rhyming *ababcc*, sounded labored, and its shifts of tone confusing. During the Romantic era, poets including Coleridge and Keats found inspiration in the poem's daring mix of earthy passions and classical themes. But it was not until the social revolutions of the late 20th century that this spirited poem earned fuller attention. Many critics regard the work as too conditioned by Elizabethan conventions to be ranked alongside its author's timeless plays and sonnets. Nevertheless, *Venus and Adonis* offers much to admire, including Shakespeare's departure from his source material. In Ovid, Venus's love for Adonis is returned. Shakespeare's more human Venus can only attempt, at times with farcical lack of success, to seduce her beloved.

LANGUAGE NOTE

EROTIC DESIRE

Many of the metaphors for sexual desire or pleasure employed in *Venus and Adonis* are conventional, such as burning, steaming, hunting, hungering, thirsting, and dying. Others are Shakespeare's striking innovations, as when Venus invites Adonis to imagine himself as a deer grazing in the parkland of her body:

'I'll be a park, and thou shalt be my deer;
Feed where thou wilt, on mountain or in dale;
Graze on my lips, and if those hills be dry,
Stray lower, where the pleasant fountains lie.'
[231–234]

The RAPE *of* LUCRECE

THE RAPE OF LUCRECE recounts the legendary violation of a virtuous wife by Tarquin, son of the Roman king. The poem's dark theme and dense language suggest that it may well have been that "graver labour" Shakespeare claimed he would undertake in his dedication to *Venus and Adonis.* Unlike Ovid's *Fasti* or "Chronicles," Shakespeare focuses on the emotions of the characters and the voices they find to articulate their tragic experience. Rhetorically spectacular, moral yet probing, Shakespeare's version is also dramatically engaging.

Titian's 'The Rape of Lucretia', painted between 1568 and 1571.

Behind the Poem

Shakespeare himself may have penned the back-story and summary to his poem, its action set in Roman antiquity. A prose "Argument" of uncertain authorship introduces *The Rape of Lucrece,* explaining that King Tarquinius Superbus murdered his way to the throne and then turned to wage war against Ardea. There, for entertainment, army leaders one night compared their wives' virtues and returned suddenly to Rome to confirm their claims. All wives were misbehaving save one: Lucrece. Consequently, Lucrece became famous for her chastity and her husband, Collatinus, won the wager. But one of the men, Sextus Tarquinius (the Tarquin of the poem that follows), the king's son, became lustful upon seeing Lucrece. After returning to camp with the others, he stole back alone to Collatium, where Lucrece politely welcomed him. The "Argument" then describes the rape and its political consequences. The poem itself takes up the story from the rape.

LANGUAGE NOTE

SEX AND POLITICS

In *The Rape of Lucrece,* sexual violence is linked to political ambition, as when Tarquin prepares to rape Lucrece. From Tarquin's perspective, his victim's body resembles political territory to be stolen from its rightful ruler, Lucrece's husband.

Her breasts like ivory globes circled with blue,
A pair of maiden worlds unconquerèd,
Save of their lord no bearing yoke they knew,
And him by oath they truly honorèd.
These worlds in Tarquin new ambition bred,
Who like a foul usurper went about
From this fair throne to heave the owner out.
[407–413]

Summary of the Poem

Tarquin hastens from Ardea to Collatium, where the chaste Lucrece is unaware that he lusts for her. Lucrece receives Tarquin warmly and, after a convivial supper, both retire. But Tarquin leaps from his bed to reflect on his planned rape [1–280]. Tortured by desire and fear, Tarquin enters Lucrece's chamber to examine her as she sleeps. He tries to repel his lust, but "His drumming heart" pressures his hand to caress the "blue veins" of Lucrece's breast [281–441]. Startled awake, Lucrece tries to reason with her attacker, but his threats of murder force her to yield [442–672]. Tarquin violates Lucrece, then flees in self-loathing, seeking daylight [673–745].

Alone, Lucrece addresses Night, her husband Collatine, Opportunity, and Time. Finally she resolves to take her own life [746–1,078]. At sunrise, Lucrece is eager to tell Collatine what happened so that he may avenge her [1,079–1,211]. She pens a letter, requesting him to return home [1,212–1,365].

Lucrece finds solace in the details of a painting depicting the fall of Troy. But when she realizes that, like Troy, she was betrayed and besieged, she uses her nails to rip at the painted figure of Sinon, the duplicitous Greek soldier who tricked the Trojans into welcoming the Trojan Horse within their city walls [1,366–1,568]. Collatine arrives with Lucrece's father and Roman lords, all astonished by the sad sight of Lucrece. She tells them what happened but, before naming the rapist, makes them promise revenge. They agree, but before she can utter the criminal's name, she stabs herself and collapses. Her father and husband debate whose grief is greater, until Collatine buries his face in Lucrece's blood. From Lucrece's expiring breath he catches the name "Tarquin." Brutus notes that Lucrece and Rome alike have been abused by Tarquin. Finally, the narrator relates that, when Lucrece's body was displayed throughout their city, the Romans banished Tarquin [1,569–1,855].

HISTORICAL SOURCES

COLLATIUM

Like Shakespeare, readers may be confused about the actual location of Collatium, where Lucrece and her husband live. In *The Rape of Lucrece,* Collatium appears to be a suburb of Rome, or close enough so that the men spying on their wives in Rome in the same night check up on Lucrece at Collatium. In fact, the setting, called "Collatia" in the Latin sources, was not next to Rome, but lay 10 miles (16 km) northeast of the capital.

Reading the poem

The Rape of Lucrece is in rhyme royal, a demanding stanza form first used in English two centuries earlier by Chaucer. Seven lines of iambic pentameter constitute each stanza, rhyming *ababbcc.* Frequently reprinted during and just following Shakespeare's lifetime, the poem was also reset in works including Thomas Heywood's 1608 play, *The Rape of Lucrece.* However, the poem was generally dismissed until the 20th century, and even then it was studied mainly to date Shakespeare's plays or to establish his budding talents. But, with its themes of political and sexual disorder, the poem gained attention in the 1960s and 70s. Its tensely-wound language influenced a new generation of poets, most notably Ted Hughes. With its bold investigation of dark emotions and its disquieting, sinewy lines, *The Rape of Lucrece* is as engrossing as it is unforgettable.

The PHOENIX *and the* TURTLE

THE PHOENIX AND THE TURTLE is Shakespeare's most enigmatic poem. First published in 1601 with Robert Chester's *Love's Martyr*, Shakespeare's contribution was the second in a series of appended poems by authors including Ben Jonson, George Chapman, and John Marston. Chester dedicated his *Love's Martyr* to his patron, Sir John Salusbury, and may have written it for Salusbury's wedding to Ursula Stanley in 1586. Shakespeare could have composed the poem just prior to Chester's 1601 publication, but an alternative view is that he wrote *The Phoenix and the Turtle* during the undocumented "lost years" (1586–91), before records show him working as a playwright in London.

Behind the Poem

In *Love's Martyr*, the phoenix and the turtle-dove mate to ensure the propagation of the phoenix's beauty. "From the sweet fire" of its parents' ashes, a new phoenix rises up. Shakespeare's elegiac poem, which begins where the phoenix and turtle-dove have been reduced to ashes, goes on to reject Chester's version.

Summary of the Poem

Invocation: a narrator invokes birds to mourn, with the swan serving as priest [1–20]. *Anthem*: the birds deliver an anthem, in which they say that Reason was unable to make sense of the singular union of the phoenix and turtle-dove; but "Love hath reason" in this instance and gives voice to a *threnos* or funeral song [21–52]. *Threnos*: Love laments the death of beauty and truth. In their "married chastity," the birds produced no offspring. Finally, Love invites all who are "true or fair" to mourn [53–67].

Reading the Poem

The Phoenix and the Turtle was generally dismissed until the arrival of Modernism, when its opaque language and haunting musicality gave it the status of a poetic masterpiece. Only 67 lines long, it is now often read as a hypnotic puzzle whose genius lies in its indecipherable mystery.

LANGUAGE NOTE

THE PHOENIX
'Phoenix' is from the Greek word for the mythical *bennu* venerated in ancient Egypt. Reborn from its own ashes, the bird symbolized the regenerative force of the rising sun. In the Christian West, the phoenix later signified Christ's resurrection and, more generally, the renewal of life.

A LOVER'S COMPLAINT

First printed in 1609 with Shakespeare's sonnets, *A Lover's Complaint* was long thought to be the work of another poet and was not solidly attributed to Shakespeare until the 1960s. It appears to have been composed around 1603–04, when public theaters were again shut to ward off the plague. Shakespeare could then have returned to sonnets begun in the 1590s and he may have written the complaint to complete the sequence, although by 1603 sonnet sequences followed by a complaint were no longer the height of fashion. Today, *A Lover's Complaint* is rarely read in isolation from the sonnets, whose themes it revisits from the viewpoint of a narrator giving voice to a young woman.

Summary of the Poem

A narrator says that he was in a valley when echoing laments drew him to the riverbank where a young maid vented her sorrow in weeping, ripping up poems, and throwing tokens of love into the mud [1–56]. An elderly cattle herder approached her to offer solace [57–70]. She told him of a young man whose charms had bewitched males and females alike. Even knowing his reputation, she fell for him [71–175]. For a long time, she resisted him. He said that, while loved by many, he never loved another. Among those who desired him, he said, was a nun prepared to give up her love of God for love of him. But, he told the maid, all the love he received from others and had never returned was now hers. He also gave her all of the tokens of love he had ever received, including gems and "deep-brained sonnets" [176–280]. She then fell for the youth's false tears and surrendered to him in love. She asks the old man "Who, young and simple, would not be so lover'd?" Finally, she answers her own question with a new lament. Were the youth to be so false again, she would be seduced by him anew [281–329].

A Stanza from the Poem

In lines 15–21, the narrator describes a maid he saw weeping on a riverbank:

Oft did she heave her napkin to her eyne,
Which on it had conceited characters,
Laund'ring the silken figures in the brine
That seasoned woe had pelleted in tears,
And often shriking undistinguish'd woe,
In clamors of all size, both high and low.

LITERARY SOURCES

THE COMPLAINT

A Lover's Complaint belongs to an Ovidian literary tradition in which speakers of high birth lament their fallen states. These "complaints" entered English love poetry through the 1559 *The Mirror for Magistrates.* As the genre evolved, the lamenter became a living lover rather than a deceased person of note. *A Lover's Complaint* makes the speakers less historical and more immediate by refusing to name both the lamenting "maid" and the youth who is the source of her grief.

The Lyric Poems

Shakespeare's lyric poems stem from the Italian tradition of the Petrarchan sonnet, which gained tremendous popularity in the 16th century throughout Europe and as far as Russia. In England, the form was particularly fashionable during the Elizabethan era. Monumental sonnet sequences, such as Philip Sidney's *Astrophil and Stella* (1591), married passionate Italian sentiments to English verse language. Shakespeare's own sonnet sequence, while probably written as the English vogue for sonnets peaked in the 1590s, was not published until 1609.

Shakespeare's lyric poems speak in the direct, first-person voice of the emotional lover. While Shakespeare appears to have overseen the publication of his major narrative poems, each of his lyric poems has raised questions about whether he intended publication. Consequently, they have been read as personal, intimate, even rigorously private compositions.

The sonnets form Shakespeare's lyric masterpiece. In fact, they represent the only lyric poems undoubtedly authored by him. *Shall I Die?*, a love lyric in jolting rhymes, is of doubtful authorship, and epitaphs said to be Shakespeare's were only linked to him by popular convention after his death. *The Passionate Pilgrim*, a miscellany by various authors, includes five Shakespeare poems, but each was pirated either from the sonnets or from *Love's Labour's Lost*. Of the Bard's non-dramatic works, the sonnets alone have engaged readers in every era.

The word 'sonnet' entered English from the Italian *sonetto*, meaning "a little song"; the sonnet was initially an Italian form. Dante composed sonnets in 1292–93, and some fifty years later Petrarch recorded more than three hundred sonnets in the *Canzoniere*. As the popularity of sonnets spread, their form was adjusted for different languages. The Petrarchan scheme was difficult to sustain in English, a language poorer in rhymes than the Romance languages. Earlier in the 16th century, the poet Henry Howard, Earl of Surrey modified the sonnet to suit English. With Surrey translating and imitating individual Italian sonnets, it was left to poets of the 1580s and 1590s to develop full cycles of original poems. Today, the form Surrey innovated is known as the "Shakespearean sonnet."

THE LYRIC POEMS AT A GLANCE

Lyric Poem	First Publication	Main Source	Form
The Passionate Pilgrim	1599? Pirated poems	Petrarchan love poetry	Various, mainly sonnets
The Sonnets	1609 Written 1590s?	Petrarchan sonnets	sonnet
Shall I Die?	None during WS's day (Authorship contested)	Petrarchan love poetry	10-line stanzas
Epitaphs	None during WS's day save on tombstones (Authorship contested)	Epitaph tradition	quatrains and sestets

The SONNETS

SHAKESPEARE'S 154 SONNETS have awakened fascination and speculation for centuries, starting even before the day they first appeared in London bookshops. *Shake-speare's Sonnets, Neuer before Published* was published in 1609, but as early as 1598, clergyman Francis Meres noted that Shakespeare was circulating "sugared sonnets among his private friends." The poems' language suggests they were at least initially composed in the early 1590s; if this is so, why were they published 15 years later, when no longer fashionable? This is just one of the mysteries surrounding the sonnets' publication. Yet these mysteries are of lesser importance than the profound truths about Time, Beauty and Verse that are charted within these much-loved poems.

BEHIND THE SONNETS

The sonnet was so popular in the Elizabethan era that around 1,200 survive in print from the 1590s alone. Many sonnets were published in a grouping known as a "sequence," which was often completed by an elegiac poem known as a "complaint." *Shake-speare's Sonnets* followed in the same tradition: the edition included Shakespeare's sonnets and *A Lover's Complaint.* Following Dante's sonnets to his dearly-departed Beatrice and Petrarch's to his Laura, most speakers in the sonnet tradition named their beloved. English poets either invented muses or named real ones. For his landmark *Astrophil and Stella,* which translates from the Latin as "star-lover and star," Philip Sidney found a muse in Elizabeth Devereux. The 1590s would see the publication of many cycles similarly named: Daniel's *Delia,* Lodge's *Phillis,* Fletcher the Elder's *Licia,* Percy's *Coelia,* Drayton's *Idea,* and Barnfield's *Cynthia. Shake-speare's Sonnets* was perhaps the publisher's rather than Shakespeare's own title. But even within the sonnets, Shakespeare never names his male or female muses.

THE SONNETS, POETRY AND TIME

Shakespeare's sonnet sequence is divided into three basic groups. Sonnets 1–126 address a young man, by convention now referred to as "the friend"; sonnets 127–152 address the so-called "dark lady"; and sonnets 153–154 treat the love god Cupid. Of the 154 sonnets, the first 17 encourage a youth to marry and have children. In fact, sonnets 1–126 are probably all addressed to the same man. Biological reproduction is initially the means Shakespeare recommends to the youth to guarantee the survival of his virtues. The first lines of the first sonnet set the theme in motion: "From fairest creatures we desire increase/That thereby beauty's rose might never die." The following 16 sonnets revisit the procreation theme, but also introduce the idea that poetry itself may, like children, preserve the young man's beauty. The final couplet of Sonnet 17 dwells on this dual fecundity, at once biological and poetic, promising to extend the young man's virtues into "the age to come," the future:

"But were some child of yours alive that time,/You should live twice, in it and in my rhyme." Like Nature itself, then, lyrics bestow a form of immortality.

Whatever Shakespeare's real-life relationships, the most central and arresting one inscribed in the sonnets is that between poetry and Time. Sonnets addressing the young man repeatedly argue that poetry, by preserving otherwise fleeting glimpses of truth, defies death. These sonnets therefore reveal the speaker's discoveries about the extraordinary power of poetry. Sonnet 18 initially delights in the fact that a poetic comparison may translate the beloved into something else: "Shall I compare thee to a summer's day?/Thou are more lovely and more temperate." The sonnet continues, "thy eternal summer shall not fade," asserting that lyrics grant the friend immortal status. The speaker's confidence is built on his certainty that poems endure because they capture truth. The final couplet claims: "So long as men can breathe or eyes can see,/So long lives this, and this gives life to thee." Thus, the ultimate subject of the sonnets is Shakespeare's poetry itself.

Love and Desire in the Sonnets

Some believe that sonnets to the friend identify Shakespeare as a homosexual. But the sonnets express no consistent experience of sexuality. In fact, the sonnets express no consistent experience of anything. Rather, they chart the evolution of feeling and thought as the poet interacts with his subjects. Judging from the poems themselves, the friend remained the sonneteer's muse for three years, over the course of which the speaker's view of the youth is anything but static. The poet's voice is at times enchanted, even worshipful; at other times confounded, disenchanted, and even combative.

With Sonnet 127, another beloved, the dark lady, gains the poet's passionate attention. Describing her dark hair and eyes as "black," the poet often relates these physical traits to moral qualities. But as the speaker's feelings for the lady change, so do his assessments of her black features. "In nothing art thou black save in thy deeds," he says in Sonnet 131, referring to their adulterous affair. But this relationship, like that with the young man, ends in frustration and deception. The speaker is ultimately revolted by his own

THE PASSIONATE PILGRIM

The Passionate Pilgrim is a collection of poems printed three times by William Jaggard: probably twice in 1599, and again in 1612. The first edition survives only in fragments, its title page and date missing. But the title page of the second edition reads "*The Passionate Pilgrim* by W. Shakespeare." In fact, only five of its 20 poems are Shakespeare's. Two are sonnets from the famous sequence that would be published in 1609 (Sonnet 138 and Sonnet 144). The remaining three poems were lifted from Act 4 of Shakespeare's 1595 play *Love's Labour's Lost.* Somehow, Jaggard managed to secure copies of the two unpublished sonnets. It is possible that Jaggard was hoping, in 1599, to mislead the public into thinking he had laid his hands on the entire collection of love poems Shakespeare was by then rumored to have been circulating privately in manuscript form. But even when reprinted in 1612, three years after the publication of the veritable sonnets, *The Passionate Pilgrim* was again attributed solely to W. Shakespeare. The 1612 edition included additional poems by Thomas Heywood, as upset to be uncredited as Shakespeare apparently was to be erroneously named the collection's author. Heywood noted in his 1612 *Apologie for Actors* that Shakespeare was "much offended with M. Jaggard (that altogether unknowne to him) presumed to make so bold with his name."

blindness, and the cruelty of his mistress, whose lips in Sonnet 145 have "Breathed forth the sound that said 'I hate.'" In Sonnet 147, the concluding couplet charts new exasperation: "For I have sworn thee fair, and thought thee bright/Who are as black as hell, as dark as night."

Within the sequence as a whole, dramatic events appear to link the male friend to the dark lady. Certain sonnets addressing the youth (34–35 and 40–42) condemn him for having an affair. And some sonnets to the dark lady suggest that she is the person having the affair with the young man. While this love triangle is already preoccupying, yet another figure enters the picture to confuse loyalties. In sonnets 78–86, the so-called rival poet has also discovered the joys of immortalizing the friend. In Sonnet 86, the speaker suspects that his own silence on the virtues of his friend can be explained by the appearance of the rival poet who now praises the youth:

Was it the proud full sail of
his great verse,
Bound for the prize of
all-too-precious you,
That did my ripe thoughts
in my brain inhearse,
Making their tomb the womb
wherein they grew?

While claiming to be silenced by the rival poet, however, the speaker in fact voices a fine sonnet. Such contradictory claims are frequent in the sonnets. The speaker may say he is too crazy, jealous, in love, or hurt to express himself, but Shakespeare nevertheless captured these and other intricate, mixed, and changing feelings in the demanding formal language of his sonnets.

How to Read a Sonnet

The sonnet is a relatively strict poetic form, striking many today as too contrived to convey natural sentiments. In its day, however, the sonnet's formality was its strength. By working within and against formal constraints, poets constructed new relationships among linked images, sounds, and ideas to produce beautiful and keenly-observed arguments. The pleasure of reading a sonnet comes from discovering how details of sound, meaning, and image are used to form the poem's basic argument. On the next page, Sonnet 54 shows the basic formal features of the Shakespearean sonnet.

Reading a sonnet involves following the speaker's train of thought and listening out for shifts of tone or direction as the poem progresses. The opening couplet of Sonnet 54 presents a general observation: integrity or loyalty (Shakespeare's *truth*) augments beauty, making it more beautiful. Next comes an example: roses look pretty, but they are even more beautiful when they smell as pretty as they look. Canker roses look like roses, *but* (the speaker is about to shift direction) canker blooms die unappreciated because appearance is their only virtue. When sweet roses die, their fragrance preserves their beauty. In the final couplet, the poet links this point to the youth he addresses: *you* are like the sweet rose because, even after your beauty vanishes, your more essential beauty remains in these very verses.

An important word in this sonnet is *sweet*. In line 2, *sweet* describes the additional beauty that "truth" brings to mere beauty. But in line 4, *sweet* describes the fragrant and pretty as opposed to the merely pretty rose. The word *sweet* links the general observation of the opening lines to the specific example developed in sonnet's core. As the sonnet progresses, the *sweet* rose evolves. This rose is more beautiful, line 4 puts it, "For that *sweet* odour which doth in it *live*." The first quatrain concludes with the word *live*, but the following line surprises the reader with the new end-rhyme *dye*, which sounds like "die." "The canker blooms have full as deep a *dye*." That is, all roses are lovely to look at, but the canker's merely visual beauty is associated with death, and is opposed to the lasting fragrance that *lives* within the *sweet* rose.

The word *die* itself appears in line 11, where canker roses "*Die* unto themselves." Death is underscored by the sudden metrical change of line 11, which also comes to an abrupt halt in mid-verse. Following this break in the music of the language and the train of thought, a pulse of life gradually resumes. "*Sweet* roses" set the sonnet back into motion, proving themselves again to be a breed apart: "*Die* unto themselves. *Sweet* roses do not so." Line 12 builds on this momentum, repeating *sweet* and then augmenting it to *sweetest*, to describe fragrances produced by sweet rose petals following their deaths. Like the distilling process used to turn sweet roses into perfume, Shakespeare's sonnet uses lyrical language to turn a *sweet* thing into the *sweetest* thing of all. The final couplet links this powerful poetic process to *you*, the *youth*, whose beauty is tied by rhyme to *truth*. The speaker proposes that the essence of the youth, his truth, will live on in these lyrics following his death. The poet uses lyrical language not only to say that such a magnificent thing can be done, but also to do it. And this sonnet has kept its promise. After all, the strength of Shakespeare's poem has allowed the fame of the youth's beauty to survive over 400 years.

METER *(see p.45)*
Each line of a sonnet consists of ten or more syllables composed in the same metre: pentameter. The majority of lines in all of the sonnets are written in iambic pentameter.

QUATRAIN
The first twelve lines of each sonnet are divided into groups of four lines, called "quatrains." Each of the three quatrains expresses a distinct idea which, linked together, form the argument of the poem. The first four lines of the sonnet rhyme *abab*. A new rhyming scheme is used for each following quatrain: *cdcd* and *efef*.

TURN
A "turn" occurs in a sonnet when the poet changes the direction of his argument. Here, the turn is signalled by the word "But." The turn does not have a fixed position; it can appear on a different line in each sonnet.

COUPLET
Each sonnet is concluded with a "couplet," two rhyming lines which shape a forceful conclusion to the poem, while at the same time often offering a new, surprising angle on the subject of the poem.

SONNET 54

O, how much more doth beauty beauteous seem *a*
By that sweet ornament which truth doth give! *b*
(truth: integrity)
The rose looks fair, but fairer we it deem *a*
For that sweet odour which doth in it live. *b*
The canker blooms have full as deep a dye *c*
(canker: a rose without odour)
As the perfumèd tincture of the roses, *d*
Hang on such thorns and play as wantonly *c*
When summer's breath their maskèd buds discloses; *d*
But for their virtue only is their show *e*
They live unwooed and unrespected fade *f*
Die to themselves. Sweet roses do not so; *e*
Of their sweet deaths are sweetest odours made. *f*
And so of you, beauteous and lovely youth, *g*
When that shall vade, by verse distils your truth. *g*
(vade: depart)

Publishing the Sonnets

A widely-held belief contends that Shakespeare's sonnets were printed without his consent. Had Shakespeare endorsed their publication, many believe he would have provided their printer with an authoritative text and a dedication. However, *Shake-speare's Sonnets* includes no dedication from the author and the text is filled with errors. Some also maintain that certain sonnets are unfinished, and that the sequence is too incoherent to have been intended for publication. Exponents of this view have argued that someone whom Shakespeare trusted betrayed him by giving the poems to their first publisher, Thomas Thorpe, or that a thief, motivated by animosity or profit, seized the poet's manuscript. Some hold that publication surely upset Shakespeare, whose poems dealt with scandalous forms of love: homoerotic and adulterous. Others variously insist that these subjects are more shocking to post-Victorian readers than to Jacobean ones; that, while the sonnets voice strong feelings, these were entirely appropriate to the form; and that emotions expressed in his sonnets do not mirror Shakespeare's own any more than those of dramatic characters in his plays.

TO THE ONLY BEGETTER
OF THESE ENSUING SONNETS
MR. W.H. ALL HAPPINESS AND
THAT ETERNITY PROMISED BY
OUR EVER-LIVING POET WISHETH
THE WELL-WISHING ADVENTURER
IN SETTING FORTH

T.T.

The dedication from *Shake-speare's Sonnets*, published by Thomas Thorpe (T.T.) in 1609. The identity of "Mr. W.H." is a mystery which has kept Shakespeare historians guessing for centuries.

Certain features of the sonnet form, not least the first-person voice and themes of love, do give the impression of offering direct access to their author's inner world. Since there has long been intense curiosity about the "youth" addressed in the sonnets, clues to his identity have also been extracted with no little strain from the frontispiece of the first edition.

STRAIGHT TALKING

When Shakespeare's sonnets were re-edited in 1640, their publisher John Benson not only inserted titles and changed the order and structure of the poems, he also altered their language so that sonnets addressing a man spoke instead to a female beloved. Since Benson's publication followed not long after Shakespeare's death in 1616, some believe that his manipulation of the poems supports the theory that Jacobeans would have been shocked to discover love sonnets addressing a man.

HENRY WRIOTHESLEY

Henry Wriothesley, Earl of Southampton, has earned a place in literary history stemming from the belief that he was the "fair youth" of Shakespeare's early sonnets. It will never be known whether Shakespeare became infatuated with the foppish young man, just 19 at the time, or whether he was merely a 'hired pen'. Wriothesley went on to have a stormy political career, as he was jailed and narrowly escaped execution after joining the Earl of Essex's failed rebellion against Elizabeth I in 1601.

Henry Wriothesley, Earl of Southampton, in *c.*1590–93.

The author of this dedication, T.T., was Thomas Thorpe, the publisher. But the identity of the "begetter" of the sonnets, "Mr. W.H.", remains a mystery. Some think this is a misprint for "Mr. W. S." or "Mr. W. Sh.," as in Mr. William Shakespeare. Others suspect that "begetter" refers to the scoundrel who may have conveyed the poems to Thorpe against Shakespeare's wishes. But the most widely held assumption is that the "begetter" must be the person who inspired the "ensuing sonnets," the majority of which address a young man.

Working from the scant evidence offered by the initials W. H., literary detectives have proposed many candidates. One is Henry Wriothesley, Earl of Southampton, to whom Shakespeare dedicated *Venus and Adonis* and *The Rape of Lucrece* in the mid-1590s. Another is William Herbert, Earl of Pembroke, whose name figures among those to whom the *First Folio* was dedicated in 1623. A third candidate is Sir William Harvey, stepfather of the Earl of Southampton, who may have commissioned lyrics urging the young man to marry and produce an heir—the first 17 sonnets of the sequence treat this theme. Of these candidates, however, two were earls and one was a gentleman, referred to as "Sir." None would have been called "Mr." save by error or to suggest intimacy. In the end, those probing these enigmas of Shakespeare's sonnets are forced to speculate; information is scarce, poor, and inconclusive.

SHALL I DIE?

THE AUTHOR OF SHALL I DIE? is as uncertain as the poem's original purpose. In nine stanzas (verses) of ten lines each, the lyrics may have been used for a musical production of a Shakespearean comedy following the playwright's death in 1616. This could explain why it was attributed to Shakespeare in one compilation dated from the 1630s. In venerable post-Petrarchan fashion, *Shall I Die?* treats love as a matter of life and death. But with its lurching rhymes and flat tone, it hardly registers the voice of a genuinely love-struck individual. The speaker first questions whether life is worth living if his love is not returned, then settles on being hopeful. Stanzas 4–6 describe a dream in which the speaker sat with the loved one in a meadow and noted her beauty. In the final stanza, the lover concludes that, since pleasures found in dreams are scant in waking life, he should act on his desires before it is too late.

Shall I Die? survives in two manuscripts containing poems compiled in the 1630s and in one of these the work is attributed to Shakespeare. But the piece is not known to have been printed during Shakespeare's lifetime, nor does anything like it appear in his plays. Nevertheless, an authorship debate arose in 1985, when US scholar Gary Taylor argued that Shakespeare probably wrote the poem in the 1590s. With the debate surrounding its authorship unresolved, *Shall I Die?* demonstrates that quests for new pieces by Shakespeare remain as alive as ever.

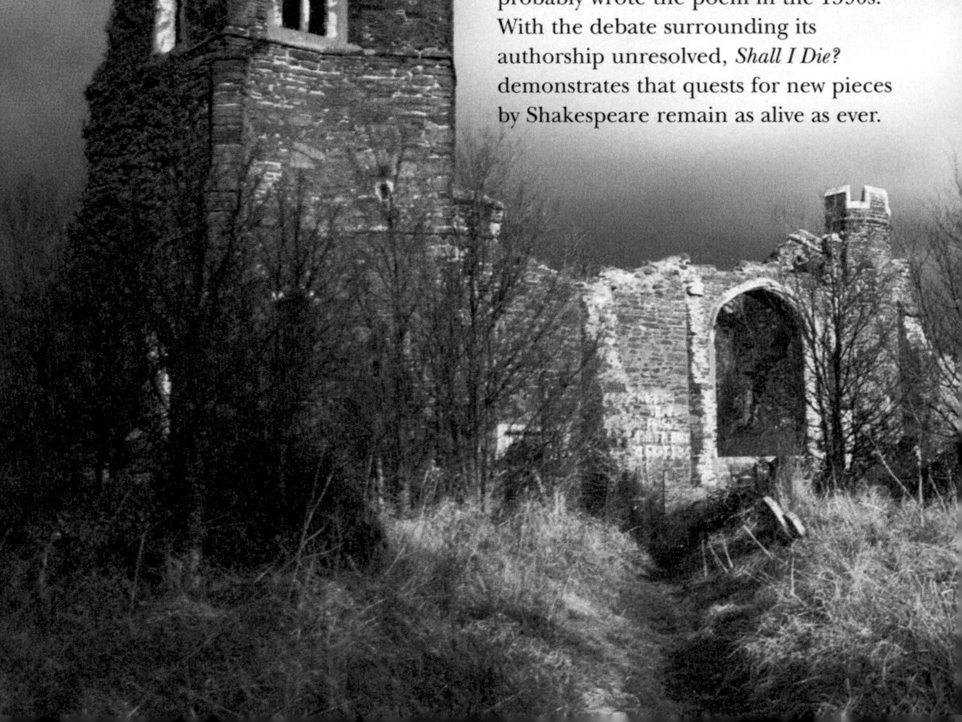

EPITAPHS

No epitaph has been proven to be by Shakespeare. But following his death in 1616, it became conventional to attribute epitaphs to the great poet. These short poems commemorate people with whom Shakespeare was associated, and at least some of them could have commissioned the poet to write their epitaphs: John Combe, Elias James, Ben Jonson, members of the Stanley family, and King James. Some of the epitaphs only appear in printed versions, while others can only be found on tombstones. Their tones vary from solemn to flippant. A couplet on the east end of the Stanley family tomb in Shropshire reads: "Ask who lies here, but do not weep;/He is not dead, he doth but sleep." But a line for moneylender John Combe jokes "'Tis a Hundred to Ten his soul is not saved."

Ben Jonson wrote epitaphs to be read as literature. But even printed epitaphs attributed to Shakespeare are of contested authorship. In 1650, Nicolas Burgh recorded the popular belief that Shakespeare and Jonson were drinking in a tavern when Jonson wrote the first line of an epitaph for his own tombstone:

Here lies Ben Jonson that was once one

Shakespeare was said to complete Jonson's epitaph with the couplet:

Who while he lived was a slow thing,
And now being dead is nothing.

But the most famous Shakespearean epitaph can be found on Shakespeare's tomb in Stratford-upon-Avon, and may have been composed by the Bard for himself:

Good friend, for Jesus' sake forbear
To dig the dust enclosèd here!
Bles't be the man that spares these stones
And Curs't be he that moves my bones!

As the sun sets over Manhattan, actors perform under the floodlights in Central Park at the opening night of the Shakespeare Festival in New York, 1961.

GLOBAL SHAKESPEARE

England's national poet has become playwright to the world. During his lifetime, Shakespeare brought the passions and politics of distant lands to the stage of the Globe. In the centuries that followed, the globe itself came under his sway. As the British Empire spread, and with it the English language, so also did devotion to England's greatest playwright. Soon Shakespeare was revered across the world. His plays were translated into more than 180 languages; they were rewritten, modernized, even parodied; and they inspired operas, ballets, paintings, and movies. No dramatist in history has wielded such influence.

Shakespeare plays are now produced around the world. Above is a Spanish poster for an Italian adaptation of *Romeo and Juliet* and a Polish poster for a Russian production of *Othello*.

What is the secret of Shakespeare's international appeal? One answer can be found in Shakespeare the universal storyteller: his plays reach beyond any single language or country. Even when set in a time and place, they often seem timeless and placeless. Their innovative structures—"high" and "low" themes, interwoven plots and subplots, penetrating soliloquies—transcend national theater conventions.

No less universal are Shakespeare's characters. In them, we find expressions of love, betrayal, greed, jealousy, ambition, loyalty, revenge, regret, solitude, or ruthlessness. These are not the emotions of one language or culture; they inform all human exchange. Many characters even have Greek, Latin, Italian, and Spanish names, names like Romeo, Iachimo, and Pericles, which evoke exotic Mediterranean lands far from England's shores.

Shakespeare also looked abroad for much of his raw material. Except in the history plays, his most important source was Italy, which offered Roman history, folk tales and age-old legends, as well as classical mythology imported from Greece. For English audiences, this represented a strange new world. Yet outside England, Shakespeare's stories often seemed familiar and were readily absorbed by new languages and cultures. Thus, even the notion that Shakespeare belonged to England became negotiable.

DISCOVERING THE BARD

Germany was the first European country to embrace Shakespeare. Goethe, Schiller, and other 18th-century German writers welcomed his natural writing style and daring plot structures as a challenge to stiff French neo-classicism. Further, while England still viewed Shakespeare primarily as a poet, German critics were the first to trumpet his genius as a dramatist. In the early 19th century, a definitive translation of the canon by August von Schlegel and Ludwig Tieck gave Shakespeare a central place in German education, a status endorsed by Heinrich Heine and Nietzsche. To this day, Shakespeare is more widely read and performed in Germany than any other playwright.

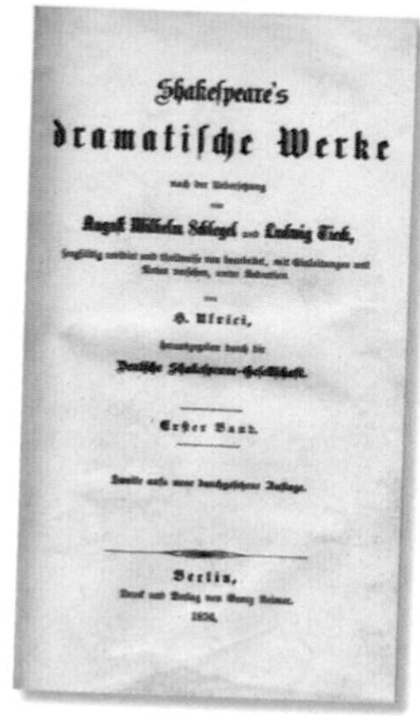

Shakespeare's
dramatische Werke
August Wilhelm Schlegel und Ludwig Tieck,
H. Ulrici,
Deutsche Shakespeare-Gesellschaft.
Erster Band.
Berlin,

Translations of Shakespeare by Schlegel and Tieck are still used by German theater companies today.

In France, Voltaire first brought Shakespeare to public attention when he returned to Paris from exile in England in the 1720's, although decades later he denounced the Englishman as "barbarous." By then the dramatist Jean-François Ducis had presented *Hamlet, Romeo and Juliet, King Lear,* and *Macbeth* on the Paris stage. However, he did Shakespeare no favor by using all-prose translations and adapting the plays to the neo-classicism of Corneille, Racine, and Molière. Only in the early 19th century, with the rise of Romanticism, did writers such as Victor Hugo recognize Shakespeare's originality. Today, his tragedies and comedies enjoy a strong following in France.

Elsewhere in Europe, the 19th century marked Shakespeare's entry into the theatrical mainstream, often in translation from non-English versions. The Russian Empress Catherine the Great had already used a German text for her 1786 adaptation of *The Merry Wives of Windsor.* Later Russian translators preferred French texts and gave the plays Russian settings. In the late 19th century, Shakespeare was still not being translated from English, although Pushkin, Turgenev, and Chekhov were among his devotees. Only

Umabatha—the Zulu version of *Macbeth*—was performed by Zulu warriors at Shakespeare's Globe in London, 1997.

This Hindi verse translation of *Macbeth* was performed in Delhi, India, in 1979.

Tolstoy was not persuaded, accusing the Bard of immorality and pomposity. Yet even Soviet Russia venerated Shakespeare.

In 19th-century Hungary, Shakespeare became a cult figure: by 1878, all his plays had been translated into Hungarian. In other European countries, individual dramas were translated for performance, with *Julius Caesar, Macbeth, King Lear,* and *Hamlet* the most popular. Unsurprisingly, it was *Hamlet* that first won over Danes to Shakespeare in 1813. Spain too embraced Shakespeare, even recognizing him as Cervantes's literary equal. In contrast, Italy at first resisted, partly out of distaste for his treatment of Roman history. But in the end, many Italians came to Shakespeare via opera, starting with Rossini's *Otello*, followed by Verdi's *Macbeth, Otello,* and *Falstaff.* And Shakespeare is now one of Italy's most popular dramatists.

By the 20th century, Shakespeare's best-known plays had been translated into most major languages. British influence spread Shakespeare through Persia and the Arab world, where his plays were often translated into literary prose, with names changed and songs added. Certain plays had special appeal. *Antony and Cleopatra* was popular in Egypt, where much of the play's action is set. Through its representation of the Moor, *Othello* stirred interest in Morocco. *Hamlet* was also presented in several Arabic versions. After World War II, the Arab League and UNESCO sponsored translation of Shakespeare's entire canon. Even today, the legend survives that Shakespeare was himself an Arab named Sheikh al Subair (meaning "prickly pear," thus 'Sheikh-pear').

In India, where Shakespeare was first introduced by colonial amateur theater groups, his plays are still performed in English. However, in 1852, *The Merchant of Venice* was staged in Bengali and, within a century, most of the canon had been translated into India's other main languages. Indeed, while Shakespeare may originally have been a colonial implant, local languages, costumes, traditions, and political context have now given him the stature of an Indian playwright.

Shakespeare arrived later in Japan, but here too his plays were molded to theater conventions. Starting with *Julius Caesar* and *The Merchant of Venice* in the 1880's, plays were adapted to the highly stylized Kabuki theater tradition. Tsubouchi Shoyo, Japan's first major translator of Shakespeare, was truer to the original texts. Later translations by Tsuneari Fukuda and Junji Kinoshita were better suited to the more realistic Shingeki—"new drama"—theater school. Today, while occasional productions conform to English practice, the preference is still to make the plays seem Japanese.

Interpreting Shakespeare

Shakespeare's universality embraces more than geography. Since the 20th century, starting with the Soviet Union's Marxist interpretation of his plays (later adopted

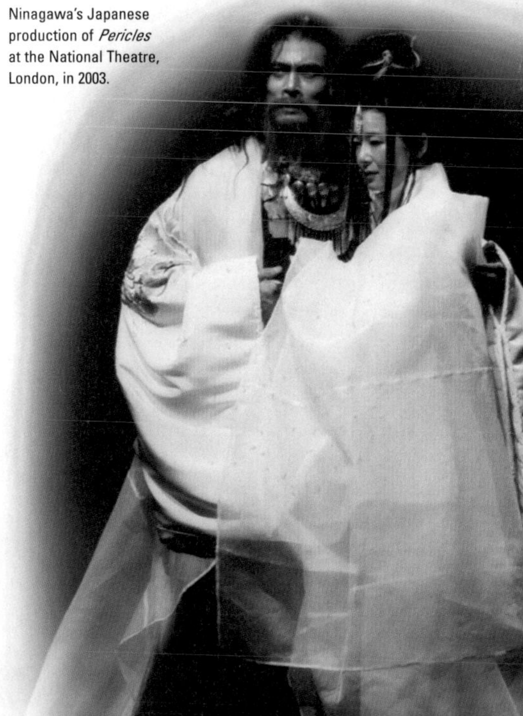

Ninagawa's Japanese production of *Pericles* at the National Theatre, London, in 2003.

Even Shakespeare's narrative poems have been dramatized for the stage. *Zohreh & Manouchehr*, a Persian adaptation of *Venus and Adonis*, was created by Shahrokh Moshkin Ghalam in Paris, 2001.

by China), scholars and theater directors around the world have explored the texts from myriad political, social, and psychological perspectives.

In 1937, Orson Welles's *Julius Caesar* in New York protested rising Fascism in Europe. After World War II, Bertolt Brecht, the German founder of the Berliner Ensemble, turned Shakespeare into a force for social change, placing restless masses at the heart of his *Coriolanus*. The Polish critic Jan Kott was no less influential. In his 1964 book *Shakespeare Our Contemporary*, he used Shakespeare's tragedies and history plays to mirror the blood-stained 20th century. Plays like *Othello* and *The Merchant of Venice* have also served to challenge racial stereotypes.

The dismantling of the British and French empires in the 1960's in turn gave rise to post-colonial interpretations of Shakespeare. *The Tempest*, inspired by England's first attempt to colonize the Americas, is the play most often viewed through this prism, with Caliban portrayed as a victim of colonialism. Some former colonies also adapted Shakespeare to their situations. In 1963, when Tanzania's first president, Julius Nyerere, translated *Julius Caesar* into Kiswahili as *Juliasi Kaizari*, he was seen to be warning against one-man dictatorship. Under South Africa's apartheid regime, with many black writers attracted by Shakespeare's image as a humanist, several of his plays were translated into the Zulu, Sechuana, and Xhosa languages. Even *Othello*, long banned for its interracial love, was finally presented in Johannesburg in 1988 with a Bantu actor in the leading role.

From the 1970's, the rise of feminism heralded radically different ways of interpreting Shakespeare. Although his plays are notoriously male-dominated, feminists found much to research in the patriarchal values represented by fathers, husbands, and lovers, and in portrayals of women as symbols of power, evil, morality, constancy, and loyalty. On stage, this has encouraged explorations of gender and of sexual variables. Gender-switching, including all-male and all-female casts, is common, with women taking on lead roles in, say, *Richard II* and *The Tempest*. The gay revolution has led to the rethinking of entire plays, with some productions of *Hamlet*, *Richard II*, *Twelfth Night*, *The Merchant of Venice*, and *Coriolanus* suggesting homoerotic relationships between key male characters.

Today, the search for new meaning in Shakespeare continues unabated, notably in American and British universities, but also in Shakespeare associations around the world and on myriad Internet web sites. Shakespeare's plays, in particular, have been examined in the light of successive academic theories: Marxism, psychoanalysis, structuralism, feminism, deconstruction, New Historicism, and Queer Theory. Similarly, every imaginable aspect of the canon has been studied, from sex and death, to astronomy and military strategy. It is said that a paper, thesis, or book on Shakespeare is published somewhere in the world every day.

Shakespeare on the Global Stage

Understandably perhaps, Britain takes a somewhat proprietorial view of Shakespeare. The Royal Shakespeare Company, based in Stratford-upon-Avon, Shakespeare's birthplace, is arguably the preeminent guardian of the Bard's legacy. In London, Shakespeare's Globe—a replica of the original open-air Globe—presents at least three Shakespeare plays each summer, while the Royal National Theatre includes Shakespeare in every season.

In North America, Shakespeare has had a Canadian home since 1953 in Stratford, Ontario, which has been the location for many acclaimed productions. In the United States, Shakespeare & Company is now constructing a replica of Philip Henslowe's 1587 Rose Theatre at its permanent base in Lenox, Massachusetts. Even the National Endowment for the Arts now promotes Shakespeare. Yet still more impressive is the plethora of Shakespeare festivals—more than 100 at last count—in American cities large and small, many of them linked to universities.

Outside the English-speaking world, Shakespeare is no less present on stage: Tokyo and Rome are among dozens of cities to build their own replicas of the Globe Theatre, although none is more unusual than the Ice Globe Theater in northern Sweden, which presents Shakespeare in Lappish in the Arctic winter. Non-English productions also enjoy the distance provided by new translations. When Shakespeare was routinely taught in schools across Europe, classical 19th century translations were favoured. Today, new productions often prefer more colloquial translations. Thus, while the English-speaking stage needs decor, costumes, and direction to suggest modernity, elsewhere it can be provided through speech.

Still, wherever performed, Shakespeare invites experimentation, such as an all-male Zimbabwean *The Taming of the Shrew*, an erotic *Macbeth* from Catalonia; *The Tempest* set in the American Civil War; a rap *Comedy of Errors* renamed *The Bomb-itty of Errors*; and the Reduced Shakespeare Company's scramble through the entire canon in 90 minutes. Some productions confront stage traditions: the French director Ariane Mnouchkine revisited *Richard II*, *Twelfth Night*, and *Henry IV Part I* as Oriental spectacles inspired by both Japan's Kabuki and India's Kathakali theater schools.

Shakespeare festivals are extremely popular in the United States, particularly among high schools. The Fall Festival of Shakespeare brought 500 teenagers from 10 schools together at the Founders' Theater. Above, Lee High School works on a scene from *Richard III*. On the right, students from Mt. Greylock High School perform *A Midsummer Night's Dream*.

Melissa Hayden (Titania) and Roland Vazquez (Bottom) in George Balanchine's balletic version of Felix Mendelssohn's orchestral score, *A Midsummer Night's Dream.*

Premier of *Hamlet* at the Ice Globe, Jukkasjarvi, Swedish Lappland, performed by the Beaivvas Sami Teahter Sami Nat.

Shakespeare in Other Art Forms

After the legendary actor-manager David Garrick introduced bardolatry to mid-18th-century England, artists quickly followed his lead by painting scenes from Shakespeare plays as well as portraits of prominent actors in dramatic poses. Reproduced as prints, works by William Hogarth, Henry Fuseli, William Blake, and, later, John Everett Millais helped to enshrine Shakespeare as England's great poet. Soon, French Romantics like Delacroix, Chassériau, and Moreau were also depicting key moments from Shakespeare plays. Yet by the end of the 19th century, the fashion for Shakespeare in art had run its course.

More lasting has been Shakespeare's association with music. A few symphonic works, like Prokofiev's ballet *Romeo and Juliet*, remain popular, but Shakespearean operas have proven more successful. Purcell's 1692 *Fairy Queen*, based on *A Midsummer Night's Dream*, was the first, but the golden age for operas inspired by Shakespeare came later. Of some 200 written in the 19th century, however, only Verdi's *Macbeth*, *Otello*, and *Falstaff* are masterpieces, while Bellini's *I Capuleti e I Montecchi*, Gounod's *Roméo et Juliette*, and Ambroise Thomas's *Hamlet* are also regularly performed. From the 20th century, Benjamin Britten's *A Midsummer Night's Dream* stands out, although composers are still drawn by Shakespeare: Philippe Boesmans recreated *The Winter's Tale* as *Wintermärchen*, Salvatore Sciarrino adapted *Macbeth*, and Thomas Adès *The Tempest*.

Undergoing still greater transformation, many of Shakespeare's plays have also been turned into musical comedies, although only three became Broadway hits. *The Comedy of Errors* gave Richard Rodgers and Lorenz Hart their story for *The Boys from Syracuse* in 1938, while a decade later Cole Porter borrowed from *The Taming of the Shrew* to write the musical *Kiss Me, Kate.* Still more popular was the 1957 *West Side Story*, in which Leonard Bernstein, Arthur Laurents, and Stephen Sondheim adapted *Romeo and Juliet* to the world of warring New York gangs.

Footsbarn Theatre's 2002 multilingual *Perchance to Dream*, which integrated scenes from four of Shakespeare's major tragedies.

It has been left to the movies, however, to carry Shakespeare to a broader public. In the three decades after Herbert Beerbohm Tree first filmed the dying scene from *King John* in 1899, scores of silent Shakespeare movies were made, including 17 versions of *Hamlet* alone. With the arrival of "talkies," Shakespeare films incorporated dialogue, music, large crowd scenes, and realistic locations. Audiences intimidated by the idea of going to the theater were suddenly given easy access to Shakespeare. Thanks to the draw of film stars, Shakespeare on screen also proved easily exportable.

Laurence Olivier's patriotic *Henry V*, filmed during World War II, was the first adaptation to exploit the screen's full potential. Olivier followed up with *Hamlet, Richard III,* and *Othello.* Orson Welles matched him with *Macbeth, Othello,* and *Chimes at Midnight*, built around Falstaff. Hollywood presented star-studded versions of *Julius Caesar* and *Antony and Cleopatra.* Non-English films won critical acclaim, notably Kozintsev's Russian *Hamlet* and *King Lear*, and Kurosawa's *Throne of Blood, The Bad Sleep Well,* and *Ran*, his Japanese versions of *Macbeth, Hamlet,* and *King Lear.*

Shakespeare has also reached large audiences through television, with some of his plots adapted for serials like *Star Trek.*

Movie directors also continue to explore fresh ways of presenting Shakespeare. Al Pacino's 1995 *Looking for Richard* shows a group of actors discussing and rehearsing *Richard III.* Oliver Parker's *Othello* and Kenneth Branagh's *Henry V, Hamlet* and *Much Ado About Nothing,* combine period costumes with modern cinematography. Other plays have been updated: Baz Luhrmann set his *Romeo + Juliet* among American drug gangs, while Richard Loncraine's *Richard III* had a Fascist Richard ruling 1930's Britain.

Curiously, though, the most successful Shakespeare film in many years—John Madden's Oscar-winning *Shakespeare in Love*—is not based on a play, but is a fictional romp about the young playwright and his mistress. Yet this is proof enough that, four centuries after he made his name in London, the Bard remains a global celebrity. For all the mystery surrounding the real Shakespeare, he has cast a spell over the world. In every language, his very name evokes beauty and enlightenment. Through his stories, characters and poetry, he has reshaped humanity's understanding of itself.

West Side Story, based on *Romeo and Juliet,* is one of the most popular screen adaptations of a Shakespeare play.

Index

Page numbers in *italic* refer to an illustration or information in a caption. Page numbers in **bold** refer to a main chapter on a subject.

Picture Credits

The publisher would like to thank the following for their kind permission to reproduce their photographs.

ABBREVIATIONS KEY:
a=above; b=below; c=center; l=left; r=right; t=top
Alamy=Alamy Images
BAL=Bridgeman Art Library, London/New York
Donald Cooper=Donald Cooper/Photostage
Mander & Mitchenson=Mander & Mitchenson Theatre Collection
MEPL=Mary Evans Picture Library
RGA=Ronald Grant Archive
Robbie Jack=Robbie Jack Photography

1 DK Images/British Library; **4-5** Corbis/Bob Krist; **5** Corbis/Fabian Cevallos (t), Shakespeare's Globe/John Tramper (cl); **8-9** Alamy/Robert Mullan; **9** AKG London/National Portrait Gallery, London (c), MEPL (br); **10** Shakespeare Birthplace Trust Records Office; **11** BAL/Haags Gemeentemuseum, Netherlands (b), MEPL (t); **12** Hulton Archive/Getty Images (b); **12-13** By permission of The British Library; **13** MEPL (cl); **14** Corbis/Ric Ergenbright; **15** Corbis/Dean Conger (b), Public Record Office (t); **16-17** AKG London/Erich Lessing; **17** AKG London (c); **18** BAL/Musee des Beaux-Arts, Rennes, France/Giraudon (b), MEPL (t); **19** BAL/Giraudon/Musee Conde, Chantilly, France; **20** BAL/Musee Massey, Tarbes, France/Lauros/Giraudon; **21** BAL/Private Collection (b); **22** AKG London (b), AKG London/Nimatallah (t); **23** BAL/Private Collection; **24-25** Shakespeare's Globe/John Tramper; **25** MEPL (b); **26** BAL/Private Collection (cl); **27** AKG London (t), BAL/Private Collection (b); **28** BAL/Dulwich Picture Gallery, London, UK (b), British Library (cl); **29** MEPL; **30** Ancient Art & Architecture Collection (b), BAL/Corpus Christi College, Cambridge, UK (t), Corbis/A & J Verkaik (l); **31** MEPL (cl); **32** Corbis/Craig Aurness; **33** MEPL; **34** BAL/Private Collection (b), Private Collection/Giraudon (t); **35** BAL/Walker Art Gallery, Liverpool, Merseyside, UK (b), MEPL (t); **36** AKG London (t), MEPL (b); **37** Donald Cooper; **38-39** Corbis/Jonathan Blair; **39** BAL/Musee de la Tapisserie, Bayeux, France/With special authorisation of the city of Bayeux; **41** BAL/British Library, London, UK (cl), MEPL (t); **43** Corbis/Archivo Iconografico, S.A.; **44** Robbie Jack Photography; **45** AKG London (b), Mander & Mitchenson (tr); **46-47** Corbis/Michael Pole; **48** Corbis/Charles Michael Murray; **50-51** Corbis/Adam Woolfitt; **52** DK Images/Wallace Collection (bc), (l); **54-55** Corbis/Adam Woolfitt; **56** Donald Cooper (tl), (tr), (b); **57** Alamy/Mick Rock; **59** Corbis/Bob Marsh/Papilio; **60** BAL/Giraudon/Centre Historique des Archives Nationales, Paris, France (cl), MEPL (tr); **61** Donald Cooper (b), MEPL (cr), The Shakespeare Theatre, Washington, DC/Carol Rosegg/Directed by Michael Kahn (tr); **62-63** Corbis/Eric and David Hosking; **64** Donald Cooper (tr), (b), Corbis/Historical Picture Archive (tl); **65** Corbis/Yann Arthus-Bertrand; **66-67** Alamy/Leamington Spa Picture Library; **68** BAL/Eton College, Windsor, UK (tr); **68** MEPL (cl); **69** Donald Cooper (b), Photofest (t); **70** James Davis Travel Photography; **72** Donald Cooper (t), The Shakespeare Theatre, Washington, DC/Carol Rosegg/1996 production, directed by Michael Kahn (b); **73** Alamy/Mick Broughton; **74-75** Alamy/John Prior Images; **76** MEPL; **77** Donald Cooper (b), The Shakespeare Theatre, Washington, DC/Carol Rosegg (t); **78** Corbis/Adam Woolfitt; **80** Donald Cooper (b), Corbis/Hulton-Deutsch Collection (t); **81** Corbis/Ludovic Maisant; **82** Getty Images/Jerry Driendl; **84** Corbis/Rebecca Emery; **85** Courtesy of the Trustees of the V&A; **86** Donald Cooper (tr), Corbis/Robbie Jack (b); **87** Aquarius Library/United Artists (tr), Moviestore Collection/London Films (b); 88-89 DK Images/Joe Cornish; **90** Donald Cooper (b), (t), Mander & Mitchenson (cl); **91** Corbis/Paul Almasy; **92-93** Corbis/Paul Almasy; **94** Corbis/Bettmann (t), MEPL (bl); **95** Donald Cooper (t), Mander & Mitchenson (b); **96-97** Corbis/So Hing-Keung; **98** Donald Cooper (tl), (cr); **99** Corbis/Michael Boys; **100** BAL/Lauros/Giraudon/Musee de l'Armee, Paris, France; **102** Corbis/Uwe Walz; **103** AKG London/British Library; **104** Knightsbridge Theatre, Los Angeles, CA/Robert Craig; **105** AKG London (t), Shakespeare Society of America, Globe Playhouse, Los Angeles (b); **106-107** Corbis/Adam Woolfitt; **108** Robbie Jack Photography (b), Mander & Mitchenson (t); **109** Corbis/W. Cody; **110-111** Corbis/Martin Jones; **112** Corbis/Jonathan Blair; **113** Corbis/Michael Nicholson (t), MEPL (b); **114** Donald Cooper (b), Photofest (t); **115** Corbis/Bettmann (t), Robbie Jack Photography (b); **116** Corbis/Sandro Vannini; **118** Donald Cooper (cr), Corbis/Abilio Lope (t), John Vickers Theatre Collection (b); **119** Corbis/Robert Estall; **121** Corbis/David Pollack; **123** MEPL; **124** Donald Cooper (b), Photofest (t); **125** RGA/New Line (b), RGA/Internacional/Alpine (t); **126-127** Arcaid/Clay Perry; **128** Robbie Jack Photography (cl), Photofest (tr); **129** Corbis/Lee Snider; **130** Corbis/Walter Rohdich/Frank Lane Picture Agency; **132** Corbis/Angelo Hornak; **133** BAL/Courtesy of the Warden and Scholars of New College, Oxford (t), Corbis/Michelle Garrett (b); **134** Aquarius Library (t), Photofest (b); **135** Robbie Jack Photography (b), Mander & Mitchenson (t); **136-137** Corbis/Peter Finger; **138** RGA/BBC/Renaissance (bl), Mander & Mitchenson (t), Photofest (cr); **139** DK Images/Joe Cornish; **140-141** Corbis/Peter Johnson; **142** Getty Images/Malcolm Piers; **143** AKG London (b); **144** Donald Cooper; **145** RGA/Two Cities (t), Moviestore Collection/Curzon/Renaissance Films (b); **146-147** Corbis/Ted Spiegel; **148** Donald Cooper (tr), MEPL (c), Photofest (b); **150** Corbis/Julio Donoso; **152** AKG London; **153** Donald Cooper (b), Corbis/Hulton-Deutsch Collection (t); **154** Corbis/Michael Freeman; **156-157** Corbis/Gavriel Jecan; **159**

Corbis/Chuck Savage (t); **160-161** Corbis/Yann Arthus-Bertrand; **162** Donald Cooper (b), Mander & Mitchenson (t); **163** Corbis/Bob Gibbons/Eye Ubiquitous; **164-165** Corbis/Wolfgang Kaehler; **166** Corbis/Richard T. Nowitz; **167** Corbis/Gianni Dagli Orti (b), MEPL (t); **168** Guy Chapman Associates/Caroline Lewis (t), Donald Cooper (b); **169** Donald Cooper (cr), RGA/Universal (tl), Mander & Mitchenson (b); **170** Corbis/Massimo Listri; **172** Donald Cooper (cr), Kobal Collection/Columbia/Bob Penn (tl), Photofest (b); **173** Corbis/Macduff Everton; **174** Corbis/Ted Spiegel; **176** Corbis/Darrell Gulin; 177 AKG London/Sotheby's; **178** Photofest; **179** RGA/MGM (bl), Kobal Collection/Columbia (tr), Photofest/Elton Productions/Pickford Productions (br); **180-181** Corbis/Gail Mooney; **182** Donald Cooper (bl), Mander & Mitchenson (br), (t); **183** Corbis/Bob Krist; **184** Corbis/John and Lisa Merrill; **186** AKG London; **187** Donald Cooper (b), Photofest (t); **190** Donald Cooper (c), (t), Robbie Jack Photography (b); **191** Corbis/Adam Woolfitt; **194** Alamy/Brigitte Thomas; **195** AKG London/VISIOARS (t), MEPL (b); **196** Donald Cooper (b), Mander & Mitchenson (t); **197** Donald Cooper (bl), MEPL (br), Royal Shakespeare Company/SBT/Tom Holte (t); **198-199** Corbis/First Light; **200** Corbis/Rune Hellestad/Sygma (cr), Robbie Jack Photography (tl), Mander & Mitchenson (bl); **201** Corbis/Pat O'Hara; **202-203** Alamy/Mediacolor's; **204** DK Images/TAP Service Archaeological Receipts Fund; **205** AKG London/Sotheby's; **206** Aquarius Library (b), Donald Cooper (tl), (tr); **207** Angence Enguerand/Bernand/Marc Enguerand (t), Lebrecht Music Collection (cr), Mander & Mitchenson (bl); **208** Corbis/Bernard Annebicque; **210** Donald Cooper (b), Photofest (t); **211** Alamy/E.J.Baumeister Jr.; **213** Alamy/Malie Rich-Griffith; **214** Getty Images/Will Crocker; **215** MEPL (t), MEPL/Weimar Archive (b); **216** Donald Cooper (b), (t); **217** Freie Volksbühne Berlin/Jlse Buhs; **218-219** Corbis/Joy Whiting/Cordaiy Photo Library Ltd; **220** Donald Cooper (cl), Corbis/Hulton-Deutsch Collection (b), The Shakespeare Theatre, Washington, DC/Carol Rosegg/1999 Free for All production at the Carter Barron Amphitheatre, directed by Daniel Fish (tr); **221** Corbis/Richard T.Nowitz; **222-223** Corbis/Frank Blackburn/Ecoscene; **224** Corbis/Michelle Garrett; **225** Corbis/Stapleton Collection (b), Inn Sign Society/Alan A.Rose (t); **226** Donald Cooper (t), Photofest (b); **227** AKG London/Joseph Martin (b), Robbie Jack Photography (cr); **228-229** Alamy/Art Kowalsky; **230** Donald Cooper (tl), Corbis/Hulton-Deutsch Collection (b), MEPL (tr); **231** Corbis/William Manning; **233** Corbis/Bob Krist; **234** Corbis/Dennis Degnan; **235** AKG London; **236** Angence Enguerand/Bernand/Vincent Pontet (b), Photofest (t); **237** Aquarius Library/Samuel Goldwyn (b), Royal Shakespeare Company/SBT/Tom Holte (t); **238-239** Corbis/Cindy Kassab; **240** Donald Cooper (tl), Photofest (b); **241** Corbis/Eric Crichton; **242-243** Alamy/Chris Andrews; **244** Corbis/Danny Lehman; **245** BAL/Birmingham Museums and Art Gallery (b), Corbis/Historical Picture Archive (t); **246** Donald Cooper (t), Angence Enguerand/Bernand/Pascal Gely (b); **247** RGA/Inter-Allied (bl), RGA/Sands Films (t), Williamstown Theatre Festival/Richard Feldman (cr); **248-249** Alamy/Robert Harding World Imagery; **250** Aquarius Library (cl), Donald Cooper (cr), Mander & Mitchenson (b); **251** Corbis/ML Sinibaldi; **254** DK Images/Joe Cornish; **255** BAL/Yales Centre for British Art, Paul Mellon Fund, USA; **256** Donald Cooper (t), Topfoto (b); **257** Donald Cooper (b), Photofest (t); **258-259** Corbis/Larry Lee Photography; **260** Donald Cooper (tl), (bl), Rex Features/Reg Wilson (cr); **261** Corbis/Roger Wood; **262-263** Corbis/Reza/Webistan; **264** Corbis/Archivo Iconografico, S.A.; **265** MEPL; **266** Photofest (t), The Shakespeare Theatre, Washington, DC/Joan Marcus (b); **267** Royal Shakespeare Company/Reg Wilson; **268-269** Alamy/Art Kowalsky; **270** Donald Cooper (cl), (b), The Shakespeare Theatre, Washington, DC/Carol Rosegg/1998 Free for All production at the Carter Barron Amphitheatre, directed by Laird Williamson (t); **271** Corbis/Araldo de Luca; **273** Corbis/Massimo Listri; **274** Corbis/Farrell Grehan; **275** MEPL; **276** Mander & Mitchenson (b), (t); **277** Angence Enguerand/Bernand/Brigitte Enguerand (c), (br); **278-279** Corbis/Mark E.Gibson; **280** Donald Cooper (br), (t), Photofest (bl); **281** Corbis/Todd A.Gipstein; **283** Alamy/Michel Arnaud; **284** Corbis/Paul Almasy; **285** MEPL; **286** Donald Cooper (t), Corbis/Hulton-Deutsch Collection (b); **287** Donald Cooper (t), Photofest (b); **288** Corbis/Neil Rabinowitz; **290-291** Getty Images/Tyler Gourey; **292** Shakespeare's Globe/John Tramper; **294-295** Corbis/Ron Watts; **296** Donald Cooper (b), RGA/Clear Blue Sky Productions (1999)/Overseas Film Group/Urania Pictures S.r.l./NDF International (t); **297** Corbis/Mimmo Jodice; **300** Corbis/Araldo de Luca; **301** Corbis/Bettmann; **302** Photofest; **303** Donald Cooper (br), Mander & Mitchenson (bl), (t); **304-305** Corbis/Wolfgang Kaehler; **306** Corbis/Bettmann (bl), RGA (br), (t); **307** Getty Images/Photodisc/Rim Light/PhotoLink; **310** Corbis/K.M.Westermann; **311** MEPL (tr), (bl); **312** ArenaPAL/Clive Barda (b), Mander & Mitchenson (cl); **313** RGA/20th Century Fox/Bazmarkfilms (cr), Photofest (bl); **314-315** Corbis/Roger Wood; **316** Donald Cooper (b), Corbis/Robbie Jack (t); **317** Corbis/Araldo de Luca; **318** Corbis/John Heseltine; **320** Corbis/Bob Krist; **321** Corbis/Bettmann (b), MEPL (t); **322** Donald Cooper (bl), Photofest (t); Piccolo Teatro di Milano, Italy (br); **323** Corbis/Condé Nast Archive (br), RGA/MGM (tl); **324-325** Alamy/Dallas and John Heaton; **326** Donald Cooper (t), Mander & Mitchenson (bl), (br); **327** Alamy/B J Gadie; **329** Getty Images/Jose Manuel; **330** Corbis/Richard Hamilton Smith; **332** Alamy/Pictor International; **333** AKG London/Erich Lessing; **334** Angence Enguerand/Bernand/Pascal Gely (b), Mander & Mitchenson (t); **335** RGA/Pilgrim/Two Cities/Rank; **336** Corbis/Angelo Hornak; **338** Donald Cooper (bl), (t), Photofest (br); **339** Corbis/Ted Horowitz; **341** Corbis/Ludovic Maisant; **342** Getty Images/James F Housel; **343** AKG London; **344** Mander & Mitchenson (b), (t); **345** Corbis/Fabian Cevallos (b), Mander & Mitchenson (t); **348** Donald Cooper (br), (t), Corbis/Robbie Jack (bl); **349** Corbis/Adam Woolfitt; **350** Alamy/The Photolibrary Wales; **352-353** Corbis/Adam Woolfitt; 354 Corbis/John Lund; **355** BAL/Harris Museum and Art Gallery, Preston, Lancashire, UK; **356** Mander & Mitchenson; **357** Donald Cooper (t), Photofest/Herald Films, Inc/Nippon Herald Films (b); **358-359** Corbis/Jim Richardson; **360** Donald Cooper (tl), (b), Corbis/Hulton-Deutsch Collection (cr); **361** Masterfile UK/Horst Klemm; **362** Corbis/Bob Krist; **364** DK Images/Angus Beare; **365** AKG London (b), MEPL (cr); **366** Piccolo Teatro di Milano, Italy/Diego e Luigi Ciminaghi (b), Schaubühne am Lehniner Platz, Berlin/Arno Declair (t); **367** RGA/Toho (b), Mander & Mitchenson (t); **368-369** DK Images/Alistair Duncan; **370** Mander & Mitchenson (cl), Photofest (t); **371** Alamy/Jon Arnold; **373** Corbis; **375** Corbis/North Carolina Museum of Art; **376** Donald Cooper (b), Photofest (t); **377** Corbis/Bettmann (t), RGA/Folio/Rank/Transac/Izaro (b); **378-379** AKG London; **380** Donald Cooper (bl), (br), The Shakespeare Theatre,Washington, DC/Carol Rosegg/2000 production directed by Michael Kahn (t); **381** Alamy/Richard W Turner; **383** Corbis/Vanni Archive; **384** Corbis/Sandro Vannini; **385** AKG London (t), MEPL (b); **386** Donald Cooper (b), Photofest (t); **387** Berliner Ensemble/Vera Tenschert (t), Donald Cooper (b); **388-389** Corbis/Clay Perry; **390** Donald Cooper (tl), (tr), (b); 391 AKG London/John Hios; **394** BAL, London New York/The Stapleton Collection; **395** Donald Cooper (t), Photofest (b); **396** Corbis/Adam Woolfitt (b), Corbis/DiMaggio/Kalish (t); **398-399** Corbis/Randy Wells; **400** Corbis/Eric Fougere; **401** DK Images/National Maritime Museum; **402-403** Corbis/Adam Woolfitt; **404** Donald Cooper (tr), (b), Photofest (tl); **405** Corbis/Sanford/Agliolo; **406-407** Corbis/Michael Maslan Historic Photographs; **408** MEPL; **409** Donald Cooper (b), Photofest (tr); **410-411** Alamy/Leslie Garland /LGPL; **412** Donald Cooper (b), (t), Mander & Mitchenson (cr); **414-415** Corbis/Layne Kennedy; **416** MEPL; **417** Donald Cooper (br), (t), RGA (bl); **418-419** Corbis/Richard Cummins; **420** Donald Cooper (tl), Photofest (tr), (b); **421** Corbis/Ludovic Maisant; **422** Getty Images/Gary Holscher; **423** Donald Cooper; **424** Corbis/Araldo de Luca; **425** AKG London; **426** Bengt Wanselius (cl), (br); **427** Donald Cooper (t), Mander & Mitchenson (bl), (br); **428-429** Getty Images/Chad Ehlers; **430** Donald Cooper (cl), (br), Kobal Collection/Boyd's Co (t); **431** Corbis/Joel W.Rogers; **433** Corbis/Michael Freeman; **434** Alamy; **435** MEPL; **436** Donald Cooper (t), Robbie Jack Photography (b); **437** Aquarius Library/MGM (bl), Moviestore Collection/Palace/Film Four (t), Photofest/Bonnie Raskin Productions/NBC (br); **438-439** Corbis/Elio Ciol; **440** Donald Cooper (bl), (br), Corbis/Hulton-Deutsch Collection (t); **441** Corbis/Marc Garanger; **443** Corbis/Paul Almasy; **444** The Art Archive/Victoria and Albert Museum London/Eileen Tweedy (cl), MEPL (tr); **445** Donald Cooper (b), (t); **446** Arcaid/Lucinda Lambton; **448** Corbis/Mimmo Jodice; **449** Corbis/Mimmo Jodice; **450** Corbis/ Christie's Images (t), Corbis/Clay Perry (b); **451** Corbis/Mimmo Jodice; **452** BAL/Giraudon/Musee des Beaux-Arts, France (t); **452-453** Corbis/Michael Freeman; **454-455** Corbis/Massimo Mastrorillo; **456-457** Corbis/Oddo & Sinibaldi; **459** Corbis/Mark A.Johnson;
460 Alamy/D J Myford; **462-463** Alamy/S J Cromwell; **463** BAL/Private Collection (t); **464-465** Corbis/Robert Estall; **466-467** Corbis/Bettmann; **467** RGA/Rank/Universalcine (c), RGA/Mosfilm (cr); **468** Lebrecht Music Collection (t); **468** Photofest (br), Topfoto/2001 PressNet (bl); **469** Royal National Theatre/Ninagawa Company, Tokyo; **470** F.Joudat; **471** Shakespeare & Company, Lenox, MA/Catherine Taylor-Williams (br), Kevin Sprague (cl); **472** Angence Enguerand/Bernand/Vincent Pontet (b), Photofest (tl); **472-473** Icehotel/Ice Globe Theatre/Harry Johansen; **473** Kobal Collection/Mirisch-7 Arts/United Artists (b).

Chapter Runners/Endpapers
8-45 MEPL; **48-153** MEPL; **155-287** Dover Publications, Inc. New York; **289-395** Dover Publications, Inc. New York; **397-445** Dover Publications, Inc. New York; **447-465** Dover Publications, Inc. New York; 467-473 Dover Publications, Inc. New York.
Picture research assistance: Carlo Ortu

The authors would like to thank Susan Deskis for her help and Marlise Simons and Ashley Rountree as well as Alexander and Jordan for their patience.

They would also like to remember with affection the Cambridge Riverside Players.